EATCS
Monographs on Theoretical Computer Science
Volume 20

Seppo Sippu
Eljas Soisalon-Soininen

# Parsing Theory

## Volume II
## LR($k$) and LL($k$) Parsing

With 110 Figures

Springer-Verlag Berlin Heidelberg New York
London Paris Tokyo Hong Kong Barcelona

*Authors*
Professor S. Sippu
Department of Computer Science, University of Jyväskylä
Seminaarinkatu 15, SF-40 100 Jyväskylä, Finland

Professor E. Soisalon-Soininen
Department of Computer Science, University of Helsinki
Teollisuuskatu 23, SF-00 510 Helsinki, Finland

*Editors*
Prof. Dr. Wilfried Brauer
Institut für Informatik, Technische Universität München
Arcisstr. 21, D-8000 München 2, Germany

Prof. Dr. Grzegorz Rozenberg
Institute of Applied Mathematics and Computer Science
University of Leiden, Niels-Bohr-Weg 1, P.O. Box 9512
NL-2300 RA Leiden, The Netherlands

Prof. Dr. Arto Salomaa
Department of Mathematics, University of Turku
SF-20 500 Turku 50, Finland

ISBN 3-540-51732-4 Springer-Verlag Berlin Heidelberg New York
ISBN 0-387-51732-4 Springer-Verlag New York Berlin Heidelberg

Library of Congress Cataloging-in-Publication Data
(Revised for vol. 2)
Sippu, Seppo, 1950-
Parsing theory.
(EATCS monographs on theoretical computer science ; v. 15, 20)
Includes bibliographical indexes.
Contents: v. 1. Languages and parsing -- v. 2. LR($k$) and LL($k$) parsing.
1. Parsing (Computer grammar) 2. Formal languages.
I. Soisalon-Soininen, Eljas, 1949- . II. Title.
III. Series: EATCS monographs on theoretical computer science ; v. 15, etc.
QA267.3.S59 1988 511.3 88-20091
ISBN 0-387-13720-3 (U.S. : v. 1)
ISBN 0-387-51732-4 (U.S. : v. 2)



Typesetting: Macmillan India Ltd, Bangalore
Offsetprinting: Color-Druck Dorfi GmbH, Berlin. Bookbinding: Lüderitz & Bauer, Berlin.
2145/3020-543210 - Printed on acid-free paper

# Preface

This work is Volume II of a two-volume monograph on the theory of deterministic parsing of context-free grammars. Volume I, "Languages and Parsing" (Chapters 1 to 5), was an introduction to the basic concepts of formal language theory and context-free parsing. Volume II (Chapters 6 to 10) contains a thorough treatment of the theory of the two most important deterministic parsing methods: LR($k$) and LL($k$) parsing. Volume II is a continuation of Volume I; together these two volumes form an integrated work, with chapters, theorems, lemmas, etc. numbered consecutively.

Volume II begins with Chapter 6 in which the classical constructions pertaining to LR($k$) parsing are presented. These include the canonical LR($k$) parser, and its reduced variants such as the LALR($k$) parser and the SLR($k$) parser. The grammar classes for which these parsers are deterministic are called LR($k$) grammars, LALR($k$) grammars and SLR($k$) grammars; properties of these grammars are also investigated in Chapter 6. A great deal of attention is paid to the rigorous development of the theory: detailed mathematical proofs are provided for most of the results presented.

Chapter 7 is devoted to the construction and implementation of LR($k$) parsers using lookahead length $k = 1$. Efficient algorithms are presented for computing parsing tables for SLR(1), canonical LR(1) and LALR(1) parsers. Special attention is paid to the optimization of LR(1) parsers. An efficient general algorithm is presented for eliminating reductions by unit rules from an LR(1) parsing table. In developing these algorithms, substantial use is made of the results of Volume I, Chapter 2, where a general algorithm for evaluating a binary relational expression was presented.

Chapter 8 deals with the theory of LL($k$) parsing. The constructions pertaining to LL($k$) parsing are developed in a way analogous to that used in LR($k$) parsing, so as to expose the dualism between these theories. For example, canonical LL($k$) parsers and LALL($k$) parsers are defined as counterparts of the canonical LR($k$) and LALR($k$) parsers. The relationship between the LL($k$) and LR($k$) grammars is studied in detail, and methods for transforming subclasses of LR($k$) grammars into LL($k$) grammars are presented.

Chapter 9 deals with the problem of syntax error handling in parsers. The nature of syntax errors is discussed, and algorithms for constructing error recovery routines for LL(1) and LR(1) parsers are presented. The treatment in this chapter is somewhat less formal than in the other chapters.

Volume II concludes with Chapter 10 that deals with the complexity of testing whether or not a given context-free grammar belongs to one of the grammar classes discussed in the previous chapters. Efficient polynomial-time algorithms are developed for LR($k$), SLR($k$), LL($k$) and SLL($k$) testing when the lookahead length $k$ is fixed. Hardness results are derived for the case in which $k$ is a parameter of the testing problems. Upper and lower bounds on the complexity of LALR($k$) and LALL($k$) testing are also established.

Jyväskylä and Helsinki, June 1990

Seppo Sippu
Eljas Soisalon-Soininen

*Acknowledgements*
The work was supported by the Academy of Finland, the Finnish Cultural Foundation, and the Ministry of Education of Finland.

# Contents

# Contents of Volume I

# 6. LR(*k*) Parsing

In this chapter we shall consider a general method for deriving deterministic right parsers for context-free grammars. The method will be called "LR(*k*) parsing". The acronym "LR(*k*)" refers to the most general deterministic parsing method in which the input string is parsed (1) in a single Left-to-right scan, (2) producing a Right parse, and (3) using lookahead of length *k*.

LR(*k*) parsers are a generalization of the nondeterministic shift-reduce parser presented in Section 5.2 and of the simple precedence parser presented in Section 5.7. The key idea in the generalization is that the stack symbols, which in the shift-reduce and simple precedence parsers are plain grammar symbols, are divided up into one or more "context-dependent" symbols. For each grammar symbol $X$ there will be as many stack symbols as there are distinct equivalence classes of the form $[\gamma X]$, where $\gamma X$ is a stack string of the shift-reduce parser. Here two stack strings $\gamma_1 X$ and $\gamma_2 X$ are called equivalent if (to put it informally) exactly the same set of parsing actions are valid in the contexts $\gamma_1 X$ and $\gamma_2 X$. In this way, replacing symbols $X$ by equivalence classes $[\gamma X]$, we can restrict the applicability of the actions of the shift-reduce parser so that a deterministic right parser is obtained for a large subclass of the context-free grammars. These grammars, called the "LR(*k*) grammars", form a powerful means of language description: any deterministic language (i.e., a language accepted by a deterministic pushdown automaton) can be generated by an LR(*k*) grammar.

In Section 6.1 we shall study the properties of the stack strings of the shift-reduce parser. The stack strings that appear in the stack in accepting computations will be called "viable prefixes". In any grammar, the viable prefixes form a regular language over the alphabet of the grammar. In Section 6.2 we shall present, for natural number *k*, an equivalence relation on the set of viable prefixes. This relation, called "LR(*k*)-equivalence", is obtained via sets of "valid *k*-items". The *k*-items are a generalization of the grammar positions used in Section 5.5 in constructing strong LL(1) parsers. The LR(*k*)-equivalence is of finite index, that is, it has only a finite number of distinct equivalence classes. Any equivalence class can be represented by a certain set of valid *k*-items. Moreover, it is possible to compute these sets from the grammar.

In Section 6.3 we shall use the concept of LR(*k*)-equivalence to define the general notion of an LR(*k*) parser, called the "canonical LR(*k*) parser". This is a right parser which uses *k*-length lookahead strings and whose stack strings consist of equivalence classes of viable prefixes. In Section 6.4 we shall study the properties of LR(*k*) grammars. In Sections 6.5 and 6.6 we shall consider some practical variations of the canonical LR($k$) parser. These variations are called "LALR($k$) parsers", "LA($k$)LR($l$) parsers", and "SLR($k$) parsers". The classes of grammars for which these parsers are deterministic are called, respectively, "LALR($k$) grammars", "LA($k$)LR($l$) grammars", and "SLR($k$) grammars". For all $k \geqslant 0$, these classes are contained in the class of LR($k$) grammars. The smallest of these classes, the class of SLR($k$) grammars, is powerful enough to generate all deterministic languages. The chapter concludes with Section 6.7, in which we shall show that any LR($k$) grammar can be transformed into an equivalent LR(1) grammar. This means that any deterministic language can in fact be generated by an SLR(1) grammar.

## 6.1 Viable Prefixes

We begin by considering the problem of constructing a deterministic right parser for the grammar $G_{ab}$:

$$S \to aA|bB \ ,$$

$$A \to c|dAd \ ,$$

$$B \to c|dBd \ .$$

$G_{ab}$ is an $s$-grammar and generates the language

$$L(G_{ab}) = \{a, b\}\{d^n c d^n | n \geqslant 0\} \ .$$

As $G_{ab}$ has two rules with the same right-hand side, it is not a simple precedence grammar, and so its simple precedence parser is nondeterministic. In fact, to any configuration of the form

$$\$\alpha c \mid y\$, \quad \text{where } \$\alpha{:}1 \in \{a, b, d\} \quad \text{and} \quad 1{:}y\$ \in \{\$, d\} \ ,$$

applies a reduce action by both $A \to c$ and $B \to c$.

We might try to make the parser deterministic by extending the lookahead and lookback symbols of the reduce actions into strings of length $k$, for some sufficiently great $k$. This would result in a parser in which the reduce actions by $A \to c$ and $B \to c$ are of the forms

$$\alpha c \mid x \to \alpha A \mid x, \qquad \beta c \mid y \to \beta B \mid y \ ,$$

where $\alpha$ and $\beta$ are certain strings in $\$V^*{:}k$ and $x$ and $y$ are certain strings in $k{:}T^*\$$. But then, in particular, there would be the pair of actions

$$d^k c \mid d^k \to d^k A \mid d^k, \qquad d^k c \mid d^k \to d^k B \mid d^k \ .$$

This is because some reduce action by $A \to c$ must be applicable to the configuration $\$ad^k c \mid d^k\$$ if the sentence $ad^k cd^k$ is to be accepted, and some reduce action by $B \rightarrow c$ must be applicable to the configuration $\$bd^kc \mid d^k\$$ if the sentence $bd^kcd^k$ is to be accepted. As the pair of actions exhibits a reduce-reduce conflict, we must conclude that it is impossible to obtain a deterministic right parser for $G_{ab}$ just by adding lookahead and lookback strings to the actions of the shift-reduce parser.

To solve the problem we take a closer look at those strings that can appear in the stack in some accepting computation of the shift-reduce parser. We call these strings *viable stack strings*. In general, a string $\gamma$ is a viable stack string of a pushdown automaton $M$ if

$$\$\gamma_s \mid w\$ \Rightarrow^* \$\gamma \mid y\$ \Rightarrow^* \$\gamma_f \mid \$ \qquad \text{in } M$$

for some input strings $w$ and $y$ and final stack contents $\gamma_f$. ($\gamma_s$ is the initial stack contents of $M$.)

Obviously, the set of viable stack strings of the shift-reduce parser for $G_{ab}$ is

$$\begin{aligned} &\{\varepsilon\} \cup \{ad^n \mid n \geq 0\} \cup \{ad^nc \mid n \geq 0\} \\ &\cup \{ad^nA \mid n \geq 0\} \cup \{ad^nAd \mid n \geq 1\} \\ &\cup \{bd^n \mid n \geq 0\} \cup \{bd^nc \mid n \geq 0\} \\ &\cup \{bd^nB \mid n \geq 0\} \cup \{bd^nBd \mid n \geq 1\} \\ &\cup \{S\} \ . \end{aligned}$$

To each stack string a number of parsing actions are applicable. However, only few of these yield a viable stack string as a result. For example, to the stack strings $ad^nc$ and $bd^nc$ a reduce action by both $A \rightarrow c$ and $B \rightarrow c$ is applicable, but among the resulting strings $ad^nA$, $bd^nB$, $ad^nB$, $bd^nA$ only the first two are viable stack strings. This means that we can resolve the reduce-reduce conflict between $A \rightarrow c$ and $B \rightarrow c$ by imposing the additional restriction that a parsing action can be applied only if it is "valid" in that it yields a viable stack string as a result.

In general, we say that an action $r$ of a pushdown automaton $M$ is *valid* for viable stack string $\gamma$ of $M$ if

$$\$\gamma \mid y\$ \overset{r}{\Rightarrow} \$\gamma' \mid y'\$ \qquad \text{in } M$$

for some input strings $y$ and $y'$ and viable stack string $\gamma'$.

As the set of viable stack strings is usually infinite, as is the case in $G_{ab}$, the reader might feel that it is impossible, in general, to find out which actions are valid for which stack strings. However, we can always divide the set of viable stack strings into a finite number of equivalence classes. Two stack strings belong to the same equivalence class if they have the same set of valid actions. Since for any grammar $G = (V, T, P, S)$ the shift-reduce parser has $|T| + |P| \leq |G|$ distinct actions, the number of distinct equivalence classes is bounded by $2^{|G|}$, the number of distinct subsets of a $|G|$-element set.

In the case of $G_{ab}$ the equivalence classes and the associated valid actions are:

| equivalence class: | valid actions: |
|---|---|
| $\{\varepsilon\}$ | shift $a$, shift $b$ |
| $\{ad^n \mid n \geqslant 0\} \cup \{bd^n \mid n \geqslant 0\}$ | shift $c$, shift $d$ |
| $\{ad^n c \mid n \geqslant 0\}$ | reduce by $A \rightarrow c$ |
| $\{aA\}$ | reduce by $S \rightarrow aA$ |
| $\{ad^n A \mid n \geqslant 1\} \cup \{bd^n B \mid n \geqslant 1\}$ | shift $d$ |
| $\{ad^n Ad \mid n \geqslant 1\}$ | reduce by $A \rightarrow dAd$ |
| $\{bd^n c \mid n \geqslant 0\}$ | reduce by $B \rightarrow c$ |
| $\{bB\}$ | reduce by $S \rightarrow bB$ |
| $\{bd^n Bd \mid n \geqslant 1\}$ | reduce by $B \rightarrow dBd$ |
| $\{S\}$ | — |

The idea is to use these equivalence classes as stack symbols of the parser. In the actions of the parser, any grammar symbol $X$ originally located to the left of the delimiter $\mid$ is replaced by an equivalence class of the form $[\delta X]$, where $\delta X$ is a viable stack string. Accordingly, for each viable stack string $\delta$ and terminal $a$ there is the shift action

(sa) $$[\delta] \mid a \rightarrow [\delta][\delta a] \mid ,$$

provided that $\delta a$ is a viable stack string. Similarly, for each stack string $\delta$ and rule $A \rightarrow X_1 \ldots X_n$, where each $X_i$ is a single symbol, $1 \leqslant i \leqslant n$, there is the reduce action

(ra) $$[\delta][\delta X_1] \ldots [\delta X_1 \ldots X_n] \mid \rightarrow [\delta][\delta A] \mid ,$$

provided that $\delta X_1, \ldots, \delta X_1 \ldots X_n$, and $\delta A$ are all viable stack strings. (In the general case, the action may also contain a lookahead string; this will be considered later.) The initial stack contents of the parser are $[\varepsilon]$, and the final stack contents are $[\varepsilon][S]$.

For example, the parser obtained in this way for $G_{ab}$ has, among others, the shift actions

$$[\varepsilon] \mid a \rightarrow [\varepsilon][ad^* \cup bd^*] \mid \quad \text{(shift } a\text{)} ,$$

$$[\varepsilon] \mid b \rightarrow [\varepsilon][ad^* \cup bd^*] \mid \quad \text{(shift } b\text{)} ,$$

and the reduce actions

$$[ad^* \cup bd^*][ad^* c] \mid \rightarrow [ad^* \cup bd^*][ad^+ A \cup bd^+ B] \mid \quad \text{(reduce by } A \rightarrow c\text{)} ,$$

$$[ad^* \cup bd^*][bd^*c] \,|\, \rightarrow [ad^* \cup bd^*][ad^+A \cup bd^+B] \,| \quad \text{(reduce by } B \rightarrow c) \ .$$

Here we have used regular expressions, rather than single members, to denote the equivalence classes. For regular expression $E$, $[E]$ means the equivalence class of any $w$ in $L(E)$, that is, $[E] = [w]$ for all $w$ in $L(E)$. Thus we have always $L(E) \subseteq [E]$. In fact we usually have $L(E) = [E]$, as is the case above. Soon we shall see that the equivalence classes are indeed regular languages, for any grammar, and can therefore always be denoted by regular expressions.

Obviously, there is no conflict between the above two reduce actions. Unfortunately, our construction has introduced some new conflicts not present in the original parser. There is a reduce-reduce conflict between two reduce actions by $A \rightarrow c$ and a reduce-reduce conflict between two reduce actions by $B \rightarrow c$. These actions (which conflict with the above two reduce actions) are:

$$[ad^* \cup bd^*][ad^*c] \,|\, \rightarrow [ad^* \cup bd^*][aA] \,| \quad \text{(reduce by } A \rightarrow c) \ ,$$

$$[ad^* \cup bd^*][bd^*c] \,|\, \rightarrow [ad^* \cup bd^*][bB] \,| \quad \text{(reduce by } B \rightarrow c) \ .$$

Note that $[aA] \neq [ad^+A \cup bd^+B] \neq [bB]$. Moreover, there is an entirely new type of conflict, a "shift-shift conflict", between the actions

$$[ad^* \cup bd^*] \,|\, c \rightarrow [ad^* \cup bd^*][ad^*c] \,| \qquad \text{(shift } c) \ ,$$

$$[ad^* \cup bd^*] \,|\, c \rightarrow [ad^* \cup bd^*][bd^*c] \,| \qquad \text{(shift } c) \ ,$$

as well as between the actions

$$[ad^+A \cup bd^+B] \,|\, d \rightarrow [ad^+A \cup bd^+B][ad^+Ad] \,| \qquad \text{(shift } d) \ ,$$

$$[ad^+A \cup bd^+B] \,|\, d \rightarrow [ad^+A \cup bd^+B][bd^+Bd] \,| \qquad \text{(shift } d) \ .$$

The reason for these new conflicts is that the division into equivalence classes is not refined enough. Consider, for example, the viable stack strings $ad^n$ and $ad^nA$, $n \geqslant 0$. For all $n \geqslant 0$, the strings $ad^n$ belong to the same equivalence class, $[ad^* \cup bd^*]$. However, the strings $ad^nA$, $n \geqslant 0$, are divided into two distinct equivalence classes: $[aA]$ and $[ad^+A \cup bd^+B]$. Similarly, $bB$ is not equivalent to $bd^nB$, $n \geqslant 1$, although all $bd^n$, $n \geqslant 0$, are equivalent. This is an anomaly, because if two stack strings $\delta_1$ and $\delta_2$ are already equivalent it is natural to assume that they remain equivalent if they are lengthened, by the same symbol $X$, to viable stack strings $\delta_1 X$ and $\delta_2 X$. In other words, the equivalence should be *right-invariant*.

Another natural requirement, closely related to right-invariance, is that two equivalent stack strings $\gamma_1$ and $\gamma_2$ should end with the same symbol, that is, $\gamma_1{:}1 = \gamma_2{:}1$. Observe that otherwise it is not clear how we can define the value of the output effect $\tau$ in the case of a reduce action

$$[\delta][\delta X_1] \ldots [\delta X_1 \ldots X_n] \,|\, \rightarrow [\delta][\delta A] \,| \ .$$

We can map this action to the rule $A \to X_1 \ldots X_n$ only if the rule is uniquely defined, that is, if there is no other rule $A' \to X'_1 \ldots X'_n$ satisfying $[\delta A'] = [\delta A]$, $[\delta X'_1] = [\delta X_1]$, ..., $[\delta X'_1 \ldots X'_n] = [\delta X_1 \ldots X_n]$. Uniqueness is clearly guaranteed if equivalent stack strings $\gamma_1$ and $\gamma_2$ always satisfy the condition $\gamma_1 : 1 = \gamma_2 : 1$.

To fulfil the above two requirements in the case of the grammar $G_{ab}$, we must refine the original equivalence as follows:

(1) The class $[ad^* \cup bd^*]$ is split into the classes $[a]$, $[ad^+]$, $[b]$, $[bd^+]$.
(2) The class $[ad^+A \cup bd^+B]$ is split into the classes $[ad^+A]$ and $[bd^+B]$.

The classes under the refined equivalence are represented in Figure 6.1 as nodes of a transition graph. The graph has an edge labeled by symbol $X$ from node $[\delta]$ to node $[\delta X]$ whenever $\delta$ and $\delta X$ are viable stack strings. The graph can be interpreted as a finite automaton, with $[\varepsilon]$ as the initial state and a given class $[\gamma]$ as the only final state. The language accepted by that automaton equals $[\gamma]$.

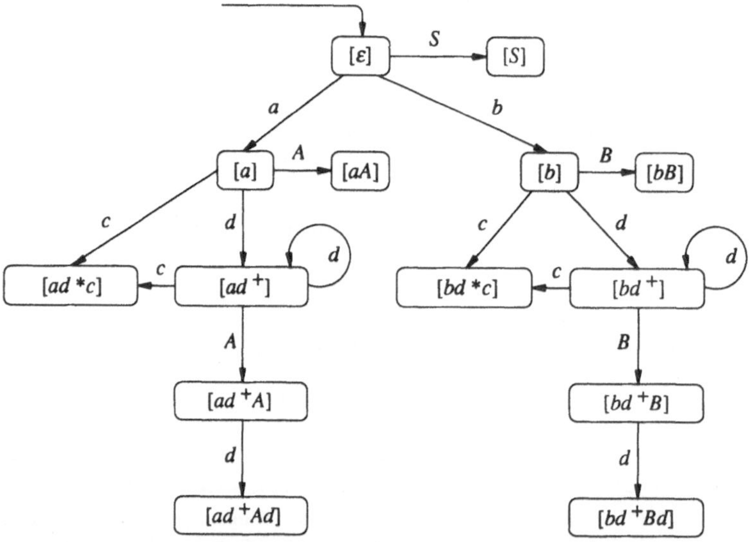


**Figure 6.1** Transition graph for the viable stack strings of the shift-reduce parser for the grammar $G_{ab}$: $S \to aA \mid bB$, $A \to c \mid dAd$, $B \to c \mid dBd$

We are now ready to write down the actions of the parser for $G_{ab}$. The shift actions are:

$$r_1 = [\varepsilon] \mid a \to [\varepsilon][a] \mid , \qquad \tau(r_1) = \varepsilon \, .$$

$$r_2 = [\varepsilon] \mid b \to [\varepsilon][b] \mid , \qquad \tau(r_2) = \varepsilon \, .$$

$$r_3 = [a] \mid c \to [a][ad^*c] \mid , \qquad \tau(r_3) = \varepsilon \, .$$

$$r_4 = [a] \mid d \rightarrow [a][ad^+] \mid , \qquad \tau(r_4) = \varepsilon \; .$$

$$r_5 = [ad^+] \mid c \rightarrow [ad^+][ad^*c] \mid , \qquad \tau(r_5) = \varepsilon \; .$$

$$r_6 = [ad^+] \mid d \rightarrow [ad^+][ad^+] \mid , \qquad \tau(r_6) = \varepsilon \; .$$

$$r_7 = [ad^+A] \mid d \rightarrow [ad^+A][ad^+Ad] \mid , \qquad \tau(r_7) = \varepsilon \; .$$

$$r_8 = [b] \mid c \rightarrow [b][bd^*c] \mid , \qquad \tau(r_8) = \varepsilon \; .$$

$$r_9 = [b] \mid d \rightarrow [b][bd^+] \mid , \qquad \tau(r_9) = \varepsilon \; .$$

$$r_{10} = [bd^+] \mid c \rightarrow [bd^+][bd^*c] \mid , \qquad \tau(r_{10}) = \varepsilon \; .$$

$$r_{11} = [bd^+] \mid d \rightarrow [bd^+][bd^+] \mid , \qquad \tau(r_{11}) = \varepsilon \; .$$

$$r_{12} = [bd^+B] \mid d \rightarrow [bd^+B][bd^+Bd] \mid , \qquad \tau(r_{12}) = \varepsilon \; .$$

The reduce actions are:

$$r_{13} = [a][ad^*c] \mid \rightarrow [a][aA] \mid , \qquad \tau(r_{13}) = A \rightarrow c \; .$$

$$r_{14} = [ad^+][ad^*c] \mid \rightarrow [ad^+][ad^+A] \mid , \qquad \tau(r_{14}) = A \rightarrow c \; .$$

$$r_{15} = [a][ad^+][ad^+A][ad^+Ad] \mid \rightarrow [a][aA] \mid ,$$
$$\tau(r_{15}) = A \rightarrow dAd \; .$$

$$r_{16} = [ad^+][ad^+][ad^+A][ad^+Ad] \mid \rightarrow [ad^+][ad^+A] \mid ,$$
$$\tau(r_{16}) = A \rightarrow dAd \; .$$

$$r_{17} = [\varepsilon][a][aA] \mid \rightarrow [\varepsilon][S] \mid , \qquad \tau(r_{17}) = S \rightarrow aA \; .$$

$$r_{18} = [b][bd^*c] \mid \rightarrow [b][bB] \mid , \qquad \tau(r_{18}) = B \rightarrow c \; .$$

$$r_{19} = [bd^+][bd^*c] \mid \rightarrow [bd^+][bd^+B] \mid , \qquad \tau(r_{19}) = B \rightarrow c \; .$$

$$r_{20} = [b][bd^+][bd^+B][bd^+Bd] \mid \rightarrow [b][bB] \mid , \qquad \tau(r_{20}) = B \rightarrow dBd \; .$$

$$r_{21} = [bd^+][bd^+][bd^+B][bd^+Bd] \mid \rightarrow [bd^+][bd^+B] \mid ,$$
$$\tau(r_{21}) = B \rightarrow dBd \; .$$

$$r_{22} = [\varepsilon][b][bB] \mid \rightarrow [\varepsilon][S] \mid , \qquad \tau(r_{22}) = S \rightarrow bB \; .$$

With these actions, the parser is deterministic. That we have indeed obtained a right parser for $G_{ab}$ is seen from the following computations.

$$\$[\varepsilon] \mid ac\$ \overset{r_1}{\Longrightarrow} \$[\varepsilon][a] \mid c\$ \overset{r_3}{\Longrightarrow} \$[\varepsilon][a][ad^*c] \mid \$$$
$$\overset{r_{13}}{\Longrightarrow} \$[\varepsilon][a][aA] \mid \$ \overset{r_{17}}{\Longrightarrow} \$[\varepsilon][S] \mid \$ \; .$$

$$\$[\varepsilon] \mid bc\$ \overset{r_2}{\Longrightarrow} \$[\varepsilon][b] \mid c\$ \overset{r_8}{\Longrightarrow} \$[\varepsilon][b][bd^*c] \mid \$$$
$$\overset{r_{18}}{\Longrightarrow} \$[\varepsilon][b][bB] \mid \$ \overset{r_{22}}{\Longrightarrow} \$[\varepsilon][S] \mid \$ \; .$$

$$\$[\varepsilon] \mid ad^n cd^n \$ \xRightarrow{r_1} \$[\varepsilon][a] \mid d^n cd^n \$ \xRightarrow{r_4} \$[\varepsilon][a][ad^+] \mid d^{n-1} cd^n \$$$

$$\xRightarrow{r_6^{n-1}} \$[\varepsilon][a][ad^+]^n \mid cd^n \$ \xRightarrow{r_5} \$[\varepsilon][a][ad^+]^n [ad^*c] \mid d^n \$$$

$$\xRightarrow{r_{14}} \$[\varepsilon][a][ad^+]^n [ad^+A] \mid d^n \$$$

$$\xRightarrow{(r_7 r_{16})^{n-1}} \$[\varepsilon][a][ad^+][ad^+A] \mid d\$$$

$$\xRightarrow{r_7} \$[\varepsilon][a][ad^+][ad^+A][ad^+Ad] \mid \$$$

$$\xRightarrow{r_{15}} \$[\varepsilon][a][aA] \mid \$ \xRightarrow{r_{17}} \$[\varepsilon][S] \mid \$, \quad \text{for all } n \geqslant 1 \ .$$

$$\$[\varepsilon] \mid bd^n cd^n \$ \xRightarrow{r_2} \$[\varepsilon][b] \mid d^n cd^n \$$$

$$\xRightarrow{r_9} \$[\varepsilon][b][bd^+] \mid d^{n-1} cd^n \$ \xRightarrow{r_{11}^{n-1}} \$[\varepsilon][b][bd^+]^n \mid cd^n \$$$

$$\xRightarrow{r_{10}} \$[\varepsilon][b][bd^+]^n [bd^*c] \mid d^n \$$$

$$\xRightarrow{r_{19}} \$[\varepsilon][b][bd^+]^n [bd^+B] \mid d^n \$$$

$$\xRightarrow{(r_{12} r_{21})^{n-1}} \$[\varepsilon][b][bd^+][bd^+B] \mid d\$$$

$$\xRightarrow{r_{12}} \$[\varepsilon][b][bd^+][bd^+B][bd^+Bd] \mid \$$$

$$\xRightarrow{r_{20}} \$[\varepsilon][b][bB] \mid \$ \xRightarrow{r_{22}} \$[\varepsilon][S] \mid \$, \quad \text{for all } n \geqslant 1 \ .$$

The parses produced are:

$$\tau(r_1 r_3 r_{13} r_{17}) = (A \to c)(S \to aA) \ .$$

$$\tau(r_2 r_8 r_{18} r_{22}) = (B \to c)(S \to bB) \ .$$

$$\tau(r_1 r_4 r_6^{n-1} r_5 r_{14} (r_7 r_{16})^{n-1} r_7 r_{15} r_{17}) = (A \to c)(A \to dAd)^n (S \to aA) \ .$$

$$\tau(r_2 r_9 r_{11}^{n-1} r_{10} r_{19} (r_{12} r_{21})^{n-1} r_{12} r_{20} r_{22}) = (B \to c)(B \to dBd)^n (S \to bB) \ .$$

The parser for $G_{ab}$ is an example of an "LR(0) parser". Here "LR" means that the input string is parsed from Left to right and that a Right parse is produced. "0" means that lookahead strings of length zero are used in the reduce actions, that is, there is no lookahead.

The procedure followed above for deriving an LR parser is more or less *ad hoc*, because of the inadequate definition of the equivalence of viable stack strings. Later in this chapter, in Section 6.2, we shall give a definition that yields the equivalence directly, and no additional refinements are needed. To this end, we give in the following a grammatical characterization for the viable stack strings of shift-reduce parsers (and prove some lemmas that will be of use in proving properties of LR parsers).

Let $G = (V, T, P, S)$ be a grammar. String $\gamma \in V^*$ is a *viable prefix* of $G$ if

$$S \underset{rm}{\Longrightarrow}^* \delta A y \underset{rm}{\Longrightarrow} \delta\alpha\beta y = \gamma\beta y$$

holds in $G$ for some strings $\delta \in V^*$ and $y \in T^*$ and rule $A \to \alpha\beta$ in $P$. $\gamma$ is a *complete viable prefix* if here $\beta = \varepsilon$.

First we note:

**Fact 6.1** Any viable prefix of grammar $G$ is a prefix of some complete viable prefix of $G$. $\square$

Most properties of viable prefixes can be derived from the following lemma.

**Lemma 6.2** *Let $G = (V, T, P, S)$ be a grammar, $\pi$ a rule string in $P^*$, $\gamma$, $\eta$, and $\delta$ strings in $V^*$, $A$ a nonterminal, and $y$ a string in $T^*$ such that*

(*a*) $$S \overset{\pi}{\underset{rm}{\Longrightarrow}} \gamma\eta y = \delta A y \quad \text{in } G, \quad \text{and} \quad \pi \neq \varepsilon\ .$$

*In other words, $\gamma$ is a prefix of some nontrivially derived right sentential form not extending over the last nonterminal. Then there are strings $\delta'$ in $V^*$ and $y'$ in $T^*$, rule strings $\pi'$ and $\pi''$ in $P^*$ and a rule $r = A' \to \alpha'\beta'$ in $P$ such that*

(*b*) $$S \overset{\pi'}{\underset{rm}{\Longrightarrow}} \delta' A' y' \overset{r}{\underset{rm}{\Longrightarrow}} \delta'\alpha'\beta' y' = \gamma\beta' y', \quad \beta' y' \overset{\pi''}{\underset{rm}{\Longrightarrow}} \eta y\ ,$$
$$\pi' r \pi'' = \pi, \quad \textit{and} \quad \alpha' : 1 = \gamma : 1\ .$$

*In other words, derivation (a) contains a segment that proves $\gamma$ to be a viable prefix, even so that the right-hand side of the rule r "cuts" $\gamma$ properly.*

*Proof.* The proof is by induction on the length of rule string $\pi$. If $|\pi| = 1$, statement (a) implies that $\pi = S \to \gamma\eta y$ is a rule in $P$. Statement (b) then holds if we choose $\delta' = y' = \varepsilon$, $\pi' = \pi'' = \varepsilon$, $r = \pi$, $\alpha' = \gamma$, and $\beta' = \eta y$. We may thus assume that $|\pi| > 1$ and, as an induction hypothesis, that the lemma holds for the rule strings shorter than $\pi$. Statement (a) then implies the existence of strings $\delta_1$ in $V^*$ and $y_1$ in $T^*$, a rule string $\pi_1$ in $P^*$, and a rule $r_1 = A_1 \to \omega_1$ such that

(1) $$S \overset{\pi_1}{\underset{rm}{\Longrightarrow}} \delta_1 A_1 y_1 \overset{r_1}{\underset{rm}{\Longrightarrow}} \delta_1\omega_1 y_1 = \gamma\eta y = \delta A y, \quad \text{and} \quad \pi_1 r_1 = \pi\ .$$

Here $y_1$ must be a suffix of $y$, that is, $y = xy_1$ for some $x$. Moreover, either $\gamma = \delta_1\alpha'$ for some $\alpha' \neq \varepsilon$ or $\delta_1 = \gamma\alpha$ for some $\alpha$. In the former case $\omega_1 = \alpha'\eta x$ and statement (b) holds if we choose $\delta' = \delta_1$, $y' = y_1$, $\pi' = \pi_1$, $\pi'' = \varepsilon$, $r = r_1$, and $\beta' = \eta x$. In the latter case, that is, when $\delta_1 = \gamma\alpha$, we may write the first derivation segment in (1) as

(2) $$S \overset{\pi_1}{\underset{rm}{\Longrightarrow}} \gamma\eta_1 y_1 = \delta_1 A_1 y_1\ ,$$

where $\eta_1$ denotes $\alpha A_1$. As here $\pi_1 \neq \varepsilon$, we can apply the induction hypothesis to $\pi_1, \gamma, \eta_1, \delta_1, A_1$, and $y_1$, and conclude that there are strings $\delta'$ in $V^*$ and $y'$ in $T^*$, rule strings $\pi'$ and $\pi_2$, and a rule $r' = A' \to \alpha'\beta'$ such that

$$S \underset{\text{rm}}{\overset{\pi'}{\Longrightarrow}} \delta'A'y' \underset{\text{rm}}{\overset{r}{\Longrightarrow}} \delta'\alpha'\beta'y' = \gamma\beta'y',\ \beta'y' \underset{\text{rm}}{\overset{\pi_2}{\Longrightarrow}} \eta_1 y_1 ,$$

(3)

$$\pi' r \pi_2 = \pi_1, \quad \text{and} \quad \alpha' :1 = \gamma :1 .$$

Here we have

(4) $$\eta_1 y_1 = \alpha A_1 y_1 \underset{\text{rm}}{\overset{r_1}{\Longrightarrow}} \alpha\omega_1 y_1 = \eta y .$$

Recall that $\delta_1 = \gamma\alpha$ and $y = xy_1$ in (1), and so $\alpha\omega_1 \doteq \eta x$. By combining (3) and (4) and choosing $\pi'' = \pi_2 r_1$ we can conclude that statement (b) holds. □

As an immediate consequence of Lemma 6.2 we have:

**Lemma 6.3** *Let $G = (V, T, P, S)$ be a grammar, $\delta$ a string in $V^*$, $y$ a string in $T^*$, and $A$ a nonterminal such that*

$$S \underset{\text{rm}}{\Longrightarrow}^{+} \delta A y \qquad \text{in } G .$$

*Then $\delta A$ is a viable prefix of $G$.*

*Proof.* Choose $\gamma = \delta A$ and $\eta = \varepsilon$ in Lemma 6.2. □

As an other application of Lemma 6.2 we prove the following important result.

**Lemma 6.4** *Any prefix of a viable prefix is a viable prefix.*

*Proof.* Let $\gamma_1$ and $\gamma_2$ be strings such that $\gamma_1\gamma_2$ is a viable prefix. We prove that $\gamma_1$ is a viable prefix. By definition,

(1) $$S \underset{\text{rm}}{\Longrightarrow}^{n} \delta A y \underset{\text{rm}}{\Longrightarrow} \delta\alpha\beta y = \gamma_1\gamma_2\beta y$$

for some $n \geq 0$, string $\delta$, terminal string $y$, and rule $A \to \alpha\beta$. Here $\delta$ is a prefix of $\gamma_1$, or $\delta \neq \varepsilon$ and $\gamma_1$ is a prefix of $\delta$. In the former case, derivation (1) proves $\gamma_1$ as a viable prefix because we may write $\alpha\beta$ as $\alpha'\beta'$, where $\delta\alpha' = \gamma_1$ and $\beta' = \gamma_2\beta$. In the latter case, we may write $\delta A y$ as $\gamma_1\eta y$ for some $\eta$. Because $\delta \neq \varepsilon$ implies $n > 0$, we can then conclude by Lemma 6.2 that $\gamma_1$ is a viable prefix. □

The following lemma states how viable prefixes rightmost derive viable prefixes.

**Lemma 6.5** *Let $G = (V, T, P, S)$ be a reduced grammar, $\gamma$ a string in $V^*$, and $A \to \alpha\beta$ a rule in $P$. If $\gamma A$ is a viable prefix of $G$, then so is $\gamma\alpha$.*

*Proof.* If

$$S \underset{rm}{\Longrightarrow}^* \delta By \underset{rm}{\Longrightarrow} \delta\alpha'\beta' y = \gamma A\beta' y \quad \text{and} \quad \beta' \Rightarrow^* x \in T^* \ ,$$

then, by Theorem 4.2,

$$S \underset{rm}{\Longrightarrow}^* \gamma Axy \underset{rm}{\Longrightarrow} \gamma\alpha\beta xy \ . \quad \square$$

**Lemma 6.6** *Let $G = (V, T, P, S)$ be a grammar and $M$ its shift-reduce parser. Further let $\gamma$ and $\eta$ be strings in $V^*$, $w$ and $y$ strings in $T^*$, and $\pi$ an action string such that*

(*a*) $$\$ \mid w\$ \stackrel{\pi}{\Longrightarrow} \$\gamma\eta \mid y\$ \quad \textit{in } M \ .$$

*Then for some action strings $\pi'$ and $\pi''$ and string $z \in T^*$*

(*b*) $$\$ \mid w\$ \stackrel{\pi'}{\Longrightarrow} \$\gamma \mid z\$ \stackrel{\pi''}{\Longrightarrow} \$\gamma\eta \mid y\$ \quad \textit{in } M, \quad \textit{and} \quad \pi'\pi'' = \pi \ .$$

*In other words, any prefix of a string appearing in the stack in a computation of M also appears in the stack in the same computation.*

*Proof.* The proof is by induction on the length of action string $\pi$. The case $\pi = \varepsilon$ is clear because then $\gamma = \eta = \varepsilon$. We may thus assume that $\pi \neq \varepsilon$ and $\eta \neq \varepsilon$. As an induction hypothesis, we assume that the lemma holds for action strings shorter than $\pi$. Derivation (a) can thus be written either as

(1) $$\$ \mid w\$ \stackrel{\pi_1}{\Longrightarrow} \$\psi \mid ay\$ \stackrel{r}{\Longrightarrow} \$\psi a \mid y\$ = \$\gamma\eta \mid y\$$$

or as

(2) $$\$ \mid w\$ \stackrel{\pi_1}{\Longrightarrow} \$\delta\omega \mid y\$ \stackrel{r}{\Longrightarrow} \$\delta A \mid y\$ = \$\gamma\eta \mid y\$ \ ,$$

depending on whether the last action in $\pi = \pi_1 r$ is a shift action or a reduce action. In case (1) $\gamma$ is a prefix of $\psi$, and in case (2) it is a prefix of $\delta$. Thus in both cases the claim follows by applying the induction hypothesis to the action string $\pi_1$. $\square$

We can now prove:

**Theorem 6.7** *Let $G = (V, T, P, S)$ be a grammar and M its shift-reduce parser. Any viable stack string of M is either S or a viable prefix of G. Conversely, any viable prefix of G is a viable stack string of M, provided that G is reduced.*

*Proof.* To prove the first part of the theorem, let $\gamma \neq S$ be a viable stack string of $M$. By definition, we have

(1) $$\$ \mid w\$ \Rightarrow^* \$\gamma \mid z\$ \stackrel{\pi}{\Longrightarrow} \$S \mid \$ \quad \text{in } M$$

for some $w$, $z$ in $T^*$ and $\pi$ in $P^*$. Since $\gamma \neq S$, $\pi$ must contain at least one reduce action. Let $r$ be the first reduce action in $\pi$. Then we can write (1) as

$$(2)\quad \begin{aligned} &\$ \mid w\$ \Rightarrow^* \$\gamma \mid z\$ = \$\gamma \mid xy\$ \xRightarrow{\pi_1} \$\gamma x \mid y\$ \\ &= \$\delta\omega \mid y\$ \xRightarrow{r} \$\delta A \mid y\$ \xRightarrow{\pi_2} \$S \mid \$ \ , \end{aligned}$$

where $\pi_1$ is an $|x|$-length string of shift actions and $\pi_1 r \pi_2 = \pi$. Lemma 5.17 now implies:

$$(3)\qquad S \underset{\text{rm}}{\Longrightarrow}^* \delta A y \ .$$

As $A \to \omega$ is a rule of $G$ and $\gamma x = \delta\omega$ we have

$$(4)\qquad S \underset{\text{rm}}{\Longrightarrow}^* \delta A y \underset{\text{rm}}{\Longrightarrow} \delta\omega y = \gamma x y \ ,$$

which means that $\gamma x$ is a viable prefix. By Lemma 6.4 so is its prefix $\gamma$.

To prove the second part of the theorem we note that by Fact 6.1 and Lemma 6.6 it suffices to prove that any complete viable prefix of $G$ is a viable stack string of $M$. Let therefore

$$(5)\qquad S \underset{\text{rm}}{\Longrightarrow}^* \delta A y \underset{\text{rm}}{\Longrightarrow} \delta\omega y = \gamma y \ ,$$

for some strings $\delta$ and $\gamma$ in $V^*$ and $y$ in $T^*$ and rule $A \to \omega$ in $P$. By Lemma 5.19

$$(6)\qquad \$\delta A \mid y\$ \Rightarrow^* \$S \mid \$ \ .$$

As $M$ has a reduce action by $A \to \omega$, we have:

$$(7)\qquad \$\delta\omega \mid y\$ \Rightarrow \$\delta A \mid y\$ \ .$$

If $G$ is reduced, here $\delta\omega$ derives some string $x$ in $T^*$. By Theorem 4.2, $\delta\omega$ rightmost derives $x$. By Lemma 5.19,

$$(8)\qquad \$ \mid xy\$ \Rightarrow^* \$\delta\omega \mid y\$ \ .$$

Combining (8), (7), and (6) we can conclude that $\gamma = \delta\omega$ is a viable stack string of $M$. □

We conclude this section by showing that for any grammar $G = (V, T, P, S)$ the set of all viable prefixes is a regular language over $V$. We do this by giving a right-linear grammar that generates the viable prefixes. Later we shall obtain (as a byproduct) another proof of the result, via finite automata.

Given a grammar $G = (V, T, P, S)$, let $G_{VP}$ denote the grammar $(V_{VP}, V, P_{VP}, [S])$, where

$$V_{VP} = \{[A] \mid A \text{ is a nonterminal in } V \setminus T\} \ ,$$

$$\begin{aligned} P_{VP} = {} & \{[A] \to \alpha \mid A \to \alpha\beta \text{ is a rule in } P\} \\ & \cup \{[A] \to \alpha[B] \mid A \to \alpha B\beta \text{ is a rule in } P,\ B \text{ is a nonterminal} \\ & \text{in } V \setminus T, \text{ and } \beta \text{ derives some string in } T^*\} \ . \end{aligned}$$

Here $[A]$, for nonterminal $A$ in $V \setminus T$, denotes a new symbol not found in $V$. The condition "$\beta$ derives some string in $T^*$" will be of importance if $G$ is not reduced.

For example, the grammar $(G_{ab})_{VP}$ for our grammar $G_{ab}$ is:

$$[S] \to \varepsilon|a|aA|b|bB|a[A]|b[B] \ ,$$

$$[A] \to \varepsilon|c|d|dA|dAd|d[A] \ ,$$

$$[B] \to \varepsilon|c|d|dB|dBd|d[B] \ .$$

**Lemma 6.8** *Let $G = (V, T, P, S)$ be a grammar. Further let*

$$S \underset{rm}{\Longrightarrow}^n \delta A y \qquad \text{in } G$$

*for some natural number $n$, string $\delta \in V^*$, nonterminal $A$ and string $y \in T^*$. Then*

$$[S] \Rightarrow^* \delta[A] \qquad \text{in } G_{VP} \ .$$

*Proof.* The proof is by induction on $n$. The case $n = 0$ is clear because then $A = S$ and $\delta = y = \varepsilon$. We can therefore assume that $n > 0$ and, as an induction hypothesis, that the lemma holds for all natural numbers $m < n$. Then, by Lemma 6.2,

$$S \underset{rm}{\Longrightarrow}^m \delta' A' y' \underset{rm}{\Longrightarrow} \delta' \alpha A \beta' y' = \delta A \beta' y'$$

for some $m < n$, $\delta'$ in $V^*$, $y'$ in $T^*$, and $A' \to \alpha A \beta'$ in $P$. By the induction hypothesis we have:

$$[S] \Rightarrow^* \delta'[A'] \qquad \text{in } G_{VP} \ .$$

By definition, $G_{VP}$ has the rule $[A'] \to \alpha[A]$. Thus,

$$[S] \Rightarrow^* \delta'[A'] \Rightarrow \delta'\alpha[A] = \delta[A] \ ,$$

as desired. □

**Lemma 6.9** *Let $G = (V, T, P, S)$ be a grammar. Further let*

$$[S] \Rightarrow^n \delta[A] \qquad \text{in } G_{VP}$$

*for some natural number $n$, string $\delta \in V^*$, and nonterminal $A \in V \setminus T$. Then*

$$S \underset{rm}{\Longrightarrow}^* \delta A y \qquad \text{in } G$$

*for some string $y \in T^*$.*

*Proof.* The proof is by induction on $n$. The case $n = 0$ is clear because then $A = S$ and $\delta = \varepsilon$. We can therefore assume that $n > 0$ and, as an induction hypothesis, that the lemma holds for $n - 1$. Then

$$[S] \Rightarrow^{n-1} \delta_1[A_1] \Rightarrow \delta_1\alpha[A] = \delta[A] \qquad \text{in } G_{VP}$$

for some strings $\delta_1$ and $\alpha$ in $V^*$ and nonterminal $A_1$ in $V$. By the induction hypothesis we have:

$$S \underset{rm}{\Longrightarrow}^* \delta_1 A_1 y_1$$

for some $y_1$ in $T^*$. As $[A_1] \rightarrow \alpha[A]$ is a rule of $G_{VP}$, $G$ must have a rule $A_1 \rightarrow \alpha A \beta$, where $\beta$ derives some $v$ in $T^*$. By Theorem 4.2, $\beta$ rightmost derives $v$, and we have:

$$S \underset{rm}{\Longrightarrow}^* \delta_1 A_1 y_1 \underset{rm}{\Longrightarrow} \delta_1 \alpha A \beta y_1 \underset{rm}{\Longrightarrow}^* \delta_1 \alpha A v y_1 = \delta A y \ ,$$

where $y$ denotes $vy_1$. □

**Theorem 6.10** *Any grammar G can be transformed into a right-linear grammar that generates the set of all viable prefixes of G.*

*Proof.* By Theorem 4.14 and Lemma 4.15, $G$ can be transformed into $G_{VP}$. Now if

(1) $$S \underset{rm}{\Longrightarrow}^* \delta A y \underset{rm}{\Longrightarrow} \delta \alpha \beta y = \gamma \beta y \qquad \text{in } G \ ,$$

then, by Lemma 6.8,

(2) $$[S] \Rightarrow^* \delta[A] \Rightarrow \delta\alpha = \gamma \qquad \text{in } G_{VP} \ .$$

Note that $[A] \rightarrow \alpha$ is a rule of $G_{VP}$. Conversely, if $[S]$ derives in $G_{VP}$ a string $\gamma$ in $V^*$, then (2) holds for some $\delta$ in $V^*$ and $A \rightarrow \alpha\beta$ in $P$. But then, by Lemma 6.9, (1) holds for some $y$. Thus $L(G_{VP})$ is the set of viable prefixes of $G$. □

By Theorems 3.24 and 6.10 we have:

**Theorem 6.11** *For any grammar $G = (V, T, P, S)$, the set of all viable prefixes of G is a regular language over V.* □

## 6.2 LR(k)-Valid Items

Let $G = (V, T, P, S)$ be a grammar. We recall from Section 5.5 that a *position* of $G$ is a dotted rule of the form $A \rightarrow \alpha \cdot \beta$, where $A \rightarrow \alpha\beta$ is a rule in $P$ and the dot is a symbol not found in $V$. A pair of the form

$$[A \rightarrow \alpha \cdot \beta, \ y]$$

is a *k-item* for $k \geqslant 0$, if $A \rightarrow \alpha \cdot \beta$ is a position of $G$ and $y$ is a string in $k\!:\!T^*$. The position $A \rightarrow \alpha \cdot \beta$ is called the *core* of the item, and the string $y$ its *lookahead string*. 0-items, that is, items of the form $[A \rightarrow \alpha \cdot \beta, \varepsilon]$, are often abbreviated to $[A \rightarrow \alpha \cdot \beta]$.

An item $[A \to \alpha \cdot \beta, y]$ is *LR(k)-valid* (or *valid*, for short) for string $\gamma \in V^*$ if

$$S \underset{rm}{\Longrightarrow}^* \delta A z \underset{rm}{\Longrightarrow} \delta\alpha\beta z = \gamma\beta z \quad \text{and} \quad k:z = y$$

hold in $G$ for some strings $\delta \in V^*$ and $z \in T^*$.

First we note:

**Fact 6.12** If $[A \to \alpha \cdot \beta, y]$ is an LR($k$)-valid item for string $\gamma$, then $\gamma$ is a viable prefix, $[A \to \alpha \cdot \beta, y]$ is a $k$-item, $\alpha$ is a suffix of $\gamma$, and $y$ belongs to $\text{FOLLOW}_k(A)$ and to $\text{FOLLOW}_k(\gamma\beta)$. Conversely, if $\gamma$ is a viable prefix, then some item is LR($k$)-valid for $\gamma$. □

As an example, consider the grammar $G_{ab}$ given in the previous section. ($G_{ab}$ has the rules $S \to aA|bB$, $A \to c|dAd$, $B \to c|dBd$.)

The items $[S \to \cdot aA, \varepsilon]$ and $[S \to \cdot bB, \varepsilon]$ are LR($k$)-valid for the empty string $\varepsilon$, for any $k \geq 0$, because

$$S \underset{rm}{\Longrightarrow}^0 S \underset{rm}{\Longrightarrow} aA \ ,$$

$$S \underset{rm}{\Longrightarrow}^0 S \underset{rm}{\Longrightarrow} bB \ ,$$

and $k:\varepsilon = \varepsilon$. The former derivation also shows that $[S \to a \cdot A, \varepsilon]$ is LR($k$)-valid for $a$ and that $[S \to aA \cdot, \varepsilon]$ is LR($k$)-valid for $aA$. Similarly, the latter derivation shows that $[S \to b \cdot B, \varepsilon]$ is LR($k$)-valid for $b$ and that $[S \to bB \cdot, \varepsilon]$ is LR($k$)-valid for $bB$.

Let $k, n \geq 0$ and $m = \min\{k, n\}$. Then $[A \to \cdot c, d^m]$ and $[A \to \cdot dAd, d^m]$ are LR($k$)-valid for $ad^n$, because

$$S \underset{rm}{\Longrightarrow}^{n+1} ad^nAd^n \underset{rm}{\Longrightarrow} ad^ncd^n \ ,$$

$$S \underset{rm}{\Longrightarrow}^{n+1} ad^nAd^n \underset{rm}{\Longrightarrow} ad^ndAdd^n \ .$$

The former derivation also shows that $[A \to c \cdot, d^m]$ is LR($k$)-valid for $ad^nc$, and the latter that $[A \to d \cdot Ad, d^m]$ is LR($k$)-valid for $ad^{n+1}$, $[A \to dA \cdot d, d^m]$ LR($k$)-valid for $ad^{n+1}A$, and $[A \to dAd \cdot, d^m]$ LR($k$)-valid for $ad^{n+1}Ad$. Similarly, the derivations

$$S \underset{rm}{\Longrightarrow}^{n+1} bd^nBd^n \underset{rm}{\Longrightarrow} bd^ncd^n \ ,$$

$$S \underset{rm}{\Longrightarrow}^{n+1} bd^nBd^n \underset{rm}{\Longrightarrow} bd^ndBdd^n$$

show that $[B \to \cdot c, d^m]$ and $[B \to \cdot dBd, d^m]$ are LR($k$)-valid for $bd^n$, $[B \to c \cdot, d^m]$ LR($k$)-valid for $bd^nc$, $[B \to d \cdot Bd, d^m]$ LR($k$)-valid for $bd^{n+1}$, $[B \to dB \cdot d, d^m]$ LR($k$)-valid for $bd^{n+1}B$, and $[B \to dBd \cdot, d^m]$ LR($k$)-valid for $bd^{n+1}Bd$.

If $G = (V, T, P, S)$ is a grammar and $\gamma$ a string in $V^*$, we denote for all $k \geq 0$:

$$\text{VALID}^G_{\text{LR}(k)}(\gamma) = \{I \mid I \text{ is an LR}(k)\text{-valid item for } \gamma\} \ .$$

If $G$ is understood, we may write $\text{VALID}_{\text{LR}(k)}$ or $\text{VALID}_k$. (Note however that later, in Chapter 8, we shall also consider LL($k$)-valid items.) If $k$ is understood, we may even write VALID.

In $G_{ab}$ we have, for all $k, n \geq 0$:

$$\text{VALID}_k(\varepsilon) = \{[S \to \cdot aA, \varepsilon], [S \to \cdot bB, \varepsilon]\} .$$

$$\text{VALID}_k(a) = \{[S \to a \cdot A, \varepsilon], [A \to \cdot c, \varepsilon], [A \to \cdot dAd, \varepsilon]\} .$$

$$\text{VALID}_k(ad^{n+1}) = \{[A \to d \cdot Ad, k{:}d^n], [A \to \cdot c, k{:}d^{n+1}], [A \to \cdot dAd, k{:}d^{n+1}]\} .$$

$$\text{VALID}_k(ad^n c) = \{[A \to c \cdot, k{:}d^n]\} .$$

$$\text{VALID}_k(aA) = \{[S \to aA \cdot, \varepsilon]\} .$$

$$\text{VALID}_k(ad^{n+1}A) = \{[A \to dA \cdot d, k{:}d^n]\} .$$

$$\text{VALID}_k(ad^{n+1}Ad) = \{[A \to dAd \cdot, k{:}d^n]\} .$$

$$\text{VALID}_k(b) = \{[S \to b \cdot B, \varepsilon], [B \to \cdot c, \varepsilon], [B \to \cdot dBd, \varepsilon]\} .$$

$$\text{VALID}_k(bd^{n+1}) = \{[B \to d \cdot Bd, k{:}d^n], [B \to \cdot c, k{:}d^{n+1}], [B \to \cdot dBd, k{:}d^{n+1}]\} .$$

$$\text{VALID}_k(bd^n c) = \{[B \to c \cdot, k{:}d^n]\} .$$

$$\text{VALID}_k(bB) = \{[S \to bB \cdot, \varepsilon]\} .$$

$$\text{VALID}_k(bd^{n+1}B) = \{[B \to dB \cdot d, k{:}d^n]\} .$$

$$\text{VALID}_k(bd^{n+1}Bd) = \{[B \to dBd \cdot, k{:}d^n]\} .$$

$$\text{VALID}_k(\gamma) = \varnothing, \text{ for all other strings } \gamma \text{ in } \{S, A, B, a, b, c, d\}^* .$$

String $\gamma_1$ is *LR(k)-equivalent* (or *equivalent*, for short) to string $\gamma_2$, written

$$\gamma_1 \rho_{\mathrm{LR}(k)} \gamma_2 \qquad (\text{or } \gamma_1 \rho_k \gamma_2, \text{ for short}) ,$$

if

$$\text{VALID}_k(\gamma_1) = \text{VALID}_k(\gamma_2) .$$

In other words, exactly those items are valid for $\gamma_2$ that are valid for $\gamma_1$. The relation $\rho_k$ is called the *LR(k)-equivalence* for $G$.

**Theorem 6.13** *For any grammar $G = (V, T, P, S)$ and natural number $k$, the LR($k$)-equivalence $\rho_k$ for $G$ is an equivalence relation on $V^*$. Moreover, $\rho_k$ is of finite index, that is, there are only a finite number of distinct equivalence classes under $\rho_k$. More specifically, the index of $\rho_k$ is at most*

$$2^{|G| \cdot (|T|+1)^k} .$$

*One of the equivalence classes under $\rho_k$ is $\{\gamma \in V^* \mid \gamma$ is not a viable prefix of $G\}$, whenever this set is nonempty.*

*Proof.* That $\rho_k$ is an equivalence relation follows immediately from the fact that it is defined by means of another equivalence relation, the identity relation on the collection of all sets of $k$-items. As $[\gamma_1]_{\rho_k} = [\gamma_2]_{\rho_k}$ if and only if VALID$(\gamma_1)$ = VALID$(\gamma_2)$, there is a bijective correspondence between equivalence classes $[\gamma]_{\rho_k}$ and $k$-item sets VALID$_k(\gamma)$. This means that the index of $\rho_k$ is the same as the number of distinct sets VALID$_k(\gamma)$. Now the number of distinct $k$-items is at most $|G|\,(|T|+1)^k$, because there are at most $|G|$ distinct item cores in $G$ and

$$|T|^k + |T|^{k-1} + \ldots + |T| + 1 \leqslant (|T|+1)^k$$

distinct strings in $k\colon T^*$. Thus, the number of distinct $k$-item sets is bounded by

$$2^{|G|\,(|T|+1)^k} .$$

By Fact 6.12, a string $\gamma$ in $V^*$ is a viable prefix of $G$ if and only if VALID$(\gamma) \neq \emptyset$. Thus, the set of all those strings in $V^*$ that are not viable prefixes of $G$ forms a single equivalence class under $\rho_k$, provided that this set is nonempty. □

For brevity, we denote $[\gamma]_{\rho_k}$ by $[\gamma]_k$ (or even $[\gamma]$, if $k$ is understood).

From the sets VALID$_k(\gamma)$ we see that in $G_{ab}$ the LR($k$)-equivalence classes of the viable prefixes $\varepsilon$, $a$, $aA$, $b$, and $bB$ are all singleton sets, containing only the viable prefix in question, independently of $k$. The viable prefixes $ad^{n+1}$, $n \geqslant 0$, in turn are all LR(0)-equivalent because VALID$_0(ad^{m+1})$ = VALID$_0(ad^{n+1})$ for all $m, n \geqslant 0$. We denote the joint LR(0)-equivalence class of $ad^{n+1}$, $n \geqslant 0$, by $[ad^+]_0$. In general, $ad^{m+1}$ and $ad^{n+1}$ are LR($k$)-equivalent whenever $m \geqslant k$ and $n \geqslant k$ because VALID$_k(ad^{m+1})$ = VALID$_k(ad^{n+1})$ whenever $m \geqslant k$ and $n \geqslant k$. We can thus conclude that $[ad^+]_0$ is the following disjoint union of LR($k$)-equivalence classes:

$$[ad^+]_0 = [ad]_k \cup \ldots \cup [ad^{k+1}d^*]_k .$$

Similarly, we conclude that the viable prefixes $ad^nc$, $ad^{n+1}A$, $ad^{n+1}Ad$, $bd^{n+1}$, $bd^nc$, $bd^{n+1}B$, and $bd^{n+1}Bd$ are divided into LR($k$)-equivalence classes as follows:

$$[ad^*c]_0 = [ac]_k \cup [adc]_k \cup \ldots \cup [ad^kd^*c]_k .$$

$$[ad^+A]_0 = [adA]_k \cup \ldots \cup [ad^{k+1}d^*A]_k .$$

$$[ad^+Ad]_0 = [adAd]_k \cup \ldots \cup [ad^{k+1}d^*Ad]_k .$$

$$[bd^+]_0 = [bd]_k \cup \ldots \cup [bd^{k+1}d^*]_k .$$

$$[bd^*c]_0 = [bc]_k \cup [bdc]_k \cup \ldots \cup [bd^kd^*c]_k .$$

$$[bd^+B]_0 = [bdB]_k \cup \ldots \cup [bd^{k+1}d^*B]_k .$$

$$[bd^+Bd]_0 = [bdBd]_k \cup \ldots \cup [bd^{k+1}d^*Bd]_k .$$

In particular, we can conclude that the LR(0)-equivalence for $G_{ab}$ is exactly the equivalence relation constructed in Section 6.1 and depicted in Figure 6.1.

From the above we also see that in $G_{ab}$ the LR($k+1$)-equivalence is a refinement of the LR($k$)-equivalence. Observe that in $G_{ab}$ each LR($k$)-equivalence class is either a single LR$(k+1)$-equivalence class or the union of two equivalence classes. For example, the LR$(k)$-equivalence class $[ad^{k+1}d^*]_k$ is the union of the LR$(k+1)$-equivalence classes $[ad^{k+1}]_{k+1}$ and $[ad^{k+2}d^*]_{k+1}$.

**Lemma 6.14** *Let $G = (V, T, P, S)$ be a grammar, $\gamma$ a string in $V^*$, and $k$, $l$ natural numbers such that $k \leqslant l$. Then*

$$\text{VALID}_k(\gamma) = \{[A \to \alpha \cdot \beta,\ k{:}y] \mid [A \to \alpha \cdot \beta,\ y] \in \text{VALID}_l(\gamma)\} \ .$$

*In other words, the set of LR$(k)$-valid items for $\gamma$ is obtained from the set of LR$(l)$-valid items for $\gamma$ by truncating the lookahead strings to length $k$.*

*Proof.* If $[A \to \alpha \cdot \beta, y]$ is an item in $\text{VALID}_l(\gamma)$, then

$$S \underset{\text{rm}}{\Longrightarrow}{}^* \delta A z \underset{\text{rm}}{\Longrightarrow} \delta\alpha\beta z = \gamma\beta z \quad \text{and} \quad l{:}z = y$$

for some strings $\delta \in V^*$ and $z \in T^*$. Then $[A \to \alpha \cdot \beta, k{:}z]$ is an item in $\text{VALID}_k(\gamma)$. Here $k{:}z = k{:}y$ since $k \leqslant l$. Conversely, if $[A \to \alpha \cdot \beta, y']$ is an item in $\text{VALID}_k(\gamma)$, then

$$S \underset{\text{rm}}{\Longrightarrow}{}^* \delta A z \underset{\text{rm}}{\Longrightarrow} \delta\alpha\beta z = \gamma\beta z \quad \text{and} \quad k{:}z = y'$$

for some strings $\delta \in V^*$ and $z \in T^*$. Then $[A \to \alpha \cdot \beta, l{:}z]$ is an item in $\text{VALID}_l(\gamma)$. Here $k{:}(l{:}z) = y'$ since $k \leqslant l$. □

**Theorem 6.15** *For any grammar $G = (V, T, P, S)$ and natural numbers $k$, $l$, $k \leqslant l$, LR$(l)$-equivalence is a refinement of LR$(k)$-equivalence. That is, each LR$(k)$-equivalence class is the union of some LR$(l)$-equivalence classes. More specifically, each LR$(k)$-equivalence class $[\gamma]_k$ is the union of all LR$(l)$-equivalence classes $[\delta]_l$ satisfying*

$$(a) \qquad \text{VALID}_k(\gamma) = \{[A \to \alpha \cdot \beta,\ k{:}y] \mid [A \to \alpha \cdot \beta,\ y] \in \text{VALID}_l(\delta)\} \ ,$$

*that is, the set of LR$(k)$-valid items for $\gamma$ is obtained from the set of LR$(l)$-valid items for $\delta$ by truncating the lookahead strings to length $k$.*

*Proof.* To show that each LR$(k)$-equivalence class $[\gamma]_k$ is contained in the union of all LR$(l)$-equivalence classes $[\delta]_l$ that satisfy statement (a), let $\delta$ be a string in $[\gamma]_k$. Then $\delta$ is in $[\delta]_l$ and $\text{VALID}_k(\gamma) = \text{VALID}_k(\delta)$. On the other hand we have, by Lemma 6.14,

$$\text{VALID}_k(\delta) = \{[A \to \alpha \cdot \beta,\ k{:}y] \mid [A \to \alpha \cdot \beta,\ y] \in \text{VALID}_l(\delta)\} \ .$$

Thus, statement (a) is true for $\gamma$ and $\delta$.

To show that, conversely, any LR$(l)$-equivalence class $[\delta]_l$ that satisfies (a) is contained in $[\gamma]_k$, let $\delta$ be a string in $V^*$ such that (a) is true and let $\delta'$ be a string in $[\delta]_l$. Then $\text{VALID}_l(\delta') = \text{VALID}_l(\delta)$ and (a) is true for $\gamma$ and $\delta$. On the other hand we have, by Lemma 6.14,

$$\text{VALID}_k(\delta') = \{[A \to \alpha\cdot\beta,\ k{:}y] \mid [A \to \alpha\cdot\beta,\ y] \in \text{VALID}_l(\delta')\}\ .$$

Thus, $\text{VALID}_k(\delta') = \text{VALID}_k(\gamma)$, which means that $\delta'$ is in $[\gamma]_k$. □

For any grammar $G = (V, T, P, S)$, the LR$(k)$-equivalence classes $[\gamma]_k$ are in a bijective correspondence with the $k$-item sets $\text{VALID}_k(\gamma)$. Hence each set $\text{VALID}_k(\gamma)$ can be regarded as a finite representation of the corresponding class $[\gamma]_k$. The collection of all sets $\text{VALID}_k(\gamma)$, $\gamma \in V^*$, can further be regarded as a finite representation of the entire LR$(k)$-equivalence. We call this collection the *canonical collection of sets of LR(k)-valid items* for $G$, or the *canonical LR(k) collection* for $G$, for short.

The canonical LR$(k)$ collection can be viewed as a finite automaton in the same way as was done in Section 6.1, where we represented the collection of equivalence classes $[\gamma]$, $\gamma \in V^*$, for $G_{ab}$ as a transition graph. The automaton is called the *canonical LR(k) machine* (or the *deterministic LR(k) machine*) for the grammar $G$. The state alphabet is the canonical LR$(k)$ collection, the input alphabet is $V$, the initial state is $\text{VALID}_k(\varepsilon)$, and the set of transitions consists of all rules of the form

$$\text{VALID}_k(\gamma)\, X \to \text{VALID}_k(\gamma X)\ ,$$

where $\gamma$ is a string in $V^*$ and $X$ is a symbol in $V$. The set of final states is usually not relevant and is therefore not fixed in the definition. We shall mostly be concerned with other properties of the machine rather than viewing it as an accepting device.

The canonical LR(0) machine is called the *LR(0) machine*, for short. In Figure 6.2 we have depicted the LR(0) machine for $G_{ab}$, using the conventional transition graph representation. We have left out the empty state $\varnothing$ and all transitions to and from it. To point out the equivalence with the transition graph of Figure 6.1 in Section 6.1, we have labeled each state $\text{VALID}_k(\gamma)$ with $[E]$, where $E$ is a regular expression denoting the LR(0)-equivalence class $[\gamma]_0$. In Figure 6.3 we have similarly depicted the canonical LR(1) machine for $G_{ab}$. Observe how several states in the LR(0) machine are "split" into two states in the canonical LR(1) machine (cf. Theorem 6.15).

We have yet to prove that the LR$(k)$-equivalence satisfies the two additional requirements imposed in Section 6.1. That is, the equivalence is right-invariant and any two equivalent viable prefixes always end with the same symbol. In proving this we shall make use of the structure of the canonical LR(1) machine. In fact we shall present an algorithm for constructing the machine from the grammar. This algorithm will then imply the desired properties of the LR$(k)$-equivalence.

Obviously, for any grammar $G$ and natural number $k$, the canonical LR$(k)$ machine is an $\varepsilon$-free, normal-form, and completely specified finite automaton. We shall show that it is deterministic and that it *induces* the LR$(k)$-equivalence, that is, strings $\gamma_1$ and $\gamma_2$ are LR$(k)$-equivalent if and only if the state accessible upon reading $\gamma_1$ coincides with the state accessible upon reading $\gamma_2$. (For equivalences induced by finite automata, see the exercises in Chapter 3.) This will readily imply the right-invariance of the LR$(k)$-equivalence. We shall also show that every

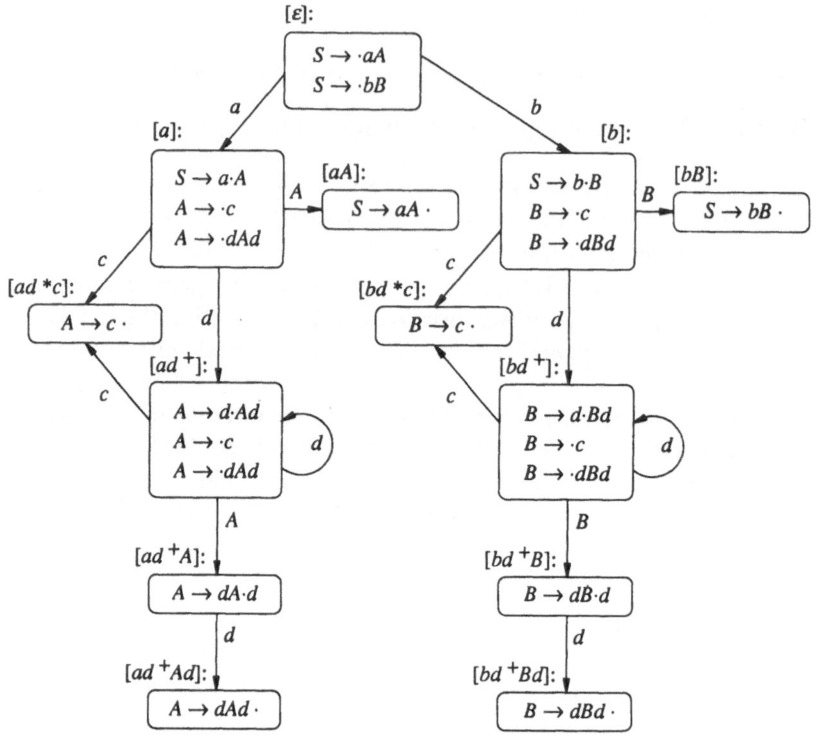


**Figure 6.2** The LR(0)-machine for the grammar $G_{ab}$: $S \to aA \mid bB$, $A \to c \mid dAd$, $B \to c \mid dBd$

nonempty state $\text{VALID}_k(\gamma)$ has a *unique entry symbol*, that is, a symbol $X$ such that all transitions to $\text{VALID}_k(\gamma)$ are on $X$. This will imply that any two LR($k$)-equivalent viable prefixes always end with the same symbol.

We begin by taking a closer look at Figures 6.2 and 6.3 and consider how an item set $\text{VALID}(\gamma)$ is composed. We observe that if $\text{VALID}(\gamma)$ contains an item of the form $[A \to \alpha \cdot B\beta, y]$, where $B$ is a nonterminal, then it also contains all items $[B \to \cdot\, \omega, z]$, where $B \to \omega$ is a rule of the grammar and $z$ is a string in $\text{FIRST}_k(\beta y)$. Conversely, each item of the form $[B \to \cdot\, \omega, z]$ in $\text{VALID}(\gamma)$, where $\gamma \neq \varepsilon$, $B \neq S$, or $z \neq \varepsilon$, is obtained in this way from some item of the form $[A \to \alpha \cdot B\beta, y]$ in $\text{VALID}(\gamma)$.

Let $G = (V, T, P, S)$ be a grammar and $k$ a natural number. We say that item $[B \to \cdot\, \omega, z]$ of $G$ is an *immediate LR($k$)-descendant* of $k$-item $[A \to \alpha \cdot B\beta, y]$ of $G$, written

$$[A \to \alpha \cdot B\beta, y]\ \mathbf{desc}_{\text{LR}(k)}\, [B \to \cdot\, \omega, z]\ ,$$

if $z$ is in $\text{FIRST}_k(\beta y)$. An item is an *LR($k$)-descendant* of $k$-item $I$ if it belongs to $\mathbf{desc}^*_{\text{LR}(k)}(I)$. Item $I_1$ is an (*immediate*) *LR($k$)-ancestor* of item $I_2$ if $I_2$ is an (immediate) LR($k$)-descendant of $I_1$.

For brevity, we often write the relation $\mathbf{desc}_{\text{LR}(k)}$ as $\mathbf{desc}_k$ (or even $\mathbf{desc}$, if $k$ is understood).

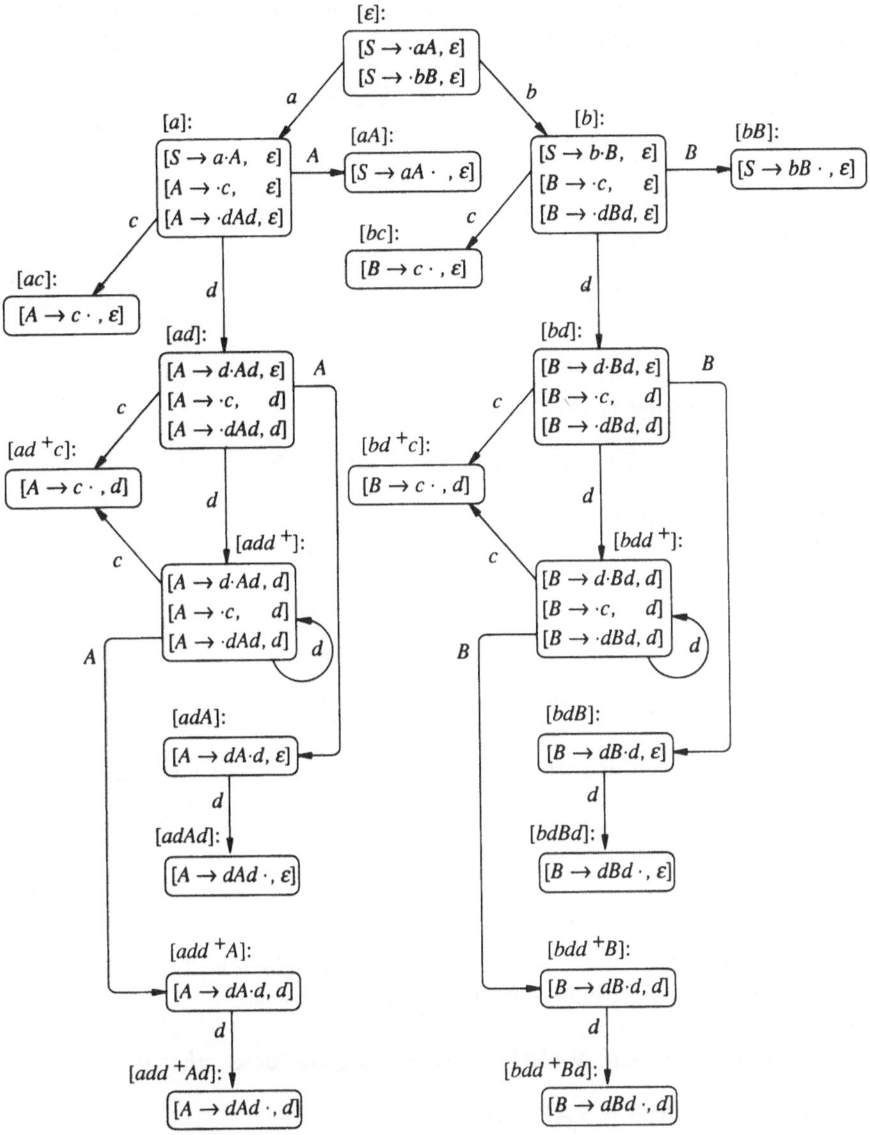


**Figure 6.3** The canonical LR(1) machine for $G_{ab}$

Later (in Chapter 10) we shall see that for any $k \geqslant 0$ the relation $\mathbf{desc}_k$ can be computed from the grammar. For $k = 0$ the computation is trivial (once the useless nonterminals have been found). For $k = 1$ the relation can be computed via a simple relational expression (see the exercises).

In the proofs that follow we often use induction on the initial derivation segment $S \underset{\text{rm}}{\Longrightarrow}^* \delta A z$ in the definition of LR($k$)-validity. Therefore it is convenient to define explicitly, for each $n \geq 0$, a set denoted by $\mathrm{VALID}_{k,n}(\gamma)$ consisting of those items $[A \rightarrow \alpha \cdot \beta, y]$ for which

$$S \underset{\mathrm{rm}}{\Longrightarrow}^n \delta A z \underset{\mathrm{rm}}{\Longrightarrow} \delta\alpha\beta z = \gamma\beta z \quad \text{and} \quad k{:}z = y$$

for some $\delta \in V^*$ and $z \in T^*$.

**Fact 6.16** For all $k \geq 0$ and $\gamma \in V^*$,

$$\mathrm{VALID}_k(\gamma) = \bigcup_{n=0}^{\infty} \mathrm{VALID}_{k,n}(\gamma) \ .$$

□

**Lemma 6.17** *If in grammar* $G = (V, T, P, S)$

$$[A \rightarrow \alpha \cdot B\beta, y] \in \mathrm{VALID}_{k,n}(\gamma) \quad \textit{and} \quad \beta \Rightarrow^m v \in T^* \ ,$$

*then for all rules* $B \rightarrow \omega$ *in* $P$

$$[B \rightarrow \cdot\,\omega, k{:}vy] \in \mathrm{VALID}_{k,n+m+1}(\gamma) \ .$$

*Proof.* By definition,

$$S \underset{\mathrm{rm}}{\Longrightarrow}^n \delta A u \underset{\mathrm{rm}}{\Longrightarrow} \delta\alpha B\beta u = \gamma B\beta u \quad \text{and} \quad k{:}u = y$$

for some $\delta \in V^*$ and $u \in T^*$. But then $\beta \Rightarrow^m v \in T^*$ implies (by Theorem 4.2) that

$$S \underset{\mathrm{rm}}{\Longrightarrow}^{n+1+m} \gamma B v u \underset{\mathrm{rm}}{\Longrightarrow} \gamma\omega v u$$

for all $B \rightarrow \omega$ in $P$. □

Lemma 6.17 implies (by Fact 6.16) that given any LR($k$)-valid item for $\gamma$, all its immediate descendants are LR($k$)-valid for $\gamma$. Thus we have:

**Lemma 6.18** *In any grammar,* $\mathrm{VALID}_k(\gamma)$ *is closed under* $\mathbf{desc}_k$, *that is,*

$$\mathbf{desc}_k^*(\mathrm{VALID}_k(\gamma)) = \mathrm{VALID}_k(\gamma) \ .$$

□

The following lemma states the converse of Lemma 6.17.

**Lemma 6.19** *If in grammar* $G = (V, T, P, S)$

$$[B \rightarrow \cdot\,\omega, z] \in \mathrm{VALID}_{k,n}(\gamma) \quad \textit{and} \quad n > 0 \ ,$$

*then for some rule* $A \rightarrow \alpha B\beta$ *in* $P$, *strings* $y$, $v$ *in* $T^*$, *and natural number* $m < n$,

$$[A \rightarrow \alpha \cdot B\beta, y] \in \mathrm{VALID}_{k,m}(\gamma),\ \beta \underset{\mathrm{rm}}{\Longrightarrow}^{n-m-1} v, \quad \textit{and} \quad k{:}vy = z \ .$$

*Proof.* By definition,

$$S \underset{rm}{\Longrightarrow}{}^n \gamma Bu \underset{rm}{\Longrightarrow} \gamma\omega u \quad \text{and} \quad k:u = z$$

for some $u \in T^*$. As $n > 0$ we can conclude by Lemma 6.2 that

$$S \underset{rm}{\Longrightarrow}{}^m \delta' Ay' \underset{rm}{\Longrightarrow} \delta'\alpha B\beta y' = \gamma B\beta y' \quad \text{and} \quad \beta y' \underset{rm}{\Longrightarrow}{}^{n-m-1} u$$

for some $\delta' \in V^*$, $y' \in T^*$, $A \to \alpha B\beta$ in $P$, and $m \leqslant n$. Then $[A \to \alpha \cdot B\beta,\ y]$ is in $\text{VALID}_{k,m}(\gamma)$ when $y = k:y'$. Moreover, $\beta \underset{rm}{\Longrightarrow}{}^{n-m-1} v$ for some $v \in T^*$ such that $vy' = u$. Here $k:vy = k:v(k:y') = k:vy' = k:u = z$, as desired. □

The following fact is an immediate consequence of the definition of $\text{VALID}_{k,0}(\gamma)$.

**Fact 6.20** In any grammar $G = (V, T, P, S)$,

$$\text{VALID}_{k,0}(\gamma) = \{[S \to \gamma \cdot \omega,\ \varepsilon] \mid S \to \gamma\omega \text{ is in } P\} .$$

□

Consider again Figures 6.2 and 6.3. Observe that any item set $\text{VALID}(\gamma X)$, where $X$ is a single symbol, contains all items of the form $[A \to \alpha X \cdot \beta,\ y]$, where $[A \to \alpha \cdot X\beta,\ y]$ is an item in $\text{VALID}(\gamma)$. In fact, these are the only items in $\text{VALID}(\gamma X)$ in which the portion of the right-hand side preceding the dot is nonempty. In addition to these items, $\text{VALID}(\gamma X)$ contains all their descendants.

We say that item $[A \to \alpha \cdot \beta,\ y]$ is *LR-essential* (or *essential*, for short), if $\alpha$ is nonempty, and *LR-inessential* (or *inessential*) otherwise. If $q$ is a set of items, we denote:

$$\text{ESS}_{\text{LR}}(q) = \{I \in q \mid I \text{ is LR-essential}\} .$$

For brevity, we may write ESS for $\text{ESS}_{\text{LR}}$.

Lemma 6.19 and Fact 6.20 imply (by Fact 6.12):

**Lemma 6.21** *Let $G = (V, T, P, S)$ be a grammar, $\gamma$ a string in $V^*$, and $I$ an item in $\text{VALID}_{k,n}(\gamma)$ for some $k, n \geqslant 0$. Then one of the following statements holds.*

(1) *$\gamma = \varepsilon$, $n = 0$, and $I = [S \to \cdot\omega,\ \varepsilon]$ for some $\omega$.*
(2) *$\gamma \neq \varepsilon$ and $I$ is essential.*
(3) *$n > 0$ and $I$ has an immediate ancestor in some $\text{VALID}_{k,m}(\gamma)$, $m < n$.*

□

**Lemma 6.22** *Let $G = (V, T, P, S)$ be a grammar and $\gamma$ a string in $V^*$. Then the following statements are true.*

$$\text{VALID}_{k,n}(\gamma) \subseteq \mathbf{desc}_k^*(\{[S \to \cdot\omega,\ \varepsilon] \mid S \to \omega \textit{ in } P\}) ,$$

*if $\gamma = \varepsilon$.*

$$\mathrm{VALID}_{k,n}(\gamma) \subseteq \mathbf{desc}_k^*(\mathrm{ESS}(\mathrm{VALID}_k(\gamma)))\ ,$$

*if* $\gamma \neq \varepsilon$.

*Proof.* The proof is by induction on $n$. If $n = 0$, Lemma 6.21 implies that $\mathrm{VALID}_{k,n}(\varepsilon)$ only contains items of the form $[S \to \cdot\omega, \varepsilon]$ and that $\mathrm{VALID}_{k,n}(\gamma)$, for $\gamma \neq \varepsilon$, only contains essential items. We may therefore assume that $n > 0$ and, as an induction hypothesis, that the lemma holds for natural numbers less than $n$. Let $I$ be an item in $\mathrm{VALID}_{k,n}(\gamma)$. By Lemma 6.21 (and Fact 6.16) either $\gamma \neq \varepsilon$ and $I$ belongs to $\mathrm{ESS}(\mathrm{VALID}_k(\gamma))$ or $I$ has an immediate ancestor $J$ in some $\mathrm{VALID}_{k,m}(\gamma)$, $m < n$. In the latter case we conclude by the induction hypothesis that $J$ belongs to $\mathbf{desc}_k^*(\{[S \to \cdot\omega,\ \varepsilon] \mid S \to \omega \text{ in } P\})$ when $\gamma = \varepsilon$ and to $\mathbf{desc}_k^*(\mathrm{ESS}(\mathrm{VALID}_k(\gamma)))$ when $\gamma \neq \varepsilon$. But then so does its immediate descendant $I$. □

Fact 6.16, Lemma 6.18, and Lemma 6.22 imply:

**Lemma 6.23** *Let* $G = (V, T, P, S)$ *be any grammar and* $\gamma$ *a string in* $V^*$. *Then* $\mathrm{VALID}_k(\gamma)$ *is spanned under* $\mathbf{desc}_k$ *by the items* $[S \to \cdot\omega,\ \varepsilon]$ *if* $\gamma = \varepsilon$, *and by the essential items in* $\mathrm{VALID}_k(\gamma)$ *if* $\gamma \neq \varepsilon$. *That is,*

$$\mathrm{VALID}_k(\varepsilon) = \mathbf{desc}_k^*(\{[S \to \cdot\omega,\ \varepsilon] \mid S \to \omega \textit{ is in } P\})\ ;$$

$$\mathrm{VALID}_k(\gamma) = \mathbf{desc}_k^*(\mathrm{ESS}(\mathrm{VALID}_k(\gamma))),\quad \textit{if}\quad \gamma \neq \varepsilon\ .$$

□

The representation of $\mathrm{VALID}_k(\varepsilon)$ by means of the relation $\mathbf{desc}_k$ implies an algorithm for constructing the initial state of the canonical LR($k$) machine: first construct the set of all items $[S \to \cdot\omega,\ \varepsilon]$ and then compute the image of this set under the relation denoted by the relational expression $\mathbf{desc}_k^*$, using the results of Chapter 2.

Let $X$ be a symbol in $V$ and let **passes-**$X$ be the relation on the set of $k$-items defined by:

$$[A \to \alpha\cdot X\beta,\ y]\ \mathbf{passes}\text{-}X\ [A \to \alpha X\cdot\beta,\ y]\ ,$$

for all rules $A \to \alpha X\beta$ in $P$ and strings $y$ in $k{:}T^*$. (Cf. the relations **passes-any** and **passes-null** defined in Chapter 5 for 0-items.)

Let $q$ be a set of $k$-items and $X$ a symbol in $V$. The $k$-item set **passes-**$X(q)$ is called the *basis of the* $X$*-successor of* $q$ and is denoted by $\mathrm{BASIS}_{\mathrm{LR}}(q, X)$. We have:

$$\mathrm{BASIS}_{\mathrm{LR}}(q, X) = \{[A \to \alpha X\cdot\beta,\ y] \mid [A \to \alpha\cdot X\beta,\ y] \in q\}\ .$$

The items in $\mathrm{BASIS}_{\mathrm{LR}}(q, X)$ are thus obtained by moving the dot over the symbol $X$ in those items $q$ in which the dot is immediately followed by $X$.

The closure of $\mathrm{BASIS}_{\mathrm{LR}}(q, X)$ under $\mathbf{desc}_k$ is called the $X$*-successor* of $q$ and it is denoted by $\mathrm{GOTO}_{\mathrm{LR}}(q, X)$. We have:

$$\mathrm{GOTO}_{\mathrm{LR}}(q, X) = \mathbf{desc}_k^*(\mathrm{BASIS}_{\mathrm{LR}}(q, X)) = \mathbf{passes}\text{-}X\ \mathbf{desc}_k^*(q)\ .$$

The set $\mathrm{GOTO_{LR}}(q, X)$ thus consists of all LR(k)-descendants of all items of the form $[A \to \alpha X \cdot \beta, y]$ for which the item $[A \to \alpha \cdot X\beta, y]$ is in $q$.

For brevity, we usually write BASIS for $\mathrm{BASIS_{LR}}$ and GOTO for $\mathrm{GOTO_{LR}}$.

The following fact is an immediate consequence of the definition of $\mathrm{VALID}_{k,n}(\gamma)$.

**Fact 6.24** If $[A \to \alpha \cdot \omega\beta, y]$ is an item in $\mathrm{VALID}_{k,n}(\gamma)$, then $\gamma\omega$ is a viable prefix and $[A \to \alpha\omega \cdot \beta, y]$ is in $\mathrm{VALID}_{k,n}(\gamma\omega)$. Conversely, if $[A \to \alpha\omega \cdot \beta, y]$ is an item in $\mathrm{VALID}_{k,n}(\delta)$, then there is a viable prefix $\gamma$ such that $\delta = \gamma\omega$ and $[A \to \alpha \cdot \omega\beta, y]$ is in $\mathrm{VALID}_{k,n}(\gamma)$. □

**Lemma 6.25** *In any grammar* $G = (V, T, P, S)$,

$$\mathrm{ESS}(\mathrm{VALID}_k(\gamma X)) = \mathrm{BASIS}(\mathrm{VALID}_k(\gamma), X)$$

*for all strings* $\gamma \in V^*$ *and symbols* $X \in V$.

*Proof.* Any item in $\mathrm{BASIS}(\mathrm{VALID}_k(\gamma), X)$ is of the form $[A \to \alpha X \cdot \beta, y]$, where $[A \to \alpha \cdot X\beta, y]$ is in $\mathrm{VALID}_k(\gamma)$. By Facts 6.16 and 6.24, $[A \to \alpha X \cdot \beta, y]$ is in $\mathrm{VALID}_k(\gamma X)$. As this item is essential, we conclude that $\mathrm{BASIS}(\mathrm{VALID}_k(\gamma), X)$ is contained in $\mathrm{ESS}(\mathrm{VALID}_k(\gamma X))$. Conversely, if $[A \to \alpha \cdot \beta, y]$ is an essential item in $\mathrm{VALID}_k(\gamma X)$, then by Facts 6.16 and 6.24 $\alpha$ is of the form $\alpha' X$ and $[A \to \alpha' \cdot X\beta, y]$ is in $\mathrm{VALID}_k(\gamma)$. Thus $[A \to \alpha' X \cdot \beta, y]$ is in $\mathrm{BASIS}(\mathrm{VALID}_k(\gamma), X)$, which means that $\mathrm{ESS}(\mathrm{VALID}_k(\gamma X))$ is contained in $\mathrm{BASIS}(\mathrm{VALID}_k(\gamma), X)$. □

Lemmas 6.23 and 6.25 imply:

**Lemma 6.26** *Let* $G = (V, T, P, S)$ *be any grammar,* $\gamma$ *a string in* $V^*$, *and* $X$ *a symbol in* $V$. *Then*

$$\mathrm{VALID}_k(\gamma X) = \mathrm{GOTO}(\mathrm{VALID}_k(\gamma), X)$$

*for all* $k \geqslant 0$. □

Lemma 6.26 implies an algorithm for constructing $\mathrm{VALID}_k(\gamma X)$ from $\mathrm{VALID}_k(\gamma)$: given $\mathrm{VALID}_k(\gamma)$ and $X$, $\mathrm{VALID}_k(\gamma X)$ is obtained as the image of $\mathrm{VALID}_k(\gamma)$ under the relation denoted by the relational expression **passes-$X$ desc$_k^*$**. If we combine this algorithm with that implied by Lemma 6.23 for constructing the initial state $\mathrm{VALID}_k(\varepsilon)$, we get an algorithm for constructing the entire canonical LR(k) machine. This algorithm is shown in Figure 6.4.

Now we can prove:

**Theorem 6.27** *Let* $G = (V, T, P, S)$ *be a grammar,* $k$ *a natural number, and* $M$ *the canonical* LR(k) *machine for* $G$. *Then the following statements hold.*

*(a)* $M$ *is deterministic.*

*(b) Each nonempty state* $q$ *in* $M$ *has a unique entry symbol, that is, there are transitions to* $q$ *on at most one symbol* $X$ *in* $V$.

Compute the relation $\mathbf{desc}_k$;
**for** all $X \in V$ **do**
  compute the relation **passes**-$X$;
$q_s := \mathbf{desc}_k^*(\{[S \to \cdot\omega, \varepsilon] \mid S \to \omega \text{ is in } P\})$;
$Q_M := \{q_s\}$;
$P_M := \varnothing$;
**repeat**
  **for** all $q \in Q_M$ and $X \in V$ **do begin**
    $q' :=$ **passes**-$X$ $\mathbf{desc}_k^*(q)$;
    $Q_M := Q_M \cup \{q'\}$;
    $P_M := P_M \cup \{qX \to q'\}$
  **end**
**until** nothing more can be added to $Q_M$ and $P_M$.

**Figure 6.4** Algorithm for constructing the canonical LR(k) machine $M$ for grammar $G = (V, T, P, S)$. $Q_M$ will contain all states of $M$, $P_M$ will contain all transitions of $M$, and $q_s$ will be the initial state of $M$

(c) *State q in M is accessible upon reading string $\gamma$ if and only if $q = \text{VALID}_k(\gamma)$.*

(d) *If a given state $\text{VALID}_k(\gamma)$ is designated as the only final state of M, then the language accepted by M is $[\gamma]_k$.*

(e) *If all nonempty states $\text{VALID}_k(\gamma)$ are designated as final states of M, then the language accepted by M is the set of viable prefixes of G.*

(f) *If all states of M are designated as final states, then the language accepted by M is $V^*$.*

*Proof.* To prove claim (a), consider a pair of transitions

$$\text{VALID}_k(\gamma_1)X_1 \to \text{VALID}_k(\gamma_1 X_1) \ ,$$
$$\text{VALID}_k(\gamma_2)X_2 \to \text{VALID}_k(\gamma_2 X_2) \ ,$$

both applicable to the same configuration. Then $\text{VALID}_k(\gamma_1) = \text{VALID}_k(\gamma_2)$ and $X_1 = X_2$. By Lemma 6.26 we then have:

$$\text{VALID}_k(\gamma_1 X_1) = \text{GOTO}(\text{VALID}_k(\gamma_1), X_1)$$
$$= \text{GOTO}(\text{VALID}_k(\gamma_2), X_2) = \text{VALID}_k(\gamma_2 X_2) \ .$$

In other words, the transitions are the same and so $M$ is deterministic.

To prove claim (b), let $q$ be a nonempty state in $M$ and let $q_1 X_1 \to q$ and $q_2 X_2 \to q$ be transitions to $q$. By definition, there are strings $\gamma_1$ and $\gamma_2$ in $V^*$ such that $q_1 = \text{VALID}_k(\gamma_1)$, $q_2 = \text{VALID}_k(\gamma_2)$, and $\text{VALID}_k(\gamma_1 X_1) = q = \text{VALID}_k(\gamma_2 X_2)$. By Lemma 6.26 we have:

$$q = \text{GOTO}(\text{VALID}_k(\gamma_1), X_1)$$
$$= \mathbf{desc}_k^*(\text{BASIS}(\text{VALID}_k(\gamma_1), X_1)),$$
$$q = \text{GOTO}(\text{VALID}_k(\gamma_2), X_2)$$
$$= \mathbf{desc}_k^*(\text{BASIS}(\text{VALID}_k(\gamma_2), X_2)) \ .$$

Since $q$ was assumed to be nonempty, BASIS(VALID$_k(\gamma_1), X_1$) and BASIS(VALID$_k(\gamma_2), X_2$) must both be nonempty. However, all items in BASIS(VALID$_k(\gamma_1), X_1$) are of the form $[A \to \alpha X_1 \cdot \beta, y]$ and all items in BASIS(VALID$_k(\gamma_2), X_2$) are of the form $[A \to \alpha X_2 \cdot \beta, y]$. Moreover, $q$ cannot contain other essential items than those in BASIS(VALID$_k(\gamma_1), X_1$) and BASIS(VALID$_k(\gamma_2), X_2$), because the closure under **desc**$_k$ only introduces inessential items. But this means that $X_1 = X_2$, as desired.

We then prove claim (c). First, a simple induction on $|\gamma_1|$ shows that

$$\text{VALID}_k(\varepsilon)\gamma_1\gamma_2 \Rightarrow^{|\gamma_1|} \text{VALID}_k(\gamma_1)\gamma_2 \qquad \text{in } M$$

for all strings $\gamma_1, \gamma_2$ in $V^*$. This implies that, for all strings $\gamma$ in $V^*$, VALID$_k(\gamma)$ is accessible upon reading $\gamma$. On the other hand, $M$ has no $\varepsilon$-transitions, and we have just shown that $M$ is deterministic. Thus, VALID$_k(\gamma)$ is the only state accessible upon reading $\gamma$.

The proof of claims (d), (e), and (f) is left to the exercises. □

**Theorem 6.28** *For any grammar $G = (V, T, P, S)$ and natural number k, the following statements hold.*

*(a) The LR(k)-equivalence of G is the equivalence induced by the canonical LR(k) machine of G, that is, strings $\gamma_1$ and $\gamma_2$ are LR(k)-equivalent if and only if the state accessible upon reading $\gamma_1$ coincides with that accessible upon reading $\gamma_2$.*

*(b) The LR(k)-equivalence of G is right-invariant, that is, whenever $\gamma_1$ and $\gamma_2$ are LR(k)-equivalent strings in $V^*$ and X is a symbol in V, then $\gamma_1 X$ and $\gamma_2 X$ are LR(k)-equivalent.*

*(c) Two LR(k)-equivalent viable prefixes always end with the same symbol, that is, whenever $\gamma_1$ and $\gamma_2$ are LR(k)-equivalent viable prefixes of G, then $\gamma_1{:}1 = \gamma_2{:}1$.*

*Proof.* To prove claim (a), let $\gamma_1$ and $\gamma_2$ be strings in $V^*$. If $\gamma_1$ and $\gamma_2$ are LR($k$)-equivalent, then VALID$_k(\gamma_1)$ = VALID$_k(\gamma_2)$, where, by Theorem 6.27, VALID$_k(\gamma_1)$ is the state accessible upon reading $\gamma_1$ and VALID$_k(\gamma_2)$ is the state accessible upon reading $\gamma_2$. Conversely, if $q_1$, the state accessible upon reading $\gamma_1$, coincides with $q_2$, the state accessible upon reading $\gamma_2$, then, by Theorem 6.27, VALID$_k(\gamma_1) = q_1 = q_2 =$ VALID$_k(\gamma_2)$, that is, $\gamma_1$ and $\gamma_2$ are LR($k$)-equivalent.

Claim (b) follows directly from claim (a), because the equivalence induced by any finite automaton is right-invariant (see the exercises in Chapter 3). However, claim (b) also follows easily from Lemma 6.26. If $\gamma_1$ and $\gamma_2$ are LR($k$)-equivalent strings in $V^*$ and $X$ is a symbol in $V$, then VALID$_k(\gamma_1)$ = VALID$_k(\gamma_2)$ and, by Lemma 6.26,

$$\begin{aligned}\text{VALID}_k(\gamma_1 X) &= \text{GOTO}(\text{VALID}_k(\gamma_1), X)\\ &= \text{GOTO}(\text{VALID}_k(\gamma_2), X) = \text{VALID}_k(\gamma_2 X)\ ,\end{aligned}$$

which means that $\gamma_1 X$ and $\gamma_2 X$ are LR($k$)-equivalent.

To prove claim (c), let $\gamma_1$ and $\gamma_2$ be LR($k$)-equivalent viable prefixes of $G$. Then $\mathrm{VALID}_k(\gamma_1) = \mathrm{VALID}_k(\gamma_2) \neq \varnothing$. If $\gamma_1 = \varepsilon$, then, by Lemma 6.23,

$$\mathrm{VALID}_k(\gamma_1) = \mathbf{desc}_k^*(\{[S \to \cdot\omega, \varepsilon] | S \to \omega \text{ is in } P\}) .$$

Thus, $\mathrm{VALID}_k(\gamma_1)$ contains no essential items. Now if $\gamma_2$ were nonempty, then, by Lemma 6.23,

$$\mathrm{VALID}_k(\gamma_2) = \mathbf{desc}_k^*(\mathrm{ESS}(\mathrm{VALID}_k(\gamma_2))) .$$

However, this is impossible because $\mathrm{VALID}_k(\gamma_2) = \mathrm{VALID}_k(\gamma_1)$ is nonempty and contains no essential items. Thus $\gamma_2 = \varepsilon$ and so at least in the case $\gamma_1 = \varepsilon$ we have $\gamma_1 : 1 = \gamma_2 : 1$. Similarly we can prove that in the case $\gamma_2 = \varepsilon$ we have $\gamma_1 = \varepsilon$ and hence $\gamma_1 : 1 = \gamma_2 : 1$. In the case $\gamma_1 \neq \varepsilon$ and $\gamma_2 \neq \varepsilon$ we can write $\gamma_1 = \gamma_1' X_1$ and $\gamma_2 = \gamma_2' X_2$ for some strings $\gamma_1'$ and $\gamma_2'$ and symbols $X_1$ and $X_2$. By Theorem 6.27, $\mathrm{VALID}_k(\gamma_1)$ is accessible upon reading $\gamma_1' X_1$ and $\mathrm{VALID}_k(\gamma_2)$ is accessible upon reading $\gamma_2' X_2$. Thus, $X_1$ is an entry symbol of $\mathrm{VALID}_k(\gamma_1)$ and $X_2$ is an entry symbol of $\mathrm{VALID}_k(\gamma_2)$. By Theorem 6.27, $X_1 = X_2$, that is, $\gamma_1 : 1 = \gamma_2 : 1$, as desired. □

## 6.3 Canonical LR($k$) Parsers

In this section we use results of the previous section to define the notion of "canonical LR($k$) parser" for grammar $G$. For convenience, we shall use the \$-augmented grammar for $G$ in the definitions (see Section 5.3). The stack alphabet of the canonical LR($k$) parser will be the collection of all LR($k$)-equivalence classes of viable prefixes of $G'$, the \$-augmented grammar for $G$. We denote this collection by $[G']_k$.

Let $G = (V, T, P, S)$ be a grammar, $G'$ its \$-augmented grammar, and $k$ a natural number. A rule of the form

$$\text{(ra)} \qquad [\delta]_k[\delta X_1]_k \ldots [\delta X_1 \ldots X_n]_k \,|\, y \to [\delta]_k[\delta A]_k \,|\, y$$

is a *canonical LR($k$) reduce action by rule* $A \to X_1 \ldots X_n$ *on lookahead* $y$ if $\delta$ is a string in $\$V^*$, $X_1, \ldots, X_n$ are symbols in $V$ ($n \geqslant 0$), $A \to X_1 \ldots X_n$ is a rule in $P$, and $y$ is a string in $k{:}T^*\$$ such that

$$[A \to X_1 \ldots X_n \cdot, y] \in \mathrm{VALID}_k(\delta X_1 \ldots X_n) .$$

Observe that $\delta$, $\delta X_1, \ldots, \delta X_1 \ldots X_n$ are all viable prefixes of $G'$. This follows from the fact that they are prefixes of $\delta X_1 \ldots X_n$, which is a viable prefix because an item, $[A \to X_1 \ldots X_n \cdot, y]$ is valid for it. Also $\delta A$ is a viable prefix of $G'$. This follows from the fact that $[A \to \cdot X_1 \ldots X_n, y]$ is valid for $\delta$ (by Fact 6.24), which in turn implies that $\mathrm{VALID}_k(\delta)$ contains an item of the form $[C \to \alpha \cdot A\beta, v]$ (see Lemma 6.19, noting that $[A \to \cdot X_1 \ldots X_n, y]$ cannot be a member of

$\text{VALID}_{k,0}(\delta)$, because $A \to X_1 \ldots X_n$ is in $P$; recall that the start rule of $G'$ is $S' \to \$S\$$).

A rule of the form

$$(sa) \qquad [\delta]_k \mid ay \to [\delta]_k[\delta a]_k \mid y$$

is a *canonical LR(k) shift action on terminal a and lookahead ay* if $\delta$ is a string in $\$V^*$, $a$ is a terminal in $T$, and $y$ is a string in $\max\{k-1, 0\}:T^*\$$ such that

$$[A \to \alpha \cdot a\beta, z] \in \text{VALID}_k(\delta) \text{ and } y \in \text{FIRST}_{\max\{k-1,0\}}(\beta z)$$

for some rule $A \to \alpha a \beta$ in $P$ and string $z$ in $k:T^*\$$. Observe that $\delta$ and $\delta a$ are viable prefixes of $G'$.

The *canonical LR(k) parser* for $G$ is the pushdown transducer with stack alphabet $[G']_k$, input alphabet $T$, initial stack contents $[\$]_k$, set of final stack contents $\{[\$]_k[\$S]_k\}$, and with set of actions consisting of all canonical LR($k$) reduce and shift actions of $G$. The output effect $\tau$ is defined to map every reduce action by rule $r$ to rule $r$ and every shift action to the empty string $\varepsilon$:

$$(1) \qquad \tau([\delta]_k[\delta X_1]_k \ldots [\delta X_1 \ldots X_n]_k \mid y \to [\delta]_k[\delta A]_k \mid y) = A \to X_1 \ldots X_n \; .$$

$$(2) \qquad \tau([\delta]_k \mid ay \to [\delta]_k[\delta a]_k \mid y) = \varepsilon \; .$$

Observe that any reduce action of the form (*ra*) defines uniquely the rule $A \to X_1 \ldots X_n$. If some reduce action is represented in two ways, say,

$$[\delta]_k[\delta X_1]_k \ldots [\delta X_1 \ldots X_n]_k \mid y \to [\delta]_k[\delta A]_k \mid y$$

and

$$[\delta]_k[\delta Y_1]_k \ldots [\delta Y_1 \ldots Y_n]_k \mid y \to [\delta]_k[\delta B]_k \mid y \; ,$$

then necessarily $X_1 = Y_1, X_2 = Y_2, \ldots, X_n = Y_n$, and $A = B$, because any two LR($k$)-equivalent viable prefixes end with the same symbol. This means that $\tau$ is well-defined.

In the case $k = 0$ the canonical LR($k$) reduce actions are of the form

$$[\delta]_0[\delta X_1]_0 \ldots [\delta X_1 \ldots X_n]_0 \mid \; \to [\delta]_0[\delta A]_0 \mid \; ,$$

where $[A \to X_1 \ldots X_n \cdot]$ is in $\text{VALID}_0(\delta X_1 \ldots X_n)$, and the canonical LR($k$) shift actions are of the form

$$[\delta]_0 \mid a \to [\delta]_0[\delta a]_0 \mid \; ,$$

where $\text{VALID}_0(\delta)$ contains an item of the form $[A \to \alpha \cdot a\beta]$ in which $\beta$ derives some terminal string. These actions are called *LR*(0) *reduce actions* and *LR*(0) *shift actions*, respectively. The canonical LR(0) parser of grammar $G$ is called the *LR*(0) *parser* for $G$.

As an example we consider the grammar $G_{ab\varepsilon}$, which has the rules

$$S \to aA \mid bB, \qquad A \to \varepsilon \mid cAd, \qquad B \to \varepsilon \mid cBd \; .$$

The grammar generates the language

$$L(G_{ab\varepsilon}) = \{ac^n d^n \mid n \geqslant 0\} \cup \{bc^n d^n \mid n \geqslant 0\} .$$

The LR(0) machine for the \$-augmented grammar for $G_{ab\varepsilon}$ is given in Figure 6.5. We have omitted the states VALID($\varepsilon$) and VALID(\$S\$), because these are not needed in the parser. We have numbered the states by positive integers. In the text we shall denote state $i$ by $q_i$. (Strictly speaking, $q_i$ will denote the equivalence class $[\gamma]$, where $i$ denotes the state VALID($\gamma$); however in examples we usually make no distinction between $[\gamma]$ and VALID($\gamma$).)

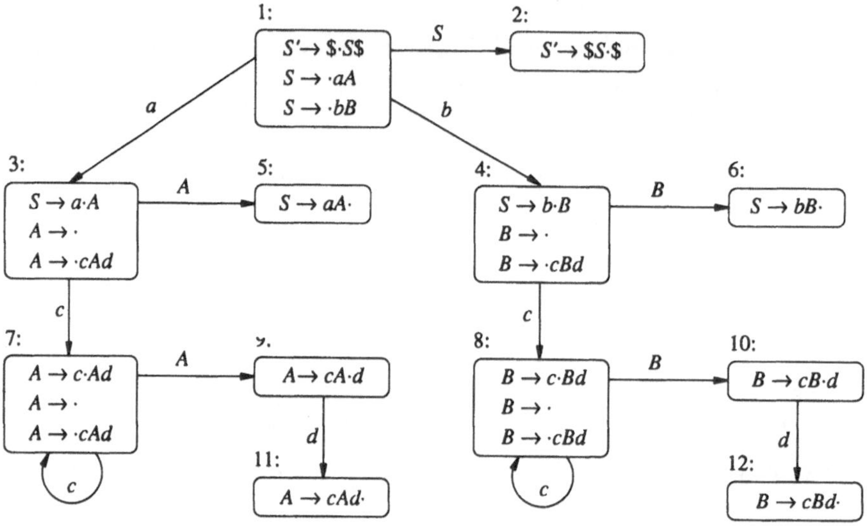


**Figure 6.5** The LR(0) machine for the \$-augmented grammar $G'_{ab\varepsilon}: S' \to \$S\$,\ S \to aA \mid bB,\ A \to \varepsilon \mid cAd,\ B \to \varepsilon \mid cBd$

The actions of the canonical LR($k$) parser can be obtained from the canonical LR($k$) machine using the algorithm depicted in Figure 6.6. The algorithm is formulated so that it also applies to reduced variants of LR($k$) parsers such as LALR($k$) parsers (to be discussed in Section 6.5). Also note that when $k \leqslant 1$ (and the grammar is reduced), the generation of shift actions can be simplified as:

**for** all $a \in T$ such that GOTO($q$, $a$) $\neq \varnothing$ **do begin**
let $q_a$ = GOTO($q$, $a$);
generate the shift action $q \mid a \to q q_a \mid$
**end** .

The LR(0) parser for $G_{ab\varepsilon}$ has the following reduce actions.

$$r_1 = q_1 q_3 q_5 \mid \to q_1 q_2 \mid , \qquad \tau(r_1) = S \to aA .$$

$$r_2 = q_1 q_4 q_6 \mid \to q_1 q_2 \mid , \qquad \tau(r_2) = S \to bB .$$

**for** all states $q$ **do begin**
  **for** all rules $A \to X_1 \ldots X_n$ of $G$ ($n \geq 0$) such that some item in $q$ has the core $A \to \cdot X_1 \ldots X_n$ **do begin**
    let $q_0, q_1, \ldots, q_n$ be the sequence of states reached from $q$ upon reading $X_1 \ldots X_n$, i.e., $q_0 = q$ and $q_i = \text{GOTO}(q, X_1 \ldots X_i)$, $i = 1, \ldots, n$;
    $q_A := \text{GOTO}(q, A)$;
    **for** all items $[A \to X_1 \ldots X_n \cdot, y]$ in $q_n$ **do**
      generate the reduce action
      $qq_1 \ldots q_n \mid y \to qq_A \mid y$
  **end**;
  **for** all items $[A \to \alpha \cdot a\beta, z]$ in $q$ such that $a \in T$ **do begin**
    $q_a := \text{GOTO}(q, a)$;
    **for** all strings $y$ in $\text{FIRST}_{\max\{k-1,\,0\}}(\beta z)$ **do**
      generate the shift action
      $q \mid ay \to qq_a \mid y$
  **end**
**end**.

**Figure 6.6** Algorithm for generating the parsing actions from an LR($k$) machine

$$r_3 = q_3 \mid \to q_3 q_5 \mid, \qquad \tau(r_3) = A \to \varepsilon .$$
$$r_4 = q_3 q_7 q_9 q_{11} \mid \to q_3 q_5 \mid, \qquad \tau(r_4) = A \to cAd .$$
$$r_5 = q_4 \mid \to q_4 q_6 \mid, \qquad \tau(r_5) = B \to \varepsilon .$$
$$r_6 = q_4 q_8 q_{10} q_{12} \mid \to q_4 q_6 \mid, \qquad \tau(r_6) = B \to cBd .$$
$$r_7 = q_7 \mid \to q_7 q_9 \mid, \qquad \tau(r_7) = A \to \varepsilon .$$
$$r_8 = q_7 q_7 q_9 q_{11} \mid \to q_7 q_9 \mid, \qquad \tau(r_8) = A \to cAd .$$
$$r_9 = q_8 \mid \to q_8 q_{10} \mid, \qquad \tau(r_9) = B \to \varepsilon .$$
$$r_{10} = q_8 q_8 q_{10} q_{12} \mid \to q_8 q_{10} \mid, \qquad \tau(r_{10}) = B \to cBd .$$

The shift actions are:

$$s_1 = q_1 \mid a \to q_1 q_3 \mid, \qquad s_5 = q_7 \mid c \to q_7 q_7 \mid ,$$
$$s_2 = q_1 \mid b \to q_1 q_4 \mid, \qquad s_6 = q_8 \mid c \to q_8 q_8 \mid ,$$
$$s_3 = q_3 \mid c \to q_3 q_7 \mid, \qquad s_7 = q_9 \mid d \to q_9 q_{11} \mid ,$$
$$s_4 = q_4 \mid c \to q_4 q_8 \mid, \qquad s_8 = q_{10} \mid d \to q_{10} q_{12} \mid .$$

To see that the parser indeed accepts all sentences in the language $L(G_{ab\varepsilon})$, consider the following computations.

$$\$q_1 \mid a\$ \overset{s_1}{\Longrightarrow} \$q_1 q_3 \mid \$ \overset{r_3}{\Longrightarrow} \$q_1 q_3 q_5 \mid \$ \overset{r_1}{\Longrightarrow} \$q_1 q_2 \mid \$ .$$

$$\$q_1 \mid b\$ \overset{s_2}{\Longrightarrow} \$q_1 q_4 \mid \$ \overset{r_5}{\Longrightarrow} \$q_1 q_4 q_6 \mid \$ \overset{r_2}{\Longrightarrow} \$q_1 q_2 \mid \$ .$$

$$\$q_1 \mid acd\$ \overset{s_1}{\Longrightarrow} \$q_1q_3 \mid cd\$ \overset{s_3}{\Longrightarrow} \$q_1q_3q_7 \mid d\$ \overset{r_7}{\Longrightarrow} \$q_1q_3q_7q_9 \mid d\$$$

$$\overset{s_7}{\Longrightarrow} \$q_1q_3q_7q_9q_{11} \mid \$ \overset{r_4}{\Longrightarrow} \$q_1q_3q_5 \mid \$ \overset{r_1}{\Longrightarrow} \$q_1q_2 \mid \$ \ .$$

$$\$q_1 \mid bcd\$ \overset{s_2}{\Longrightarrow} \$q_1q_4 \mid cd\$ \overset{s_4}{\Longrightarrow} \$q_1q_4q_8 \mid d\$ \overset{r_9}{\Longrightarrow} \$q_1q_4q_8q_{10} \mid d\$$$

$$\overset{s_8}{\Longrightarrow} \$q_1q_4q_8q_{10}q_{12} \mid \$ \overset{r_6}{\Longrightarrow} \$q_1q_4q_6 \mid \$ \overset{r_2}{\Longrightarrow} \$q_1q_2 \mid \$ \ .$$

$$\$q_1 \mid ac^nd^n\$ \overset{s_1}{\Longrightarrow} \$q_1q_3 \mid c^nd^n\$ \overset{s_3}{\Longrightarrow} \$q_1q_3q_7 \mid c^{n-1}d^n\$$$

$$\overset{s_5^{n-1}}{\Longrightarrow} \$q_1q_3q_7^n \mid d^n\$ \overset{r_7}{\Longrightarrow} \$q_1q_3q_7^nq_9 \mid d^n\$ \overset{s_7}{\Longrightarrow} \$q_1q_3q_7^nq_9q_{11} \mid d^{n-1}\$$$

$$\overset{(r_8s_7)^{n-1}}{\Longrightarrow} \$q_1q_3q_7q_9q_{11} \mid \$ \overset{r_4}{\Longrightarrow} \$q_1q_3q_5 \mid \$ \overset{r_1}{\Longrightarrow} \$q_1q_2 \mid \$ \ ,$$

for all $n \geqslant 1$.

$$\$q_1 \mid bc^nd^n\$ \overset{s_2}{\Longrightarrow} \$q_1q_4 \mid c^nd^n\$ \overset{s_4}{\Longrightarrow} \$q_1q_4q_8 \mid c^{n-1}d^n\$$$

$$\overset{s_6^{n-1}}{\Longrightarrow} \$q_1q_4q_8^n \mid d^n\$ \overset{r_9}{\Longrightarrow} \$q_1q_4q_8^nq_{10} \mid d^n\$$$

$$\overset{s_8}{\Longrightarrow} \$q_1q_4q_8^nq_{10}q_{12} \mid d^{n-1}\$ \overset{(r_{10}s_8)^{n-1}}{\Longrightarrow} \$q_1q_4q_8q_{10}q_{12} \mid \$$$

$$\overset{r_6}{\Longrightarrow} \$q_1q_4q_6 \mid \$ \overset{r_2}{\Longrightarrow} \$q_1q_2 \mid \$, \quad \text{for all } n \geqslant 1 \ .$$

The parses produced are:

For $a$: $\tau(s_1r_3r_1) = (A \to \varepsilon)(S \to aA)$ .

For $b$: $\tau(s_2r_5r_2) = (B \to \varepsilon)(S \to bB)$ .

For $acd$: $\tau(s_1s_3r_7s_7r_4r_1) = (A \to \varepsilon)(A \to cAd)(S \to aA)$ .

For $bcd$: $\tau(s_2s_4r_9s_8r_6r_2) = (B \to \varepsilon)(B \to cBd)(S \to bB)$ .

For $ac^nd^n$, $n \geqslant 1$: $\tau(s_1s_3s_5^{n-1}r_7s_7(r_8s_7)^{n-1}r_4r_1)$

$= (A \to \varepsilon)(A \to cAd)^{n-1}(A \to cAd)(S \to aA)$

$= (A \to \varepsilon)(A \to cAd)^n(S \to aA)$ .

For $bc^nd^n$, $n \geqslant 1$: $\tau(s_2s_4s_6^{n-1}r_9s_8(r_{10}s_8)^{n-1}r_6r_2)$

$= (B \to \varepsilon)(B \to cBd)^{n-1}(B \to cBd)(S \to bB)$

$= (B \to \varepsilon)(B \to cBd)^n(S \to bB)$ .

The parser is nondeterministic, because there is a "shift-reduce conflict" at states $q_3$, $q_4$, $q_7$, and $q_8$. The conflict is between a reduce action by rule $A \to \varepsilon$ and a shift action on terminal $c$. At state $q_3$ the conflicting pair of actions is

$$r_3 = q_3 \mid \to q_3q_5 \mid , \qquad s_3 = q_3 \mid c \to q_3q_7 \mid \ .$$

Both actions are applicable to any configuration of the form $\$\phi q_3 \mid cy\$$.

The canonical LR(1) parser for $G_{ab\varepsilon}$ is deterministic. The actions of the canonical parses are the following (obtained from the canonical LR(1) machine given in Figure 6.7):

$$
\begin{array}{ll}
r_1 = q_1q_3q_5 \mid \$ \to q_1q_2 \mid \$, & \tau(r_1) = S \to aA\ . \\
r_2 = q_1q_4q_6 \mid \$ \to q_1q_2 \mid \$, & \tau(r_2) = S \to bB\ . \\
r_3 = q_3 \mid \$ \to q_3q_5 \mid \$, & \tau(r_3) = A \to \varepsilon\ . \\
r_4 = q_3q_7q_9q_{11} \mid \$ \to q_3q_5 \mid \$, & \tau(r_4) = A \to cAd\ . \\
r_5 = q_4 \mid \$ \to q_4q_6 \mid \$, & \tau(r_5) = B \to \varepsilon\ . \\
r_6 = q_4q_8q_{10}q_{12} \mid \$ \to q_4q_6 \mid \$, & \tau(r_6) = B \to cBd\ . \\
r_7 = q_7 \mid d \to q_7q_9 \mid d, & \tau(r_7) = A \to \varepsilon\ . \\
r_8 = q_7q_{13}q_{15}q_{17} \mid d \to q_7q_9 \mid d, & \tau(r_8) = A \to cAd\ . \\
r_9 = q_8 \mid d \to q_8q_{10} \mid d, & \tau(r_9) = B \to \varepsilon\ . \\
r_{10} = q_8q_{14}q_{16}q_{18} \mid d \to q_8q_{10} \mid d, & \tau(r_{10}) = B \to cBd\ . \\
r_{11} = q_{13} \mid d \to q_{13}q_{15} \mid d, & \tau(r_{11}) = A \to \varepsilon\ . \\
r_{12} = q_{13}q_{13}q_{15}q_{17} \mid d \to q_{13}q_{15} \mid d & \tau(r_{12}) = A \to cAd\ . \\
r_{13} = q_{14} \mid d \to q_{14}q_{16} \mid d, & \tau(r_{13}) = B \to \varepsilon\ . \\
r_{14} = q_{14}q_{14}q_{16}q_{18} \mid d \to q_{14}q_{16} \mid d, & \tau(r_{14}) = B \to cBd\ . \\
s_1 = q_1 \mid a \to q_1q_3 \mid\ , & \\
s_2 = q_1 \mid b \to q_1q_4 \mid\ , & \\
s_3 = q_3 \mid c \to q_3q_7 \mid\ , & \\
s_4 = q_4 \mid c \to q_4q_8 \mid\ , & \\
s_5 = q_7 \mid c \to q_7q_{13} \mid\ , & \\
s_6 = q_8 \mid c \to q_8q_{14} \mid\ , & \\
s_7 = q_9 \mid d \to q_9q_{11} \mid\ , & \\
s_8 = q_{10} \mid d \to q_{10}q_{12} \mid\ , & \\
s_9 = q_{13} \mid c \to q_{13}q_{13} \mid\ , & \\
s_{10} = q_{14} \mid c \to q_{14}q_{14} \mid\ , & \\
s_{11} = q_{15} \mid d \to q_{15}q_{17} \mid\ , & \\
s_{12} = q_{16} \mid d \to q_{16}q_{18} \mid\ . &
\end{array}
$$

Observe that there are no longer any conflicts between reduce actions by $A \to \varepsilon$ and shift actions on $c$. The lookahead symbol in any reduce action by rule $A \to \varepsilon$ is either \$ or $d$. That the parser still accepts all sentences in $L(G_{ab\varepsilon})$, is seen from the

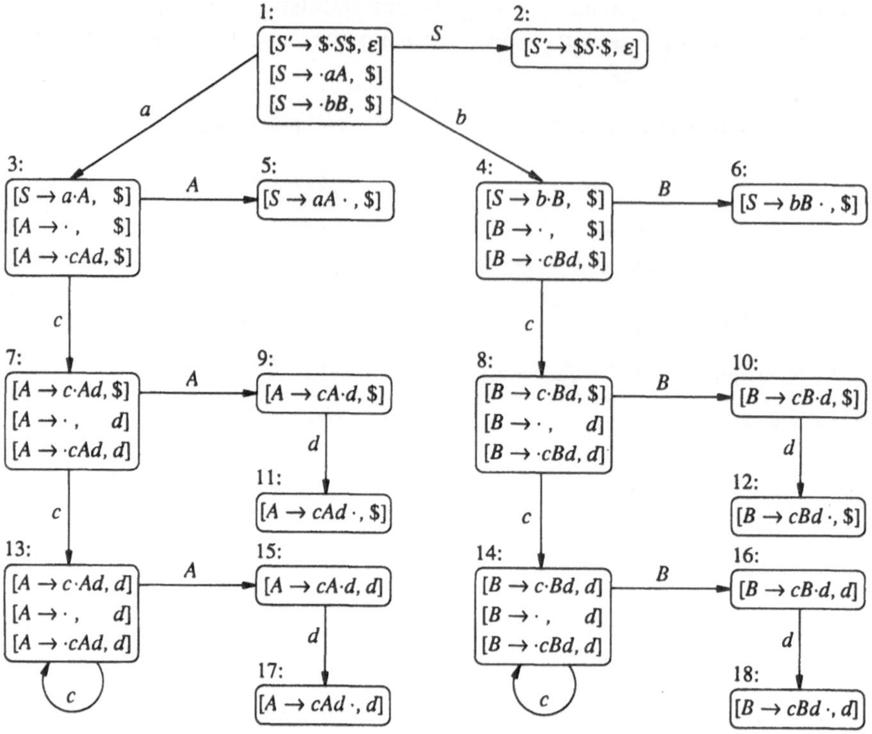


**Figure 6.7** Canonical LR(1) machine for the \$-augmented grammar $G'_{abc}$: $S' \to \$S\$$, $S \to aA|bB$, $A \to \varepsilon|cAd$, $B \to \varepsilon|cBd$

computations:

$$\$q_1 \mid a\$ \overset{s_1}{\Longrightarrow} \$q_1q_3 \mid \$ \overset{r_3}{\Longrightarrow} \$q_1q_3q_5 \mid \$ \overset{r_1}{\Longrightarrow} \$q_1q_2 \mid \$ \;.$$

$$\$q_1 \mid b\$ \overset{s_2}{\Longrightarrow} \$q_1q_4 \mid \$ \overset{r_5}{\Longrightarrow} \$q_1q_4q_6 \mid \$ \overset{r_2}{\Longrightarrow} \$q_1q_2 \mid \$ \;.$$

$$\$q_1 \mid acd\$ \overset{s_1}{\Longrightarrow} \$q_1q_3 \mid cd\$ \overset{s_3}{\Longrightarrow} \$q_1q_3q_7 \mid d\$$$

$$\overset{r_7}{\Longrightarrow} \$q_1q_3q_7q_9 \mid d\$ \overset{s_7}{\Longrightarrow} \$q_1q_3q_7q_9q_{11} \mid \$ \overset{r_4}{\Longrightarrow} \$q_1q_3q_5 \mid \$$$

$$\overset{r_1}{\Longrightarrow} \$q_1q_2 \mid \$ \;.$$

$$\$q_1 \mid bcd\$ \overset{s_2}{\Longrightarrow} \$q_1q_4 \mid cd\$ \overset{s_4}{\Longrightarrow} \$q_1q_4q_8 \mid d\$$$

$$\overset{r_9}{\Longrightarrow} \$q_1q_4q_8q_{10} \mid d\$ \overset{s_8}{\Longrightarrow} \$q_1q_4q_8q_{10}q_{12} \mid \$ \overset{r_6}{\Longrightarrow} \$q_1q_4q_6 \mid \$$$

$$\overset{r_2}{\Longrightarrow} \$q_1q_2 \mid \$ \;.$$

$$\$q_1 \mid accdd\$ \xRightarrow{s_1 s_3} \$q_1 q_3 q_7 \mid cdd\$ \xRightarrow{s_5} \$q_1 q_3 q_7 q_{13} \mid dd\$$$

$$\xRightarrow{r_{11}} \$q_1 q_3 q_7 q_{13} q_{15} \mid dd\$ \xRightarrow{s_{11}} \$q_1 q_3 q_7 q_{13} q_{15} q_{17} \mid d\$$$

$$\xRightarrow{r_8} \$q_1 q_3 q_7 q_9 \mid d\$ \xRightarrow{s_7} \$q_1 q_3 q_7 q_9 q_{11} \mid \$ \xRightarrow{r_4} \$q_1 q_3 q_5 \mid \$$$

$$\xRightarrow{r_1} \$q_1 q_2 \mid \$ \ .$$

$$\$q_1 \mid bccdd\$ \xRightarrow{s_2 s_4} \$q_1 q_4 q_8 \mid cdd\$ \xRightarrow{s_6} \$q_1 q_4 q_8 q_{14} \mid dd\$$$

$$\xRightarrow{r_{13}} \$q_1 q_4 q_8 q_{14} q_{16} \mid dd\$ \xRightarrow{s_{12}} \$q_1 q_4 q_8 q_{14} q_{16} q_{18} \mid d\$$$

$$\xRightarrow{r_{10}} \$q_1 q_4 q_8 q_{10} \mid d\$ \xRightarrow{s_8} \$q_1 q_4 q_8 q_{10} q_{12} \mid \$$$

$$\xRightarrow{r_6} \$q_1 q_4 q_6 \mid \$ \xRightarrow{r_2} \$q_1 q_2 \mid \$ \ .$$

$$\$q_1 \mid ac^n d^n \$ \xRightarrow{s_1 s_3 s_5} \$q_1 q_3 q_7 q_{13} \mid c^{n-2} d^n \$$$

$$\xRightarrow{s_9^{n-2}} \$q_1 q_3 q_7 q_{13}^{n-1} \mid d^n \$ \xRightarrow{r_{11}} \$q_1 q_3 q_7 q_{13}^{n-1} q_{15} \mid d^n \$$$

$$\xRightarrow{s_{11}} \$q_1 q_3 q_7 q_{13}^{n-1} q_{15} q_{17} \mid d^{n-1} \$$$

$$\xRightarrow{(r_{12} s_{11})^{n-2}} \$q_1 q_3 q_7 q_{13} q_{15} q_{17} \mid d\$ \xRightarrow{r_8} \$q_1 q_3 q_7 q_9 \mid d\$$$

$$\xRightarrow{s_7} \$q_1 q_3 q_7 q_9 q_{11} \mid \$ \xRightarrow{r_4} \$q_1 q_3 q_5 \mid \$ \xRightarrow{r_1} \$q_1 q_2 \mid \$ \ ,$$

for all $n \geqslant 2$ .

$$\$q_1 \mid bc^n d^n \$ \xRightarrow{s_2 s_4 s_6} \$q_1 q_4 q_8 q_{14} \mid c^{n-2} d^n \$$$

$$\xRightarrow{s_{10}^{n-2}} \$q_1 q_4 q_8 q_{14}^{n-1} \mid d^n \$ \xRightarrow{r_{13}} \$q_1 q_4 q_8 q_{14}^{n-1} q_{16} \mid d^n \$$$

$$\xRightarrow{s_{12}} \$q_1 q_4 q_8 q_{14}^{n-1} q_{16} q_{18} \mid d^{n-1} \$$$

$$\xRightarrow{(r_{14} s_{12})^{n-2}} \$q_1 q_4 q_8 q_{14} q_{16} q_{18} \mid d\$ \xRightarrow{r_{10}} \$q_1 q_4 q_8 q_{10} \mid d\$$$

$$\xRightarrow{s_8} \$q_1 q_4 q_8 q_{10} q_{12} \mid \$ \xRightarrow{r_6} \$q_1 q_4 q_6 \mid \$ \xRightarrow{r_2} \$q_1 q_2 \mid \$ \ ,$$

for all $n \geqslant 2$ .

As a further example, we consider the canonical LR(2) parser for $G_{ab\varepsilon}$. The canonical LR(2) machine for the \$-augmented grammar for $G_{ab\varepsilon}$ is given in Figure 6.8. The parser has the following reduce actions.

$$r_1 = q_1 q_3 q_5 \mid \$ \to q_1 q_2 \mid \$, \qquad \tau(r_1) = S \to aA \ .$$

$$r_2 = q_1 q_4 q_6 \mid \$ \to q_1 q_2 \mid \$, \qquad \tau(r_2) = S \to bB \ .$$

$$r_3 = q_3 \mid \$ \to q_3 q_5 \mid \$, \qquad \tau(r_3) = A \to \varepsilon \ .$$

$$r_4 = q_3 q_7 q_9 q_{11} \mid \$ \to q_3 q_5 \mid \$, \qquad \tau(r_4) = A \to cAd \ .$$

$$r_5 = q_4 \mid \$ \to q_4 q_6 \mid \$, \qquad \tau(r_5) = B \to \varepsilon \ .$$

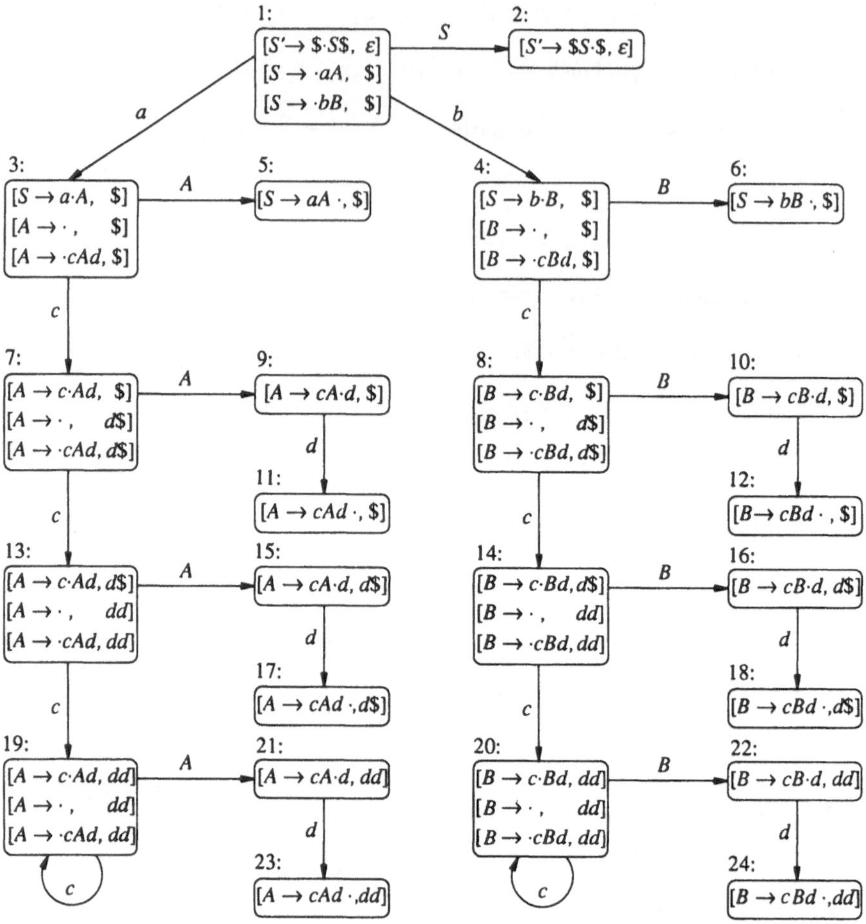


**Figure 6.8** The canonical LR(2) machine for the $-augmented grammar $G'_{ab\varepsilon}$: $S' \to \$S\$$, $S \to aA|bB$, $A \to \varepsilon|cAd$, $B \to \varepsilon|cBd$

$$r_6 = q_4q_8q_{10}q_{12} \mid \$ \to q_4q_6 \mid \$, \qquad \tau(r_6) = B \to cBd \ .$$

$$r_7 = q_7 \mid d\$ \to q_7q_9 \mid d\$, \qquad \tau(r_7) = A \to \varepsilon \ .$$

$$r_8 = q_7q_{13}q_{15}q_{17} \mid d\$ \to q_7q_9 \mid d\$, \qquad \tau(r_8) = A \to cAd \ .$$

$$r_9 = q_8 \mid d\$ \to q_8q_{10} \mid d\$, \qquad \tau(r_9) = B \to \varepsilon \ .$$

$$r_{10} = q_8q_{14}q_{16}q_{18} \mid d\$ \to q_8q_{10} \mid d\$, \qquad \tau(r_{10}) = B \to cBd \ .$$

$$r_{11} = q_{13} \mid dd \to q_{13}q_{15} \mid dd, \qquad \tau(r_{11}) = A \to \varepsilon \ .$$

$$r_{12} = q_{13}q_{19}q_{21}q_{23} \mid dd \to q_{13}q_{15} \mid dd, \qquad \tau(r_{12}) = A \to cAd \ .$$

$$r_{13} = q_{14} \mid dd \to q_{14}q_{16} \mid dd, \qquad \tau(r_{13}) = B \to \varepsilon \ .$$

$r_{14} = q_{14}q_{20}q_{22}q_{24} \mid dd \rightarrow q_{14}q_{16} \mid dd,$ $\tau(r_{14}) = B \rightarrow cBd$ .

$r_{15} = q_{19} \mid dd \rightarrow q_{19}q_{21} \mid dd,$ $\tau(r_{15}) = A \rightarrow \varepsilon$ .

$r_{16} = q_{19}q_{19}q_{21}q_{23} \mid dd \rightarrow q_{19}q_{21} \mid dd,$ $\tau(r_{16}) = A \rightarrow cAd$ .

$r_{17} = q_{20} \mid dd \rightarrow q_{20}q_{22} \mid dd,$ $\tau(r_{17}) = B \rightarrow \varepsilon$ .

$r_{18} = q_{20}q_{20}q_{22}q_{24} \mid dd \rightarrow q_{20}q_{22} \mid dd,$ $\tau(r_{18}) = B \rightarrow cBd$ .

Now that $k > 1$ the determining of the shift actions is more complicated than in the case $k \leqslant 1$. We need the following sets.

$$\mathrm{FIRST}_1(A\$) = \{\$, c\} = \mathrm{FIRST}_1(B\$) \ .$$

$$\mathrm{FIRST}_1(Ad\$) = \{d, c\} = \mathrm{FIRST}_1(Bd\$) \ .$$

$$\mathrm{FIRST}_1(\$) = \{\$\} \ .$$

$$\mathrm{FIRST}_1(Add\$) = \{d, c\} = \mathrm{FIRST}_1(Bdd\$) \ .$$

$$\mathrm{FIRST}_1(d\$) = \{d\} \ .$$

$$\mathrm{FIRST}_1(Addd) = \{d, c\} = \mathrm{FIRST}_1(Bddd) \ .$$

$$\mathrm{FIRST}_1(dd) = \{d\} \ .$$

The shift actions are:

$s_1 = q_1 \mid a\$ \rightarrow q_1q_3 \mid \$$ ,

$s_2 = q_1 \mid ac \rightarrow q_1q_3 \mid c$ ,

$s_3 = q_1 \mid b\$ \rightarrow q_1q_4 \mid \$$ ,

$s_4 = q_1 \mid bc \rightarrow q_1q_4 \mid c$ ,

$s_5 = q_3 \mid cd \rightarrow q_3q_7 \mid d$ ,

$s_6 = q_3 \mid cc \rightarrow q_3q_7 \mid c$ ,

$s_7 = q_4 \mid cd \rightarrow q_4q_8 \mid d$ ,

$s_8 = q_4 \mid cc \rightarrow q_4q_8 \mid c$ ,

$s_9 = q_7 \mid cd \rightarrow q_7q_{13} \mid d$ ,

$s_{10} = q_7 \mid cc \rightarrow q_7q_{13} \mid c$ ,

$s_{11} = q_8 \mid cd \rightarrow q_8q_{14} \mid d$ ,

$s_{12} = q_8 \mid cc \rightarrow q_8q_{14} \mid c$ ,

$s_{13} = q_9 \mid d\$ \rightarrow q_9q_{11} \mid \$$ ,

$s_{14} = q_{10} \mid d\$ \rightarrow q_{10}q_{12} \mid \$$ ,

$s_{15} = q_{13} \mid cd \rightarrow q_{13}q_{19} \mid d$ ,

$s_{16} = q_{13} \mid cc \rightarrow q_{13}q_{19} \mid c$ ,

$$s_{17} = q_{14} \mid cd \to q_{14}q_{20} \mid d \ ,$$

$$s_{18} = q_{14} \mid cc \to q_{14}q_{20} \mid c \ ,$$

$$s_{19} = q_{15} \mid dd \to q_{15}q_{17} \mid d \ ,$$

$$s_{20} = q_{16} \mid dd \to q_{16}q_{18} \mid d \ ,$$

$$s_{21} = q_{19} \mid cd \to q_{19}q_{19} \mid d \ ,$$

$$s_{22} = q_{19} \mid cc \to q_{19}q_{19} \mid c \ ,$$

$$s_{23} = q_{20} \mid cd \to q_{20}q_{20} \mid d \ ,$$

$$s_{24} = q_{20} \mid cc \to q_{20}q_{20} \mid c \ ,$$

$$s_{25} = q_{21} \mid dd \to q_{21}q_{23} \mid d \ ,$$

$$s_{26} = q_{22} \mid dd \to q_{22}q_{24} \mid d \ .$$

We leave to the reader the task of verifying that the parser works properly. In the case of correct input strings, that is, sentences in $L(G_{ab\varepsilon})$, the behavior of the parser is completely analogous to that of the canonical LR(1) parser. However, in the case of incorrect input strings, that is, nonsentences, the behaviors of the two parsers might be different. This is because the LR(2) parser, thanks to its longer lookahead strings, may detect an error and halt earlier than the LR(1) parser. For example, when given as input the nonsentence *aa*, the LR(1) parser proceeds one step until it detects the error:

$$\$q_1 \mid aa\$ \overset{s_1}{\Longrightarrow} \$q_1q_3 \mid a\$ \ .$$

In the LR(2) parser the initial configuration $\$q_1 \mid aa\$$ is already an error configuration.

Next we shall establish the correctness of the canonical LR($k$) parser: we shall show that it is indeed a right parser of the grammar. As in Chapter 5 in proving the correctness of the shift-reduce parser and the simple procedence parser we give two lemmas that relate rightmost derivations in the grammar with derivations in the parser.

In the first lemma (which is the easier one) we show that any derivation in the parser yields a rightmost derivation in the grammar. Actually, this is not much more than a restatement of Lemma 5.17 (for shift-reduce parsers) or Lemma 5.60 (for simple precedence parsers). This is because there is a homomorphism from the set of action strings of the canonical LR($k$) parser for grammar $G$ to the set of action strings of the shift-reduce parser for $G$. This homomorphism is defined as follows:

$$h([\delta]_k[\delta X_1]_k \dots [\delta X_1 \dots X_n]_k \mid y \to [\delta]_k[\delta A]_k \mid y)$$

$$= X_1 \dots X_n \mid \ \to A \mid \ .$$

$$h([\delta]_k \mid ay \to [\delta]_k[\delta a]_k \mid y) = \ \mid a \to a \mid \ .$$

The homomorphism $h$ maps reduce actions by rule $r$ to reduce actions by rule $r$ and shift actions on terminal $a$ to shift actions on terminal $a$. Moreover, whenever action $r'$ is applicable to a configuration

$$(c1) \qquad \$[\$]_k[\$Y_1]_k \ldots [\$Y_1 \ldots Y_n]_k \mid w\$$$

of the canonical LR($k$) parser, then $h(r')$ is applicable to the configuration

$$(c2) \qquad \$Y_1 \ldots Y_n \mid w\$$$

of the shift-reduce parser. Also, if the application of $r'$ to ($c$1) yields the configuration

$$\$[\$]_k[\$X_1]_k \ldots [\$X_1 \ldots X_m]_k \mid w'\$ \ ,$$

then the application of $h(r')$ to ($c$2) yields the configuration

$$\$X_1 \ldots X_m \mid w'\$ \ .$$

This means that whenever

$$\$[\$]_k[\$Y_1]_k \ldots [\$Y_1 \ldots Y_n]_k \mid w\$$$

$$\stackrel{\pi'}{\Longrightarrow} \$[\$]_k[\$X_1]_k \ldots [\$X_1 \ldots X_m]_k \mid y\$$$

holds in the canonical LR($k$) parser, then

$$\$Y_1 \ldots Y_n \mid w\$ \stackrel{h(\pi')}{\Longrightarrow} \$X_1 \ldots X_m \mid y\$$$

holds in the shift-reduce parser.

**Lemma 6.29** *Let $G = (V, T, P, S)$ be a grammar and $(M, \tau)$ its canonical LR(k) parser. Further let $Y_1, \ldots, Y_n$ be symbols in $V$ ($n \geq 0$), $w$ a string in $T^*$, $\Phi$ a string over the alphabet of $M$, and $\pi'$ an action string such that*

$$(a) \qquad \begin{array}{l} \$Y_1 \ldots Y_n \text{ is a viable prefix of the \$-augmented grammar } G' \text{ and} \\ \$[\$]_k[\$Y_1]_k \ldots [\$Y_1 \ldots Y_n]_k \mid w\$ \stackrel{\pi'}{\Longrightarrow} \Phi \qquad \text{in } M \ . \end{array}$$

*Then for some strings $x$ and $y$ and symbols $X_1, \ldots, X_m$ ($m \geq 0$)*

$$(b) \qquad \begin{array}{l} w = xy, \$X_1 \ldots X_m \text{ is a viable prefix of } G' \ , \\ \Phi = \$[\$]_k[\$X_1]_k \ldots [\$X_1 \ldots X_m]_k \mid y\$, \qquad |\pi'| = |\tau(\pi')| + |x| \ , \\ \text{and } X_1 \ldots X_m \xRightarrow[\text{rm}]{\tau(\pi')^R} Y_1 \ldots Y_n x \qquad \text{in } G \ . \end{array}$$

*Proof.* As in Lemma 5.17, the proof is by induction on the length of action string $\pi'$. If $\pi' = \varepsilon$, then

$$\Phi = \$[\$]_k[\$Y_1]_k \ldots [\$Y_1 \ldots Y_n]_k \mid w\$ \ , \tag{1}$$

and statements (*b*) hold when we choose $x = \varepsilon$, $y = w$, $m = n$, $X_1 = Y_1, \ldots, X_n = Y_n$. This proves the base case.

To prove the induction step, we assume that $\pi'$ is of the form $r'\pi''$, where $r'$ is a single action. As an induction hypothesis, we assume that the lemma holds for the action string $\pi''$. If $r'$ is a reduce action, then for some $p$, $1 \leqslant p \leqslant n+1$, and nonterminal $A$

$$\begin{aligned} &\$[\$]_k[\$Y_1]_k \ldots [\$Y_1 \ldots Y_n]_k \mid w\$ \\ &\overset{r'}{\Rightarrow} \$[\$]_k[\$Y_1]_k \ldots [\$Y_1 \ldots Y_{p-1}]_k[\$Y_1 \ldots Y_{p-1}A]_k \mid w\$ \\ &\overset{\pi''}{\Rightarrow} \Phi \quad \text{in } M \ , \end{aligned} \tag{2}$$

where $\$Y_1 \ldots Y_{p-1}A$ is a viable prefix of the \$-augmented grammar $G'$ for $G$ and $\tau(r') = A \to Y_p \ldots Y_n$. Then

$$Y_1 \ldots Y_{p-1}A \underset{\text{rm}}{\overset{\tau(r')}{\Longrightarrow}} Y_1 \ldots Y_n \qquad \text{in } G \ . \tag{3}$$

On the other hand, because $\$Y_1 \ldots Y_{p-1}A$ is a viable prefix of $G'$, we can apply the induction hypothesis to the latter derivation segment in (2) and conclude that for some strings $x$ and $y$ and symbols $X_1, \ldots, X_m$ $(m \geqslant 0)$

$$\begin{aligned} &w = xy, \qquad \$X_1 \ldots X_m \text{ is a viable prefix of } G' \ , \\ &\Phi = \$[\$]_k[\$X_1]_k \ldots [\$X_1 \ldots X_m]_k \mid y\$, \qquad |\pi''| = |\tau(\pi'')| + |x| \ , \\ &\text{and } X_1 \ldots X_m \underset{\text{rm}}{\overset{\tau(\pi'')^R}{\Longrightarrow}} Y_1 \ldots Y_{p-1}Ax \qquad \text{in } G \ . \end{aligned} \tag{4}$$

By combining (3) and (4) it is then easy to see that statements (*b*) hold. Note that $\tau(\pi'')^R\tau(r') = (\tau(r')\tau(\pi''))^R = \tau(r'\pi'')^R = \tau(\pi')$.

We have yet to consider the case in which $r'$ is a shift action on some terminal $a$. Then for some string $z$

$$\begin{aligned} &\$[\$]_k[\$Y_1]_k \ldots [\$Y_1 \ldots Y_n]_k \mid w\$ \\ &= \$[\$]_k[\$Y_1]_k \ldots [\$Y_1 \ldots Y_n]_k \mid az\$ \\ &\overset{r'}{\Rightarrow} \$[\$]_k[\$Y_1]_k \ldots [\$Y_1 \ldots Y_n]_k[\$Y_1 \ldots Y_na]_k \mid z\$ \\ &\overset{\pi''}{\Rightarrow} \Phi \quad \text{in } M \ , \end{aligned} \tag{5}$$

where $\$Y_1 \ldots Y_na$ is a viable prefix of $G'$ and $\tau(r') = \varepsilon$. Then we can apply the induction hypothesis to the latter derivation segment in (5) and conclude that for some strings $x'$ and $y$ and symbols $X_1 \ldots X_m$ ($m \geqslant 0$)

$$z = x'y, \qquad \$X_1 \ldots X_m \text{ is a viable prefix of } G' ,$$

(6) $$\Phi = \$[\$]_k[\$X_1]_k \ldots [\$X_1 \ldots X_m]_k \,|\, y\$, \qquad |\pi''| = |\tau(\pi'')| + |x'| ,$$

$$\text{and } X_1 \ldots X_m \xRightarrow[\text{rm}]{\tau(\pi'')} Y_1 \ldots Y_n ax' \qquad \text{in } G .$$

Statements (*b*) then hold if we choose $x = ax'$. Note that $\tau(r') = \varepsilon$ and that $w = az$. □

Corresponding to Lemmas 5.18 and 5.61 we have:

**Lemma 6.30** *If $(M, \tau)$ is the canonical LR(k) parser for grammar G, then $L(M) \subseteq L(G)$, and $\tau(\pi')$ is a right parse of sentence w in G whenever $\pi'$ is a parse of w in M. Moreover,* $\text{TIME}_G(w) \leqslant \text{TIME}_M(w) - |w|$.

*Proof.* Choose $n = 0$ and $\Phi = \$[\$]_k[\$S]_k \,|\, \$$ in Lemma 6.29. □

Next we shall establish the more difficult part of the correctness proof of the canonical LR(*k*) parser. The essence of this part of the proof is a lemma that corresponds to Lemma 5.19 (for shift-reduce parsers) and Lemma 5.63 (for simple precedence parsers). First we need a lemma that states when the parser can perform a sequence of successive shift actions.

**Lemma 6.31** *Let $G = (V, T, P, S)$ be a grammar and M its canonical LR(k) parser. Further let $\gamma$ be a viable prefix of the \$-augmented grammar $G'$ for G, $[A \to \alpha \cdot \beta, z]$ an item of $G'$, y a string in $T^*$, and $a_1, \ldots, a_n$ terminals in T ($n \geqslant 0$) such that*

(*a*) $$[A \to \alpha \cdot \beta, z] \in \text{VALID}_k(\gamma a_1 \ldots a_n) \text{ , and}$$
$$k{:}y\$ \in \text{FIRST}_k(\beta z).$$

*Then there is an n-length string $\pi'$ of shift actions of M such that*

(*b*) $$\$\Phi[\gamma]_k \,|\, a_1 \ldots a_n y\$ \overset{\pi'}{\Rightarrow} \$\Phi[\gamma]_k[\gamma a_1]_k \ldots [\gamma a_1 \ldots a_n]_k \,|\, y\$ \quad \text{in } M ,$$

*for any string $\Phi$ in $[G']_k^*$.*

*Proof.* We show that, for all $i = 1, \ldots, n$, $M$ has the shift action

$$r_i' = [\gamma a_1 \ldots a_{i-1}]_k \,|\, a_i z_i \to [\gamma a_1 \ldots a_{i-1}]_k[\gamma a_1 \ldots a_i]_k \,|\, z_i ,$$

where $a_i z_i = \max\{k, 1\}: a_i \ldots a_n y\$$. Observe that then, for any string $\Phi$ in $[G']_k^*$,

$$\$\Phi[\gamma]_k \mid a_1 \ldots a_n y\$$$

$$\overset{r_1'}{\Longrightarrow} \$\Phi[\gamma]_k[\gamma a_1]_k \mid a_2 \ldots a_n y\$$$

$$\vdots$$

$$\overset{r_{n-1}'}{\Longrightarrow} \$\Phi[\gamma]_k[\gamma a_1]_k \ldots [\gamma a_1 \ldots a_{n-1}]_k \mid a_n y\$$$

$$\overset{r_n'}{\Longrightarrow} \$\Phi[\gamma]_k[\gamma a_1]_k \ldots [\gamma a_1 \ldots a_{n-1}]_k[\gamma a_1 \ldots a_n]_k \mid y\$ \; .$$

Statement (*b*) then holds if we choose $\pi' = r_1' \ldots r_n'$.

To show that $M$ indeed has the shift actions $r_1', \ldots, r_n'$, let $i$ be any integer such that $1 \leqslant i \leqslant n$. Because $[A \to \alpha \cdot \beta, z]$ is an item in $\text{VALID}_k(\gamma a_1 \ldots a_n)$, we have, for some $\delta$ and $z'$,

$$S' \underset{\text{rm}}{\Longrightarrow}{}^* \delta A z' \underset{\text{rm}}{\Longrightarrow} \delta\alpha\beta z' = \gamma a_1 \ldots a_n \beta z', \quad \text{and}$$

$$k{:}z' = z \; .$$

We have two cases to consider: (1) $a_i$ is contained in $\alpha$, that is, $\alpha$ is of the form $\alpha' a_i \ldots a_n$; (2) $a_i$ is not contained in $\alpha$, that is, $\delta = \gamma a_1 \ldots a_{j-1}$ and $\alpha = a_j \ldots a_n$ for some $j > i$. In case (1) we have:

$$[A \to \alpha' \cdot a_i \ldots a_n \beta, z] \in \text{VALID}_k(\gamma a_1 \ldots a_{i-1}) \; .$$

Moreover, the condition $k{:}y\$ \in \text{FIRST}_k(\beta z)$ implies that

$$\max\{k, 1\}: a_i \ldots a_n y\$ \in \text{FIRST}_{\max\{k,\,1\}}(a_i \ldots a_n \beta z) \; ,$$

which means that $M$ has the shift action $r_i'$. In case (2), we can apply Lemma 6.2 to the derivation

$$S' \underset{\text{rm}}{\Longrightarrow}{}^+ \delta A z' = \gamma a_1 \ldots a_i \ldots a_{j-1} A z'$$

and conclude that for some strings $\delta'$ and $y'$ and rule $A' \to \alpha'' a_i \beta'$

$$S' \underset{\text{rm}}{\Longrightarrow}{}^* \delta' A' y' \underset{\text{rm}}{\Longrightarrow} \delta' \alpha'' a_i \beta' y' = \gamma a_1 \ldots a_i \beta' y', \text{ and}$$

$$\beta' y' \underset{\text{rm}}{\Longrightarrow}{}^* a_{i+1} \ldots a_{j-1} A z' \; .$$

Here we have:

$$[A' \to \alpha'' \cdot a_i \beta', k{:}y'] \in \text{VALID}_k(\gamma a_1 \ldots a_{i-1}) \; .$$

Moreover, the conditions $k{:}z' = z$ and $k{:}y\$ \in \text{FIRST}_k(\beta z)$ imply that

$$\max\{k, 1\}: a_i \ldots a_n y\$ \in \text{FIRST}_{\max\{k,\,1\}}(a_i \beta'(k{:}y')) \; ,$$

because

$$a_i\beta' y' \Rightarrow^* a_i \ldots a_{j-1} A z' \Rightarrow a_i \ldots a_n \beta z' .$$

Thus even in this case $M$ has the shift action $r_i'$. □

Now we can prove the lemma that corresponds to Lemmas 5.19 and 5.63:

**Lemma 6.32** *Let $G = (V, T, P, S)$ be a grammar and $(M, \tau)$ its canonical LR(k) parser. Further let $X_1, \ldots, X_m, Y_1, \ldots, Y_n$ be symbols in $V$ ($m, n \geq 0$), $x$ and $y$ strings in $T^*$, $\pi$ a rule string in $P^*$, and $[A \to \alpha \cdot \beta, z]$ a k-item of the \$-augmented grammar $G'$ for $G$ such that*

$$(a) \quad \begin{cases} X_1 \ldots X_m \overset{\pi^R}{\underset{\text{rm}}{\Longrightarrow}} Y_1 \ldots Y_n x & \text{in } G , \\ [A \to \alpha \cdot \beta, z] \in \text{VALID}_k(\$X_1 \ldots X_m) , \\ k{:}y\$ \in \text{FIRST}_k(\beta z), \text{ and} \\ \text{either } Y_1 \ldots Y_n = \varepsilon \text{ or } Y_n \text{ is a nonterminal} . \end{cases}$$

*Then for some action string $\pi'$*

$$(b) \quad \begin{cases} \tau(\pi') = \pi, |\pi'| = |\pi| + |x|, \text{ and} \\ \$[\$]_k[\$Y_1]_k \ldots [\$Y_1 \ldots Y_n]_k \mid xy\$ \\ \overset{\pi'}{\Longrightarrow} \$[\$]_k[\$X_1]_k \ldots [\$X_1 \ldots X_m]_k \mid y\$ \quad \text{in } M . \end{cases}$$

*Proof.* The proof is by induction on the length of rule string $\pi$. In the base case we have $\pi = \varepsilon$ and hence $X_1 \ldots X_m = Y_1 \ldots Y_n x$. Then

$$(1) \quad \begin{array}{l} [A \to \alpha \cdot \beta, z] \in \text{VALID}_k(\$Y_1 \ldots Y_n x) \text{ and} \\ k{:}y\$ \in \text{FIRST}_k(\beta z) , \end{array}$$

which implies, by Lemma 6.31, the existence of $\pi'$, an $|x|$-length string of shift actions of $M$, such that

$$(2) \quad \begin{array}{l} \$[\$]_k[\$Y_1]_k \ldots [\$Y_1 \ldots Y_n]_k \mid xy\$ \\ \overset{\pi'}{\Rightarrow} \$[\$]_k[\$Y_1]_k \ldots [\$Y_1 \ldots Y_n]_k \ldots [\$Y_1 \ldots Y_n x]_k \mid y\$ . \end{array}$$

As $\tau(\pi') = \varepsilon$, we can conclude that statements (*b*) hold.

To prove the induction step, we assume that $\pi$ is of the form $r\pi_1$, where $r$ is a rule $B \to \omega$. As an induction hypothesis, we assume that the lemma holds for the rule string $\pi_1$. We have:

$$(3) \quad X_1 \ldots X_m \overset{\pi_1^R}{\underset{\text{rm}}{\Longrightarrow}} Z_1 \ldots Z_p B x_1 \overset{r}{\underset{\text{rm}}{\Longrightarrow}} Z_1 \ldots Z_p \omega x_1 = Y_1 \ldots Y_n x \quad \text{in } G$$

for some symbols $Z_1, \ldots, Z_p$ in $V (p \geq 0)$ and string $x_1$ in $T^*$. Here $x = vx_1$ and

$Z_1 \dots Z_p\omega = Y_1 \dots Y_n v$ for some $v$, because $Y_1 \dots Y_n$ is empty or ends with a nonterminal. As $Z_1 \dots Z_p B$ ends with a nonterminal we can apply the induction hypothesis to the first derivation segment in (3) and conclude that for some action string $\pi'_1$

(4)
$$\tau(\pi'_1) = \pi_1, \quad |\pi'_1| = |\pi_1| + |x_1|, \text{ and}$$
$$\$[\$]_k[\$Z_1]_k \dots [\$Z_1 \dots Z_p]_k[\$Z_1 \dots Z_p B]_k \mid x_1 y\$$$
$$\overset{\pi'_1}{\Longrightarrow} \$[\$]_k[\$X_1]_k \dots [\$X_1 \dots X_m]_k \mid y\$ \qquad \text{in } M\ .$$

On the other hand, because $[A \to \alpha \cdot \beta, z]$ is an item in $\text{VALID}_k(\$X_1 \dots X_m)$, we have

(5)
$$S' \underset{\text{rm}}{\Longrightarrow}^* \delta A z' \underset{\text{rm}}{\Longrightarrow} \delta\alpha\beta z' = \$X_1 \dots X_m \beta z' \qquad \text{in } G'\ ,$$
$$\text{and } k{:}z' = z$$

for some strings $\delta$ and $z'$. The condition $k{:}y\$ \in \text{FIRST}_k(\beta z)$ implies (by Theorem 4.2) the existence of a string $u$ in $T^*$ such that

(6)
$$\beta \underset{\text{rm}}{\Longrightarrow}^* u \quad \text{and} \quad k{:}uz = k{:}y\$\ .$$

By (5), (6), and (3) we then have:

(7)
$$S' \underset{\text{rm}}{\Longrightarrow}^* \$Z_1 \dots Z_p B x_1 u z' \underset{\text{rm}}{\Longrightarrow} \$Z_1 \dots Z_p \omega x_1 u z' \qquad \text{in } G'\ .$$

Here $k{:}x_1 uz' = k{:}x_1 uz = k{:}x_1 y\$$ (by (5) and (6)), which means that

(8)
$$[B \to \omega\cdot, k{:}x_1 y\$] \in \text{VALID}_k(\$Z_1 \dots Z_p\omega)\ .$$

As here $\$Z_1 \dots Z_p\omega = \$Y_1 \dots Y_n v$, where $v$ is in $T^*$, we may conclude by Lemma 6.31 that

(9)
$$\$[\$]_k[\$Y_1]_k \dots [\$Y_1 \dots Y_n]_k \mid xy\$$$
$$= \$[\$]_k[\$Y_1]_k \dots [\$Y_1 \dots Y_n]_k \mid vx_1 y\$$$
$$\overset{\pi'_2}{\Longrightarrow} \$[\$]_k[\$Y_1]_k \dots [\$Y_1 \dots Y_n]_k \dots [\$Y_1 \dots Y_n v]_k \mid x_1 y\$$$
$$= \$[\$]_k[\$Z_1]_k \dots [\$Z_1 \dots Z_p]_k \dots [\$Z_1 \dots Z_p\omega]_k \mid x_1 y\$ \quad \text{in } M\ ,$$

for some $|v|$-length shift action string $\pi'_2$. Moreover, (8) implies that $M$ has the reduce action

(10)
$$r' = [\$Z_1 \dots Z_p]_k \dots [\$Z_1 \dots Z_p\omega]_k \mid y' \to$$
$$[\$Z_1 \dots Z_p]_k[\$Z_1 \dots Z_p B]_k \mid y'\ ,$$

where $y' = k{:}x_1 y\$$. This means that

$$(11)\qquad \begin{aligned} &\$[\$]_k[\$Z_1]_k \ldots [\$Z_1 \ldots Z_p]_k \ldots [\$Z_1 \ldots Z_p\omega]_k \mid x_1 y\$ \\ &\overset{r'}{\Rightarrow} \$[\$]_k[\$Z_1]_k \ldots [\$Z_1 \ldots Z_p]_k[\$Z_1 \ldots Z_p B]_k \mid x_1 y\$ \quad \text{in } M\ . \end{aligned}$$

Combining (9), (11), and (4) we then have:

$$(12)\qquad \begin{aligned} &\$[\$]_k[\$Y_1]_k \ldots [\$Y_1 \ldots Y_n]_k \mid xy\$ \\ &\overset{\pi'}{\Rightarrow} \$[\$]_k[\$X_1]_k \ldots [\$X_1 \ldots X_m]_k \mid y\$ \quad \text{in } M\ , \end{aligned}$$

where $\pi' = \pi'_2 r' \pi'_1$. Here

$$(13)\qquad \begin{aligned} &\tau(\pi') = \tau(\pi'_2)\tau(r')\tau(\pi'_1) = r\pi_1 = \pi, \text{ and} \\ &|\pi'| = |\pi'_2| + |r'| + |\pi'_1| = |v| + 1 + |\pi_1| + |x_1| = |r\pi_1| + |vx_1| \\ &= |\pi| + |x|\ , \end{aligned}$$

as claimed. □

Corresponding to Lemmas 5.20 and 5.64 we have:

**Lemma 6.33** *If* $(M, \tau)$ *is the canonical LR(k) parser for grammar G, then* $L(G) \subseteq L(M)$, *and for any right parse* $\pi$ *of sentence w in G,* $\tau(\pi') = \pi$ *for some parse* $\pi'$ *of w in M. Moreover,* $\text{TIME}_M(w) \leqslant \text{TIME}_G(w) + |w|$.

*Proof.* Choose $m = 1$, $n = 0$, $X_1 = S$, $x = w$, $[A \to \alpha \cdot \beta, z] = [S' \to \$S \cdot \$, \varepsilon]$, and $y = \varepsilon$ in Lemma 6.32. □

By Lemmas 6.30 and 6.33 we now have:

**Theorem 6.34** *The canonical LR(k) parser M for grammar G is a right parser for G. Moreover, for each sentence w in L(G), M produces all right parses of w in G, and* $\text{TIME}_M(w) = \text{TIME}_G(w) + |w|$. □

## 6.4 LR(*k*) Grammars

We say that a grammar $G = (V, T, P, S)$ is *LR(k)* if its canonical LR($k$) parser is deterministic and if, in addition, $S \Rightarrow^+ S$ is impossible in $G$. A language over alphabet $T$ is *LR(k)* if it is the language generated by some LR($k$) grammar with terminal alphabet $T$.

As in the definition of simple precedence grammars (Section 5.7), we require that the start symbol must not nontrivially derive itself. Otherwise some ambiguous grammars might be called LR($k$) grammars, for example the grammar $S \rightarrow a|S$, which has a deterministic LR(0) parser.

First we note:

**Theorem 6.35** *Any LR($k$) grammar is unambiguous.*

*Proof.* The proof is completely analogous to that for simple precedence grammars (Theorem 5.66). Let $M$ be the canonical LR($k$) parser for an LR($k$) grammar $G$. By definition, $M$ is deterministic. Moreover, $S \Rightarrow^+ S$ is not possible in $G$. Thus, by Lemma 6.29,

$$\$[\$]_k[\$S]_k \mid \$ \Rightarrow^+ \$[\$]_k[\$S]_k \mid \$$$

is not possible in $M$. Together with determinism, this means that $M$ has exactly one accepting computation on each $w$ in $L(G)$ and hence produces for each $w$ exactly one right parse in $G$. On the other hand, by Theorem 6.34, $M$ produces all the right parses. So each $w$ in $L(G)$ has exactly one right parse in $G$, which means, by Theorem 4.12, that $G$ is unambiguous. □

Next we shall derive a grammatical characterization for LR($k$) grammars, one that resembles the characterization of SLL($k$) grammars given in Theorem 5.34($d$). To this end we shall first prove a lemma that relates the nondeterminism of the canonical LR($k$) parser with the occurrence of "reduce-reduce conflicts" and "shift-reduce conflicts" between pairs of items in states of the canonical LR($k$) machine.

Let $G = (V, T, P, S)$ be a grammar, $G'$ its \$-augmented grammar, and $k$ a natural number. We say that $k$-items $[A_1 \rightarrow \omega_1 \cdot, y_1]$ and $[A_2 \rightarrow \omega_2 \cdot, y_2]$ of $G'$ *exhibit a reduce-reduce-conflict* if $y_1 = y_2$ and $A_1 \rightarrow \omega_1$ and $A_2 \rightarrow \omega_2$ are distinct rules. We say that $k$-items $[A \rightarrow \alpha \cdot a\beta, z]$ and $[B \rightarrow \omega \cdot, y]$ of $G'$ *exhibit a shift-reduce conflict* if $a$ is a terminal in $T$ and $y$ is in $\mathrm{FIRST}_k(a\beta z)$.

**Lemma 6.36** *The canonical LR($k$) parser for grammar $G = (V, T, P, S)$ is nondeterministic if and only if some state in the canonical LR($k$) machine contains a pair of items exhibiting a reduce-reduce or shift-reduce conflict.*

*Proof.* First assume that for some viable prefix $\gamma$ of $G'$, $\mathrm{VALID}_k(\gamma)$ contains a pair of items $I_1, I_2$ exhibiting a reduce-reduce or a shift-reduce conflict. Then either

(1) $\quad I_1 = [A \rightarrow X_1 \ldots X_n \cdot, y]$ and $I_2 = [B \rightarrow Y_1 \ldots Y_m \cdot, y]$

for some distinct rules $A \rightarrow X_1 \ldots X_n$ and $B \rightarrow Y_1 \ldots Y_m$ and string $y$, or

(2) $\quad I_1 = [A \rightarrow X_1 \ldots X_n \cdot a\beta, z]$, $I_2 = [B \rightarrow Y_1 \ldots Y_m \cdot, y]$, and $y \in \mathrm{FIRST}_k(a\beta z)$

for some rules $A \rightarrow X_1 \ldots X_n a\beta$ and $B \rightarrow Y_1 \ldots Y_m$, terminal $a$ in $T$, and strings $z$ and $y$. First we note by Fact 6.24 that both $X_1 \ldots X_n$ and $Y_1 \ldots Y_m$ are suffixes of $\gamma$. We assume that $m \leqslant n$ (the case $n < m$ is handled analogously). Then

$Y_1 \ldots Y_m = X_i \ldots X_n$, where $i = n - m + 1$. By definition, the parser has in case (1) the pair of reduce actions

$$\text{(3)} \quad \begin{aligned} &[\delta]_k[\delta X_1]_k \ldots [\delta X_1 \ldots X_n]_k \mid y \to [\delta]_k[\delta A]_k \mid y \ , \\ &[\delta X_1 \ldots X_{i-1}]_k[\delta X_1 \ldots X_i]_k \ldots [\delta X_1 \ldots X_n]_k \mid y \\ &\to [\delta X_1 \ldots X_{i-1}]_k[\delta X_1 \ldots X_{i-1} B]_k \mid y \ , \end{aligned}$$

and in case (2) the pair of shift and reduce actions

$$\text{(4)} \quad \begin{aligned} &[\delta X_1 \ldots X_n]_k \mid ay' \to [\delta X_1 \ldots X_n]_k[\delta X_1 \ldots X_n a]_k \mid y' \ , \\ &[\delta X_1 \ldots X_{i-1}]_k[\delta X_1 \ldots X_i]_k \ldots [\delta X_1 \ldots X_n]_k \mid y \\ &\to [\delta X_1 \ldots X_{i-1}]_k[\delta X_1 \ldots X_{i-1} B]_k \mid y \ , \end{aligned}$$

where $\delta X_1 \ldots X_n = \gamma$ and $k{:}ay' = y$. But the pair of actions (3) are both applicable to any configuration

$$\text{(5)} \quad \$[\delta]_k[\delta X_1]_k \ldots [\delta X_1 \ldots X_n]_k \mid w\$ \ ,$$

where $ay'$ is a prefix of $w\$$, and so are (4). This means that the parser is nondeterministic.

To prove the converse, assume that the parser is nondeterministic. Then there is a pair of distinct actions $r_1$, $r_2$ both applicable to the same configuration. We have to consider three cases: (a) $r_1$ and $r_2$ are both reduce actions, (b) $r_1$ is a shift action and $r_2$ is a reduce action, and (c) both $r_1$ and $r_2$ are shift actions. First we note that case (c) can never happen because if two shift actions are applicable to the same configuration, then they have to be of the form

$$\text{(6)} \quad \begin{aligned} &[\gamma]_k \mid ay \to [\gamma]_k[\gamma a]_k \mid y \ , \\ &[\gamma]_k \mid ayv \to [\gamma]_k[\gamma a]_k \mid yv \ , \end{aligned}$$

where for some items $[A_1 \to \alpha_1 \cdot a\beta_1, z_1]$ and $[A_2 \to \alpha_2 \cdot a\beta_2, z_2]$ in $\text{VALID}_k(\gamma)$,

$$\text{(7)} \quad \begin{aligned} &y \in \text{FIRST}_{\max\{k-1,\,0\}}(\beta_1 z_1), \quad \text{and} \\ &yv \in \text{FIRST}_{\max\{k-1,\,0\}}(\beta_2 z_2) \ . \end{aligned}$$

Because $A_1 \to \alpha_1, a\beta_1$, and $A_2 \to \alpha_2 a\beta_2$ are distinct from $S' \to \$S\$$, neither $\beta_1$ nor $\beta_2$ can derive a string containing \$. On the other hand, the lookahead strings $z_1$ and $z_2$ can contain \$ only as the last symbol. Hence $y$ and $yv$ can contain \$ only as the last symbol. Moreover, $y$ can be shorter than $yv$ only if $y$ ends with \$. But then $v$ must be $\varepsilon$. So the actions in (6) are in fact identical. In the same way, we can conclude that in case (a) the lookahead strings in both reduce actions must be the same and that in case (b) the lookahead string of the shift action $r_1$ must be of the form $ay'$, where $k{:}ay'$ is the lookahead string of the reduce action $r_2$.

In case (a) we have

$$\text{(8)} \quad \begin{aligned} &r_1 = [\delta]_k[\delta X_1]_k \ldots [\delta X_1 \ldots X_n]_k \mid y \to [\delta]_k[\delta A]_k \mid y \ , \\ &r_2 = [\gamma]_k[\gamma Y_1]_k \ldots [\gamma Y_1 \ldots Y_m]_k \mid y \to [\gamma]_k[\gamma B]_k \mid y \ , \end{aligned}$$

for some strings $\delta$ and $\gamma$ and distinct rules $A \to X_1 \ldots X_n$ and $B \to Y_1 \ldots Y_m$ such that one of the strings $[\delta]_k[\delta X_1]_k \ldots [\delta X_1 \ldots X_n]_k$ and $[\gamma]_k[\gamma Y_1]_k \ldots [\gamma Y_1 \ldots Y_m]_k$ is a suffix of the other. In particular,

(9) $$[\delta X_1 \ldots X_n]_k = [\gamma Y_1 \ldots Y_m]_k \ .$$

On the other hand, we conclude by definition that $\mathrm{VALID}_k(\delta X_1 \ldots X_n)$ contains the item $[A \to X_1 \ldots X_n \cdot, y]$ and $\mathrm{VALID}_k(\gamma Y_1 \ldots Y_m)$ contains the item $[B \to Y_1 \ldots Y_m \cdot, y]$. Thus, a state in the canonical LR($k$) machine contains a pair of items exhibiting a reduce-reduce conflict.

In case (b) we have:

(10) $$\begin{aligned} r_1 &= [\delta]_k \mid ay' \to [\delta]_k[\delta a]_k \mid y' \ , \\ r_2 &= [\gamma]_k[\gamma X_1]_k \ldots [\gamma X_1 \ldots X_n]_k \mid y \to [\gamma]_k[\gamma B]_k \mid y \end{aligned}$$

for some strings $\delta$ and $\gamma$, terminal $a$, strings $y'$ and $y$, and rule $B \to X_1 \ldots X_n$ such that

(11) $$[\delta]_k = [\gamma X_1 \ldots X_n]_k \quad \text{and} \quad y = k{:}ay' \ .$$

By definition, $\mathrm{VALID}_k(\delta)$ contains an item $[A \to \alpha \cdot a\beta, z]$, where $y'$ is in $\mathrm{FIRST}_{\max\{k-1,\,0\}}(\beta z)$, and $\mathrm{VALID}_k(\gamma X_1 \ldots X_n)$ contains the item $[B \to X_1 \ldots X_n \cdot, y]$. Then $y$ is in $\mathrm{FIRST}_k(a\beta z)$. Thus a state in the canonical LR($k$) machine contains a pair of actions exhibiting a shift-reduce conflict. □

The grammar $G_{ab\varepsilon}$ considered in Section 6.3 is not an LR(0) grammar because the LR(0) machine has states that contain pairs of items exhibiting a shift-reduce conflict. (See Figure 6.5, the item pair $[A \to \cdot]$, $[A \to \cdot cAd]$ in states $q_3$ and $q_7$ and the item pair $[B \to \cdot]$, $[B \to \cdot cBd]$ in states $q_4$ and $q_8$.)

As an example of a grammar which is not LR(1) due to a reduce-reduce conflict, consider the grammar

$$\begin{array}{ll} S \to AB, & C \to ab \ , \\ A \to a, & D \to b \ , \\ B \to CDb \mid aEb, & E \to b \ . \end{array}$$

The canonical LR(1) machine for the \$-augmented grammar is shown in Figure 6.9. The item pair $[C \to ab \cdot, b]$, $[E \to b \cdot, b]$ in state $q_{12}$ ($= \mathrm{VALID}_1$ (\$$Aab$)) exhibits a reduce-reduce conflict. Thus the grammar is not LR(1). Observe however that the grammar is LR(2), because in the canonical LR(2) machine the state $\mathrm{VALID}_2(\$Aab)$ consists of the items $[C \to ab \cdot, bb]$ and $[E \to b \cdot, b\$]$, which do not exhibit any conflict.

Consider then a variation of the above grammar in which the rule $E \to b$ has been replaced by $E \to bba$. The canonical LR(1) machine for the augmented grammar is depicted in Figure 6.10. State $q_{12}$ now contains the item pair $[E \to b \cdot ba, b]$, $[C \to ab \cdot, b]$, which exhibits a shift-reduce conflict. In the

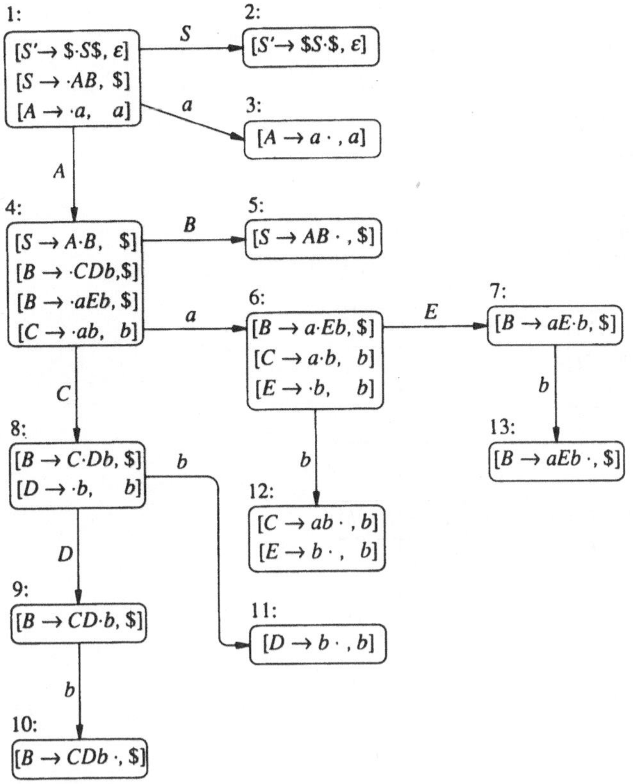


**Figure 6.9** The canonical LR(1) machine for the \$-augmented grammar $S' \to \$S\$$, $S \to AB$, $A \to a$, $B \to CDb|aEb$, $C \to ab$, $D \to b$, $E \to b$. State $q_{12}$ contains a pair of items exhibiting a reduce-reduce conflict

canonical LR(2) machine the state $\mathrm{VALID}_2(\$Aab)$ consists of the non-conflicting items $[E \to b \cdot ba, b\$]$ and $[C \to ab \cdot, bb]$ and so the grammar is LR(2).

**Lemma 6.37** *Let M be the canonical LR(k) parser for a grammar $G = (V, T, P, S)$ and let $\gamma$ be a viable prefix of the \$-augmented grammar $G'$ for G. Then $\mathrm{VALID}_k(\gamma)$ contains a pair of items exhibiting a reduce-reduce conflict if and only if the statements*

$$(a)\ S' \underset{rm}{\Longrightarrow}^* \delta_1 A_1 y_1 \underset{rm}{\Longrightarrow} \delta_1 \omega_1 y_1 = \gamma y_1 \ ,$$

$$(b)\ S' \underset{rm}{\Longrightarrow}^* \delta_2 A_2 y_2 \underset{rm}{\Longrightarrow} \delta_2 \omega_2 y_2 = \gamma y_2 \ ,$$

*(c)* $k{:}y_1 = k{:}y_2$, *and*

*(d)* $A_1 \to \omega_1 \neq A_2 \to \omega_2$

*hold in $G'$ for some strings $\delta_1, \delta_2 \in \$V^*$, $y_1, y_2 \in T^*\$$, and rules $A_1 \to \omega_1$, $A_2 \to \omega_2$ in P.*

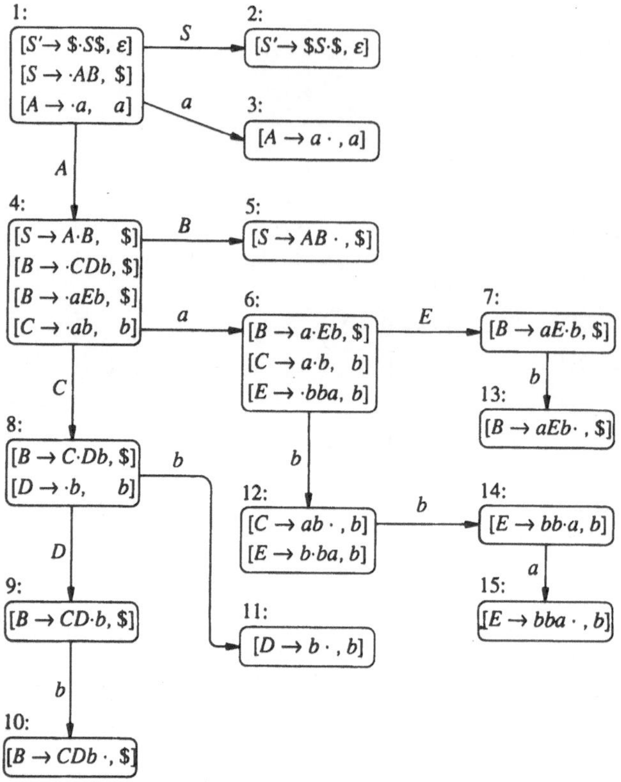


**Figure 6.10** The canonical LR(1) machine for the \$-augmented grammar $S' \to \$S\$$, $S \to AB$, $A \to a$, $B \to CDb|aEb$, $C \to ab$, $D \to b$, $E \to bba$. State $q_{12}$ contains a pair of items exhibiting a shift-reduce conflict

*Proof.* The lemma follows directly from the definition of a reduce-reduce conflict and the definition of LR($k$)-validity. Note that in (a) and (b) the items $[A_1 \to \omega_1\cdot, k{:}y_1]$ and $[A_2 \to \omega_2\cdot, k{:}y_2]$ belong to VALID$_k(\gamma)$. Also note that $\delta_1$, $\delta_2$ are in $\$V^*$, $y_1, y_2$ are in $T^*\$$, and $A_1 \to \omega_1$, $A_2 \to \omega_2$ are in $P$, because $A_1 \to \omega_1$ and $A_2 \to \omega_2$ are, by (d), distinct rules and because VALID$_k(\$S\$)$ contains only the item $[S' \to \$S\$\cdot, \varepsilon]$. □

For example, in the grammar of Figure 6.9 we have:

$$S' \underset{\text{rm}}{\Longrightarrow}^4 \$ACbb\$ \underset{\text{rm}}{\Longrightarrow} \$Aabbb\$ = \delta_1\omega_1 bb\$ = \gamma bb\$ \ ,$$

$$S' \underset{\text{rm}}{\Longrightarrow}^3 \$AaEb\$ \underset{\text{rm}}{\Longrightarrow} \$Aabb\$ = \delta_2\omega_2 b\$ = \gamma b\$ \ ,$$

where $\delta_1 = \$A$, $\delta_2 = \$Aa$, $\omega_1 = ab$, $\omega_2 = b$, and $\gamma = \delta_1\omega_1 = \delta_2\omega_2 = \$Aab$.

**Lemma 6.38** *Let $M$ be the canonical LR(k) parser for a grammar $G = (V, T, P, S)$ and let $\gamma$ be a viable prefix of the \$-augmented grammar $G'$ for $G$. Then* $\text{VALID}_k(\gamma)$ *contains a pair of items exhibiting a shift-reduce conflict if and only if the statements*

(a) $S' \underset{rm}{\Rightarrow}^* \delta_1 A_1 y_1 \underset{rm}{\Rightarrow} \delta_1 \omega_1 y_1 = \gamma y_1$ ,

(b) $S' \underset{rm}{\Rightarrow}^* \delta_2 A_2 y_2 \underset{rm}{\Rightarrow} \delta_2 \omega_2 y_2 = \gamma v y_2$ ,

(c) $v \neq \varepsilon$, *and*

(d) $k{:}y_1 = k{:}vy_2$

*hold in $G'$ for some strings $\delta_1, \delta_2 \in \$V^*$, strings $y_1, y_2 \in T^*\$$, string $v \in T^*$, and rules $A_1 \to \omega_1$ and $A_2 \to \omega_2$ in $P$.*

*Proof.* We first assume that $[A \to \alpha \cdot a\beta, z]$ and $[B \to \omega \cdot, y]$ are items in $\text{VALID}_k(\gamma)$ exhibiting a shift-reduce conflict. By definition, we then have in $G'$:

$$S' \underset{rm}{\Rightarrow}^* \delta_1 B y_1 \underset{rm}{\Rightarrow} \delta_1 \omega y_1 = \gamma y_1 ,$$

$$S' \underset{rm}{\Rightarrow}^* \delta_2' A y_2' \underset{rm}{\Rightarrow} \delta_2' \alpha a \beta y_2' = \gamma a \beta y_2' ,$$

$$k{:}y_1 = y, \quad k{:}y_2' = z, \quad \text{and}$$

$$y \in \text{FIRST}_k(a\beta z) ,$$

for some strings $\delta_1$ and $\delta_2'$ and terminal strings $y_1$ and $y_2'$. The condition $a \in T$ implies that here $A \to \alpha a \beta$ and $B \to \omega$ are distinct from $S' \to \$S\$$ and that $\delta_1, \delta_2'$ are strings in $\$V^*$ and $y_1, y_2'$ strings in $T^*\$$. Now if $\beta$ is in $T^*$, statements (a) to (d) readily hold for $A_1 = B, \omega_1 = \omega, A_2 = A, \omega_2 = \alpha a \beta, \delta_2 = \delta_2', y_2 = y_2'$, and $v = a\beta$. If, on the contrary, $\beta$ contains nonterminals, then the condition $y \in \text{FIRST}_k(a\beta z)$ implies, by Lemma 4.1 and Theorem 4.2, that

$$\beta \underset{rm}{\Rightarrow}^* \alpha' A_2 y' \underset{rm}{\Rightarrow} \alpha' \omega_2 y' = v' y', \text{ and}$$

$$y = k{:}av'y'z ,$$

for some string $\alpha' \in V^*$, $y', v' \in T^*$, and rule $A_2 \to \omega_2$ in $P$. Then

$$S' \underset{rm}{\Rightarrow}^* \gamma a \alpha' A_2 y' y_2' \underset{rm}{\Rightarrow} \gamma a \alpha' \omega_2 y' y_2' = \gamma a v' y' y_2' .$$

If we choose $v = av'$, then $v \neq \varepsilon$,

$$k{:}y_1 = y = k{:}av'y'z = k{:}vy'z = k{:}vy'(k{:}y_2') = k{:}vy'y_2' ,$$

and (b) holds for $\delta_2 = \gamma a \alpha'$ and $y_2 = y' y_2$.

To prove the converse, we assume that statements (a) to (d) hold. In (a), $[A_1 \to \omega_1 \cdot, k{:}\ y_1]$ is an item in $\text{VALID}_k(\gamma)$. In (b), we have to consider two cases: (1) $v$ is a suffix of $\omega_2$, or (2) $\omega_2$ is a proper suffix of $v$. In case (1), $\omega_2$ is of the form $\alpha v$, and so $[A_2 \to \alpha \cdot v, k\!:\!y_2]$ is an item in $\text{VALID}_k(\gamma)$. By (c) and (d), $[A_2 \to \alpha \cdot v, k\!:\!y_2]$ and $[A_1 \to \omega_1 \cdot, k\!:\!y_1]$ then exhibit a shift-reduce conflict. In case (2), $v$ is of the form $az\omega_2$, for some $a$ in $T$ and $z$ in $T^*$. By (b), we then have:

$$S' \underset{\text{rm}}{\Longrightarrow}^* \delta_2 A_2 y_2 = \gamma a z A_2 y_2 \ .$$

Here we can apply Lemma 6.2 and conclude that

$$S' \underset{\text{rm}}{\Longrightarrow}^* \alpha' A' y' \underset{\text{rm}}{\Longrightarrow} \alpha'\alpha'' a\beta' y' = \gamma a \beta' y', \quad \beta' y' \Rightarrow^* z A_2 y_2 \ ,$$

for some strings $\alpha'$, $y'$ and rule $A' \to \alpha'' a \beta'$. Then $[A' \to \alpha'' \cdot a\beta', k\!:\!y']$ is an item in $\text{VALID}_k(\gamma)$. Moreover,

$$a\beta' y' \Longrightarrow^* a z A_2 y_2 \Rightarrow a z \omega_2 y_2 = v y_2 \ ,$$

which means that $k\!:\!vy_2$ is in $\text{FIRST}_k(a\beta'(k\!:\!y'))$. By (d), $[A' \to \alpha'' \cdot a\beta', k\!:\!y']$ and $[A_1 \to \omega_1 \cdot, k\!:\!y_1]$ exhibit a shift-reduce conflict. □

For example, in the grammar of Figure 6.10 we have:

$$S' \underset{\text{rm}}{\Longrightarrow}^4 \$ACbb\$ \underset{\text{rm}}{\Longrightarrow} \$Aabbb\$ = \delta_1 \omega_1 bb\$ = \gamma bb\$ \ ,$$

$$S' \underset{\text{rm}}{\Longrightarrow}^3 \$AaEb\$ \underset{\text{rm}}{\Longrightarrow} \$Aabbab\$ = \delta_2 \omega_2 b\$ = \gamma bab\$ \ ,$$

where $\delta_1 = \$A$, $\delta_2 = \$Aa$, $\omega_1 = ab$, $\omega_2 = bba$, $\gamma = \delta_1\omega_1 = \$Aab$, $y_1 = bb\$$, $v = ba$, and $y_2 = b\$$.

**Theorem 6.39** (*Characterizations of LR(k) Grammars*) *The following statements are logically equivalent for all grammars $G = (V, T, P, S)$ and natural numbers $k$.*

(a) *The canonical LR(k) parser of G is deterministic.*

(b) *In the canonical LR(k) machine of the \$-augmented grammar G′ no state contains a pair of items exhibiting a reduce-reduce or a shift-reduce conflict.*

(c) *The conditions*

$$S \underset{\text{rm}}{\Longrightarrow}^* \delta_1 A_1 y_1 \underset{\text{rm}}{\Longrightarrow} \delta_1 \omega_1 y_1 = \gamma y_1 \qquad \textit{in } G \ ,$$

$$S \underset{\text{rm}}{\Longrightarrow}^* \delta_2 A_2 y_2 \underset{\text{rm}}{\Longrightarrow} \delta_2 \omega_2 y_2 = \gamma v y_2 \qquad \textit{in } G \ ,$$

*and* $k\!:\!y_1 = k\!:\!vy_2$

*always imply that $\delta_1 = \delta_2$, $A_1 = A_2$, and $\omega_1 = \omega_2$.*

*Proof.* The equivalence of statements (a) and (b) is stated in Lemma 6.36. The equivalence of statements (b) and (c) follows from Lemmas 6.37 and 6.38. Note that (c) is clearly equivalent to the following statement:

(c′) The conditions

$$S' \underset{rm}{\Longrightarrow}^{*} \delta_1 A_1 y_1 \underset{rm}{\Longrightarrow} \delta_1 \omega_1 y_1 = \gamma y_1 \qquad \text{in } G' ,$$

$$S' \underset{rm}{\Longrightarrow}^{*} \delta_2 A_2 y_2 \underset{rm}{\Longrightarrow} \delta_2 \omega_2 y_2 = \gamma v y_2 \qquad \text{in } G' ,$$

and $k{:}y_1 = k{:}vy_2$

always imply that $\delta_1 = \delta_2$, $A_1 = A_2$, and $\omega_1 = \omega_2$.

Here $G'$ is the \$-augmented grammar for $G$. Now Lemma 6.37 says that when $v = \varepsilon$, statement ($c'$) is equivalent to the nonexistence of pairs of items in $\text{VALID}_k(\gamma)$ exhibiting a reduce-reduce conflict. Similarly, Lemma 6.38 says that when $v \neq \varepsilon$, statement ($c'$) is equivalent to the nonexistence of pairs of items in $\text{VALID}_k(\gamma)$ exhibiting a shift-reduce conflict. □

As was the case with SLL($k$) grammars (see Section 5.4), the LR($k$) grammars, $k \geqslant 0$, form a properly increasing hierarchy:

**Theorem 6.40** *For all $k \geqslant 0$, the class of LR($k$) grammars is properly contained in the class of LR($k$ + 1) grammars.*

*Proof.* That every LR($k$) grammar is an LR($k$ + 1) grammar follows directly from Theorem 6.39, characterization (c). The grammar $S \to ab^kc \mid Ab^kd$, $A \to a$ is an example of an LR($k$ + 1) grammar which is not LR($k$). □

By definition, any LR($k$) language is a deterministic language, that is, can be accepted by some deterministic pushdown automaton. In fact also the converse is true, that is, any deterministic language can be generated by an LR($k$) grammar:

**Proposition 6.41** *Any pushdown automation $M$ with input alphabet $T$ can be transformed into an equivalent grammar $G$ with terminal alphabet $T$ such that $M$ is deterministic if and only if $G$ is LR($k$) for some $k \geqslant 0$.* □

In Section 6.7 we shall show that any LR($k$) language, $k \geqslant 0$, is in fact an LR(1) language. So the family of deterministic languages coincides with the family of LR(1) languages.

Next we shall show that the canonical LR($k$) parser of any LR($k$) grammar has the desirable property that it *detects an error* in any nonsentence, that is, given any input string $w$ not in the language, the parser has on $w$ a computation that ends with an error configuration. At the end of Section 5.4 we noted that any practical parser should possess this property. In fact we can prove more than just the error detection property of canonical LR($k$) parsers of LR($k$) grammars. First, it turns out that the error detection property is possessed by the canonical LR($k$) parser of *any* grammar, provided that $k \geqslant 1$. Second, in the case of an LR($k$) grammar, the canonical LR($k$) parser does not loop forever on any input string. Recall that this is a stronger property than mere error detection.

**Lemma 6.42** *Let $G = (V, T, P, S)$ be a grammar and $M$ its canonical LR(k) parser. Further let $x$ and $y$ be strings in $T^*$ and $\psi$ a string in $[G']_k^*$ such that*

$$\$[\$]_k \mid xy\$ \Rightarrow^* \$\psi \mid y\$ \ .$$

*If the condition $xy' \in L(G)$ always implies that $k{:}y \neq k{:}y'$, then $\$\psi \mid y\$$ is an error configuration.*

*Proof.* By lemma 6.29, $\psi$ is of the form $[\$]_k[\$X_1]_k \ldots [\$X_1 \ldots X_n]_k$, where $X_1 \ldots X_n \Rightarrow^* x$. If $\$\psi \mid y\$$ were not an error configuration, then, by definition, some action of $M$ would be applicable to it. Then $\text{VALID}_k(\$X_1 \ldots X_n)$ would contain an item $[A \to \alpha \cdot \beta, z]$, where $\text{FIRST}_k(\beta z)$ contains $k{:}y\$$. This would imply that

$$S' \underset{\text{rm}}{\Longrightarrow^*} \$\delta A z'\$ \underset{\text{rm}}{\Longrightarrow} \$\delta\alpha\beta z'\$ = \$X_1 \ldots X_n \beta z'\$ \ ,$$

$$k{:}z'\$ = z, \quad \beta \Rightarrow^* v, \quad \text{and} \quad k{:}y\$ = k{:}vz$$

for some strings $\delta \in V^*$ and $z', v \in T^*$. But then $xvz'$ would belong to $L(G)$ although obviously $k{:}y = k{:}vz'$. □

Now we can prove:

**Theorem 6.43** *Let $G = (V, T, P, S)$ be a grammar and $M$ its canonical LR(k) parser, where $k \geqslant 1$. Then $M$ detects an error in any input string in $T^* \setminus L(G)$.*

*Proof.* Let $w$ be a string in $T^* \setminus L(G)$. We consider two cases: (1) $k{:}w \neq k{:}w'$ for all $w' \in L(G)$; (2) $k{:}w = k{:}w'$ for some $w' \in L(G)$.

In case (1) the claim follows immediately from Lemma 6.42. Then the initial configuration for $w$ is an error configuration.

In case (2) $T^*$ contains strings $x$, $y$, and $y'$ such that the following statements are true.

(a) $w = xy$.

(b) $k{:}y = k{:}y'$ and $xy' \in L(G)$.

(c) For all $y''$ in $T^*$, $xy'' \in L(G)$ implies $k + 1{:}y \neq k + 1{:}y''$.

Now $y \neq y'$ because $xy \notin L(G)$ and $xy' \in L(G)$. The conditions $k > 0$, $k{:}y = k{:}y'$, and $y \neq y'$ together imply that $y = ay_1$ and $y' = ay'_1$ for some $a \in T$ and $y_1, y'_1 \in T^*$. Since $xay'_1 = xy'$ is in $L(G) = L(M)$, then $M$, when started at the initial configuration for $xay'_1$, must enter, after zero or more moves, a configuration in which the remaining input string is $ay'_1$ and to which a shift action on terminal $a$ and lookahead $k{:}ay'_1\$$ is applicable. That is, for some $\psi$ and $\psi'$

$$\$[\$]_k \mid xay'_1\$ \Rightarrow^* \$\psi \mid ay'_1\$ \Rightarrow \$\psi' \mid y'_1\$ \qquad \text{in } M \ .$$

By Lemma 6.29, $\psi$ is of the form $[\$]_k[\$X_1]_k \ldots [\$X_1 \ldots X_n]_k$, where $X_1 \ldots X_n \underset{\text{rm}}{\Longrightarrow^*} x$. By the definition of a shift action, $\psi'$ is $\psi[\$X_1 \ldots X_n a]_k$

and $\text{VALID}_k(\$X_1 \ldots X_n)$ contains an item $[A \rightarrow \alpha \cdot a\beta,\ z]$, where $k{:}ay_1'\$ \in \text{FIRST}_k(a\beta z)$. Because $k{:}ay_1\$ = k{:}ay_1'\$$, we can apply Lemma 6.32 and conclude that

$$\$[\$]_k \mid xay_1\$ \Rightarrow^* \$[\$]_k[\$X_1]_k \ldots [\$X_1 \ldots X_n]_k \mid ay_1\$ = \$\psi \mid ay_1\$ \ .$$

The shift action applied to $\$\psi \mid ay_1'\$$ also applies here, because $k{:}ay_1\$ = k{:}ay_1'\$$. So we have:

$$\$[\$]_k \mid xay_1\$ \Rightarrow^* \$\psi \mid ay_1\$ \Rightarrow \$\psi' \mid y_1\$ \ .$$

By statement (c), $xay_1'' \in L(G)$ always implies that $k{:}y_1 \neq k{:}y_1''$. This means, by Lemma 6.42, that $\$\psi' \mid y_1\$$ is an error configuration. □

Theorem 6.43 does not hold for $k = 0$. This is seen by considering the LR(0) parser for the ambiguous grammar

$$S \rightarrow S \mid a \ .$$

The LR(0) parser of this grammar has the actions

$$[\$]_0 \mid a \rightarrow [\$]_0[\$a]_0 \mid \ ,$$

$$[\$]_0[\$a]_0 \mid \ \rightarrow [\$]_0[\$S]_0 \mid \ ,$$

$$[\$]_0[\$S]_0 \mid \ \rightarrow [\$]_0[\$S]_0 \mid \ .$$

Although the parser is deterministic it does not detect an error in the nonsentence *aa*. The parser loops forever on *aa*:

$$\$[\$]_0 \mid aa\$ \Rightarrow \$[\$]_0[\$a]_0 \mid a\$ \Rightarrow \$[\$]_0[\$S]_0 \mid a\$$$

$$\Rightarrow^n \$[\$]_0[\$S]_0 \mid a\$, \quad \text{for all } n \geqslant 0 \ .$$

In the case $k \geqslant 1$ Theorem 6.43 guarantees that on any nonsentence there is some computation ending with an error configuration. This does not, of course, exclude the possibility that the parser may also loop forever on that nonsentence. This may happen when the grammar is not LR($k$), as is the case with the grammar

$$S \rightarrow a^{k+1} \mid ASb^k \ ,$$

$$A \rightarrow \varepsilon \ .$$

A portion of the canonical LR($k$) machine for this grammar is shown in Figure 6.11. The grammar is unambiguous but not LR($k$). The canonical LR($k$) parser loops forever on any input string of the form $a^k w$:

$$\$[\$]_k \mid a^k w\$$$

$$\Rightarrow \$[\$]_k[\$A]_k \mid a^k w\$$$

$$\Rightarrow \$[\$]_k[\$A]_k[\$AA^+]_k \mid a^k w\$$$

$$\Rightarrow^n \$[\$]_k[\$A]_k[\$AA^+]_k^n \mid a^k w\$, \quad \text{for all } n \geqslant 0 \ .$$

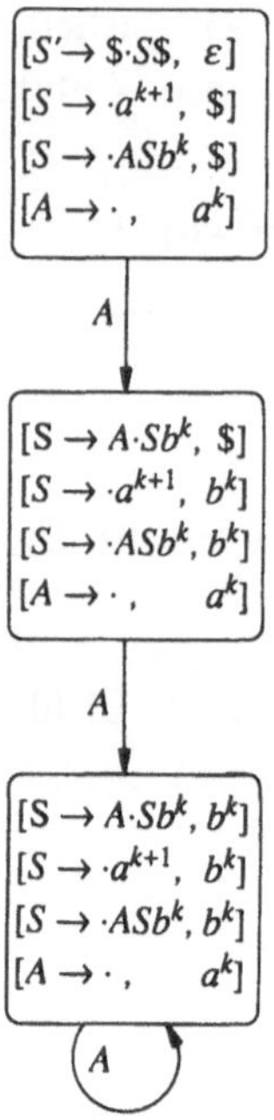


**Figure 6.11** Portion of the canonical LR($k$) machine for the grammar $S' \to \$S\$$, $S \to a^{k+1} | ASb^k$, $A \to \varepsilon$

We conclude this section by showing that in the case of an LR($k$) grammar the canonical LR($k$) parser does not loop forever on any input string.

**Theorem 6.44** *Let $G = (V, T, P, S)$ be an LR(k) grammar and M its canonical LR(k) parser, $k \geqslant 0$. Then M does not loop forever on any input string.*

*Proof.* For the sake of contradiction, assume that $M$ loops forever on some $w$ in $T^*$. Then there are strings $x, y \in T^*$ and $\psi_i \in [G']_k^*$, $i \geqslant 1$, and reduce actions $r_i$, $i \geqslant 1$, such that

(1)
$$\$[\$]_k \mid w\$ = \$[\$]_k \mid xy\$ \Rightarrow^* \$\psi_1 \mid y\$ \quad \text{in } M, \quad \text{and}$$
$$\$\psi_i \mid y\$ \xRightarrow{r_i} \$\psi_{i+1} \mid y\$ \qquad \text{in } M \quad \text{for all } i \geqslant 1 \ .$$

By Lemma 6.29,

(2) $\psi_i = [\$]_k \ldots [\$\gamma_i]_k$, for all $i \geqslant 1$ ,

where

(3) $\gamma_1 \underset{\text{rm}}{\Longrightarrow}^* x$ and $\gamma_{i+1} \underset{\text{rm}}{\Longrightarrow} \gamma_i$ in $G$ for all $i \geqslant 1$ .

Moreover, for all $i \geqslant 1$ there is a rule $A_i \to \omega_i$ such that

(4) $[A_i \to \omega_i \cdot, k{:}y\$] \in \text{VALID}_k(\$\gamma_i)$ .

By definition, we have, for all $i \geqslant 1$,

(5) $$S' \underset{rm}{\Longrightarrow} \$S\$ \underset{rm}{\Longrightarrow}^* \$\delta_i A_i z_i \$ \underset{rm}{\Longrightarrow} \$\delta_i \omega_i z_i \$ = \$\gamma_i z_i \$ \quad \text{in } G' ,$$

$$\text{and } k{:}z_i\$ = k{:}y\$ ,$$

where $z_i$ is a string in $T^*$ and $\delta_i$ is a string in $V^*$. By (3) we then have:

(6) $$xz_i \in L(G) \quad \text{for all } i \geqslant 1 .$$

Because $\gamma_1 \underset{rm}{\Longrightarrow}^* x$ and $[A_1 \to \omega_1 \cdot, k{:}z_i\$]$ is in $\text{VALID}_k(\$\gamma_1)$ for all $i \geqslant 1$, we can conclude by Lemma 6.32 that

(7) $$\$[\$]_k \mid xz_i\$ \Rightarrow^* \$\psi_1 \mid z_i\$ \quad \text{in } M \quad \text{for all } i \geqslant 1 .$$

The reduce actions $r_i$, $i \geqslant 1$, applied in (1) have all $k{:}y\$$ as the lookahead string. Thus, for example, $r_1$ applies to the configuration $\$\psi_1 \mid z_i\$$, producing $\$\psi_2 \mid z_i\$$. More generally,

(8) $$\$\psi_n \mid z_i\$ \xRightarrow{r_n} \$\psi_{n+1} \mid z_i\$ \quad \text{in } M \quad \text{for all } i, n \geqslant 1 .$$

(For $n \geqslant 2$, this result also follows from Lemma 6.32, because $\gamma_{n+1} \underset{rm}{\Longrightarrow} \gamma_n$, $[A_{n+1} \to \omega_{n+1} \cdot, k{:}z_i\$]$ is in $\text{VALID}_k(\$\gamma_{n+1})$, and $\gamma_n{:}1 = A_{n-1}$ is a nonterminal.) All in all, statements (7) and (8) mean that $M$ loops forever on all $xz_i$, $i \geqslant 1$. But then $z_i$ must be the empty string $\varepsilon$ for all $i \geqslant 1$, because $M$ is deterministic and accepts the sentence $xz_i$ for all $i \geqslant 1$. This implies further, by (5) and (3), that for $n \geqslant 1$

(9) $$S \underset{rm}{\Longrightarrow}^* \delta_{n+1} A_{n+1} \underset{rm}{\Longrightarrow} \delta_{n+1} \omega_{n+1} = \gamma_{n+1} \underset{rm}{\Longrightarrow}^n \gamma_1 \underset{rm}{\Longrightarrow}^* x .$$

In other words, $x$ has arbitrarily long rightmost derivations from $S$. By Theorem 4.12, $G$ is ambiguous. This is a contradiction, because an LR($k$) grammar is always unambiguous (Theorem 6.35). □

## 6.5 LALR($k$) Parsing

We start this section by analyzing the canonical LR($k$) approach to parser construction from the point of view of the size of the parsers it produces. First we note that it is easy to derive an upper bound on the size of the canonical LR($k$) parser for a given grammar:

**Theorem 6.45** *The size of the canonical LR($k$) parser for grammar $G = (V, T, P, S)$ is*

$$O(2^{|T|^k |G| + k \log |T| + \log |G|}) .$$

*Proof.* The number of distinct $k$-items of $G$ is at most $(|T| + 1)^k|G|$, because there are at most $|G|$ distinct item cores $A \to \alpha \cdot \beta$ in $G$ and at most $(|T| + 1)^k$ lookahead strings in $k:T^*$. Thus the number of distinct LR($k$)-equivalence classes $[\delta]_k$ in $[G']_k$ is bounded by $2^{(|T|+1)^k|G'|}$, where $G'$ is the \$-augmented grammar for $G$. This means that the sum of the lengths of all reduce actions

$$[\delta]_k[\delta X_1]_k \ldots [\delta X_1 \ldots X_n]_k \,|\, y \to [\delta]_k[\delta A]_k \,|\, y$$

is

$$O(2^{(|T|+1)^k|G'|} \cdot |G| \cdot (|T| + 1)^k) \; .$$

This proves the lemma, because $|G'|$ is $O(|G|)$ and because the size of the canonical LR($k$) parser is clearly dominated by the reduce actions. □

The size bound given in Lemma 6.45 is one-level exponential in $|G|$ and two-level exponential in $k$. So a canonical LR($k$) parser seems to be, and indeed often is, essentially larger than the strong LL($k$) or simple precedence parser for the same grammar. Recall that the size of the strong LL($k$) parser for grammar $G$ is only polynomial in $|G|$ and one-level exponential in $k$ (Fact 5.45). The size of the simple precedence parser is also polynomial in $|G|$.

One might wish to know whether or not the bound in Lemma 6.45 actually is sometimes reached. That is, are there constants $c$, $n_0 > 0$ and a sequence of grammars $G_n = (V_n, T_n, P_n, S_n)$ such that the size of the canonical LR($k$) parser for any $G_n$, $n \geqslant n_0$, is at least

$$c2^{|Tn|^k|Gn| + k\log|Tn| + \log|Gn|} \; .$$

It is not known whether or not such a sequence of grammars exists. For $k = 0$ the bound is $c2^{|G| + \log|G|}$. However, one can prove:

**Proposition 6.46** *For each $n \geqslant 0$, let $G_n$ be the grammar with nonterminal alphabet $\{A_0, A_1, \ldots, A_n\}$, terminal alphabet $\{0, 1, a, a_0, a_1, \ldots, a_n\}$, start symbol $A_0$, and rules*

$$A_{i-1} \to 1A_ia_{i-1} \qquad \text{for all } i,\ 1 \leqslant i \leqslant n \; ;$$

$$A_n \to 1A_0a_n \; ;$$

$$A_i \to 0A_ia_i \qquad \text{for all } i,\ 1 \leqslant i \leqslant n \; ;$$

$$A_i \to 0A_0a_i \qquad \text{for all } i,\ 1 \leqslant i \leqslant n \; ;$$

$$A_0 \to a \; .$$

*Then there is a constant $c > 0$ such that the size of the canonical LR(0) collection for $G_n$ is at least $2^{c|G_n|}$ for all $n \geqslant 0$.* □

Fortunately, for grammars of conventional programming languages the size of the canonical LR($k$) parser seems to remain within reasonable limits when $k = 0$. However, when $k$ increases, the number of states in the canonical LR($k$) machine tends to grow steadily.

Consider, for example, the grammar $G_{ab\varepsilon}$ given in Section 6.3. The canonical LR(0), LR(1), and LR(2) machines for the corresponding \$-augmented grammar were given in Figures 6.5, 6.7, and 6.8. For arbitrary $k$, $n \geqslant 0$ we have:

$$\begin{aligned}
\mathrm{VALID}_k(\$ac^{n+1}) &= \{[A \to c \cdot Ad,\ k{:}d^n\$],\ [A \to \cdot,\ k{:}d^{n+1}\$]\ ,\\
&\qquad [A \to \cdot cAd,\ k{:}d^{n+1}\$]\}\ ,\\
\mathrm{VALID}_k(\$ac^{n+1}A) &= \{[A \to cA \cdot d,\ k{:}d^n\$]\}\ ,\\
\mathrm{VALID}_k(\$ac^{n+1}Ad) &= \{[A \to cAd \cdot,\ k{:}d^n\$]\}\ ,\\
\mathrm{VALID}_k(\$bc^{n+1}) &= \{[B \to c \cdot Bd,\ k{:}d^n\$],\ [B \to \cdot,\ k{:}d^{n+1}\$]\ ,\\
&\qquad [B \to \cdot cBd,\ k{:}d^{n+1}\$]\}\ ,\\
\mathrm{VALID}_k(\$bc^{n+1}B) &= \{[B \to cB \cdot d,\ k{:}\ d^n\$]\}\ ,\\
\mathrm{VALID}_k(\$bc^{n+1}Bd) &= \{[B \to cBd \cdot,\ k{:}d^n\$]\}\ .
\end{aligned}$$

Now, for fixed $k$, two states of the form $\mathrm{VALID}_k(\$ac^{n+1})$, $n \geqslant 0$, are different if and only if $n < k$. The same holds for the states $\mathrm{VALID}_k(\$ac^{n+1}A)$, $\mathrm{VALID}_k(\$ac^{n+1}Ad)$, $\mathrm{VALID}_k(\$bc^{n+1})$, $\mathrm{VALID}_k(\$bc^{n+1}B)$, and $\mathrm{VALID}_k(\$bc^{n+1}Bd)$. For all $n \geqslant k$ we have:

$$\begin{aligned}
\mathrm{VALID}_k(\$ac^{n+1}) &= \mathrm{VALID}_k(\$ac^{k+1})\ ,\\
\mathrm{VALID}_k(\$ac^{n+1}A) &= \mathrm{VALID}_k(\$ac^{k+1}A)\ ,\\
\mathrm{VALID}_k(\$ac^{n+1}Ad) &= \mathrm{VALID}_k(\$ac^{k+1}Ad)\ ,\\
\mathrm{VALID}_k(\$bc^{n+1}) &= \mathrm{VALID}_k(\$bc^{k+1})\ ,\\
\mathrm{VALID}_k(\$bc^{n+1}B) &= \mathrm{VALID}_k(\$bc^{k+1}B)\ ,\\
\mathrm{VALID}_k(\$bc^{n+1}Bd) &= \mathrm{VALID}_k(\$bc^{k+1}Bd)\ .
\end{aligned}$$

In addition to these states the canonical LR($k$) machine for $G'_{ab\varepsilon}$ has the states $\mathrm{VALID}_k(\$)$, $\mathrm{VALID}_k(\$S)$, $\mathrm{VALID}_k(\$a)$, $\mathrm{VALID}_k(\$aA)$, $\mathrm{VALID}_k(\$b)$, and $\mathrm{VALID}_k(\$bB)$. Thus the total number of states in the canonical LR($k$) machine is

$$6(k+1) + 6 = 6k + 12\ ,$$

which means a growth rate linear in $k$.

The growth of the canonical LR($k$) machine with $k$ is due to the fact that long lookahead strings give rise to several states having the same set of item cores. In the canonical LR($k$) machine for $G'_{ab\varepsilon}$ the set of cores $\{A \to c \cdot .Ad,\ A \to \cdot,\ A \to \cdot cAd\}$, for example, appears $k+1$ times, so that there are $k+1$ distinct states having exactly these item cores. In terms of LR($k$)-equivalence, this means that any LR(0)-equivalence class $[\gamma]_0$ is partitioned into one or more LR($k$)-equivalence classes $[\gamma_1]_k, \ldots, [\gamma_n]_k$, when $k \geqslant 0$. Recall Theorem 6.15, saying that any LR($k$)-equivalence class is the union of one or more LR($l$)-equivalence classes, whenever $k \leqslant l$.

In the case of $G'_{ab\varepsilon}$ the partitions of the LR(0)-equivalence classes into LR(k) equivalence classes are the following (the unions are all disjoint):

$$[\$]_0 = [\$]_k \, ,$$

$$[\$S]_0 = [\$S]_k \, ,$$

$$[\$a]_0 = [\$a]_k \, .$$

$$[\$aA]_0 = [\$aA]_k \, .$$

$$[\$ac^+]_0 = [\$ac]_k \cup \ldots \cup [\$ac^k]_k \cup [\$ac^kc^+]_k \, .$$

$$[\$ac^+A]_0 = [\$acA]_k \cup \ldots \cup [\$ac^kA]_k \cup [\$ac^kc^+A]_k \, .$$

$$[\$ac^+Ad]_0 = [\$acAd]_k \cup \ldots \cup [\$ac^kAd]_k \cup [\$ac^kc^+Ad]_k \, .$$

$$[\$b]_0 = [\$b]_k \, .$$

$$[\$bB]_0 = [\$bB]_k \, .$$

$$[\$bc^+]_0 = [\$bc]_k \cup \ldots \cup [\$bc^k]_k \cup [\$bc^kc^+]_k .$$

$$[\$bc^+B]_0 = [\$bcB]_k \cup \ldots \cup [\$bc^kB]_k \cup [\$bc^kc^+B]_k \, .$$

$$[\$bc^+Bd]_0 = [\$bcBd]_k \cup \ldots \cup [\$bc^kBd]_k \cup [\$bc^kc^+Bd]_k \, .$$

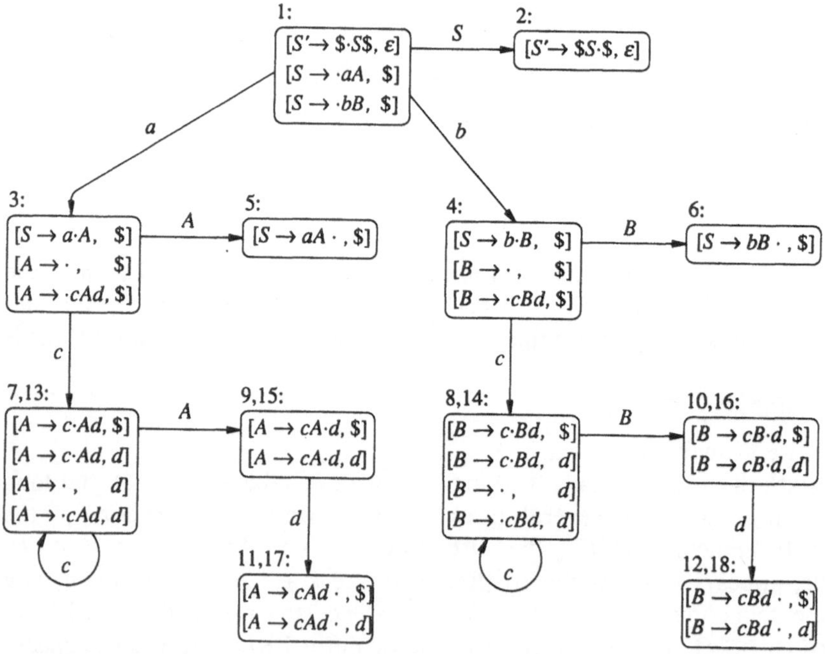


**Figure 6.12** The LALR(1) machine for the \$-augmented grammar $G'_{ab\varepsilon}: S' \to \$S\$$, $S \to aA|bB$, $A \to \varepsilon|cAd$, $B \to \varepsilon|cBd$. The doubly labeled states have been obtained by uniting two states in the canonical LR(1) machine (see Figure 6.7)

One obvious way to reduce the size of the canonical LR($k$) machine is to prevent the proliferation of states by uniting all states that have the same set of item cores. More specifically, in the canonical LR(0) machine every state $q$ is replaced by the union

$$q_1 \cup \ldots \cup q_n ,$$

where

$$\{q_1, \ldots, q_n\} = \{q' \mid q' \text{ is a state in the canonical LR}(k) \text{ machine such that } q' \text{ has the same set of item cores as } q\} .$$

This procedure produces a finite automaton which is isomorphic to the LR(0) machine. The automation is called the *LALR(k) machine* for the grammar, "LALR($k$)" being an acronym for "Look-Ahead LR($k$)".

For example, to get the LALR(1) machine for the grammar $G'_{ab\varepsilon}$ from its canonical LR(1) machine (Figure 6.7) one must unite states $q_7$ and $q_{13}$, states $q_8$ and $q_{14}$, states $q_9$ and $q_{15}$, states $q_{10}$ and $q_{16}$, states $q_{11}$ and $q_{17}$, and states $q_{12}$ and $q_{18}$. The resulting machine is shown in Figure 6.12. The LALR(2) machine, obtained similarly from the canonical LR(2) machine (Figure 6.8) is shown in Figure 6.13. Note the isomorphism of both these automata with the LR(0) machine (Figure 6.5).

The known properties of the canonical LR($k$) machine imply immediately:

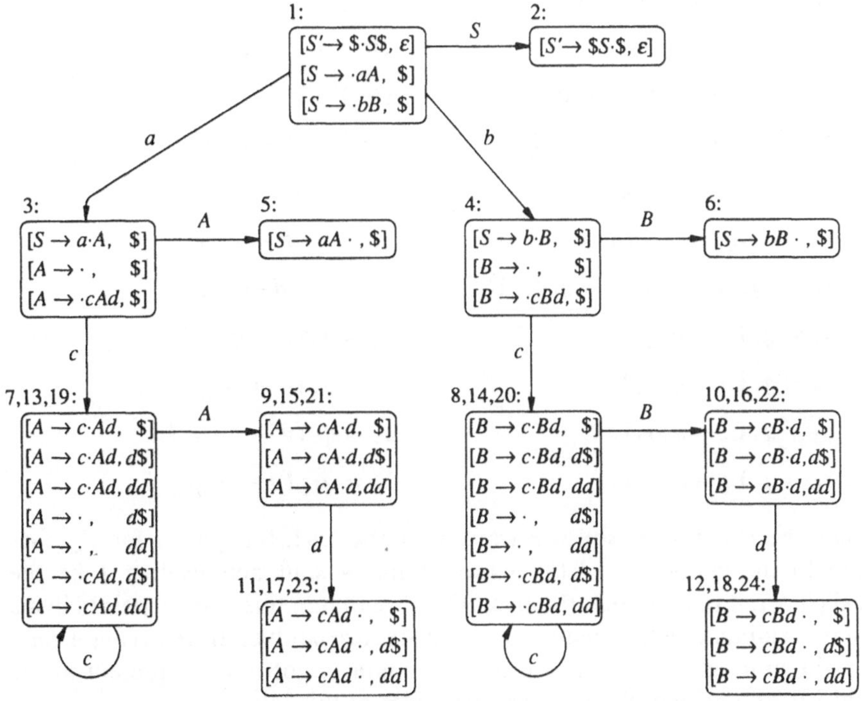


**Figure 6.13** The LALR(2) machine for $G'_{ab\varepsilon}$. The triply labeled states have been obtained by uniting three states in the canonical LR(2) machine (see Figure 6.8)

**Theorem 6.47** *Let $q$ be a state in the LALR(k) machine for grammar $G$ accessible upon reading string $\delta$. Then $\delta$ is a viable prefix of $G$, and each item in $q$ is LR(k)-valid for some viable prefix LR(0)-equivalent to $\delta$. Conversely, if an item $I$ is LR(k)-valid for a viable prefix $\gamma$, then there is a state $q$ in the LALR(k) machine such that $q$ contains $I$ and is accessible upon reading any viable prefix LR(0)-equivalent to $\gamma$.* □

The algorithm given in Figure 6.6 was used in Section 6.3 to generate the parsing actions of the canonical LR($k$) parser from the canonical LR($k$) machine. We can readily apply this algorithm to the LALR($k$) machine. In the case of the LALR(1) machine for $G'_{ab\varepsilon}$ we get the following set of actions:

$$r_1 = q_1q_3q_5 \mid \$ \to q_1q_2 \mid \$, \qquad \tau(r_1) = S \to aA \ .$$
$$r_2 = q_1q_4q_6 \mid \$ \to q_1q_2 \mid \$, \qquad \tau(r_2) = S \to bB \ .$$
$$r_3 = q_3 \mid \$ \to q_3q_5 \mid \$, \qquad \tau(r_3) = A \to \varepsilon \ .$$
$$r_4 = q_3q_7q_9q_{11} \mid \$ \to q_3q_5 \mid \$, \qquad \tau(r_4) = A \to cAd \ .$$
$$r'_4 = q_3q_7q_9q_{11} \mid d \to q_3q_5 \mid d, \qquad \tau(r'_4) = A \to cAd \ .$$
$$r_5 = q_4 \mid \$ \to q_4q_6 \mid \$, \qquad \tau(r_5) = B \to \varepsilon \ .$$
$$r_6 = q_4q_8q_{10}q_{12} \mid \$ \to q_4q_6 \mid \$, \qquad \tau(r_6) = B \to cBd \ .$$
$$r'_6 = q_4q_8q_{10}q_{12} \mid d \to q_4q_6 \mid d, \qquad \tau(r'_6) = B \to cBd \ .$$
$$r_7 = q_7 \mid d \to q_7q_9 \mid d, \qquad \tau(r_7) = A \to \varepsilon \ .$$
$$r_8 = q_7q_7q_9q_{11} \mid d \to q_7q_9 \mid d, \qquad \tau(r_8) = A \to cAd \ .$$
$$r'_8 = q_7q_7q_9q_{11} \mid \$ \to q_7q_9 \mid \$, \qquad \tau(r'_8) = A \to cAd \ .$$
$$r_9 = q_8 \mid d \to q_8q_{10} \mid d, \qquad \tau(r_9) = B \to \varepsilon \ .$$
$$r_{10} = q_8q_8q_{10}q_{12} \mid d \to q_8q_{10} \mid d, \qquad \tau(r_{10}) = B \to cBd \ .$$
$$r'_{10} = q_8q_8q_{10}q_{12} \mid \$ \to q_8q_{10} \mid \$, \qquad \tau(r'_{10}) = B \to cBd \ .$$
$$s_1 = q_1 \mid a \to q_1q_3 \mid, \qquad s_5 = q_7 \mid c \to q_7q_7 \mid,$$
$$s_2 = q_1 \mid b \to q_1q_4 \mid, \qquad s_6 = q_8 \mid c \to q_8q_8 \mid,$$
$$s_3 = q_3 \mid c \to q_3q_7 \mid, \qquad s_7 = q_9 \mid d \to q_9q_{11} \mid,$$
$$s_4 = q_4 \mid c \to q_4q_8 \mid, \qquad s_8 = q_{10} \mid d \to q_{10}q_{12} \mid .$$

We call the resulting pushdown transducer the LALR(1) parser for $G_{ab\varepsilon}$. As compared to the canonical LR(1) parser, it has 4 shift actions less. Like the canonical parser, it remains deterministic. Observe that in this case no pair of items in any state exhibits a reduce-reduce or a shift-reduce conflict. In the general case, however, the uniting of states may introduce conflicts not initially present in the canonical LR($k$) machine. We shall see examples of this later.

We have yet to verify that the above method to reduce the size of the canonical LR($k$) parser indeed works. First of all, we must give a precise definition of the LALR($k$) parser.

Let $G = (V, T, P, S)$ be a grammar, $G'$ its \$-augmented grammar, and $k$ a natural number. A rule of the form

$$(ra) \qquad [\delta]_0[\delta X_1]_0 \ldots [\delta X_1 \ldots X_n]_0 \mid y \to [\delta]_0[\delta A]_0 \mid y$$

is an *LALR(k) reduce action by rule $A \to X_1 \ldots X_n$ on lookahead $y$* if $\delta$ is a string in $\$V^*$, $X_1, \ldots, X_n$ are symbols in $V$ $(n \geqslant 0)$, $A \to X_1 \ldots X_n$ is a rule in $P$, and $y$ is a string in $k{:}T^*\$$ such that

$$[A \to X_1 \ldots X_n\cdot, y] \in \text{VALID}_k(\gamma) \quad \text{and} \quad [\gamma]_0 = [\delta X_1 \ldots X_n]_0 \ ,$$

for some string $\gamma$ in $\$V^*$. In other words, $[A \to X_1 \ldots X_n\cdot, y]$ is LR($k$)-valid for some viable prefix LR(0)-equivalent to $\delta X_1 \ldots X_n$.

A rule of the form

$$(sa) \qquad [\delta]_0 \mid ay \to [\delta]_0[\delta a]_0 \mid y$$

is an *LALR(k) shift action on terminal a and lookahead ay* if $\delta$ is a string in $\$V^*$, $a$ is a terminal in $T$, and $y$ is a string in $\max\{k-1, 0\}{:}T^*\$$ such that

$$[A \to \alpha\cdot a\beta, z] \in \text{VALID}_k(\gamma), \quad [\gamma]_0 = [\delta]_0, \quad \text{and}$$
$$y \in \text{FIRST}_{\max\{k-1,\,0\}}(\beta z) \ ,$$

for some rule $A \to \alpha a\beta$, string $z$ in $k{:}T^*\$$, and string $\gamma$ in $\$V^*$. In other words, for some viable prefix $\gamma$ LR(0)-equivalent to $\delta$, $\text{VALID}_k(\gamma)$ contains an item of the form $[A \to \alpha\cdot a\beta, z]$, where $y$ is in $\text{FIRST}_{\max\{k-1,\,0\}}(\beta z)$.

The *LALR(k) parser* for $G$ is the pushdown transducer with stack alphabet $[G']_0$, input alphabet $T$, initial stack contents $[\$]_0$, set of final stack contents $\{[\$]_0[\$S]_0\}$, and with set of actions consisting of all LALR($k$) reduce and shift actions of $G$. The output effect $\tau$ is defined in the usual way, mapping all reduce actions by rule $r$ to $r$ and all shift actions to the empty string.

Theorem 6.47 implies that the LALR($k$) parser can be constructed from the LALR($k$) machine using the algorithm of Figure 6.6.

The upper bound on the size of the LALR($k$) parser is considerably smaller than the size of the canonical parser:

**Theorem 6.48** *The size of the LALR(k) parser for grammar $G = (V, T, P, S)$ is*

$$O(2^{|G| + k\log|T| + \log|G|}) \ .$$

*Proof.* Cf. the proof of Theorem 6.45. □

Next we present the usual pair of lemmas needed in the correctness proof of a right parser. Again, the result stated in the first lemma is immediate; in this case it follows from the corresponding result for LR(0) parsers (Lemma 6.29), because the actions of an LALR($k$) parser differ from those of an LR(0) parser only in that some lookahead has been added. The result stated in the second lemma is a straightforward modification of the corresponding result for canonical LR($k$) parsers (Lemma 6.32); we leave the details of the proof for the exercises.

**Lemma 6.49** *Let $G = (V, T, P, S)$ be a grammar and $(M, \tau)$ its LALR($k$) parser. Further let $Y_1, \ldots, Y_n$ be symbols in $V$ ($n \geq 0$), $w$ a string in $T^*$, $\Phi$ a string over the alphabet of $M$, and $\pi'$ an action string such that*

(a) $\$Y_1 \ldots Y_n$ *is a viable prefix of the \$-augmented grammar $G'$ and*
$\$[\$]_0[\$Y_1]_0 \ldots [\$Y_1 \ldots Y_n]_0 \mid w\$ \overset{\pi'}{\Longrightarrow} \Phi$ *in $M$ .*

*Then for some strings $x$ and $y$ and symbols $X_1, \ldots, X_m$ ($m \geq 0$)*

$w = xy$, $\$X_1 \ldots X_m$ *is a viable prefix of $G'$ .*

(b) $\Phi = \$[\$]_0[\$X_1]_0 \ldots [\$X_1 \ldots X_m]_0 \mid y\$, \quad |\pi'| = |\tau(\pi')| + |x|$ ,

*and* $X_1 \ldots X_m \underset{\text{rm}}{\overset{\tau(\pi')^R}{\Longrightarrow}} Y_1 \ldots Y_n x$ *in $G$ .*

□

**Lemma 6.50** *Let $G = (V, T, P, S)$ be a grammar and $(M, \tau)$ its LALR($k$) parser. Further let $X_1, \ldots, X_m$, $Y_1 \ldots, Y_n$ be symbols in $V$($m, n \geq 0$), $x$ and $y$ strings in $T^*$, $\pi$ a rule string in $P^*$, and $[A \to \alpha \cdot \beta, z]$ a $k$-item of the \$-augmented grammar $G'$ for $G$ such that*

$X_1 \ldots X_m \underset{\text{rm}}{\overset{\pi^R}{\Longrightarrow}} Y_1 \ldots Y_n x$ *in $G$ ,*

(a) $[A \to \alpha \cdot \beta, z] \in \text{VALID}_k(\$X_1 \ldots X_m)$ ,
$k{:}y\$ \in \text{FIRST}_k(\beta z)$, *and*

*either $Y_1 \ldots Y_n = \varepsilon$ or $Y_n$ is a nonterminal .*

*Then for some action string $\pi'$*

$\tau(\pi') = \pi, \quad |\pi'| = |\pi| + |x|$, *and*

(b) $\$[\$]_0[\$Y_1]_0 \ldots [\$Y_1 \ldots Y_n]_0 \mid xy\$$

$\overset{\pi'}{\Longrightarrow} \$[\$]_0[\$X_1]_0 \ldots [\$X_1 \ldots X_n]_0 \mid y\$$ *in $M$ .*

□

By Lemmas 6.49 and 6.50 we can prove in the usual way:

**Theorem 6.51** *The LALR($k$) parser $M$ for grammar $G$ is a right parser for $G$. Moreover, for each sentence $w$ in $L(G)$, $M$ produces all right parses of $w$ in $G$, and* $\text{TIME}_M(w) = \text{TIME}_G(w) + |w|$. □

In the above we have derived the concepts of the LALR(1) machine and the LALR($k$) parser from that of the canonical LR($k$) machine. Another way to arrive at the same concepts is to start from the LR(0) machine and to consider the problem of adding suitable $k$-length lookahead strings to the 0-items in the states of the machine. Indeed, it is the latter approach we shall use in Chapter 7, when we consider the efficient construction of LALR(1) parsers.

Theorem 6.51 says that the adding of LALR($k$) lookahead to the 0-items is sufficient in that the resulting pushdown transducer remains a valid right parser of the grammar, that is, still accepts the whole language and produces all the right parses it is supposed to produce. (Note that the adding of lookahead can only reduce the language accepted and the set of parses produced.) The following theorem says that the adding of LALR($k$) lookahead is also minimal in that every item in every state of the LALR($k$) machine is actually "used" in the parsing of some input string.

**Theorem 6.52** *Let $G$ be a reduced grammar and $M$ its LALR($k$) parser. Further let $q$ be a state in the LALR($k$) machine for $G'$, the \$-augmented grammar for $G$, and $[A \to \alpha \cdot \beta, z]$ an item in $q$. Then there are terminal strings $x$ and $y$ and symbols $X_1, \ldots, X_m$ ($m \geq 0$) such that*

$$\$[\$]_0 \mid xy\$ \Rightarrow^* \$[\$]_0[\$X_1]_0 \ldots [\$X_1 \ldots X_m]_0 \mid y\$ \qquad \text{in } M \ ,$$

*where the set of item cores in* $\text{VALID}_0(\$X_1 \ldots X_m)$ *is the same as in $q$ and $k{:}y\$$ is in* $\text{FIRST}_k(\beta z)$.

*Proof.* Since $q$ is a union of one or more $\text{VALID}_k(\gamma)$, where $\gamma$ is a viable prefix of $G'$, there are symbols $X_1, \ldots, X_m$ such that $[A \to \alpha \cdot \beta, z]$ is in $\text{VALID}_k(\$X_1 \ldots X_m)$. Moreover, the set of item cores in $\text{VALID}_0(\$X_1 \ldots X_m)$ is the same as in $q$. Since $G$ was assumed to be a reduced grammar, $X_1 \ldots X_m$ derives some terminal string $x$. By Theorem 4.2, $X_1 \ldots X_m$ rightmost derives $x$. Also, there is a terminal string $y$ such that $k{:}y\$$ is in $\text{FIRST}_k(\beta z)$. But then we can apply Lemma 6.50 and conclude that

$$\$[\$]_0 \mid xy\$ \Rightarrow^* \$[\$]_0[\$X_1]_0 \ldots [\$X_1 \ldots X_m]_0 \mid y\$ \qquad \text{in } M \ ,$$

as claimed. □

Observe that for the canonical LR($k$) parser we can prove the following: If $q$ is a state in the canonical LR($k$) machine and $[A \to \alpha \cdot \beta, z]$ is an item in $q$, then, for *any* symbols $X_1, \ldots, X_m$ satisfying $\text{VALID}_k(\$X_1 \ldots X_m) = q$, $k{:}y\$$ is in $\text{FIRST}_k(\beta z)$ and

$$\$[\$]_k \mid xy\$ \Rightarrow^* \$[\$]_k[\$X_1]_k \ldots [\$X_1 \ldots X_m]_k \mid y\$$$

for some $x$ and $y$. This follows directly from Lemma 6.32 when it is applied to some derivation $X_1 \ldots X_m \underset{rm}{\Rightarrow}^* x$. Thus in the canonical LR($k$) parser every item $[A \to \alpha \cdot \beta, z]$ in any state $q$ can be "used" in the parsing of *all* terminal strings of the form $xy$, where $k{:}y\$$ is in $\text{FIRST}_k(\beta z)$ and $x$ is derived by some viable prefix $\gamma$ satisfying $\text{VALID}_k(\$\gamma) = q$.

The difference between the behaviors of the canonical LR($k$) parser and the LALR($k$) parser only becomes visible in the parsing of some nonsentences. The LALR($k$) parser may detect the error somewhat later than the canonical parser. For example, the canonical LR(1) parser for $G_{ab\varepsilon}$ detects an error in the nonsentence *acdd* as soon as the second $d$ becomes the current input symbol:

$$\$q_1 \mid acdd\$$$

$$\overset{s_1}{\Longrightarrow} \$q_1q_3 \mid cdd\$$$
$$\overset{s_3}{\Longrightarrow} \$q_1q_3q_7 \mid dd\$$$
$$\overset{r_7}{\Longrightarrow} \$q_1q_3q_7q_9 \mid dd\$$$
$$\overset{s_7}{\Longrightarrow} \$q_1q_3q_7q_9q_{11} \mid d\$ \ .$$

The LALR(1) parser, on the contrary, makes one further move before it enters an error configuration:

$$\$q_1 \mid acdd\$$$
$$\overset{s_1}{\Longrightarrow} \$q_1q_3 \mid cdd\$$$

$$\overset{s_3}{\Longrightarrow} \$q_1q_3q_7 \mid dd\$$$

$$\overset{r_7}{\Longrightarrow} \$q_1q_3q_7q_9 \mid dd\$$$

$$\overset{s_7}{\Longrightarrow} \$q_1q_3q_7q_9q_{11} \mid d\$$$

$$\overset{r'_4}{\Longrightarrow} \$q_1q_3q_5 \mid d\$ \ .$$

We say that grammar $G = (V, T, P, S)$ is *LALR*($k$) if its LALR($k$) parser is deterministic and $S \Rightarrow^+ S$ is impossible in $G$. A language over alphabet $T$ is *LALR*($k$) if it is the language generated by an LALR($k$) grammar.

**Theorem 6.53** (*Characterization of LALR(k) Grammars*). *The LALR(k) parser of grammar G is deterministic if and only if in the LALR(k) machine of the \$-augmented grammar for G no state contains a pair of items exhibiting a reduce-reduce or a shift-reduce conflict.*

*Proof.* The proof is completely analogous to that of Lemma 6.36. The details are left to the exercises. □

For example $G_{ab\varepsilon}$ is an LALR(1) grammar.

**Theorem 6.54** *The class of LALR*(0) *grammars coincides with the class of LR*(0) *grammars. For* $k \geqslant 1$ *the class of LALR(k) grammars is properly contained in the class of LR(k) grammars.*

*Proof.* That the class of LALR(0) grammars coincides with the class of LR(0) grammars follows directly from the fact that the LALR(0) machine, by definition, coincides with the canonical LR(0) machine. That the class of LALR($k$) grammars is always contained in the class of LR($k$) grammars follows from Theorem 6.53, because the uniting of states in the canonical LR($k$) machine can only increase the number of pairs of items exhibiting reduce-reduce or shift-reduce conflicts. That for $k \geqslant 1$ not all LR($k$) grammars are LALR($k$) grammars follows from the fact that the uniting of states can actually introduce conflicts not present in the original machine. This happens, for example, in the case of the grammar

$$S \to aAa \,|\, bAb \,|\, aBb \,|\, bBa \ ,$$

$$A \to c \ ,$$

$$B \to c \ .$$

This grammar is LR(1) but is not LALR($k$) for any $k$. The canonical LR($k$) machine

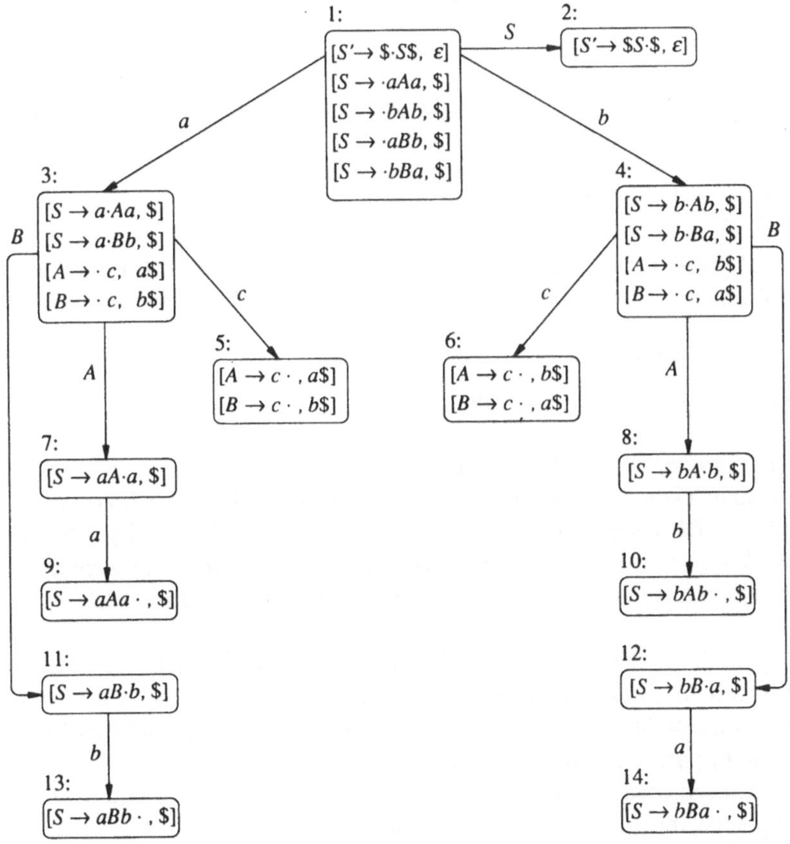


**Figure 6.14** The canonical LR($k$) machine ($k \geqslant 2$) for the grammar $S' \to \$S\$$, $S \to aAa|bAb|aBb|bBa$, $A \to c$, $B \to c$. The grammar is an example of an LR(1) grammar which is not LALR($k$) for any $k$

($k \geqslant 2$) for its \$-augmented grammar is shown in Figure 6.14. (To obtain the LR(1) machine, just truncate the lookahead strings.) In the LALR($k$) machine the states $q_5$ and $q_6$ are united, which introduces two reduce-reduce conflicts. □

The concepts of an LALR($k$) machine and an LALR($k$) parser can be generalized to yield machines and parsers that lie "between" the canonical LR($k$) and the LALR($k$) machines and parsers. Instead of uniting two states $q_1$ and $q_2$ whenever the sets of item cores coincide we can unite $q_1$ and $q_2$ whenever the truncating of the $k$-length lookahead strings to length $l$, $l \leqslant k$, yields the same set of $l$-items. That is, $q_1$ and $q_2$ are united whenever

$$\mathrm{TRUNC}_l(q_1) = \mathrm{TRUNC}_l(q_2) \ ,$$

where, for $k$-item set $q$,

$$\mathrm{TRUNC}_l(q) = \{[A \to \alpha \cdot \beta, l{:}y] \mid [A \to \alpha \cdot \beta, y] \in q\} \ .$$

The finite automaton obtained from the canonical LR($l$) machine by replacing every state $q$ by the union

$$q_1 \cup \ldots \cup q_n \ ,$$

where

$$\{q_1, \ldots, q_n\} = \{q' \mid q' \text{ is a state in the canonical LR}(k) \text{ machine such that } \mathrm{TRUNC}_l(q') = q\} \ ,$$

is called the *LA(k)LR(l) machine* for $G$.

**Fact 6.55** The LA($k$)LR($k$) machine is the same as the canonical LR($k$) machine. The LA($k$)LR(0) machine is the same as the LALR($k$) machine. □

The LA(2)LR(1) machine for $G'_{ab\varepsilon}$ is shown in Figure 6.15.
Corresponding to Theorem 6.47 we have:

**Theorem 6.56** *Let q be a state in the LA(k)LR(l) machine for grammar G accessible upon reading string δ. Then δ is a viable prefix of G, and each item in q is LR(k)-valid for some viable prefix LR(l)-equivalent to δ. Conversely, if an item I is LR(k)-valid for a viable prefix γ, then there is a state q in the LA(k)LR(l) machine such that q contains I and is accessible upon reading any viable prefix LR(l)-equivalent to γ.* □

As in the case of the LALR($k$) machine, the algorithm of Figure 6.6 can be used to produce a parser from the LA($k$)LR($l$) machine. In the following we give a formal definition of the concept of "LA($k$)LR($l$) parser". The definition is obtained from that of the LALR($k$) parser by just replacing "0" by "$l$".

Let $G = (V, T, P, S)$ be a grammar, $G'$ its \$-augmented grammar, and $k$ and $l$ natural numbers such that $k \geqslant l$. A rule of the form

$$(ra) \qquad [\delta]_l[\delta X_1]_l \ldots [\delta X_1 \ldots X_n]_l \mid y \to [\delta]_l[\delta A]_l \mid y$$

is an *LA(k)LR(l) reduce action by rule $A \to X_1 \ldots X_n$ on lookahead y* if $\delta$ is a string

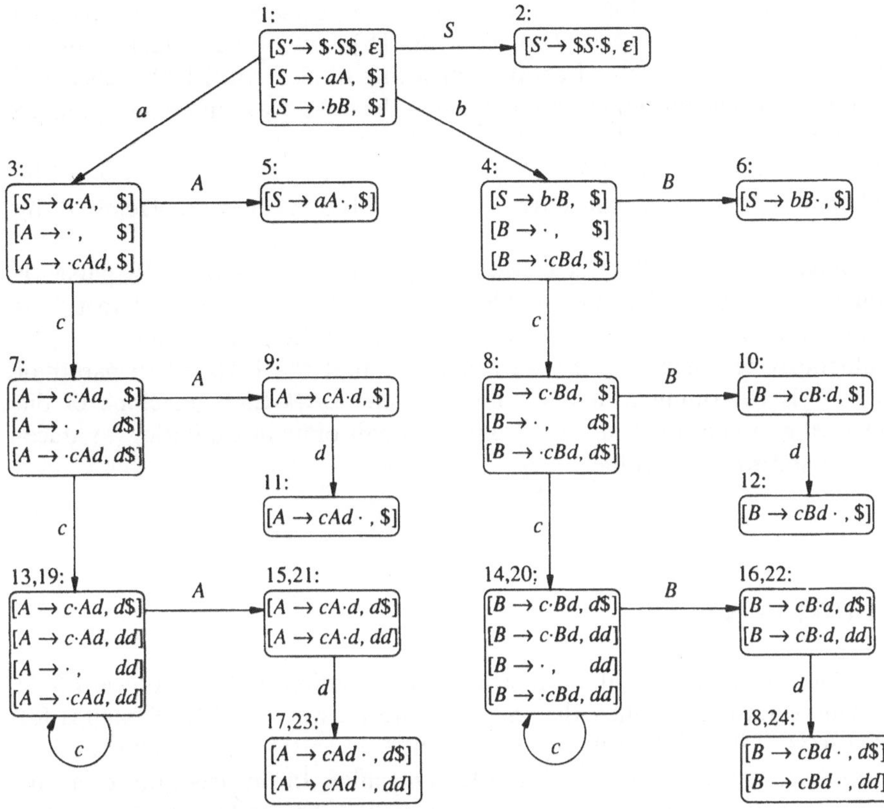


**Figure 6.15** The LA(2)LR(1) machine for the \$-augmented grammar $G'_{ab\varepsilon}: S' \rightarrow \$S\$,\ S \rightarrow aA|bB,$ $A \rightarrow \varepsilon|cAd,\ B \rightarrow \varepsilon|cBd$. Doubly labeled states have been obtained by uniting two states in the canonical LR(2) machine (see Figure 6.8)

in $\$V^*$, $X_1, \ldots, X_n$ are symbols in $V$ ($n \geqslant 0$), $A \rightarrow X_1 \ldots X_n$ is a rule in $P$, and $y$ is a string in $k{:}T^*\$$ such that

$$[A \rightarrow X_1 \ldots X_n \cdot, y] \in \mathrm{VALID}_k(\gamma) \quad \text{and} \quad [\gamma]_l = [\delta X_1 \ldots X_n]_l \ ,$$

for some string $\gamma$ in $\$V^*$. In other words, $[A \rightarrow X_1 \ldots X_n \cdot, y]$ is LR($k$)-valid for some viable prefix LR($l$)-equivalent to $\delta X_1 \ldots X_n$.

A rule of the form

$$(sa) \qquad [\delta]_l \mid ay \rightarrow [\delta]_l [\delta a]_l \mid y$$

is an *LA(k)LR(l) shift action on terminal a and lookahead ay* if $\delta$ is a string in $\$V^*$, $a$ is a terminal in $T$, and $y$ is a string in $\max\{k-1, 0\}{:}T^*\$$ such that

$$[A \rightarrow \alpha \cdot a\beta, z] \in \mathrm{VALID}_k(\gamma),\ [\gamma]_l = [\delta]_l, \quad \text{and}$$

$$y \in \mathrm{FIRST}_{\max\{k-1,\,0\}}(\beta z) \ ,$$

for some rule $A \rightarrow \alpha a \beta$, string $z$ in $k{:}\ T^*\$$, and string $\gamma$ in $\$V^*$.

The *LA(k)LR(l) parser* for $G$ is the pushdown transducer with stack alphabet $[G']_l$, input alphabet $T$, initial stack contents $[\$]_l$, set of final stack contents $\{[\$]_l[\$S]_l\}$, and with the set of actions consisting of all LA($k$)LR($l$) reduce and shift actions of $G$. The output effect is defined in the usual way, mapping all reduce actions by rule $r$ to $r$ and all shift actions to the empty string.

The correctness of the LA($k$)LR($l$) parser can be proved in the usual way. The pair of Lemmas needed is obtained from Lemmas 6.49 and 6.50 by replacing "0" by "$l$".

Grammar $G = (V, T, P, S)$ is called *LA(k)LR(l)* if its LA($k$)LR($l$) parser is deterministic and $S \Rightarrow^+ S$ is impossible in $G$. A language over alphabet $T$ is *LA(k)LR(l)* if it is the language generated by an LA($k$)LR($l$) grammar.

Analogously to Theorem 6.53 we can prove that the LA($k$)LR($l$) parser of grammar $G$ is deterministic if and only if in the LA($k$)LR($l$) machine of the \$-augmented grammar for $G$ no state contains a pair of items exhibiting a reduce-reduce or a shift-reduce conflict.

## 6.6 SLR(k) Parsing

In this section we shall present another practical variation of the canonical LR($k$) parser. This variation is called the "SLR($k$) parser", where "SLR($k$)" stands for "Simple LR($k$)". Like the LALR($k$) parser, the SLR($k$) parser is the result of adding $k$-length lookahead to the items of the LR(0) machine. In this case, however, the adding is done in a crude, simple way, which means that, unlike the case of the LALR($k$) lookahead, the result is seldom minimal.

The lookahead is added to the 0-items as follows. Each item $[A \to \alpha \cdot \beta]$ in state $q$ of the LR(0) machine is replaced by the set of $k$-items

$$[A \to \alpha \cdot \beta, y_1], \ldots, [A \to \alpha \cdot \beta, y_n] \ ,$$

where

$$\{y_1, \ldots, y_n\} = \text{FOLLOW}'_k(A) \ .$$

That is, any string in $\text{FOLLOW}'_k(A)$ is considered a legal lookahead string for all items of the nonterminal $A$, regardless of the context, state $q$, in which the item appears.

It is clear that this way of adding lookahead is always sufficient in the sense that the resulting parser is guaranteed to accept the whole language $L(G)$. Observe that the added lookahead strings form a superset of the lookahead strings of the LALR($k$) parser, because whenever $[A \to \alpha \cdot \beta, y]$ is an item in some state of the LALR($k$) machine, then by definition it belongs to some state of the canonical LR($k$) machine and thus, by Fact 6.12, $y$ belongs to $\text{FOLLOW}'_k(A)$.

For a formal definition of the SLR($k$) parser, let $G = (V, T, P, S)$ be a grammar, $G'$ its \$-augmented grammar, and $k$ a natural number. A rule of the form

(*ra*) $\quad [\delta]_0[\delta X_1]_0 \ldots [\delta X_1 \ldots X_n]_0 \mid y \to [\delta]_0[\delta A]_0 \mid y$

is an *SLR(k) reduce action by rule* $A \to X_1 \dots X_n$ *on lookahead* $y$ if $\delta$ is a string in $\$V^*$, $X_1, \dots, X_n$ are symbols in $V$ $(n \geqslant 0)$, $A \to X_1 \dots X_n$ is a rule in $P$, and $y$ is a string in $k{:}T^*\$$ such that

$$[A \to X_1 \dots X_n \cdot] \in \mathrm{VALID}_0(\delta X_1 \dots X_n) \quad \text{and} \quad y \in \mathrm{FOLLOW}'_k(A) \ .$$

A rule of the form

$$(sa) \qquad [\delta]_0 \mid ay \to [\delta]_0[\delta a]_0 \mid y$$

is an *SLR(k) shift action on terminal a and lookahead ay* if $\delta$ is a string in $\$V^*$, $a$ is a terminal in $T$, and $y$ is a string in $\max\{k-1, 0\}{:}T^*\$$ such that

$$[A \to \alpha \cdot a\beta] \in \mathrm{VALID}_0(\delta) \quad \text{and}$$

$$y \in \mathrm{FIRST}_{\max\{k-1,\,0\}}(\beta \mathrm{FOLLOW}'_k(A)) \ ,$$

for some rule $A \to \alpha a \beta$.

The *SLR(k) parser* for $G$ is the pushdown transducer with stack alphabet $[G']_0$, input alphabet $T$, initial stack contents $[\$]_0$, set of final stack contents $\{[\$]_0[\$S]_0\}$, and set of actions consisting of all SLR$(k)$ reduce and shift actions of $G$. The output effect $\tau$ is defined in the usual way, mapping all reduce actions by rule $r$ to $r$ and all shift actions to the empty string.

As an example consider the SLR(1) parser for $G_{ab\varepsilon}$. The $\mathrm{FOLLOW}'_1$ sets for the nonterminals are:

$$\mathrm{FOLLOW}'_1(S) = \{\$\} \ .$$

$$\mathrm{FOLLOW}'_1(A) = \{\$, d\} = \mathrm{FOLLOW}'_1(B) \ .$$

This means that in addition to the actions of the LALR(1) parser, the SLR(1) parser has the following actions.

$$r'_3 = q_3 \mid d \to q_3 q_5 \mid d, \qquad \tau(r'_3) = A \to \varepsilon \ .$$

$$r'_5 = q_4 \mid d \to q_4 q_6 \mid d, \qquad \tau(r'_5) = B \to \varepsilon \ .$$

$$r'_7 = q_7 \mid \$ \to q_7 q_9 \mid \$, \qquad \tau(r'_7) = A \to \varepsilon \ .$$

$$r'_9 = q_8 \mid \$ \to q_8 q_{10} \mid \$, \qquad \tau(r'_9) = B \to \varepsilon \ .$$

The correctness of the SLR$(k)$ parser is easily established. The fact that the actions of the SLR$(k)$ parser are obtained from the actions of the LR(0) parser by adding some lookahead implies that Lemma 6.49 is still valid for the SLR$(k)$ parser. On the other hand, since the set of actions of the SLR$(k)$ parser forms a superset of the set of actions of the LALR$(k)$ parser, we conclude that Lemma 6.50 is still valid for the SLR$(k)$ parser. Thus we can state:

**Theorem 6.57** *The SLR(k) parser M for grammar G is a right parser for G. Moreover, for each sentence w in L(G), M produces all right parses of w in G, and* $\mathrm{TIME}_M(w) = \mathrm{TIME}_G(w) + |w|$. □

Grammar $G = (V, T, P, S)$ is *SLR(k)* if its SLR($k$) parser is deterministic and $S \Rightarrow^+ S$ is impossible in $G$. A language over alphabet $T$ is *SLR(k)* if it is the language generated by an SLR($k$) grammar.

For example, $G_{ab\varepsilon}$ is an SLR(1) grammar: the adding of the extra reduce actions to the LALR(1) parser does not make the parser nondeterministic.

**Theorem 6.58** (*Characterization of SLR(k) Grammars*). *The SLR(k) parser of grammar G is deterministic if and only if the following two statements are true for all states q in the LR(0) machine for the \$-augmented grammar for G.*

(1) *Whenever q contains a pair of distinct items* $[A_1 \to \omega_1 \cdot]$, $[A_2 \to \omega_2 \cdot]$, *then*

$$\text{FOLLOW}_k(A_1) \cap \text{FOLLOW}_k(A_2) = \varnothing \ .$$

(2) *Whenever q contains a pair of items* $[A \to \alpha \cdot a\beta]$, $[B \to \omega \cdot]$, *where a is a terminal, then*

$$\text{FIRST}_k(a\beta\text{FOLLOW}_k(A)) \cap \text{FOLLOW}_k(B) = \varnothing \ .$$

*Proof.* Obviously, the SLR($k$) parser has two distinct reduce actions both applicable to the same configuration if and only if some state $q$ in the LR(0) machine contains a pair of distinct items $[A_1 \to \omega_1 \cdot]$ and $[A_2 \to \omega_2 \cdot]$, where $\text{FOLLOW}'_k(A_1)$ and $\text{FOLLOW}'_k(A_2)$ contain a common lookahead string $y$. Similarly, the SLR($k$) parser has a shift action and a reduce action both applicable to the same configuration if and only if some state $q$ contains a pair of items $[A \to \alpha \cdot a\beta]$, $[B \to \omega \cdot]$, where $\text{FIRST}'_k(a\beta\text{FOLLOW}'_k(A))$ and $\text{FOLLOW}'_k(B)$ contain a common lookahead string $y$. The details of the proof are left to the exercises. □

**Theorem 6.59** *The class of SLR(0) grammars coincides with the class of LR(0) grammars. For* $k \geqslant 1$ *the class of SLR(k) grammars is properly contained in the class of LALR(k) grammars.*

*Proof.* That the class of SLR(0) grammars coincides with the class of LR(0) grammars follows directly from the fact that the SLR(0) parser coincides with the LR(0) parser. That the class of SLR($k$) grammars is always contained in the class of LALR($k$) grammars follows from the fact that the SLR($k$) parser contains every action of the LALR($k$) parser. That for $k \geqslant 1$ not all LALR($k$) grammars are SLR($k$) follows from the fact that usually not all strings in $\text{FOLLOW}'_k(A)$ are valid followers of $A$ in every context. This is the case, for example, with the grammar $G_{nslr}$:

$$S \to Ac \mid bA \mid bc \ ,$$

$$A \to \varepsilon \ .$$

This grammar is LALR(1) but is not SLR($k$) for any $k$. The canonical LR(1) machine for its \$-augmented grammar is shown in Figure 6.16. The machine

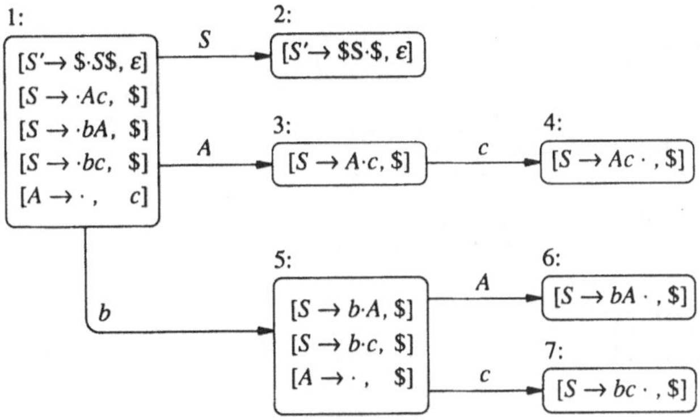


**Figure 6.16** The canonical LR(1) machine for the grammar $G'_{ns1r}$: $S' \to \$S\$$, $S \to Ac|bA|bc$, $A \to \varepsilon$. The grammar is LALR(1) but not SLR($k$) for any $k$

coincides with the LALR(1) machine and is free from conflicts. However, for items $[S \to b \cdot c]$ and $[A \to \cdot]$ in VALID$_0$($b),

$$\text{FIRST}'_k(c\text{FOLLOW}'_k(S)) \cap \text{FOLLOW}'_k(A)$$
$$= \{k{:}c\$\} \cap \{k{:}c\$, k{:}\$\} \neq \varnothing$$

for all $k \geqslant 0$. □

Theorems 6.54 and 6.59 say that an SLR($k$) grammar is always an LALR($k$) grammar, which in turn is always an LR($k$) grammar. If a grammar is SLR($k$), the behavior of the three parsers, the SLR($k$) parser, the LALR($k$) parser, and the canonical LR($k$) parser, differ only in the way some nonsentences are processed. The SLR($k$) parser may detect the error somewhat later than the LALR($k$) parser, which in turn may detect the error somewhat later than the canonical LR($k$) parser.

As an example, consider the SLR(1) grammar

$$S \to aA|Ac|Bd \;,$$
$$A \to B \;,$$
$$B \to b \;.$$

The canonical LR(1) machine for its \$-augmented grammar is shown in Figure 6.17. In the LALR(1) machine states $q_6$ and $q_7$ are united. The SLR(1), LALR(1), and canonical LR(1) parsers all behave differently in the case of the nonsentence $abc$. The canonical LR(1) parser detects the error as soon as $c$ becomes the current input symbol:

$$\$q_1 \mid abc\$$$
$$\Rightarrow \$q_1q_3 \mid bc\$$$
$$\Rightarrow \$q_1q_3q_6 \mid c\$ \;.$$

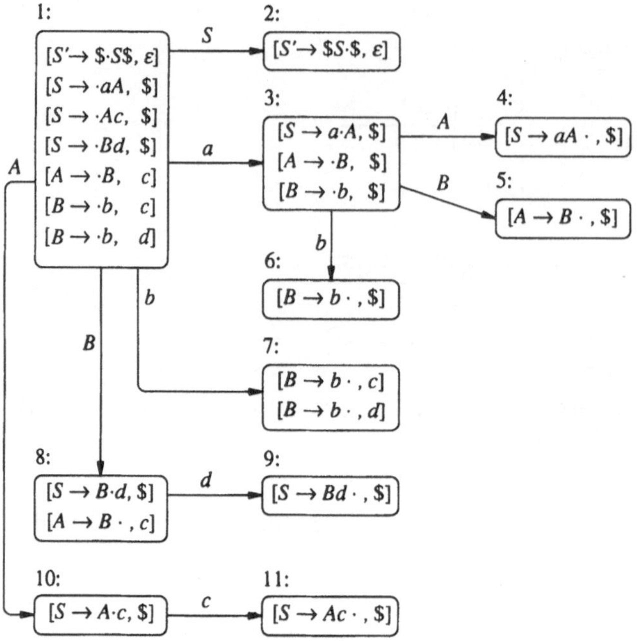


**Figure 6.17** The canonical LR(1) machine for the SLR(1) grammar $S' \to \$S\$$, $S \to aA|Ac|Bd$, $A \to B$, $B \to b$. In the case of this grammar, the canonical LR(1), LALR(1), and SLR(1) parsers all behave differently on the erroneous string *abc*

The LALR(1) parser reduces by $B \to b$ on lookahead $c$ before it detects the error:

$$\$q_1 \mid abc\$$$
$$\Rightarrow \$q_1q_3 \mid bc\$$$
$$\Rightarrow \$q_1q_3q_{6,7} \mid c\$$$
$$\Rightarrow \$q_1q_3q_5 \mid c\$ \ ,$$

where $q_{6,7}$ denotes the union of $q_6$ and $q_7$. Because $c$ belongs to $\text{FOLLOW}'_1(A)$, the SLR(1) parser even reduces by $A \to B$ before it detects the error:

$$\$q_1 \mid abc\$$$
$$\Rightarrow \$q_1q_3 \mid bc\$$$
$$\Rightarrow \$q_1q_3q_{6,7} \mid c\$$$
$$\Rightarrow \$q_1q_3q_5 \mid c\$$$
$$\Rightarrow \$q_1q_3q_4 \mid c\$ \ .$$

The concept of LALR($k$) parsing was motivated by the fact that it yields parsers that are smaller than the canonical LR($k$) parser, when $k \geqslant 1$. The reader may wonder what is the motivation for the concept of SLR($k$) parsing, which seems to be nothing more than an inferior simplification of the concept of LALR($k$) parsing. The SLR($k$) parser is no smaller than the LALR($k$) parser (on the contrary, it is often somewhat larger), and it is deterministic for a smaller class of grammars than the LALR($k$) parser is. However, compared with the LALR($k$) parser, the SLR($k$) parser is easier to construct from the LR(0) machine: the lookahead strings for all items in any state are obtained from the "context-independent" sets $\mathrm{FOLLOW}'_k(A)$, whereas in the case of the LALR($k$) parser the lookahead strings depend on the context and are only obtained via difficult computations on the LR(0) machine (see Chapter 7). Also, it is possible to test an arbitrary context-free grammar $G$ for the SLR($k$) property in deterministic time polynomial in the size of $|G|$, whereas testing $G$ for the (non)-LALR($k$) property is PSPACE-complete (see Chapter 10).

The SLR($k$) grammars are also practical in that they are equivalent in descriptional power to the LR($k$) grammars. That is, any LR($k$) language can be generated by an SLR($k$) grammar. We shall show this by giving a grammatical transformation that transforms any grammar $G$ into a grammar $T_k(G)$ which is SLR($k$) if and only if $G$ is LR($k$). The idea behind the transformation is to replace each nonterminal $A$ in the original grammar by the set of all pairs of the form $([\gamma]_k, A)$, where $\gamma$ is a viable prefix of the \$-augmented grammar for $G$. Each new nonterminal $([\gamma]_k, A)$ will generate the same language as $A$ does. The difference is that in rightmost derivations the nonterminal $([\gamma]_k, A)$ can only be used in contexts equivalent to $\gamma$, that is, only when the original grammar has a right sentential form $\delta A y$, where $[\$\delta]_k = [\gamma]_k$. The set $\mathrm{FOLLOW}'_k(([\gamma]_k, A))$ will then contain only those strings in $\mathrm{FOLLOW}'_k(A)$ that are legal followers of $A$ in contexts equivalent to $\gamma$, that is, strings $k{:}y$, where $\delta A y$ is a right sentential form and $[\$\delta]_k = [\gamma]_k$. This will mean that the transformed grammar is in fact SLR($k$) whenever it is LR($k$).

Now let $G = (V, T, P, S)$ be a grammar, $G'$ its \$-augmented grammar, and $k$ a natural number. We define $T_k(G)$ to be the grammar with nonterminal alphabet $[G']_k \times (V \setminus T)$, terminal alphabet $T$, start symbol $([\$]_k, S)$, and the set of rules consisting of all rules of the form

$$([\$\gamma]_k, A) \to U_1 \ldots U_m \ ,$$

where $\gamma A$ and $\gamma X_1 \ldots X_m$ are viable prefixes of $G$, $A \to X_1 \ldots X_m$ is a rule in $P$, $X_1, \ldots, X_m$ are symbols in $V$ ($m \geqslant 0$). and

$$U_i = \begin{cases} ([\$\gamma X_1 \ldots X_{i-1}]_k, X_i), & \text{when } X_i \text{ is a nonterminal ;} \\ X_i, \quad \text{when } X_i \text{ is a terminal .} \end{cases}$$

Observe that here $\$\gamma X_1 \ldots X_i$ is a viable prefix of $G'$ for all $i = 0, \ldots, m$.

As an example, consider the non-SLR ($k$) grammar $G_{nslr}$ given in the proof of Theorem 6.59. Using the canonical LR(1) machine shown in Figure 6.16 we can write the transformed grammar $T_1(G_{nslr})$:

$$(q_1, S) \to (q_1, A)c \,|\, b(q_5, A) \,|\, bc \ ,$$

$$(q_1, A) \to \varepsilon \ ,$$

$$(q_5, A) \to \varepsilon \ .$$

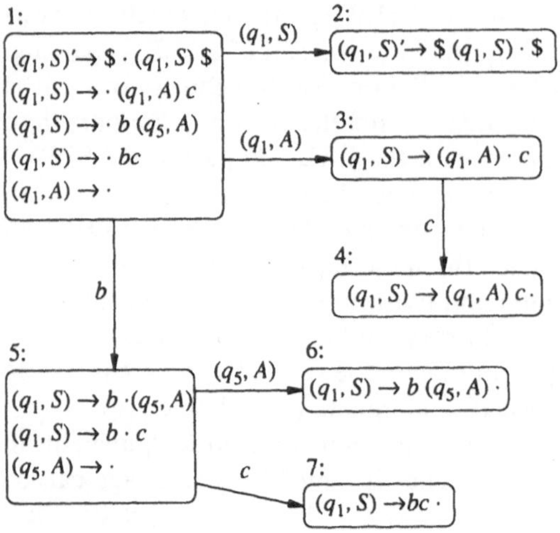


**Figure 6.18** The LR(0) machine for the \$-augmented grammar of the transformed grammar $T_1(G_{nslr})$, where $G_{nslr}$ is the non-SLR(k) grammar $S \to Ac|bA|bc$, $A \to \varepsilon$ (see Figure 6.16)

The LR(0) machine for the \$-augmented grammar of $T_1(G_{nslr})$ is shown in Figure 6.18. Observe that now, for the items $[(q_1, S) \to b \cdot c]$ and $[(q_5, A) \to \cdot]$ in state $q_5$,

$$\mathrm{FIRST}'_1(c\mathrm{FOLLOW}'_1((q_1, S))) \cap \mathrm{FOLLOW}'_1((q_5, A))$$
$$= \{c\} \cap \{\$\} = \varnothing \ ,$$

which means that $T_1(G_{nslr})$ is SLR(1).

Grammatical transformations are often used in parsing theory when we are given a grammar which is not parsable by means of the chosen parsing method (e.g., the strong LL(1) method) but which can be transformed into an equivalent grammar to which this parsing method applies. These transformations should possess the property that from a parse of a sentence in the transformed grammar one can recover a parse of the sentence in the original grammar. Then the parser of the transformed grammar can act as a parser of the original grammar. This is important because it is usually the parse of the sentence in the original, user-provided grammar one is interested in, not the parse of some automatically constructed transformed grammar. For example, in compiling a program one must recover the derivation tree of the program in the original syntax of the language, because it is in accordance with this tree that the semantics of the program are defined. Indeed, the original grammar is often referred to as the "semantic grammar", while the transformed grammar is referred to as the "parsing grammar".

We shall show that the transformation $T_k$, besides actually producing for an LR(k) grammar an equivalent SLR(k) grammar, possesses the desired property that the parses in the original grammar can be recovered from parses in the transformed grammar. More specifically, we shall show that $T_k(G)$ "right-to-right covers" $G$, which means that right parses in $T_k(G)$ are mapped, by a homomorphism, to right parses in $G$. Then a right parser of $T_k(G)$ can act as a right parser of $G$. In fact $T_k(G)$ also "left-to-left covers" $G$, that is, left parses in $T_k(G)$ are mapped homomorphically to left parses in $G$. Indeed, $T_k$ produces a very strong form of "cover", one that is structurally equivalent to the original grammar. Two grammars $G_1$ and $G_2$ are said to be *structurally equivalent* if $L(G_1) = L(G_2)$ and if for any sentence $w$ the derivation trees of $w$ in $G_1$ and $G_2$ have the same structure, that is, are the same except perhaps for the labeling of nonterminal nodes. The derivation trees of the sentences in the structurally equivalent grammars $G_{nslr}$ and $T_1(G_{nslr})$ are given in Figure 6.19.

In the following we give the definition of a "cover" in a general form. Besides "right-to-right covers" and "left-to-left covers", also "left-to-right covers" and "right-to-left covers" are defined. Left-to-right covers will be studied in Chapter 8, where some subclasses of LR($k$) grammars are transformed into LL($k$) grammars.

Let $x$ and $y$ be words in {"left", "right"}. An *x-to-y cover* of a grammar $G = (V, T, P, S)$ is a pair $(\hat{G}, h)$, where $\hat{G} = (\hat{V}, T, \hat{P}, \hat{S})$ is a grammar and $h$ is a homomorphism from $\hat{P}^*$ to $P$ such that the following statements hold.

(1) $h$ maps $x$ parses to $y$ parses, that is, for all $w$ in $L(\hat{G})$ and $x$ parses $\hat{\pi}$ of $w$ in $\hat{G}$, $h(\hat{\pi})$ is a $y$ parse of $w$ in $G$.

(2) Any $y$ parse in $G$ is an image of some $x$ parse in $\hat{G}$, that is, for all $w$ in $L(G)$ and $y$ parses $\pi$ of $w$ in $G$, $w$ has in $\hat{G}$ an $x$ parse $\hat{\pi}$ such that $h(\hat{\pi}) = \pi$.

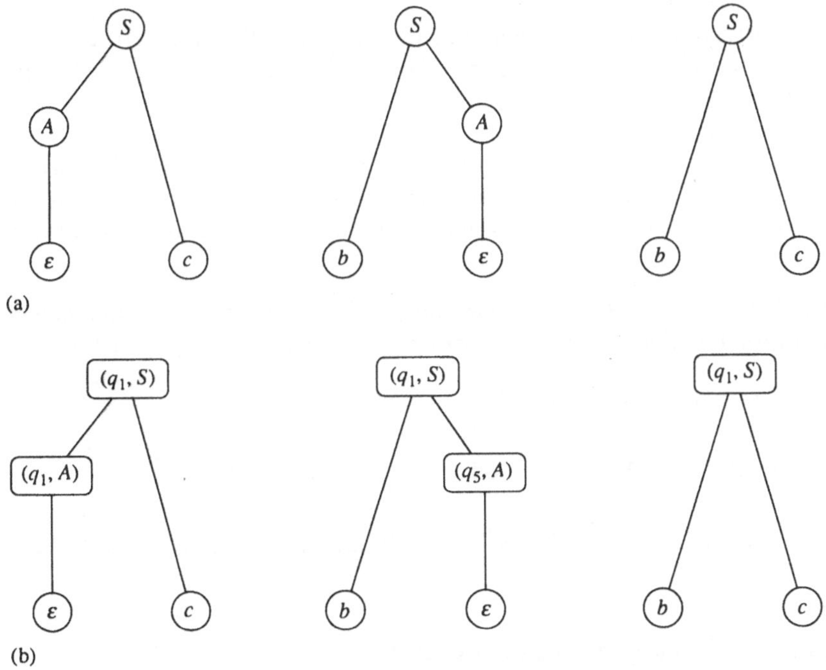


**Figure 6.19** Derivation trees of sentences in the structurally equivalent grammars $G_{nslr}$ (**a**) and $T_1(G_{nslr})$ (**b**)

If $(\hat{G}, h)$ is an $x$-to-$y$ cover of $G$, we say that *$\hat{G}$ $x$-to-$y$ covers $G$ with respect to $h$*. If $\hat{G}$ $x$-to-$y$ covers $G$ with respect to some $h$, we say that *$\hat{G}$ $x$-to-$y$ covers $G$*.

By Theorem 4.2 we have:

**Fact 6.60** If grammar $\hat{G}$ $x$-to-$y$ covers grammar $G$, then $L(\hat{G}) = L(G)$. □

The definitions of parsers and covers imply immediately:

**Fact 6.61** If $(M, \tau)$ is an $x$ parser of grammar $\hat{G}$ and if $\hat{G}$ $x$-to-$y$ covers grammar $G$ with respect to homomorphism $h$, then $(M, \tau h)$ is a $y$ parser of $G$. □

In the case of the transformation $T_k$ the covering homomorphism, denoted by $h_k$, is defined by:

$$h_k(U \to U_1 \ldots U_m) = A \to X_1 \ldots X_m \ ,$$

where $U = ([\$\gamma]_k, A)$ and, for all $i = 1, \ldots, m$,

$$U_i = \begin{cases} ([\$\gamma X_1 \ldots X_{i-1}]_k, X_i), & \text{when } X_i \text{ is a nonterminal ;} \\ X_i, & \text{when } X_i \text{ is a terminal .} \end{cases}$$

First we show that $(T_k(G), h_k)$ right-to-right covers $G$. This will readily imply that $T_k(G)$ and $G$ are structurally equivalent. Observe that for any right parse $\pi'$ in $T_k(G)$ the derivation tree corresponding to $h_k(\pi')$ has the same structure as the derivation tree corresponding to $\pi'$. This is because $h_k$ maps each rule $U \to U_1 \ldots U_m$ of $T_k(G)$ to a single, equally long rule $A \to X_1 \ldots X_m$, where $U_i$ is a nonterminal if and only if $X_i$ is.

The following two lemmas relate rightmost derivations in $T_k(G)$ with those in $G$. The techniques used in the formulation of the results as well as in their proofs are similar to those we have used frequently in proving the correctness of right parsers.

**Lemma 6.62** *Let $G = (V, T, P, S)$ be a grammar, $\gamma$ a string in $V^*$, $A$ a nonterminal of $G$, $\Phi$ a string over the alphabet of $T_k(G)$, and $\pi'$ a rule string of $T_k(G)$ such that*

(a) *$\gamma A$ is a viable prefix of $G$ and*

$$([\$\gamma]_k, A) \xRightarrow[\text{rm}]{\pi'} \Phi \quad \text{in } T_k(G) \ .$$

*Then there are symbols $X_1, \ldots, X_m$ in $V$ $(m \geq 0)$ and a string $y$ in $T^*$ such that*

$$\Phi = U_1 \ldots U_m y \ ,$$

(b) *$\gamma X_1 \ldots X_m$ is a viable prefix of $G$, and*

$$A \xRightarrow[\text{rm}]{h_k(\pi')} X_1 \ldots X_m y \quad \text{in } G \ ,$$

*where, for all* $i = 1, \ldots, m$,

(c) $$U_i = \begin{cases} ([\$\gamma X_1 \ldots X_{i-1}]_k, X_i), & \textit{when } X_i \textit{ is a nonterminal ;} \\ X_i, & \textit{when } X_i \textit{ is a terminal .} \end{cases}$$

*Proof.* The proof is by induction on the length of the rule string $\pi'$. In the base case $\pi' = \varepsilon$ and $\Phi = ([\$\gamma]_k, A)$. Statements ($b$) and ($c$) then hold if we choose $m = 1$, $X_1 = A$, $U_1 = ([\$\gamma]_k, A)$, and $y = \varepsilon$.

To prove the induction step we assume that $\pi'$ is of the form $\pi'_1 r'$, where $r'$ is a rule of $T_k(G)$. As an induction hypothesis, we assume that the lemma holds for the rule string $\pi'_1$. Then we have:

(1) $$([\$\gamma]_k, A) \xRightarrow[\text{rm}]{\pi'_1} U_1 \ldots U_n U' y \xRightarrow[\text{rm}]{r'} U_1 \ldots U_n W_1 \ldots W_p y = \Phi$$

in $T_k(G)$, for some symbols $U_1, \ldots, U_n, U', W_1, \ldots, W_p$ of $T_k(G)$ and string $y \in T^*$. By definition, $G$ has a viable prefix $\delta$ and a rule $B \to Z_1 \ldots Z_p$ such that $U' = ([\$\delta]_k, B)$, $\delta Z_1 \ldots Z_p$ is a viable prefix and, for all $i = 1, \ldots, p$,

(2) $$W_i = \begin{cases} ([\$\delta Z_1 \ldots Z_{i-1}]_k, Z_i), & \text{when } Z_i \text{ is a nonterminal ;} \\ Z_i, & \text{when } Z_i \text{ is a terminal .} \end{cases}$$

The induction hypothesis implies the existence of symbols $X_1, \ldots, X_n \in V$ such that

(3) $\gamma X_1 \ldots X_n B$ is a viable prefix of $G$, and

$$A \xRightarrow[\text{rm}]{h_k(\pi'_1)} X_1 \ldots X_n B y \quad \text{in } G ,$$

where, for all $i = 1, \ldots, n$,

(4) $$U_i = \begin{cases} ([\$\gamma X_1 \ldots X_{i-1}]_k, X_i), & \text{when } X_i \text{ is a nonterminal ;} \\ X_i, & \text{when } X_i \text{ is a terminal .} \end{cases}$$

Moreover, $U' = ([\$\gamma X_1 \ldots X_n]_k, B)$. Then $[\$\gamma X_1 \ldots X_n]_k = [\$\delta]_k$, which implies, by the right invariance of LR($k$)-equivalence, that

(5) $$[\$\delta Z_1 \ldots Z_{i-1}]_k = [\$\gamma X_1 \ldots X_n Z_1 \ldots Z_{i-1}]_k ,$$

for all $i = 1, \ldots, p$. If we choose $m = n + p$ and, for all $i = 1, \ldots, p$, $U_{n+i} = W_i$ and $X_{n+i} = Z_i$, then we can conclude that statements ($b$) and ($c$) hold. □

**Lemma 6.63** *Let* $G = (V, T, P, S)$ *be a grammar,* $\gamma$ *a string in* $V^*$, $y$ *a string in* $T^*$, $A$ *a nonterminal of* $G$, $X_1, \ldots, X_m$ *symbols in* $V$ $(m \geqslant 0)$, *and* $\pi$ *a rule string in* $P^*$ *such* *that*

$$\text{(a)}\quad \begin{array}{l} \gamma A \textit{ is a viable prefix of } G \ , \\ A \overset{\pi}{\underset{\text{rm}}{\Longrightarrow}} X_1 \ldots X_m y \textit{ in } G, \textit{ and} \\ \textit{either } X_1 \ldots X_m = \varepsilon \textit{ or } X_m \textit{ is a nonterminal} \ . \end{array}$$

*Then* $T_k(G)$ *has a rule string* $\pi'$ *such that*

$$\text{(b)}\quad \begin{array}{l} h_k(\pi') = \pi \textit{ and} \\ ([\$\gamma]_k, A) \overset{\pi'}{\underset{\text{rm}}{\Longrightarrow}} U_1 \ldots U_m y \qquad \textit{in } T_k(G) \ , \end{array}$$

*where, for all* $i = 1, \ldots, m$,

$$\text{(c)}\quad U_i = \begin{cases} ([\$\gamma X_1 \ldots X_{i-1}]_k, X_i), & \textit{when } X_i \textit{ is a nonterminal} \ ; \\ X_i, & \textit{when } X_i \textit{ is a terminal} \ . \end{cases}$$

*Proof.* The proof is by induction on the length of rule string $\pi$. In the base case we have $\pi = \varepsilon$. Then $m = 1$, $A = X_1$, and $y = \varepsilon$. Statements $(b)$ and $(c)$ then hold if we choose $\pi' = \varepsilon$ and $U_1 = ([\$\gamma]_k, A)$.

To prove the induction step we assume that $\pi$ is of the form $\pi_1 r$, where $r$ is a rule $B \to Z_1 \ldots Z_p$. As an induction hypothesis, we assume that the lemma holds for the rule string $\pi_1$. We have:

$$\text{(1)}\quad \begin{array}{l} A \overset{\pi_1}{\underset{\text{rm}}{\Longrightarrow}} Y_1 \ldots Y_n B y_1 \overset{r}{\underset{\text{rm}}{\Longrightarrow}} Y_1 \ldots Y_n Z_1 \ldots Z_p y_1 \\ = X_1 \ldots X_m y \qquad \text{in } G \end{array}$$

for some symbols $Y_1, \ldots, Y_n \in V \ (n \geq 0)$ and string $y_1 \in T^*$. Here $y = zy_1$ and $Y_1 \ldots Y_n Z_1 \ldots Z_p = X_1 \ldots X_m z$ for some $z$, because $X_1 \ldots X_m$ is empty or ends with a nonterminal. We can apply the induction hypothesis to the first derivation segment in (1) and conclude that for some rule string $\pi'_1$ of $T_k(G)$

$$\text{(2)}\quad \begin{array}{l} h_k(\pi'_1) = \pi_1 \text{ and} \\ ([\$\gamma]_k, A) \overset{\pi'_1}{\underset{\text{rm}}{\Longrightarrow}} U_1 \ldots U_n([\$\gamma Y_1 \ldots Y_n]_k, B) y_1 \qquad \text{in } T_k(G) \ , \end{array}$$

where, for all $i = 1, \ldots, n$,

$$\text{(3)}\quad U_i = \begin{cases} ([\$\gamma Y_1 \ldots Y_{i-1}]_k, Y_i), & \text{when } Y_i \text{ is a nonterminal} \ ; \\ Y_i, & \text{when } Y_i \text{ is a terminal} \ . \end{cases}$$

By definition, $T_k(G)$ has the rule

$$\text{(4)}\quad r' = ([\$\gamma Y_1 \ldots Y_n]_k, B) \to U_{n+1} \ldots U_{n+p} \ ,$$

where, for all $i = n + 1, \ldots, n + p$,

(5) $$U_i = \begin{cases} ([\$\gamma Y_1 \ldots Y_n Z_1 \ldots Z_{i-1}]_k, Z_i), & \text{when } Z_i \text{ is a nonterminal ;} \\ Z_i, & \text{when } Z_i \text{ is a terminal .} \end{cases}$$

Then we have:

$$h_k(\pi'_1 r') = h_k(\pi'_1)\, h_k(r') = \pi_1 r = \pi \text{ and}$$

(6) $$([\$\gamma]_k, A) \underset{\text{rm}}{\overset{\pi'_1 r'}{\Longrightarrow}} U_1 \ldots U_{n+p} y_1 = U_1 \ldots U_m z y_1 = U_1 \ldots U_m y \ .$$

Note that $m = n + p - |z|$ and $U_{n+p-|z|} \ldots U_{n+p} = z$. Statements ($b$) and ($c$) thus hold if we choose $\pi' = \pi'_1 r'$. □

**Theorem 6.64** *Let $G = (V, T, P, S)$ be a grammar and $k$ a natural number. Then $T_k(G)$ right-to-right covers $G$ with respect to the homomorphism $h_k$.*

*Proof.* In proving that right parses in $T_k(G)$ are mapped by $h_k$ to right parses in $G$, choose $\gamma = \varepsilon$, $A = S$, and $\Phi = w$ in Lemma 6.62. In proving that right parses in $G$ are images under $h_k$ of right parses in $T_k(G)$, choose $\gamma = \varepsilon$, $A = S$, $m = 0$, and $y = w$ in Lemma 6.63. □

**Corollary 6.65** *If $(M, \tau)$ is a right parser of $T_k(G)$, then $(M, \tau h_k)$ is a right parser of $G$.* □

**Lemma 6.66** *Let $G = (V, T, P, S)$ be a grammar, $\gamma$ a viable prefix of $G$, $y$ a string in $T^*$, $A$ a nonterminal of $G$, and $l$ a natural number. Then*

($a$) $$y \in \text{FOLLOW}_l(([\$\gamma]_k, A)) \quad \textit{in } T_k(G)$$

*if and only if for some strings $\delta \in V^*$ and $z \in T^*$*

($b$) $$S \underset{\text{rm}}{\Longrightarrow^*} \delta A z \quad \textit{in } G, \quad [\$\delta]_k = [\$\gamma]_k, \quad \textit{and} \quad l{:}z = y \ .$$

*In other words, $y$ is a legal follower of nonterminal $([\$\gamma]_k, A)$ in $T_k(G)$ if and only if $y$ is a legal follower of $A$ in $G$ in some context LR($k$)-equivalent to $\gamma$.*

*Proof.* By Exercise 5.17 (cf. Lemma 5.32), $y$ is a string in $\text{FOLLOW}_l(([\$\gamma]_k, A))$ if and only if for some string $\Phi$ and terminal string $z$

$$([\$]_k, S) \underset{\text{rm}}{\Longrightarrow^*} \Phi([\$\gamma]_k, A)z \quad \text{in } T_k(G) \quad \text{and} \quad l{:}z = y \ .$$

By Lemmas 6.62 and 6.63 this is true if and only if

$$S \underset{\text{rm}}{\Longrightarrow^*} X_1 \ldots X_m A z \quad \text{in } G, \quad l{:}z = y, \text{ and}$$

$$[\$X_1 \ldots X_m]_k = [\$\gamma]_k \ ,$$

for some symbols $X_1, \ldots, X_m$ in $V$. □

**Lemma 6.67** *Let $G = (V, T, P, S)$ be a grammar, $y$ a string in $T^*$, $U_1, \ldots, U_p$ symbols of $T_k(G)$, $U \rightarrow U_m \ldots U_p$ a rule of $T_k(G)$ $(m \leqslant p+1)$, and $l$ a natural number. Then*

$$[U \rightarrow U_m \ldots U_i \cdot U_{i+1} \ldots U_p, y] \in \mathrm{VALID}_l(\$U_1 \ldots U_i)$$

*if and only if $G$ has symbols $X_1, \ldots, X_p$ and a nonterminal $A$ such that*

$$[A \rightarrow X_m \ldots X_i \cdot X_{i+1} \ldots X_p, y] \in \mathrm{VALID}_l(\$X_1 \ldots X_i) ,$$

*where $U = ([\$X_1 \ldots X_{m-1}]_k, A)$ and, for all $j = 1, \ldots, p$,*

$$U_j = \begin{cases} ([\$X_1 \ldots X_{j-1}]_k, X_j), & \text{when } X_j \text{ is a nonterminal ;} \\ X_j, & \text{when } X_j \text{ is a terminal .} \end{cases}$$

*Proof.* The proof is similar to that of Lemma 6.66. The details are left to the exercises. □

**Lemma 6.68** *If grammar $G$ is non-LR($k$), then so is $T_k(G)$.*

*Proof.* In a non-LR($k$) grammar, either $S \Rightarrow^+ S$, or some set $\mathrm{VALID}_k(\$X_1 \ldots X_i)$ contains a pair of items exhibiting a reduce-reduce or a shift-reduce conflict. In the former case Lemma 6.63 implies that $([\$]_k, S) \Rightarrow^+ ([\$]_k, S)$, that is, $T_k(G)$ is non-LR($k$). In the latter case we have:

$$[A \rightarrow X_m \ldots X_i \cdot, y] \in \mathrm{VALID}_k(\$X_1 \ldots X_i) ,$$

(1) $$[B \rightarrow X_n \ldots X_i \cdot X_{i+1} \ldots X_p, u] \in \mathrm{VALID}_k(\$X_1 \ldots X_i), \text{ and}$$

$$y \in \mathrm{FIRST}_k(X_{i+1} \ldots X_p u) ,$$

for some $m, n \leqslant i+1$, $p \geqslant i$, symbols $X_{i+1}, \ldots, X_p$, nonterminals $A$ and $B$, and terminal strings $y$ and $u$, where $X_{i+1}$ is a terminal whenever $i+1 \leqslant p$. Moreover, the item cores are distinct, that is, $A \neq B$ or $m \neq n$ or $i+1 \leqslant p$. By Lemma 6.67 we then have:

(2) $$[U \rightarrow U_m \ldots U_i \cdot, y] \in \mathrm{VALID}_k(\$U_1 \ldots U_i), \text{ and}$$
$$[W \rightarrow U_n \ldots U_i \cdot U_{i+1} \ldots U_p, u] \in \mathrm{VALID}_k(\$U_1 \ldots U_i) ,$$

where $U = ([\$X_1 \ldots X_{m-1}]_k, A)$, $W = ([\$X_1 \ldots X_{n-1}]_k, B)$, and, for all $j = 1, \ldots, p$,

(3) $$U_j = \begin{cases} ([\$X_1 \ldots X_{j-1}]_k, X_j), & \text{when } X_j \text{ is a nonterminal ;} \\ X_j, & \text{when } X_j \text{ is a terminal .} \end{cases}$$

Here $U_{i+1}$ is a terminal whenever $i+1 \leqslant p$. Moreover, the item cores are distinct, that is, $U \neq W$ or $m \neq n$ or $i+1 \leqslant p$. On the other hand, the condition $y \in \mathrm{FIRST}_k(X_{i+1} \ldots X_p u)$ implies that $y$ also belongs to $\mathrm{FIRST}_k(U_{i+1} \ldots U_p u)$. Observe that if $X_j$ rightmost derives terminal string $v$, then so does $U_j$, by

Lemma 6.63. We conclude that item pair (2) exhibits a reduce-reduce or a shift-reduce conflict. □

**Lemma 6.69** *If the grammar $T_k(G)$ is non-SLR($k$), then G is non-LR($k$).*

*Proof.* If $([\$]_k, S) \Rightarrow^+ ([\$]_k, S)$, then, by Lemma 6.62, $S \Rightarrow^+ S$. Otherwise, if $T_k(G)$ is non-SLR($k$), we have, by Theorem 6.58,

$$[U \to U_m \dots U_i \cdot] \in \text{VALID}_0(\$U_1 \dots U_i) ,$$

$$[W \to U_n \dots U_i \cdot U_{i+1} \dots U_p] \in \text{VALID}_0(\$U_1 \dots U_i), \text{ and}$$

$$y \in \text{FOLLOW}_k(U) \cap \text{FIRST}_k(U_{i+1} \dots U_p \text{FOLLOW}_k(W)) ,$$

where the item cores are distinct, and in addition, $U_{i+1}$ is a terminal whenever $i + 1 \leqslant p$. By Lemma 6.67 there are symbols $X_1, \dots, X_p$ and nonterminals $A$ and $B$ such that $U = ([\$X_1 \dots X_{m-1}]_k, A)$, $W = ([\$X_1 \dots X_{n-1}]_k, B)$ and, for all $j = 1, \dots, p$,

$$U_j = \begin{cases} ([\$X_1 \dots X_{j-1}]_k, X_j), & \text{when } X_j \text{ is a nonterminal ;} \\ X_j, & \text{when } X_j \text{ is a terminal .} \end{cases}$$

By Lemma 6.66 we have:

$$S \underset{\text{rm}}{\Longrightarrow}^* \gamma Az, [\$\gamma]_k = [\$X_1 \dots X_{m-1}]_k, \quad k{:}z = y ,$$

$$S \underset{\text{rm}}{\Longrightarrow}^* \delta Bu, [\$\delta]_k = [\$X_1 \dots X_{n-1}]_k, \quad k{:}xu = y, \text{ and}$$

$$x \in \text{FIRST}_k(U_{i+1} \dots U_p) ,$$

for some strings $\gamma$ and $\delta$ and terminal strings $x$, $u$, and $z$. Here the condition $x \in \text{FIRST}_k(U_{i+1} \dots U_p)$ implies that $x$ also belongs to $\text{FIRST}_k(X_{i+1} \dots X_p)$. Observe that if $U_j$ rightmost derives terminal string $v$, then so does $X_j$, by Lemma 6.62. Thus the items $[A \to X_m \dots X_i \cdot, k{:}z\$]$ and $[B \to X_n \dots X_i \cdot X_{i+1} \dots X_p, k{:}u\$]$ exhibit a conflict. On the other hand we have:

$$S \underset{\text{rm}}{\Longrightarrow}^* \gamma Az \underset{\text{rm}}{\Longrightarrow} \gamma X_m \dots X_i z, \text{ and}$$

$$S \underset{\text{rm}}{\Longrightarrow}^* \delta Bu \underset{\text{rm}}{\Longrightarrow} \delta X_n \dots X_p u,$$

which means that $[A \to X_m \dots X_i \cdot, k{:}z\$]$ is LR($k$)-valid for $\$\gamma X_m \dots X_i$ and that $[B \to X_n \dots X_i \cdot X_{i+1} \dots X_p, k{:}u\$]$ is LR($k$)-valid for $\$\delta X_n \dots X_i$. Moreover, the right invariance of the LR($k$)-equivalence implies that $\$\gamma X_m \dots X_i$ and $\$\delta X_n \dots X_i$ are LR($k$)-equivalent, because $\$\gamma$ is LR($k$)-equivalent to $\$X_1 \dots X_{m-1}$ and $\$\delta$ is LR($k$)-equivalent to $\$X_1 \dots X_{n-1}$. □

We can now state:

**Theorem 6.70** *Let $k$ be a natural number. Any grammar $G$ can be transformed into a structurally equivalent grammar which is $SLR(k)$ if and only if $G$ is $LR(k)$.* □

By Theorems 6.54, 6.59, and 6.70 we have:

**Theorem 6.71** *For any fixed $k \geqslant 0$, the families of $LR(k)$ languages, $LALR(k)$ languages, and $SLR(k)$ languages are all equal.* □

## 6.7 Covering LR($k$) Grammars by LR(1) Grammars

In this section we shall show that for any $k \geqslant 1$ the family of LR($k$) languages coincides with the family of LR(1) languages. That is, for any LR($k$) grammar there is an equivalent LR(1) grammar. More specifically, we shall show tnat any LR($k$) grammar can be transformed into an LR(1) grammar that right-to-right covers (and left-to-left covers) the original grammar. This means that in right parsing any deterministic language we can always avoid using lookahead strings of length $k > 1$; single lookahead symbols will do. This is in contrast to the fact that in left parsing the shortening of lookahead is not possible: as noted in Section 5.4, the families of SLL($k$) languages, $k \geqslant 0$, form a properly increasing hierarchy. As any LR(1) grammar can further be transformed into an equivalent SLR(1) grammar that right-to-right covers the original grammar, we conclude that we can right parse any deterministic language by means of an SLR(1) parser.

Let $G = (V, T, P, S)$ be a grammar and $k$ a natural number. We shall transform $G$ into a grammar $T_{k,1}(G)$ which is LR(1) if and only if $G$ is LR($k + 1$). The idea behind the transformation is to "shift" the derivation trees in $G$ $k$ symbols to the right; in the parser this will mean that reduce actions are postponed until 1-symbol lookahead is sufficient to resolve uniquely the parsing action to be performed. To achieve this, any nonterminal $A$ of $G$ is replaced by a set of nonterminals of the form $(x, A, y)$, where $y$ is a string in $\text{FOLLOW}_k(A)$ and $x$ is a string in $\text{FIRST}_k(Ay)$. The language generated by the new nonterminal $(x, A, y)$ will be:

$$\{z \in T^* \mid xz = vy,\ A \Rightarrow^* v, \text{ and } k{:}vy = x\} .$$

In other words, the derivation tree of the prefix $v$ in $vy$ is shifted $k$ symbols to the right so that it becomes a derivation tree of the suffix $z$ in $vy = xz$ (see Figure 6.20). The start symbol of the transformed grammar will be a new symbol $S_0$, which has rules of the form $S_0 \to x(x, S, \varepsilon)$ (see Figure 6.21).

Formally, $T_{k,1}(G)$ is defined as the grammar with terminal alphabet $T$, nonterminal alphabet

$$\{S_0\} \cup \{(x, X, y) \mid X \in V,\ y \in \text{FOLLOW}_k(X),\ x \in \text{FIRST}_k(Xy)\} ,$$

start symbol $S_0$, and set of rules

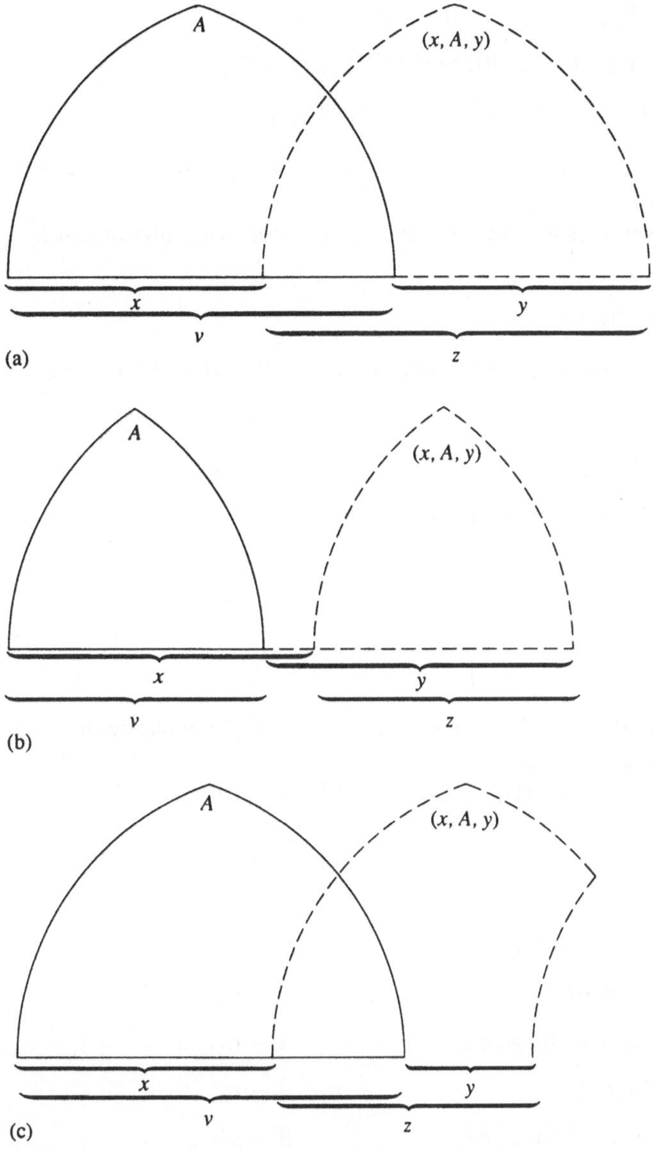


**Figure 6.20** Derivation trees in $G$ and in $T_{k,1}(G)$. In all cases $vy = xz$, where $A \Rightarrow^* v$, $(x, A, y) \Rightarrow^* z$, and $k{:}vy = x$. In (**a**) $|v| > k$. In (**b**) $|v| < k$. In (**c**) $|y| < k$

$$\{S_0 \to x(x, S, \varepsilon) \mid x \in \mathrm{FIRST}_k(S)\}$$
$$\cup \{(y_0, A, y_m) \to (y_0, X_1, y_1)\,(y_1, X_2, y_2) \ldots (y_{m-1}, X_m, y_m) \mid \ m \geqslant 0\ ,$$
$$X_1, \ldots, X_m \in V, A \to X_1 \ldots X_m \in P, y_m \in \mathrm{FOLLOW}_k(A)\ ,$$

$$y_i \in \text{FIRST}_k(X_{i+1}y_{i+1}) \text{ for all } i = 0, \ldots, m-1\}$$
$$\cup \{(ax, a, xb) \to b \mid a, b \in T, xb \in \text{FOLLOW}_k(a) \cap T^k\}$$
$$\cup \{(ax, a, x) \to \varepsilon \mid a \in T, x \in \text{FOLLOW}_k(a) \setminus T^k\} \ .$$

Here $(y_0, A, y_m) \to (y_0, X_1, y_1)\ (y_1, X_2, y_2) \ldots (y_{m-1}, X_m, y_m)$ denotes the rule $(y_0, A, y_0) \to \varepsilon$ when $m = 0$.

The right-to-right cover will be obtained by means of a homomorphism $h_{k,1}$ defined as follows:

$$h_{k,1}(S_0 \to x(x, S, \varepsilon)) = \varepsilon \ ,$$
$$h_{k,1}((y_0, A, y_m) \to (y_0, X_1, y_1) \ldots (y_{m-1}, X_m, y_m)) = A \to X_1 \ldots X_m \ ,$$
$$h_{k,1}((ax, a, xb) \to b) = \varepsilon \ ,$$
$$h_{k,1}((ax, a, x) \to \varepsilon) = \varepsilon \ .$$

As an example, consider the grammar $G_{\text{LR2}}$:

$$S \to Abb \mid Bb \ ,$$
$$A \to aA \mid a \ ,$$
$$B \to aB \mid a \ .$$

The grammar is SLR(2) but not LR(1) (see the canonical LR(1) machine depicted in Figure 6.24). The language generated is $\{a\}^+\{bb, b\}$ .

The transformed grammar $T_{1,1}(G_{\text{LR2}})$ has the following rules.

| rule $r$: | $h_{1,1}(r)$: |
|---|---|
| $r_1 = S_0 \to a(a, S, \varepsilon)$, | $\varepsilon$ . |
| $r_2 = (a, S, \varepsilon) \to (a, A, b)\ (b, b, b)\ (b, b, \varepsilon)$, | $S \to Abb$ . |
| $r_3 = (a, S, \varepsilon) \to (a, B, b)\ (b, b, \varepsilon)$, | $S \to Bb$ . |
| $r_4 = (a, A, b) \to (a, a, a)\ (a, A, b)$, | $A \to aA$ . |
| $r_5 = (a, A, b) \to (a, a, b)$, | $A \to a$ . |
| $r_6 = (a, B, b) \to (a, a, a)\ (a, B, b)$, | $B \to aB$ . |
| $r_7 = (a, B, b) \to (a, a, b)$, | $B \to a$ . |
| $r_8 = (a, a, a) \to a$, | $\varepsilon$ . |
| $r_9 = (a, a, b) \to b$, | $\varepsilon$ . |
| $r_{10} = (b, b, b) \to b$, | $\varepsilon$ . |
| $r_{11} = (b, b, \varepsilon) \to \varepsilon$, | $\varepsilon$ . |

Figure 6.22 shows the derivation trees of the sentence *aabb* in $G_{\text{LR2}}$ and in $T_{1,1}(G_{\text{LR2}})$. Figure 6.23 shows the derivation trees of the sentence *aab*.

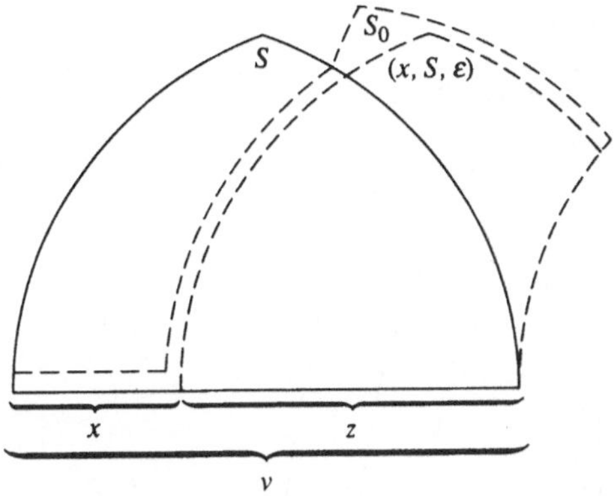


**Figure 6.21** Derivation trees in $G$ and in $T_{k,1}(G)$. Here $v = xz$, where $S \Rightarrow^* v$, $(x, S, \varepsilon) \Rightarrow^* z$, $S_0 \Rightarrow^* v$, and $k{:}v = x$

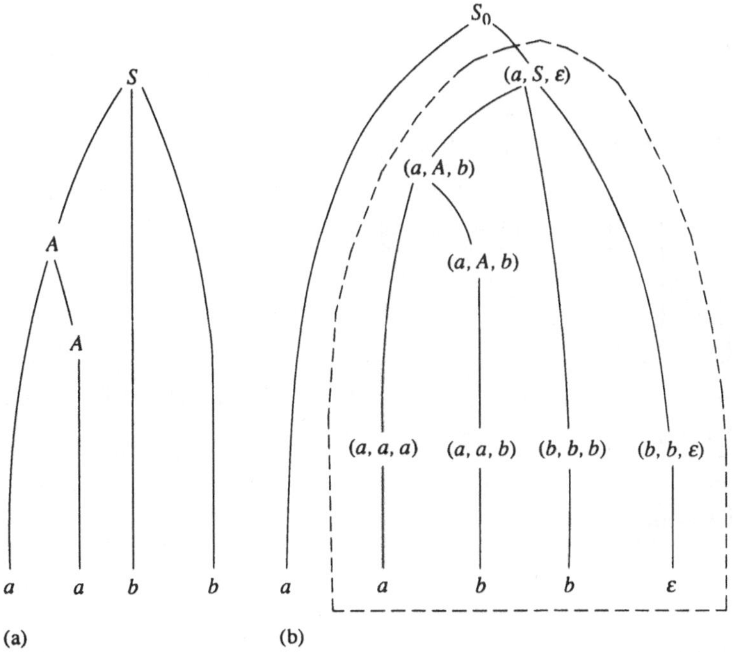


**Figure 6.22** Derivation trees of the sentence *aabb*: (**a**) in the LR(2) grammar $G_{LR2}$: $S \to Abb \mid Bb$, $A \to aA \mid a$, $B \to aB \mid a$; (**b**) in the transformed LR(1) grammar $T_{1,1}(G_{LR2})$

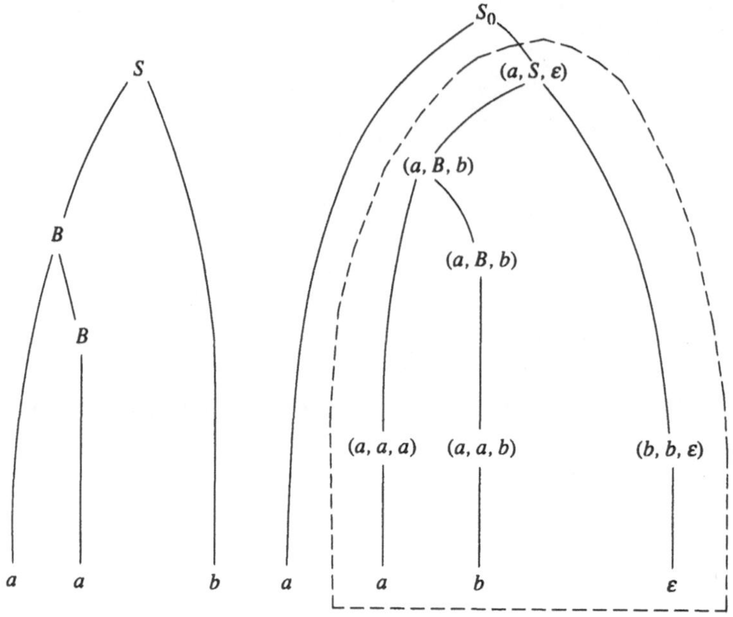


(a) (b)

**Figure 6.23** Derivation trees of the sentence *aab*: (**a**) in the LR(2) grammar $G_{LR2}$; (**b**) in the transformed grammar $T_{1,1}(G_{LR2})$

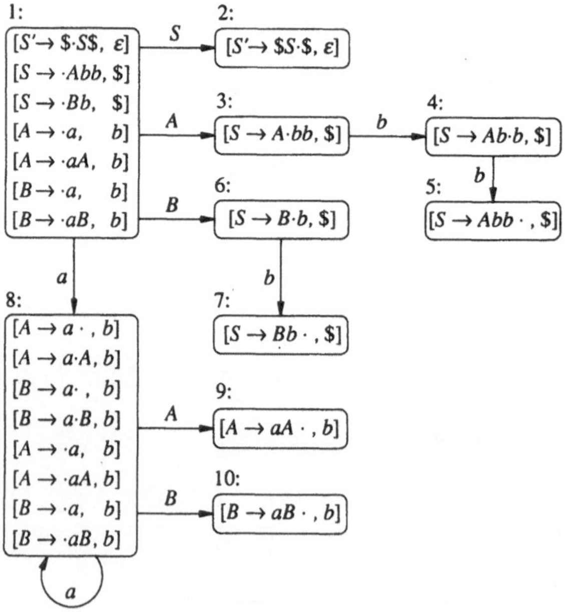


**Figure 6.24** The canonical LR(1) machine for the $-augmented LR(2) grammar $G'_{LR2}$: $S' \to \$S\$$, $S \to Abb \mid Bb$, $A \to a \mid aA$, $B \to a \mid aB$. The grammar is SLR(2) but not LR(1). The pair of items $[A \to a\cdot, b]$, $[B \to a\cdot, b]$ in state 8 exhibit a reduce-reduce conflict

To see that $T_{1,1}(G_{LR2})$ indeed right-to-right covers $G_{LR2}$ with respect to $h_{1,1}$, consider the following derivations.

$$\begin{aligned}
S_0 &\overset{r_1}{\underset{rm}{\Longrightarrow}} a(a, S, \varepsilon) \\
&\overset{r_2}{\underset{rm}{\Longrightarrow}} a(a, A, b)\,(b, b, b)\,(b, b, \varepsilon) \\
&\overset{r_{11}}{\underset{rm}{\Longrightarrow}} a(a, A, b)\,(b, b, b) \\
&\overset{r_{10}}{\underset{rm}{\Longrightarrow}} a(a, A, b)b \\
&\overset{r_4^n}{\underset{rm}{\Longrightarrow}} a(a, a, a)^n\,(a, A, b)b \\
&\overset{r_5}{\underset{rm}{\Longrightarrow}} a(a, a, a)^n\,(a, a, b)b \\
&\overset{r_9}{\underset{rm}{\Longrightarrow}} a(a, a, a)^n bb \\
&\overset{r_8^n}{\underset{rm}{\Longrightarrow}} aa^n bb, \quad \text{for all } n \geqslant 0\ .
\end{aligned}$$

Here $S$ rightmost derives $aa^nbb$ using the rule string $h_{1,1}(r_1r_2r_{11}r_{10}r_4^nr_5r_9r_8^n) = (S \rightarrow Abb)\,(A \rightarrow aA)^n(A \rightarrow a)$ .

$$\begin{aligned}
S_0 &\overset{r_1}{\underset{rm}{\Longrightarrow}} a(a, S, \varepsilon) \\
&\overset{r_3}{\underset{rm}{\Longrightarrow}} a(a, B, b)\,(b, b, \varepsilon) \\
&\overset{r_{11}}{\underset{rm}{\Longrightarrow}} a(a, B, b) \\
&\overset{r_6^n}{\underset{rm}{\Longrightarrow}} a(a, a, a)^n\,(a, B, b) \\
&\overset{r_7}{\underset{rm}{\Longrightarrow}} a(a, a, a)^n(a, a, b) \\
&\overset{r_9}{\underset{rm}{\Longrightarrow}} a(a, a, a)^n b \\
&\overset{r_8^n}{\underset{rm}{\Longrightarrow}} aa^n b, \quad \text{for all } n \geqslant 0\ .
\end{aligned}$$

Here $S$ rightmost derives $aa^nb$ using the rule string $h_{1,1}(r_1r_3r_{11}r_6^nr_7r_9r_8^n) = (S \rightarrow Bb)\,(B \rightarrow aB)^n(B \rightarrow a)$.

That the transformed grammar $T_{1,1}(G_{LR2})$ is indeed LR(1) is seen from Figure 6.25, which shows the canonical LR(1) machine of the \$-augmented grammar $T_{1,1}(G_{LR2})'$. For brevity we have denoted the nonterminals by

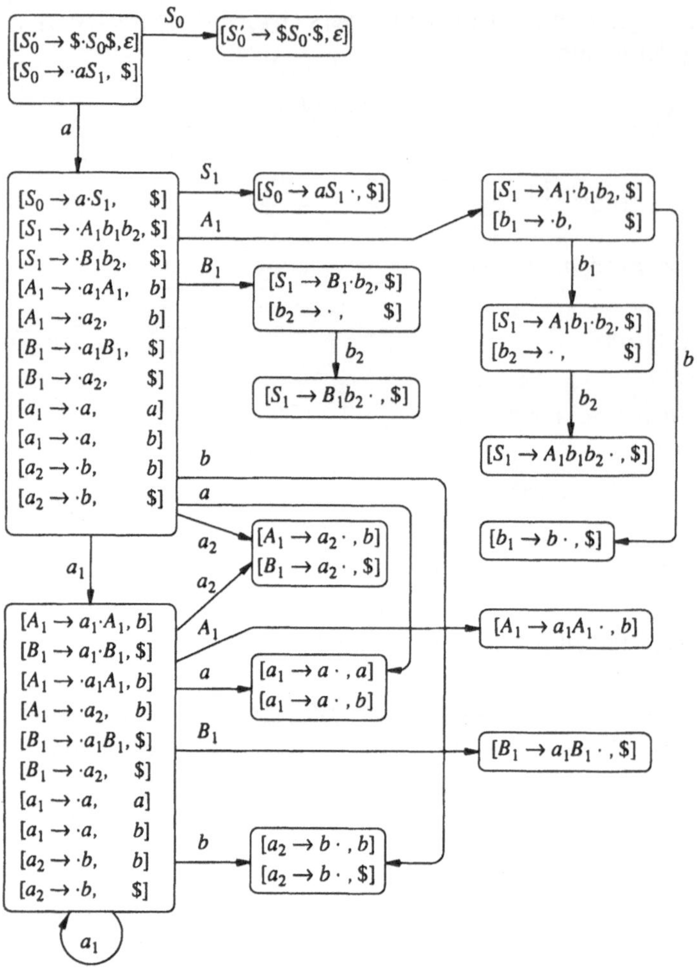

**Figure 6.25** The canonical LR(1) machine for the \$-augmented transformed LR(1) grammar $T_{1,1}(G_{LR2})'$: $S'_0 \to \$S_0\$$, $S_0 \to aS_1$, $S_1 \to A_1b_1b_2 \mid B_1b_2$, $A_1 \to a_1A_1 \mid a_2$, $B_1 \to a_1B_1 \mid a_2$, $a_1 \to a$, $a_2 \to b$, $b_1 \to b$, $b_2 \to \varepsilon$

single subscripted letters as follows: $(a, S, \varepsilon) = S_1$, $(a, A, b) = A_1$, $(a, B, b) = B_1$, $(a, a, a) = a_1$, $(a, a, b) = a_2$, $(b, b, b) = b_1$, $(b, b, \varepsilon) = b_2$.

For $k = 2$ the transformed grammar $T_{k,1}(G_{LR2})$ has the following rules.

| rule $r$: | $h_{2,1}(r)$: |
|---|---|
| $r_1 = S_0 \to aa(aa, S, \varepsilon)$, | $\varepsilon$ . |
| $r_2 = S_0 \to ab(ab, S, \varepsilon)$, | $\varepsilon$ . |
| $r_3 = (aa, S, \varepsilon) \to (aa, A, bb)\ (bb, b, b)\ (b, b, \varepsilon)$, | $S \to Abb$ . |
| $r_4 = (aa, S, \varepsilon) \to (aa, B, b)\ (b, b, \varepsilon)$, | $S \to Bb$ . |

| rule $r$: | $h_{2,1}(r)$: |
|---|---|
| $r_5 = (ab, S, \varepsilon) \to (ab, A, bb)\,(bb, b, b)\,(b, b, \varepsilon)$, | $S \to Abb$ . |
| $r_6 = (ab, S, \varepsilon) \to (ab, B, b)\,(b, b, \varepsilon)$, | $S \to Bb$ . |
| $r_7 = (aa, A, bb) \to (aa, a, aa)\,(aa, A, bb)$, | $A \to aA$ . |
| $r_8 = (aa, A, bb) \to (aa, a, ab)\,(ab, A, bb)$, | $A \to aA$ . |
| $r_9 = (ab, A, bb) \to (ab, a, bb)$, | $A \to a$ . |
| $r_{10} = (aa, B, b) \to (aa, a, aa)\,(aa, B, b)$, | $B \to aB$ . |
| $r_{11} = (aa, B, b) \to (aa, a, ab)\,(ab, B, b)$, | $B \to aB$ . |
| $r_{12} = (ab, B, b) \to (ab, a, b)$, | $B \to a$ . |
| $r_{13} = (aa, a, aa) \to a$, | $\varepsilon$ . |
| $r_{14} = (aa, a, ab) \to b$, | $\varepsilon$ . |
| $r_{15} = (ab, a, bb) \to b$, | $\varepsilon$ . |
| $r_{16} = (ab, a, b) \to \varepsilon$, | $\varepsilon$ . |
| $r_{17} = (b, b, \varepsilon) \to \varepsilon$, | $\varepsilon$ . |
| $r_{18} = (bb, b, b) \to \varepsilon$, | $\varepsilon$ . |

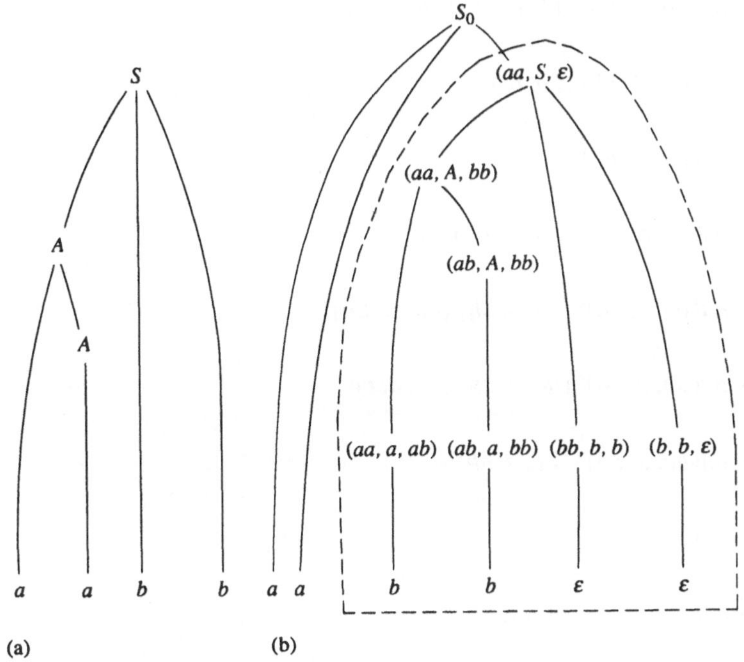


**Figure 6.26** Derivation trees of the sentence *aabb*: (**a**) in the LR(2) grammar $G_{LR2}$; (**b**) in the transformed LR(1) grammar $T_{2,1}(G_{LR2})$

The derivation tree of the sentence *aabb* in this grammar is depicted in Figure 6.26. The sentences $a^n bb$, $n \geqslant 1$, are derived as follows.

$$
\begin{aligned}
S_0 &\overset{r_2}{\underset{\text{rm}}{\Longrightarrow}} ab(ab, S, \varepsilon) \\
&\overset{r_5}{\underset{\text{rm}}{\Longrightarrow}} ab(ab, A, bb)\,(bb, b, b)\,(b, b, \varepsilon) \\
&\overset{r_{17}}{\underset{\text{rm}}{\Longrightarrow}} ab(ab, A, bb)\,(bb, b, b) \\
&\overset{r_{18}}{\underset{\text{rm}}{\Longrightarrow}} ab(ab, A, bb) \\
&\overset{r_9}{\underset{\text{rm}}{\Longrightarrow}} ab(ab, a, bb) \\
&\overset{r_{15}}{\underset{\text{rm}}{\Longrightarrow}} abb\ .
\end{aligned}
$$

Here $S$ rightmost derives *abb* using the rule string $h_{2,1}(r_2 r_5 r_{17} r_{18} r_9 r_{15}) = (S \to Abb)\,(A \to a)$ .

$$
\begin{aligned}
S_0 &\overset{r_1}{\underset{\text{rm}}{\Longrightarrow}} aa(aa, S, \varepsilon) \\
&\overset{r_3}{\underset{\text{rm}}{\Longrightarrow}} aa(aa, A, bb)\,(bb, b, b)\,(b, b, \varepsilon) \\
&\overset{r_{17}}{\underset{\text{rm}}{\Longrightarrow}} aa(aa, A, bb)\,(bb, b, b) \\
&\overset{r_{18}}{\underset{\text{rm}}{\Longrightarrow}} aa(aa, A, bb) \\
&\overset{r_7^n}{\underset{\text{rm}}{\Longrightarrow}} aa(aa, a, aa)^n\,(aa, A, bb) \\
&\overset{r_8}{\underset{\text{rm}}{\Longrightarrow}} aa(aa, a, aa)^n\,(aa, a, ab)\,(ab, A, bb) \\
&\overset{r_9}{\underset{\text{rm}}{\Longrightarrow}} aa(aa, a, aa)^n\,(aa, a, ab)\,(ab, a, bb) \\
&\overset{r_{15}}{\underset{\text{rm}}{\Longrightarrow}} aa(aa, a, aa)^n\,(aa, a, ab)b \\
&\overset{r_{14}}{\underset{\text{rm}}{\Longrightarrow}} aa(aa, a, aa)^n bb \\
&\overset{r_{13}^n}{\underset{\text{rm}}{\Longrightarrow}} aaa^n bb, \quad \text{for all } n \geqslant 0\ .
\end{aligned}
$$

Here $S$ rightmost derives $aaa^n bb$ using the rule string $h_{2,1}(r_1 r_3 r_{17} r_{18} r_7^n r_8 r_9 r_{15} r_{14} r_{13}^n) = (S \to Abb)\,(A \to aA)^n\,(A \to aA)\,(A \to a)$.

One might be tempted to think that when applied to an LR($k$) grammar the transformation $T_{k,1}$ would produce an LR(0) grammar, since the transformation $T_{k-1,1}$ produces an LR(1) grammar. This is not true in the general case because not all LR(1) languages are LR(0) languages. However, if the language generated by an LR($k$) grammar $G$ is *prefix-free*, that is, no proper prefix of a sentence is a sentence, then the transformed grammar $T_{k,1}(G)$ is indeed LR(0) (see the exercises).

We now show that the transformation always produces a right-to-right cover no matter what the original grammar is. As usual, we derive the result from two major lemmas that relate derivations in the transformed grammar with derivations in the original grammar and vice versa.

**Lemma 6.72** *Let $G = (V, T, P, S)$ be a grammar, $k$ a positive natural number, $A$ a nonterminal of $G$, $y$ a string in $\text{FOLLOW}_k(A)$, $x$ a string in $\text{FIRST}_k(Ay)$, $\Phi$ a string over the alphabet of $T_{k,1}(G)$, and $\pi'$ a rule string of $T_{k,1}(G)$ such that*

$$\text{(a)} \qquad (x, A, y) \xRightarrow[\text{rm}]{\pi'} \Phi \qquad \text{in } T_{k,1}(G)\ .$$

*Then there is a natural number $m$ and there are strings $y_0, \ldots, y_m, z, v \in T^*$ and symbols $X_1, \ldots, X_m \in V$ such that*

$$\Phi = (y_0, X_1, y_1)(y_1, X_2, y_2) \ldots (y_{m-1}, X_m, y_m)z\ ,$$

$$\text{(b)} \qquad y_0 = x, \quad y_m z = vy, \quad \text{and}$$

$$A \xRightarrow[\text{rm}]{h_{k,1}(\pi')} X_1 \ldots X_m v \qquad \text{in } G\ .$$

*Moreover, if $|y_m| < k$, then $z = \varepsilon$ .*

*Proof.* The proof is by induction on the length of rule string $\pi'$. In the base case we have $\pi' = \varepsilon$. Then $\Phi = (x, A, y)$ and so statements ($b$) hold if we choose $m = 1$, $y_0 = x$, $y_m = y$, $z = v = \varepsilon$, and $X_1 = A$.

To prove the induction step we assume that $\pi'$ is of the form $\pi'_1 r'$, where $r'$ is a rule of $T_{k,1}(G)$. As an induction hypothesis we assume that the lemma holds for the rule string $\pi'_1$. Then we have in $T_{k,1}(G)$:

$$(x, A, y) \xRightarrow[\text{rm}]{\pi'_1} (y_0, X_1, y_1) \ldots (y_{n-2}, X_{n-1}, y_{n-1})(y_{n-1}, X, y'_n)z_1$$

$$\xRightarrow[\text{rm}]{r'} (y_0, X_1, y_1) \ldots (y_{n-2}, X_{n-1}, y_{n-1})\omega z_1 = \Phi\ ,$$

where $n$ is a natural number, $y_0, \ldots, y_{n-1}, y'_n, z_1$ are strings in $T^*$, $X_1, \ldots, X_{n-1}, X$ are symbols in $V$, $(y_{n-1}, X, y'_n) \to \omega$ is the rule $r'$, and $|y'_n| < k$ implies $z_1 = \varepsilon$. Moreover, there is a string $v_1$ in $T^*$ such that

$$y_0 = x, \quad y'_n z_1 = v_1 y, \text{ and } A \xRightarrow[\text{rm}]{h_{k,1}(\pi'_1)} X_1 \ldots X_{n-1} X v_1 \quad \text{in } G\ .$$

We have to consider three cases, depending on the form of the rule $r'$.

*Case 1*: $r' = (y_{n-1}, X, y'_n) \to (y_{n-1}, X_n, y_n) \ldots (y_{m-1}, X_m, y_m)$ for some natural number $m \geqslant n-1$, strings $y_n, \ldots, y_m$ in $T^*$, and symbols $X_n, \ldots, X_m$ in $V$. By definition, $y_m = y'_n$ and $h_{k,1}(r') = X \to X_n \ldots X_m$ is a rule of $G$. Then we have:

$$\Phi = (y_0, X_1, y_1) \ldots (y_{m-1}, X_{m}, y_m)z_1 \ ,$$

$$y_0 = x,\ y_m z_1 = y'_n z_1 = v_1 y, \text{ and}$$

$$A \xrightarrow[\text{rm}]{h_{k,1}(\pi'_1)} X_1 \ldots X_{n-1} X v_1 \xrightarrow[\text{rm}]{h_{k,1}(r')} X_1 \ldots X_m v_1 \qquad \text{in } G \ ,$$

which means that statements $(b)$ hold if we choose $z = z_1$ and $v = v_1$.

*Case 2*: $r' = (au, a, ub) \to b$ for some terminals $a, b$ in $T$ and string $u$ in $T^{k-1}$. By definition, $h_{k,1}(r') = \varepsilon$. If we choose $m = n-1$, $z = bz_1$, *and* $v = av_1$, we then have:

$$\Phi = (y_0, X_1, y_1) \ldots (y_{n-2}, X_{n-1}, y_{n-1})bz_1$$

$$= (y_0, X_1, y_1) \ldots (y_{m-1}, X_m, y_m)z \ ,$$

$$y_0 = x,\ y_m z = y_{n-1} bz_1 = aubz_1 = ay'_n z_1 = av_1 y = vy, \text{ and}$$

$$A \xrightarrow[\text{rm}]{h_{k,1}(\pi'_1 r')} X_1 \ldots X_{n-1} X v_1 = X_1 \ldots X_m av_1 = X_1 \ldots X_m v \qquad \text{in } G \ .$$

Moreover, the implication $|y_m| < k$ implies $z = \varepsilon$ holds trivially, because $y_m = y_{n-1} = au \in T^k$.

*Case 3*: $r' = (ay'_n, a, y'_n) \to \varepsilon$ for some terminal $a \in T$. By definition, $|y'_n| < k$ and $h_{k,1}(r') = \varepsilon$. If we choose $m = n-1$, $z = z_1$, and $v = av_1$, we then have:

$$\Phi = (y_0, X_1, y_1) \ldots (y_{n-2}, X_{n-1}, y_{n-1})z_1$$

$$= (y_0, X_1, y_1) \ldots (y_{m-1}, X_m, y_m)z \ ,$$

$$y_0 = x,\ y_m z = y_{n-1} z_1 = ay'_n z_1 = av_1 y = vy, \text{ and}$$

$$A \xrightarrow[\text{rm}]{h_{k,1}(\pi'_1 r')} X_1 \ldots X_{n-1} X v_1 = X_1 \ldots X_m av_1 = X_1 \ldots X_m v \qquad \text{in } G \ .$$

Also in this case the implication $|y_m| < k$ implies $z = \varepsilon$ holds trivially, because $z = \varepsilon$. (Note that $|y'_n| < k$ implies, by the induction hypothesis, that $z_1 = \varepsilon$.) □

**Lemma 6.73** *If*

$$(x, A, y) \xrightarrow[\text{rm}]{\pi'} z \in T^* \qquad \text{in } T_{k,1}(G) \ ,$$

*then*

$$A \xrightarrow[\text{rm}]{h_{k,1}(\pi')} v \qquad \text{in } G \ ,$$

*where* $vy = xz$.

*Proof.* Choose $\Phi = z$ in Lemma 6.72. □

**Lemma 6.74** *If $\pi'$ is a right parse of sentence w in $T_{k,1}(G)$, then $h_{k,1}(\pi')$ is a right parse of w in G.*

*Proof.* If

$$S_0 \underset{\text{rm}}{\overset{r'}{\Longrightarrow}} x(x, S, \varepsilon) \underset{\text{rm}}{\overset{\pi'_1}{\Longrightarrow}} xz = w \in T^* \qquad \text{in } T_{k,1}(G) \;,$$

then $h_{k,1}(r'\pi'_1) = h_{k,1}(\pi'_1)$ and, by Lemma 6.73,

$$S \underset{\text{rm}}{\overset{h_{k,1}(\pi'_1)}{\Longrightarrow}} xz \qquad \text{in } G \;.$$

□

**Lemma 6.75** *Let $G = (V, T, P, S)$ be a grammar, k a positive natural number, A a nonterminal of G, $X_1, \ldots, X_m$ symbols in V ($m \geqslant 0$), $y_0, \ldots, y_m, v, y, z$ strings in $T^*$, and $\pi$ a rule string in $P^*$ such that*

$$A \underset{\text{rm}}{\overset{\pi}{\Longrightarrow}} X_1 \ldots X_m v \qquad \textit{in } G \;,$$

$$m = 0 \textit{ or } X_m \textit{ is a nonterminal} \;,$$

(*a*)
$$y \in \text{FOLLOW}_k(A),\ y_m = k\!:\!vy,\ y_m z = vy, \textit{ and}$$

$$y_i \in \text{FIRST}_k(X_{i+1} y_{i+1}) \textit{ for all } i = 0, \ldots, m-1 \;.$$

*Then there is a rule string $\pi'$ of $T_{k,1}(G)$ such that*

(*b*)
$$h_{k,1}(\pi') = \pi, \textit{ and}$$

$$(y_0, A, y) \underset{\text{rm}}{\overset{\pi'}{\Longrightarrow}} (y_0, X_1, y_1)(y_1, X_2, y_2) \ldots (y_{m-1}, X_m, y_m)z$$

*in $T_{k,1}(G)$ .*

*Proof.* The proof is by induction on the length of rule string $\pi$. In the base case we have $\pi = \varepsilon$. Then $m = 1$, $X_1 = A$, $v = \varepsilon$, $y_m = y$, $z = \varepsilon$, and $y_0$ is in $\text{FIRST}_k(Ay)$. Thus $(y_0, A, y)$ is a nonterminal of $T_{k,1}(G)$ and statements (*b*) hold trivially for $\pi' = \varepsilon$.

To prove the induction step we assume that $\pi$ is of the form $\pi_1 r$, where $r$ is a rule of $G$. As an induction hypothesis, we assume that the lemma holds for the rule string $\pi_1$. We have:

(1)
$$A \underset{\text{rm}}{\overset{\pi_1}{\Longrightarrow}} X_1 \ldots X_n B v_1 \underset{\text{rm}}{\overset{r}{\Longrightarrow}} X_1 \ldots X_n X_{n+1} \ldots X_p v_1$$

$$= X_1 \ldots X_m v \qquad \text{in } G$$

for some natural number $n \geqslant 0$, symbols $X_{m+1}, \ldots, X_p$ ($p \geqslant m$), and string $v_1$ in

$T^*$. Observe that $v_1$ is a suffix of $v$ because $X_1 \ldots X_m$ is empty or ends with a nonterminal. We have $r = B \to X_{n+1} \ldots X_p$ and $v = X_{m+1} \ldots X_p v_1$. If $p > m$, let $y_p = k{:}v_1 y$. Then in any case $y_p = k{:}v_1 y$. Now let $z_1$ be the suffix of $v_1 y$ for which $y_p z_1 = v_1 y$ and let $y_i = k{:}X_{i+1} y_{i+1}$ for all $i = m+1, \ldots, p-1$. Then $y_m = k{:}vy = k{:}X_{m+1} \ldots X_p v_1 y = k{:}X_{m+1} y_{m+1}$ if $p > m$. Moreover, $y_n$ is always in $\text{FIRST}_k(By_p)$. This means that we can apply the induction hypothesis to the first derivation segment in (1) and conclude that for some rule string $\pi'_1$ of $T_{k,1}(G)$

(2) $$h_{k,1}(\pi'_1) = \pi_1, \text{ and}$$
$$(y_0, A, y) \underset{\text{rm}}{\overset{\pi'_1}{\Longrightarrow}} (y_0, X_1, y_1) \ldots (y_{n-1}, X_n, y_n)(y_n, B, y_p) z_1$$

in $T_{k,1}(G)$. Because $y_i$ is in $\text{FIRST}_k(X_{i+1} y_{i+1})$ for all $i = n, \ldots, p-1$, $T_{k,1}(G)$ has the rule

(3) $$r' = (y_n, B, y_p) \to (y_n, X_{n+1}, y_{n+1}) \ldots (y_{p-1}, X_p, y_p) \ .$$

Here $h_{k,1}(r') = B \to X_{n+1} \ldots X_p = r$. By (2) we then have:

(4) $$(y_0, A, y) \underset{\text{rm}}{\overset{\pi'_1 r'}{\Longrightarrow}} (y_0, X_1, y_1) \ldots (y_{p-1}, X_p, y_p) z_1 \quad \text{in } T_{k,1}(G) \ .$$

Since $X_{m+1}, \ldots, X_p$ are terminals, each $(y_i, X_{i+1}, y_{i+1})$, $i = m, \ldots, p-1$, is of the form $(ax, a, xb)$ or $(ax, a, x)$. Thus we have:

(5) $$(y_m, X_{m+1}, y_{m+1}) \ldots (y_{p-1}, X_p, y_p) \underset{\text{rm}}{\overset{\pi'_2}{\Longrightarrow}} u \in T^* \qquad \text{in } T_{k,1}(G) \ ,$$

where $\pi'_2$ consists of $p - m$ rules of the forms $(ax, a, xb) \to b$ or $(ax, a, x) \to \varepsilon$. By (4) and (5) we have:

(6) $$(y_0, A, y) \underset{\text{rm}}{\overset{\pi'_1 r' \pi'_2}{\Longrightarrow}} (y_0, X_1, y_1) \ldots (y_{m-1}, X_m, y_m) u z_1 \text{ in } T_{k,1}(G) \ .$$

Let $\pi' = \pi'_1 r' \pi'_2$. Then $h_{k,1}(\pi') = \pi$. (Note that $h_{k,1}(\pi'_2) = \varepsilon$.) We have yet to show that $uz_1 = z$. By applying Lemma 6.72 to derivation (6) we may conclude that

(7) $$A \underset{\text{rm}}{\overset{\pi}{\Longrightarrow}} X_1, \ldots X_m v' \qquad \text{in } G \ ,$$

where $y_m u z_1 = v'y$. However, we assumed in $(a)$ that the string rightmost derived from $A$ using $\pi$ is $X_1 \ldots X_m v$. Hence $v' = v$, and we have $y_m u z_1 = v'y = vy = y_m z$, implying $uz_1 = z$, as claimed. □

**Lemma 6.76** *If*

$$A \underset{\text{rm}}{\overset{\pi}{\Longrightarrow}} v \in T^* \qquad \textit{in } G \ ,$$

$$y \in \text{FOLLOW}_k(A), \quad x = k{:}vy, \quad \textit{and} \quad xz = vy \ ,$$

*then for some rule string* $\pi'$ *of* $T_{k,1}(G)$

$$h_{k,1}(\pi') = \pi, \text{ and}$$

$$(x, A, y) \underset{rm}{\overset{\pi'}{\Longrightarrow}} z \qquad \text{in } T_{k,1}(G) .$$

*Proof.* Choose $m = 0$ and $y_0 = x$ in Lemma 6.75. □

**Lemma 6.77** *If* $\pi$ *is a right parse of sentence* $w$ *in* $G$, *then* $w$ *has in* $T_{k,1}(G)$ *a right parse* $\pi'$ *such that* $h_{k,1}(\pi') = \pi$.

*Proof.* If

$$S \underset{rm}{\overset{\pi}{\Longrightarrow}} w \in T^* \qquad \text{in } G ,$$

then, by Lemma 6.76, we have for some $\pi'_1$:

$$h_{k,1}(\pi'_1) = \pi, \text{ and}$$

$$(x, S, \varepsilon) \underset{rm}{\overset{\pi'_1}{\Longrightarrow}} z \qquad \text{in } T_{k,1}(G) ,$$

where $x = k{:}w$ and $xz = w$. Because $x$ is in $\text{FIRST}_k(S)$, $T_{k,1}(G)$ has the rule $r' = S_0 \rightarrow x(x, S, \varepsilon)$ and so

$$S_0 \underset{rm}{\overset{r'}{\Longrightarrow}} x(x, S, \varepsilon) \underset{rm}{\overset{\pi'_1}{\Longrightarrow}} xz = w \qquad \text{in } T_{k,1}(G) .$$

Here we have for $\pi' = r'\pi'_1$: $h_{k,1}(\pi') = \pi$, because, by definition, $h_{k,1}(r') = \varepsilon$. □

By Lemmas 6.74 and 6.77 we have:

**Theorem 6.78** *For all grammars* $G$ *and positive natural numbers* $k$, $T_{k,1}(G)$ *right-to-right covers* $G$ *with respect to the homomorphism* $h_{k,1}$. □

We next show that $T_{k,1}(G)$ is LR(1) if and only if $G$ is LR($k$).

**Lemma 6.79** *Let* $n$ *be a natural number,* $(y_0, X_1, y_1), \ldots, (y_{n-1}, X_n, y_n)$ *nonterminals of* $T_{k,1}(G)$, *and* $z$ *a string in* $T^*$ *such that*

(*a*) $\qquad (y_0, X_1, y_1) \ldots (y_{n-1}, X_n, y_n) \Rightarrow^* z \qquad$ *in* $T_{k,1}(G)$ .

*Then there is a string* $v \in T^*$ *such that*

(*b*) $\qquad X_1 \ldots X_n \Rightarrow^* v \qquad$ *in* $G$ *and* $vy_n = y_0 z$ .

*Proof.* There are strings $z_1, \ldots, z_n$ in $T^*$ such that $z_1 \ldots z_n = z$ and $(y_{i-1}, X_i, y_i)$ derives $z_i$, for all $i = 1, \ldots, n$ (Lemma 4.1). Whenever $X_i$ is a nonterminal of $G$, we can conclude by Lemma 6.73 that

(1) $X_i \Rightarrow^* v_i$ and $v_i y_i = y_{i-1} z_i$ ,

for some $v_i \in T^*$. Whenever $X_i$ is a terminal, then, by definition, one of the following is true: (i) $y_i$ is of the form $xb$, $y_{i-1} = X_i x$, and $z_i = b$; (ii) $y_{i-1} = X_i y_i$ and $z_i = \varepsilon$. In both cases (1) is true for $v_i = X_i$. Thus, for all $i = 1, \ldots, n$, (1) is true for some $v_i$. Then

(2) $$X_1 \ldots X_n \Rightarrow^* v_1 \ldots v_n \text{ and}$$
$$y_0 z = y_0 z_1 z_2 \ldots z_n = v_1 y_1 z_2 \ldots z_n = \ldots = v_1 v_2 \ldots v_n y_n ,$$

which means that statement $(b)$ is true for $v = v_1 \ldots v_n$. □

**Lemma 6.80** *Let $G = (V, T, P, S)$ be a grammar, $G'$ its \$-augmented grammar, and $k$ a positive natural number. Further let $U \rightarrow \phi\psi$ be a rule of $T_{k,1}(G)$, $d$ a terminal in $T \cup \{\$\}$, and $\Phi$ a string over the alphabet of $T_{k,1}(G)'$, the \$-augmented grammar for $T_{k,1}(G)$, such that*

$$[U \rightarrow \phi \cdot \psi, d] \in \text{VALID}_1(\Phi) .$$

*Then one of the following statements is true.*

(i) *$\Phi$ is of the form $\$x$ and $[U \rightarrow \phi \cdot \psi, d]$ is of the form $[S_0 \rightarrow x \cdot y(xy, S, \varepsilon), \$]$.*

(ii) *$\Phi$ is of the form $\$x(x, S, \varepsilon)$ and $[U \rightarrow \phi \cdot \psi, d]$ is of the form $[S_0 \rightarrow x(x, S, \varepsilon)\cdot, \$]$ .*

(iii) *$\Phi$ is of the form $\$y_0(y_0, X_1, y_1) \ldots (y_{r-1}, X_r, y_r)$ and $[U \rightarrow \phi \cdot \psi, d]$ is of the form*

$$[(y_m, A, y_n) \rightarrow (y_m, X_{m+1}, y_{m+1}) \ldots (y_{r-1}, X_r, y_r) \cdot (y_r, X_{r+1}, y_{r+1}) \ldots (y_{n-1}, X_n, y_n), d] ,$$

*where*

$$[A \rightarrow X_{m+1} \ldots X_r \cdot X_{r+1} \ldots X_n, y_n d] \in \text{VALID}_{k+1}(\$X_1 \ldots X_r)$$

*and $|y_n| < k$ implies $d = \$$ .*

(iv) *$\Phi$ is of the form $\$y_0(y_0, X_1, y_1) \ldots (y_{r-1}, X_r, ax)$ and $[U \rightarrow \phi \cdot \psi, d]$ is of the form $[(ax, a, xb) \rightarrow \cdot b, d]$, where*

$$[A \rightarrow \alpha \cdot a\beta, y'] \in \text{VALID}_{k+1}(\$X_1 \ldots X_r) \text{ and}$$
$$xbd \in \text{FIRST}_{k+1}(\beta y')$$

*for some $(k+1)$-item $[A \rightarrow \alpha \cdot a\beta, y']$ of $G'$ .*

(v) *$\Phi$ is of the form $\$y_0(y_0, X_1, y_1) \ldots (y_{r-1}, X_r, ax)b$ and $[U \rightarrow \phi \cdot \psi, d]$ is of the form $[(ax, a, xb) \rightarrow b\cdot, d]$, where*

$$[A \rightarrow \alpha \cdot a\beta, y'] \in \text{VALID}_{k+1}(\$X_1 \ldots X_r) \text{ and}$$
$$xbd \in \text{FIRST}_{k+1}(\beta y')$$

*for some $(k+1)$-item $[A \rightarrow \alpha \cdot a\beta, y']$ of $G'$ .*

*(vi) $\Phi$ is of the form* $\$y_0(y_0, X_1, y_1) \ldots (y_{r-1}, X_r, ax)$ *and* $[U \to \phi \cdot \psi, d]$ *is of the form* $[(ax, a, x) \to \cdot, \$]$, *where*

$$[A \to \alpha \cdot a\beta, y'] \in \text{VALID}_{k+1}(\$X_1 \ldots X_r) \text{ and}$$
$$x\$ \in \text{FIRST}_{k+1}(\beta y')$$

*for some* $(k+1)$*-item* $[A \to \alpha \cdot a\beta, y']$ *of* $G'$ .

*Proof.* We have to consider four cases, depending on the form of the nonterminal $U$.

*Case 1*: $U = S_0$. Then one of the statements (i) and (ii) is true.

*Case 2*: $U$ is of the form $(x, A, y)$ where $A$ is a nonterminal of $G$. Then we have:

$$S'_0 \underset{rm}{\Longrightarrow} \$S_0\$ \underset{rm}{\Longrightarrow} \$y_0(y_0, S, \varepsilon)\$ \underset{rm}{\Longrightarrow^*} \$y_0\gamma(x, A, y)z\$$$

(1) $$\underset{rm}{\Longrightarrow} \$y_0\gamma\phi\psi z\$ = \Phi\psi z\$ \qquad \text{in } T_{k,1}(G)'$$

and $1{:}z\$ = d$ ,

for some $y_0$ in FIRST$_k(S)$, $z$ in $T^*$, and string $\gamma$ over the alphabet of $T_{k,1}(G)$. This implies:

(2) $$(y_0, S, \varepsilon) \underset{rm}{\Longrightarrow^*} \gamma(x, A, y)z \qquad \text{in } T_{k,1}(G) .$$

Now Lemma 6.72 implies the existence of a natural number $m$, strings $y_1, \ldots, y_{m-1}$ in $T^*$, and symbols $X_1, \ldots, X_m$ in $V$ such that

(3) $$\gamma(x, A, y)z = (y_0, X_1, y_1) \ldots (y_{m-1}, X_m, x)\,(x, A, y)z$$
$$\text{and } S \underset{rm}{\Longrightarrow^*} X_1 \ldots X_m Ayz \qquad \text{in } G .$$

Moreover, $|y| < k$ implies $z = \varepsilon$. By the definition of $T_{k,1}(G)$, there is a natural number $n \geqslant m$, strings $y_m, \ldots, y_n \in T^*$, and symbols $X_{m+1}, \ldots, X_n \in V$ such that

(4) $$y_m = x,\ y_n = y,\ A \to X_{m+1} \ldots X_n \text{ is a rule in } P \text{ and}$$
$$U \to \phi\psi = (y_m, A, y_n) \to (y_m, X_{m+1}, y_{m+1}) \ldots (y_{n-1}, X_n, y_n) .$$

Then we have:

(5) $$\Phi = \$y_0\gamma\phi = \$y_0(y_0, X_1, y_1) \ldots (y_{r-1}, X_r, y_r) ,$$

where $r = m + |\phi|$, and

(6) $$S' \underset{rm}{\Longrightarrow^*} \$X_1 \ldots X_m Ayz\$ \underset{rm}{\Longrightarrow} \$X_1 \ldots X_m X_{m+1} \ldots X_n yz\$ \quad \text{in } G' ,$$

which means that

$$\text{(7)}\qquad [A \to X_{m+1} \ldots X_r \cdot X_{r+1} \ldots X_n,\, k+1{:}yz\$] \in \text{VALID}_{k+1}(\$X_1 \ldots X_r) .$$

Here $k+1{:}yz\$ = yd = y_n d$. Recall that $1{:}z\$ = d$ and $y = y_n$ and that $|y| < k$ implies $z = \varepsilon$. Then $|y| < k$ also implies $d = \$$. We conclude that statement (iii) is true.

*Case 3*: $U$ is of the form $(ax, a, xb)$, where $a$ and $b$ are terminals in $T$. As in Case 2 we can conclude the existence of a natural number $r$, strings $y_0, \ldots, y_{r-1}, z \in T^*$, and symbols $X_1, \ldots, X_r \in V$ such that

$$\text{(8)}\qquad \Phi = \$y_0(y_0, X_1, y_1) \ldots (y_{r-1}, X_r, ax)\phi ,$$

where $\phi\psi = b$ and

$$\text{(9)}\qquad (y_0, S, \varepsilon) \underset{\text{rm}}{\Longrightarrow}^{+} (y_0, X_1, y_1) \ldots (y_{r-1}, X_r, ax)\,(ax, a, xb)z$$

in $T_{k,1}(G)$, where $1{:}z\$ = d$. Here we can apply Lemma 6.2 and conclude that there are natural numbers $i \leqslant r$ and $n > r$, nonterminal $A'$, symbols $X_{r+1}, \ldots, X_n \in V$, and strings $y_r, \ldots, y_n, u \in T^*$ such that $X_{r+1} = a$, $y_r = ax$, $y_{r+1} = xb$, and

$$\text{(10)}\qquad \begin{aligned} &(y_0, S, \varepsilon) \underset{\text{rm}}{\Longrightarrow}^{*} (y_0, X_1, y_1) \ldots (y_{i-1}, X_i, y_i)\,(y_i, A', y_n)u \\ &\underset{\text{rm}}{\Longrightarrow} (y_0, X_1, y_1) \ldots (y_{i-1}, X_i, y_i)\,(y_i, X_{i+1}, y_{i+1}) \ldots \\ &\qquad\qquad (y_{n-1}, X_n, y_n)u , \end{aligned}$$

where $A' \to X_{i+1} \ldots X_n$ is a rule of $G$ and

$$\text{(11)}\qquad (y_{r+1}, X_{r+2}, y_{r+2}) \ldots (y_{n-1}, X_n, y_n)u \underset{\text{rm}}{\Longrightarrow}^{*} z .$$

By Lemma 6.72 we have:

$$\text{(12)}\qquad S \underset{\text{rm}}{\Longrightarrow}^{*} X_1 \ldots X_i A' y_n u \qquad \text{in } G .$$

Thus, we have in $G'$

$$\text{(13)}\qquad S' \underset{\text{rm}}{\Longrightarrow}^{*} \$X_1 \ldots X_i A' y_n u\$ \underset{\text{rm}}{\Longrightarrow} \$X_1 \ldots X_i X_{i+1} \ldots X_n y_n u\$$$

which means, since $i+1 \leqslant r+1 \leqslant n$ and $X_{r+1} = a$, that

$$\text{(14)}\qquad [A' \to X_{i+1} \ldots X_r \cdot a X_{r+2} \ldots X_n,\, k+1{:}y_n u\$] \in \text{VALID}_{k+1}(\$X_1 \ldots X_r) .$$

On the other hand, (11) implies by Lemma 6.79 the existence of a string $v$ in $T^*$ such that

$$(15) \qquad X_{r+2} \cdots X_n \underset{rm}{\Longrightarrow}{}^* v \quad \text{in } G \text{ and } vy_n u = y_{r+1} z .$$

Because here $y_{r+1} = xb$, $|xb| = k$, and $1{:}z\$ = d$, we have:

$$(16) \qquad \begin{aligned} xbd &= k+1{:}y_{r+1}z\$ \in \mathrm{FIRST}_{k+1}(X_{r+2} \cdots X_n y_n u\$) \\ &= \mathrm{FIRST}_{k+1}(X_{r+2} \cdots X_n(k+1{:}y_n u\$)) . \end{aligned}$$

By (8), (14), and (16) we conclude that one of statements (iv) and (v) is true. (Choose $A = A'$, $\alpha = X_{i+1} \cdots X_r$, $\beta = X_{r+2} \cdots X_n$, and $y' = k+1{:}y_n u\$$.)
*Case 4*: $U$ is of the form $(ax, a, x)$, where $a$ is a terminal in $T$. The proof is similar to that of Case 3. In (8) we have $\phi = \varepsilon$, in (9) $z = \varepsilon$ and $(ax, a, x)$ in place of $(ax, a, xb)$. Thus $d = \$$. In (10) and (11) $u = \varepsilon$. In (15) $y_{r+1} = x$. In (16) $x\$$ is in place of $xbd$. This means that statement (vi) is true. □

**Lemma 6.81** *Let $G = (V, T, P, S)$ be a grammar and k a positive natural number. If $T_{k,1}(G)$ is non-LR(1), then G is non-LR($k+1$) .*

*Proof.* First we note that $S_0 \Rightarrow^+ S_0$ is always impossible in $T_{k,1}(G)$. Then we show that if some state in the canonical LR(1) machine of the augmented grammar $T_{k,1}(G)'$ contains a pair of 1-items exhibiting a reduce-reduce conflict or a shift-reduce conflict, then either $S \Rightarrow^+ S$ is true in $G$ or some state in the canonical LR($k+1$) machine of the augmented grammar $G'$ contains a pair of ($k+1$)-items exhibiting a reduce-reduce conflict or a shift-reduce conflict. Therefore let $\Phi$ be a string over the alphabet of $T_{k,1}(G)'$ and let $I$ and $J$ be distinct items in $\mathrm{VALID}_1(\Phi)$ exhibiting a reduce-reduce conflict or a shift-reduce conflict. In principle we should consider any combination of the six forms (i) to (vi) that the items $I$ and $J$ can take according to Lemma 6.80. However, most of the combinations can be discarded immediately because in fact they cannot occur at all. Only five cases remain to be considered:

*Case 1*: $\Phi = \$x(x, S, \varepsilon)$, $I = [S_0 \to x(x, S, \varepsilon)\cdot, \$]$, and $J = [(x, A, \varepsilon) \to (x, S, \varepsilon)\cdot, \$]$. Then $[A \to S\cdot, \$]$ is LR($k+1$)-valid for $\$S$, which means that

$$S' \underset{rm}{\Longrightarrow} \$S\$ \underset{rm}{\Longrightarrow}{}^* \$A\$ \underset{rm}{\Longrightarrow} \$S\$ \quad \text{in } G' .$$

But then $S \Rightarrow^+ S$ in $G$.

*Case 2*: $\Phi = \$x(x, S, \varepsilon)$, $I = [S_0 \to x(x, S, \varepsilon)\cdot, \$]$, and $J = [(\varepsilon, A, \varepsilon) \to \cdot, \$]$. Then $[A \to \cdot, \$]$ is LR($k+1$)-valid for $\$S$, which means that

$$S' \underset{rm}{\Longrightarrow} \$S\$ \underset{rm}{\Longrightarrow}{}^* \$SA\$ \underset{rm}{\Longrightarrow} \$S\$ \quad \text{in } G' .$$

Also in this case $S \Rightarrow^+ S$ in $G$.

*Case 3*: $\Phi = \$y_0(y_0, X_1, y_1) \ldots (y_{r-1}, X_r, y_r)$, $I = [(y_m, A, y_r) \to (y_m, X_{m+1}, y_{m+1}) \ldots (y_{r-1}, X_r, y_r)\cdot, d]$, and $J = [(y_p, B, y_r) \to (y_p, X_{p+1}, y_{p+1}) \ldots (y_{r-1}, X_r, y_r)\cdot, d]$. Then $[A \to X_{m+1} \ldots X_r\cdot, y_r d]$ and $[B \to X_{p+1} \ldots X_r\cdot, y_r d]$ are distinct $(k+1)$-items in $\text{VALID}_{k+1}(\$X_1 \ldots X_r)$ exhibiting a reduce-reduce conflict.

*Case 4*: $\Phi = \$y_0(y_0, X_1, y_1) \ldots (y_{r-1}, X_r, ax)$, $I = [(y_m, A, ax) \to (y_m, X_{m+1}, y_{m+1}) \ldots (y_{r-1}, X_r, ax)\cdot, b]$, and $J = [(ax, a, xb) \to \cdot b, d]$. Then $\text{VALID}_{k+1}(\$X_1 \ldots X_r)$ contains the item $[A \to X_{m+1} \ldots X_r\cdot, axb]$ and some item $[B \to \alpha \cdot a\beta, y']$, where $xbd$ is in $\text{FIRST}_{k+1}(\beta y')$. These two items exhibit a shift-reduce conflict.

*Case 5*: $\Phi = \$y_0(y_0, X_1, y_1) \ldots (y_{r-1}, X_r, ax)$, $I = [(y_m, A, ax) \to (y_m, X_{m+1}, y_{m+1}) \ldots (y_{r-1}, X_r, ax)\cdot, \$]$, and $J = [(ax, a, x) \to \cdot, \$]$. Then $\text{VALID}_{k+1}(\$X_1 \ldots X_r)$ contains the item $[A \to X_{m+1} \ldots X_r\cdot, ax\$]$ and some item $[B \to \alpha \cdot a\beta, y']$, where $x\$$ is in $\text{FIRST}_{k+1}(\beta y')$. These two items exhibit a shift-reduce conflict. □

**Lemma 6.82** *Let $n$ be a natural number, $X_1, \ldots, X_n$ symbols in $V$, $v_1, \ldots, v_n$ strings in $T^*$*, and *$y_0, \ldots, y_n$ strings in $k{:}T^*$ such that in $G$*

(*a*) $X_i \Rightarrow^* v_i$, $y_i \in \text{FOLLOW}_k(X_i)$, *and* $y_{i-1} = k{:}v_i y_i$

*for all $i = 1, \ldots, n$. Then in $T_{k,1}(G)$*

(*b*) $(y_0, X_1, y_1) \ldots (y_{n-1}, X_n, y_n) \Rightarrow^* z$ ,

*where $v_1 \ldots v_n y_n = y_0 z$. (Observe that here $v_1 \ldots v_n$ is derived by $X_1 \ldots X_n$; cf. Lemma* 6.79.)

*Proof.* For all $i = 1, \ldots, n$, let $z_i$ be the unique suffix of $v_i y_i$ satisfying $y_{i-1} z_i = v_i y_i$. We show that for all $i = 1, \ldots, n$

(1) $(y_{i-1}, X_i, y_i) \Rightarrow^* z_i$ in $T_{k,1}(G)$ .

Whenever $X_i$ is a nonterminal, (1) follows immediately from Lemma 6.75. (Choose $A = X_i$, $m = 0$, $v = v_i$.) Whenever $X_i$ is a terminal, $v_i = X_i$ and we have two cases to consider: (i) $|y_i| = k$, and (ii) $|y_i| < k$. In case (i) $(y_{i-1}, X_i, y_i)$ is of the form $(v_i x, v_i, xb)$. Here $b = z_i$, because $v_i x z_i = y_{i-1} z_i = v_i y_i = v_i x b$. On the other hand, $(v_i x, v_i, xb)$ directly derives $b$, by definition. In case (ii) $(y_{i-1}, X_i, y_i)$ is of the form $(v_i x, v_i, x)$, which, by definition, directly derives $\varepsilon$. On the other hand, $z_i = \varepsilon$ because $y_{i-1} z_i = v_i y_i = v_i x = y_{i-1}$. We conclude that (1) is true for all $i = 1, \ldots, n$. Now (*b*) holds when we choose $z = z_1 \ldots z_n$. Moreover,

$$y_0 z = y_0 z_1 z_2 \ldots z_n = v_1 y_1 z_2 \ldots z_n = \ldots = v_1 \ldots v_n y_n ,$$

as claimed. □

**Lemma 6.83** *Let $G = (V, T, P, S)$ be a grammar, $G'$ its \$-augmented grammar, and $k$ a positive natural number. Further let $A$ be a nonterminal of $G$, $X_1, \ldots, X_n$ symbols in $V$ $(n \geq 0)$, $v_1, \ldots, v_n$ strings in $T^*$, $y_0, \ldots, y_n$ strings in $k{:}T^*$, and $d$ a terminal in $T \cup \{\$\}$ such that*

(a)
$$[A \to X_{m+1} \ldots X_r \cdot X_{r+1} \ldots X_n, y_n d] \in \mathrm{VALID}_{k+1}(\$X_1 \ldots X_r) ,$$
$$X_i \Rightarrow^* v_i \text{ and } y_{i-1} = k{:}v_i y_i \quad \text{for all } i = 1, \ldots, n ,$$

*where $0 \leq m \leq r \leq n$. Then the following is true in $T_{k,1}(G)'$, the \$-augmented grammar for $T_{k,1}(G)$:*

(b)
$$[(y_m, A, y_n) \to (y_m, X_{m+1}, y_{m+1}) \ldots (y_{r-1}, X_r, y_r) \cdot (y_r, X_{r+1}, y_{r+1}) \ldots (y_{n-1}, X_n, y_n), d]$$
$$\in \mathrm{VALID}_1(\$y_0(y_0, X_1, y_1) \ldots (y_{r-1}, X_r, y_r)) .$$

*Moreover, if $r < n$ and $(y_r, X_{r+1}, y_{r+1})$ is of the form $(ax, a, xb)$, then*

(c)
$$[(ax, a, xb) \to \cdot b, 1{:}ud]$$
$$\in \mathrm{VALID}_1(\$y_0(y_0, X_1, y_1) \ldots (y_{r-1}, X_r, y_r)) ,$$

*where $xbu = v_{r+2} \ldots v_n y_n$. Similarly, if $r < n$ and $(y_r, X_{r+1}, y_{r+1})$ is of the form $(ax, a, x)$, then $d = \$$ and*

(d) $[(ax, a, x) \to \cdot, \$] \in \mathrm{VALID}_1(\$y_0(y_0, X_1, y_1) \ldots (y_{r-1}, X_r, y_r))$ .

*Proof.* By definition, there is a string $v$ in $T^*$ such that in $G'$

$$S' \underset{rm}{\Longrightarrow} \$S\$ \underset{rm}{\Longrightarrow^*} \$X_1 \ldots X_m A v\$$$

(1)
$$\underset{rm}{\Longrightarrow} \$X_1 \ldots X_m X_{m+1} \ldots X_n v\$$$
and $k + 1{:}v\$ = y_n d$ .

Here $v$ is of the form $y_n z$ where $y_n = k{:}v$ and $d = 1{:}z\$$. Because $\varepsilon$ is in $\mathrm{FOLLOW}_k(S)$ and $y_i$ is in $\mathrm{FIRST}_k(X_{i+1} y_{i+1})$ for all $i = 0, \ldots, m-1$ and because $y_m = k{:}v_{m+1} \ldots v_n y_n$ is in $\mathrm{FIRST}_k(A y_n)$, we can conclude by Lemma 6.75 that

(2)
$$(y_0, S, \varepsilon) \underset{rm}{\Longrightarrow^*} (y_0, X_1, y_1) \ldots (y_{m-1}, X_m, y_m)(y_m, A, y_n) z$$

in $T_{k,1}(G)$. Because $y_n$ is in $\mathrm{FOLLOW}_k(A)$ (in $G$) and because $y_i$ is in $\mathrm{FIRST}_k(X_{i+1} y_{i+1})$ for all $i = m, \ldots, n-1$, $T_{k,1}(G)$ has the rule

(3)
$$(y_m, A, y_n) \to (y_m, X_{m+1}, y_{m+1}) \ldots (y_{n-1}, X_n, y_n) .$$

Then we have in $T_{k,1}(G)'$:

$$S'_0 \underset{rm}{\Longrightarrow} \$S_0\$ \underset{rm}{\Longrightarrow} \$y_0(y_0, S, \varepsilon)\$$$

(4) $$\underset{rm}{\Longrightarrow}^* \$y_0(y_0, X_1, y_1) \dots (y_{m-1}, X_m, y_m)(y_m, A, y_n)z\$$$

$$\underset{rm}{\Longrightarrow} \$y_0(y_0, X_1, y_1) \dots (y_{m-1}, X_m, y_m)(y_m, X_{m+1}, y_{m+1}) \dots$$

$$(y_{n-1}, X_n, y_n)z\$ \ .$$

Because here $1{:}z\$ = d$, we conclude that statement ($b$) is true.

Assume next that $r < n$ and $(y_r, X_{r+1}, y_{r+1})$ is of the form $(ax, a, xb)$. Then $T_{k,1}(G)$ has the rule $(ax, a, xb) \to b$. On the other hand, because for all $i = r + 2, \dots, n$, $X_i \Longrightarrow^* v_i$, $y_i = k{:}v_{i+1} \dots v_n y_n$ is in $\text{FOLLOW}_k(X_i)$, and $y_{i-1} = k{:}v_i y_i$, we can conclude by Lemma 6.82 that

(5) $$(y_{r+1}, X_{r+2}, y_{r+2}) \dots (y_{n-1}, X_n, y_n) \Rightarrow^* u \ ,$$

where $v_{r+2} \dots v_n y_n = y_{r+1} u = xbu$. But then statement ($b$) implies, by Lemma 6.17, that statement ($c$) is true.

Assume now that $r < n$ and $(y_r, X_{r+1}, y_{r+1})$ is of the form $(ax, a, x)$. Then $T_{k,1}(G)$ has the rule $(ax, a, x) \to \varepsilon$. As above, we can conclude by Lemma 6.82 that

(6) $$(y_{r+1}, X_{r+2}, y_{r+2}) \dots (y_{n-1}, X_n, y_n) \Rightarrow^* u \ ,$$

where $v_{r+2} \dots v_n y_n = y_{r+1} u = xu$. Because $|y_{r+1}| < k$ and because $y_i$ is in $\text{FIRST}_k(X_{i+1} y_{i+1})$ for all $i$, we have $|y_i| < k$ for all $i = r + 1, \dots, n$. This implies, by (6), that $u = \varepsilon$, and, by (1), that $d = \$$. But then, by Lemma 6.17, statement ($d$) is true. □

**Lemma 6.84** *Let $G = (V, T, P, S)$ be a reduced grammar and $k$ a positive natural number. If $G$ is non-LR($k + 1$), then $T_{k,1}(G)$ is non-LR(1).*

*Proof.* First we show that if $S \Rightarrow^+ S$ holds in $G$, then $T_{k,1}(G)$ is ambiguous. The condition $S \Rightarrow^+ S$ implies that for some nonterminals $A_1, \dots, A_m$ of $G (m \geq 0)$,

(1) $$S \underset{rm}{\Longrightarrow}^+ A_1 \dots A_m S \quad \text{and} \quad A_i \Rightarrow^* \varepsilon \quad \text{for } i = 1, \dots m \ .$$

Since $G$ was assumed to be reduced, $\text{FIRST}_k(S)$ contains some string $x$. By applying Lemma 6.75 to the derivation from $S$ in (1) we may conclude that

(2) $$(x, S, \varepsilon) \Rightarrow^+ (x, A_1, x) \dots (x, A_m, x)(x, S, \varepsilon)$$

holds in $T_{k,1}(G)$. By applying Lemma 6.75 to the derivations $A_i \Rightarrow^* \varepsilon$ we may conclude that

(3) $$(x, A_i, x) \Rightarrow^* \varepsilon \quad \text{for } i = 1, \dots, m \ .$$

Thus $(x, S, \varepsilon)$ nontrivially derives itself in $T_{k,1}(G)$.

Next we show that if some state in the canonical LR($k+1$) machine of the augmented grammar $G'$ contains a pair of ($k+1$)-items exhibiting a reduce-reduce conflict, then some state in the canonical LR(1) machine of $T_{k,1}(G)'$ contains a pair of 1-items exhibiting a reduce-reduce conflict. Let $[A \to X_{m+1} \ldots X_r\cdot, w']$ and $[B \to X_{p+1} \ldots X_r\cdot, w']$ be distinct ($k+1$)-items in $\text{VALID}_{k+1}(\$X_1 \ldots X_r)$. Let $y_r$ be the unique string in $k{:}T^*$ and $d$ the unique terminal in $T \cup \{\$\}$ for which $y_r d = w'$. Because $G$ is reduced, each $X_i$ derives some terminal string $v_i$. Let $y_i = k{:}v_{i+1}y_{i+1}$ for all $i = 0, \ldots, r-1$. Then we can conclude by Lemma 6.83 that

$$(4)\quad \begin{aligned} &[(y_m, A, y_r) \to (y_m, X_{m+1}, y_{m+1}) \ldots (y_{r-1}, X_r, y_r)\cdot, d] \\ &[(y_p, B, y_r) \to (y_p, X_{p+1}, y_{p+1}) \ldots (y_{r-1}, X_r, y_r)\cdot, d] \end{aligned}$$

are distinct 1-items in $\text{VALID}_1(\$y_0(y_0, X_1, y_1) \ldots (y_{r-1}, X_r, y_r))$.

Finally we show that if some state in the canonical LR($k+1$) machine of $G'$ contains a pair of ($k+1$)-items exhibiting a shift-reduce conflict, then some state in the canonical LR(1) machine of $T_{k,1}(G)'$ contains a pair of 1-items exhibiting a shift-reduce or reduce-reduce conflict. Let $[A \to X_{m+1} \ldots X_r\cdot, w'_1]$ and $[B \to X_{p+1} \ldots X_r\cdot X_{r+1} \ldots X_n, w'_2]$ be ($k+1$)-items in $\text{VALID}_{k+1}(\$X_1 \ldots X_r)$ such that $n > r$, $X_{r+1}$ is a terminal in $T$, and $w'_1$ is in $\text{FIRST}_{k+1}(X_{r+1} \ldots X_n w'_2)$. Then there are strings $v_{r+1}, \ldots, v_n \in T^*$ such that

$$(5)\quad \begin{aligned} &k+1{:}v_{r+1} \ldots v_n w'_2 = w'_1 \text{ and} \\ &X_i \Rightarrow^* v_i \quad \text{for all } i = r+1, \ldots, n\ . \end{aligned}$$

On the other hand, since $G$ is reduced, each $X_i$, $1 \leqslant i \leqslant r$, derives some terminal string $v_i$. Now let $y_n$ be the unique string in $T^*$ and $d_2$ the unique terminal in $T \cup \{\$\}$ for which $y_n d_2 = w'_2$. Further let $y_i = k{:}v_{i+1}y_{i+1}$ for all $i = 0, \ldots, n-1$. Then we have:

$$(6)\quad \begin{aligned} &y_r = k{:}v_{r+1}y_{r+1} = k{:}v_{r+1}v_{r+2}y_{r+2} = \ \ldots\ = k{:}v_{r+1} \ldots v_n y_n \\ &\text{and } w'_1 = k+1{:}v_{r+1} \ldots v_n w'_2 = k+1{:}v_{r+1} \ldots v_n y_n d_2\ , \end{aligned}$$

which means that $w'_1$ is of the form $y_r d_1$, for some $d_1$ in $T \cup \{\$\}$. By Lemma 6.83 we conclude that

$$(7)\quad \begin{aligned} &[(y_m, A, y_r) \to (y_m, X_{m+1}, y_{m+1}) \ldots (y_{r-1}, X_r, y_r)\cdot, d_1] \\ &\in \text{VALID}_1(\$y_0(y_0, X_1, y_1) \ldots (y_{r-1}, X_r, y_r))\ . \end{aligned}$$

If $(y_r, X_{r+1}, y_{r+1})$ is of the form $(ax, a, xb)$, we also have:

$$(8)\quad \begin{aligned} &[(ax, a, xb) \to \cdot b, 1{:}ud_2] \\ &\in \text{VALID}_1(\$y_0(y_0, X_1, y_1) \ldots (y_{r-1}, X_r, y_r))\ , \end{aligned}$$

where $xbu = v_{r+2} \ldots v_n y_n$. Then

$$(9)\quad \begin{aligned} w'_1 &= k+1{:}v_{r+1} \ldots v_n y_n d_2 = k+1{:}av_{r+2} \ldots v_n y_n d_2 \\ &= k+1{:}axbud_2 = k+1{:}y_r bud_2\ , \end{aligned}$$

which implies $d_1 = b$, since $w_1' = y_r d_1$ and $|y_r| = k$. But this means that the items in (7) and (8) exhibit a shift-reduce conflict. If on the contrary $(y_r, X_{r+1}, y_{r+1})$ is of the form $(ax, a, x)$, we have, by Lemma 6.83, $d_2 = \$$ and

(10) $$[(ax, a, x) \to \cdot, \$] \\ \in \text{VALID}_1(\$y_0(y_0, X_1, y_1) \ldots (y_{r-1}, X_r, y_r)) \ .$$

Now because $|y_{r+1}| = |x| < k$ and $y_{r+1} = k{:}v_{r+2} \ldots v_n y_n$, we have $y_{r+1} = v_{r+2} \ldots v_n y_n$ and hence $y_r = ay_{r+1} = v_{r+1} \ldots v_n y_n$. This implies further that $d_1 = \$$, because

(11) $$y_r d_1 = w_1' = k + 1{:}v_{r+1} \ldots v_n y_n \$ = k + 1{:}y_r \$ = y_r \$ \ .$$

But then the items in (7) and (10) exhibit a reduce-reduce conflict. □

By Lemmas 6.81 and 6.84 we have:

**Theorem 6.85** *For any reduced grammar $G = (V, T, P, S)$ and positive natural number k, the grammar, $T_{k,1}(G)$ is LR(1) if and only if G is LR(k + 1).* □

For any $k \geqslant 1$, the grammar $T_{k,1}(G)$ can be constructed from $G$, because the sets $\text{FIRST}_k(X)$ and $\text{FOLLOW}_k(X)$ can be computed for all symbols $X$. Hence by Theorems 6.78 and 6.85 we have:

**Theorem 6.86** *Let $k \geqslant 1$. Any reduced grammar can be transformed into an equivalent grammar that right-to-right covers the original grammar, and is LR(1) if and only if the original grammar is LR(k).* □

Theorem 6.85 says that any LR($k$) language, $k \geqslant 0$, is an LR(1) language. In Section 6.6 we showed (Theorem 6.71) that any LR($k$) language is always an SLR($k$) language. By Proposition 6.41 we can now state:

**Theorem 6.87** *For any alphabet T, the family of deterministic languages over T coincides with the family of SLR(1) languages over T.* □

## Exercises

6.1 Show that $\gamma$ is a viable prefix of grammar $G = (V, T, P, S)$ if and only if there is a string $\delta$ in $V^*$, a rule $A \to \omega$ in $P$, and a string $y$ in $T^*$ such that

$$S \underset{rm}{\Longrightarrow}^* \delta A y \underset{rm}{\Longrightarrow} \delta \omega y \qquad \text{in } G$$

and $\gamma$ is a prefix of $\delta\omega$.

6.2 Give regular expressions to denote the sets of viable prefixes of the following grammars.

a) $E \to T|E + T, T \to F|T*F, F \to a|(E)$.
b) $E \to T|T + E, T \to F|F*T, F \to a|(E)$.
c) $S \to \varepsilon|SaSb$.
d) $S \to \varepsilon|a|$ **if** $B$ **then** $SC, B \to b, C \to \varepsilon|$**else** $S$.
e) $S \to \varepsilon|aAbS|bBaS, A \to \varepsilon|aAbA, B \to \varepsilon|bBaB$.

6.3 Give right-linear grammars to generate the sets of viable prefixes of the grammars of the previous exercise.

6.4 Show that the set of complete viable prefixes of any grammar $G = (V, T, P, S)$ is a regular language over $V$.

6.5 Evaluate the complexity of the transformation presented in Section 6.1 to produce a right-linear grammar for the viable prefixes of a given grammar $G$. Can you obtain an $O(|G|)$ time-bounded transformation?

6.6 Give the LR(0) machine for the \$-augmented grammars of the grammars of Exercise 6.2.

6.7 Give the canonical LR(1) machines for the \$-augmented grammars of the grammars of Exercise 6.2.

6.8 Give the canonical LR(2) machines for the \$-augmented grammars of the grammars of Exercise 6.2.

6.9 Evaluate the complexity of computing for grammar $G$ the relation $\mathbf{desc}_k$, when (a) $k = 0$, (b) $k = 1$.

6.10 Evaluate the complexity of constructing for grammar $G$: (a) the LR(0) machine, (b) the canonical LR(1) machine.

6.11 Prove claims (d), (e), and (f) of Theorem 6.27.

6.12 Is $[\varepsilon]_k = \{\varepsilon\}$ true for all grammars $G$ and natural numbers $k$?

6.13 Show that (noninitial) states $q_1$ and $q_2$ in the canonical LR($k$) machine are the same if and only if their bases are the same.

6.14 Give the LR(0) parsers for the grammars of Exercise 6.2. Simulate the parsers on typical sentences of the languages. Identify pairs of actions that cause non-determinism.

6.15 Give the canonical LR(1) parsers for the grammars of Exercise 6.2. Are the parsers deterministic?

6.16 Give the canonical LR(2) parsers for the grammars of Exercise 6.2. Compare the behavior of the canonical LR(2) parser with that of the canonical LR(1) parser and of the LR(0) parser on some nonsentences.

6.17 In proving the correctness of the canonical LR($k$) parser we have used for Lemma 6.32 a most general formulation, one that corresponds closely to Lemma 5.19. This is because we wish to derive from a single technical result as many properties as possible. Besides proving that the canonical LR($k$) parser of grammar $G$ is a right parser of $G$, we have for example derived from Lemma 6.32 that the canonical LR($k$) parser of an LR($k$) grammar does not loop forever on any input string (Theorem 6.44). If we only wished to prove that the canonical LR($k$) parser is a right parser, then a somewhat simpler formulation of Lemma 6.32 would do. This formulation reads as follows:

Let $X$ be a symbol in $V$, $x$ and $y$ strings in $T^*$, $\pi$ a rule string in $P^*$, $\gamma$ a string in $V^*$, and $[A \rightarrow \alpha \cdot X\beta, z]$ an item of $G'$ such that

$$X \underset{\text{rm}}{\overset{\pi^R}{\Longrightarrow}} x, [A \rightarrow \alpha \cdot X\beta, z] \in \text{VALID}_k(\$\gamma), \quad \text{and}$$

$$k : y\$ \in \text{FIRST}_k(\beta z) \; .$$

Then there is an action string $\pi'$ such that

$$\tau(\pi') = \pi, \quad |\pi'| = |\pi| + |x|, \quad \text{and}$$

$$\$\Phi[\$\gamma]_k \mid xy\$ \overset{\pi'}{\Longrightarrow} \$\Phi[\$\gamma]_k[\$\gamma X]_k \mid y\$$$

for any string $\Phi$ in $[G']_k^*$.
Prove this and use the result to prove Lemma 6.33.

6.18 Show that the grammar $S \rightarrow Aa \mid a$, $A \rightarrow S$ is an LR(0) grammar.

6.19 Consider the grammars of Exercise 6.2. Which of these are LR($k$) for some $k$? Give the smallest such $k$.

6.20 Let $G = (V, T, P, S)$ be a grammar, $\phi$ a string in $V^*$, $A \rightarrow \omega$ a rule in $P$, and $i$ a natural number. The pair $(A \rightarrow \omega, i)$ is called a *handle* of $\phi$ if

$$S \underset{\text{rm}}{\Longrightarrow}{}^* \delta A y \underset{\text{rm}}{\Longrightarrow} \delta \omega y = \phi \quad \text{and} \quad |\delta\omega| = i$$

hold for some strings $\delta \in V^*$ and $y \in T^*$. Show that a reduced grammar is unambiguous if and only if $S \Rightarrow^+ S$ is impossible and no right sentential form has more than one handle.

6.21 Let $G = (V, T, P, S)$ be a grammar in which $S \Rightarrow^+ S$ is impossible. Further let $k$ be a natural number. Show that $G$ is LR($k$) if and only if the following statement holds for all right sentential forms $\gamma y_1$ and $\gamma y_2$, rules $A_1 \rightarrow \omega_1$ and

$A_2 \to \omega_2$, and natural numbers $i$: If $(A_1 \to \omega_1, |\gamma|)$ is a handle of $\gamma y_1$ and $(A_2 \to \omega_2, i)$ is a handle of $\gamma y_2$ and $k{:}y_1 = k{:}y_2$, then $(A_1 \to \omega_1, |\gamma|) = (A_2 \to \omega_2, i)$.

6.22 Consider the grammars of Figures 6.9 and 6.10 (see Section 6.4). Using the concept of a handle show that these grammars are not LR(1).

6.23 Consider the left-linear grammar

$$S \to Ab\,|\,Bc, \quad A \to \varepsilon\,|\,Aa, \quad B \to \varepsilon\,|\,Ba \ .$$

Show that the grammar is not LR($k$) for any $k$. Base your proof (a) on the definition of LR($k$) grammars, (b) on Theorem 6.39(b), (c) on Theorem 6.39 (c), (d) on the concept of a handle (see Exercise 6.21).

6.24 Consider the right-linear grammar

$$S \to C\,|\,D, \quad C \to b\,|\,aC, \quad D \to c\,|\,aD \ .$$

(Observe that the grammar generates the same language as the grammar of the previous exercise.) Show that the grammar is LR(1). Base your proof (a) on the definition of LR(1) grammars, (b) on Theorem 6.39(b), (c) on the concept of a handle.

6.25 Consider the grammar

$$S \to AB, \quad A \to a, \quad B \to CD\,|\,aE, \quad C \to ab \ ,$$

$$D \to bb, \quad E \to bba \ .$$

Show that the grammar is LR(2) but not LR(1). Base your proof (a) on the definition of LR($k$) grammars, (b) on Theorem 6.39(b), (c) on Theorem 6.39(c), (d) on the concept of a handle.

6.26 Let $G = (V, T, P, S)$ be a grammar, $\alpha$ a string in $V^*$, and $k$ a natural number. Define:

$$\mathrm{EFF}_k(\alpha) = \{k{:}x \,|\, \text{either } \alpha = x \in T^* \text{ or, for some } \beta \text{ in } V^*\backslash(V\backslash T)x, \alpha \underset{\mathrm{rm}}{\Longrightarrow}{}^* \beta \underset{\mathrm{rm}}{\Longrightarrow} x \in T^*\} \ .$$

In other words, $\mathrm{EFF}_k(\alpha)$ consists of all strings $x$ in $\mathrm{FIRST}_k(\alpha)$ that are obtained via rightmost derivations that do not use an $\varepsilon$-rule in front of $x$ at the last step. Give $\mathrm{FIRST}_2(X)$ and $\mathrm{EFF}_2(X)$ for the symbols of the grammar

$$S \to AB, \quad A \to Ba\,|\,\varepsilon, \quad B \to Cb\,|\,C, \quad C \to c\,|\,\varepsilon.$$

6.27 Show that for all symbols $X$ and strings $\alpha$,

$$\mathrm{EFF}_k(X\alpha) = k{:}\mathrm{EFF}_k(X)\mathrm{FIRST}_k(\alpha) \ .$$

6.28 Show that a canonical LR($k$) parser is nondeterministic if and only if some state in the canonical LR($k$) machine contains a pair of items

$$[A \to \omega\cdot, x], \quad [B \to \alpha\cdot\beta, y] ,$$

where $x$ belongs to $\text{EFF}_k(\beta y)$.

6.29 Give a relational expression to compute $\text{EFF}_1(X)$.

6.30 Call a grammar $G = (V, T, P, S)$ an *LLR(k) grammar* if the following statements hold.
(i) $G$ is unambiguous.
(ii) The conditions

$$S \Rightarrow^* xAy_1 \Rightarrow^* xwy_1 ,$$

$$S \Rightarrow^* xwy_2, \text{ and}$$

$$k{:}y_1 = k{:}y_2$$

always imply

$$S \Rightarrow^* xAy_2 .$$

Show the following:

a) Any reduced LR(0) grammar is LLR(1).
b) Any reduced LR($k$) grammar, when $k \geqslant 1$, is LLR($k$).
c) For any $k \geqslant 0$, there is a grammar which is LLR(0) but not LR($k$).

6.31 Show that for right-linear grammars $G$ the following statements are equivalent.

a) $G$ is LR($k$)
b) $G$ is LR(1).
c) $G$ is unambiguous.

6.32 Show that any regular language is LR(1).

6.33 Consider situations in which the canonical LR($k$) parser of a non-LR($k$) grammar loops forever on some input. Can you give an exact grammatical characterization for these situations? Is it solvable whether or not the canonical LR($k$) parser for a given grammar $G$ loops forever on some input string?

6.34 Prove Proposition 6.46.

6.35 Show that if $G$ is a non-right-recursive grammar, the canonical LR($k$) machine has at most $|G|^{k|G|} \cdot 2^{|G|}$ states.

6.36 For each $n \geqslant 1$, let $G_n$ be the grammar with the following rules:

$$S \to A_i \qquad (1 \leqslant i \leqslant n) ,$$
$$A_i \to a_j A_i \qquad (1 \leqslant i \neq j \leqslant n) ,$$
$$A_i \to a_i B_i | b_i \qquad (1 \leqslant i \leqslant n) ,$$
$$B_i \to a_j B_i | b_i \qquad (1 \leqslant i, j \leqslant n) .$$

Show the following:

a) $G_n$ is an LR(0) grammar.
b) $|G_n|$ is $O(n^2)$.
c) There is a constant $c > 0$ such that the size of the canonical LR(0) machine for $G_n$ is at least $2^{cn}$ for all $n \geqslant 1$.
d) There is a constant $c > 0$ and a natural number $n_0$ such that when $n > n_0$ any deterministic right parser for $G_n$ has size at least $2^{cn}$.

Claim (d) means that LR($k$) grammars are exponentially more succinct language descriptions than deterministic right parsers.

6.37 Give the LALR(1) parsers for the grammars of Exercise 6.2. Compare the size and the behavior of the LALR(1) parser with the size and the behavior of the canonical LR(1) parser. Are the grammars LALR(1)?

6.38 Show that for $k = 1$ no state in the LALR($k$) machine of an LR($k$) grammar can contain a pair of items exhibiting a shift-reduce conflict. Does this hold for $k > 1$?

6.39 Prove Lemmas 6.49 and 6.50.

6.40 Prove Theorem 6.53.

6.41 Derive an upper bound on the size of an LA($k$)LR($l$) parser.

6.42 Prove or disprove the following characterization of LA($k$)LR($l$) grammars: The LA($k$)LR($l$) parser of grammar $G = (V, T, P, S)$ is deterministic if and only if the conditions

$$S \underset{\text{rm}}{\Longrightarrow}^* \delta_1 A_1 y_1 \underset{\text{rm}}{\Longrightarrow} \delta_1 \omega_1 y_1 = \gamma_1 y_1 ,$$

$$S \underset{\text{rm}}{\Longrightarrow}^* \delta_2 A_2 y_2 \underset{\text{rm}}{\Longrightarrow} \delta_2 \omega_2 y_2 = \gamma_2 v y_2 ,$$

$[\gamma_1]_l = [\gamma_2]_l$, and $k{:}y_1 = k{:}vy_2$

always imply $[\delta_1\omega_1]_l = [\delta_2\omega_2]_l$, $A_1 = A_2$, and $\omega_1 = \omega_2$.

6.43 Show that the LA($k$)LR($l$) parser of an LA($k$)LR($l$) grammar does not loop forever on any input string.

6.44 The way we have defined the notion of an LALR($k$) parser may introduce actions that are extraneous in that they are never used in the parsing of any sentence in the language. For example, in the LALR(1) parser for the grammar $G_{ab\varepsilon}$ (see Section 6.5) reduce actions $r'_4$, $r'_6$, $r'_8$, $r'_{10}$ are extraneous. Can you redefine LALR($k$) parsers so that extraneous actions would be eliminated? Apply your definition to the grammar $G_{ab\varepsilon}$. Do you get a valid right parser in the general case? Does your definition change the class of LALR($k$) grammars?

6.45 Give the SLR(1) parsers for the grammars of Exercise 6.2. Compare the behavior of the SLR(1) parser with that of the LALR(1) parser and of the canonical LR(1) parser. Are the grammars SLR(1)?

6.46 Show that any simple precedence grammar is an SLR(1) grammar. Give an SLR(1) grammar which is not simple precedence.

6.47 Can you give a grammatical characterization, similar to Theorem 6.39(c), for SLR($k$) grammars?

6.48 Show that the SLR($k$) parser of an SLR($k$) grammar does not loop forever on any input string.

6.49 Consider the grammar $G$ with the rules

$$S \to Aa|dAb|cb|dca \ ,$$
$$A \to c \ .$$

a) Show that $G$ is LR(1).
b) Show that $G$ is not SLR($k$) for any $k$.
c) Is $G$ LALR($k$) for some $k$?
d) Give the transformed SLR(1) grammar $T_1(G)$ for $G$.
e) Give the derivation trees of the sentences in $L(G)$, both in $G$ and in $T_1(G)$.

6.50 Prove Lemma 6.67.

6.51 Consider transforming LR($k$) grammars into SLR($k$) grammars. One might be tempted to resort to the following transformation. For each viable prefix $\delta A$ and rule $A \to X_1 \dots X_n$ of the original grammar, the transformed grammar has the rule

$$[\$\delta A]_k \to Y_1 \dots Y_n \ ,$$

where $Y_i = [\$\delta X_1 \dots X_i]$ when $X_i$ is a nonterminal and $Y_i = X_i$ when $X_i$ is a terminal ($i = 1, \dots, n$). The start symbol of the transformed grammar is $[\$S]_k$. Show that this transformation does not work.

6.52 The transformation of LR($k$) grammars into SLR($k$) grammars presented in Section 6.6 has an exponential time and space complexity. Is the exponential growth of the grammar necessary? That is, is there a sequence of LR($k$) grammars $G_n$ of size polynomial in $n$ and constants $c$, $n_0 > 0$ such that when $n > n_0$ the size of any SLR($k$) grammar equivalent to $G_n$ has size at least $2^{cn}$?

6.53 Consider the grammar $G$:

$$S \to Abb \mid Bb \ ,$$

$$A \to \varepsilon \mid aA \ ,$$

$$B \to \varepsilon \mid aB \ .$$

a) Show that $G$ is SLR(2) but not LR(1).
b) Give the transformed grammar $T_{1,1}(G)$.
c) Give the transformed grammar $T_{2,1}(G)$. Is it LR(0)?

6.54 Consider the grammar $G$:

$$S \to Abb \mid Bbc \ ,$$

$$A \to aA \mid a \ ,$$

$$B \to aB \mid a \ .$$

a) Show that $G$ is SLR(2) but not LR(1).
b) Give the transformed grammar $T_{1,1}(G)$.
c) Give the transformed grammar $T_{2,1}(G)$. Show that it is LR(0).

6.55 Consider the grammar $G$:

$$S \to a \mid aac \mid bSS \ .$$

a) Show that $G$ is SLR(2) but not LR(1).
b) Give the transformed grammar $T_{1,1}(G)$.
c) Give the transformed grammar $T_{2,1}(G)$. Is it LR(0)?

6.56 Show that language $L$ is LR(0) if and only if it is LR($k$) and the conditions

$$w \in L, \quad wx \in L, \quad y \in L$$

always imply

$$yx \in L \ .$$

6.57 A language is *prefix-free* if no proper prefix of any of its sentences is a sentence. Show that any prefix-free LR($k$) language is LR(0).

6.58 Let $L$ be an LR($k$) language over alphabet $T$ and let $\#$ be a symbol not in $T$. Show that $L\#$ is an LR(0) language over $T \cup \{\#\}$

6.59 Show that the transformed grammar $T_{k,1}(G)$ is LR(0) if $G$ is LR($k$) and $L(G)$ is prefix-free. Does the converse hold? That is, is $L(G)$ prefix-free whenever $T_{k,1}(G)$ is LR(0)?

6.60 What can you say about the transformed grammar $T_{k,1}(G)$ when $G$ is SLR($k+1$), LALR($k+1$), or LA($k+1$)LR($l$)? Is $T_{k,1}(G)$ SLR(1), LALR(1), or LA(1)LR($l$), respectively?

6.61 Evaluate the complexity of the transformation of LR($k$) grammars into LR(1) grammars.

6.62 Does the transformed grammar $T_{k,1}(G)$ left-to-left cover $G$?

6.63 The concept of an LA($k$) LR($l$) parser can be generalized by using in place of the LR($l$)-equivalence $\rho_l$ any relation $\rho$ on $V^*$ satisfying the following conditions:

(i) $\rho$ is an equivalence.
(ii) $\rho$ is of finite index.
(iii) $\rho$ is right-invariant.
(iv) $\gamma_1{:}1 = \gamma_2{:}1$ whenever $\gamma_1$ and $\gamma_2$ are $\rho$-equivalent viable prefixes.

Define formally the concept of an *LA(k) LR(ρ) parser*, that is, an LR-like parser that uses $k$-length lookahead and in which the stack alphabet is the collection of all $\rho$-equivalence classes.

6.64 Formulate and prove the counterpart of Lemma 6.32 for LA($k$)LR($\rho$) parsers.

6.65 Call a relation $\lambda$ on $2^{\Sigma^*}$ a *lookahead operator* over alphabet $\Sigma$ if the following conditions are satisfied:

(i) $\lambda(2^{\Sigma^*})$ is finite.
(ii) Each set in $\lambda(2^{\Sigma^*})$ is finite.
(iii) If $W_1 \lambda W_2$, then $W_2 \subseteq \text{PREFIX}(W_1)$.
(iv) If $y \in W_1 \subseteq \Sigma^*$, then for some $W_2$, $W_1 \lambda W_2$ and $\text{PREFIX}(y) \cap W_2 \neq \varnothing$.
(v) If $W_1 W W_2 \lambda W_3$ and $W' \lambda W$, then $W_1 W' W_2 \lambda W_3$.
(vi) If $W_1 W' W_2 \lambda W_3$, then, for some $W$, $W' \lambda W$ and $W_1 W W_2 \lambda W_3$.

For natural number $k$ define relations $\lambda_k$ and $\hat{\lambda}_k$ by setting:

(1) $W \lambda_k \{y\}$ whenever $W \subseteq \Sigma^*$ and $y \in k{:}W$.
(2) $W_1 \hat{\lambda}_k W_2$ whenever $W_1 \subseteq \Sigma^*$ and $W_2 = k{:}W_1$.

Show that $\lambda_k$ and $\hat{\lambda}_k$ are lookahead operators.

6.66 Let $G = (V, T, P, S)$ be a grammar and $\lambda$ a lookahead operator over $T$. Call a pair $[A \to \alpha \cdot \beta, W]$, where $A \to \alpha\beta$ is a rule in $P$ and $W$ is a set in $\lambda(2^{T^*})$, a $\lambda$-*item* of $G$. Say that $\lambda$-item $[A \to \alpha \cdot \beta, W]$ is *LR*($\lambda$)-*valid for* string $\gamma$ if

$$\{y \in T^* \mid S \underset{rm}{\Longrightarrow}^* \delta A y \underset{rm}{\Longrightarrow} \delta\alpha\beta y = \gamma\beta y\} \,\lambda\, W \ .$$

Denote by $\text{VALID}_\lambda(\gamma)$ the set of all LR($\lambda$)-valid items for $\gamma$. Define relation $\mathbf{desc}_\lambda$ such that $\text{VALID}_\lambda(\gamma X)$ will be obtained as GOTO ($\text{VALID}_\lambda(\gamma), X$). Prove the necessary lemmas to obtain this result.

6.67 Define and prove the correctness of the general notion of an LA($\lambda$) LR($\rho$) parser, that is, an LR-like parser that uses lookahead strings appearing in sets in $\lambda(2^{T^*})$ and in which the stack alphabet is the collection of all $\rho$-equivalence classes. Consider applications that might benefit from this general notion of an LR parser.

6.68 The context-free grammar is the basic notation used to describe the syntax of programming languages. However, most programming language manuals use some richer syntactic notation so as to make possible syntax descriptions that are more succinct and easier to read than those obtained via ordinary context-free grammars. One widely used notation is the *extended context-free grammar*, which is like an ordinary context-free grammar but allows regular expressions to be used on the right-hand sides of the rules:

$E \to T(\text{'+'}\,T)^*$,

$T \to F(\text{'*'}\,F)^*$,

$F \to a \cup \text{'('}E\text{')'}$.

This "extended grammar" describes the same language as does the ordinary context-free grammar

$E \to T \mid E\ \text{'+'}\ T$,

$T \to F \mid T\ \text{'*'}\ E$,

$F \to a \mid \text{'('}E\text{')'}$.

Formally, an extended context-free grammar is a quadruple $G = (V, T, P, S)$ in which $V$, $T$, and $S$ are (as in an ordinary context-free grammar) the alphabet, the terminal alphabet, and the start symbol, respectively, and $P$ is a finite set of rules, of the form $A \to E$ where $A$ is a nonterminal in $V$ and $E$ is a regular expression over $V$. A rule $A \to E$ can be thought of as denoting a (usually infinite) set of ordinary context-free rules, called *instances* of $A \to E$. An instance of $A \to E$ is any rule of the form $A \to \omega$ in which $\omega$ is a string in $L(E)$, the language denoted by the regular expression $E$. For example, the rule $F \to a \cup \text{'('}E\text{')'}$ has two instances: $F \to a$ and $F \to \text{'('}E\text{')'}$, while the rules $E \to T(\text{'+'}\,T)^*$ and $T \to F(\text{'*'}\,F)^*$ both have an infinite number of instances:

$E \to T, E \to T$ '+'$T, E \to T$'+'$T$ '+'$T, \ldots,$ and $T \to F,$ $T \to F$'*'$F, T \to$ $F$'*'$F$'*'$F, \ldots$. The *directly-derives* relation of an extended grammar $G = (V, T, P, S)$ is defined as the relation on $V^*$ given by the set of all rule instances:

$$\underset{G}{\Longrightarrow} = \{(\alpha A \beta, \alpha \omega \beta) | \alpha \text{ and } \beta \text{ are strings in } V^* \text{ and}$$

$$A \to \omega \text{ is an instance of some rule in } P\} \ .$$

The language generated by $G$ is then defined in the usual way:

$$L(G) = \{w \in T^* | S \underset{G}{\Longrightarrow}^* w\} \ .$$

Show that any extended context-free grammar $(V, T, P, S)$ can be transformed in linear time into an equivalent ordinary context-free grammar $(V', T, P', S)$.

6.69 The *viable prefixes* of an extended context-free grammar can be defined as in a conventional grammar, by means of the "rightmost derives" relation induced by the instances of the rules. The *items* of an extended grammar are obtained in the usual way by inserting a dot between subexpressions in the right-hand sides of the rules. Examples of 0-items of the extended grammar given in the previous exercise are: $E \to \cdot T$('+'$T)^*$, $E \to T(\cdot$'+'$T)^*$, $E \to T$('+'$\cdot T)^*$, $F \to \cdot(a \cup$ '('$E$')'). Define formally the notion of an "LR($k$)-valid item for viable prefix $\gamma$" in an extended grammar.

6.70 Give an algorithm for constructing VALID$_k(\gamma)$, the set of LR($k$)-valid items for viable prefix $\gamma$, in an extended context-free grammar. Apply your algorithm to the case of the grammar given in Exercise 6.68.

*Hint*: Observe that if $[E \to T\cdot$('+'$T)^*, y]$ is in VALID$_k(\gamma)$, then so are $[E \to T(\cdot$'+'$T)^*, y]$ and $[E \to T$('+'$T)^* \cdot, y]$, and if $[E \to T$('+'$T \cdot)^*, y]$ is in VALID$_k(\gamma)$, then so are $[E \to T(\cdot$'+'$T)^*, y]$ and $[E \to T$('+'$T)^* \cdot, y]$. Also observe that if $[F \to \cdot(a \cup$ '('$E$')'$), y]$ is in VALID$_k(\gamma)$, then so are $[F \to \cdot a \cup$ '('$E$')'$, y]$ and $[F \to a \cup \cdot$'('$E$')'$, y]$, and if $[F \to a \cdot \cup$ '('$E$')'$, y]$ is in VALID$_k(\gamma)$, then so is $[F \to (a \cup$ '('$E$')'$)\cdot, y]$.

6.71 A *right parse* of a sentence $w$ in an extended context-free grammar $G = (V, T, P, S)$ is any string

$$(r_1, i_1)(r_2, i_2) \ldots (r_n, i_n)$$

of rule-instance pairs such that $S$ rightmost derives $w$ in $G$ using instance string $i_1 i_2 \ldots i_n$. A *right parser* for $G$ is any pushdown transducer $M$ that accepts $L(G)$ and produces for each sentence $w$ in $L(G)$ a right parse in $G$.

The collection of all sets VALID$_k(\gamma)$ can be used to construct an "LR($k$) parser" for $G$. The construction is not, however, so straightforward as it is in the case of conventional grammars. The fact that rules can have instances of arbitrary length makes it difficult to determine the "handle" in reduce actions. For example, in a state containing the item $[T \to F(\text{'}*\text{'}F)^* \cdot,\ +]$ the portion of the stack to be reduced to $T$ depends upon how many $F$'s have been recognized. Find ways to solve this problem. Define formally the notion of a "canonical LR($k$) parser" for an extended grammar.

6.72 Define the notion of an "extended LR($k$) grammar", that is, the LR($k$) property of an extended context-free grammar. Reconsider the transformation of extended grammars to conventional grammars suggested in Exercise 6.68. Does your transformation produce an LR($k$) grammar (in the usual sense) if and only if the original grammar is LR($k$) (according to your definition)?

## Bibliographic Notes

The theory of LR($k$) parsing was introduced by Knuth (1965). Most of the properties of LR($k$) parsers and LR($k$) grammars already appear in Knuth's original paper. These include the observation that the viable prefixes form a regular language (Theorem 6.11), the "item technique" used to construct the canonical LR($k$) machine (Section 6.2), the idea of how the LR($k$) parser operates (Section 6.3), and the characterization of LR($k$) grammars by means of the notion of a "handle" (Exercise 6.20). Knuth (1965) also showed how LR($k$) languages can be recognized by deterministic (normal-form) pushdown automata and, conversely, how deterministic (normal-form) pushdown automata can be transformed into equivalent LR(1) grammars, thus proving that the family of deterministic languages coincides with the family of LR(1) languages (cf. Proposition 6.41). Aho and Ullman (1972b, 1973a) developed further the theory of LR($k$) parsing and established the notation and terminology now used in the literature. From them come, among other things, the grammatical characterization of LR($k$) grammars (Theorem 6.39(c)) and the terms "viable prefix", "valid LR($k$) item", and "canonical collection".

Geller and Harrison (1977a) have analyzed in detail the different definitions of LR($k$) grammars encountered in the literature (see also Harrison, 1978). From them comes the characterization of LR(0) languages given in Exercise 6.56. The "LLR($k$) grammars" considered in Exercise 6.30 are the grammars defined by Lewis and Stearns (1968) (see Geller and Harrison, 1977a).

The size of LR($k$) parsers has been studied by Earley (1968), Purdom (1974), Pittl (1981a), and by Ukkonen (1981, 1983, 1985). The sequence of grammars given in Exercise 6.36, showing that the size of LR($k$) parsers can grow non-polynomially in the size of the grammar, is from Earley (1968) (who attributed it to J. Reynolds). The sequence of grammars given in Proposition 6.46, yielding a true exponential lower bound, is from Ukkonen (1985). That LR($k$) grammars can indeed be exponentially more succinct language descriptors than deterministic right parsers (i.e. that exponential growth is necessary for any right parser) was proved by

Ukkonen (1981, 1983) and independently by Pittl (1981a) (see Exercise 6.36(d)). The result of Exercise 6.35 comes from Ukkonen (1985). Purdom (1974) argues that grammars describing real programming languages have LR parsers whose size grows only linearly.

The notions of LALR($k$) and SLR($k$) parsing come from DeRemer (1969, 1971). Most of the properties of LALR($k$) and SLR($k$) parsers and grammars can be found in DeRemer (1969). The notion of LA($k$)LR($l$) parsing comes from Anderson (1972) (see also LaLonde, 1976b). Geller and Harrison (1977b) and Heilbrunner (1981) have proposed general approaches to LR($k$) parsing that yield canonical LR($k$), LALR($k$), SLR($k$), and other kinds of LR($k$) parser variants as special cases.

The notion of grammatical covering is attributed to J. Reynolds and R. Haskell (see Gray and Harrison, 1972). The terminology used in Sections 6.6 and 6.7 follows Nijholt (1980a, 1980b). The covering of LR($k$) grammars by LR(1) grammars has been studied by Mickunas, Lancaster and Schneider (1976), Mickunas (1976), and by Nijholt (1977). The transformation presented in Section 6.7 is essentially that given by Mickunas (1976). Another solution to the covering problem of LR($k$) grammars is presented by Nijholt (1977), who derives the result via the technique of transforming normal-form pushdown transducers into equivalent LR(1) grammars, using the fact that LR($k$) parsers can be implemented by normal-form pushdown transducers. Transformations of LR($k$) grammars into bounded context or precedence grammars are considered by Graham (1970, 1971, 1974), Mickunas, Lancaster and Schneider (1976), and by Wyrostek (1986).

Various extensions of the LR($k$) parsing method have been proposed. The LR($k$) parsing of "extended context-free grammars", also called "regular right-part grammars" (see Exercises 6.68 to 6.72) is studied by Madsen and Kristensen (1976), LaLonde (1977, 1979, 1981), Heilbrunner (1979), Purdom and Brown (1981), Chapman (1984), and by Nakata and Sassa (1986). LR-like parsers using unbounded lookahead are considered by Čulik and Cohen (1973) and Baker (1981). Szymanski (1973), Szymanski and Williams (1976), and Tai (1979) have considered "noncanonical" extensions of LR($k$) parsing techniques. Harris (1987) considers LR-like parsing of non-context-free grammars.

The development of syntax-directed editors has given rise to "incremental" parsing techniques. Incremental LR parsing is studied by Celentano (1978), Ghezzi and Mandrioli (1979, 1980), Wegman (1980), Jalili and Gallier (1982), and Degano, Mannucci and Mojana (1988).

The monograph of Aho and Ullman (1972b, 1973a) is a comprehensive general source for the fundamentals of LR($k$) parsing. Many surveys and introductory texts on LR($k$) parsing exist. Among them are Aho and Johnson (1974), Aho and Ullman (1977), Waite and Goos (1984), and Aho, Sethi and Ullman (1986). An extensive bibliography on LR($k$) parsing is given in Nijholt (1983a).

# 7. Construction and Implementation of LR(1) Parsers

This chapter is devoted to the practical issues involved in the construction and use of deterministic LR(1) parsers. We shall show how the practical versions of LR(1) parsers, most notably the LALR(1) parsers, can be constructed efficiently, and we shall present methods for encoding LR(1) parsers as efficient RAM programs. Two versions of RAM program implementation are considered: in the first implementation the parsing program is table-driven, that is, the rules of the parser are encoded in a two-dimensional array which is simulated by a program body; in the other implementation the tabular information is further transformed into a set of program statements.

Special attention is paid to developing ways to optimize LR(1) parsers. We shall give an efficient algorithm for determining those entries in the parsing table which can never be consulted. These "inessential (or don't care) error entries" are important in several methods for optimizing LR(1) parsers. An effect similar to that achieved with optimization is often obtained by using a short ambiguous grammar for language description instead of a more complicated LR(1) grammar, and by augmenting the ambiguous grammar with rules for resolving the parsing conflicts.

In Section 7.1 we consider the construction of LR(0) and SLR(1) parsers, and in Section 7.2 the construction of canonical LR(1) parsers. The LALR(1) parser construction is considered in Section 7.3, where in particular, an efficient algorithm is given for determining the lookahead symbols for the reduce actions of an LALR(1) parser. In Section 7.4 the concept of an LR(0)-based LR(1) parser of a grammar is defined; this is a generalization of an LALR(1) parser and allows some simple compressions. The implementation of any LR(0)-based LR(1) parser as a RAM program is considered. Section 7.5 is devoted to the development of methods for optimizing LR(0)-based LR(1) parsers on the basis of inessential error entries. Detailed algorithms are given for determining inessential error entries, and these are used to merge compatible states of the parser and to eliminate reductions by unit rules from the parser. Finally, the use of ambiguous grammars together with disambiguating rules as a means of producing deterministic parsers is considered in Section 7.6.

## 7.1 Construction of SLR(1) Parsers

In this section we shall derive a practical algorithm for constructing SLR(1) parsers. First of all, we have to construct the canonical LR(0) collection and the deterministic, or canonical, LR(0) machine for the grammar. Although the size of the deterministic LR(0) machine is exponential in the worst case (Theorem 6.45), there is motivation for trying to make the construction process as efficient as possible, because the exponential size of the LR(0) machine does not occur very often. In fact, the LR(0) machine is seldom unreasonably large for practical grammars.

In a practical algorithm for constructing the LR(0) collection each 0-item $[A \to \alpha \cdot X\beta]$ is represented by a link pointing to the location where symbol $X$ in rule $A \to \alpha X\beta$ is stored in the representation of the grammar (Figure 4.2). Note that item $[A \to \omega \cdot]$ then needs a special notation because no symbol appears after the dot.

By Lemma 6.23 the initial state $\text{VALID}_0(\varepsilon)$ of the deterministic LR(0) machine for grammar $G = (V, T, P, S)$ is obtained by constructing the reflexive transitive closure of the set $\{[S \to \cdot\omega] \mid S \to \omega \in P\}$ under the relation **desc**. The other states are then constructed by the rule (Lemma 6.26):

$$\text{GOTO}(\text{VALID}_0(\gamma), X) = \text{VALID}_0(\gamma X) .$$

This construction can be viewed as the construction of a deterministic finite automaton from a nondeterministic one.

Let $I_0$ be the set of all 0-items of grammar $G = (V, T, P, S)$. We define a nondeterministic finite automaton $M_{\text{LR}(0)}$ ($M_0$, for short) with state alphabet $I_0 \cup \{q_s\}$, $q_s \notin I_0$, input alphabet $V$, initial state $q_s$, and set of final states $I_0$. The set of transitions of $M_0$ consists of all rules of the forms

(a) $q_s \to [S \to \cdot\omega]$ ,

(b) $[A \to \alpha \cdot X\beta]X \to [A \to \alpha X \cdot \beta]$, $X \in V$, and

(c) $[A \to \alpha \cdot B\beta] \to [B \to \cdot\omega]$ ,

where $\beta$ derives some terminal string.

In other words, $M_0$ has a transition on symbol $X$ from any state $[A \to \alpha \cdot X\beta]$ to state $[A \to \alpha X \cdot \beta]$, and transitions on the empty string $\varepsilon$ from the initial state to each state $[S \to \cdot\omega]$ and from any state $[A \to \alpha \cdot B\beta]$ to all states $[B \to \cdot\omega]$. The automaton $M_0$ is called the *nondeterministic LR(0) machine for G.*

Clearly, the nondeterministic LR(0) machine for grammar $G$ is of size $O(|G|^2)$, and it can be computed in time $O(|G|^2)$.

As an example consider the grammar

$$E \to E + T \mid T ,$$

$$T \to a \mid (E) .$$

The nondeterministic LR(0) machine for this grammar is given in Figure 7.1.

**Lemma 7.1** *The set of viable prefixes of G is the language accepted by the nondeterministic LR(0) machine $M_0$ for G, and for any viable prefix $\gamma$,*

$$\text{VALID}_0(\gamma) = \{q \mid q \in I_0 \text{ and } q \text{ is accessible upon reading } \gamma \text{ in } M_0\} .$$

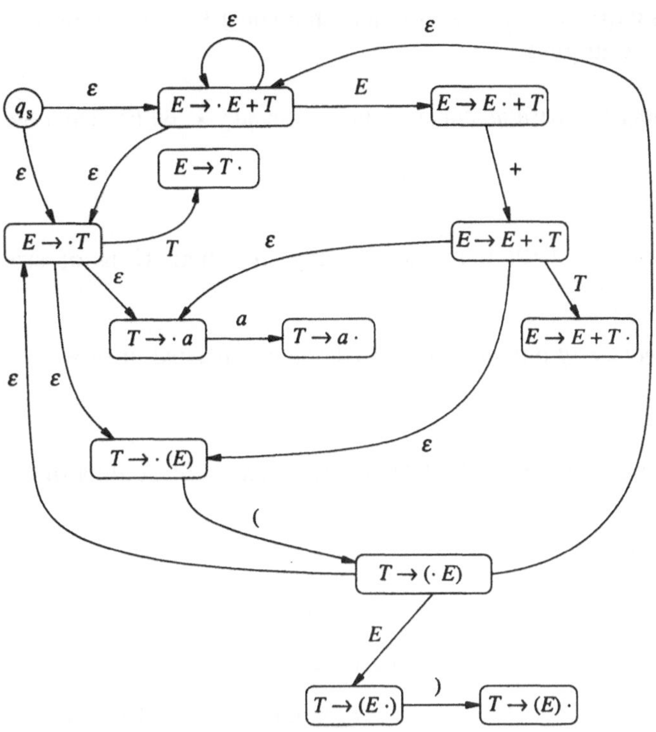


**Figure 7.1** The nondeterministic LR(0) machine for the grammar $E \to E + T \mid T$, $T \to a \mid (E)$

*Proof.* By construction, the set

$$\{q \mid q \in I_0 \text{ and } q \text{ is accessible upon reading } \varepsilon\}$$

equals the set $\mathbf{desc}^*(\{[S \to \cdot\omega] \mid S \to \omega \in P\}) = \text{VALID}_0(\varepsilon)$.

Assume as an induction hypothesis that for any string $\gamma$ of length $n$, $n \geqslant 0$, the set

$$I = \{q \mid q \in I_0 \text{ and } q \text{ is accessible upon reading } \gamma\}$$

is nonempty if and only if $\gamma$ is a viable prefix and $I = \text{VALID}_0(\gamma)$. Then, by the construction of $M_0$, for any $X$ in $V$,

$$I' = \{q \mid q \in I_0 \text{ and } q \text{ is accessible upon reading } \gamma X\}$$

is nonempty if and only if $\gamma$ is a viable prefix and $I' = \text{GOTO}(\text{VALID}_0(\gamma), X) \neq \varnothing$. Since, by Lemma 6.26, $\text{GOTO}(\text{VALID}_0(\gamma), X) = \text{VALID}_0(\gamma X)$, and by Fact 6.12, $\text{VALID}_0(\gamma X) \neq \varnothing$ if and only if $\gamma X$ is a viable prefix, we conclude that $I'$ is nonempty if and only if $\gamma X$ is a viable prefix and $I' = \text{VALID}_0(\gamma X)$. Hence we obtain the lemma. □

Lemma 7.1. implies that we obtain the deterministic LR(0) machine for $G$ by making the nondeterministic LR(0) machine deterministic. This can be done using the algorithm given in Figure 3.9. As the nondeterministic LR(0) machine has $O(|G|)$ states, Theorem 3.30 implies:

**Theorem 7.2** *The deterministic LR(0) machine for any grammar G can be computed in time*

$$O(2^{|G| + 2\log|G|}) \ . \quad \square$$

Because the deterministic LR(0) machine for any grammar $G$ is of size $O(2^{|G| + \log|G|})$, we get:

**Theorem 7.3** *The LR(0) parser of any grammar G can be constructed in time*

$$O(2^{|G| + 2\log|G|}) \ . \quad \square$$

We now turn to the construction of SLR(1) parsers. The shift actions of an SLR(1) parser are of the form

$$[\delta] \mid a \rightarrow [\delta][\delta a] \mid$$

and the reduce actions are of the form

$$[\delta][\delta X_1] \ldots [\delta X_1 \ldots X_m] \mid a \rightarrow [\delta][\delta A] \mid a \ ,$$

where $[A \rightarrow X_1 \ldots X_m \cdot]$ is in $\text{VALID}_0(\delta X_1 \ldots X_m)$ and $a$ is in $\text{FOLLOW}'_1(A)$. Thus, in constructing the SLR(1) parser from the LR(0) parser, we first need to compute the sets $\text{FOLLOW}'_1(A)$ for all nonterminals $A$. This takes time $O(|T| \cdot |G|)$ (see Section 5.5). Then we simply add the lookahead symbols to the rules of the LR(0) parser. We have:

**Theorem 7.4** *The SLR(1) parser of any grammar $G = (V, T, P, S)$ can be constructed in time*

$$O(2^{|G| + 2\log|G| + \log|T|}) \ . \quad \square$$

Whether or not a grammar $G$ is SLR(1) can be tested directly by inspecting the LR(0) collection of sets of items constructed for the \$-augmented grammar $G'$ for $G$. A (reduced) grammar $G$ is not SLR(1) if and only if some set of items contains two distinct items

$$[A_1 \rightarrow \omega_1 \cdot] \quad \text{and} \quad [A_2 \rightarrow \omega_2 \cdot]$$

where $\text{FOLLOW}'_1(A_1) \cap \text{FOLLOW}'_1(A_2) \neq \varnothing$, or two distinct items

$$[A_1 \rightarrow \alpha \cdot a\beta] \quad \text{and} \quad [A_2 \rightarrow \omega \cdot] \ ,$$

where $a$ is in $\text{FOLLOW}'_1(A_2)$. This testing can be done efficiently, if we first compute the relation denoted by the relational expression $\textbf{follows}^{-1}\textbf{follows}$, where **follows** is defined by:

$$a \ \textbf{follows} \ A \ ,$$

if $a$ is in $\mathrm{FOLLOW}'_1(A)$. By the results of Section 5.5. the relation **follows** can be described by a relational expression of size $O(|G|)$. Thus by Theorem 2.29 the relation denoted by $\mathbf{follows}^{-1}\mathbf{follows}$ can be computed in time $O(|G|^2)$.

Using the relation denoted by $\mathbf{follows}^{-1}\mathbf{follows}$ it can be checked in time $O(|G|^2)$ whether a given set of 0-items causes a reduce-reduce conflict, that is, whether this set of items contains two items $[A_1 \to \omega_1 \cdot]$ and $[A_2 \to \omega_2 \cdot]$, such that $\mathrm{FOLLOW}'_1(A_1) \cap \mathrm{FOLLOW}'_1(A_2) \neq \varnothing$. A possible shift-reduce conflict can be found in time $O(|G|^2)$ using the relation **follows**. Thus the whole SLR(1) test can be performed in time $O(|G|^2 \cdot 2^{|G| + \log|G|}) = O(2^{|G| + 3\log|G|})$.

In Section 10.1 we shall present a polynomial time-bounded algorithm for SLR(1) testing. In practice, however, it may be better to use the above algorithm because the LR(0) collection of sets of times is seldom too large for practical grammars.

## 7.2 Construction of Canonical LR(1) Parsers

In the previous section we considered algorithms for constructing deterministic LR(0) machines. In this section these methods will be generalized to the construction of deterministic LR(1) machines. We want to point out, however, that the deterministic LR(1) machine is often too large for implementation, as the experiments with practical grammars have shown. Thus, special techniques for making the construction process a little more efficient may not be of much use.

In representing a set of 1-items notice that the core of a 1-item will be represented as a 0-item. Moreover, a set of 1-items $\{[A \to \alpha \cdot \beta, a_1], \ldots, [A \to \alpha \cdot \beta, a_n]\}$ will be represented as $[A \to \alpha \cdot \beta, \{a_1, \ldots, a_n\}]$, and internally by a pair of pointers the first of which denotes the core and the second the set of lookahead symbols.

We can define the nondeterministic LR(1) machine for a grammar in the same way as the nondeterministic LR(0) machine. Let $G = (V, T, P, S)$ be a grammar and $I_1$ the set of all 1-items for $G$. We define the *nondeterministic LR(1) machine for G* as a nondeterministic finite automaton $M_1$ with state alphabet $I_1 \cup \{q_s\}$, $q_s \notin I_1$, input alphabet $V$, initial state $q_s$ and set of final states $I_1$. The set of transitions of $M_1$ consists of all rules of the forms

(a) $\quad q_s \to [S \to \cdot\omega, \varepsilon]$ ,

(b) $\quad [A \to \alpha \cdot X\beta, y]X \to [A \to \alpha X \cdot \beta, y], \quad X \in V$ ,

and

(c) $\quad [A \to \alpha \cdot B\beta, y] \to [B \to \cdot\omega, z]$ ,

where $z \in \mathrm{FIRST}_1(\beta y)$.

The size of the deterministic LR(1) machine of grammar $G$ is $O(|T|^2 \cdot |G|^2)$, and it can also be constructed in time $O(|T|^2 \cdot |G|^2)$.

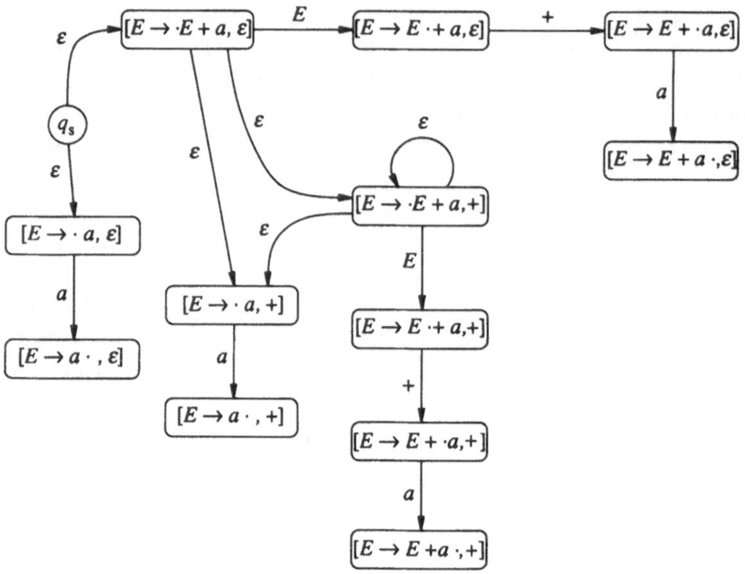


**Figure 7.2** The nondeterministic LR(1) machine for the grammar $E \to E + a | a$

As an example, the nondeterministic LR(1) machine for the grammar $E \to E + a | a$ is given in Figure 7.2.

The following lemma is proved in the same way as Lemma 7.1.

**Lemma 7.5** *The set of viable prefixes of grammar G is the language accepted by the nondeterministic LR(1) machine $M_1$ for G, and for any viable prefix $\gamma$,*

$$\text{VALID}_1(\gamma) = \{q \mid q \in I_1 \text{ and } q \text{ is accessible upon reading } \gamma \text{ in } M_1\} \ . \quad \square$$

Lemma 7.5 implies that we obtain the deterministic LR(1) machine for $G$ by making the nondeterministic LR(1) machine deterministic using the algorithm given in Figure 3.9. The deterministic LR(1) machine is of size $O(2^{|G|^2 + 2\log|G|})$ (Theorem 6.45). Thus the proof of Theorem 3.30 implies that the algorithm of Figure 3.9, when applied to the nondeterministic LR(1) machine for $G$, takes time $O(2^{|G|^2 + 2\log|G|} \cdot |Q|)$, where $Q$ is the set of states in the nondeterministic LR(1) machine. The set $Q$ is of size $O(|T| \cdot |G|)$, and thus we obtain:

**Theorem 7.6** *The deterministic LR(1) machine for any grammar G can be constructed in time*

$$O(2^{|G|^2 + 4\log|G|}) \ . \quad \square$$

As the deterministic LR(1) machine for grammar $G$ is of size $O(2^{|G|^2 + 2\log|G|})$, we also have:

**Theorem 7.7** *The canonical LR(1) parser of any grammar G can be constructed in time*

$$O(2^{|G|^2 + 4\log|G|}) . \quad \square$$

Testing whether or not a grammar $G$ is LR(1) can be done directly by inspecting the LR(1) collection of sets of items constructed for the \$-augmented grammar $G'$. Grammar $G$ is not LR(1) if and only if some set of items contains two distinct items

$$[A_1 \to \omega_1 \cdot, a] \text{ and } [A_2 \to \omega_2 \cdot, a] ,$$

or two distinct items

$$[A_1 \to \alpha \cdot a\beta, b] \quad \text{and} \quad [A_2 \to \omega \cdot, a] ,$$

where $a$ is in $T \cup \{\$\}$. Thus we need $O(|T| \cdot |G|)$ time for each LR(1) state in order to perform the LR(1) test. Hence the total time needed is bounded by $O(|G|^2 \cdot 2^{|G|^2 + 2\log|G|})$. We have:

**Theorem 7.8** *A grammar G with terminal alphabet T can be tested for the LR(1) property in deterministic time* $O(2^{|G|^2 + 4\log|G|})$. $\square$

Finally we note that in Section 10.1 we shall present a polynomial algorithm for LR(1) testing.

## 7.3 Construction of LALR(1) Parsers

In this section we shall develop a practical method for constructing LALR(1) parsers. By Theorem 6.47 the LALR(1) parser for a grammar can be constructed by first computing the canonical LR(1) collection and then unioning all sets with equal core sets. This method is certainly unnecessarily inefficient because we have to construct the LR(1) collection first. In the following, we shall first construct the LR(0) collection and then add lookahead symbols in appropriate places.

Let $G = (V, T, P, S)$ be a reduced grammar and $G' = (V \cup \{\$\}, T \cup \{\$\}, P \cup \{S' \to \$S\$\}, S')$ its \$-augmented grammar. For state $q$ in the LR(0) collection for $G'$ and rule $A \to \omega$ of $G$ we define the *LALR(1) lookahead set for the reduce action by rule $A \to \omega$ at state $q$*, denoted by $\text{LALR}(q, A \to \omega)$, to be the union of all sets

$$\{a \in T \cup \{\$\} \mid [A \to \omega \cdot, a] \in \text{VALID}_1(\gamma) \text{ for some } \gamma \text{ such that } \text{VALID}_0(\gamma) = q\} .$$

In the following we shall show that the LALR(1) lookahead sets can be determined directly from the transitions of the deterministic LR(0) machine. This means that not even the item sets forming the LR(0) collection need be present during the construction process. We denote by $Q$ the set of states of the deterministic LR(0) machine for the \$-augmented grammar $G'$ for grammar

$G = (V, T, P, S)$. We define some relations involving states in $Q$, symbols in $V \cup \{\$\}$, and pairs $(q, A)$ in $Q \times (V \setminus T)$ and $(q, A \to \omega)$ in $Q \times P$. In pair $(q, A)$ the state $q$ has a transition on the nonterminal $A$ and in pair $(q, A \to \omega)$ the state $q$ contains the item $[A \to \omega \cdot]$. The relations are defined by:

$(q, A)$ **goes-to** GOTO$(q, A)$, if state $q$ has a transition on nonterminal $A$;

$q$ **has-transition-on** $X$, if $q$ has a transition on symbol $X$ in $V$;

$q$ **has-null-transition** $(q, A)$, if state $q$ has a transition on nonterminal $A$ and $A$ is nullable;

(GOTO$(q, \alpha)$, $A$) **includes** $(q, B)$, if state $q$ has a transition on nonterminal $B$ and $G$ has a rule $B \to \alpha A \beta$, where $\beta$ is nullable;

(GOTO$(q, \omega)$, $A \to \omega$) **lookback** $(q, A)$, if state $q$ has a transition on $A$.

The relations **goes-to, has-transition-on, has-null-transition, includes**, and **lookback** are clearly of size $O(|G| \cdot |Q|)$ and can be computed in time $O(|G| \cdot |Q|)$.

**Lemma 7.9** *Let $q$ be a state in $Q$ that has a transition on a nonterminal $B$. and let $A$ be a nonterminal and $\alpha$ a string in $V^*$ such that $B \underset{rm}{\Longrightarrow}^n \alpha A$. Then* GOTO$(q, \alpha A) \neq \varnothing$ *and*

$$(\text{GOTO}(q, \alpha), A) \ \textbf{includes*} \ (q, B) \ .$$

*Proof.* We prove the lemma by induction on $n$. The base case $n = 0$ is clear. In the case $n > 0$ we can conclude by Lemma 6.2 that for some $m < n$, string $\delta'$ and rule $A' \to \alpha' A \beta'$:

$$B \underset{rm}{\Longrightarrow}^m \delta' A' \underset{rm}{\Longrightarrow} \delta' \alpha' A \beta' = \alpha A \beta', \quad \beta' \Rightarrow^* \varepsilon \ .$$

By the induction hypothesis, GOTO$(q, \delta' A') \neq \varnothing$, and

$$(\text{GOTO}(q, \delta'), A') \ \textbf{includes*} \ (q, B) \ .$$

Then also GOTO$(q, \delta' \alpha' A) \neq \varnothing$ and

$$(\text{GOTO}(q, \delta' \alpha'), A) \ \textbf{includes} \ (\text{GOTO}(q, \delta'), A') \ ,$$

which means that the claim holds. □

**Lemma 7.10** *If for $n \geqslant 0$*

$$(q, A) \ \textbf{includes}^n \ (q', B) \ ,$$

*then, for some $\alpha$ in $V^*$, $q =$ GOTO$(q', \alpha)$ and $B \underset{rm}{\Longrightarrow}^* \alpha A$.*

*Proof.* An easy induction on $n$. □

We then define the relational expressions

**directly-reads = goes-to has-transition-on terminal** ,

and

**reads = goes-to has-null-transition** .

**Fact 7.11** For $n > 0$, $(q, A)$ **reads**$^n$ $(q', B)$ if and only if $B$ is nullable and there is a nullable string $\delta$ of length $(n - 1)$ such that $q' = \mathrm{GOTO}(q, A\delta)$ and $q'$ has a transition on $B$. □

For the relational expression

**has-LALR-lookahead = lookback includes* reads* directly-reads** ,

we shall show that

$(q, A \to \omega)$ **has-LALR-lookahead** $a$

if and only if $a$ is in $\mathrm{LALR}(q, A \to \omega)$. In other words,

$\mathrm{LALR}(q, A \to \omega) =$ **has-LALR-lookahead**$((q, A \to \omega))$ .

Before giving a formal proof of this statement we illustrate the relation denoted by **has-LALR-lookahead**. Consider the situation depicted in Figure 7.3. After reducing at state $q$ by rule $A \to \omega$, the next input symbol may be $a$ whenever $\beta$ is nullable. This demonstrates that if

$(q, A \to \omega)$ **lookback reads* directly-reads** $a$ ,

then for some $\gamma\omega$ such that $\mathrm{VALID}_0(\gamma\omega) = q$, $[A \to \omega\cdot, a]$ is in $\mathrm{VALID}_1(\gamma\omega)$, that is, $a$ is in $\mathrm{LALR}(q, A \to \omega)$. The origin of a lookahead symbol may, however, be even more complicated as is demonstrated in Figure 7.4. The situation given in

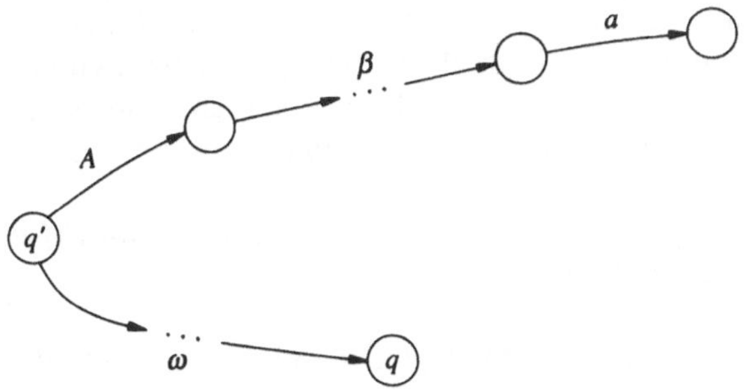


**Figure 7.3** Portion of a deterministic LR(0) machine. Here $A \to \omega$ is a rule and $\beta$ is nullable. Now $a$ belongs to $\mathrm{LALR}(q, A \to \omega)$ and $(q, A \to \omega)$ **lookback** $(q', A)$ **reads* directly-reads** $a$

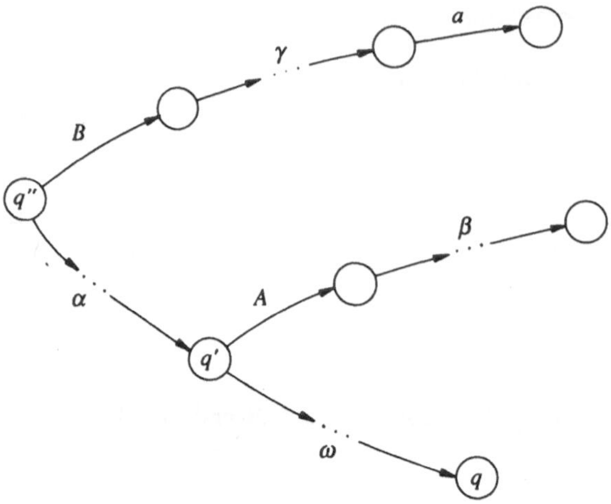


**Figure 7.4** Portion of a deterministic LR(0) machine. Here $A \to \omega$ and $B \to \alpha A\beta$ are rules and $\beta$ and $\gamma$ are nullable. Now $a \in \mathrm{LALR}(q, A \to \omega)$ and $(q, A \to \omega)$ **lookback** $(q', A)$ **includes** $(q'', B)$ **reads* directly-reads** $a$

Figure 7.4 illustrates that if

$(q, A \to \omega)$ **lookback includes**$^+$ **reads* directly-reads** $a$ ,

then $a$ is in $\mathrm{LALR}(q, A \to \omega)$.

We next give some lemmas that are necessary in proving the desired result.

**Lemma 7.12** *If $\gamma\beta$ is a viable prefix of a reduced grammar and $\beta \Rightarrow^n az$, where $n \geq 0$, $a$ is a terminal and $z$ a terminal string, then there is a viable prefix $\gamma\delta a$, where $\delta$ is nullable.*

*Proof.* The proof is by induction on $n$. If $\beta$ is of the form $\delta a\psi$, where $\delta$ is nullable, the claim follows directly from the fact that any prefix of a viable prefix is viable. In particular, this is the case when $n = 0$. We may thus assume that $n > 0$ and that $\beta$ is of the form $\delta' B\psi$, where $\delta'$ is nullable and $B \Rightarrow \beta' \Rightarrow^{n-1} az'$ for some $\beta'$ and $z'$. Because $\gamma\delta' B$, being a prefix of a viable prefix, is viable, then so is $\gamma\delta'\beta'$ (by Lemma 6.5, since the grammar is reduced). As $\beta' \Rightarrow^{n-1} az'$, the claim then follows by applying the induction hypothesis to the viable prefix $\gamma'\beta'$, where $\gamma' = \gamma\delta'$. □

**Lemma 7.13** *In a reduced grammar,* $(q, A)$ **reads* directly-reads** $a$ *if and only if $q$ contains an item $[B \to \alpha \cdot A\beta]$ with $a \in \mathrm{FIRST}_1(\beta)$.*

*Proof.* Let $\gamma$ be a viable prefix such that $q = \mathrm{VALID}_0(\gamma)$. To prove the "only if" part, assume that

$(q, A)$ **reads* directly-reads** $a$.

By Fact 7.11, there is a nullable string $\delta$ such that GOTO($q$, $A\delta a$) is nonempty. Thus $\gamma A\delta a$ is a viable prefix of $G'$ and

$$S' \underset{rm}{\Longrightarrow}^* \gamma' By \underset{rm}{\Longrightarrow} \gamma'\alpha'\beta' y = \gamma A\delta a\beta' y$$

for some string $\gamma'$, rule $B \to \alpha'\beta'$, and terminal string $y$. We consider two cases: (1) $A$ is contained in $\alpha'$, (2) $A$ is not contained in $\alpha'$. In case (1), $\alpha'$ is of the form $\alpha A\delta a$, where $\alpha$ is a suffix of $\gamma$. Then

$$S' \underset{rm}{\Longrightarrow}^* \gamma' By \underset{rm}{\Longrightarrow} \gamma'\alpha A\beta y = \gamma A\beta y \ ,$$

where we have written $\delta a\beta' = \beta$. Thus $[B \to \alpha \cdot A\beta] \in \text{VALID}_0(\gamma)$ and $a \in \text{FIRST}_1(\beta)$, as desired. In case (2), $\gamma'$ is of the form $\gamma A\eta$ and

$$S' \underset{rm}{\Longrightarrow}^* \gamma' By = \gamma A\eta By \ ,$$

where $a \in \text{FIRST}_1(\eta B)$. By Lemma 6.2,

$$S' \underset{rm}{\Longrightarrow}^* \delta' B' y' \underset{rm}{\Longrightarrow} \delta'\alpha'' A\beta'' y' = \gamma A\beta'' y' \ ,$$

$$\beta'' y' \Rightarrow^* \eta By$$

for some string $\delta'$, rule $B' \to \alpha'' A\beta''$, and terminal string $y'$. Thus $[B' \to \alpha'' \cdot A\beta''] \in \text{VALID}_0(\gamma)$. Moreover, the condition $\beta'' y' \Rightarrow^* \eta By$ implies that $\beta''$ derives some $\eta Bz$, where $z$ is a prefix of $y$. Thus $a \in \text{FIRST}_1(\beta'')$, as desired.

To prove the "if" part of the lemma, assume that $q$ contains an item $[B \to \alpha \cdot A\beta]$ such that $a \in \text{FIRST}_1(\beta)$. By Fact 6.24, $\gamma A\beta$ is a viable prefix. By Lemma 7.12, there is a viable prefix $\gamma A\delta a$, where $\delta$ is nullable. This means that GOTO($q$, $A\delta a$) is nonempty, and hence (by Fact 7.11) that

($q$, $A$) **reads* directly-reads** $a$ ,

as desired. □

Next we shall show that the symbols in LALR($q$, $A \to \omega$) are obtained from the items in those states $q'$ for which the condition ($q$, $A \to \omega$) **lookback includes*** ($q'$, $B$) holds. To prove this we need the following technical lemma which is similar to Lemma 5.50.

**Lemma 7.14** *Let $G = (V, T, P, S)$ be a grammar. Further let $A$ be a nonterminal, $X$ and $Y$ symbols in $V$, $\gamma$ and $\psi$ strings in $V^*$, $y$ a string in $T^*$, and $\pi$ a rule string in $P^*$ such that*

(a) $$A \overset{\pi}{\underset{rm}{\Longrightarrow}} \gamma X\psi Yy \quad \text{and} \quad \psi \Rightarrow^* \varepsilon \ .$$

*Then there are symbols $X'$ and $Y'$ in $V$, a rule $r' = B \to \alpha X'\psi' Y'\beta$ in $P$, and strings*

*$\gamma'$, $\alpha'$, $\beta'$ in $V^*$ and $y'$ in $T^*$ such that*

$$\text{(b)}\quad \begin{aligned} &A \underset{rm}{\overset{\pi'}{\Longrightarrow}} \gamma' B y' \underset{rm}{\overset{r'}{\Longrightarrow}} \gamma'\alpha X'\psi' Y'\beta y', \quad \gamma'\alpha\alpha' = \gamma \ , \\ &X' \underset{rm}{\Longrightarrow}^* \alpha' X, \quad \psi' \Rightarrow^* \varepsilon, \quad \text{and} \quad Y' \underset{lm}{\Longrightarrow}^* Y\beta' \ , \end{aligned}$$

*where $\pi' r'$ is a prefix of $\pi$. In other words, in the rightmost derivation of $\gamma X\psi Yy$ from $A$ there is a step showing that the symbols $X$ and $Y$ "originate" from a pair of adjoining symbols in the right-hand side of the same rule.*

*Proof.* Cf. the proof of Lemma 5.50. The details of the proof are left as an exercise. □

Now we are ready to prove:

**Lemma 7.15** *In a reduced grammar, terminal $a$ belongs to* LALR$(q, A \to \omega)$ *if and only if there is a rule $C \to \alpha B\beta$ and state $q'$ such that*

$$(q, A \to \omega)\ \textbf{lookback includes*}\ (q', B) \ ,$$

$$[C \to \alpha \cdot B\beta] \in q', \quad \textit{and} \quad a \in \text{FIRST}_1(\beta) \ .$$

*Proof.* Assume first that $a$ belongs to LALR$(q, A \to \omega)$. The definition of LALR$(q, A \to \omega)$ implies that for some viable prefix $\gamma$ of $G'$ and terminal string $y$,

$$S' \underset{rm}{\Longrightarrow}^* \gamma A a y \underset{rm}{\Longrightarrow} \gamma\omega a y \ ,$$

where VALID$_0(\gamma\omega) = q$. Choosing, in Lemma 7.14, $X = A$, $\psi = \varepsilon$, and $Y = a$ we can conclude that for some nonterminal $B$, rule $C \to \alpha B\beta$, strings $\alpha'$, $\beta'$, $\gamma'$, and terminal string $y'$,

$$S' \underset{rm}{\Longrightarrow}^* \gamma' C y' \underset{rm}{\Longrightarrow} \gamma'\alpha B\beta y', \quad \gamma'\alpha\alpha' = \gamma \ ,$$

$$B \underset{rm}{\Longrightarrow}^* \alpha' A, \quad \text{and} \quad \beta \Rightarrow^* a\beta' \ .$$

Here $[C \to \alpha \cdot B\beta] \in \text{VALID}_0(\gamma'\alpha)$ and $a \in \text{FIRST}_1(\beta)$. Denote $q' = \text{VALID}_0(\gamma'\alpha)$. As $\gamma'\alpha B$ is a viable prefix and $B \underset{rm}{\Longrightarrow}^* \alpha' A$, we conclude by Lemma 7.9 that GOTO$(q', \alpha' A) \neq \varnothing$ and

$$(\text{GOTO}(q', \alpha'), A)\ \textbf{includes*}\ (q', B) \ .$$

Here GOTO$(q', \alpha') = \text{VALID}_0(\gamma'\alpha\alpha') = \text{VALID}_0(\gamma)$. On the other hand, $\gamma A$ is a viable prefix and $A \to \omega$ a rule, and so

$$(\text{VALID}_0(\gamma\omega), A \to \omega)\ \textbf{lookback}\ (\text{VALID}_0(\gamma), A) \ .$$

Here $\text{VALID}_0(\gamma\omega) = q$, which means that

$$(q, A \to \omega) \textbf{ lookback includes* } (q', B) \ ,$$

as desired.

To prove the converse, assume that for some rule $C \to \alpha B\beta$ and state $q'$,

$$(q, A \to \omega) \textbf{ lookback includes* } (q', B) \ ,$$

$$[C \to \alpha \cdot B\beta] \in q', \quad \text{and} \quad a \in \text{FIRST}_1(\beta) \ .$$

The condition $[C \to \alpha \cdot B\beta] \in q'$ implies that for some string $\delta$ and terminal string $y$,

$$S' \underset{\text{rm}}{\Longrightarrow}^* \delta C y \underset{\text{rm}}{\Longrightarrow} \delta\alpha B\beta y \quad \text{and} \quad \text{VALID}_0(\delta\alpha) = q' \ .$$

As $a \in \text{FIRST}_1(\beta)$, we have, by Theorem 4.2, $\beta \underset{\text{rm}}{\Longrightarrow}^* az$ for some terminal string $z$. So we have:

$$S' \underset{\text{rm}}{\Longrightarrow}^* \delta\alpha B\beta y \underset{\text{rm}}{\Longrightarrow}^* \delta\alpha Bazy \ .$$

The definitions of **lookback** and **includes** imply that

$$(q, A \to \omega) \textbf{ lookback } (q_1, A) \textbf{ includes* } (q', B) \ ,$$

where $\text{GOTO}(q_1, \omega) = q$. By Lemma 7.10, there is a string $\alpha'$ such that $q_1 = \text{GOTO}(q', \alpha')$ and $B \underset{\text{rm}}{\Longrightarrow}^* \alpha' A$. We have:

$$S' \underset{\text{rm}}{\Longrightarrow}^* \delta\alpha Bazy \underset{\text{rm}}{\Longrightarrow}^* \delta\alpha\alpha' Aazy \underset{\text{rm}}{\Longrightarrow} \delta\alpha\alpha'\omega azy \ ,$$

where $\text{VALID}_0(\delta\alpha\alpha'\omega) = \text{GOTO}(q', \alpha'\omega) = \text{GOTO}(q_1, \omega) = q$. This means that $a \in \text{LALR}(q, A \to \omega)$. □

Lemmas 7.13 and 7.15 together imply:

**Theorem 7.16** *Let G be a reduced grammar and G' its \$-augmented grammar. Terminal a of G' is in the LALR(1) lookahead set for the reduce action by rule $A \to \omega$ of G at state q in the deterministic LR(0) machine for G' if and only if*

$$(q, A \to \omega) \textbf{ has-LALR-lookahead } a \ . \quad \square$$

Let $DM$ be the deterministic LR(0) machine for the \$-augmented grammar $G'$ for the grammar $G = (V, T, P, S)$, and let $Q$ be the set of states of $DM$. The relations **includes** and **lookback** are of size $O(|G| \cdot |Q|)$ and can be computed from $G$ and $DM$ in time $O(|G| \cdot |Q|)$. The relations denoted by **directly-reads** and **reads** are of size $O(|G| \cdot |DM|)$, but the relational expressions

**directly-reads = goes-to has-transition-on terminal** ,

**reads = goes-to has-null-transition** ,

and **goes-to, has-transition-on**, and **has-null-transition** are of size $O(|G|\cdot|Q|)$ and the relations in them can be computed in time $O(|G|\cdot|Q|)$. Thus we conclude that the relational expression **has-LALR-lookahead** is of size $O(|G|\cdot|Q|)$ and, from Theorem 2.29, that the relation denoted by it can be computed in time $O(|T|\cdot|G|\cdot|Q|)$, or, more specifically, in time $O(t\cdot|G|\cdot|Q|)$, where $t$ is the time taken by one set operation on subsets of $T$.

**Theorem 7.17** *Let DM be the deterministic LR(0) machine for the \$-augmented grammar $G'$ for a reduced grammar $G = (V, T, P, S)$. The collection of all LALR(1) lookahead sets* LALR$(q, A \rightarrow \omega)$, *where $q$ is a state of DM and $A \rightarrow \omega$ is a rule of $G$, can be computed in time $O(t\cdot|G|\cdot|Q|)$, where $Q$ is the set of states of DM and $t$ is the time taken by one set operation (assignment or union) on subsets of $T$.* □

The following fact is an immediate consequence of the definition of LALR(1) lookahead sets and of the definition of an LALR(1) parser.

**Fact 7.18** The LALR(1) reduce actions by rule $A \rightarrow X_1 \ldots X_m$ of grammar $G$ are of the form

$$[\delta]_0[\delta X_1]_0 \ldots [\delta X_1 \ldots X_m]_0 \mid a \rightarrow [\delta]_0[\delta A]_0 \mid a \ ,$$

where $\delta A$ is a viable prefix of $G'$ and

$$a \in \mathrm{LALR}(\mathrm{VALID}_0(\delta X_1 \ldots X_m), A \rightarrow X_1 \ldots X_m) \ . \quad \square$$

As the size of the deterministic LR(0) machine for any grammar $G$ is $O(2^{|G| + \log|G|})$, and by Theorem 7.2 it can be constructed in time $O(2^{|G| + 2\log|G|})$, we get from Theorem 7.17 and Fact 7.18:

**Theorem 7.19** *The LALR(1) parser of any grammar $G = (V, T, P, S)$ can be constructed in time*

$$O(2^{|G| + 2\log|G| + \log|T|}) \ . \quad \square$$

A (reduced) grammar $G$ is not LALR(1) if and only if some state $q$ in the LR(0) collection for $G'$ contains two distinct items $[A_1 \rightarrow \omega_1 \cdot]$ and $[A_2 \rightarrow \omega_2 \cdot]$ such that

$$\mathrm{LALR}(q, A_1 \rightarrow \omega_1) \cap \mathrm{LALR}(q, A_2 \rightarrow \omega_2) \neq \varnothing \ ,$$

or $q$ contains two distinct items $[A_1 \rightarrow \alpha \cdot a\beta]$ and $[A_2 \rightarrow \omega \cdot]$, where $a \in \mathrm{LALR}(q, A_2 \rightarrow \omega)$. Thus, after having computed the LALR(1) lookahead sets, the time needed for the LALR(1) test is $O(|T|\cdot|G|)$ for each set of items in the LR(0) collection. Because the size of the LR(0) collection is $O(2^{|G| + \log|G|})$ and computing the LALR(1) lookahead sets takes time $O(2^{|G| + 2\log|G| + \log|T|})$, the whole LALR(1) test takes time $O(2^{|G| + 2\log|G| + \log|T|})$. In Section 10.4 we shall show that the question of whether a given grammar is LALR(1) is PSPACE-complete. Thus it is most likely that there does not exist a polynomial time algorithm for LALR(1) testing.

As an example of the LALR(1) parser construction process we apply the above techniques to the grammar:

$$S \to aABa \ ,$$

$$B \to \varepsilon \ ,$$

$$A \to bCB \mid d \ ,$$

$$C \to bA \mid bDb \ ,$$

$$D \to d \ .$$

The deterministic LR(0) machine for the corresponding \$-augmented grammar is given in Figure 7.5. Let us first consider the computation of the LALR(1) look-ahead sets. By Theorem 7.16 these are obtained directly from the relation denoted

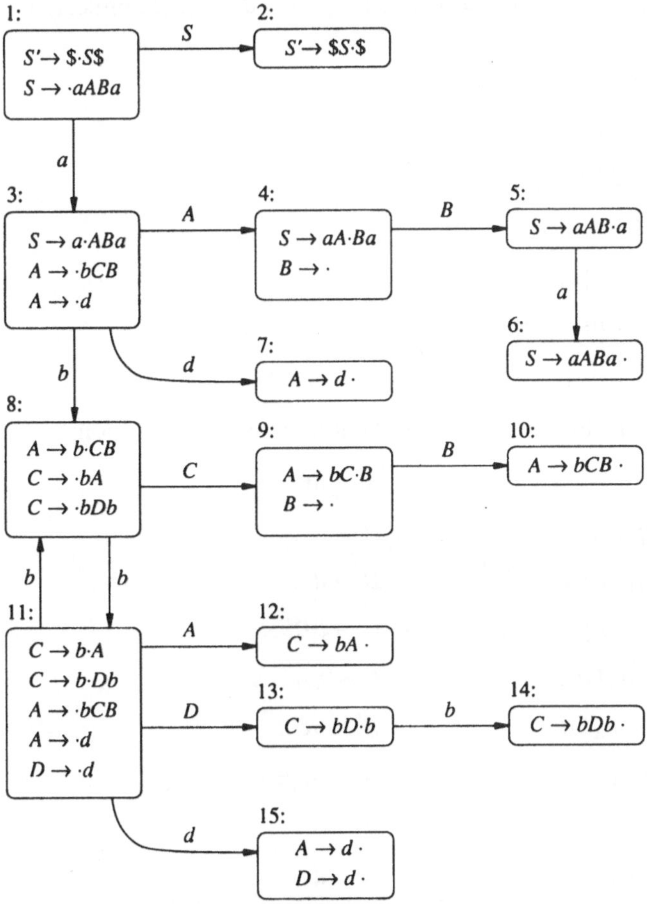


**Figure 7.5** The deterministic LR(0) machine for the grammar $S' \to \$S\$$, $S \to aABa$, $B \to \varepsilon$, $A \to bCB \mid d$, $C \to bA \mid bDb$, $D \to d$

by the relational expression **has-LALR-lookahead.** In order to compute this relation consider first the state $q_{15}$ in the LR(0) machine:

$$\textbf{lookback}(q_{15}, A \to d) = \{(q_{11}, A)\} \ ,$$

$$\textbf{includes*}(q_{11}, A) = \{(q_8, C), (q_{11}, A), (q_3, A)\} \ ,$$

$$\textbf{reads* directly-reads}\ (\{(q_8, C), (q_{11}, A)\}) = \emptyset \ ,$$

$$\textbf{reads* directly-reads}\ (q_3, A) = \{a\} \ .$$

Thus **has-LALR-lookahead** $(q_{15}, A \to d) = \text{LALR}(q_{15}, A \to d) = \{a\}$.

$$\textbf{lookback}\ (q_{15}, D \to d) = \{(q_{11}, D)\} \ ,$$

$$\textbf{includes*}\ (q_{11}, D) = \{(q_{11}, D)\} \ ,$$

$$\textbf{reads* directly-reads}\ (q_{11}, D) = \{b\} \ .$$

Thus **has-LALR-lookahead** $(q_{15}, D \to d) = \text{LALR}(q_{15}, D \to d) = \{b\}$. Similarly we obtain:

$$\text{LALR}(q_{14}, C \to bDb) = \{a\} \ ,$$

$$\text{LALR}(q_{12}, C \to bA) = \{a\} \ ,$$

$$\text{LALR}(q_{10}, A \to bCB) = \{a\} \ ,$$

$$\text{LALR}(q_9, B \to \varepsilon) = \{a\} \ ,$$

$$\text{LALR}(q_7, A \to d) = \{a\} \ ,$$

$$\text{LALR}(q_6, S \to aABa) = \{\$\} \ ,$$

$$\text{LALR}(q_4, B \to \varepsilon) = \{a\} \ .$$

Thus the LALR(1) parser of this grammar has the following reduce actions.

| rule: | output: |
|---|---|
| $q_{11}q_{15} \mid a \to q_{11}q_{12} \mid a$ , | $A \to d$ . |
| $q_{11}q_{15} \mid b \to q_{11}q_{13} \mid b$ , | $D \to d$ . |
| $q_8q_{11}q_{13}q_{14} \mid a \to q_8q_9 \mid a$ , | $C \to bDb$ . |
| $q_8q_{11}q_{12} \mid a \to q_8q_9 \mid a$ , | $C \to bA$ . |
| $q_3q_8q_9q_{10} \mid a \to q_3q_4 \mid a$ , | $A \to bCB$ . |
| $q_{11}q_8q_9q_{10} \mid a \to q_{11}q_{12} \mid a$ , | $A \to bCB$ . |
| $q_9 \mid a \to q_9q_{10} \mid a$ , | $B \to \varepsilon$ . |
| $q_3q_7 \mid a \to q_3q_4 \mid a$ , | $A \to d$ . |
| $q_1q_3q_4q_5q_6 \mid \$ \to q_1q_2 \mid \$$ , | $S \to aABa$ . |
| $q_4 \mid a \to q_4q_5 \mid a$ , | $B \to \varepsilon$ . |

The shift actions are:

$$q_1 \mid a \to q_1 q_3 \mid ,$$
$$q_3 \mid d \to q_3 q_7 \mid ,$$
$$q_3 \mid b \to q_3 q_8 \mid ,$$
$$q_5 \mid a \to q_5 q_6 \mid ,$$
$$q_8 \mid b \to q_8 q_{11} \mid ,$$
$$q_{11} \mid b \to q_{11} q_8 \mid ,$$
$$q_{13} \mid b \to q_{13} q_{14} \mid ,$$
$$q_{11} \mid d \to q_{11} q_{15} \mid .$$

## 7.4 Implementation of LR(1) Parsers

In this section we shall demonstrate how to implement deterministic SLR(1), LALR(1), and canonical LR(1) parsers as RAM programs; the general term *LR*(1) *parser* is used for any of these parsers. We shall give formal schemes for generating for any deterministic LR(1) parser a parsing program that simulates the parser. There are two basically different ways to do this. In both cases the parsing program contains a body that is independent of the underlying grammar and parser. Then we may create a parsing program by augmenting the body by program statements that correspond to the rules of the underlying LR(1) parser. The other possibility is that the parsing program is table-driven, so that the rules of the LR(1) parser in question are encoded as a matrix, called a parsing table, which is then interpreted by the parsing program body. In both cases the stack of the underlying pushdown automaton is implemented explicitly as a stack of states of the parsing machine.

An important observation in deriving an efficient implementation of an LR(1) parser is that in performing a reduce action it is not necessary to match the whole left-hand side of the rule with the top portion of the stack. In fact, when making a reduce action by rule $A \to X_1 \ldots X_m$, $m \geqslant 2$, at state $[\delta X_1 \ldots X_m]$ it is not necessary to verify that the states $[\delta X_1], \ldots, [\delta X_1 \ldots X_{m-1}]$ are actually on top of the parsing stack.

**Fact 7.20** Let $M$ be an LR(1) parser of grammar $G = (V, T, P, S)$, and let $q_1 = [\$]$, and $q_2, \ldots, q_n$, $n \geqslant 2$, be states (stack symbols) of $M$ such that

$$\$q_1 \mid w\$ \underset{M}{\Longrightarrow^*} \$q_1 q_2 \ldots q_n \mid y\$$$

for some terminal strings $w$ and $y$. If $M$ has a reduce action

$$q'_i \ldots q'_{n-1} q_n \mid a \to q'_i q \mid a, \qquad 1 \leqslant i < n, \text{ by rule } A \to X_{i+1} \ldots X_n ,$$

then $M$ also has a reduce action

$$q_i \ldots q_n \,|\, a \to q_i q \,|\, a, \qquad \text{by the rule } A \to X_{i+1} \ldots X_n \,. \quad \square$$

For the following discussion it is helpful to define a table, called Goto, indexed by the equivalence classes of viable prefixes and by the symbols of the underlying grammar:

$$\text{Goto}[[\delta], X] = [\delta X] \,.$$

A reduce action by rule $A \to \omega$ applies to a configuration

$$\$q_1 \ldots q_n \,|\, y\$$$

accessible from an initial configuration, whenever the parser has a reduce action $\phi q_n \,|\, 1{:}y\$ \to \phi' \,|\, 1{:}y\$$ by rule $A \to \omega$. The reduce action is performed by popping the states $q_{n-|\omega|+1}, \ldots, q_n$ from the stack and then pushing the state $\text{Goto}[q_{n-|\omega|}, A]$ onto the stack.

A shift action applies to a configuration $\$q_1 \ldots q_n \,|\, y\$$, if $\text{Goto}[q_n, 1{:}y\$] \neq \varnothing$, and it is performed by pushing the state $\text{Goto}[q_n, 1{:}y\$]$ onto the stack and by deleting the first symbol from the input string.

Thus we may implement a deterministic LR(1) parser by using a parsing action table, called Action, which is defined for the states and the input symbols of the parser as follows.

$$\text{Action}[q, a] = \text{“reduce by } A \to X_1 \ldots X_m\text{”} \,,$$

meaning that a reduce action by rule $A \to X_1 \ldots X_m$ is to be applied, whenever the parser has an action

$$[\delta][\delta X_1] \ldots [\delta X_1 \ldots X_m] \,|\, a \to [\delta][\delta A] \,|\, a$$

$$\text{where } [\delta X_1 \ldots X_m] = q \,;$$

$$\text{Action}[q, a] = \text{“shift Goto}[q, a]\text{”} \,,$$

whenever $\text{Goto}[q, a] \neq \varnothing$;

$$\text{Action}[q, a] = \text{“accept”} \,,$$

if $q = [\$S]$ and $a = \$$, where $S$ is the start symbol of the grammar. Otherwise,

$$\text{Action}[q, a] = \text{“error”} \,.$$

Clearly, the Action table is well-defined for any deterministic LR(1) parser.

For any deterministic LR(1) parser the *LR(1) parsing table*, indexed by state and grammar symbol, means the combination of the Goto and Action tables, such that the entries for terminal symbols in the Goto table are not repeated, as they are already included in the Action table. Similarly, any variation of an LR(1) parser to be defined in the sequel may be represented by a parsing table composed of the Goto table and an Action table corresponding to the rules of the parser in question.

In the implementation we assume, as in Section 5.6, that the terminal alphabet $T$ of the grammar consists of token class names in some lexical description. The special token class name *eof-token* is reserved for the representation of the end marker \$. We also assume that a scanner has been constructed for the lexical description. The scanner is organized as a subroutine of the parser, and the parser calls the scanner whenever the current input symbol has been shifted and a new one must be read. A call

*scan*

in the parser has the effect that the next token is extracted from the input string and stored in a global variable, *token*. The variable token has two fields. The field denoted by

*token.kind*

contains the token class name of the token, and the other field (not considered here) contains the actual character string of the token.

In Figures 7.6 to 7.8 a general scheme for a table-driven parsing program is given that corresponds to an LR(1) parser. The Goto table defining the transitions of the underlying deterministic parsing machine and the parsing action table Action are available as corresponding arrays.

The implementation involves a stack that can contain any stack symbols of the parser, and also the end marker \$ (*eof-token*). The stack is operated using the operations *empty*, *push*, *pop*, and *top*. The operation *empty* initializes the stack as empty. The operation *push*($q$) pushes symbol $q$ onto the stack. The operation *pop*($l$) pops from the stack $l$ topmost symbols. The top of the stack is denoted by *top*. Initially the symbol \$ and the initial stack contents are pushed onto the stack.

For handling the correct termination of the parsing program we use a global boolean variable *accept*. The initial value of *accept* is **false**, and the value **true** is

```
empty;
push (eof-token);
push (initial-state);
accept:= false;
scan;
repeat
    if Action[top, token.kind] = "reduce by A → X1 ... Xm"
    then reduce(A, m) else
    if Action[top, token.kind] = "shift q"
    then shift(q) else
    if Action[top, token.kind] = "accept"
    then accept:= true else
    error
until accept ;
```

**Figure 7.6** Program body for a table-driven implementation of an LR(1) parser. The actual output of grammar rules has been left out. The procedures *reduce*(**nonterminal** $A$, **length** $m$) and *shift*(**state** $q$) are shown in Figures 7.7 and 7.8, respectively

```
procedure reduce (nonterminal A, length m);
begin
    pop(m);
    push(Goto[top, A]) ;
end;
```

**Figure 7.7** Procedure *reduce* that simulates a reduce action by rule $A \to X_1 \ldots X_m$. Notice that the right-hand side of the rule is not itself needed as a parameter, only its length

```
procedure shift(state q);
begin
    push(q);
    scan;
end;
```

**Figure 7.8** Procedure *shift* that simulates a shift action of an LR(1) parser

assigned to *accept* when the topmost state of the stack is $[\$S]$ and the current scanned token is *eof-token*.

The effect of the actions of the LR(1) parser is obtained by simulation in the obvious way. To determine which action to apply next the parsing action table Action is used. If for the topmost state $q$ in the stack and for the current input symbol $a$ the action is "reduce by $A \to X_1 \ldots X_m$", then the effect of the corresponding reduce action is obtained by first popping $m$ topmost states from the stack. The state which now becomes visible in the stack is $[\gamma]$ for some viable prefix $\gamma$ such that

$$[\gamma][\gamma X_1] \ldots [\gamma X_1 \ldots X_m] \mid a \to [\gamma][\gamma A] \mid a \ ,$$

where $[\gamma X_1 \ldots X_m] = q$, is a reduce action. Thus to complete the effect the state $\text{Goto}[[\gamma], A] = [\gamma A]$ is pushed onto the stack.

If for the topmost state $q$ and the current input symbol $a$ the Action table contains the value "shift Goto$[q, a]$", the effect of the shift action

$$q \mid a \to q \ \text{Goto}[q, a] \mid$$

is obtained by pushing the state Goto$[q, a]$ onto the stack and by calling the procedure *scan*.

The simulation goes on until one of the following statements is true: (1) the topmost state of the stack is $[\$S]$ and the current input sumbol is *eof-token*; (2) no action is applicable in a situation in which the topmost state of the stack is not $[\$S]$, or the current input symbol is not *eof-token*. In case (1) the accepting configuration of the parser is reached and the parser accepts its input. In this case the stack contents must be $[\$][\$S]$, which is the final stack contents of an LR(1) parser. In case (2) an error handling procedure, *error*, is called for. A call

*error*

terminates the processing (or, preferably, performs some recovery action in order to make possible the continuation of the parsing, see Chapter 9).

As an example consider the grammar $G_{\text{block2}}$:

$$S \to \varepsilon \mid a := E \mid \textbf{begin}\ C\ \textbf{end}\ ,$$

$$C \to C;\ S \mid S\ ,$$

$$E \to E + T \mid T\ ,$$

$$T \to a \mid (E)\ .$$

In the lexical description, ':= ', 'begin', 'end', ';', '+', '(','), and '*a*' all form a token class. The names for these token classes are, respectively, *becomes, begin-token, end-token, semicolon, plus, left-par, right-par, a-token.*

The deterministic LR(0) machine for the \$-augmented grammar for $G_{\text{block2}}$ is given in Figure 7.9. We shall give the LALR(1) parser as a parsing table. First, the LALR(1) lookahead sets are given in Figure 7.10. The Action and Goto tables are given in Figure 7.11. In the Action table the rules are numbered as follows: (1) $S \to \varepsilon$, (2) $S \to a := E$, (3) $S \to$ **begin** $C$ **end**, (4) $C \to C; S$, (5) $C \to S$, (6) $E \to E + T$, (7) $E \to T$, (8) $T \to a$, (9) $T \to (E)$.

The rows in the Action table usually contain only a few different types of values. Thus it is often reasonable to encode the Action table as program statements in the following way. A row in the Action table, say corresponding to state $q$, has a list of statements the first of which is labeled by the state name. The last statement in the list is a call for the error procedure, and the other statements are constructed by the following rules. For each entry $(q, a)$ such that Action$[q, a]$ = "shift $q'$", there is a statement

**if** *token.kind* $= a$ **then** *shift*$(q')$ ,

and for all rules $A \to X_1 \ldots X_m$ of the grammar and for all terminals $a_1, \ldots, a_n$ such that

$$\text{Action}[q, a_1] = \ \ldots\ = \text{Action}[q, a_n] = \text{"reduce by } A \to X_1 \ldots X_m\text{"}\ ,$$

there is a statement

**if** *token.kind* **in** $\{a_1, \ldots, a_n\}$ **then** *reduce*$(A, m)$ .

(If $n = 1$ here, the condition "*token.kind* **in** $\{a_1, \ldots, a_n\}$" is replaced by "*token.kind* $= a_1$".)

The Goto table is needed only for the nonterminal transitions in the procedure reduce. Moreover, whenever the value Goto$[q, A]$ is determined, $[\delta A]$ is a state, that is, $\delta A$ is a viable prefix, for all $\delta$ such that $[\delta] = q$. Thus the error entries of the Goto table need never be consulted. Also, there are usually rather few different states for one nonterminal in the Goto table. This means that it is reasonable to encode the Goto table as program statements with respect to the columns, not with respect to the rows. Any column in the Goto table, say corresponding to nonterminal $A$, has a list of statements the first of which is labeled by the nonterminal name. The last statement in the list is not a call for an error procedure because the

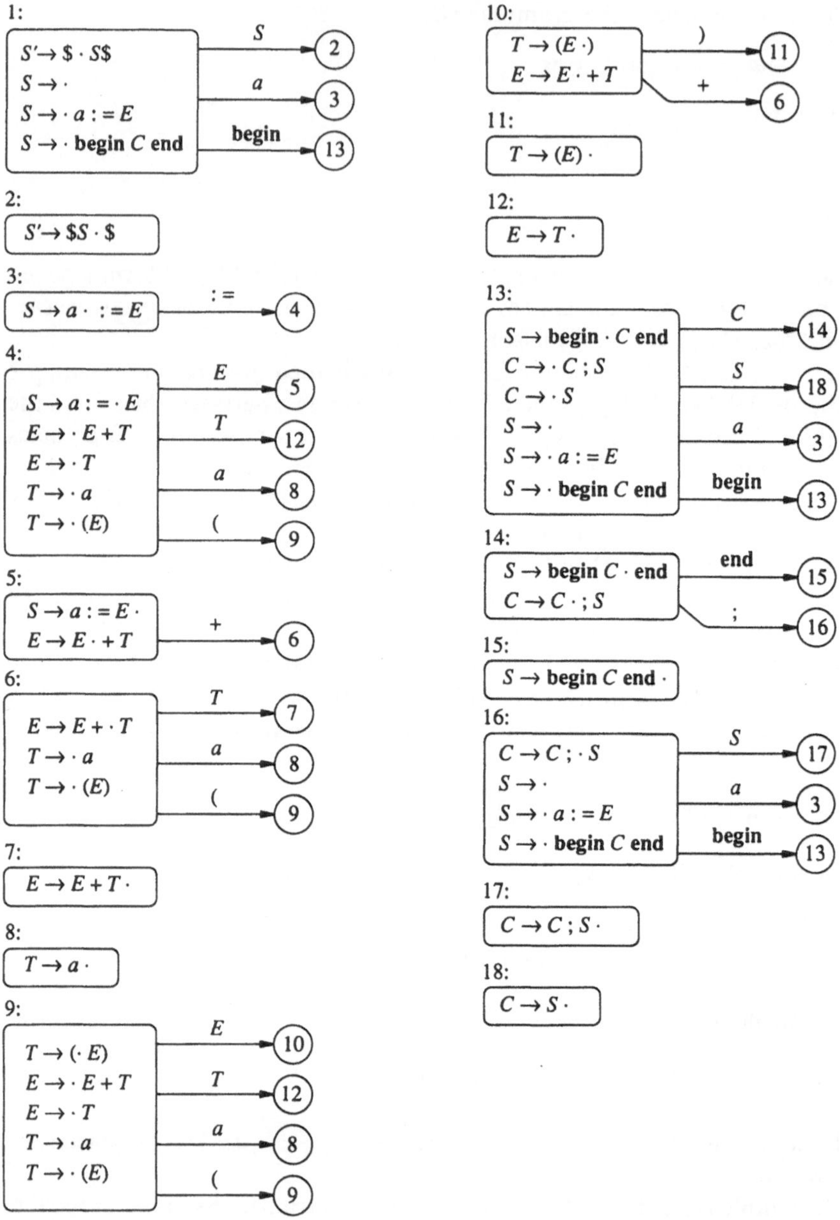


**Figure 7.9** The deterministic LR(0) machine for the \$-augmented grammar for $G_{\text{block2}}$

$\text{LALR}(q_1, S \rightarrow \varepsilon) = \{\$\}$,
$\text{LALR}(q_5, S \rightarrow a := E) = \{\$, \textbf{end}, ;\}$,
$\text{LALR}(q_7, E \rightarrow E + T) = \{\$, \textbf{end}, ;, +, )\}$,
$\text{LALR}(q_8, T \rightarrow a) = \{\$, \textbf{end}, ;, +, )\}$,
$\text{LALR}(q_{11}, T \rightarrow (E)) = \{\$, \textbf{end}, ;, +, )\}$,
$\text{LALR}(q_{12}, E \rightarrow T) = \{\$, \textbf{end}, ;, +, )\}$,
$\text{LALR}(q_{13}, S \rightarrow \varepsilon) = \{\textbf{end}, ;\}$,
$\text{LALR}(q_{15}, S \rightarrow \textbf{begin}\ C\ \textbf{end}) = \{\$, \textbf{end}, ;\}$,
$\text{LALR}(q_{16}, S \rightarrow \varepsilon) = \{\textbf{end}, ;\}$,
$\text{LALR}(q_{17}, C \rightarrow C ; S) = \{\textbf{end}, ;\}$,
$\text{LALR}(q_{18}, C \rightarrow S) = \{\textbf{end}, ;\}$

**Figure 7.10** The LALR(1) lookahead sets $\text{LALR}(q, A \rightarrow \omega)$, where $A \rightarrow \omega$ is a rule of the grammar $G_{\text{block2}}$, and $q$ is a state of the deterministic LR(0) machine for the \$-augmented grammar for $G_{\text{block2}}$

| | Action | | | | | | | | | Goto | | | |
|---|---|---|---|---|---|---|---|---|---|---|---|---|---|
| | *a* | := | **begin** | **end** | ; | + | ( | ) | \$ | *S* | *E* | *C* | *T* |
| 1 | s3 | | s13 | | | | | | *r*1 | 2 | | | |
| 2 | | | | | | | | | *a* | | | | |
| 3 | | s4 | | | | | | | | | | | |
| 4 | s8 | | | | | | s9 | | | | 5 | | 12 |
| 5 | | | | *r*2 | *r*2 | s6 | | | *r*2 | | | | |
| 6 | s8 | | | | | | s9 | | | | | | 7 |
| 7 | | | | *r*6 | *r*6 | *r*6 | | *r*6 | *r*6 | | | | |
| 8 | | | | *r*8 | *r*8 | *r*8 | | *r*8 | *r*8 | | | | |
| 9 | s8 | | | | | | s9 | | | | 10 | | 12 |
| 10 | | | | | | s6 | | s11 | | | | | |
| 11 | | | | *r*9 | *r*9 | *r*9 | | *r*9 | *r*9 | | | | |
| 12 | | | | *r*7 | *r*7 | *r*7 | | *r*7 | *r*7 | | | | |
| 13 | s3 | | s13 | *r*1 | *r*1 | | | | | 18 | | 14 | |
| 14 | | | | s15 | s16 | | | | | | | | |
| 15 | | | | *r*3 | *r*3 | | | | *r*3 | | | | |
| 16 | s3 | | s13 | *r*1 | *r*1 | | | | | 17 | | | |
| 17 | | | | *r*4 | *r*4 | | | | | | | | |
| 18 | | | | *r*5 | *r*5 | | | | | | | | |

**Figure 7.11** The LALR(1) parsing table for the grammar $G_{\text{block2}}$: (1) $S \rightarrow \varepsilon$, (2) $S \rightarrow a := E$, (3) $S \rightarrow \textbf{begin}\ C\ \textbf{end}$, (4) $C \rightarrow C ; S$, (5) $C \rightarrow S$, (6) $E \rightarrow E + T$, (7) $E \rightarrow T$, (8) $T \rightarrow a$, (9) $T \rightarrow (E)$. In the Action table, *a* denotes "accept", *ri* denotes "reduce by rule *i*", *sq* denotes "shift *q*", and "error" is denoted by blank. In the Goto table, blank for entry $(q, A)$ means that $\text{Goto}[q, A] = \varnothing$

error entries are irrelevant. Instead, the last statement is

$$push(q)\ ,$$

where $q$ is a state that appears most often in the $A$-column in question. For all other non-error entries in the $A$-column, that is, for entries $(q', A)$ such that

$\text{Goto}[q', A] = q'' \neq \emptyset$ and $q'' \neq q$, there is a statement

$$\textbf{if } \text{top} = q' \textbf{ then } push(q'') .$$

In Figures 7.12 and 7.13 the above method for implementing a deterministic LR(1) parser as a parsing program is applied to the LALR(1) parser of our example grammar $G_{\text{block2}}$. If the statements for two or more different states are the same, then the corresponding program segments can be merged, as is done in Figure 7.12. Notice that the calls for the procedure *error* have error message texts as parameters.

```
empty;
push (eof-token);
push (initial-state);
accept:= false;
scan;
repeat
    case top of begin
        1: if token.kind = a-token then
              shift (3) else
           if token.kind = begin-token then
              shift(13) else
           if token.kind = eof-token then
              reduce(S, 0) else
           error("No S can start with this");
        2: if token.kind = eof-token then
              accept:= true else
           error ("eof-token expected");
        3: if token.kind = becomes then
              shift(4) else
           error(":= expected");
    9:6:4: if token.kind = a-token then
              shift(8) else
           if token.kind = left-par then
              shift(9) else
           error("No E can start with this");
        5: if token.kind = plus then
              shift(6) else
           if token.kind in {eof-token, end-token, semicolon} then
              reduce(S, 3) else
           error("No E can be followed by this");
        7: if token.kind in {eof-token, end-token, semicolon, plus, right-par} then
              reduce(E, 3) else
           error ("No E can be followed by this");
        8: if token.kind in {eof-token, end-token, semicolon, plus, right-par} then
              reduce(T, 1) else
           error("No T can be followed by this");
       10: if token.kind = plus then
              shift(6) else
```

**Figure 7.12** Parsing program that simulates the LALR(1) parser of the grammar $G_{\text{block2}}$: $S \to \varepsilon \mid a{:=}\ E \mid \textbf{begin}\ C\ \textbf{end},\ C \to C\ ;\ S \mid S,\ E \to E + T \mid T,\ T \to a \mid (E)$

```
        if token.kind = right-par then
           shift(11) else
        error(" + or expected");
    11: if token.kind in {eof-token, end-token, semicolon, plus, right-par} then
           reduce(T, 3) else
        error("No T can be followed by this");
    12: if token.kind in {eof-token, end-token, semicolon, plus, right-par} then
           reduce(E, 1) else
        error("No E can be followed by this");
 16:13: if token.kind = a-token then
           shift(3) else
        if token.kind = begin-token then
           shift(13) else
        if token.kind in {end-token, semicolon} then
           reduce(S, 0) else
        error("No S can start with this");
    14: if token.kind = end-token then
           shift(15) else
        if token.kind = semicolon then
           shift(16) else
        error("end or ; expected");
    15: if token.kind in {eof-token, end-token, semicolon} then
           reduce(S, 3) else
        error("No S can be followed by this");
    17: if token.kind in {end-token, semicolon} then
           reduce(C, 3) else
        error("No C can be followed by this");
    18: if token.kind in {end-token, semicolon} then
           reduce(C, 1) else
        error("No C can be followed by this");
   end case;
until accept.
```

**Figure 7.12** (cont.)

```
procedure reduce (nonterminal A, length m);
begin
   pop(m);
   case A of begin
      S: if top = 1 then push(2) else
         if top = 13 then push(18) else
         push(17);
      E: if top = 4 then push(5) else
         push(10);
      C: push(14);
      T: if top = 6 then push(7) else
         push(12);
   end case;
end reduce;
```

**Figure 7.13** Procedure *reduce* in the case of the grammar $G_{\text{block2}}$; the Goto table for nonterminals is encoded as program statements

The parsing program of Figure 7.12 simulates exactly the behavior of the corresponding LALR(1) parser. In practice, however, exact simulation is not feasible because of the large size of the program. The parsing program that simulates the LR(0) parser of the same grammar is considerably smaller (and also allows some further simplifications, as we shall see shortly), because then it is not necessary to check the validity of the next input symbol when performing a reduce action. However, the LR(0) parser is usually nondeterministic for practical grammars, as is the case for our example grammar $G_{\text{block2}}$. The solution is to resort to a parser in which the next input symbol is checked in conjunction with a reduce action only if it is necessary for achieving determinism. Such a parser is deterministic, whenever the underlying grammar is LALR(1), and it shares the parsing properties of an LR(0) parser. This is stated formally in the following.

Let $G = (V, T, P, S)$ be a grammar and let $M$ be the LALR(1) parser of $G$. Let $M'$ be a pushdown transducer with stack alphabet $[G']$, where $G'$ is the \$-augmented grammar for $G$, and with initial stack contents [\$] and final stack contents [\$][\$$S$]. The set of actions of $M'$ contains all actions of $M$, but it may contain some additional reduce actions: if

$$[\delta][\delta X_1] \ldots [\delta X_1 \ldots X_m] \mid a \to [\delta][\delta A] \mid a$$

is a reduce action of $M$ by rule $A \to X_1 \ldots X_m$, then $M'$ may contain, for any $b$ in $T \cup \{\$\}$, the reduce action

$$[\delta][\delta X_1] \ldots [\delta X_1 \ldots X_m] \mid b \to [\delta][\delta A] \mid b$$

by rule $A \to X_1 \ldots X_m$. The output effect $\tau'$ of $M'$ maps all shift actions to $\varepsilon$ and all reduce action by rule $A \to X_1 \ldots X_m$ to $A \to X_1 \ldots X_m$. Any pushdown transducer $M'$ satisfying the above conditions is called an *(LR(0)-based) LR(1) parser* of grammar $G$.

**Fact 7.21** Let $G$ be a grammar, and $M_0$ and $M_1$ its LR(0) and LALR(1) parsers, respectively. Further let $M'$ be any LR(0)-based LR(1) parser of $G$. Then

$$\underset{M_1}{\Longrightarrow} \subseteq \underset{M'}{\Longrightarrow} \subseteq \underset{M_0}{\Longrightarrow} . \quad \square$$

Fact 7.21 and Theorems 6.34, 6.44, and 6.51 imply:

**Theorem 7.22** *Let G be a grammar and M′ its LR(0)-based LR(1) parser. Then M′ is a right parser of G, and*

$$\text{TIME}_{M'}(w) = \text{TIME}_G(w) + |w|$$

*for all sentences w in L(G). Moreover, if G is LR(1) and M′ is deterministic, then M′ detects an error in every nonsentence.* □

An *LR(1)-based LR(1) parser* is defined by adding reduce actions to the canonical LR(1) parser in the same way as we added reduce actions to the LALR(1) parser in defining an LR(0)-based LR(1) parser. It is easy to see that also any LR(1)-based LR(1) parser $M''$ of $G$ is a right parser of $G$ and $\mathrm{TIME}_{M''}(w) = \mathrm{TIME}_G(w) + |w|$ for all sentences $w$ in $L(G)$. Moreover, $M''$ detects an error in every nonsentence, whenever $G$ is LR(1) and $M''$ is deterministic.

The following fact is immediate from the definition of an LR(0)-based LR(1) parser.

**Fact 7.23** For any LALR(1) grammar $G$ there is a deterministic LR(0)-based LR(1) parser $M$ such that if $M$ has a reduce action

$$\phi q \mid a \rightarrow \phi' \mid a \ ,$$

then, for all $b$ in $T \cup \{\$\}$, $M$ has a rule the left-hand side of which is of the form $\psi q \mid b$. That is, $M$ has either a shift action

$$q \mid b \rightarrow qq' \mid \ ,$$

or a reduce action of the form

$$\psi q \mid b \rightarrow \psi' \mid b \ .$$

$M$ is called an *(LR(0)-based) LR(1) parser using default reductions* of grammar $G$. □

Fact 7.23 together with Theorem 7.22 imply that we obtain a correct right parser if the parsing program scheme for implementing LALR(1) or SLR(1) parsers is modified as follows (notice that the SLR(1) parser of grammar $G$ is an LR(0)-based LR(1) parser of $G$; see the exercises). In any state involving reduce actions, one reduce action is chosen as a *default reduce action* (or *default reduction*) which is performed in case no other action can be applied. The default reduction then replaces the call for the error procedure. The error detection is, of course, delayed by the use of default reductions but notice that, by Fact 7.21, the resulting parsing program has the error detection capability of the LR(0) parser, at least. This implementation method is called the *parsing program for an LR(1) parser using default reductions.*

As an example, we give in Figure 7.14 the parsing program for the (uniquely defined) LR(1) parser using default reductions of our example grammar $G_{\mathrm{block2}}$.

An LR(1) parser often contains states at which a reduce action is the only possible non-error action. Such a state is called a *unique reduce state.* In the parsing program for an LR(1) parser using default reductions a unique reduce state $q$ corresponds to a program segment of the form

$q$: *reduce*$(A, m)$ ;

This means, because no checking of symbols is made at a unique reduce state, that the unique reduce action could be combined with the previous action. This implies that the unique reduce states become inaccessible and can thus be deleted altogether.

```
empty;
push(eof-token);
push(initial-state);
accept := false;
scan;
repeat
      case top of begin
  16:13:1: if token.kind = a-token then
                 shift(3) else
            if token.kind = begin-token then
                 shift(13) else
            reduce(S, 0);
         2: if token.kind = eof-token then
                 accept := true else
            error("eof-token expected");
         3: if token.kind = becomes then
                 shift(4) else
            error(":= expected");
    9:6:4: if token.kind = a-token then
                 shift(8) else
            if token.kind = left-par then
                 shift(9) else
            error("No E can start with this");
         5: if token.kind = plus then
                 shift(6) else
            reduce(S, 3) ;
         7: reduce(E, 3);
         8: reduce(T, 1);
        10: if token.kind = plus then
                 shift(6) else
            if token.kind = right-par then
                 shift(11) else
            error(" + or ) expected");
        11: reduce(T, 3);
        12: reduce(E, 1);
        14: if token.kind = end-token then
                 shift(15) else
            if token.kind = semicolon then
                 shift(16) else
            error ("end or ; expected");
        15: reduce(S, 3);
        17: reduce(C, 3);
        18: reduce(C, 1);
      end case;
until accept.
```

**Figure 7.14** Parsing program for the LR(1) parser using default reductions of the grammar $G_{\text{block2}}$: $S \to \varepsilon | a := E |$ **begin** $C$ **end**, $C \to C ; S | S$, $E \to E + T | T$, $T \to a | (E)$

When entering a unique reduce state the preceding action may be a shift action or a reduce action. If the preceding action is a shift action,

$$shift(q) \;,$$

where $q$ is a unique reduce state, then this action may be replaced by the action

$$shiftreduce(A, m - 1)\ ,$$

where $A$ and $m$ are the parameters for the procedure *reduce* at state $q$. The effect of a call *shiftreduce*$(A, m - 1)$ is the same as the effect of a call *reduce*$(A, m)$, except that a call *shiftreduce*$(A, m - 1)$ also causes the scanning of the next input symbol. The procedure shiftreduce in the case of our example grammar is given in Figure 7.16.

If a unique reduce state $q$ is entered by a reduce action, then this happens by the operation *push*($q$)

```
empty;
push(eof-token);
push(initial-state);
accept := false;
scan;
repeat
    case top of begin
  16:13:1: if token.kind = a-token then
                 shift(3) else
           if token.kind = begin-token then
                 shift(13) else
           reduce(S, 0);
         2: if token.kind = eof-token then
                 accept := true else
           error("eof-token expected");
         3: if token.kind = becomes then
                 shift(4) else
           error(":= expected");
   9:6:4: if token.kind = a-token then
                 shiftreduce(T, 0) else
           if token.kind = left-par then
                 shift(9) else
           error("No E can start with this");
       5: if token.kind = plus then
                 shift(6) else
           reduce(S, 3);
      10: if token.kind = plus then
                 shift(6) else
           if token.kind = right-par then
                 shiftreduce(T, 2) else
           error(" + or ) expected");
      14: if token.kind = end-token then
                 shiftreduce(S, 2) else
           if token.kind = semicolon then
                 shift(16) else
           error("end or ; expected");
    end case;
until accept.
```

**Figure 7.15** Parsing program for the LR(1) parser using default reductions of the grammar $G_{block2}$, when the unique reduce states have been eliminated

in the procedure *reduce* (or *shiftreduce*). This operation may simply be replaced by the call

$$reduce(A, m-1) \ ,$$

where $A$ and $m$ are the parameters for the procedure reduce at state $q$.

When the above modifications have been made for all *shift*($q$) and *push*($q$), where $q$ is a unique reduce state, we can delete from the parsing program all program segments labeled by a unique reduce state. We give the result in the case of our example parser in Figures 7.15 to 7.17.

The above method for eliminating unique reduce states may make the procedure *reduce* recursive, as for example the procedure given in Figure 7.17. The recursion may, of course, be eliminated by replacing a recursive call by statements that pop an appropriate number of states from the stack, assign an appropriate value to the variable $A$, and pass the control back to the beginning of the **case**-statement.

In the table-driven implementation of an LR(1) parser using default reductions the unique reduce states are eliminated as follows: whenever an entry ($q$, $X$) in the

```
procedure shiftreduce (nonterminal A, length m) ;
begin
    scan;
    pop(m);
    case A of begin
        S: if top = 1 then push(2) else
           if top = 13 then reduce(C, 0) else
           reduce(C, 2);
        T: if top = 6 then reduce(E, 2) else
           reduce(E, 0);
    end case;
end shiftreduce;
```

**Figure 7.16** Procedure *shiftreduce* for the parsing program given in Figure 7.15

```
procedure reduce (nonterminal A, length m) ;
begin
    pop(m);
    case A of begin
        S: if top = 1 then push(2) else
           if top = 13 then reduce(C, 0) else
           reduce(C, 2);
        E: if top = 4 then push(5) else
           push(10);
        C: push(14);
        T: if top = 6 then reduce(E, 2) else
           reduce(E, 0);
    end case;
end reduce;
```

**Figure 7.17** Procedure *reduce* for the parsing program given in Figure 7.15

Action or Goto table entails entering a unique reduce state, then an indication of this reduction is added to the entry $(q, X)$. The details of this mode of implementation are left as exercises.

## 7.5 Optimization of LR(1) Parsers

In this section we shall consider the optimization of deterministic LR(1) parsers. Our main concern are the LR(0)-based LR(1) parsers, SLR(1) and LALR(1) parsers. The LR(0)-based LR(1) parsers form a class of LR(1) parsers of great practical importance and are thus worthy of further optimization. Our results, however, apply also to canonical LR(1) parsers and their variations. We shall present methods for reducing the number of states of the parser, and we shall also investigate ways to speed up the parser.

The effect of speeding up the parser is achieved by eliminating reduce actions by semantically insignificant unit rules of the form $A \to B$, where $B$ is a nonterminal of the grammar. "Semantically insignificant" means that no reduce action by rule $A \to B$ causes any semantic action in the compilation process. That is, if we leave out the reductions by semantically insignificant unit rules, we still produce enough information for further compilation. More specifically, we are able to construct for the sentence to be parsed an *abstract syntax tree*, which contains the essential information on the structure of the sentence with respect to the grammar. It should be noted, however, that the elimination of reduce actions by unit rules produces a parser which is not, according to a strict interpretation of the definition, a right parser of the underlying grammar.

As an illustration of the usefulness of the elimination of reductions by unit rules consider the usual rudimentary grammar $G_{exp}$ for arithmetic expressions:

$$E \to E + T \mid T \ ,$$

$$T \to T * F \mid F \ ,$$

$$F \to a \mid (E) \ .$$

A normal parser produces for the sentence $a + a$ the derivation tree given in Figure 7.18. Clearly, the reductions by rules $E \to T$ and $T \to F$ are unimportant for further considerations. A parser that leaves out the reductions by $E \to T$ and $T \to F$ produces for $a + a$ the tree structure shown in Figure 7.19.

### *Inessential error entries*

An important observation in reducing the number of states and in eliminating reduce actions by unit rules is that some *error entries* in the parsing table, namely, pairs $(q, X)$ such that Action$[q, X]$ = "error" or Goto$[q, X] = \varnothing$, are never consulted. The Goto table is needed only for nonterminals and clearly no error entries for nonterminals can be consulted. The case of the Action table

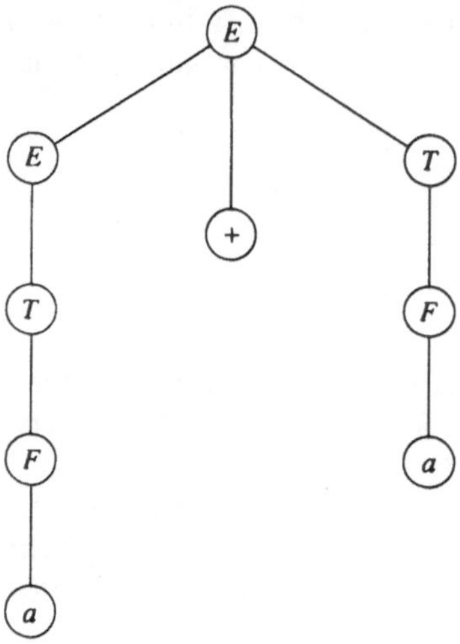


**Figure 7.18** Derivation tree for sentence $a + a$ in the grammar $G_{exp}$: $E \to E + T|T$, $T \to T * F|F$, $F \to a|(E)$

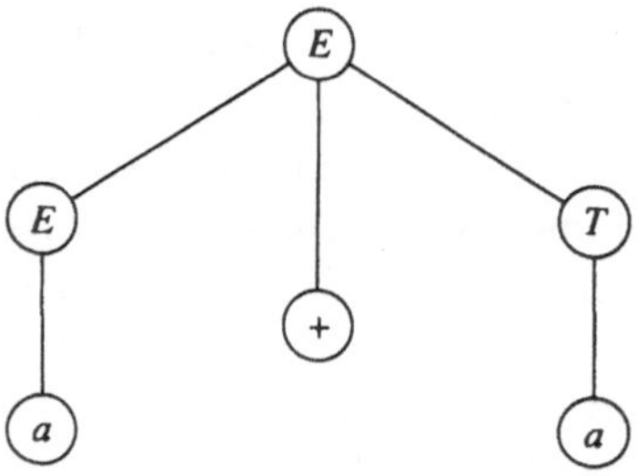


**Figure 7.19.** Tree structure for sentence $a + a$ corresponding to the derivation tree of Figure 7.18, when the parser leaves out the reductions by rules $E \to T$ and $T \to F$

is more subtle, but indeed there might exist a state $q$ and terminal $a$ such that Action$[q, a]$ = "error" but such that no configuration $\$\phi q \mid aw$ is accessible from any initial configuration. We demonstrate this by the LR(1) parsing of the grammar

$$S \to ab|Ac \ ,$$

$$A \to a \ .$$

The deterministic LR(0) machine for the corresponding \$-augmented grammar is given in Figure 7.20. For any deterministic LR(0)-based LR(1) parser of this grammar, Action$[[\$A], b]$ = "error", but no configuration $\$[\$][\$A] \mid bw$ is accessible. The reason for this is that a configuration

$$\$[\$][\$A] \mid y\$$$

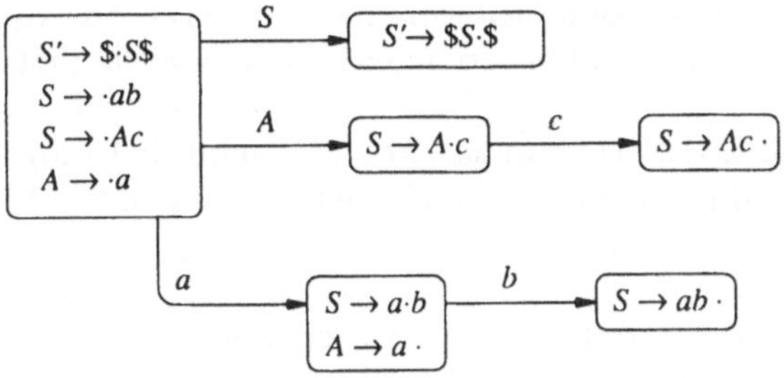


**Figure 7.20** The deterministic LR(0) machine for the grammar $S' \to \$S\$$, $S \to ab|Ac$, $A \to a$. At the state $[\$A]$ the next input symbol cannot be $b$, and thus the error entry $([\$A], b)$ is never consulted

is accessed only after a reduce action by rule $A \to a$, that is, when the stack contents are $[\$][\$a]$. But for any configuration $\$[\$][\$a] \mid bw$ and for any LR(0)-based LR(1) parser $M$,

$$\$[\$][\$a] \mid bw \underset{M}{\Longrightarrow} \$[\$][\$a][\$ab] \mid w \ .$$

Thus $\$[\$][\$A] \mid bw$ is never accessed.

Let $G = (V, T, P, S)$ be a reduced LR(1) grammar and $M$ a deterministic LR(1) parser of $G$. Further, let Action be the parsing action table corresponding to $M$. For state $q$ and terminal $a$ such that Action$[q, a]$ = "error", we define the entry $(q, a)$ to be an *essential error entry*, if

$$\$[\$] \mid w\$ \underset{M}{\Longrightarrow}{}^{*} \$\phi q \mid y\$, \quad 1{:}y\$ = a \ ,$$

for some $w$ and $y$ in $T^*$ and stack string $\phi$. Otherwise the error entry $(q, a)$ is *inessential* (or *don't care*).

Some basic conclusions from the above definitions are in order. First:

**Fact 7.24** For state $q = [\gamma b]$, where $\gamma b$ is a viable prefix ending with a terminal, all error entries $(q, a)$, $a \in T \cup \{\$\}$, are essential (in a reduced grammar). □

Fact 7.24 implies further:

**Fact 7.25** Let $q = [\delta A]$ for some viable prefix $\delta A$ ending with a nonterminal and let $a$ be a terminal in $T \cup \{\$\}$ such that $(q, a)$ is an error entry. The error entry $(q, a)$ is essential if and only if

$$\$\phi' q' \mid ay \underset{M}{\Longrightarrow}{}^{*} \$\phi q \mid ay \ ,$$

where $q' = [\gamma b]$ for some terminal $b$ in $T \cup \{\$\}$, and the configuration $\$\phi' q' \mid ay$ is accessible from some initial configuration. □

In the following we shall show how the inessential error entries of the parsing action table for a deterministic LR(0)-based LR(1) parser can be determined.

(Recall that an (LR(0)-based) LR(1) parser is obtained from the LALR(1) parser of the grammar by adding new lookahead symbols to reduce actions such that conflicts do not arise.)

Let $G = (V, T, P, S)$ be a reduced LALR(1) grammar, $M$ a deterministic LR(0)-based LR(1) parser of $G$, and Action the parsing action table corresponding to $M$. We shall define relations on the set of pairs of the forms $(q, A \rightarrow \alpha \cdot \beta)$, $(q, \cdot B)$, and $(q, B \cdot)$, where $q$ is a state of $M$, $[A \rightarrow \alpha \cdot \beta]$ a 0-item of $G$, and $B \in V \backslash T$. For pair $(q, A \rightarrow \alpha \cdot \beta)$, the set VALID($\gamma$), where $[\gamma] = q$, always contains the item $[A \rightarrow \cdot \alpha\beta]$, and for pairs $(q, \cdot B)$ and $(q, B \cdot)$, VALID($\gamma$) always contains some item of the form $[A \rightarrow \alpha \cdot B\beta]$.

We shall first define some relations which may be used to derive a sufficient condition for an error entry to be essential. This condition is also a good approximation to a necessary condition for practical grammars. Later on we shall sharpen the condition and give an exact characterization of essential error entries.

Let **symbol-in**, **points**, **expands**, and **entered-by** be relations defined by:

$$(\text{Goto}[q, \alpha], B \cdot) \ \textbf{symbol-in} \ (q, A \rightarrow \alpha B \cdot \beta) \ ;$$

$$(q, A \rightarrow \alpha \cdot B\beta) \ \textbf{points} \ (\text{Goto}[q, \alpha], \cdot B) \ ;$$

$$(q, \cdot B) \ \textbf{expands} \ (q, B \rightarrow \cdot \omega) \ ;$$

$$(q, A \rightarrow \alpha X \cdot \beta) \ \textbf{entered-by} \ X \ ,$$

where $X \in V$. These relations are illustrated in Figure 7.21.

**Fact 7.26** The relations **symbol-in**, **points**, **expands**, and **entered-by** are of size $O(|G| \cdot n)$ and can be computed from $G$ and $M$ in time $O(|G| \cdot n)$, where $n$ is the number of states in $M$. □

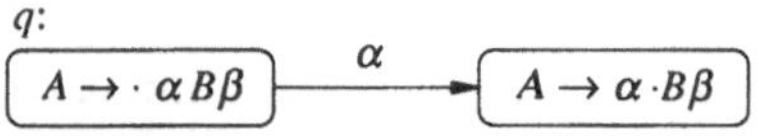


(a) (Goto[$q$, $\alpha$], $B \cdot$) **symbol-in** ($q, A \rightarrow \alpha B \cdot \beta$),
($q, A \rightarrow \alpha \cdot B\beta$) **points** (Goto[$q$, $\alpha$], $\cdot B$).

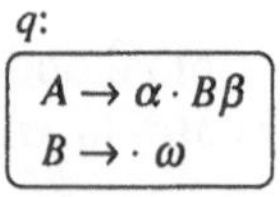


(b) ($q$, $\cdot B$) **expands** ($q, B \rightarrow \cdot \omega$).

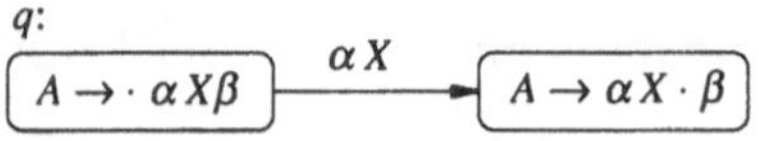


(c) ($q, A \rightarrow \alpha X \cdot \beta$) **entered-by** $X$.

**Figure 7.21** Illustration of the relations **symbol-in**, **points**, **expands** and **entered-by**

Then let $a$ be a terminal in $T \cup \{\$\}$ and let **on-$a$-reduces-to, directly-on-$a$-passes-null**, and **error-entry-on-$a$** be relations defined by:

$(q, B \rightarrow \omega\cdot)$ **on-$a$-reduces-to** $(q, B\cdot)$,
whenever Action[Goto[$q$, $\omega$], $a$] = "reduce by $B \rightarrow \omega$" ;

$(q, A \rightarrow \alpha\cdot B\beta)$ **directly-on-$a$-passes-null** $(q, A \rightarrow \alpha B\cdot\beta)$,
whenever Action[Goto[$q$, $\alpha$], $a$] = "reduce by $B \rightarrow \varepsilon$" ;

$(q, A \rightarrow \alpha\cdot\beta)$ **error-entry-on-$a$** (Goto[$q$, $\alpha$], $a$),
whenever Action[Goto[$q$, $\alpha$], $a$] = "error" .

**Fact 7.27** For any terminal $a \in TU\{\$\}$, the relations **on-$a$-reduces-to, directly-on-$a$-passes-null**, and **error-entry-on-$a$** are of size $O(|G|\cdot n)$ and can be computed from $G$ and $M$ in time $O(|G|\cdot n)$, where $n$ is the number of states in $M$. □

Consider then the relational expression

**directly-descends = points expands** ,

and, for terminal $a \in T \cup \{\$\}$, the relational expressions

**may-on-$a$-access = (on-$a$-reduces-to symbol-in $\cup$ directly-descends* · directly-on-$a$-passes-null)*** ,

**may-imply-$a$-essential = terminal entered-by$^{-1}$ · may-on-$a$-access error-entry-on-$a$** .

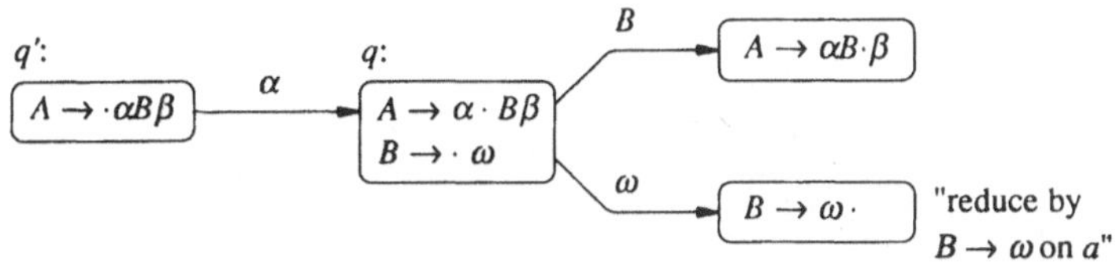


(a) $(q, B \rightarrow \omega\cdot)$ **on-$a$-reduces-to symbol-in** $(q', A \rightarrow \alpha B\cdot\beta)$.

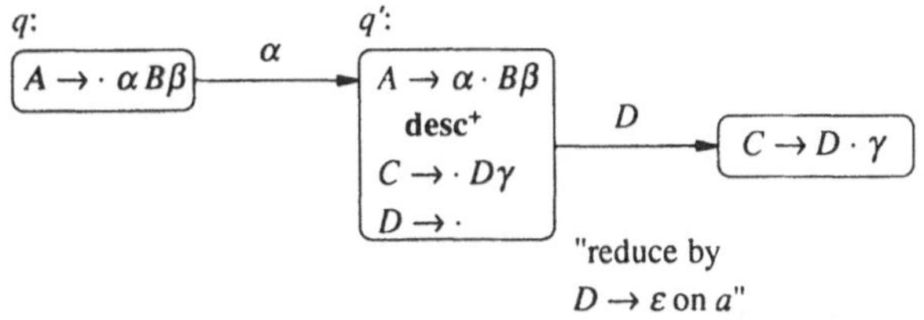


(b) $(q, A \rightarrow \alpha\cdot B\beta)$ **directly-descends$^+$ · directly-on-$a$-passes-null** $(q', C \rightarrow D\cdot\gamma)$.

**Figure 7.22** Illustration of the relational expressions **on-$a$-reduces-to symbol-in** and **directly-descends$^+$ · directly-on-$a$-passes-null**

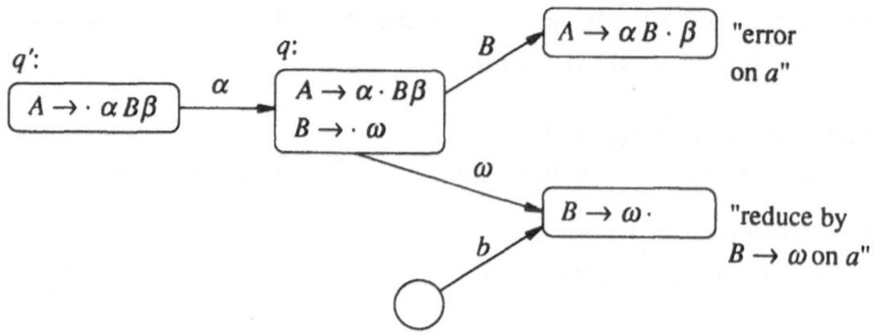


**Figure 7.23** $b$ **terminal entered-by**$^{-1}$ $(q, B \to \omega\cdot)$ **on-$a$-reduces-to symbol-in** $(q', A \to \alpha B \cdot \beta)$ **error-entry-on-$a$** (Goto$[q', \alpha B]$, $a$), that is,

$b$ **may-imply-$a$-essential** (Goto$[q', \alpha B]$, $a$)

The relational expressions **on-$a$-reduces-to symbol-in** and **directly-descends* directly-on-$a$-passes-null**, which are the essential elements in **may-on-$a$-access**, are illustrated in Figure 7.22. The relational expression **may-imply-$a$-essential** is illustrated in Figure 7.23.

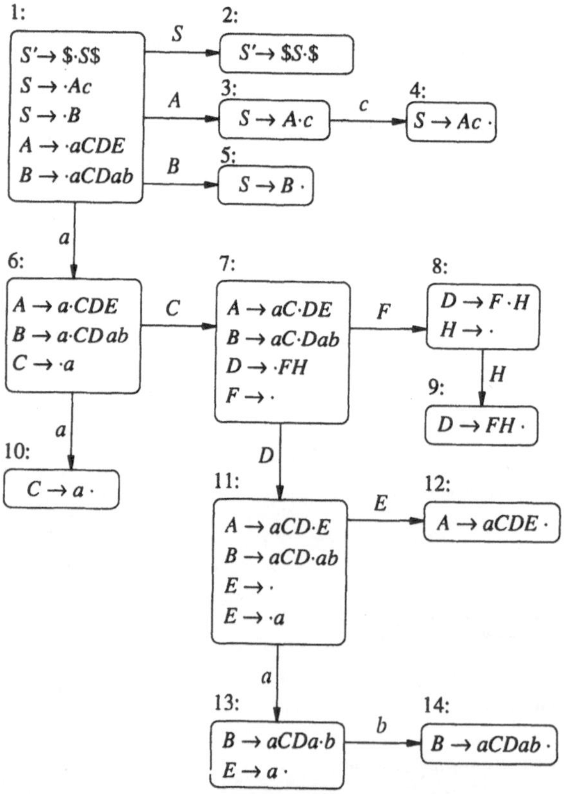


**Figure 7.24** The deterministic LR(0) machine for the grammar $S' \to \$S\$$, $S \to Ac|B$, $A \to aCDE$, $B \to aCDab$, $C \to a$, $D \to FH$, $E \to \varepsilon|a$, $F \to \varepsilon$, $H \to \varepsilon$

We shall show that whenever $(q, a)$ is an essential error entry, then

$$b \textbf{ may-imply-}a\textbf{-essential } (q, a)$$

for some $b \in T \cup \{\$\}$. Before going into details of the proof of this statement we give some examples that illustrate its correctness, and also in some sense the quality of this condition as an approximation of an exact characterization of essential error entries.

We shall consider an LR(0)-based LR(1) parser of the LALR(1) grammar

$$\begin{array}{ll} S \to Ac \mid B, & D \to FH\ , \\ A \to aCDE, & E \to \varepsilon \mid a\ , \\ B \to aCDab, & F \to \varepsilon\ , \\ C \to a, & H \to \varepsilon\ . \end{array}$$

The deterministic LR(0) machine for the corresponding \$-augmented grammar is given in Figure 7.24. The parsing table for the LR(1) parser using default reductions is given in Figure 7.25.

Let us then consider the error entry $(q_3, b)$ in Figure 7.25. At first one might think that $(q_3, b)$ is an inessential error entry because Action$[q_{13}, b]$ = "shift $q_{14}$" and thus after reducing at the state $q_{13}$ by $E \to a$ the symbol $b$ is no longer possible as the next input symbol at the state $q_{12}$. Because the state $q_3$ can be accessed only via the reduction by the rule $A \to aCDE$ at the state $q_{12}$, we might be tempted to conclude that $b$ is impossible as the next input symbol at the state $q_3$, too. However,

| | Action | | | | Goto | | | | | | | |
|---|---|---|---|---|---|---|---|---|---|---|---|---|
| | $a$ | $b$ | $c$ | \$ | $S$ | $A$ | $B$ | $C$ | $D$ | $E$ | $F$ | $H$ |
| 1 | s6 | | | | 2 | 3 | 5 | | | | | |
| 2 | | | | $a$ | | | | | | | | |
| 3 | | | s4 | | | | | | | | | |
| 4 | r1 | r1 | r1 | r1 | | | | | | | | |
| 5 | r2 | r2 | r2 | r2 | | | | | | | | |
| 6 | s10 | | | | | | | 7 | | | | |
| 7 | r9 | r9 | r9 | r9 | | | | | 11 | | 8 | |
| 8 | r10 | r10 | r10 | r10 | | | | | | | | 9 |
| 9 | r6 | r6 | r6 | r6 | | | | | | | | |
| 10 | r5 | r5 | r5 | r5 | | | | | | | | |
| 11 | s13 | r7 | r7 | r7 | | | | | | 12 | | |
| 12 | r3 | r3 | r3 | r3 | | | | | | | | |
| 13 | r8 | s14 | r8 | r8 | | | | | | | | |
| 14 | r4 | r4 | r4 | r4 | | | | | | | | |

**Figure 7.25** The parsing table for the LR(1) parser using default reductions of the grammar (1) $S \to Ac$, (2) $S \to B$, (3) $A \to aCDE$, (4) $B \to aCDab$, (5) $C \to a$, (6) $D \to FH$, (7) $E \to \varepsilon$, (8) $E \to a$, (9) $F \to \varepsilon$, (10) $H \to \varepsilon$

$$
\begin{aligned}
\$q_1q_6q_{10} \mid b &\Rightarrow \$q_1q_6q_7 \mid b \\
&\Rightarrow \$q_1q_6q_7q_8 \mid b \\
&\Rightarrow \$q_1q_6q_7q_8q_9 \mid b \\
&\Rightarrow \$q_1q_6q_7q_{11} \mid b \\
&\Rightarrow \$q_1q_6q_7q_{11}q_{12} \mid b \\
&\Rightarrow \$q_1q_3 \mid b \ .
\end{aligned}
$$

Thus by Fact 7.25 the error entry $(q_3, b)$ is essential. Also

$a$ **may-imply-$b$-essential** $(q_3, b)$ ,

because

$a$ **terminal entered-by**$^{-1}$ $(q_6, C \to a\cdot)$
**on-$b$-reduces-to symbol-in** $(q_1, A \to aC\cdot DE)$
**directly-descends* directly-on-$b$-passes-null**
$(q_7, D \to F\cdot H)$ **directly-on-$b$-passes-null**
$(q_7, D \to FH\cdot)$ **on-$b$-reduces-to symbol-in**
$(q_1, A \to aCD\cdot E)$ **directly-on-$b$-passes-null**
$(q_1, A \to aCDE\cdot)$ **on-$b$-reduces-to symbol-in**
$(q_1, S \to A\cdot c)$ **error-entry-on-$b$** $(q_3, b)$ ,

Informally, first notice that at the state $q_7$ the terminal $b$ can be the next input symbol. Then the possibility to reduce the empty string $\varepsilon$ to $DE$ implies that $b$ can also be the next input symbol at the state $q_{12}$. Thus the reduction by $A \to aCDE$ makes it possible that $b$ can be the next input symbol at the state $q_3$.

Consider then a slight modification of the above example grammar:

$$
\begin{aligned}
&S \to Ac \mid B, && D \to FH \mid Fb \ , \\
&A \to aCDE, && E \to \varepsilon \mid a \ , \\
&B \to aCDab, && F \to \varepsilon \ , \\
&C \to a, && H \to \varepsilon \ .
\end{aligned}
$$

The deterministic LR(0) machine for the corresponding \$-augmented grammar is given in Figure 7.26. Notice that in the parsing table for the LR(1) parser using default reductions of this grammar the error entry $(q_3, b)$ is indeed inessential. For example,

$a$ **terminal entered-by**$^{-1}$ $(q_6, C \to a\cdot)$
**on-$b$-reduces-to symbol-in** $(q_1, A \to aC\cdot DE)$
**directly-descends* directly-on-$b$-passes-null**
$(q_7, D \to F\cdot H)$ ,

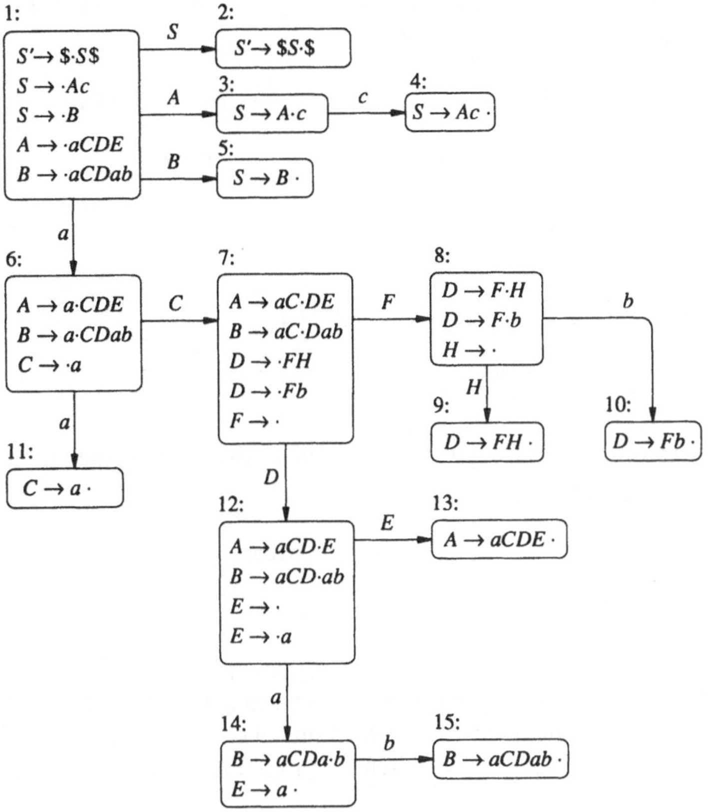


**Figure 7.26** The deterministic LR(0) machine for the grammar $S' \to \$S\$$, $S \to Ac|B$, $A \to aCDE$, $B \to aCDab$, $C \to a$, $D \to FH|Fb$, $E \to \varepsilon|a$, $F \to \varepsilon$, $H \to \varepsilon$

but $(q_7, D \to F \cdot H)$ **directly-on-$b$-passes-null** $(q_7, D \to FH \cdot)$ does not hold any more because Action$[q_8, b]$ = "shift $q_{10}$".

**Lemma 7.28** *Let $n \geqslant 0$ and*

$$\$[X_1][X_1X_2]\ldots[X_1\ldots X_m]\,|\,a \underset{M}{\Longrightarrow}^n$$

$$\$[Y_1][Y_1Y_2]\ldots[Y_1\ldots Y_p]\,|\,a\ .$$

*Then for all* $[B \to Y_{j+1}\ldots Y_p \cdot \beta] \in \mathrm{VALID}(Y_1\ldots Y_p), j < p$, *there is an item* $[A \to X_{i+1}\ldots X_m \cdot \alpha] \in \mathrm{VALID}(X_1\ldots X_m)$ *such that*

$$([X_1\ldots X_i], A \to X_{i+1}\ldots X_m \cdot \alpha)\ \textbf{may-on-}a\textbf{-access}$$

$$([Y_1\ldots Y_j], B \to Y_{j+1}\ldots Y_p \cdot \beta).$$

*Proof.* We prove the lemma by induction on $n$. For $n = 0$ the lemma holds immediately. If $n > 0$, then either

$$\$[X_1]\ldots[X_1\ldots X_m]\,|\,a \underset{M}{\Longrightarrow}^{n-1} \$[Y_1]\ldots[Y_1\ldots Y_{p-1}]\,|\,a$$

$$\underset{M}{\Longrightarrow} \$[Y_1]\ldots[Y_1\ldots Y_p]\,|\,a\ ,$$

or for $l \geqslant 1$

$$\$[X_1]\ldots[X_1\ldots X_m]\,|\,a$$

$$\underset{M}{\Longrightarrow}^{n-1} \$[Y_1]\ldots[Y_1\ldots Y_{p-1}Z_1\ldots Z_l]\,|\,a$$

$$\underset{M}{\Longrightarrow} \$[Y_1]\ldots[Y_1\ldots Y_p]\,|\,a\ .$$

In the former case the induction hypothesis implies that for some item $[A \to X_{i+1}\ldots X_m \cdot \alpha] \in \text{VALID}(X_1\ldots X_m)$,

$([X_1\ldots X_i], A \to X_{i+1}\ldots X_m \cdot \alpha)$ **may-on-*a*-access**

$([Y_1\ldots Y_k], C \to Y_{k+1}\ldots Y_{p-1} \cdot \gamma)$,

for all $[C \to Y_{k+1}\ldots Y_{p-1} \cdot \gamma] \in \text{VALID}(Y_1\ \ldots Y_{p-1})$, $k < (p-1)$. Further because in this case Action$[[Y_1\ldots Y_{p-1}], a] = Y_p \to \varepsilon$ and thus the item $[Y_p \to \cdot]$ is in VALID($Y_1\ldots Y_{p-1}$), we conclude by the definitions of **directly-descends** and **directly-on-*a*-passes-null** that for any item $[B + Y_{j+1}\ldots Y_p \cdot \beta]$ in VALID($Y_1\ldots Y_p$), $j < p$, there is an item $[C \to Y_{k+1}\ldots Y_{p-1} \cdot \gamma]$ such that

$([Y_1\ldots Y_k], C \to Y_{k+1}\ldots Y_{p-1} \cdot \gamma)$

**directly-descends* directly-on-*a*-passes-null**

$([Y_1\ldots Y_j], B \to Y_{j+1}\ldots Y_p \cdot \beta)$ .

Thus in this case we obtain the desired result.

In the latter case the induction hypothesis implies that for some item $[A \to X_{i+1}\ldots X_m \cdot \alpha] \in \text{VALID}(X_1\ldots X_m)$,

$([X_1\ldots X_i], A \to X_{i+1}\ldots X_m \cdot \alpha)$ **may-on-*a*-access**

$([\beta], B \to \gamma \cdot \delta)$,

for all $[\beta]$ and $[B \to \gamma \cdot \delta]$ such that $\beta\gamma = Y_1\ldots Y_{p-1}Z_1\ldots Z_l$, $|\gamma| \geqslant 1$, and $[B \to \gamma \cdot \delta] \in \text{VALID}(\beta\gamma)$. Because in this case Action$[[Y_1\ldots Y_{p-1}Z_1\ldots Z_l], a] = Y_p \to Z_1\ldots Z_l$ and thus the item $[Y_p \to Z_1\ldots Z_l \cdot]$ is in VALID($Y_1\ldots Y_{p-1}Z_1\ldots Z_l$), we conclude in particular that

$([X_1\ldots X_i],\ A \to X_{i+1}\ldots X_m \cdot \alpha)$ **may-on-*a*-access**

$([Y_1\ldots Y_{p-1}], Y_p \to Z_1\ldots Z_l \cdot)$ .

Further, by the definitions of **on-$a$-reduces-to** and **symbol-in**

$$([Y_1 \ldots Y_{p-1}], Y_p \rightarrow Z_1 \ldots Z_l \cdot)$$

**on-$a$-reduces-to symbol-in**

$$([Y_1 \ldots Y_j], B \rightarrow Y_{j+1} \ldots Y_p \cdot \beta)$$

for all $[B \rightarrow Y_{j+1} \ldots Y_p \cdot \beta] \in \text{VALID}(Y_1 \ldots Y_p), j < p$. □

Lemma 7.28 and Fact 7.25 imply:

**Lemma 7.29** *If an error entry* $(q, a)$ *is essential, then*

$b$ **may-imply-$a$-essential** $(q, a)$

*for some* $b \in T \cup \{\$\}$. □

The fact that the converse of Lemma 7.29 does not hold true is shown by the following example. Consider the LALR(1) grammar

$$S \rightarrow bABb \mid bba \mid cAB \ ,$$

$$A \rightarrow b \ ,$$

$$B \rightarrow CD \ ,$$

$$C \rightarrow \varepsilon \ ,$$

$$D \rightarrow E \ ,$$

$$E \rightarrow \varepsilon \ .$$

The deterministic LR(0) machine for the corresponding \$-augmented grammar is given in Figure 7.27. The parsing table for the LR(0)-based LR(1) parser using default reductions of this grammar is given in Figure 7.28. With respect to this parser we have:

$b$ **terminal entered-by**$^{-1}$ $(q_{12}, A \rightarrow b \cdot)$

**on-$a$-reduces-to symbol-in** $(q_1, S \rightarrow cA \cdot B)$

**directly-descends** $(q_{13}, B \rightarrow \cdot CD)$

**directly-on-$a$-passes-null** $(q_{13}, B \rightarrow C \cdot D)$

**directly-descends** $(q_9, D \rightarrow \cdot E)$

**directly-on-$a$-passes-null** $(q_9, D \rightarrow E \cdot)$

**on-$a$-reduces-to symbol-in** $(q_6, B \rightarrow CD \cdot)$

**on-$a$-reduces-to symbol-in** $(q_1, S \rightarrow bAB \cdot b)$

**error-entry-on-$a$** $(q_7, a)$ .

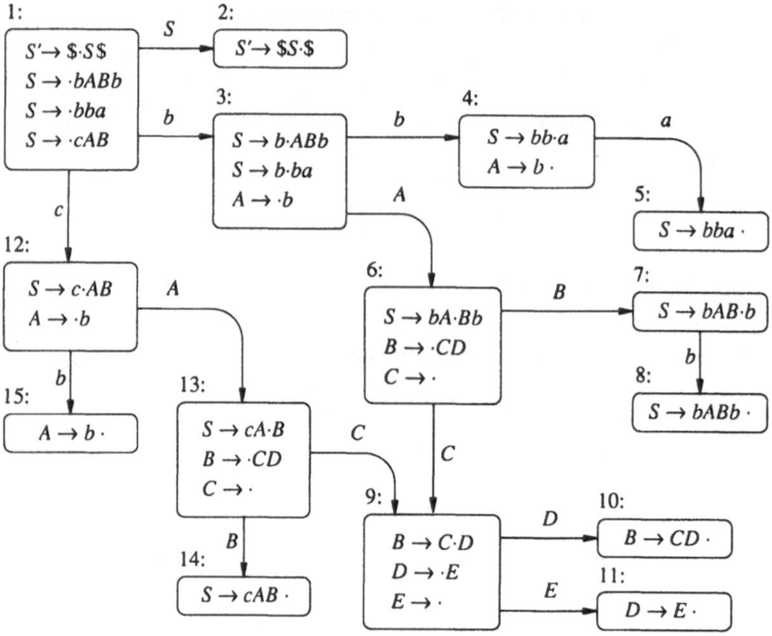


**Figure 7.27** The deterministic LR(0) machine for the grammar $S' \to \$S\$$, $S \to bABb|bba|cAB$, $A \to b$, $B \to CD$, $C \to \varepsilon$, $D \to E$, $E \to \varepsilon$

| | Action | | | | Goto | | | | | |
|---|---|---|---|---|---|---|---|---|---|---|
| | *a* | *b* | *c* | $ | *S* | *A* | *B* | *C* | *D* | *E* |
| 1 | | s3 | s12 | | 2 | | | | | |
| 2 | | | | *a* | | | | | | |
| 3 | | s4 | | | | 6 | | | | |
| 4 | s5 | *r*4 | *r*4 | *r*4 | | | | | | |
| 5 | *r*2 | *r*2 | *r*2 | *r*2 | | | | | | |
| 6 | *r*6 | *r*6 | *r*6 | *r*6 | | | 7 | 9 | | |
| 7 | | s8 | | | | | | | | |
| 8 | *r*1 | *r*1 | *r*1 | *r*1 | | | | | | |
| 9 | *r*8 | *r*8 | *r*8 | *r*8 | | | | | 10 | 11 |
| 10 | *r*5 | *r*5 | *r*5 | *r*5 | | | | | | |
| 11 | *r*7 | *r*7 | *r*7 | *r*7 | | | | | | |
| 12 | | s15 | | | | 13 | | | | |
| 13 | *r*6 | *r*6 | *r*6 | *r*6 | | | 14 | 9 | | |
| 14 | *r*3 | *r*3 | *r*3 | *r*3 | | | | | | |
| 15 | *r*4 | *r*4 | *r*4 | *r*4 | | | | | | |

**Figure 7.28** The parsing table for the LR(1) parser using default reductions of the grammar (1) $S \to bABb$, (2) $S \to bba$, (3) $S \to cAB$, (4) $A \to b$, (5) $B \to CD$, (6) $C \to \varepsilon$, (7) $D \to E$, (8) $E \to \varepsilon$

However, the error entry $(q_7, a)$ is not essential, because the configuration $\$q_1q_3q_6q_7 \mid x\$$ for any $x$ in $T^*$ is accessible only via the configuration $\$q_1q_3q_4 \mid x\$$. But if here $x = aw$, then

$$\$q_1q_3q_4 \mid aw\$ \Rightarrow \$q_1q_3q_4q_5 \mid w\$$$

and thus $\$q_1q_3q_6q_7 \mid aw\$$ is not accessible.

Now define:

$$\textbf{may-imply-essential} = \textbf{may-imply-}a_1\textbf{-essential} \cup \ldots \cup \textbf{may-imply-}a_n\textbf{-essential} ,$$

where $\{a_1, \ldots, a_n\} = T \cup \{\$\}$.

By Lemma 7.29 we have:

**Lemma 7.30** *The set of essential error entries is included in the set* **may-imply-essential** $(T \cup \{\$\})$. □

By Facts 7.26 and 7.27 the relational expression **may-imply-essential** is of size $O(|T| \cdot |G| \cdot n)$, has domain $T$, and can be constructed from $G$ and $M$ in time $O(|T| \cdot |G| \cdot n)$. Here $n$ denotes the number of states in $M$. By Theorem 2.28 we have:

**Lemma 7.31** *The set* **may-imply-essential** $(T \cup \{\$\})$ *can be computed in time* $O(|T| \cdot |G| \cdot n)$, *where n is the number of states in M.* □

The result of Lemma 7.30 implies, by Lemma 7.31, a practical algorithm for determining most of the inessential error entries. To determine exactly the set of inessential error entries we need some additional relations on the set of pairs of the forms $(q, A \to \alpha \cdot \beta)$, $(q, \cdot B)$, and $(q, B \cdot)$. Recall that if $q = [\gamma]$, then for pair $(q, A \to \alpha \cdot \beta)$, VALID($\gamma$) always contains $[A \to \cdot \alpha\beta]$, and for pairs $(q, \cdot B)$, and $(q, B \cdot)$, VALID($\gamma$) contains some item of the form $[A \to \alpha \cdot B\beta]$.

Define

$$(q, B \cdot) \ \textbf{left-corner-in} \ (q, A \to B \cdot \beta)$$

and, for all $a \in T$,

$$(q, A \to \alpha \cdot B\beta) \ \textbf{on-}a\textbf{-passes-null} \ (q, A \to \alpha B \cdot \beta) ,$$

whenever $(q, A \to \alpha \cdot B\beta)$ **may-on-*a*-access** $(q, A \to \alpha B \cdot \beta)$. Thus **on-*a*-passes-null** is a subrelation of that denoted by **may-on-*a*-access** and a superrelation of **directly-on-*a*-passes-null**.

**Fact 7.32** The relation **left-corner-in** is of size $O(|G| \cdot n)$ and can be computed in time $O(|G| \cdot n)$, where $n$ is the number of states in $M$. □

By Facts 7.26 and 7.27 and Theorem 2.29 the relation denoted by **may-on-*a*-access** can be computed in time $O(|G|^2 \cdot n^2)$, for any fixed $a$. We have:

**Lemma 7.33** *For any terminal $a \in T \cup \{\$\}$, the relation* **on-$a$-passes-null** *is of size $O(|G| \cdot n)$ and can be computed from $G$ and $M$ in time $O(|G|^2 \cdot n^2)$, where $n$ is the number of states in $M$.* □

Now consider, for terminal $a \in T \cup \{\$\}$, the relational expressions

**on-$a$-accesses** = (**on-$a$-reduces-to symbol-in** ∪ **on-$a$-passes-null**)* ·

(**on-$a$-reduces-to left-corner-in** ∪

**directly-descends** ∪ **on-$a$-passes-null**)*

and

**implies-$a$-essential** = **terminal entered-by**$^{-1}$ ·

**on-$a$-accesses error-entry-on-$a$** .

We shall show that $(q, a)$ is an essential error entry if and only if $b$ **implies-$a$-essential** $(q, a)$ for some $b \in T \cup \{\$\}$. We shall first show that all essential error entries are indeed accessed by the relation denoted by **implies-$a$-essential.**

**Lemma 7.34** *Let $n \geqslant 0$ and*

$$\$[X_1][X_1X_2]\ldots[X_1\ldots X_m] \mid a \underset{M}{\Longrightarrow}{}^n \$[Y_1][Y_1Y_2]\ldots[Y_1\ldots Y_p] \mid a\ .$$

*Then for all $[B \to Y_{j+1} \ldots Y_p \cdot \beta] \in \text{VALID}(Y_1 \ldots Y_p)$, $j < p$, there is an item $[A \to X_{i+1} \ldots X_m \cdot \alpha] \in \text{VALID}(X_1 \ldots X_m)$ such that*

$([X_1 \ldots X_i], A \to X_{i+1} \ldots X_m \cdot \alpha)$ **on-$a$-accesses**

$([Y_1 \ldots Y_j], B \to Y_{j+1} \ldots Y_p \cdot \beta)$.

*Proof.* Exactly as in the proof of Lemma 7.28 we may show by induction on $n$ *that* for all $[B \to Y_{j+1} \ldots Y_p \cdot \beta] \in \text{VALID}(Y_1 \ldots Y_p)$, $j < p$, there is $[A \to X_{i+1} \ldots X_m \cdot \alpha]$ in $\text{VALID}(X_1 \ldots X_m)$ such that

$([X_1 \ldots X_i], A \to X_{i+1} \ldots X_m \cdot \alpha)$

**on-$a$-accesses directly-descends* directly-on-$a$-passes-null**

$([Y_1 \ldots Y_j], B \to Y_{j+1} \ldots Y_p \cdot \beta)$

or for some $([Y_1 \ldots Y_{p-1}], Y_p \to Z_1 \ldots Z_l \cdot)$, $l \geqslant 1$,

$([X_1 \ldots X_i], A \to X_{i+1} \ldots X_m \cdot \alpha)$ **on-$a$-accesses**

$([Y_1 \ldots Y_{p-1}], Y_p \to Z_1 \ldots Z_l \cdot)$ **on-$a$-reduces-to symbol-in**

$([Y_1 \ldots Y_j], B \to Y_{j+1} \ldots Y_p \cdot \beta)$.

In the former case we conclude the lemma because

$$\textbf{directly-descends* directly-on-}a\textbf{-passes-null}$$
$$\subseteq (\textbf{directly-descends} \cup \textbf{on-}a\textbf{-passes-null})^* \ .$$

In the latter case first notice that if

$$([X_1 \ldots X_i], A \to X_{i+1} \ldots X_m \cdot \alpha)$$
$$(\textbf{on-}a\textbf{-reduces-to symbol-in} \cup \textbf{on-}a\textbf{-passes-null})^*$$
$$([Y_1 \ldots Y_{p-1}], Y_p \to Z_1 \ldots Z_l \cdot) \ ,$$

then the lemma immediately holds. Assume then that this is not the case. Then we have, whenever $|Y_{j+1} \ldots Y_{p-1}| \geqslant 1$,

$$([X_1 \ldots X_i], A \to X_{i+1} \ldots X_m \cdot \alpha) \ \textbf{on-}a\textbf{-accesses}$$
$$([Y_1 \ldots Y_j], B \to Y_{j+1} \ldots Y_{p-1} \cdot Y_p\beta)$$
$$\textbf{directly-descends on-}a\textbf{-passes-null}^l$$
$$([Y_1 \ldots Y_{p-1}], Y_p \to Z_1 \ldots Z_l \cdot) \ .$$

This means that $([Y_1 \ldots Y_j], B \to Y_{j+1} \ldots Y_{p-1} \cdot Y_p\beta)$ **on-*a*-passes-null** $([Y_1 \ldots Y_j], B \to Y_{j+1} \ldots Y_p \cdot \beta)$, which implies the lemma. If $|Y_{j+1} \ldots Y_{p-1}| = 0$, then

$$([Y_1 \ldots Y_{p-1}], Y_p \to Z_1 \ldots Z_l \cdot)$$
$$\textbf{on-}a\textbf{-reduces-to left-corner-in}$$
$$([Y_1 \ldots Y_j], B \to Y_{j+1} \ldots Y_p \cdot \beta)$$

implying the lemma. □

Lemma 7.34 together with Fact 7.25 imply that if an error entry $(q, a)$ is essential, then $b$ **implies-*a*-essential** $(q, a)$ for some $b \in T \cup \{\$\}$. We shall next prove the converse of this statement by a sequence of lemmas.

The proof of the following lemma is left as an exercise.

**Lemma 7.35** *Let* $Y_1 \ldots Y_p$, $p > 0$, *be a viable prefix of* $G'$ *and* $[B \to Y_{j+1} \ldots Y_p \cdot Z\beta]$, $j < p$, *be an item in* VALID$(Y_1 \ldots Y_p)$. *If*

$$([Y_1 \ldots Y_j], B \to Y_{j+1} \ldots Y_p \cdot Z\beta) \ \textbf{on-}a\textbf{-passes-null}$$
$$([Y_1 \ldots Y_j], B \to Y_{j+1} \ldots Y_p Z \cdot \beta) \ ,$$

*then*

$$\$[Y_1] \ldots [Y_1 \ldots Y_p] \mid a \underset{M}{\Rightarrow}{}^* \$[Y_1] \ldots [Y_1 \ldots Y_p][Y_1 \ldots Y_p Z] \mid a.$$

□

The converse of Lemma 7.34 is obtained from the following two lemmas.

**Lemma 7.36** *Let $n \geq 0$, and*

$$(q, A \to \alpha \cdot \beta) \text{ (on-}a\text{-reduces-to symbol-in} \cup \text{on-}a\text{-passes-null})^n \ (q', B \to \gamma \cdot \delta) \ .$$

*where $\alpha \neq \varepsilon$ and $\gamma \neq \varepsilon$. Then for any viable prefix $Y_1 \ldots Y_p$, $p \geq 1$, of $G'$ and $j < p$ such that*

$$[Y_1 \ldots Y_j] = q' \quad \text{and} \quad Y_{j+1} \ldots Y_p = \gamma \ ,$$

*there is a viable prefix $X_1 \ldots X_m$, $m \geq 1$, and $i < m$ such that*

$$[X_1 \ldots X_i] = q, X_{i+1} \ldots X_m = \alpha$$

*and*

$$\$[X_1] \ldots [X_1 \ldots X_m] \mid a \underset{M}{\Longrightarrow}^* \$[Y_1] \ldots [Y_1 \ldots Y_p] \mid a \ .$$

*Proof.* The proof is by induction on $n$. The base case $n = 0$ is clear. Assume then that $n > 0$. Then either

$$(q, A \to \alpha \cdot \beta) \text{ (on-}a\text{-reduces-to symbol-in} \cup \text{on-}a\text{-passes-null})^{n-1}$$
$$(q'', C \to \omega \cdot) \text{ on-}a\text{-reduces-to symbol-in } (q', B \to \gamma \cdot \delta) \ ,$$

for some pair $(q'', C \to \omega \cdot)$ where $\omega \neq \varepsilon$, or

$$(q, \ A \to \alpha \cdot \beta) \text{ (on-}a\text{-reduces-to symbol-in} \ \cup \ \text{on-}a\text{-passes-null})^{n-1}$$
$$(q', B \to \gamma' \cdot Y\delta) \text{ on-}a\text{-passes-null } (q', B \to \gamma' Y \cdot \delta) = (q', B \to \gamma \cdot \delta) \ .$$

In the former case the definitions of **on-$a$-reduces-to** and **symbol-in** imply that for any viable prefix $Y_1 \ldots Y_p$, $p \geq 1$, of $G'$ and $j < p$ such that

$$[Y_1 \ldots Y_j] = q' \quad \text{and} \quad Y_{j+1} \ldots Y_p = \gamma$$

there is a viable prefix $Z_1 \ldots Z_l$ and $k < l$ such that

$$[Z_1 \ldots Z_k] = q'', Z_{k+1} \ldots Z_l = \omega, \text{ and}$$
$$\$[Z_1] \ldots [Z_1 \ldots Z_l] \mid a \underset{M}{\Longrightarrow} \$[Y_1] \ldots [Y_1 \ldots Y_p] \mid a \ .$$

(Here $Z_1 \ldots Z_k = Y_1 \ldots Y_{p-1}$.) Further, the induction hypothesis implies that there is a viable prefix $X_1 \ldots X_m$, $m \geq 1$, of $G'$ and $i < m$ such that

$$[X_1 \ldots X_i] = q, X_{i+1} \ldots X_m = \alpha$$

and

$$\$[X_1] \ldots [X_1 \ldots X_m] \mid a \underset{M}{\Longrightarrow}^* \$[Z_1] \ldots [Z_1 \ldots Z_l] \mid a \ .$$

As $\$[Z_1] \ldots [Z_1 \ldots Z_l] \mid a \underset{M}{\Longrightarrow} \$[Y_1] \ldots [Y_1 \ldots Y_p] \mid a$, we obtain the desired result.

In the latter case the induction hypothesis and Lemma 7.35 immediately imply the desired result. □

**Lemma 7.37** *Let $n \geqslant 0$, and*

$$(q, A \to \alpha \cdot \beta)$$

$$(\textbf{on-}a\textbf{-reduces-to left-corner-in} \cup$$

$$\textbf{directly-descends} \cup \textbf{on-}a\textbf{-passes-null})^n$$

$$(q', B \to \gamma \cdot \delta) \ .$$

*Then there is a viable prefix $Y_1 \ldots Y_p$, $p \geqslant 1$, of $G'$ and $j \leqslant p$, $k \leqslant j$ such that*

$$[Y_1 \ldots Y_j] = q',\ Y_{j+1} \ldots Y_p = \gamma \ ,$$

$$[Y_1 \ldots Y_k] = q \ ,$$

*and*

$$\$[Y_1] \ldots [Y_1 \ldots Y_k\alpha] \mid a \underset{M}{\Longrightarrow}{}^* \$[Y_1] \ldots [Y_1 \ldots Y_p] \mid a \ .$$

*Proof.* The proof is by induction on $n$. In the base case $n = 0$ we have $q = q'$ and $A \to \alpha \cdot \beta = B \to \gamma \cdot \delta$. The lemma then holds if we choose any viable prefix $Y_1 \ldots Y_p$ and $j \leqslant p$ such that $[Y_1 \ldots Y_j] = q'$ and $Y_{j+1} \ldots Y_p = \gamma$.

Assume then that $n > 0$. We have three cases to consider.

*Case 1*: $(j + 1) = p$ and

$$(q, A \to \alpha \cdot \beta)$$

$$(\textbf{on-}a\textbf{-reduces-to left-corner-in} \cup$$

$$\textbf{directly-descends} \cup \textbf{on-}a\textbf{-passes-null})^{n-1}$$

$$(q', C \to \omega \cdot)$$

$$\textbf{on-}a\textbf{-reduces-to left-corner-in}$$

$$(q', B \to C \cdot \delta) = (q', B \to \gamma \cdot \delta) \ ,$$

where $C = \gamma$ and Action[Goto[$q'$, $\omega$], $a$] $= C \to \omega$. The induction hypothesis implies that there is a viable prefix $Y_1 \ldots Y_r$ and $j \leqslant r$, $k \leqslant j$ such that

$$[Y_1 \ldots Y_j] = q',\quad Y_{j+1} \ldots Y_r = \omega \ ,\quad [Y_1 \ldots Y_k] = q \ ,$$

and

$$\$[Y_1] \ldots [Y_1 \ldots Y_k\alpha] \mid a \underset{M}{\Longrightarrow}{}^* \$[Y_1] \ldots [Y_1 \ldots Y_r] \mid a \ .$$

Here

$$\begin{aligned} &\$[Y_1] \ldots [Y_1 \ldots Y_r] \mid a \\ &= \$[Y_1] \ldots [Y_1 \ldots Y_k] \ldots [Y_1 \ldots Y_j] \ldots [Y_1 \ldots Y_j\omega] \mid a \\ &\underset{M}{\Longrightarrow} \$[Y_1] \ldots [Y_1 \ldots Y_k] \ldots [Y_1 \ldots Y_j][Y_1 \ldots Y_jC] \mid a \ . \end{aligned}$$

The lemma then holds for the viable prefix $Y_1 \ldots Y_j C$ and $p = (j + 1)$.

*Case 2*: $\gamma = \varepsilon$ and

$$(q, A \to \alpha \cdot \beta)$$

$$(\textbf{on-}a\textbf{-reduces-to left-corner-in} \cup$$

$$\textbf{directly-descends} \cup \textbf{on-}a\textbf{-passes-null})^{n-1}$$

$$(q'', C \to \eta \cdot B\psi)$$

$$\textbf{directly-descends}$$

$$(\text{Goto}[q'', \eta], B \to \cdot \delta) = (q', B \to \gamma \cdot \delta) \ ,$$

where $q''$ is a state and $[C \to \eta \cdot B\psi]$ an item in Goto$[q'', \eta]$. The induction hypothesis implies that there is a viable prefix $Y_1 \ldots Y_p$ and natural numbers $l \leqslant p$, $k \leqslant l$ such that

$$[Y_1 \ldots Y_l] = q'', \quad Y_{l+1} \ldots Y_p = \eta \ , \quad [Y_1 \ldots Y_k] = q \ ,$$

and

$$\$[Y_1] \ldots [Y_1 \ldots Y_k \alpha] \mid a \underset{M}{\Longrightarrow}{}^{*} \$[Y_1] \ldots [Y_1 \ldots Y_p] \mid a \ .$$

This means that the lemma holds when choosing $j = p$, because $q' = \text{Goto}[q'', \eta] = [Y_1 \ldots Y_p]$ and $\gamma = \varepsilon$.

*Case 3*: The proof of the case

$$(q, A \to \alpha \cdot \beta)$$

$$(\textbf{on-}a\textbf{-reduces-to left-corner-in} \cup$$

$$\textbf{directly-descends} \cup \textbf{on-}a\textbf{-passes-null})^{n-1} \cdot$$

$$\textbf{on-}a\textbf{-passes-null}$$

$$(q', B \to \gamma \cdot \delta)$$

is left as an exercise. □

Lemmas 7.36 and 7.37 imply the following lemma.

**Lemma 7.38** *Let $q$ and $q'$ be states of $M$ and $[A \to \alpha \cdot \beta]$ and $[B \to \gamma \cdot \delta]$ items such that*

$$(q, A \to \alpha \cdot \beta) \ \textbf{on-}a\textbf{-accesses} \ (q', B \to \gamma \cdot \delta) \ ,$$

*Then there are viable prefixes $X_1 \ldots X_m$, $m \geqslant 1$, and $Y_1 \ldots Y_p$, $p \geqslant 1$, of $G'$ and natural numbers $i \leqslant m$ and $j \leqslant p$ such that*

$$[X_1 \ldots X_i] = q, X_{i+1} \ldots X_m = \alpha \ ,$$

$$[Y_1 \ldots Y_j] = q', Y_{j+1} \ldots Y_p = \gamma$$

*and*

$$\$[X_1]\ldots[X_1\ldots X_m] \mid a \underset{M}{\Longrightarrow}{}^{*} \$[Y_1]\ldots[Y_1\ldots Y_p] \mid a\ .$$

□

Lemmas 7.34 and 7.38 and Fact 7.25 imply (a detailed proof is left as an exercise):

**Lemma 7.39** *An error entry* $(q, a)$ *is essential if and only if*

$b$ **implies-$a$-essential** $(q, a)$

*for some* $b \in T \cup \{\$\}$. □

Finally consider the relational expression

**implies-essential** = **implies-$a_1$-essential** $\cup \ldots \cup$ **implies-$a_n$-essential** ,

where $\{a_1, \ldots, a_n\} = T \cup \{\$\}$.

Lemma 7.39 implies:

**Lemma 7.40** *The set of essential error entries is obtained as the set* **implies-essential** $(T \cup \{\$\})$. □

By Facts 7.26, 7.27 and 7.32 and by Lemma 7.33 the relational expression **implies-essential** is of size $O(|T| \cdot |G| \cdot n)$, has domain $T$, and can be constructed from $G$ and $M$ in time $O(|T| \cdot |G|^2 \cdot n^2)$. By Theorem 2.28 we have:

**Lemma 7.41** *The set* **implies-essential**$(T \cup \{\$\})$ *can be computed in time* $O(|T| \cdot |G|^2 \cdot n^2)$, *where* $n$ *is the number of states in* $M$. □

Thus we get from Lemmas 7.40 and 7.41:

**Theorem 7.42** *The set of inessential error entries in any LR(0)-based LR(1) parser* $M$ *for a reduced LALR(1) grammar* $G = (V, T, P, S)$ *can be computed in time* $O(|T| \cdot |G|^2 \cdot n^2)$, *where* $n$ *is the number of states in* $M$. □

### *Reducing the number of states in an LR(1) parser*

We shall now show how inessential error entries in a parsing table representing an LR(1) parser may be used to produce a smaller parser. Where there exist inessential error entries, we may merge rows (states) in a parsing table without affecting the behavior of the parser.

As an example, consider the grammar

$$E \to E + T | T * F | a \ ,$$

$$T \to T * F | a \ ,$$

$$F \to a \ ,$$

which has been obtained from the grammar

$$E \to E + T | T \ ,$$

$$T \to T * F | F \ ,$$

$$F \to a$$

by eliminating the unit rules $E \to T$ and $T \to F$. The deterministic LR(0) machine for the corresponding \$-augmented grammar is shown in Figure 7.29, and the parsing table for an LR(1) parser using default reductions is shown in Figure 7.30. Consider then the error entries $(q_8, \$)$, $(q_8, +)$, and $(q_8, a)$. The state $q_8$ can only be accessed by reducing by the rule $T \to a$ at the state $q_7$, or by reducing by the rule

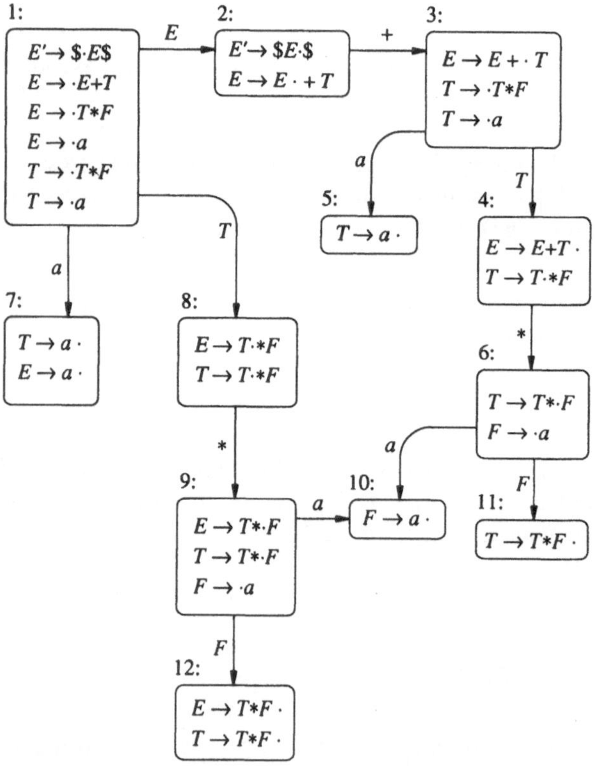


**Figure 7.29** The deterministic LR(0) machine for the grammar $E' \to \$E\$$, $E \to E + T | T * F | a$, $T \to T * F | a$, $F \to a$

| | Action | | | | Goto | | |
|---|---|---|---|---|---|---|---|
| | $a$ | $+$ | $*$ | $\$$ | $E$ | $T$ | $F$ |
| 1 | s7 | | | | 2 | 8 | |
| 2 | | s3 | | $a$ | | | |
| 3 | s5 | | | | | 4 | |
| 4 | $r1$ | $r1$ | s6 | $r1$ | | | |
| 5 | $r5$ | $r5$ | $r5$ | $r5$ | | | |
| 6 | s10 | | | | | | 11 |
| 7 | $r3$ | $r3$ | $r5$ | $r3$ | | | |
| 8 | | | s9 | | | | |
| 9 | s10 | | | | | | 12 |
| 10 | $r6$ | $r6$ | $r6$ | $r6$ | | | |
| 11 | $r4$ | $r4$ | $r4$ | $r4$ | | | |
| 12 | $r2$ | $r2$ | $r4$ | $r2$ | | | |

**Figure 7.30** The parsing table for an LR(1) parser using default reductions of the grammar (1) $E \rightarrow E + T$, (2) $E \rightarrow T * F$, (3) $E \rightarrow a$, (4) $T \rightarrow T * F$, (5) $T \rightarrow a$, (6) $F \rightarrow a$

| | Action | | | | Goto | | |
|---|---|---|---|---|---|---|---|
| | $a$ | $+$ | $*$ | $\$$ | $E$ | $T$ | $F$ |
| 1 | s7 | | | | 2 | 2 | |
| 2,8 | | s3 | s9 | $a$ | | | |
| 3 | s5 | | | | | 4 | |
| 4 | $r1$ | $r1$ | s6 | $r1$ | | | |
| 5 | $r5$ | $r5$ | $r5$ | $r5$ | | | |
| 6 | s10 | | | | | | 11 |
| 7 | $r3$ | $r3$ | $r5$ | $r3$ | | | |
| 9 | s10 | | | | | | 12 |
| 10 | $r6$ | $r6$ | $r6$ | $r6$ | | | |
| 11 | $r4$ | $r4$ | $r4$ | $r4$ | | | |
| 12 | $r2$ | $r2$ | $r4$ | $r2$ | | | |

**Figure 7.31** The parsing table obtained from that shown in Figure 7.30 by merging rows 2 and 8

$T \rightarrow T * F$ at the state $q_{12}$. Thus, as is easily seen from the parsing table, these error entries are all inessential. Similarly, it is easy to see that the error entry $(q_2, *)$ is inessential. This means, because no error entry $(q, A)$ where $A$ is a nonterminal can ever be consulted, that the rows for $q_2$ and $q_8$ in the parsing table can be merged without affecting the behavior of the parser by any means. The resulting parsing table, given in Figure 7.31, is simulated exactly in the same way as the original table, and it can also be implemented as a parsing program.

Let $G = (V, T, P, S)$ be an LALR(1) grammar, and consider the parsing table for a deterministic LR(0)-based LR(1) parser $M$ of $G$. We say that two states $q_1$ and $q_2$ are *compatible*, if

(1) $\text{Action}[q_1, a] = \text{Action}[q_2, a]$, or either $(q_1, a)$ or $(q_2, a)$ is an inessential error entry, for all $a \in T \cup \{\$\}$, and

(2) $\text{Goto}[q_1, A] = \text{Goto}[q_2, A]$, or either $(q_1, A)$ or $(q_2, A)$ is an error entry, for all $A \in V \setminus T$.

The states $q_2$ and $q_8$ of the parser given in Figure 7.30 are compatible.

Compatibility is not always an equivalence relation on $[G']$, the set of states of $M$. Let $\rho = \{Q_1, \ldots, Q_m\}$ be some partition of $[G']$ such that each $Q_i$ in $\rho$ contains only pairwise compatible states. Such a partition is called a *compatible partition.* The proof of the following theorem is left as an exercise.

**Theorem 7.43** *Let $G = (V, T, P, S)$ be an LALR(1) grammar and M its deterministic LR(0)-based LR(1) parser represented by a parsing table (composed of* Action *and* Goto). *Further let $\rho$ be a compatible partition of the set of states of M, and let* Action′ *and* Goto′ *be tables defined by: for all $Q \in \rho$ and $a \in T \cup \{\$\}$,*

$$\text{Action}'[Q, a] = \begin{cases} \text{“error”}, & \textit{if all entries } (q, a), \\ & q \in Q, \textit{ are error entries}, \\ \text{Action}[q, a], & \textit{where } q \in Q \textit{ and } (q, a) \textit{ is not} \\ & \textit{an error entry, otherwise}; \end{cases}$$

*for all $X \in V$,*

$$\text{Goto}'[Q, X] = \bigcup_{q \in Q} \text{Goto}[q, X] .$$

*Then Action′ and Goto′ form a parsing table that represents a right parser of G which behaves exactly in the same way as M.* □

If no ambiguity arises the tables Action′ and Goto′ as above are denoted by Action and Goto.

We are interested, of course, in finding a smallest compatible partition of $[G']$. In general, this is a computationally difficult problem, but there exist efficient approximation algorithms that “usually” produce a compatible partition which is close to a smallest one. In the following we shall describe an approximation

Let $([G'], R)$ be an undirected graph, where $R$ contains an edge $(q_1, q_2)$ whenever $q_1$ and $q_2$ are not compatible. We shall *color* the graph such that no two nodes $q_1$ and $q_2$ have the same color if $(q_1, q_2)$ is in $R$. In the colored graph each color corresponds to an element in a compatible partition, that is, nodes with the same color form one element in the partition. An algorithm for graph coloring is given in Figure 7.32. Initially all nodes are uncolored.

As an illustration of the behavior of the given algorithm consider a hypothetical situation where the states are $q_1$, $q_2$, $q_3$, and $q_4$, and the compatible pairs are $(q_1, q_3)$, $(q_1, q_4)$, and $(q_2, q_4)$. The corresponding graph is given in Figure 7.33. Now the algorithm may first, for example, choose node $q_1$ and color it by color 1.

**repeat**
  Choose an uncolored node $v$ with a maximum number of nodes $v'$ such that $(v, v')$ is in $R$ and $v'$ is colored;
  Color node $v$ with the least possible color, that is, the least color which is not the color of any adjacent node of $v$
**until** all nodes are colored.

**Figure 7.32** An algorithm for graph coloring

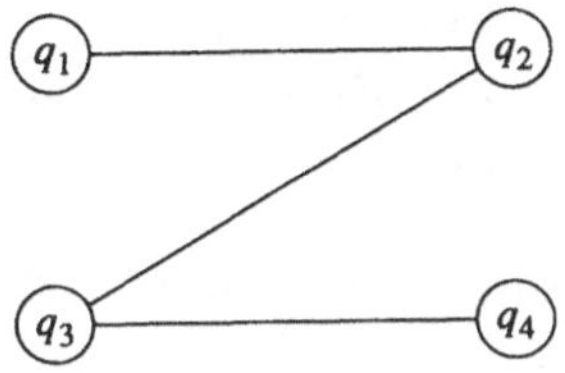


**Figure 7.33** Graph corresponding to the situation in which the compatible pairs of states are $(q_1, q_3)$, $(q_1, q_4)$, and $(q_2, q_4)$

Then the next node to be handled is $q_2$ and it will be colored by 2. The node $q_3$ will be colored by the least possible color, that is, 1, and the node $q_4$ will get color 2. The compatible partition corresponding to this coloring is $\{\{q_1, q_3\}, \{q_2, q_4\}\}$.

Finally we note that the applicability of the described method for reducing the size of the parser by merging compatible states is rather restricted: there are usually only a few compatible states. However, we could treat the Action and Goto tables separately and thereby get more compatible rows. When doing this the old state names must be preserved (see the exercises). In a corresponding way columns may also be merged.

We can also factor out an error matrix from the Action table and thus make all error entries in the Action table inessential. The error matrix has the same set of entries as the Action table. Each non-error entry in the Action table has the value **true** in the error matrix, and each error entry in the Action table the value **false**. Now the error checking is done by consulting the error matrix, and if the action to be performed is not "error", then the correct action is found in the Action table. Thus no error entry in the Action table will ever be consulted, and it can be compressed accordingly. This method of implementing LR(1) parsers is treated in the exercises.

### *Eliminating reductions by unit rules*

We shall describe how an LR(1) parser can be caused to avoid making reductions by *unit rules* of the form $A \to B$, where $B$ is a nonterminal. We want to bypass the reductions by those unit rules that are semantically insignificant. In the following we assume that all rules $A \to B$ are such; the case in which some unit rules have semantic significance is handled by simply treating them as non-unit rules.

We shall first consider an elimination method that cannot increase the number of states (stack symbols) of the parser but may leave some reductions by unit rules uneliminated. However, for typical grammars with unit rules, such as grammars that describe expressions and contain unit rules to indicate precedence levels, all reductions by unit rules will be eliminated.

Secondly, we shall describe an algorithm that eliminates all reductions by unit rules but may enlarge the parser considerably. However, in this case the parser size can again be reduced by merging compatible states.

Let $G$ be an LALR(1) grammar, and consider the parsing table for a deterministic LR(0)-based LR(1) parser $M$ of $G$. Further let $A \to B$, where $B \in V \setminus T$, be a unit rule of $G$, and let $q$ be a state such that $\text{Goto}[q, A] \neq \varnothing$ and $\text{Goto}[q, B] \neq \varnothing$ (there must exist at least one such state $q$ for any unit rule $A \to B$). We say that $q_1 = \text{Goto}[q, A]$ and $q_2 = \text{Goto}[q, B]$ are $(A, B)$-*compatible*, if

(1) for all $a \in T \cup \{\$\}$, either $\text{Action}[q_1, a] = \text{Action}[q_2, a]$ or one of the following three statements is true:
  (a) $\text{Action}[q_2, a] =$ "reduce by $A \to B$",
  (b) $(q_2, a)$ is an inessential error entry, or
  (c) $(q_1, a)$ is an inessential error entry,

and

(2) for all $C \in V \setminus T$, one of the following statements is true:
  (d) $\text{Goto}[q_1, C] = \text{Goto}[q_2, C]$,
  (e) $\text{Goto}[q_1, C] = \varnothing$, or
  (f) $\text{Goto}[q_2, C] = \varnothing$.

We eliminate reductions by the rule $A \to B$ as follows. For any state $q$ such that $q_1 = \text{Goto}[q, A] \neq \varnothing$ and $q_2 = \text{Goto}[q, B] \neq \varnothing$, and $q_1$ and $q_2$ are $(A, B)$-compatible,

(1) replace $\text{Goto}[q, B]$ by $q_1$ ,

and, for all $a \in T \cup \{\$\}$, whenever $\text{Action}[q_1, a] =$ "error" and $\text{Action}[q_2, a] \neq$ "reduce by $A \to B$",

(2) replace $\text{Action}[q_1, a]$ by $\text{Action}[q_2, a]$ .

Moreover, if after this modification $\text{Goto}[q', B] = q_2$ for no state $q'$, then the state $q_2$ can be deleted altogether.

It is clear that the resulting parser behaves exactly in the same way as the original parser, except that it possibly bypasses some reductions by unit rules.

As an example consider the grammar

$$E \to E + T \mid T \ ,$$

$$T \to T * a \mid a \ .$$

The deterministic LR(0) machine for the corresponding \$-augmented grammar is shown in Figure 7.34, and the LR(0)-based LR(1) parser using default reductions is shown in Figure 7.35.

Now because reducing by $E \rightarrow T$ at the state $q_7$ or reducing by $E \rightarrow E + T$ at the state $q_4$ are the only ways to reach the state $q_2$, and, moreover, Goto$[q_7, *] \neq \varnothing$ and Goto$[q_4, *] \neq \varnothing$, we conclude that the error entry $(q_2, *)$ is inessential. Thus the states $q_2$ and $q_7$ are $(E, T)$-compatible and the reduction by $E \rightarrow T$ can be eliminated by the method just described. The resulting parser that bypasses the reductions by $E \rightarrow T$ is shown in Figure 7.36.

Consider then how the new parser behaves when parsing the string $a + a{*}a$:

| *configuration* | *output* |
|---|---|
| $\$q_1 \mid a + a{*}a\$$ | |
| $\Rightarrow \$q_1q_5 \mid + a{*}a\$$ | |
| $\Rightarrow \$q_1q_2 \mid + a{*}a\$$ | $T \rightarrow a$ |
| $\Rightarrow \$q_1q_2q_3 \mid a{*}a\$$ | |
| $\Rightarrow \$q_1q_2q_3q_5 \mid {*}a\$$ | |
| $\Rightarrow \$q_1q_2q_3q_4 \mid {*}a\$$ | $T \rightarrow a$ |
| $\Rightarrow \$q_1q_2q_3q_4q_6 \mid a\$$ | |
| $\Rightarrow \$q_1q_2q_3q_4q_6q_8 \mid \$$ | |
| $\Rightarrow \$q_1q_2q_3q_4 \mid \$$ | $T \rightarrow T{*}a$ |
| $\Rightarrow \$q_1q_2 \mid \$$ | $E \rightarrow E + T$ |

Hence the output produced by the parser of Figure 7.36 for the sentence $a + a{*}a$ is

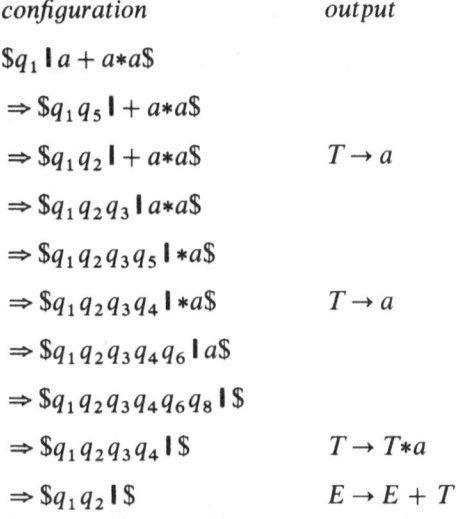

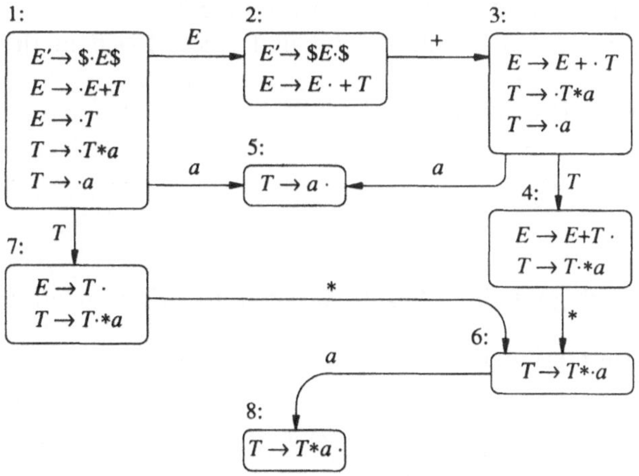


**Figure 7.34** The deterministic LR(0) machine for the grammar $E' \rightarrow \$E\$$, $E \rightarrow E + T|T$, $T \rightarrow T * a|a$

| | Action | | | | Goto | |
|---|---|---|---|---|---|---|
| | $a$ | $+$ | $*$ | $\$$ | $E$ | $T$ |
| 1 | s5 | | | | 2 | 7 |
| 2 | | s3 | | $a$ | | |
| 3 | s5 | | | | | 4 |
| 4 | r1 | r1 | s6 | r1 | | |
| 5 | r4 | r4 | r4 | r4 | | |
| 6 | s8 | | | | | |
| 7 | r2 | r2 | s6 | r2 | | |
| 8 | r3 | r3 | r3 | r3 | | |

**Figure 7.35** An LR(1) parser using default reductions of the grammar (1) $E \to E + T$, (2) $E \to T$, (3) $T \to T*a$, (4) $T \to a$

| | Action | | | | Goto | |
|---|---|---|---|---|---|---|
| | $a$ | $+$ | $*$ | $\$$ | $E$ | $T$ |
| 1 | s5 | | | | 2 | 2 |
| 2, 7 | | s3 | s6 | $a$ | | |
| 3 | s5 | | | | | 4 |
| 4 | r1 | r1 | s6 | r1 | | |
| 5 | r4 | r4 | r4 | r4 | | |
| 6 | s8 | | | | | |
| 8 | r3 | r3 | r3 | r3 | | |

**Figure 7.36** The parser obtained from the parser shown in Figure 7.35 by eliminating the reductions by the rule $E \to T$. Notice that now the columns for $E$ and $T$ have become compatible and can be merged

$(T \to a)$ $(T \to a)$ $(T \to T*a)$ $(E \to E + T)$ instead of the output $(T \to a)$ $(E \to T)$ $(T \to a)$ $(T \to T*a)$ $(E \to E + T)$ produced by the parser of Figure 7.35.

We extend the above algorithm to handle several unit rules $A \to B$ in the following way.

Let $<$ be a relation on $V \backslash T$ defined by:

$$A < B \ ,$$

if $A \to B$ is a rule of $G$.

**Fact 7.44** For any reduced unambiguous (and thus LR($k$)) grammar $G$, the relation

$$< \cup \ \{(A, A) | A \text{ is a nonterminal}\}$$

is a partial order. □

We apply the above algorithm in the order given by $<$ with respect to the left-hand sides of the unit rules. That is, we treat a unit rule $A \to B$ after all unit rules

```
Create an ordering A_1, ..., A_m of nonterminals appearing in unit rules
of the LALR(1) grammar G such that if A_i → A_j is a rule then i < j;
for i = 1 to m do
begin
    for all unit rules A_i → A_j do
        for all states q such that q_1 = Goto[q, A_i] ≠ ∅ and q_2 = Goto[q, A_j] ≠ ∅,
            and q_1 and q_2 are (A_i, A_j)-compatible with respect to the modified
            Action and Goto tables produced thus far do
        begin
            Replace Goto[q, A_j] by q_1;
            for all a ∈ T ∪ {$} do
                if Action[q_1, a] = "error" and
                   Action[q_2, a] ≠ "reduce by A_i → A_j" then
                     Replace Action[q_1, a] by Action[q_2, a]
        end
end;
Delete all states to which there is no reference.
```

**Figure 7.37** An algorithm for eliminating unit rules

$A' \to B'$ where $A' < A$ have already been treated. A formulation of the algorithm is given in Figure 7.37.

The proof of the following theorem is straightforward and is left as an exercise.

**Theorem 7.45** *Let $G = (V, T, P, S)$ be an $LALR(1)$ grammar and $M$ its deterministic $LR(0)$-based $LR(1)$ parser represented by a parsing table (composed of* Action *and* Goto*). Then the algorithm of Figure 7.37 modifies* Action *and* Goto *such that the resulting table represents a pushdown transducer that behaves exactly as $M$ but bypasses some reductions by unit rules.* □

By the definition of $(A, B)$-compatibility a unit rule $A \to B$ is always eliminated by the algorithm of Figure 7.37, if the item $[A \to B\cdot]$ appears only in the singleton state $\{[A \to B\cdot]\}$ of $M$. This is the case for all unit rules for the LALR(1) parser of Figure 7.11. The parser after eliminating the unit rules is shown in Figure 7.38. Notice that the elimination effect is obtained by simply leaving out the rows where reductions by unit rules are performed, and also all references to these rows.

As a note of the applicability of the algorithm of Figure 7.37 consider the grammar describing expressions with $n \geqslant 1$ binary operators and precedence levels:

$$E_0 \to E_0 b_1 E_1 \mid E_1 \ ,$$

$$E_1 \to E_1 b_2 E_2 \mid E_2 \ ,$$

$$\vdots$$

$$E_{n-1} \to E_{n-1} b_n E_n \mid E_n \ ,$$

$$E_n \to (E_0) \mid a \ .$$

| | Action | | | | | | | | | Goto | | | |
|---|---|---|---|---|---|---|---|---|---|---|---|---|---|
| | $a$ | := | **begin** | **end** | ; | + | ( | ) | $ | $S$ | $E$ | $C$ | $T$ |
| 1 | s3 | | s13 | | | | | | r1 | 2 | | | |
| 2 | | | | | | | | | a | | | | |
| 3 | | s4 | | | | | | | | | | | |
| 4 | s8 | | | | | | s9 | | | | 5 | | |
| 5 | | | | r2 | r2 | s6 | | | r2 | | | | |
| 6 | s8 | | | | | | s9 | | | | | | 7 |
| 7 | | | | r6 | r6 | r6 | | r6 | r6 | | | | |
| 8 | | | | r8 | r8 | r8 | | r8 | r8 | | | | |
| 9 | s8 | | | | | | s9 | | | | 10 | | |
| 10 | | | | | | s6 | | s11 | | | | | |
| 11 | | | | r9 | r9 | r9 | | r9 | r9 | | | | |
| 13 | s3 | | s13 | r1 | r1 | | | | | | | 14 | |
| 14 | | | | s15 | s16 | | | | | | | | |
| 15 | | | | r3 | r3 | | | | r3 | | | | |
| 16 | s3 | | s13 | r1 | r1 | | | | | 17 | | | |
| 17 | | | | r4 | r4 | | | | | | | | |

**Figure 7.38** The parsing table for the LALR(1) parser of the grammar (1) $S \to \varepsilon$, (2) $S \to a := E$, (3) $S \to$ **begin** $C$ **end**, (4) $C \to C ; S$, (5) $C \to S$, (6) $E \to E + T$, (7) $E \to T$, (8) $T \to a$, (9) $T \to (E)$, after the reductions by the rules $C \to S$ and $E \to T$ have been eliminated. Now $q_{13}$ and $q_{16}$ are compatible, as well as $q_4$ and $q_6$, and also $q_6$ and $q_9$. Thus $q_{13}$ and $q_{16}$, and either $q_4$ and $q_6$, or $q_6$ and $q_9$ can be merged. Also notice that all Goto columns have become compatible, but the merging of the columns for $E$ and $T$ conflicts with the merging of $q_6$ with $q_4$ or $q_9$, if the Action and Goto tables are not compressed separately

It can be shown that the algorithm of Figure 7.37 eliminates all reductions by unit rules from any deterministic LR(1) parser of this grammar.

In order to develop our second method to eliminate reductions by unit rules we assume that the LALR(1) grammar $G = (V, T, P, S)$ to be considered does not contain a nonterminal that derives only the empty string. Consider the parsing table for the LALR(1) parser of $G$, and let

$$A_1 \to A_2,\ A_2 \to A_3, \ldots, A_{p-1} \to A_p,\ p \geqslant 2 \ ,$$

be a sequence of unit rules of $G$, and $q$ and $q_1, \ldots, q_p$ states such that

$$q_1 = \text{Goto}[q, A_1], \ldots, q_p = \text{Goto}[q, A_p] \ .$$

Moreover, we assume that at $q_1$ no reduction by a unit rule is possible. Thus if we enter some state $q_i$, $1 < i \leqslant p$, consecutive reductions by unit rules may be performed until state $q_1$ is entered.

The construction of the LALR(1) parser implies immediately:

**Lemma 7.46** *Let $A_1, \ldots, A_p$ and $q_1, \ldots, q_p$ be as above. For all i, $i = 1, \ldots, p-1$, and for all $a \in T \cup \{\$\}$, if $(q_i, a)$ is not an error entry, then* Action$[q_{i+1}, a]$ = *"reduce by $A_i \to A_{i+1}$".* □

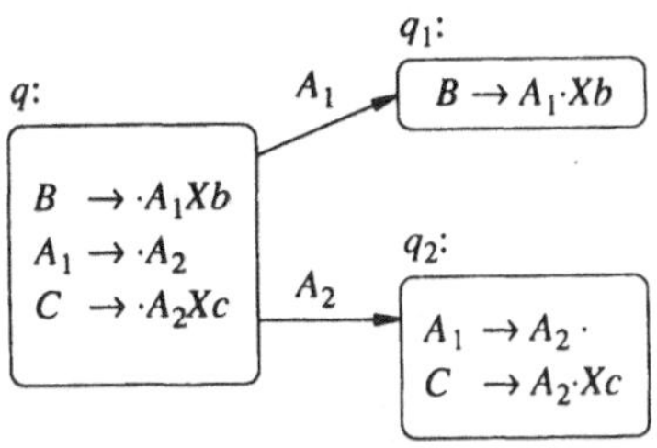


**Figure 7.39** The state $q_2$ is bound to have a parsing conflict whenever $X$ derives a nonempty terminal string

Lemma 7.46 implies that, when the reductions by unit rules $A_1 \to A_2, \ldots, A_{p-1} \to A_p$ are omitted, then for any two distinct states $q_i$ and $q_j$, $1 \leqslant i, j \leqslant p$, the corresponding sets of terminals on which there is a non-error parsing action are disjoint.

The proof of the following lemma is left as an exercise. The role of the requirement that all nonterminals derive nonempty terminal strings is illustrated in Figure 7.39.

**Lemma 7.47** *Let $A_1, \ldots, A_p$ and $q_1, \ldots, q_p$ be as above. For any two distinct states $q_i$ and $q_j$, $1 \leqslant i, j \leqslant p$, and for any $X \in V$,* $\text{Goto}[q_i, X] = \varnothing$ *or* $\text{Goto}[q_j, X] = \varnothing$. □

Lemmas 7.46 and 7.47 imply that by adding for each $q_i$, $2 \leqslant i \leqslant p$, a new state $q_i'$ which is the union of all states $q_j$, $j \leqslant i$, except that the items $[A_1 \to A_2\cdot], \ldots, [A_{i-1} \to A_i\cdot]$ are omitted, and which is accessed by $A_i$ from the state $q$, we obtain a parser that bypasses the reductions by the unit rules $A_1 \to A_2, \ldots, A_{p-1} \to A_p$.

Formally, each new state $q_i'$, $2 \leqslant i \leqslant p$, is defined by extending the Action and Goto tables as follows. For all $a \in T \cup \{\$\}$,

$$\text{Action}[q_i', a] = \begin{cases} \text{Action}[q_1, a], \text{ if Action}[q_1, a] \neq \text{"error"}, \\ \text{Action}[q_j, a], \text{ where } 1 < j < i, \text{ if} \\ \qquad \text{Action}[q_j, a] \notin \{\text{"error"}, \\ \qquad\qquad \text{"reduce by } A_{j-1} \to A_j\text{"}\}, \\ \text{Action}[q_i, a], \text{ otherwise}, \end{cases}$$

and for all $X \in V$,

$$\text{Goto}[q_i', X] = \begin{cases} \text{Goto}[q_j, X], \text{ where } 1 \leqslant j < i, \text{ if} \\ \qquad \text{Goto}[q_j, X] \neq \varnothing, \\ \text{Goto}[q_i, X], \text{ otherwise}. \end{cases}$$

Lemmas 7.46 and 7.47 imply that $\text{Action}[q_i', a]$ and $\text{Goto}[q_i', X]$ are well-defined. In addition, for all $i$, $2 \leqslant i \leqslant p$, $\text{Goto}[q, A_i]$ is replaced by $q_i'$, and if after these

**for** all sequences $A_1 \to A_2, \ldots, A_{i-1} \to A_i$, $i \geqslant 2$,
 of unit rules, and all states $q$ and $q_1, \ldots, q_i$
 such that Goto$[q, A_1] = q_1, \ldots,$ Goto$[q, A_i] = q_i$
 and Action$[q_1, a]$ is not
 a reduction by a unit rule for any $a \in T \cup \{\$\}$ **do**
 **if** no new state that is the combination of
  $q_1, \ldots, q_i$ has been created yet **then**
   Construct the combination of $q_1, \ldots, q_i$;
**for** each newly constructed state $q'$ **do**
 **if** $q'$ is the combination of the states Goto$[q, A_1], \ldots,$ Goto$[q, A_i]$ **then**
   Goto$[q, A_i] := q'$;
Delete all states to which there is no reference.

**Figure 7.40** An algorithm that eliminates all reductions by unit rules from a deterministic LALR(1) parser, provided that all nonterminals of the grammar derive nonempty terminal strings

replacements there is no reference.to a state $q_i$, then this state can be deleted. We say that the state $q_i'$ defined as above is the *combination of* the states $q_1, \ldots, q_i$ (*without unit rules*).

The above elimination method can be generalized to handle all possible sequences of reductions by unit rules. A formulation of a general algorithm is given in Figure 7.40.

We state without proof:

**Theorem 7.48** *Let G be an LALR(1) grammar and let M be its LALR(1) parser, and assume that all nonterminals of G derive nonempty terminal strings. Then the algorithm given in Figure 7.40 eliminates all reductions by unit rules from M, that is, the resulting table represents a pushdown transducer that behaves exactly as M but bypasses all reductions by unit rules.* □

The algorithm of Figure 7.40 creates new states and thus it may increase the size of the parser. We shall estimate the possible increase in the number of states. Let $n$ be the number of states in the original parser. For a sequence $A_1 \to A_2, \ldots, A_{p-1} \to A_p$ of unit rules and states $q$ and $q_1, \ldots, q_p$ such that Goto$[q, A_i] = q_i$, $i = 1, \ldots, p$, we might need $p$ new states. Moreover, we may have $p$ new states for every sequence $A_1' \to A_2, \ldots, A_{p-1} \to A_p$, where $A_1' \neq A_1$ and Goto$[q, A_1'] \neq \varnothing$. Thus for any nonterminal entry in the Goto table there may be $|G|$ new states. We conclude that the number of states in the new parser is bounded by $O(n \cdot |G|^2)$.

The algorithm of Figure 7.40 is applied—for simplicity—to the LALR(1) parser of an LALR(1) grammar and not to an arbitrary deterministic LR(1) parser of the grammar. However, in the same way for example as an LR(1) parser using default reductions is constructed from the LALR(1) parser, we may modify the parser produced by the algorithm of Figure 7.40.

It is important to observe that the inessential error entries in the original parser remain as such after performing the algorithm of Figure 7.40. In fact, significant savings of space are usually obtained by merging compatible states in the resulting parsing table.

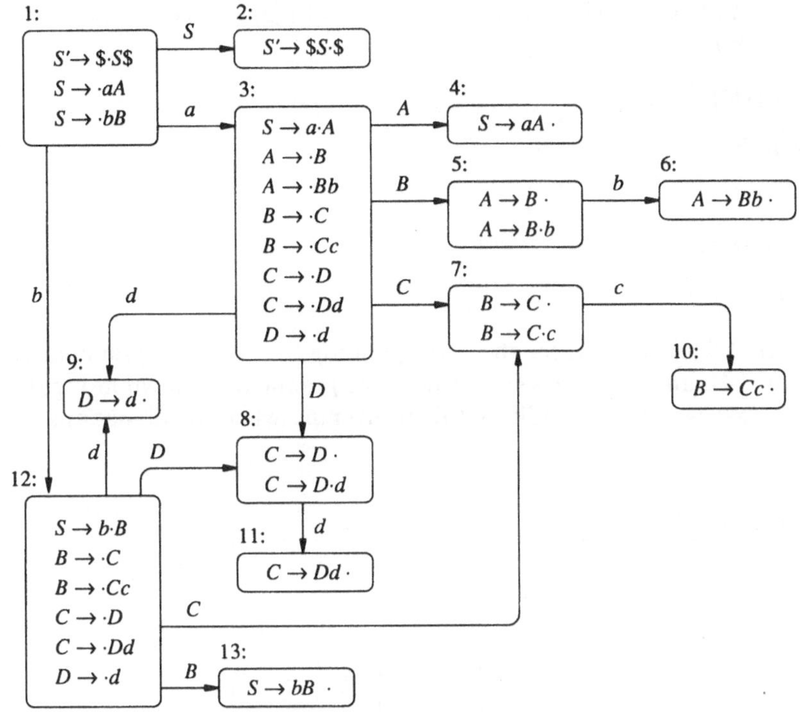


**Figure 7.41** The deterministic LR(0) machine for the grammar $S' \to \$S\$$, $S \to aA \mid bB$, $A \to B \mid Bb$, $B \to C \mid Cc$, $C \to D \mid Dd$, $D \to d$

| | Action | | | | | Goto | | | | |
|---|---|---|---|---|---|---|---|---|---|---|
| | *a* | *b* | *c* | *d* | $ | *S* | *A* | *B* | *C* | *D* |
| 1 | s3 | s12 | | | | 2 | | | | |
| 2 | | | | | *a* | | | | | |
| 3 | | | | s9 | | | 4 | 5 | 7 | 8 |
| 4 | | | | | r1 | | | | | |
| 5 | | s6 | | | r3 | | | | | |
| 6 | | | | | r4 | | | | | |
| 7 | | r5 | s10 | | r5 | | | | | |
| 8 | | r7 | r7 | s11 | r7 | | | | | |
| 9 | | r9 | r9 | r9 | r9 | | | | | |
| 10 | | r6 | | | r6 | | | | | |
| 11 | | r8 | r8 | | r8 | | | | | |
| 12 | | | | s9 | | | | 13 | 7 | 8 |
| 13 | | | | | r2 | | | | | |

**Figure 7.42** The LALR(1) parser of the grammar (1) $S \to aA$, (2) $S \to bB$, (3) $A \to B$, (4) $A \to Bb$, (5) $B \to C$, (6) $B \to Cc$, (7) $C \to D$, (8) $C \to Dd$, (9) $D \to d$

Let us demonstrate the behavior of the algorithm of Figure 7.40 by an example. Consider the grammar

$$S \to aA \mid bB \ ,$$

$$A \to B \mid Bb \ ,$$

$$B \to C \mid Cc \ ,$$

$$C \to D \mid Dd \ ,$$

$$D \to d \ .$$

The deterministic LR(0) machine for the corresponding \$-augmented grammar is shown in Figure 7.41, and the LALR(1) parser of the grammar is shown in Figure 7.42. In Figure 7.43 we give a modified LR(0) machine where combinations of

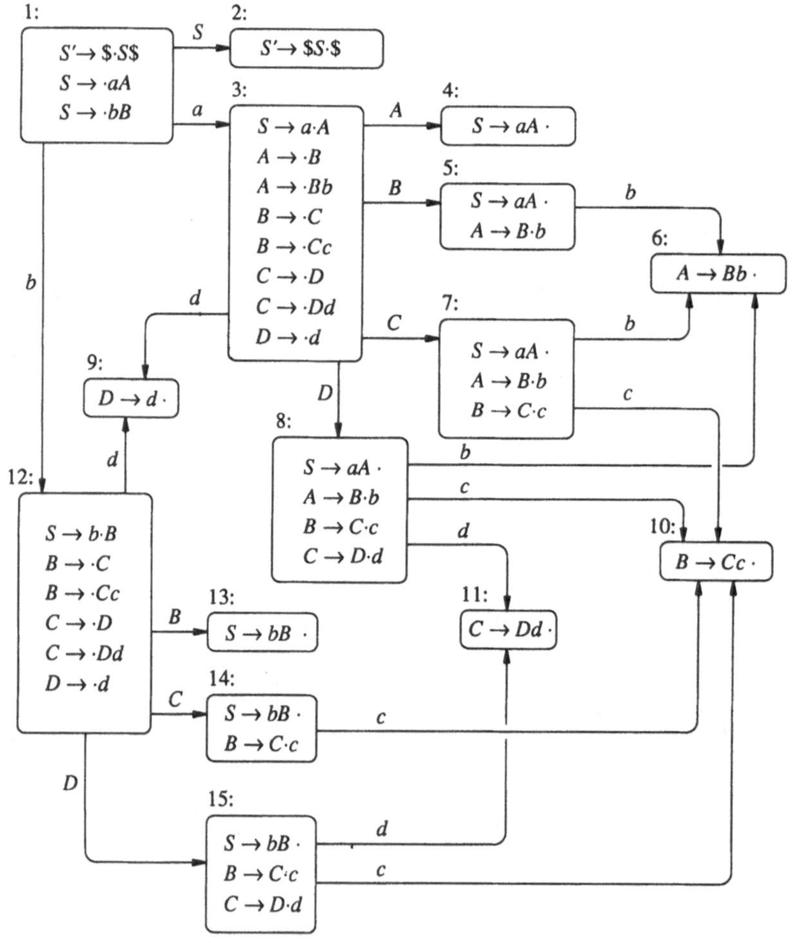


**Figure 7.43** The modified LR(0) machine

states without unit rules are given as respective item sets; this modified machine is a representation of the modified Goto table produced by the algorithm of Figure 7.40. The complete parser yielded by the algorithm of Figure 7.40 that bypasses all reductions by unit rules is given in Figure 7.44. Finally, Figure 7.45 shows the parser obtained from the parser of Figure 7.44 by merging compatible states.

We close this section by noting that there is no conceptual difficulty in generalizing the above methods for eliminating reductions by unit rules to handle also rules of the form $A \to a$, where $a$ is a terminal. We have excluded these rules in

| | Action | | | | | Goto | | | | |
|---|---|---|---|---|---|---|---|---|---|---|
| | *a* | *b* | *c* | *d* | $ | *S* | *A* | *B* | *C* | *D* |
| 1 | s3 | s12 | | | | 2 | | | | |
| 2 | | | | | *a* | | | | | |
| 3 | | | | s9 | | | 4 | 5 | 7 | 8 |
| 4 | | | | | *r*1 | | | | | |
| 5 | | s6 | | | *r*1 | | | | | |
| 6 | | | | | *r*4 | | | | | |
| 7 | | s6 | s10 | | *r*1 | | | | | |
| 8 | | s6 | s10 | s11 | *r*1 | | | | | |
| 9 | | *r*9 | *r*9 | *r*9 | *r*9 | | | | | |
| 10 | | *r*6 | | | *r*6 | | | | | |
| 11 | | *r*8 | *r*8 | | *r*8 | | | | | |
| 12 | | | | s9 | | | | 13 | 14 | 15 |
| 13 | | | | | *r*2 | | | | | |
| 14 | | | s10 | | *r*2 | | | | | |
| 15 | | | s10 | s11 | *r*2 | | | | | |

**Figure 7.44** The parser obtained from the parser of Figure 7.42 by eliminating all reductions by unit rules using the algorithm of Figure 7.40. The numbering of states corresponds to Figure 7.43

| | Action | | | | | Goto | | | | |
|---|---|---|---|---|---|---|---|---|---|---|
| | *a* | *b* | *c* | *d* | $ | *S* | *A* | *B* | *C* | *D* |
| 1 | s3 | s12 | | | | 2 | | | | |
| 2 | | | | | *a* | | | | | |
| 3 | | | | s9 | | | 4 | 4 | 4 | 4 |
| 4, 5, 7, 8 | | s6 | s10 | s11 | *r*1 | | | | | |
| 6 | | | | | *r*4 | | | | | |
| 9 | | *r*9 | *r*9 | *r*9 | *r*9 | | | | | |
| 10 | | *r*6 | | | *r*6 | | | | | |
| 11 | | *r*8 | *r*8 | | *r*8 | | | | | |
| 12 | | | | s9 | | | | 13 | 13 | 13 |
| 13, 14, 15 | | | s10 | s11 | *r*2 | | | | | |

**Figure 7.45** The parser obtained from the parser of Figure 7.44 by merging compatible states. Observe that now the columns for all nonterminals have become compatible and can be merged

the above discussion for simplicity and because these rules often do have semantic significance and thus should not be eliminated.

## 7.6 Parsing Ambiguous Grammars

Often a "natural" grammar for describing a language is ambiguous; then the grammar designer prefers one way to derive sentences and ignores the others. Simple verbal rules fix a unique way to parse the sentences. A common example is

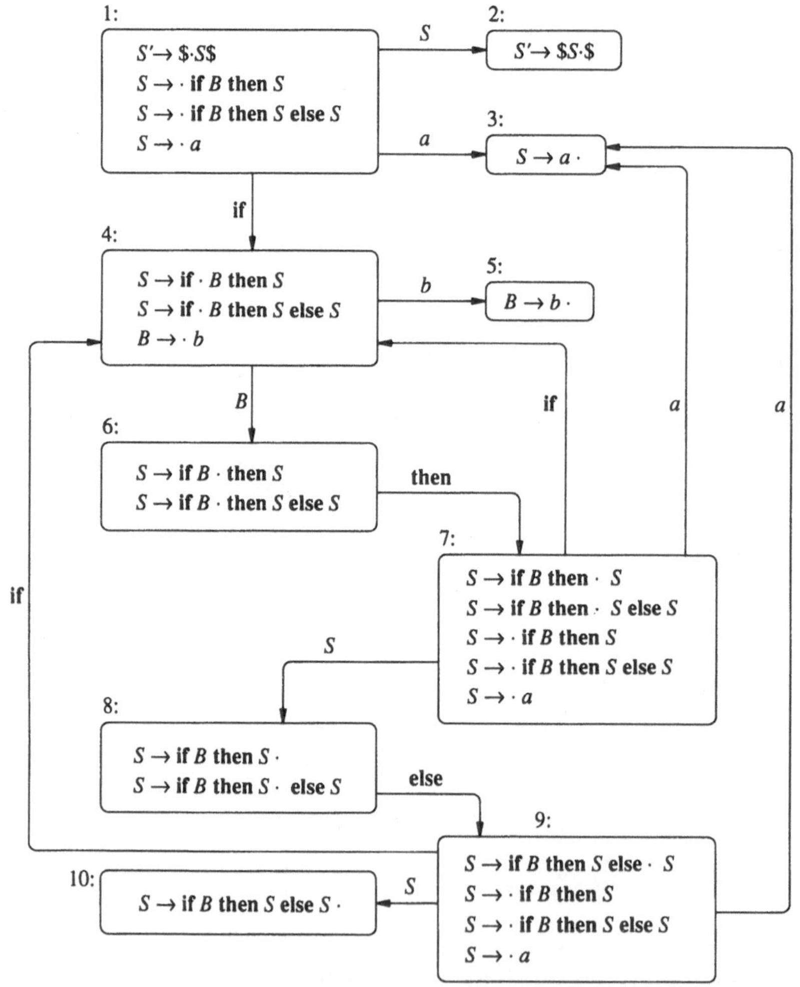


**Figure 7.46** The deterministic LR(0) machine for the grammar $S' \to \$S\$$, $S \to$ **if** $B$ **then** $S\,|\,$**if** $B$ **then** $S$ **else** $S\,|\,a$, $B \to b$

the "dangling-else" description of conditional statements by the grammar $G_{\text{delse}}$:

$$S \to \textbf{if } B \textbf{ then } S \mid \textbf{if } B \textbf{ then } S \textbf{ else } S \mid a \ ,$$

$$B \to b \ .$$

But $G_{\text{delse}}$ is ambiguous: for example, in the case of the sentence

**if** $b$ **then if** $b$ **then** $a$ **else** $a$

the keyword **else** may be associated either with the first or the second **then**. The common solution would choose the second **then**, following the general rule to leave the first **then** unassociated whenever some **then** must be left unassociated.

In this section we shall consider LR(1) parsers of ambiguous grammars. By definition, no LR(1) parser of an ambiguous grammar can be deterministic, but our intention is to investigate ways to make LR(1) parsers deterministic so that the desired parse is obtained. In some cases nondeterminism caused by ambiguities can be disposed of by deleting some actions in such a way that the resulting parser is still a right parser of the grammar or parses a desired subset of the language. To demonstrate this we consider the LALR(1) parsing of the grammar $G_{\text{delse}}$. The deterministic LR(0) machine for the \$-augmented grammar for $G_{\text{delse}}$ is given in Figure 7.46. The LALR(1) (and SLR(1)) parser of $G_{\text{delse}}$ has the following reduce actions.

| action: | output: |
|---|---|
| $q_1q_3 \mid \$ \to q_1q_2 \mid \$$, | $S \to a$ . |
| $q_1q_3 \mid \textbf{else} \to q_1q_2 \mid \textbf{else}$, | $S \to a$ . |
| $q_4q_5 \mid \textbf{then} \to q_4q_6 \mid \textbf{then}$, | $B \to b$ . |
| $q_1q_4q_6q_7q_8 \mid \$ \to q_1q_2 \mid \$$, | $S \to \textbf{if } B \textbf{ then } S$ . |
| $q_7q_4q_6q_7q_8 \mid \$ \to q_7q_8 \mid \$$, | $S \to \textbf{if } B \textbf{ then } S$ . |
| $q_9q_4q_6q_7q_8 \mid \$ \to q_9q_{10} \mid \$$, | $S \to \textbf{if } B \textbf{ then } S$ . |
| $q_1q_4q_6q_7q_8 \mid \textbf{else} \to q_1q_2 \mid \textbf{else}$, | $S \to \textbf{if } B \textbf{ then } S$ . |
| $q_7q_4q_6q_7q_8 \mid \textbf{else} \to q_7q_8 \mid \textbf{else}$, | $S \to \textbf{if } B \textbf{ then } S$ . |
| $q_9q_4q_6q_7q_8 \mid \textbf{else} \to q_9q_{10} \mid \textbf{else}$, | $S \to \textbf{if } B \textbf{ then } S$ . |
| $q_1q_4q_6q_7q_8q_9q_{10} \mid \$ \to q_1q_2 \mid \$$, | $S \to \textbf{if } B \textbf{ then } S \textbf{ else } S$ . |
| $q_7q_4q_6q_7q_8q_9q_{10} \mid \$ \to q_7q_8 \mid \$$, | $S \to \textbf{if } B \textbf{ then } S \textbf{ else } S$ . |
| $q_9q_4q_6q_7q_8q_9q_{10} \mid \$ \to q_9q_{10} \mid \$$, | $S \to \textbf{if } B \textbf{ then } S \textbf{ else } S$ . |
| $q_1q_4q_6q_7q_8q_9q_{10} \mid \textbf{else} \to q_1q_2 \mid \textbf{else}$, | $S \to \textbf{if } B \textbf{ then } S \textbf{ else } S$ . |
| $q_7q_4q_6q_7q_8q_9q_{10} \mid \textbf{else} \to q_7q_8 \mid \textbf{else}$, | $S \to \textbf{if } B \textbf{ then } S \textbf{ else } S$ . |
| $q_9q_4q_6q_7q_8q_9q_{10} \mid \textbf{else} \to q_9q_{10} \mid \textbf{else}$, | $S \to \textbf{if } B \textbf{ then } S \textbf{ else } S$ . |

The shift actions are:

$$q_1 \mid a \to q_1 q_3 \mid ,$$

$$q_1 \mid \textbf{if} \to q_1 q_4 \mid ,$$

$$q_4 \mid b \to q_4 q_5 \mid ,$$

$$q_6 \mid \textbf{then} \to q_6 q_7 \mid ,$$

$$q_7 \mid a \to q_7 q_3 \mid ,$$

$$q_7 \mid \textbf{if} \to q_7 q_4 \mid ,$$

$$q_8 \mid \textbf{else} \to q_8 q_9 \mid ,$$

$$q_9 \mid a \to q_9 q_3 \mid ,$$

$$q_9 \mid \textbf{if} \to q_9 q_4 \mid .$$

The nondeterminism of the LALR(1) parser of $G_{\mathbf{delse}}$ arises from the actions

$$q_8 \mid \textbf{else} \to q_8 q_9 \mid$$

and

$$q_1 q_4 q_6 q_7 q_8 \mid \textbf{else} \to q_1 q_2 \mid \textbf{else} ,$$

$$q_7 q_4 q_6 q_7 q_8 \mid \textbf{else} \to q_7 q_8 \mid \textbf{else} ,$$

$$q_9 q_4 q_6 q_7 q_8 \mid \textbf{else} \to q_9 q_{10} \mid \textbf{else} .$$

Now it is easy to verify that solving this shift-reduce conflict in favor of shifting corresponds to the requirement that each **else** is associated with the closest possible **then**. It is also clear that deleting the reduce actions

$$q_1 q_4 q_6 q_7 q_8 \mid \textbf{else} \to q_1 q_2 \mid \textbf{else} ,$$

$$q_7 q_4 q_6 q_7 q_8 \mid \textbf{else} \to q_7 q_8 \mid \textbf{else} ,$$

$$q_9 q_4 q_6 q_7 q_8 \mid \textbf{else} \to q_9 q_{10} \mid \textbf{else}$$

from the parser indeed yields a deterministic right parser of the grammar (a formal proof of this fact is left as an exercise). The resulting parser can be expressed as a parsing program (or a parsing table) in exactly the same way as in a usual deterministic LR(1) parser.

The above example nicely demonstrates the usefulness of allowing ambiguous descriptions. The ambiguous grammar $G_{\mathbf{delse}}$ is easy, but an unambiguous grammar defining the correct parse is rather complicated to construct. However, what we need are formal rules, called *disambiguating rules*, which are attached to grammar rules in order to resolve ambiguities. We shall consider only shift-reduce conflicts arising from ambiguities, and we shall ignore the question of whether the resulting deterministic pushdown transducer is indeed a parser of the grammar; at least it parses the sentences of some subset of the language described by the grammar, which may in fact be the intention of the grammar designer.

Let $A \to \omega$ be a rule of the grammar and $b$ a terminal such that at some state $q$ of the LR(1) parser there is a shift-reduce conflict between reducing by $A \to \omega$ and shifting $b$, that is, at state $q$ it is possible to reduce by $A \to \omega$ on $b$ and to shift on $b$. To resolve this conflict we may write either

$$A \to \omega, \ < b$$

or

$$A \to \omega, \ > b \ ,$$

where $<$ and $>$ may be interpreted as precedence relations between $\omega$ and $b$. If $A \to \omega, \ < b$, then shifting on $b$ has higher precedence than reducing by $A \to \omega$ and thus at any state this conflict is resolved in favor of shifting. If $A \to \omega, \ > b$, then reducing by $A \to \omega$ has higher precedence and the conflict is resolved accordingly. Of course, there may be several terminals causing a shift-reduce conflict when reducing by rule $A \to \omega$. Then all these terminals must be listed. For example,

$$A \to \omega, \ < b, \ < c, \ > d$$

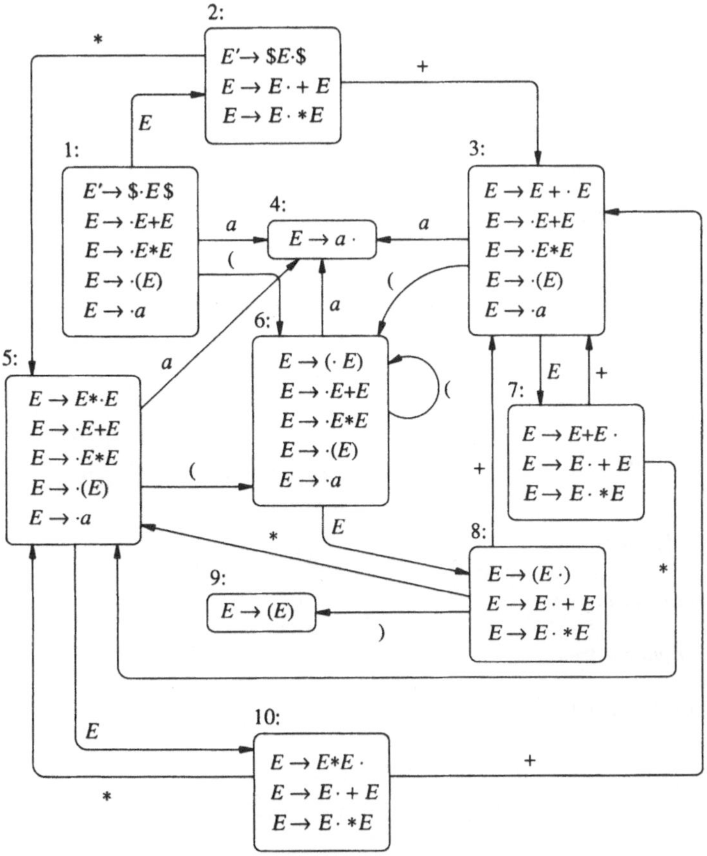


**Figure 7.47** The deterministic LR(0) machine for the grammar $E' \to \$E\$$, $E \to E + E|E * E|(E)|a$

means that the conflicts caused by $b$ and $c$ are resolved in favor of shifting and the conflict caused by $d$ in favor of reducing by $A \to \omega$.

As another example consider the ambiguous grammar

$$E \to E + E \mid E * E \mid (E) \mid a \ ,$$

which describes expressions with addition and multiplication as operators. Let us make the usual assumption that addition and multiplication are left-associative operators, so that for example $E + E + E$ is to be interpreted as $(E + E) + E$. We also assume, as usual, that multiplication has higher precedence than addition, so that for example $E + E * E$ is interpreted as $E + (E * E)$. Now these rules define ways to resolve the ambiguities:

$$E \to E + E, \ > + , \ < * \ ,$$

$$E \to E * E, \ > + , \ > * \ ,$$

```
empty;
push(eof-token);
push(initial-state);
accept := false;
scan;
repeat
     case top of begin
  6:5:3:1: if token.kind = a-token then
               shift(4) else
           if token.kind = left-par then
               shift (6) else
           error ("No E can start with this");
        2: if token.kind = eof-token then
               accept := true else
           if token.kind = plus then
               shift(3) else
           if token.kind = star then
               shift(5) else
           error ("eof, +, or * expected");
        4: reduce(E, 1);
        7: if token.kind = star then
               shift(5) else
           reduce (E, 3);
        8: if token.kind = plus then
               shift(3) else
           if token.kind = star then
               shift(5) else
           if token.kind = right-par then
               shift(9) else
           error (" +, *, or) expected");
        9: reduce(E, 3);
       10: reduce(E, 3);
     end case;
until accept.
```

**Figure 7.48** A deterministic right parser of the grammar $E \to E + E \mid E * E \mid (E) \mid a$ implemented as a parsing program

$$E \to (E) \ ,$$

$$E \to a \ .$$

From these rules a deterministic right parser of the grammar can be constructed. In Figure 7.47 we give the deterministic LR(0) machine, and the deterministic parser with conflicts resolved according to the above rules is shown in Figure 7.48 as a parsing program (see Section 7.4).

Finally we note that as the ambiguous grammar is short, the resulting parsing table is often small compared to the table obtained from the unambiguous grammar. It is especially noteworthy that for any grammar of the form

$$E_0 \to E_0 b_1 E_1 | E_1 \ ,$$

$$E_1 \to E_1 b_2 E_2 | E_2 \ ,$$

$$\vdots$$

$$E_{n-1} \to E_{n-1} b_n E_n | E_n \ ,$$

$$E_n \to (E_0) | a \ ,$$

$n \geqslant 1$, the parsing table obtained using the algorithm of Figure 7.37 for eliminating unit rules is of the same size as the corresponding parsing table for the ambiguous grammar

$$E \to Eb_1 E | \ldots | Eb_n E \ ,$$

$$E \to (E) | a \ .$$

## Exercises

7.1 Construct the nondeterministic LR(0) machine for the grammar $G_{\text{exp}}$:

$$E \to E + T | T \ ,$$

$$T \to T * F | F \ ,$$

$$F \to a | (E) \ ,$$

and construct the corresponding deterministic automaton by using the algorithm of Figure 3.9.

7.2 The algorithm of Figure 3.9 for making a nondeterministic finite automaton deterministic could be made more practical in the following way. When forming the set of states of the deterministic automaton, each new state accessible by, say, string $x$ is identified in the present algorithm by the union of all states accessible by $x$ in the nondeterministic automaton. This new state of the deterministic automaton could, however, be identified by the union of those states that are accessible by $x$ but in such a way that the last move is not an ε-move. Storing the constructed new states in this way saves space and makes it easier to search for, when a new candidate state has been created, whether or not it has already been constructed.

a) Write an algorithm which is a modification of the algorithm of Figure 3.9 as suggested above.

b) Design an implementation for constructing the deterministic LR(0) machine from a nondeterministic one, which is based on this modification of the algorithm of Figure 3.9.

7.3 Write a detailed algorithm that, given a set of items in the LR(0) collection for a \$-augmented grammar, tests whether or not this set of items violates the SLR(1) condition. The time bound of the algorithm should be $O(n^2)$, where $n$ is the size of the grammar.

7.4 Prove Lemma 7.5.

7.5 Construct the nondeterministic LR(1) machine for the grammar

$$E \to E + T \mid T \ ,$$

$$T \to a \mid (E) \ .$$

Construct the corresponding deterministic automaton by applying the algorithm of Figure 3.9.

7.6 Write a detailed algorithm that, given a set of items in the LR(1) collection for a \$-augmented grammar, tests whether or not this set of items violates the LR(1) condition. The time bound of the algorithm should be $O(m \cdot n)$, where $m$ is the size of the terminal alphabet and $n$ the size of the grammar.

7.7 Construct the deterministic LR(0) machine for the \$-augmented grammar for the grammar

$$S \to aAb \mid bba \mid bBE \ ,$$

$$A \to aBC \ ,$$

$$B \to b \ ,$$

$$C \to d \mid \varepsilon \ ,$$

$$E \to \varepsilon \ .$$

Give the relations **directly-reads, reads, includes,** and **lookback** for this LR(0) machine, and compute the relation denoted by **has-LALR-lookahead**. Give the LALR(1) parser of the grammar. Is it deterministic?

7.8 Prove Lemma 7.10.

7.9 Prove Fact 7.11.

7.10 Prove Lemma 7.14.

7.11 Define for state $q$ in the deterministic LR(0) machine for the \$-augmented grammar $G'$ for a grammar $G$:

$$(q, A) \textbf{ receives } (q', B) \ ,$$

if $\text{GOTO}(q, A) \neq \varnothing$ and for some rule $B \to \omega$ of $G$ $(\text{GOTO}(q, A), B \to \omega)$ **lookback** $(q', B)$. Show that

$$\textbf{lookback} \cdot \textbf{receives}^* \cdot \textbf{directly-reads} \neq \textbf{has-LALR-lookahead}.$$

7.12 Prove Fact 7.18.

7.13 Consider the scheme for implementing LR(1) parsers as parsing programs given in Section 7.4. Design an extension of the parsing program implementation (table-driven or the tables encoded as program instructions) such that the parsing program produces as output the derivation tree of the string to be parsed.

7.14 Give the SLR(1) parser of the grammar $G_{\text{exp}}$:

$$E \to E + T \mid T \ ,$$

$$T \to T * F \mid F \ ,$$

$$F \to a \mid (E) \ ,$$

a) as a parsing program,
b) as a parsing table.

7.15 Plan the implementation of deterministic LR(2) parsers (SLR(2), LALR(2), canonical LR(2) parsers). Notice that you cannot combine the Action and Goto tables for terminals in the same way as in the case of implementing LR(1) parsers.

7.16 Why is an SLR(1) parser an LR(0)-based LR(1) parser?

7.17 Prove Fact 7.21.

7.18 Let $G$ be a grammar and $M''$ its LR(1)-based LR(1) parser. Show that $M''$ is a right parser of $G$ and $\text{TIME}_{M''}(w) = \text{TIME}_G(w) + |w|$ for all sentences $w$ in $L(G)$.

7.19 Consider the parsing program given in Figures 7.15 to 7.17 that illustrates the elimination of unique reduce states. Modify the procedure *reduce* given in Figure 7.17 so that it is no longer recursive.

7.20 Consider the table-driven implementation of an LR(1) parser using default reductions. Modify the parsing scheme given in Figures 7.6 to 7.8 so that unique reduce states are eliminated. As an example construct the new Action and Goto tables having this elimination effect in the case of the grammar $G_{\text{block2}}$: $S \to \varepsilon | a := E |$ **begin** $C$ **end**, $C \to C \text{ ; } S | S$, $E \to E + T | T$, $T \to a | (E)$.

7.21 Construct an LR(0)-based LR(1) parser using default reductions (as a parsing program) from which unique reduce states have been eliminated for the grammar

$$
\begin{array}{ll}
S \to A | I, & T \to T * P | P \ , \\
A \to a := E, & P \to a | (E) \ , \\
I \to \textbf{if } B \textbf{ then } A\ L, & B \to B \textbf{ or } a | a \ , \\
E \to E + T | T, & L \to \textbf{else } S | \varepsilon \ .
\end{array}
$$

Consider a parsing program implementation of an LR(1) parser in which the rules are encoded as program statements (see for example Figure 7.15). Assume then that such a parsing program has two program segments as follows:

$$
\begin{array}{l}
q\text{: } \textbf{if } \textit{token.kind} = a_1 \textbf{ then } \textit{shift}(q_1) \textbf{ else} \\
\quad \textbf{if } \textit{token.kind} = a_2 \textbf{ then } \textit{shift}(q_2) \textbf{ else} \\
\qquad \vdots \\
\quad \textbf{if } \textit{token.kind} = a_n \textbf{ then } \textit{shift}(q_n) \textbf{ else} \\
\quad \textit{error} \ ;
\end{array}
$$

and for some $i$, $1 < i \leqslant n$,

$$
\begin{array}{l}
q'\text{: } \textbf{if } \textit{token.kind} = a_i \textbf{ then } \textit{shift}(q_i) \textbf{ else} \\
\qquad \vdots \\
\quad \textbf{if } \textit{token.kind} = a_n \textbf{ then } \textit{shift}(q_n) \textbf{ else} \\
\quad \textit{error} \ ;
\end{array}
$$

Clearly, the latter segment can be placed as a part of the first:

$$
\begin{array}{l}
q\text{: } \textbf{if } \textit{token.kind} = a_1 \textbf{ then } \textit{shift}(q_1) \textbf{ else} \\
\qquad \vdots \\
q'\text{: } \textbf{if } \textit{token.kind} = a_i \textbf{ then } \textit{shift}(q_i) \textbf{ else} \\
\qquad \vdots \\
\quad \textbf{if } \textit{token.kind} = a_n \textbf{ then } \textit{shift}(q_n) \textbf{ else} \\
\quad \textit{error} \ ;
\end{array}
$$

In general, there may exist several states which could be merged as described above. Notice that if a program segment for a state $q$ contains only shift statements then these can be ordered arbitrarily. In order to find an optimal placement (that is, with minimal number of statements) of program segments containing only shift statements we define a labeled directed graph $(A, R)$, called the *shift graph*, in the following way. The set $A$ of nodes consists of one designated node, say $r$, and of those states of the underlying LR(1) parser at which only shift actions are possible. Pair $(q, q')$, where $q, q' \in A \setminus \{r\}$, is in $R$, if $q \neq q'$ and $q'$ *covers* $q$, that is, each shift statement in the program segment labeled by $q$ appears in the program segment labeled by $q'$. Pair $(q, q')$ is labeled by the number of those shift statements that appear in the program segment for $q'$ but not in the program segment for $q$. For all $q \in A$, $q \neq r$, pair $(r, q)$ is in $R$, and $(r, q)$ is labeled by the number of shift statements in the program segment for $q$.

7.22 Show that the shift graph $(A, R)$ as defined above is acyclic and that there is a *directed spanning tree* (a subset of the edges which forms a tree, with all nodes included) with root $r$ for $(A, R)$.

7.23 Give an algorithm that constructs a minimum cost directed spanning tree $(A, R')$ with root $r$ for the shift graph $(A, R)$, that is, a directed spanning tree with the least possible sum of the labels of the edges in the tree. What is the time complexity of your algorithm?

7.24 Show that an optimal placement of program segments for states having only shift actions can be derived from a minimum cost spanning tree with root $r$ for the shift graph $(A, R)$.

7.25 Extend the above technique for subsuming states to be applicable also in the case of states with reduce actions.

7.26 In the parsing program implementation methods for LR(1) parsers suggested in Section 7.4 no attention was paid to the special structure of the reductions by the $\varepsilon$-rules. Add a feature to the parsing program schemes which allows the efficient handling of $\varepsilon$-reductions by simply pushing a state onto the stack.

7.27 Prove Fact 7.24.

7.28 Prove Fact 7.25.

7.29 Let $G = (V, T, P, S)$ be a reduced LR(1) grammar, $M$ its canonical LR(1) parser, and Action the parsing action table corresponding to $M$. Let $q$ be any state of $M$ entered by a nonterminal, that is, $q = [\delta A]$ for some viable prefix $\delta A$ of $G'$ where $A$ is a nonterminal, and let $a$ be a terminal in $T \cup \{\$\}$ such that $(q, a)$ is an error entry. Show that $(q, a)$ is an inessential error entry.

7.30 Let $G = (V, T, P, S)$ be a reduced SLR(1) grammar and $M$ its SLR(1) parser represented by a parsing table. Let $q$ be any state of $M$ entered by a nonterminal and $a$ any terminal in $T \cup \{\$\}$ such that $(q, a)$ is an error entry. Show that $(q, a)$ is an essential error entry if and only if for some rule $A \to \omega$ and state $q'$ such that Goto$[q', A] = q$ the condition Action[Goto$[q', \omega]$, $a$] = "reduce by $A \to \omega$" holds.

7.31 Let $G = (V, T, P, S)$ be an $\varepsilon$-free LALR(1) grammar, and consider a deterministic LR(0)-based LR(1) parser of $G$ represented by a parsing table. Show that whenever $(q, a)$ is an error entry, then $(q, a)$ is an essential error entry if and only if

$b$ **terminal entered-by**$^{-1}$ **(on-*a*-reduces-to symbol-in)***

**error-entry-on-*a*** $(q, a)$

for some $b \in T \cup \{\$\}$.

7.32 Give a reasonable condition for a grammar under which an error entry $(q, a)$ is essential if and only if

$b$ **may-imply-*a*-essential** $(q, a)$

for some terminal $b$.

7.33 Prove Lemma 7.35.

7.34 Complete the proof of Lemma 7.37. That is, give a proof for Case 3.

7.35 Prove Lemma 7.39.

7.36 Formalize the concept of a "general" LR(1) parser, that is, an LR(1) parser that behaves "exactly in the same way" as some LR(0)-based LR(1) parser of the given grammar but has perhaps fewer stack symbols. Use your formalization to prove Theorem 7.43.

7.37 Show that the graph coloring algorithm given in Figure 7.32 can indeed be used to produce a compatible partition of states of an LR(1) parser. In other words, show that the sets of nodes with equal color can be taken as elements for a compatible partition. What is the time complexity of the algorithm of Figure 7.32?

7.38 Develop a method for optimizing LR(1) parsers represented by a parsing table so that the Action and Goto tables can be compressed separately. Now the compatibility of states is defined with respect to one table only. In the compressed parser the states may not have the same indexes in different tables and thus a conversion vector is needed. Then apply this approach to optimize an LR(1) parser of the grammar $G_{\text{block2}}$: $S \to \varepsilon | a := E |$ **begin** $C$ **end**, $C \to C$ ; $S | S$, $E \to E + T | T$, $T \to a | (E)$. Also eliminate unique reduce states from this parser.

7.39 A table-driven LR(1) parser has a form which is especially amenable for compression if the Action table is divided into two parts in the following way. The first part, called the error checking part, handles error checking by a Boolean array, and in the second part, the action part, the corresponding action is found whenever the current input symbol was not erroneous. Give a detailed description of this kind of table-driven implementation including the program for table simulation. Take into account that the error checking and action parts are compressed separately as described in the previous exercise. Apply this method for producing a compact LR(1) parser for the grammar $E \to E + T | T * F | a$, $T \to T * F | a$, $F \to a | (E)$. Merge compatible states separately in the error checking part and in the action part. Notice that all error entries in the action part are inessential and that the inessential error entries in the error checking part are those which were inessential in the original Action table. Eliminate unique reduce states.

7.40 What is the time complexity of the algorithm given in Figure 7.37 with respect to the size $|G|$ of the underlying grammar $G$ and the number of states of the parser?

7.41 Consider the parser given in Figure 7.38. Compress the Action and Goto tables by

a) using default reductions and eliminating unique reduce states,
b) merging compatible rows and columns separately in the Action and Goto tables.

7.42 Formalize the concept of an "LR(1) parser bypassing unit reductions" meaning a pushdown transducer which behaves "in exactly the same way" as a true LR(1) parser but bypasses some reductions by unit rules. Use your formalization to prove Theorem 7.45.

7.43 Give an example which demonstrates that the algorithm of Figure 7.37 does not remove all reductions by unit rules even if for all states $q$, $q_1$, and $q_2$ and unit rules $A \to B$ such that $\text{Goto}[q, A] = q_1$ and $\text{Goto}[q, B] = q_2$ the states $q_1$ and $q_2$ are initially $(A, B)$-compatible.

7.44 Let $n \geqslant 1$ and $G_n$ be the grammar

$$E_0 \to E_0 b_1 E_1 | E_1 ,$$

$$E_1 \to E_1 b_2 E_2 | E_2 ,$$

$$\vdots$$

$$E_{n-1} \to E_{n-1} b_n E_n | E_n ,$$

$$E_n \to (E_0) | a .$$

Show that the algorithm of Figure 7.37 eliminates all reductions by unit rules from any LR(0)-based LR(1) parser of $G_n$.

7.45 The algorithm of Figure 7.37 cannot increase the number of states of the parser because it does not create new states but only merges existing states. However, the number of non-error entries in the Action and Goto tables, and hence the actual size of the parser, may increase. Can you devise any reasonable bound for this increase? What can you say about this increase in the case of the grammars $G_n$ given in the previous exercise?

7.46 a) Show that Lemma 7.46 does not hold for all deterministic LR(0)-based LR(1) parsers of the given LALR(1) grammar.
b) Show that Lemma 7.46 holds for the SLR(1) parser of an SLR(1) grammar.

7.47 Prove Lemma 7.47. Can you find an example which shows that the assumption of Lemma 7.47 that no nonterminal derives only the empty string is really needed?

7.48 Consider the algorithm given in Figure 7.40 for eliminating reductions by unit rules. In many cases two new states $q'$ and $q''$ created by the algorithm, such that $q'$ is a combination of $q_1, \ldots, q_i$ and $q''$ is a combination of $q_1, \ldots, q_j$, $j < i$, are compatible and can be merged. Show that any two such states $q'$ and $q''$ can be merged if the original parser is the SLR(1) parser of an SLR(1) grammar, provided that no nonterminal derives only the empty string.

7.49 Apply the algorithm of Figure 7.40 for eliminating the reductions by unit rules from the LR(1) parser constructed in Exercise 7.21. Merge all compatible states.

7.50 Consider the LALR(1) parser of the grammar $G_{\text{delse}}$: $S \to \textbf{if } B \textbf{ then } S \mid \textbf{if } B \textbf{ then } S \textbf{ else } S \mid a$, $B \to b$ given in Section 7.6. Show that by deleting the actions

$$q_1 q_4 q_6 q_7 q_8 \mid \textbf{else} \to q_1 q_2 \mid \textbf{else} ,$$

$$q_7 q_4 q_6 q_7 q_8 \mid \textbf{else} \to q_7 q_8 \mid \textbf{else}, \text{ and}$$

$$q_9 q_4 q_6 q_7 q_8 \mid \textbf{else} \to q_9 q_{10} \mid \textbf{else}$$

a deterministic right parser of the grammar is obtained.

7.51 When using ambiguous grammars for language description it is often reasonable to have special disambiguating rules for error detection. Design a mechanism for error detection using disambiguating rules. Give an ambiguous grammar with disambiguating rules for expressions having addition, subtraction, multiplication, division, and equality as operators. We assume that the equality operation is not associative and has the lowest precedence. Otherwise the standard associativity and precedence rules are preferred.

7.52 A reduce-reduce conflict could be resolved by simply choosing the rule that appears first in the given list of rules. However, it may be desirable to have different preferences on different terminals which cause the conflict. Taking this into account design a disambiguating rule mechanism for resolving reduce-reduce conflicts.

## Bibliographic Notes

LaLonde (1971) was the first to design an efficient algorithm for constructing LALR(1) parsers. Later on, many implementations for the construction of LALR(1) lookahead sets have been presented, among which the most prominent are the algorithms by Kristensen and Madsen (1981), DeRemer and Pennello (1982), Park, Choe and Chang (1985), and Bermudez and Logothetis (1989). Our presentation follows DeRemer and Pennello (1982) (also see Sager, 1986).

The table-driven implementation of LR(1) parsers originates from Knuth (1965). Encoding the parsing tables as program statements has been suggested e.g. by Aho and Johnson (1974) and Aho and Ullman (1977). The use of default reductions and the elimination of unique reduce states have been suggested in several sources, perhaps first by DeRemer (1969). The method for subsuming rows in a parsing program considered in Exercises 7.22 to 7.25 originates from Ichbiah and Morse (1970), who used it for precedence parser optimization.

Algorithms for determining inessential error entries in the parsing table for canonical LR(1) and SLR(1) parsers have been devised by Aho and Ullman (1972a, 1973a, 1973b). Soisalon-Soininen (1982) presented an algorithm for determining inessential error entries for any LR(0)-based LR(1) parser. The first efficient algorithm for determining all inessential error entries for any LR(0)-based LR(1) parser is given in Sippu and Soisalon-Soininen (1985). Joliat (1973, 1974) was the first to suggest the error matrix factoring from the parsing table, thus making all error entries inessential. This approach is favored by Dencker, Durre and Heuft (1984) based on a detailed experimental analysis. Determining the true inessential error entries remains important, however, for the compression of the error matrix and for the elimination of reductions by unit rules.

The idea of making use of inessential error entries in parsing table compression comes from Pager (1970), who, however, considered all error entries inessential and thus sacrificed some essential features of LR($k$) parsing: the correctness of the parser was preserved by storing the stack string in the parsing stack and by matching the stack string with the right-hand side of the rule by which a reduce action was to be performed. Pager's idea was used by Aho and Ullman (1972a, 1973a) and by Joliat (1973, 1974) but now retaining the properties of LR($k$) parsing. The approximation algorithm for graph coloring given in Figure 7.32 and its use for parsing table compression was proposed by Dencker et al. (1984).

The elimination of reductions by unit rules has been studied in many sources, e.g. Anderson, Eve and Horning (1973), Aho and Ullman (1973a, 1973b), Demers (1974, 1975), Pager (1974, 1977b), LaLonde (1976a), Soisalon-Soininen (1977a,

1980a, 1982), Koskimies and Soisalon-Soininen (1979), Rushby (1977), Tokuda (1981), Drossopoulou (1982), Schmitz (1984), LaLonde (1984), and by Heilbrunner (1985). The algorithm given in Figure 7.37 is the one suggested by Aho and Ullman (1973b), and the algorithm of Figure 7.40 is from Anderson et al. (1973). The method indicated in Exercise 7.48 for SLR(1) parsers is the basic method of Pager (1974, 1977b). In the work of Rushby (1977) the whole LR($k$) theory is developed in conjunction with unit rule elimination. Drossopoulou (1982) considers the general question of combining consecutive reduce actions.

LR($k$) parsing of ambiguous grammars is considered in Demers (1974) and in Aho, Johnson and Ullman (1975). Johnson (1975) describes a compiler writing system that employs ambiguous grammars with disambiguating rules; also see Aho and Ullman (1977) and Aho, Sethi and Ullman (1986). The formalism for disambiguating rules used in Section 7.6 is from Koskimies, Paakki, Nurmi and Sippu (1988).

Finally we would like to mention the work of Pager (1977a) which generalizes in a practical way the construction of LALR(1) parsers to produce a deterministic LR(1) parser for any LR(1) grammar. Heilbrunner (1981) formalizes this and other algorithms for constructing LR(1) parsers.

# 8. LL($k$) Parsing

In this chapter we shall generalize the notion of strong LL($k$) parsing presented in Chapter 5 and consider a method for deterministic left parsing that applies to a slightly wider class of context-free grammars than does the strong LL($k$) parsing method. This method will be called "canonical LL($k$) parsing". As in strong LL($k$) parsing, the acronym "LL($k$)" means that the input string is parsed (1) in a single Left-to-right scan, (2) producing a Left parse, and (3) using lookahead of length $k$.

The concept of a canonical LL($k$) parser can be viewed as a dual of the concept of a canonical LR($k$) parser. A canonical LL($k$) parser will be obtained as a generalization of a strong LL($k$) parser in a way analogous to that in which a canonical LR($k$) parser was obtained as a generalization of a shift-reduce or a simple precedence parser. As we recall, a canonical LR($k$) parser uses as stack symbols certain equivalence classes of viable prefixes, that is, valid stack strings of a shift-reduce or a simple precedence parser. The equivalence relation in question was called an LR($k$)-equivalence. Analogously, a canonical LL($k$) parser will use as stack symbols certain equivalence classes of valid stack strings of a strong LL($k$) parser. These stack strings will be called "viable suffixes" and the equivalence relation will be called an "LL($k$)-equivalence". To construct the LL($k$)-equivalence for a given grammar, we shall use the concept of an "LL($k$)-valid item", a dual of the concept of an LR($k$)-valid item. Indeed, the entire theory of canonical LL($k$) parsing can be regarded as a dual theory of the theory of canonical LR($k$) parsing. To exhibit this duality, we shall persist in a treatment that follows closely the treatment of canonical LR($k$) parsing in Chapter 6. Most lemmas and theorems presented in Chapter 6 will have their natural counterparts in this chapter.

In Section 8.1 we shall define the notion of a "viable suffix" and prove lemmas that state the basic properties of viable suffixes. In Section 8.2 we shall introduce the notions of an "LL($k$)-valid item", "LL($k$)-equivalence", and a "canonical LL($k$) machine" and show how the canonical LL($k$) machine for a grammar can be constructed. In Section 8.3 we shall define, and prove the correctness of, the notion of a "canonical LL($k$) parser". We shall also see how the notion of a canonical LL($k$) parser implies in a natural way parser variants that can be regarded as duals of the LALR($k$) parsers and the LA($k$)LR($l$) parsers. These parser variants will be called "LALL($k$) parsers" and "LA($k$)LL($l$) parsers". In Section 8.4 we shall study the properties of "LL($k$) grammars", that is, grammars for which the canonical LL($k$) parser is deterministic. In particular, we shall give a rigorous proof of the fact that any (reduced) LL($k$) grammar is also an LR($k$) grammar. In Section 8.5 we shall derive an efficient algorithm for constructing canonical LL(1) parsers and

LALL(1) parsers. In Sections 8.6 and 8.7 we shall consider the problem of transforming grammars into a form to which left parsing can be applied. First we review the traditional method for removing left recursion from grammars so that a covering grammar is obtained (Section 8.6). Then we present a one-pass transformation that produces covering LL($k$) grammars for a subclass of LR($k$) grammars called "PLR($k$) grammars" (Section 8.7).

## 8.1 Viable Suffixes

In Section 6.1 we showed that there are grammars whose shift-reduce parser cannot be made deterministic by adding lookahead and lookback strings to the actions of the parser, although a deterministic right parser does exist and can be algorithmically constructed from the grammar. In this section we shall show that the same is true for produce-shift parsers: for some grammars the produce-shift parser cannot be made deterministic by adding lookahead and lookback strings, but there may, however, be a natural way to construct a deterministic left parser.

We shall consider the grammar $G_{abL}$:

$$S \rightarrow aAab \mid bAb \ ,$$

$$A \rightarrow cAB \mid \varepsilon \mid a \ ,$$

$$B \rightarrow \varepsilon \ .$$

$G_{abL}$ is an SLR(2) grammar and generates the regular language

$$L(G_{abL}) = a\{c\}^*\{\varepsilon, a\}ab \cup b\{c\}^*\{\varepsilon, a\}b \ .$$

First we show that $G_{abL}$ is not SLL($k$) for any natural number $k$. This comes from the fact that

$$\mathrm{FIRST}_k(\varepsilon\,\mathrm{FOLLOW}_k(A)) = \{k{:}ab, k{:}b\}$$

and

$$\mathrm{FIRST}_k(a\ \mathrm{FOLLOW}_k(A)) = \{k{:}aab, k{:}ab\} \ ,$$

and thus

$$k{:}ab \in \mathrm{FIRST}_k(\varepsilon\ \mathrm{FOLLOW}_k(A)) \cap \mathrm{FIRST}_k(a\ \mathrm{FOLLOW}_k(A))$$

for any $k$. Hence at a configuration

$$\$\gamma A \mid ab\$$$

of the SLL($k$) parser of $G_{abL}$ we are not able to decide whether to use the produce action by the rule $A \rightarrow a$ or the produce action by the rule $A \rightarrow \varepsilon$.

We might try to make the parser deterministic by using a lookback string for the produce actions by the rules $A \rightarrow a$ and $A \rightarrow \varepsilon$. That is, instead of the actions

$$A \mid y \rightarrow a \mid y \quad \text{and} \quad A \mid y \rightarrow \ \mid y \ ,$$

we would have several actions of the forms

$$\alpha A \mid y \to \alpha a \mid y \quad \text{and} \quad \beta A \mid y \to \beta \mid y \ ,$$

where $\alpha$ and $\beta$ are strings in $\$V^*{:}m$ for $m > 0$. Now if we were able to use this kind of actions in such a way that

$$\{\alpha \mid \alpha A \mid y \to \alpha a \mid y \text{ is an action}\}$$
$$\cap \{\beta \mid \beta A \mid y \to \beta \mid y \text{ is an action}\} = \varnothing \ ,$$

then we would have created a deterministic left parser for $G_{abL}$. However, we must have the actions

$$B^m A \mid y \to B^m a \mid y \quad \text{and} \quad B^m A \mid y \to B^m \mid y \ ,$$

because some produce action by the rule $A \to a$ must be applicable to the configuration $\$bB^m A \mid ab\$$, if the sentence $bc^m ab$ is to be accepted, and some produce action by the rule $A \to \varepsilon$ must be applicable to the configuration $\$baB^m A \mid ab\$$, if the sentence $ac^m ab$ is to be accepted. As this pair of produce actions exhibits a produce-produce conflict, we conclude that it is impossible to obtain a deterministic left parser for $G_{abL}$ just by adding lookback strings to the actions of the SLL($k$) parser.

We can, however, make the SLL($k$) parser ($k > 1$) of $G_{abL}$ deterministic by classifying the viable stack strings in a way reminiscent to that we used in Section 6.1 to create a deterministic right parser for the grammar $G_{ab}$. The set of viable stack strings of the SLL($k$) parser of $G_{abL}$ is

$$\{S\} \cup \{baAa\} \cup \{bAb\}$$
$$\cup \{baB^n Ac \mid n \geq 1\} \cup \{baB^n A \mid n \geq 0\}$$
$$\cup \{baB^n a \mid n \geq 0\} \cup \{baB^n \mid n \geq 0\}$$
$$\cup \{\varepsilon\}$$
$$\cup \{bB^n Ac \mid n \geq 1\} \cup \{bB^n A \mid n \geq 0\}$$
$$\cup \{bB^n a \mid n \geq 1\} \cup \{bB^n \mid n \geq 0\} \ .$$

We say that an action $r$ of an SLL($k$) parser is *valid* for viable stack string $\gamma$ if

$$\$\gamma' \mid y'\$ \overset{r}{\Rightarrow} \$\gamma \mid y\$$$

holds for some input strings $y$ and $y'$ and viable stack string $\gamma'$ such that $k{:}y\$$.is in $\text{FIRST}_k(\gamma^R\$)$. Observe that unlike in the LR($k$) case an action is defined to be valid for viable stack strings resulting from the application of the action, not for viable stack strings to which the action is applied.

We divide the set of viable stack strings of an SLL($k$) parser into a finite number of equivalence classes in the following way. Two stack strings belong to the same equivalence class if they have the same set of valid actions. Since for any grammar

$G = (V, T, P, S)$ the SLL($k$) parser has at most $|T| + |T|^k \cdot |P| \leqslant |G|^{k+1}$ distinct actions, the number of distinct equivalence classes is bound by $2^{|G|^{k+1}}$.

For the SLL(2) parser of $G_{abL}$ the equivalence classes and the associated valid actions are:

| equivalence class: | valid actions: |
|---|---|
| $\{\varepsilon, bA\}$ | $b\,\vert\,b \to \,\vert$ |
| $\{S\}$ | — |
| $\{bB^n \vert n \geqslant 0\}$ | $A\,\vert\,b\$ \to \,\vert\,b\$$ |
| | $B\,\vert\,b\$ \to \,\vert\,b\$$ |
| | $a\,\vert\,a \to \,\vert$ |
| $\{ba\}$ | $A\,\vert\,ab \to a\,\vert\,ab$ |
| | $A\,\vert\,ab \to \,\vert\,ab$ |
| | $B\,\vert\,ab \to \,\vert\,ab$ |
| | $a\,\vert\,a \to \,\vert$ |
| $\{bB^n a \vert n \geqslant 1\}$ | $A\,\vert\,ab \to a\,\vert\,ab$ |
| $\{bB^n A \vert n \geqslant 1\} \cup \{baB^n A \vert n \geqslant 1\}$ | $c\,\vert\,c \to \,\vert$ |
| $\{bB^n Ac \vert n \geqslant 1\}$. | $A\,\vert\,ca \to BAc\,\vert\,ca$ |
| | $A\,\vert\,cb \to BAc\,\vert\,cb$ |
| | $A\,\vert\,cc \to BAc\,\vert\,cc$ |
| $\{baB^n \vert n \geqslant 1\}$ | $A\,\vert\,ab \to \,\vert\,ab$ |
| | $B\,\vert\,ab \to \,\vert\,ab$ |
| | $a\,\vert\,a \to \,\vert$ |
| $\{baB^n a \vert n \geqslant 0\}$ | $A\,\vert\,aa \to a\,\vert\,aa$ |
| $\{baA\}$ | $a\,\vert\,a \to \,\vert$ |
| $\{baB^n Ac \vert n \geqslant 1\}$ | $A\,\vert\,ca \to BAc\,\vert\,ca$ |
| | $A\,\vert\,cc \to BAc\,\vert\,cc$ |
| $\{baAa\}$ | $S\,\vert\,aa \to baAa\,\vert\,aa$ |
| | $S\,\vert\,ac \to baAa\,\vert\,ac$ |
| $\{bAb\}$ | $S\,\vert\,ba \to bAb\,\vert\,ba$ |
| | $S\,\vert\,bb \to bAb\,\vert\,bb$ |
| | $S\,\vert\,bc \to bAb\,\vert\,bc$ |

To obtain the desired property that the equivalence should be right-invariant and that any two equivalent viable stack strings should end with the same symbol, we must further make the following refinements:

1) $\{\varepsilon, bA\}$ is split into $\{\varepsilon\}$ and $\{bA\}$.
2) $\{bB^n | n \geq 0\}$ is split into $\{b\}$ and $\{bB^n | n \geq 1\}$.
3) $\{bB^nA | n \geq 1\} \cup \{baB^nA | n \geq 1\}$ is split into $\{bB^nA | n \geq 1\}$ and $\{baB^nA | n \geq 1\}$.

As in Section 6.1 we can represent the resulting right-invariant equivalence as a transition graph that has a transition on symbol $X$ from class $[\gamma]$ to class $[\gamma X]$ whenever $\gamma X$ is a viable stack string (see Figure 8.1). As was the case with viable prefixes, that is, viable stack strings of the shift-reduce parser, we shall see that the viable stack strings of the SLL($k$) parser always form a regular language.

We may use equivalence classes as stack symbols thus creating a new kind of parser which may be deterministic in some cases in which the SLL($k$) parser is not. The new produce actions are of the form

$$[\delta A] \mid y \to Y_n \ldots Y_1 \mid y \ ,$$

where $\delta A$ is a viable stack string, and for some symbols $X_1, \ldots, X_n$ in $V$, $A \to X_1 \ldots X_n$ is a rule, $y$ is a string in $\text{FIRST}_k(X_1 \ldots X_n \delta^R \$)$, and

$$Y_i = \begin{cases} [\delta X_n \ldots X_i] & \text{when } X_i \text{ is a nonterminal ;} \\ X_i & \text{when } X_i \text{ is a terminal .} \end{cases}$$

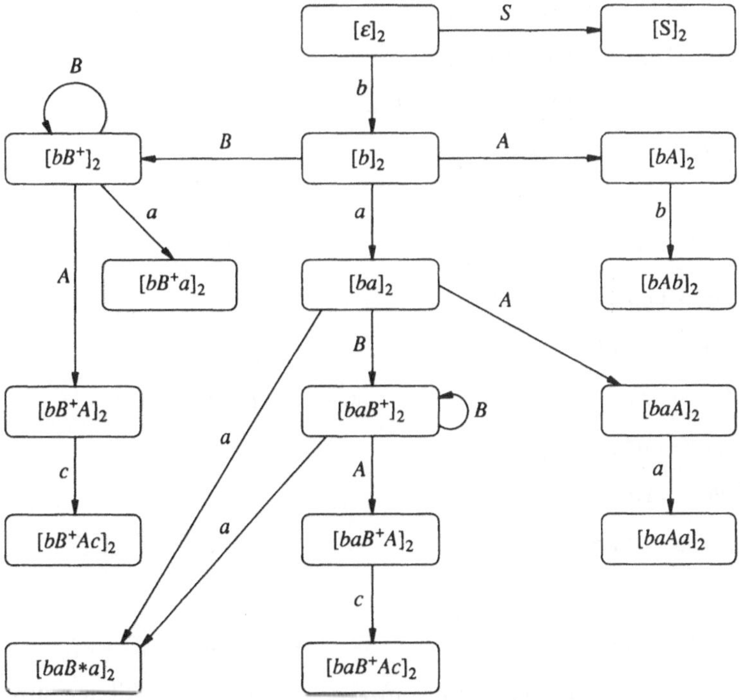


**Figure 8.1** Transition graph for the viable stack strings of the SLL(2) parser of the grammar $G_{abL}$: $S \to aAab | bAb$, $A \to cAB | \varepsilon | a$, $B \to \varepsilon$

The shift actions are as in the SLL($k$) parser. The initial stack contents are $[S]$ and the final stack contents are empty.

For example, the parser obtained in this way from the SLL(2) parser of $G_{abL}$ has the following produce actions.

| action $r$: | $\tau(r)$: |
|---|---|
| $[S]_2 \mid aa \to ba[baA]_2 a \mid aa$ | $S \to aAab$ |
| $[S]_2 \mid ac \to ba[baA]_2 a \mid ac$ | ” |
| $[S]_2 \mid ba \to b[bA]_2 b \mid ba$ | $S \to bAb$ |
| $[S]_2 \mid bb \to b[bA]_2 b \mid bb$ | ” |
| $[S]_2 \mid bc \to b[bA]_2 b \mid bc$ | ” |
| $[bA]_2 \mid ca \to [bB^+]_2[bB^+A]_2 c \mid ca$ | $A \to cAB$ |
| $[bA]_2 \mid cb \to [bB^+]_2[bB^+A]_2 c \mid cb$ | ” |
| $[bA]_2 \mid cc \to [bB^+]_2[bB^+A]_2 c \mid cc$ | ” |
| $[bB^+A]_2 \mid ca \to [bB^+]_2[bB^+A]_2 c \mid ca$ | ” |
| $[bB^+A]_2 \mid cb \to [bB^+]_2[bB^+A]_2 c \mid cb$ | ” |
| $[bB^+A]_2 \mid cc \to [bB^+]_2[bB^+A]_2 c \mid cc$ | ” |
| $[baA]_2 \mid ca \to [baB^+]_2[baB^+A]_2 c \mid ca$ | ” |
| $[baA]_2 \mid cc \to [baB^+]_2[baB^+A]_2 c \mid cc$ | ” |
| $[baB^+A]_2 \mid ca \to [baB^+]_2[baB^+A]_2 c \mid ca$ | ” |
| $[baB^+A]_2 \mid cc \to [baB^+]_2[baB^+A]_2 c \mid cc$ | ” |
| $[bA]_2 \mid b\$ \to \mid b\$$ | $A \to \varepsilon$ |
| $[bB^+A]_2 \mid b\$ \to \mid b\$$ | ” |
| $[baA]_2 \mid ab \to \mid ab$ | ” |
| $[baB^+A]_2 \mid ab \to \mid ab$ | ” |
| $[bA]_2 \mid ab \to a \mid ab$ | $A \to a$ |
| $[bB^+A]_2 \mid ab \to a \mid ab$ | ” |
| $[baA]_2 \mid aa \to a \mid aa$ | ” |
| $[baB^+A]_2 \mid aa \to a \mid aa$ | ” |
| $[bB^+]_2 \mid b\$ \to \mid b\$$ | $B \to \varepsilon$ |
| $[baB^+]_2 \mid ab \to \mid ab$ | ” |

In the above produce actions no produce-produce conflict is exhibited any longer. This is because the conflicting pair of actions

$$A \mid ab \to a \mid ab, \quad A \mid ab \to \mid ab$$

in the SLL(2) parser has now been replaced by the actions

$$[bA]_2 \mid ab \to a \mid ab, \qquad [bB^+A]_2 \mid ab \to a \mid ab, \qquad [baA]_2 \mid ab \to \mid ab,$$
$$[baB^+A]_2 \mid ab \to \mid ab \ .$$

The parser accepts the sentences $ac^nab$ and $bc^nab$, $n > 0$, in the following way:

$$\$[S]_2 \mid ac^nab\$$$
$$\Rightarrow \$ba[baA]_2a \mid ac^nab\$$$
$$\Rightarrow \$ba[baA]_2 \mid c^nab\$$$
$$\Rightarrow^{2n} \$ba[baB^+]_2^n[baB^+A]_2 \mid ab\$$$
$$\Rightarrow \$ba[baB^+]_2^n \mid ab\$$$
$$\Rightarrow^n \$ba \mid ab\$$$
$$\Rightarrow^2 \$ \mid \$.$$
$$\$[S]_2 \mid bc^nab\$$$
$$\Rightarrow \$b[bA]_2b \mid bc^nab\$$$
$$\Rightarrow \$b[bA]_2 \mid c^nab\$$$
$$\Rightarrow^{2n} \$b[bB^+]_2^n[bB^+A]_2 \mid ab\$$$
$$\Rightarrow \$b[bB^+]_2^na \mid ab\$$$
$$\Rightarrow \$b[bB^+]_2^n \mid b\$$$
$$\Rightarrow^n \$b \mid b\$$$
$$\Rightarrow \$ \mid \$ \ .$$

The deterministic left parser constructed above for $G_{abL}$ is a simplified version of a canonical LL(2) parser. Later we shall see that this simplified parser may not be deterministic for all LL($k$) grammars, that is, grammars for which the true canonical LL($k$) parser is deterministic. The error detection capability of the simplified parser may also be worse than that of the true canonical parser, when $k > 1$.

In the following we give a grammatical characterization for the viable stack strings of the SLL($k$) parser and study the properties of these strings. We follow the presentation used in Section 6.1 in order to facilitate comparison and to make the dualism more apparent.

Let $G = (V, T, P, S)$ be a grammar. String $\gamma \in V^*$ is a *viable suffix* of $G$ if

$$S \underset{\text{lm}}{\Longrightarrow^*} xA\delta \underset{\text{lm}}{\Longrightarrow} x\alpha\beta\delta = x\alpha\gamma^R$$

holds in $G$ for some strings $x \in T^*$ and $\delta \in V^*$ and rule $A \to \alpha\beta$ in $P$. $\gamma$ is a *complete viable suffix* if here $\alpha = \varepsilon$. Thus, viable suffixes are reversals of certain suffixes of left sentential forms, whereas viable prefixes are certain prefixes of right sentential forms.

**Fact 8.1** Any viable suffix of grammar $G$ is a prefix of some complete viable suffix of $G$. □

It turns out that the set of viable suffixes of a grammar $G$ coincides with the set of viable prefixes of the reversal $G^R$ of $G$. Recall that $G^R$ is the grammar obtained from $G$ by replacing each rule $r = A \to \omega$ by its reversal $r^R$, that is, by the rule $A \to \omega^R$ in which $\omega^R$ is the reversal of the string $\omega$.

**Lemma 8.2** *For rule string $r_1 \ldots r_n$, $n \geq 0$, of grammar $G = (V, T, P, S)$ and strings $\phi_1$ and $\phi_2$ in $V^*$, (a)*

$$\phi_1 \xrightarrow[\text{rm}]{r_1 \ldots r_n} \phi_2 \quad \text{in } G$$

*if and only if*

$$\phi_1^R \xrightarrow[\text{lm}]{r_1^R \ldots r_n^R} \phi_2^R \quad \text{in } G^R,$$

*and (b)*

$$\phi_1 \xrightarrow[\text{lm}]{r_1 \ldots r_n} \phi_2 \quad \text{in } G$$

*if and only if*

$$\phi_1^R \xrightarrow[\text{rm}]{r_1^R \ldots r_n^R} \phi_2^R \quad \text{in } G^R,$$

*Proof.* An induction on $n$. A detailed proof is left as an exercise. □

From Lemma 8.2 we obtain:

**Lemma 8.3** (*a*) *String $\gamma \in V^*$ is a (complete) viable prefix of $G$ if and only if $\gamma$ is a (complete) viable suffix of $G^R$.*

(*b*) *String $\gamma \in V^*$ is a (complete) viable suffix of $G$ if and only if $\gamma$ is a (complete) viable prefix of $G^R$.*

*Proof.* The "only if" part of (a) follows from the fact that if

$$S \xRightarrow[\text{rm}]{}{}^* \delta A y \xRightarrow[\text{rm}]{} \delta\alpha\beta y = \gamma\beta y$$

holds in $G$, then, by Lemma 8.2,

$$S \xRightarrow[\text{lm}]{}{}^* (\delta A y)^R = y^R A \delta^R \xRightarrow[\text{lm}]{} y^R(\alpha\beta)^R\delta^R = y^R\beta^R(\delta\alpha)^R = y^R\beta^R\gamma^R$$

holds in $G^R$. The "only if" part of (b) follows analogously. Finally, the "if" parts of both (a) and (b) follow from the fact that $(G^R)^R = G$. □

From Lemma 8.3 and Theorem 6.11 we have:

**Theorem 8.4** *For any grammar $G = (V, T, P, S)$, the set of all viable suffixes of G is a regular language over V.* □

The following lemma states a result similar to Lemma 6.2 but now for leftmost derivations and viable suffixes instead of rightmost derivations and viable prefixes.

**Lemma 8.5** *Let $G = (V, T, P, S)$ be a grammar, $\pi$ a rule string in $P^*$, x a string in $T^*$, $\eta$, $\gamma$, and $\delta$ strings in $V^*$, and A a nonterminal such that*

$$(a) \qquad S \underset{\mathrm{lm}}{\overset{\pi}{\Longrightarrow}} x\eta\gamma = xA\delta \quad \text{in } G, \quad \text{and} \quad \pi \neq \varepsilon \ .$$

*In other words, $\gamma$ is a suffix of some nontrivially derived left sentential form not extending over the first nonterminal. Then there are strings x' in $T^*$ and $\delta'$ in $V^*$, rule strings $\pi'$ and $\pi''$ in $P^*$, and a rule $r = A' \to \alpha'\beta'$ in P such that*

$$(b) \qquad S \underset{\mathrm{lm}}{\overset{\pi'}{\Longrightarrow}} x'A'\delta' \underset{\mathrm{lm}}{\overset{r}{\Longrightarrow}} x'\alpha'\beta'\delta' = x'\alpha'\gamma, \quad x'\alpha' \underset{\mathrm{lm}}{\overset{\pi''}{\Longrightarrow}} x\eta \ ,$$

$$\pi' r \pi'' = \pi, \quad \text{and} \quad 1:\beta' = 1:\gamma \ .$$

*In other words, derivation (a) contains a segment that proves $\gamma^R$ to be a viable suffix, even so that the right-hand side of the rule r "cuts" $\gamma$ properly.*

*Proof.* Analogous to that of Lemma 6.2. Another proof is obtained using Lemma 6.2 together with Lemma 8.2. □

The following lemma is an immediate consequence of Lemma 8.5.

**Lemma 8.6** *Let $G = (V, T, P, S)$ be a grammar, x a string in $T^*$ and $\delta$ a string in $V^*$, and A a nonterminal such that*

$$S \underset{\mathrm{lm}}{\Longrightarrow}^+ xA\delta \quad \text{in } G \ .$$

*Then $\delta^R A$ is a viable suffix of G.*

*Proof.* Choose $\gamma = A\delta$ *and* $\eta = \varepsilon$ in Lemma 8.5. □

The following lemma also follows from Lemma 8.5.

**Lemma 8.7** *Any prefix of a viable suffix is a viable suffix.*

*Proof.* We base the proof on Lemma 6.4 and Lemma 8.3. Another proof is obtained using Lemma 8.5 (see the exercises). Let $\gamma_1$ and $\gamma_2$ be strings such that $\gamma_1\gamma_2$ is a viable suffix. Then by Lemma 8.3(*b*) $\gamma_1\gamma_2$ is a viable prefix of $G^R$. Thus, by Lemma 6.4, $\gamma_1$ is a viable prefix of $G^R$, and therefore, by Lemma 8.3(*a*), a viable suffix of $(G^R)^R = G$. □

Corresponding to Lemma 6.5 we have:

**Lemma 8.8** *Let $G = (V, T, P, S)$ be a reduced grammar, $\delta$ a string in $V^*$, and $A \to \alpha\beta$ a rule in P. If $\delta A$ is a viable suffix of G, then so is $\delta\beta^R$.* □

Now we shall demonstrate that in any reduced grammar $G$ the viable suffixes are the same as the viable stack strings of the SLL($k$) parser of $G$ (except possibly the start symbol $S$, which need not be a viable suffix). This will be done in a way analogous to that used in Section 6.1 to show the correspondence between viable prefixes and viable stack strings of shift-reduce parsers.

**Lemma 8.9** *Let $G = (V, T, P, S)$ be a grammar and M its SLL(k) parser for some $k \geqslant 0$. Further let $\gamma$ and $\eta$ be strings in $V^*$, y a string in $T^*$, and $\pi$ an action string such that*

$$\$\gamma\eta \mid y\$ \stackrel{\pi}{\Longrightarrow} \$ \mid \$ \quad \textit{in } M \ .$$

*Then for some action strings $\pi'$ and $\pi''$ and string $z \in T^*$*

$$\$\gamma\eta \mid y\$ \stackrel{\pi'}{\Longrightarrow} \$\gamma \mid z\$ \stackrel{\pi''}{\Longrightarrow} \$ \mid \$ \quad \textit{in } M, \quad \textit{and} \quad \pi'\pi'' = \pi \ .$$

*Proof.* A simple induction on the length of action string $\pi$. Cf. the proof of Lemma 6.6. A detailed proof is left as an exercise. □

Lemma 8.9 implies immediately:

**Lemma 8.10** *Any prefix of a viable stack string of an SLL(k) parser is a viable stack string.* □

Using Lemma 8.10 and Lemmas 5.27 and 5.29 we can now prove:

**Theorem 8.11** *Let $G = (V, T, P, S)$ be a grammar and M its SLL(k) parser for some $k \geqslant 0$. Any viable stack string of M is either S or a viable suffix of G. Conversely, any viable suffix of G is a viable stack string of M, provided that G is reduced.*

*Proof.* To prove the first part of the theorem, let $\gamma \neq S$ be a viable stack string of $M$. By definition,

(1) $$\$S \mid w\$ \stackrel{\pi}{\Longrightarrow} \$\gamma \mid z\$ \Rightarrow^* \$ \mid \$ \quad \text{in } M$$

for some $w, z \in T^*$ and action string $\pi$. Since $\gamma \neq S$, $\pi$ must contain at least one produce action. Let $r$ be the last produce action in $\pi$. Then we can write (1) as

$$\$S \mid w\$ \xRightarrow{\pi_1} \$\delta A \mid yz\$ \xRightarrow{r} \$\delta\omega^R \mid yz\$ = \$\gamma y^R \mid yz\$ \xRightarrow{\pi_2} \$\gamma \mid z\$ \ ,$$

where $\pi_2$ is a $|y|$-length string of shift actions and $\pi_1 r \pi_2 = \pi$. Lemma 5.27 now implies that for some $x \in T^*$, $w = xyz$ and

$$S \underset{\text{lm}}{\Longrightarrow^*} xA\delta^R \quad \text{in } G \ .$$

As $A \to \omega$ is a rule of $G$ and $\gamma y^R = \delta\omega^R$, we have:

$$S \underset{\text{lm}}{\Longrightarrow^*} xA\delta^R \underset{\text{lm}}{\Longrightarrow} x\omega\delta^R = x(\gamma y^R)^R \ ,$$

which means that $\gamma y^R$ is a viable suffix. By Lemma 8.7, so is its prefix $\gamma$.

To prove the second part of the theorem we note that by Fact 8.1 and Lemma 8.10 it suffices to prove that any complete viable suffix of $G$ is a viable stack string of $M$. Therefore let

$$S \underset{\text{lm}}{\Longrightarrow^*} xA\delta \underset{\text{lm}}{\Longrightarrow} x\omega\delta = x\gamma^R$$

for some strings $x \in T^*$, and $\delta$ and $\gamma \in V^*$, and rule $A \to \omega$ in $P$. If $G$ is reduced, there is a string $y \in T^*$ such that $\gamma^R \Rightarrow^* y$. Then $k{:}y$ is in $\text{FIRST}_k(A\delta)$ and hence, by Lemma 5.29,

(2) $\quad \$S \mid xy\$ \Rightarrow^* \$\delta^R A \mid y\$ \quad \text{in } M$ .

As $k{:}y\$$ is in $\text{FIRST}'_k(\omega\text{FOLLOW}'_k(A))$, $M$ has the produce action $A \mid (k{:}y\$) \to \omega^R \mid (k{:}y\$)$. We have:

(3) $\quad \$\delta^R A \mid y\$ \Rightarrow \$\delta^R\omega^R \mid y\$ = \$\gamma \mid y\$$ .

Further, as $\gamma^R \Rightarrow^* y$, we conclude by Lemma 5.29 that

(4) $\quad \$\gamma \mid y\$ \Rightarrow^* \$ \mid \$$ .

Combining (2), (3), and (4) we can conclude that $\gamma$ is a viable stack string of $M$. □

## 8.2 LL($k$)-Valid Items

Let $G = (V, T, P, S)$ be a grammar. We recall from Section 6.2 that a *k-item*, for $k \geqslant 0$, is a pair of the form $[A \to \alpha \cdot \beta, y]$, where $A \to \alpha \cdot \beta$ is a position (or item core) of $G$, that is, $A \to \alpha\beta$ is a rule of $G$, and $y$ in $k{:}T^*$ is a lookahead string.

An item $[A \to \alpha \cdot \beta, y]$ is *LL(k)-valid* (or *valid*, for short) for string $\gamma \in V^*$ if

$$S \underset{\text{lm}}{\Longrightarrow^*} xA\delta \underset{\text{lm}}{\Longrightarrow} x\alpha\beta\delta = x\alpha\gamma^R \quad \text{and} \quad y \in \text{FIRST}_k(\gamma^R)$$

hold in $G$ for some strings $x \in T^*$ and $\delta \in V^*$.

We have:

**Fact 8.12** If $[A \to \alpha \cdot \beta, y]$ is an LL($k$)-valid item for string $\gamma$, then $\gamma$ is a viable suffix, $[A \to \alpha \cdot \beta, y]$ is a $k$-item, $\beta^R$ is a suffix of $\gamma$, and $y$ belongs to $\text{FIRST}_k(\beta\text{FOLLOW}_k(A))$. Conversely, if $\gamma$ is a viable suffix, then some $k$-item is LL($k$)-valid for $\gamma$, provided that the grammar is reduced. □

As an example, consider $G_{abL}$, the example grammar of Section 8.1: $S \to aAab \mid bAb$, $A \to cAB \mid \varepsilon \mid a$, $B \to \varepsilon$. The items $[S \to aAab\cdot, \varepsilon]$ and $[S \to bAb\cdot, \varepsilon]$ are LL($k$)-valid for the empty string $\varepsilon$, for any $k \geqslant 0$, because

$$S \underset{lm}{\Longrightarrow}^0 S \underset{lm}{\Longrightarrow} aAab \ ,$$

$$S \underset{lm}{\Longrightarrow}^0 S \underset{lm}{\Longrightarrow} bAb \ ,$$

and $\varepsilon$ is in $\text{FIRST}_k(\varepsilon^R)$. These derivations also show that (1) $[S \to aAa\cdot b, k{:}b]$ and $[S \to bA\cdot b, k{:}b]$ are LL($k$)-valid for $b$, (2) $[S \to aA\cdot ab, k{:}ab]$ is LL($k$)-valid for $ba$, and for $n \geqslant 0$ (3) $[S \to a\cdot Aab, k{:}c^nab]$ and $[S \to a\cdot Aab, k{:}c^naab]$ are LL($k$)-valid for $baA$, (4) $[S \to b\cdot Ab, k{:}c^nb]$ and $[S \to b\cdot Ab, k{:}c^nab]$ are LL($k$)-valid for $bA$, (5) $[S \to \cdot aAab, k{:}ac^nab]$ and $[S \to \cdot aAab, k{:}ac^naab]$ LL($k$)-valid for $baAa$, and that (6) $[S \to \cdot bAb, k{:}bc^nb]$ and $[S \to \cdot bAb, k{:}bc^nab]$ are LL($k$)-valid for $bAb$.

Consider then the derivations

$$S \underset{lm}{\Longrightarrow}^* ac^nAB^nab \underset{lm}{\Longrightarrow} ac^nB^nab \ ,$$

$$S \underset{lm}{\Longrightarrow}^* ac^nAB^nab \underset{lm}{\Longrightarrow} ac^naB^nab \ ,$$

$$S \underset{lm}{\Longrightarrow}^* ac^nAB^nab \underset{lm}{\Longrightarrow} ac^ncABB^nab \ ,$$

where $n \geqslant 0$. These derivations show that (1) $[A \to \cdot, k{:}ab]$, $[A \to a\cdot, k{:}ab]$, and $[A \to cAB\cdot, k{:}ab]$ are LL($k$)-valid for $baB^n$, (2) $[A \to \cdot a, k{:}aab]$ is LL($k$)-valid for $baB^na$, (3) $[A \to cA\cdot B, k{:}ab]$ is LL($k$)-valid for $baB^{n+1}$, (4) $[A \to c\cdot AB, y]$ is LL($k$)-valid for $baB^{n+1}A$, for all $y$ in $k{:}\{c\}^*\{\varepsilon, a\}ab$, and (5) $[A \to \cdot cAB, y]$ is LL($k$)-valid for $baB^{n+1}Ac$, for all $y$ in $k{:}\{c\}^+\{\varepsilon, a\}ab$.

Correspondingly, for $n \geqslant 0$ the derivations

$$S \underset{lm}{\Longrightarrow}^* bc^nAB^nb \underset{lm}{\Longrightarrow} bc^nB^nb \ ,$$

$$S \underset{lm}{\Longrightarrow}^* bc^nAB^nb \underset{lm}{\Longrightarrow} bc^naB^nb \ ,$$

$$S \underset{lm}{\Longrightarrow}^* bc^nAB^nb \underset{lm}{\Longrightarrow} bc^ncABB^nb$$

show that (1) $[A \to \cdot, k{:}b]$, $[A \to a\cdot, k{:}b]$, and $[A \to cAB\cdot, k{:}b]$ are LL($k$)-valid for $bB^n$, (2) $[A \to \cdot a, k{:}ab]$ is LL($k$)-valid for $bB^na$, (3) $[A \to cA\cdot B, k{:}b]$ is LL($k$)-valid for $bB^{n+1}$, (4) $[A \to c\cdot AB, y]$ is LL($k$)-valid for $bB^{n+1}A$, for all $y$ in $k{:}\{c\}^*\{\varepsilon, a\}b$, and (5) $[A \to \cdot cAB, y]$ is LL($k$)-valid for $bB^{n+1}Ac$, for all $y$ in $k{:}\{c\}^+\{\varepsilon, a\}b$.

Finally, $[B \to \cdot,\ k{:}ab]$ is LL($k$)-valid for $baB^n$, and $[B \to \cdot,\ k{:}b]$ for $bB^n$, for $n \geqslant 0$, because

$$S \underset{\text{lm}}{\Longrightarrow}^* ac^{n+1}B^{n+1}ab \underset{\text{lm}}{\Longrightarrow} ac^{n+1}B^n ab, \quad \text{and}$$

$$S \underset{\text{lm}}{\Longrightarrow}^* bc^{n+1}B^{n+1}b \underset{\text{lm}}{\Longrightarrow} bc^{n+1}B^n b\ .$$

If $G = (V, T, P, S)$ is a grammar and $\gamma$ is a string in $V^*$, we denote for all $k \geqslant 0$:

$$\text{VALID}^G_{\text{LL}(k)}(\gamma) = \{I \mid I \text{ is an LL}(k)\text{-valid item for } \gamma\}\ .$$

If $G$ is understood, we may write $\text{VALID}_{\text{LL}(k)}$. If it is clear that LL($k$)-valid items are meant and not LR($k$)-valid items, we may write $\text{VALID}_k$. Finally, if $k$ is also understood, we may even write VALID.

In $G_{abL}$ we have for all $k, n \geqslant 0$:

$$\text{VALID}_k(baAa) = \{[S \to \cdot aAab,\ y] \mid y \in k{:}a\{c\}^*\{\varepsilon, a\}ab\}\ .$$

$$\text{VALID}_k(bAb) = \{[S \to \cdot bAb,\ y] \mid y \in k{:}b\{c\}^*\{\varepsilon, a\}b\}\ .$$

$$\text{VALID}_k(baB^{n+1}Ac) = \{[A \to \cdot cAB,\ y] \mid y \in k{:}\{c\}^+\{\varepsilon, a\}ab\}\ .$$

$$\text{VALID}_k(baB^{n+1}A) = \{[A \to c \cdot AB,\ y] \mid y \in k{:}\{c\}^*\{\varepsilon, a\}ab\}\ .$$

$$\text{VALID}_k(baB^n a) = \{[A \to \cdot a,\ k{:}aab]\}\ .$$

$$\text{VALID}_k(baB^{n+1}) = \{[A \to cA \cdot B,\ k{:}ab], [A \to cAB \cdot,\ k{:}ab],$$
$$[A \to \cdot,\ k{:}ab], [A \to a \cdot,\ k{:}ab], [B \to \cdot,\ k{:}ab]\}\ .$$

$$\text{VALID}_k(ba) = \{[S \to aA \cdot ab,\ k{:}ab], [A \to \cdot a,\ k{:}ab],$$
$$[A \to cAB \cdot,\ k{:}ab], [A \to \cdot,\ k{:}ab], [A \to a \cdot,\ k{:}ab],$$
$$[B \to \cdot,\ k{:}ab]\}\ .$$

$$\text{VALID}_k(baA) = \{[S \to a \cdot Aab,\ y] \mid y \in k{:}\{c\}^*\{\varepsilon, a\}ab\}\ .$$

$$\text{VALID}_k(b) = \{[S \to aAa \cdot b,\ k{:}b], [S \to bA \cdot b,\ k{:}b],$$
$$[A \to cAB \cdot,\ k{:}b], [A \to \cdot,\ k{:}b], [A \to a \cdot,\ k{:}b],$$
$$[B \to \cdot,\ k{:}b]\}\ .$$

$$\text{VALID}_k(\varepsilon) = \{[S \to aAab \cdot,\ \varepsilon], [S \to bAb \cdot,\ \varepsilon]\}\ .$$

$$\text{VALID}_k(bB^{n+1}Ac) = \{[A \to \cdot cAB,\ y] \mid y \in k{:}\{c\}^+\{\varepsilon, a\}b\}\ .$$

$$\text{VALID}_k(bB^{n+1}A) = \{[A \to c \cdot AB,\ y] \mid y \in k{:}\{c\}^*\{\varepsilon, a\}b\}\ .$$

$$\text{VALID}_k(bB^{n+1}a) = \{[A \to \cdot a,\ k{:}ab]\}\ .$$

$$\text{VALID}_k(bB^{n+1}) = \{[A \to cA \cdot B,\ k{:}b], [A \to cAB \cdot,\ k{:}b],$$
$$[A \to \cdot,\ k{:}b], [A \to a \cdot,\ k{:}b], [B \to \cdot,\ k{:}b]\}\ .$$

$$\text{VALID}_k(bA) = \{[S \to b \cdot Ab,\ y] \mid y \in \{c\}^*\{\varepsilon, a\}b\}\ .$$

In grammar $G$, string $\gamma_1$ is *LL(k)-equivalent* (or *equivalent*, for short) to string $\gamma_2$, written

$$\gamma_1 \rho_{LL(k)} \gamma_2 \quad \text{(or } \gamma_1 \rho_k \gamma_2 \text{, for short)} ,$$

if

$$\text{VALID}_k(\gamma_1) = \text{VALID}_k(\gamma_2) .$$

The relation $\rho_k$ is called the *LL(k)-equivalence* for $G$.

The definition of a viable suffix implies immediately:

**Fact 8.13** Let $G = (V, T, P, S)$ be a grammar, $k$ a natural number, and $\gamma$ a string in $V^*$. For all items $[A_1 \to \alpha_1 \cdot \beta_1, y_1]$ and $[A_2 \to \alpha_2 \cdot \beta_2, y_2]$ in $\text{VALID}_k(\gamma)$,

$$\begin{aligned} &\{z \mid [A_1 \to \alpha_1 \cdot \beta_1, z] \in \text{VALID}_k(\gamma)\} \\ &= \{z \mid [A_2 \to \alpha_2 \cdot \beta_2, z] \in \text{VALID}_k(\gamma)\} \\ &= \text{FIRST}_k(\gamma^R) . \end{aligned}$$

□

From Fact 8.13 we obtain an upper bound for the number of distinct LL($k$)-equivalence classes.

**Theorem 8.14** *For any grammar $G = (V, T, P, S)$ and natural number $k$, the LL(k)-equivalence $\rho_k$ for $G$ is an equivalence relation on $V^*$. Moreover, $\rho_k$ is of finite index, that is, there are only a finite number of distinct equivalence classes under $\rho_k$. More specifically, the index of $\rho_k$ is at most*

$$2^{|G| + (|T|+1)^k} .$$

*Proof.* The number of distinct subsets of $k\!:\!T^*$ is at most $2^{(|T|+1)^k}$. By Fact 8.13, each of these subsets may occur in at most $2^{|G|}$ sets $\text{VALID}_0(\gamma)$. Hence we obtain the bound $2^{|G|} \cdot 2^{(|T|+1)^k} = 2^{|G|+(|T|+1)^k}$. □

Instead of $[\gamma]_{\rho_k}$ we write $[\gamma]_k$ or even $[\gamma]$, if $k$ is understood.

In our example grammar $G_{abL}$ the LL($k$)-equivalence classes of the viable suffixes $\varepsilon$, $b$, $ba$, $bA$, $baA$, $bAb$, and $baAa$ are all singleton sets, containing only the viable suffix in question, independently of $k$. The viable suffixes $baB^{n+1}Ac$, $n \geqslant 0$, are all LL($k$)-equivalent for any $k$, as are the viable suffixes $bB^{n+1}Ac$. Moreover, $baB^{n+1}Ac$ and $bB^{n+1}Ac$ are LL(1)- and LL(0)-equivalent for all $n \geqslant 0$. Similarly, each of the sets

$$\{baB^{n+1}A \mid n \geqslant 0\}, \quad \{bB^{n+1}A \mid n \geqslant 0\}, \quad \{baB^n a \mid n \geqslant 0\} ,$$
$$\{bB^{n+1}a \mid n \geqslant 0\}, \quad \{baB^{n+1} \mid n \geqslant 0\}, \quad \{bB^{n+1} \mid n \geqslant 0\}$$

forms a distinct LL($k$)-equivalence class for $k \geqslant 2$, but for $k = 1$ the equivalence classes are

$$\{baB^{n+1}A \mid n \geqslant 0\}, \quad \{bB^{n+1}A \mid n \geqslant 0\} ,$$
$$\{baB^n a \mid n \geqslant 0\} \cup \{bB^{n+1} a \mid n \geqslant 0\},$$
$$\{baB^{n+1} \mid n \geqslant 0\}, \quad \{bB^{n+1} \mid n \geqslant 0\} ,$$

and for $k = 0$ the equivalence classes are

$$\{baB^{n+1}A \mid n \geqslant 0\} \cup \{bB^{n+1}A \mid n \geqslant 0\} ,$$
$$\{baB^n a \mid n \geqslant 0\} \cup \{bB^{n+1} a \mid n \geqslant 0\} ,$$
$$\{baB^{n+1} \mid n \geqslant 0\} \cup \{bB^{n+1} \mid n \geqslant 0\} .$$

Corresponding to Lemma 6.14 we have:

**Lemma 8.15** *For all strings $\gamma \in V^*$ and natural numbers $k$, $l$ ($k \leqslant l$),*

$$\text{VALID}_k(\gamma) = \{[A \to \alpha \cdot \beta, k{:}y] \mid [A \to \alpha \cdot \beta, y] \in \text{VALID}_l(\gamma)\} .$$

*In other words, the set of LL(k)-valid items for $\gamma$ is obtained from the set of LL(l)-valid items for $\gamma$ by truncating the lookahead strings to length k.*

*Proof.* Exercise. □

Using Lemma 8.15 we can prove:

**Theorem 8.16** *For any grammar $G = (V, T, P, S)$ and natural numbers $k$, $l$, $k \leqslant l$, LL(l)-equivalence is a refinement of LL(k)-equivalence. That is, each LL(k)-equivalence class is the union of some LL(l)-equivalence classes. More specifically, each LL(k)-equivalence class $[\gamma]_k$ is the union of all LL(l)-equivalence classes $[\delta]_l$ satisfying*

$$\text{VALID}_k(\gamma) = \{[A \to \alpha \cdot \beta, k{:}y] \mid [A \to \alpha \cdot \beta, y] \in \text{VALID}_l(\delta)\} ,$$

*that is, the set of LL(k)-valid items for $\gamma$ is obtained from the set of LL(l)-valid items for $\delta$ by truncating the lookahead strings to length k.*

*Proof.* Exercise. □

As was the case with the LR($k$)-equivalence considered in Section 6.2, we can regard each set $\text{VALID}_k(\gamma)$ as a finite representation of the LL($k$)-equivalence class $[\gamma]_k$, and the collection of all sets $\text{VALID}_k(\gamma)$, $\gamma \in V^*$, as a finite representation of the entire LL($k$)-equivalence. We call this collection the *canonical collection of sets of LL(k)-valid items*, or the *canonical LL(k) collection*, for short.

The *canonical LL(k) machine* (or the *deterministic LL(k) machine*) for grammar $G = (V, T, P, S)$ is the finite automaton in which the state alphabet is the canonical

LL($k$) collection for $G$, the input alphabet is $V$, the initial state is $\text{VALID}_k(\varepsilon)$, and the set of transitions consists of all rules of the form

$$\text{VALID}_k(\gamma)X \rightarrow \text{VALID}_k(\gamma X),$$

where $\gamma$ is a string over $V^*$ and $X$ is a symbol in $V$. The set of final states is not fixed in the definition.

Figures 8.2 and 8.3 show the canonical LL(1) and LL(2) machines for the \$-augmented grammar for $G_{abL}$. (As in the case of LR($k$) parsers, it is the canonical machine for the \$-augmented grammar we shall use in the construction of LL($k$) parsers.) As usual, we have left out the empty state $\varnothing$, as well as the states $\text{VALID}(\varepsilon)$ $(= \{[S' \rightarrow \$S\$\cdot,\ \varepsilon]\})$ and $\text{VALID}(\$S\$)$ $(= \{[S' \rightarrow \cdot\$S\$, y] \mid y \in \text{FIRST}_k(\$S\$)\})$.

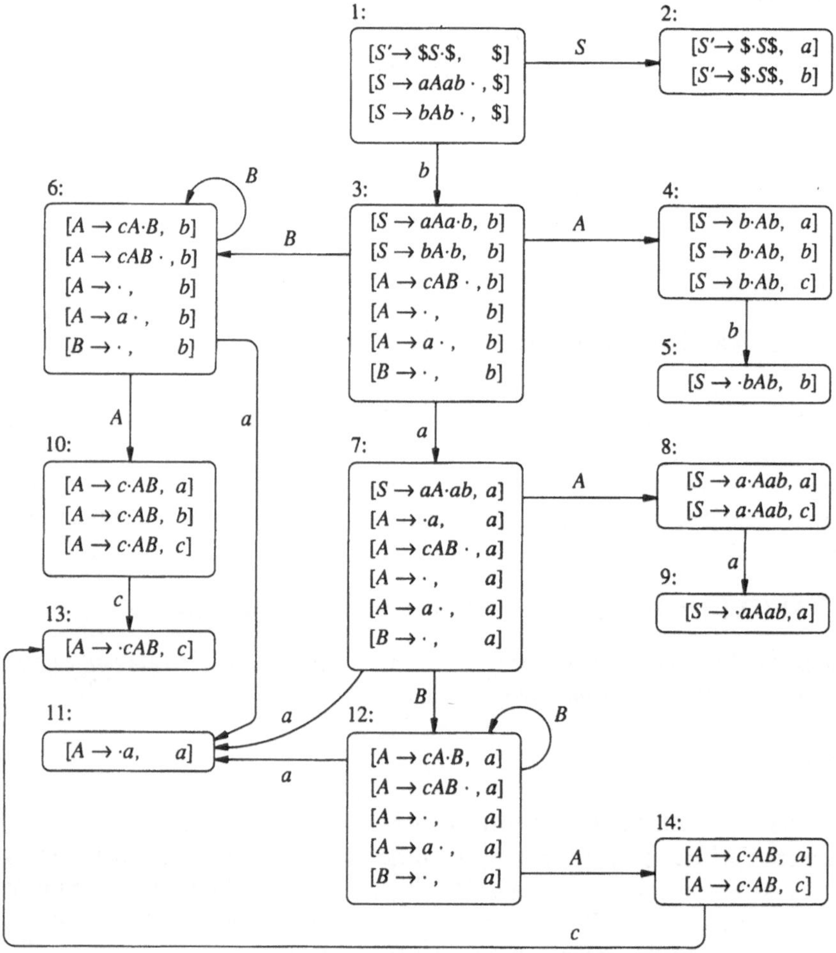


**Figure 8.2** The canonical LL(1) machine for the \$-augmented grammar $G'_{abL}$: $S' \rightarrow \$S\$$, $S \rightarrow aAab \mid bAb$, $A \rightarrow cAB \mid \varepsilon \mid a$, $B \rightarrow \varepsilon$

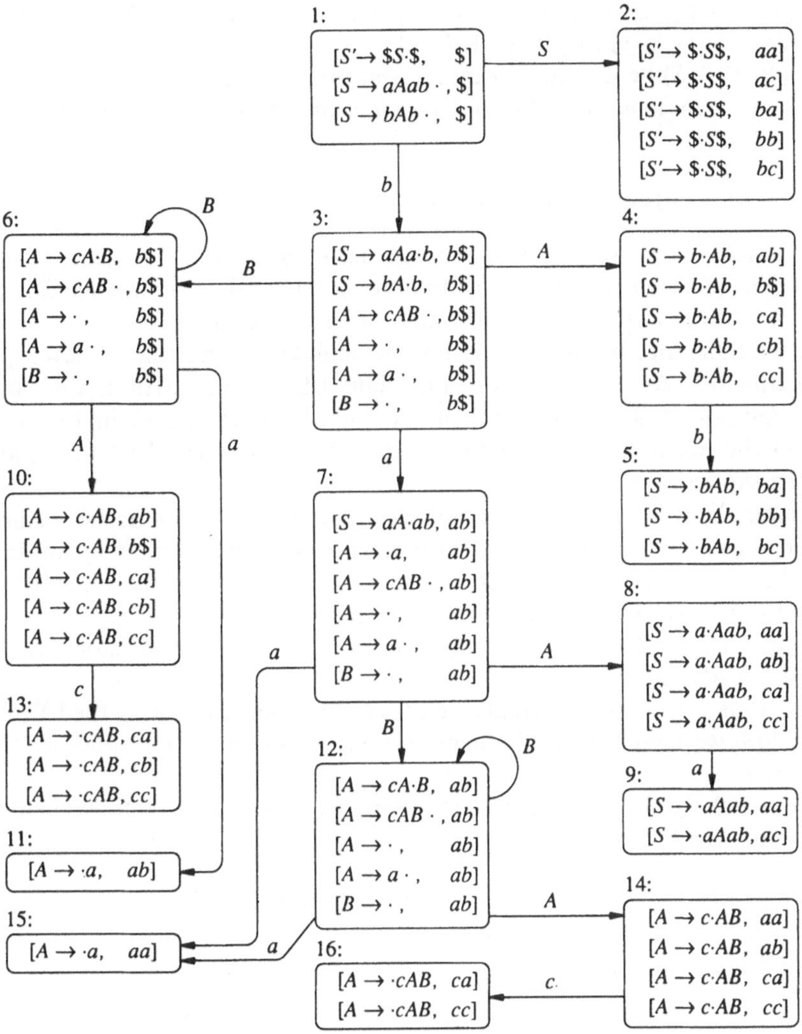


**Figure 8.3** The canonical LL(2) machine for $G'_{abL}$

In the following we shall derive an algorithm for constructing the canonical LL($k$) machine for a grammar. We shall proceed in a way completely analogous to that taken in Section 6.2 to construct the canonical LR($k$) machine. Again, the construction algorithm will imply the desired properties of the equivalence relation being considered, that is, LL($k$)-equivalence is right-invariant, and two LL($k$)-equivalent viable suffixes always end with the same symbol.

From Figures 8.2 and 8.3 we observe that whenever VALID($\gamma$) contains an item of the form $[A \to \alpha B \cdot \beta, y]$, where $B$ is a nonterminal, then it also contains all items $[B \to \omega \cdot, y]$, where $B \to \omega$ is a rule of the grammar. Conversely, for each item of the form $[B \to \omega\cdot, y]$ in VALID($\gamma$), where $\gamma \neq \varepsilon$, $B \neq S$, or $y \neq \varepsilon$, there is some item of the form $[A \to \alpha B\cdot\beta, y]$ in VALID($\gamma$).

Let $G = (V, T, P, S)$ be a grammar and $k$ a natural number. We say that any item $[B \to \omega\cdot, y]$ is an *immediate LL(k)-descendant* of $k$-item $[A \to \alpha B\cdot\beta, y]$ of $G$, written

$$[A \to \alpha B\cdot\beta, y]\,\mathbf{desc}_{\mathrm{LL}(k)}\,[B \to \omega\cdot, y] \ ,$$

if $B \to \omega$ is a rule of $G$ and $\alpha$ derives some terminal string. An item is an *LL(k)-descendant* of $k$-item $I$ if it belongs to $\mathbf{desc}^*_{\mathrm{LL}(k)}(I)$. Item $I_1$ is an *(immediate) LL(k)-ancestor* of item $I_2$ if $I_2$ is an (immediate) LL($k$)-descendant of $I_1$.

Observe the difference between the definition of $\mathbf{desc}_{\mathrm{LL}(k)}$ and that of $\mathbf{desc}_{\mathrm{LR}(k)}$ given in Section 6.2. An item has an immediate LL($k$)-descendant if the dot immediately follows some nonterminal in the right-hand side, and in the descendant item the dot is placed at the extreme right. Moreover, the lookahead strings are the same in both items.

The requirement that the string $\alpha$ in $[A \to \alpha B\cdot\beta, y]$ should derive some terminal string has only been introduced so as to allow grammars that may not be reduced. Without this additional requirement the main theorems at the end of this section would not hold unless the grammar is reduced.

For brevity, we write the relation $\mathbf{desc}_{\mathrm{LL}(k)}$ as $\mathbf{desc}_k$ if "LL" is understood, and just as **desc** if $k$ is also understood.

The proofs that follow are very similar to the corresponding proofs in the LR($k$) theory. Therefore we merely state the necessary facts and lemmas and leave the proofs as exercises.

For all $k, n \geqslant 0$ we define $\mathrm{VALID}_{k,n}(\gamma)$ as the set consisting of those items $[A \to \alpha\cdot\beta, y]$ for which

$$S \underset{\mathrm{lm}}{\Longrightarrow}^n xA\delta \underset{\mathrm{lm}}{\Longrightarrow} x\alpha\beta\delta = x\alpha\gamma^R \quad \text{and} \quad y \in \mathrm{FIRST}_k(\gamma^R)$$

for some $\delta \in V^*$ and $x \in T^*$.

**Fact 8.17** For all $k \geqslant 0$ and $\gamma \in V^*$,

$$\mathrm{VALID}_k(\gamma) = \bigcup_{n=0}^{\infty} \mathrm{VALID}_{k,n}(\gamma) \ .$$

□

**Lemma 8.18** *If in grammar* $G = (V, T, P, S)$

$$[A \to \alpha B\cdot\beta, y] \in \mathrm{VALID}_{k,n}(\gamma) \quad \textit{and} \quad \alpha \Rightarrow^m v \in T^* \ ,$$

*then for all rules* $B \to \omega$ *in* $P$

$$[B \to \omega\cdot, y] \in \mathrm{VALID}_{k,n+m+1}(\gamma) \ .$$

□

From Lemma 8.18 (and Fact 8.17) we conclude that all immediate LL($k$)-descendants of an LL($k$)-valid item for $\gamma$ are LL($k$)-valid for $\gamma$. Thus we have:

**Lemma 8.19** *In any grammar,* $\text{VALID}_k(\gamma)$ *is closed under* **desc**, *that is,*

$$\mathbf{desc}^*(\text{VALID}_k(\gamma)) = \text{VALID}_k(\gamma) .$$

□

The converse of Lemma 8.18 is stated in the following:

**Lemma 8.20** *If in grammar* $G = (V, T, P, S)$

$$[B \to \omega\cdot, y] \in \text{VALID}_{k,n}(\gamma) \quad \textit{and} \quad n > 0 ,$$

*then for some rule* $A \to \alpha B\beta$ *in* $P$, *string* $v$ *in* $T^*$, *and natural number* $m < n$

$$[A \to \alpha B\cdot\beta, y] \in \text{VALID}_{k,m}(\gamma) \quad \textit{and} \quad \alpha \Rightarrow^{n-m-1} v .$$

□

The definition of $\text{VALID}_{k,0}(\gamma)$ implies immediately:

**Fact 8.21** *In any grammar* $G = (V, T, P, S)$

$$\text{VALID}_{k,0}(\gamma) = \{[S \to \omega\cdot\gamma^R, \varepsilon] \mid S \to \omega\gamma^R \in P\} .$$

□

Consider again Figures 8.2 and 8.3. We observe that any item set $\text{VALID}(\gamma X)$, where $X$ is a single symbol, contains the item $[A \to \alpha\cdot X\beta, z]$ whenever $\text{VALID}(\gamma)$ contains an item of the form $[A \to \alpha X\cdot\beta, y]$ satisfying $z \in \text{FIRST}_k(Xy)$. Conversely, any item in $\text{VALID}(\gamma X)$ in which the portion of the right-hand side following the dot is nonempty is obtained in this way from some item in $\text{VALID}(\gamma)$. In addition to these items, $\text{VALID}(\gamma X)$ contains all their descendants.

We say that item $[A \to \alpha\cdot\beta, y]$ is *LL-essential* (or *essential*, for short), if $\beta$ is nonempty, and *LL-inessential* (or *inessential*) otherwise. If $q$ is a set of items, we denote:

$$\text{ESS}_{\text{LL}}(q) = \{I \in q \mid I \text{ is LL-essential}\} .$$

For brevity we may write ESS for $\text{ESS}_{\text{LL}}$.

Lemma 8.20 and Fact 8.21 imply (by Fact 8.12):

**Lemma 8.22** *Let* $G = (V, T, P, S)$ *be a grammar,* $\gamma$ *a string in* $V^*$, *and* $I$ *an item in* $\text{VALID}_{k,n}(\gamma)$ *for some* $k, n \geq 0$. *Then one of the following statements holds.*

(*a*) $\gamma = \varepsilon$, $n = 0$, *and* $I = [S \to \omega\cdot, \varepsilon]$ *for some* $\omega$.
(*b*) $\gamma \neq \varepsilon$ *and* $I$ *is essential.*
(*c*) $n > 0$ *and* $I$ *has an immediate ancestor in some* $\text{VALID}_{k,m}(\gamma)$, $m < n$.

□

**Lemma 8.23** *Let $G = (V, T, P, S)$ be a grammar and $\gamma$ a string in $V^*$. Then the following statements are true.*

$$\mathrm{VALID}_{k,n}(\gamma) \subseteq \mathbf{desc}^*(\{[S \to \omega\cdot, \varepsilon] \mid S \to \omega \in P\}), \quad \text{if } \gamma = \varepsilon .$$

$$\mathrm{VALID}_{k,n}(\gamma) \subseteq \mathbf{desc}^*(\mathrm{ESS}(\mathrm{VALID}_k(\gamma))), \quad \text{if } \gamma \neq \varepsilon .$$

□

Fact 8.17, Lemma 8.19, and Lemma 8.23 imply:

**Lemma 8.24** *Let $G = (V, T, P, S)$ be any grammar and $\gamma$ a string in $V^*$. Then $\mathrm{VALID}_k(\gamma)$ is spanned under* **desc** *by the items $[S \to \omega\cdot, \varepsilon]$ if $\gamma = \varepsilon$, and by the essential items in $\mathrm{VALID}_k(\gamma)$ if $\gamma \neq \varepsilon$. That is,*

$$\mathrm{VALID}_k(\varepsilon) = \mathbf{desc}^*(\{[S \to \omega\cdot, \varepsilon] \mid S \to \omega \in P\}) ;$$

$$\mathrm{VALID}_k(\gamma) = \mathbf{desc}^*(\mathrm{ESS}(\mathrm{VALID}_k(\gamma))), \quad \text{if } \gamma \neq \varepsilon .$$

□

Let $X$ be a symbol in $V$ and let $\mathbf{passes}_k$-$X$ be the relation on the set of $k$-items defined by:

$$[A \to \alpha X \cdot \beta, y] \quad \mathbf{passes}_k\text{-}X \quad [A \to \alpha \cdot X\beta, z]$$

for all rules $A \to \alpha X\beta$ in $P$, strings $y$ in $k{:}T^*$, and strings $z$ in $\mathrm{FIRST}_k(Xy)$.

In Chapter 10 we shall see that for any $k \geqslant 0$ the relation $\mathbf{passes}_k$-$X$ can be computed from the grammar. For $k = 0$ the computation is trivial (once the useless nonterminals have been found). For $k = 1$ the relation can be computed via a single relational expression (see the exercises).

Let $q$ be a set of $k$-items and $X$ a symbol in $V$. The $k$-item set $\mathbf{passes}_k$-$X(q)$ is called the *basis of the $X$-successor of $q$* and is denoted by $\mathrm{BASIS}_{\mathrm{LL}(k)}(q, X)$. We have:

$$\mathrm{BASIS}_{\mathrm{LL}(k)}(q, X) = \{[A \to \alpha \cdot X\beta, z] \mid [A \to \alpha X \cdot \beta, y] \in q \text{ and } z \in \mathrm{FIRST}_k(Xy)\} .$$

Recall the corresponding definition in the LR($k$) theory and notice the difference: Here the dot is moved from right to left and not from left to right as in the LR($k$) case. Moreover, the lookahead string is now changed from $y$ to any $z$ in $\mathrm{FIRST}_k(Xy)$.

The closure of $\mathrm{BASIS}_{\mathrm{LL}(k)}(q, X)$ under **desc** is called the *$X$-successor* of $q$ and is denoted by $\mathrm{GOTO}_{\mathrm{LL}(k)}(q, X)$. We have:

$$\mathrm{GOTO}_{\mathrm{LL}(k)}(q, X) = \mathbf{desc}^*(\mathrm{BASIS}_{\mathrm{LL}(k)}(q, X)) = \mathbf{passes}_k\text{-}X\ \mathbf{desc}^*(q) .$$

The set $\mathrm{GOTO}_{\mathrm{LL}(k)}(q, X)$ thus consists of all LL($k$)-descendants of all items $[A \to \alpha \cdot X\beta, z]$ for which $q$ contains an item $[A \to \alpha X \cdot \beta, y]$ where $\mathrm{FIRST}_k(Xy)$ contains $z$.

For brevity, we may write $\text{BASIS}_k$ (or even BASIS) for $\text{BASIS}_{\text{LL}(k)}$, and $\text{GOTO}_k$ (or even GOTO) for $\text{GOTO}_{\text{LL}(k)}$.

**Lemma 8.25** *If* $[A \to \alpha\omega \cdot \beta, y]$ *is an item in* $\text{VALID}_{k,n}(\gamma)$, *then* $\gamma\omega^R$ *is a viable suffix and* $[A \to \alpha \cdot \omega\beta, z]$ *is in* $\text{VALID}_{k,n}(\gamma\omega^R)$ *for all* $z \in \text{FIRST}_k(\omega y)$. *Conversely, if* $[A \to \alpha \cdot \omega\beta, z]$ *is an item in* $\text{VALID}_{k,n}(\delta)$, *then there is a viable suffix* $\gamma$ *such that* $\delta = \gamma\omega^R$ *and* $\text{VALID}_{k,n}(\gamma)$ *contains an item* $[A \to \alpha\omega \cdot \beta, y]$ *where* $\text{FIRST}_k(\omega y)$ *contains* $z$. □

**Lemma 8.26** *In any grammar* $G = (V, T, P, S)$,

$$\text{ESS}(\text{VALID}_k(\gamma X)) = \text{BASIS}_k(\text{VALID}_k(\gamma), X)$$

*for all strings* $\gamma \in V^*$ *and symbols* $X \in V$. □

Lemmas 8.24 and 8.26 imply:

**Lemma 8.27** *Let* $G = (V, T, P, S)$ *be any grammar,* $\gamma$ *a string in* $V^*$, *and* $X$ *a symbol in* $V$. *Then for all* $k \geqslant 0$

$$\text{VALID}_k(\gamma X) = \text{GOTO}_k(\text{VALID}_k(\gamma), X)\ . \quad \square$$

Lemmas 8.24 and 8.27 imply an algorithm for constructing the canonical LL($k$) machine. This algorithm is shown in Figure 8.4.

Corresponding to Theorem 6.27 we have:

**Theorem 8.28** *Let* $G = (V, T, P, S)$ *be a grammar,* $k$ *a natural number, and* $M$ *the canonical LL(k) machine for G. Then the following statements hold.*

(*a*) *M is deterministic.*

(*b*) *Each nonempty state q in M has a unique entry symbol, that is, there are transitions to q on at most one symbol* $X \in V$.

```
Compute the relation desc;
for all X ∈ V do
    compute the relation passes_k-X;
q_s := desc*({[S → ω·, ε] | S → ω ∈ P});
Q_M := {q_s};
P_M := ∅;
repeat
    for all q ∈ Q_M and X ∈ V do begin
            q' := passes_k-X desc*(q) ;
            Q_M := Q_M ∪ {q'} ;
            P_M := P_M ∪ {q X → q'}
    end
until nothing more can be added to Q_M and P_M.
```

**Figure 8.4** Algorithm for constructing the canonical LL($k$) machine for grammar $G = (V, T, P, S)$. $Q_M$ will contain all states of $M$, $P_M$ will contain all transitions of $M$, and $q_s$ will be the initial state of $M$

(c) *State q is accessible upon reading* $\gamma$ *if and only if* $q = \mathrm{VALID}_k(\gamma)$.

(d) *If a given state* $\mathrm{VALID}_k(\gamma)$ *is designated as the only final state of M, then the language accepted by M is* $[\gamma]_k$.

(e) *If all nonempty states* $\mathrm{VALID}_k(\gamma)$ *are designated as final states of M, then the language accepted by M is the set of viable suffixes of G.*

(*f*) *If all states of M are designated as final states, then the language accepted by M is* $V^*$. □

Corresponding to Theorem 6.28 we have:

**Theorem 8.29** *For any grammar* $G = (V, T, P, S)$ *and natural number k, the following statements hold.*

(a) *The LL(k)-equivalence of G is the equivalence induced by the canonical LL(k) machine of G, that is, strings* $\gamma_1$ *and* $\gamma_2$ *are LL(k)-equivalent if and only if the state accessible upon reading* $\gamma_1$ *coincides with the state accessible upon reading* $\gamma_2$.

(b) *The LL(k)-equivalence of G is right-invariant, that is, whenever* $\gamma_1$ *and* $\gamma_2$ *are LL(k)-equivalent strings in* $V^*$ *and X is a symbol in V, then* $\gamma_1 X$ *and* $\gamma_2 X$ *are LL(k)-equivalent.*

(c) *Two LL(k)-equivalent viable suffixes always end with the same symbol, that is, whenever* $\gamma_1$ *and* $\gamma_2$ *are LL(k)-equivalent viable suffixes, then* $\gamma_1{:}1 = \gamma_2{:}1$.
□

## 8.3 Canonical LL(*k*) Parsers

In this section we shall use the results of the previous sections to define the notion of a "canonical LL($k$) parser" for grammar $G = (V, T, P, S)$. Later in the section we shall also briefly consider reduced variants of the canonical parser, called LALL($k$) and LA($k$)LL($l$) parsers, the analogs of the LALR($k$) and LA($k$)LR($l$) parsers. The stack alphabet of the canonical LL($k$) parser will be the collection of all LL($k$)-equivalence classes of viable suffixes of $G'$, the \$-augmented grammar for $G$. We denote this collection by $[G']_k$.

A rule of the form

$$(pa) \qquad [\delta]_k[\delta A]_k \mid y \to [\delta]_k[\delta X_n]_k \ldots [\delta X_n \ldots X_1]_k \mid y$$

is a *canonical LL(k) produce action by rule* $A \to X_1 \ldots X_n$ *on lookahead y* if $\delta$ is a string in $\$V^*$, $X_1, \ldots X_n$ are symbols in $V$ $(n \geq 0)$, $A \to X_1 \ldots X_n$ is a rule in $P$, and $y$ is a string in $k{:}T^*\$$ such that

$$[A \to \cdot X_1 \ldots X_n, y] \in \mathrm{VALID}_k(\delta X_n \ldots X_1) .$$

The results of the previous section imply that here the strings $\delta$, $\delta X_n, \ldots,$ $\delta X_n \ldots X_1$, and $\delta A$ are all viable suffixes of $G'$.

A rule of the form

$$(sa) \qquad [\delta a]_k \mid ay \to \mid y$$

is a *canonical LL($k$) shift action on terminal $a$ and lookahead $ay$* if $\delta$ is a string in $\$V^*$, $a$ is a terminal in $T$, and $y$ is a string in $\max\{k-1, 0\}:T^*\$$ such that

$$[A \to \alpha \cdot a\beta, k:ay] \in \text{VALID}_k(\delta a)$$

for some rule $A \to \alpha a \beta$ in $P$. (Observe that $\delta a$ is then a viable suffix of $G'$.)

The *canonical LL($k$) parser* for $G$ is the pushdown transducer with stack alphabet $[G']_k$, input alphabet $T$, initial stack contents $[\$]_k[\$S]_k$, set of final stack contents $\{[\$]_k\}$, and with set of actions consisting of all canonical LL($k$) produce and shift actions of $G$. As usual, the output effect $\tau$ is defined to map every produce action by rule $r$ to rule $r$ and every shift action to the empty string $\varepsilon$. The fact that any two LL($k$)-equivalent viable suffixes always end with the same symbol guarantees that $\tau$ is well-defined.

The actions of the canonical LL($k$) parser can be obtained from the canonical LL($k$) machine using the algorithm depicted in Figure 8.5. As usual, we identify

```
for all states q do begin
    for all rules A → X_1 . . . X_n of G(n ≥ 0) such that some
    item in q has the core A → X_1 . . . X_n· do begin
        let q_{n+1}, q_n, . . . , q_1 be the sequence of states
        reached from q upon reading X_n . . . X_1, i.e., q_{n+1} = q and
        q_i = GOTO(q, X_n . . . . X_i), i = n, . . . , 1;
        q_A: = GOTO(q, A);
        for all items [A → ·X_1 . . . X_n, y] in q_1 do
            generate the produce action
            qq_A | y → qq_n . . . q_1 | y
    end;
    for all items [A → α·aβ, ay] in q such that
    a ∈ T do
        generate the shift action q | ay → | y
end.
```

**Figure 8.5** Algorithm for generating the parsing actions from an LL($k$) machine ($k \geq 1$)

an LL($k$)-equivalence class $[\gamma]_k$ with the state VALID$_k(\gamma)$. The algorithm will also apply to LALL($k$) and LA($k$)LL($l$) parsers.

As an example consider the grammar $G_{abL}: S \to aAab \mid bAb$, $A \to cAB \mid \varepsilon \mid a$, $B \to \varepsilon$ (given in the previous section). The canonical LL(2) machine for its \$-augmented grammar was shown in Figure 8.3. The canonical LL(2) parser has the following produce actions ($q_i$ denotes state $i$).

$$r_1 = q_1q_2 \mid aa \to q_1q_3q_7q_8q_9 \mid aa, \qquad \tau(r_1) = S \to aAab\ .$$

$$r_2 = q_1q_2 \mid ac \to q_1q_3q_7q_8q_9 \mid ac, \qquad \tau(r_2) = S \to aAab\ .$$

$$r_3 = q_1q_2 \mid ba \to q_1q_3q_4q_5 \mid ba, \qquad \tau(r_3) = S \to bAb\ .$$

$$r_4 = q_1q_2 \mid bb \to q_1q_3q_4q_5 \mid bb, \qquad \tau(r_4) = S \to bAb\ .$$

$$r_5 = q_1q_2 \mid bc \to q_1q_3q_4q_5 \mid bc, \qquad \tau(r_5) = S \to bAb\ .$$

$$r_6 = q_3q_4 \mid ca \to q_3q_6q_{10}q_{13} \mid ca, \qquad \tau(r_6) = A \to cAB\ .$$

$r_7 = q_3q_4 \mid cb \to q_3q_6q_{10}q_{13} \mid cb,$ $\tau(r_7) = A \to cAB$ .

$r_8 = q_3q_4 \mid cc \to q_3q_6q_{10}q_{13} \mid cc,$ $\tau(r_8) = A \to cAB$ .

$r_9 = q_3q_4 \mid b\$ \to q_3 \mid b\$,$ $\tau(r_9) = A \to \varepsilon$ .

$r_{10} = q_3q_4 \mid ab \to q_3q_7 \mid ab,$ $\tau(r_{10}) = A \to a$ .

$r_{11} = q_3q_6 \mid b\$ \to q_3 \mid b\$,$ $\tau(r_{11}) = B \to \varepsilon$ .

$r_{12} = q_6q_{10} \mid ca \to q_6q_6q_{10}q_{13} \mid ca,$ $\tau(r_{12}) = A \to cAB$ .

$r_{13} = q_6q_{10} \mid cb \to q_6q_6q_{10}q_{13} \mid cb,$ $\tau(r_{13}) = A \to cAB$ .

$r_{14} = q_6q_{10} \mid cc \to q_6q_6q_{10}q_{13} \mid cc,$ $\tau(r_{14}) = A \to cAB$ .

$r_{15} = q_6q_{10} \mid b\$ \to q_6 \mid b\$,$ $\tau(r_{15}) = A \to \varepsilon$ .

$r_{16} = q_6q_{10} \mid ab \to q_6q_{11} \mid ab,$ $\tau(r_{16}) = A \to a$ .

$r_{17} = q_6q_6 \mid b\$ \to q_6 \mid b\$,$ $\tau(r_{17}) = B \to \varepsilon$ .

$r_{18} = q_7q_8 \mid ca \to q_7q_{12}q_{14}q_{16} \mid ca,$ $\tau(r_{18}) = A \to cAB$ .

$r_{19} = q_7q_8 \mid cc \to q_7q_{12}q_{14}q_{16} \mid cc,$ $\tau(r_{19}) = A \to cAB$ .

$r_{20} = q_7q_8 \mid ab \to q_7 \mid ab,$ $\tau(r_{20}) = A \to \varepsilon$ .

$r_{21} = q_7q_8 \mid aa \to q_7q_{15} \mid aa,$ $\tau(r_{21}) = A \to a$ .

$r_{22} = q_7q_{12} \mid ab \to q_7 \mid ab,$ $\tau(r_{22}) = B \to \varepsilon$ .

$r_{23} = q_{12}q_{14} \mid ca \to q_{12}q_{12}q_{14}q_{16} \mid ca,$ $\tau(r_{23}) = A \to cAB$ .

$r_{24} = q_{12}q_{14} \mid cc \to q_{12}q_{12}q_{14}q_{16} \mid cc,$ $\tau(r_{24}) = A \to cAB$ .

$r_{25} = q_{12}q_{14} \mid ab \to q_{12} \mid ab,$ $\tau(r_{25}) = A \to \varepsilon$ .

$r_{26} = q_{12}q_{14} \mid aa \to q_{12}q_{15} \mid aa,$ $\tau(r_{26}) = A \to a$ .

$r_{27} = q_{12}q_{12} \mid ab \to q_{12} \mid ab,$ $\tau(r_{27}) = B \to \varepsilon$ .

The shift actions are:

$s_1 = q_3 \mid b\$ \to \mid \$$ ,

$s_2 = q_5 \mid ba \to \mid a$ ,

$s_3 = q_5 \mid bb \to \mid b$ ,

$s_4 = q_5 \mid bc \to \mid c$ ,

$s_5 = q_7 \mid ab \to \mid b$ ,

$s_6 = q_9 \mid aa \to \mid a$ ,

$s_7 = q_9 \mid ac \to \mid c$ ,

$s_8 = q_{11} \mid ab \to \mid b$ ,

$$s_9 = q_{13} \mid ca \to \mid a \ ,$$

$$s_{10} = q_{13} \mid cb \to \mid b \ ,$$

$$s_{11} = q_{13} \mid cc \to \mid c \ ,$$

$$s_{12} = q_{15} \mid aa \to \mid a \ ,$$

$$s_{13} = q_{16} \mid ca \to \mid a \ ,$$

$$s_{14} = q_{16} \mid cc \to \mid c \ ,$$

The sentences $ac^n ab$, $n \geqslant 2$, are accepted as follows.

$$\$q_1 q_2 \mid ac^n ab\$$$

$$\overset{r_2}{\Longrightarrow} \$q_1 q_3 q_7 q_8 q_9 \mid ac^n ab\$$$

$$\overset{s_7}{\Longrightarrow} \$q_1 q_3 q_7 q_8 \mid c^n ab\$$$

$$\overset{r_{19}}{\Longrightarrow} \$q_1 q_3 q_7 q_{12} q_{14} q_{16} \mid c^n ab\$$$

$$\xrightarrow{s_{14}(r_{24}s_{14})^{n-2}r_{23}} \$q_1 q_3 q_7 q_{12}^n q_{14} q_{16} \mid cab\$$$

$$\overset{s_{13}}{\Longrightarrow} \$q_1 q_3 q_7 q_{12}^n q_{14} \mid ab\$$$

$$\overset{r_{25}}{\Longrightarrow} \$q_1 q_3 q_7 q_{12}^n \mid ab\$$$

$$\overset{r_{27}^{n-1}}{\Longrightarrow} \$q_1 q_3 q_7 q_{12} \mid ab\$$$

$$\overset{r_{22}}{\Longrightarrow} \$q_1 q_3 q_7 \mid ab\$$$

$$\overset{s_5}{\Longrightarrow} \$q_1 q_3 \mid b\$$$

$$\overset{s_1}{\Longrightarrow} \$q_1 \mid \$ \ .$$

The parse produced is $\tau(r_2 s_7 r_{19} s_{14}(r_{24}s_{14})^{n-2} r_{23} s_{13} r_{25} r_{27}^{n-1} r_{22} s_5 s_1) = (S \to aAab)\,(A \to cAB)^n (A \to \varepsilon)(B \to \varepsilon)^n$.

In Section 8.1 we presented, as an introductory example, a simplified version of the canonical LL($k$) parser. In that parser the left-hand sides of produce actions were of the form $[\delta A]_k \mid y$, whereas in the true canonical LL($k$) parser they are of the form $[\delta]_k [\delta A]_k \mid y$. Also, in the right-hand sides of produce actions terminal $a$ was used in place of equivalence class $[X_n \ldots X_i a]_k$. As we shall see in the following, the role of the additional symbol $[\delta]_k$ is essential in that removing it will make the parser nondeterministic in some cases. The presence of $[\delta]_k$ in the actions of the canonical LL($k$) parser is also in accordance with the definition of the canonical LR($k$) parser and makes these two kinds of parser perfect analogs of each other. The effect of using terminal $a$ in place of class $[X_n \ldots X_i a]_k$, on the contrary, is not so significant: error detection may only be somewhat delayed in the case $k \geqslant 2$ (see the exercises).

As an example, consider the SLL(1) grammar

$$S \to aB \mid Bd \mid cad \ ,$$
$$A \to a \ ,$$
$$B \to bA \ .$$

The canonical LL(1) machine for the corresponding \$-augmented grammar is shown in Figure 8.6. The canonical LL(1) parser has two produce actions that are mapped by the output effect $\tau$ to the rule $A \to a$:

$$q_1 q_7 \mid a \to q_1 q_{11} \mid a, \qquad q_5 q_7 \mid a \to q_5 q_9 \mid a \ .$$

If the stack symbols $q_1$ and $q_5$ were left out of these actions, nondeterminism would arise:

$$q_7 \mid a \to q_{11} \mid a, \qquad q_7 \mid a \to q_9 \mid a \ .$$

This is due to the fact that $[\$A]_1 = q_7 = [\$dA]_1$ although $[\$a]_1 = q_{11} \neq q_9 = [\$da]_1$.

The usual methods for implementing left parsers (e.g., the recursive descent method, see Section 5.6) require that the produce actions only consult the topmost symbol in the stack. It might be inconvenient (although not impossible) to arrange the implementation so that the symbol next below the topmost could also be

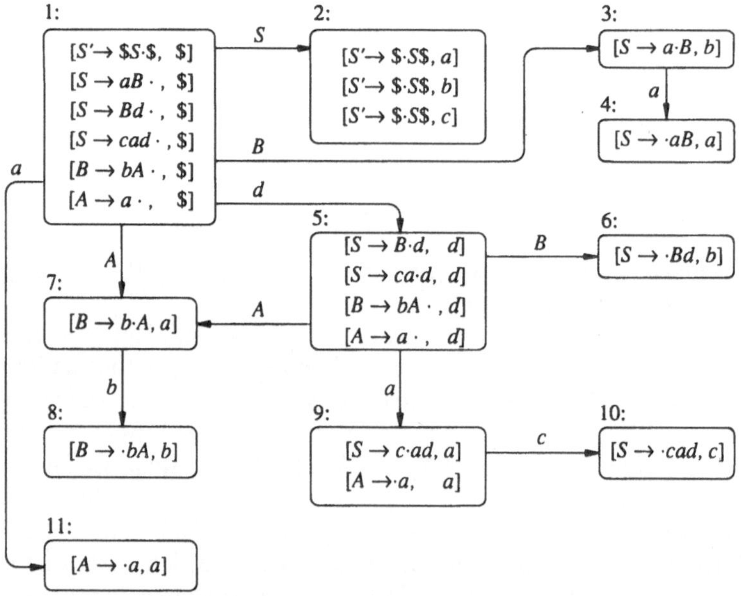


**Figure 8.6** The canonical LL(1) machine for the grammar $S' \to \$S\$$, $S \to aB \mid Bd \mid cad$, $A \to a$, $B \to bA$

consulted. Fortunately, situations like the above do not occur very often. In most cases we can factor out the symbol $[\delta]_k$ from the produce action

$$[\delta]_k[\delta A]_k \mid y \to [\delta]_k[\delta X_n]_k \dots [\delta X_n \dots X_1]_k \mid y$$

and use the action

$$[\delta A]_k \mid y \to [\delta X_n]_k \dots [\delta X_n \dots X_1]_k \mid y \ .$$

We leave it to the reader to verify that this factoring out is possible whenever either (1) the right-hand side $X_1 \dots X_n$ is empty or (2) $[\gamma X_n]_k = [\delta X_n]_k$ for all strings $\gamma$ satisfying $[\gamma A]_k = [\delta A]_k$. To overcome the problem completely one must resort to another formulation of the canonical LL($k$) parser (see Exercise 8.32).

We now return to our original definition of a canonical LL($k$) parser and prove that it does indeed yield a valid left parser for the grammar. As in Chapter 5 in the case of produce-shift and SLL($k$) parsers, we base the proof on two major lemmas, one that states how derivations in the parser are mapped to leftmost derivations in the grammar, and one that states how leftmost derivations in the grammar are mapped to derivations in the parser. As regards the details of the formulation and the proof of the lemmas, the reader should observe the analogy with the proof of the correctness of the canonical LR($k$) parser presented in Chapter 6. Again, it is the latter of these two lemmas that needs a conscientious treatment, while the former is more or less evident.

**Lemma 8.30** *Let $G = (V, T, P, S)$ be a grammar and $(M, \tau)$ its canonical LL($k$) parser. Further let $X_1, \dots, X_m$ be symbols in $V$ ($m \geq 0$), $w$ a string in $T^*$, $\Phi$ a string over the alphabet of $M$, and $\pi'$ an action string such that*

(*a*)
$\$X_1 \dots X_m$ *is a viable suffix of the \$-augmented grammar $G'$ and*

$$\$[\$]_k[\$X_1]_k \dots [\$X_1 \dots X_m]_k \mid w\$ \xRightarrow{\pi'} \Phi \quad \text{in } M \ .$$

*Then for some strings $x$ and $y$ and symbols $Y_1, \dots, Y_n$ ($n \geq 0$)*

(*b*)
$w = xy$, $\$Y_1 \dots Y_n$ *is a viable suffix of $G'$* ,

$\Phi = \$[\$]_k[\$Y_1]_k \dots [\$Y_1 \dots Y_n]_k \mid y\$, \quad |\pi'| = |\tau(\pi')| + |x|$ ,

*and* $X_m \dots X_1 \xRightarrow[\text{lm}]{\tau(\pi')} xY_n \dots Y_1$ *in $G$* .

*Proof.* The proof is not much more than a restatement of Lemma 5.12 (for produce-shift parsers) and 5.27 (for SLL($k$) parsers). It can be proved by a straightforward induction on the length of action string $\pi'$. We leave the details to the exercises. □

**Lemma 8.31** *If $(M, \tau)$ is the canonical LL($k$) parser for grammar $G$, then $L(M) \subseteq L(G)$, and $\tau(\pi')$ is a left parse of sentence $w$ in $G$ whenever $\pi'$ is a parse of $w$ in $M$. Moreover,* $\text{TIME}_G(w) \leq \text{TIME}_M(w) - |w|$.

*Proof.* Choose $m = 1$, $X_1 = S$, and $\Phi = \$[\$]_k \mid \$$ in Lemma 8.30. □

The following lemma is an analog to Lemma 6.31 and states when the canonical LL($k$) parser can perform a sequence of successive shift actions.

**Lemma 8.32** *Let $G = (V, T, P, S)$ be a grammar, $G'$ its \$-augmented grammar, and $M$ the canonical LL($k$) parser for $G$. Further let $\gamma$ be a string in $\$V^*$, $y$ a string in $T^*$, and $a_1, \ldots, a_n$ terminals in $T$ ($n \geqslant 0$) such that*

$$(a) \qquad \begin{array}{l} \gamma a_n \ldots a_1 \textit{ is a viable suffix of } G' \quad \textit{and} \\ k{:}y\$ \in \mathrm{FIRST}_k(\gamma^R) \ . \end{array}$$

*Then there is an $n$-length string $\pi'$ of shift actions of $M$ such that*

$$(b) \qquad \$\Phi[\gamma]_k[\gamma a_n]_k \ldots [\gamma a_n \ldots a_1]_k \mid a_1 \ldots a_n y\$ \overset{\pi'}{\Longrightarrow} \$\Phi[\gamma]_k \mid y\$ \quad \textit{in } M$$

*for any string $\Phi$ in $[G']_k^*$.*

*Proof.* We show that for all $i = 1, \ldots, n$, $M$ has the shift action

$$r_i' = [\gamma a_n \ldots a_i]_k \mid a_i z_i \to \mid z_i \ ,$$

where $a_i z_i = \max\{k, 1\}{:}a_i \ldots a_n y\$$. Observe that then, for any string $\Phi \in [G']_k^*$,

$$\begin{array}{l} \$\Phi[\gamma]_k[\gamma a_n]_k \ldots [\gamma a_n \ldots a_1]_k \mid a_1 \ldots a_n y\$ \\ \overset{r_1'}{\Longrightarrow} \$\Phi[\gamma]_k[\gamma a_n]_k \ldots [\gamma a_n \ldots a_2]_k \mid a_2 \ldots a_n y\$ \\ \quad \vdots \\ \overset{r_{n-1}'}{\Longrightarrow} \$\Phi[\gamma]_k[\gamma a_n]_k \mid a_n y\$ \\ \overset{r_n'}{\Longrightarrow} \$\Phi[\gamma]_k \mid y\$ \ . \end{array}$$

Statement ($b$) then holds if we choose $\pi' = r_1' \ldots r_n'$.

To show that $M$ does indeed have these shift actions, let $i$ be any natural number such that $1 \leqslant i \leqslant n$. Because $\gamma a_n \ldots a_1$ is a viable suffix of $G'$, we have, for some $x$ and $\delta$,

$$\begin{array}{l} S' \underset{\mathrm{lm}}{\Longrightarrow^*} xA\delta \underset{\mathrm{lm}}{\Longrightarrow} x\alpha\beta\delta = x\alpha(\gamma a_n \ldots a_1)^R \\ = x\alpha a_1 \ldots a_{i-1}(\gamma a_n \ldots a_i)^R \ . \end{array}$$

We have two cases to consider: (1) $a_i$ is contained in $\beta$, that is, $\beta$ is of the form $a_1 \ldots a_i\beta'$; (2) $a_i$ is not contained in $\beta$, that is, $\beta = a_1 \ldots a_j$ and $\delta = a_{j+1} \ldots a_n\gamma^R$

for some $j < i$. In case (1) we have:

$$[A \rightarrow \alpha a_1 \ldots a_{i-1} \cdot a_i \beta', k{:}a_i \ldots a_n y\$] \in \mathrm{VALID}_k(\gamma a_n \ldots a_i) \ ,$$

because $k{:}a_i \ldots a_n y\$ \in \mathrm{FIRST}_k(a_i \ldots a_n \gamma^R)$. This means that $M$ has the shift action $r_i'$. In case (2), we can apply Lemma 8.5 to the derivation

$$S' \underset{\mathrm{lm}}{\Longrightarrow}^{+} xA\delta = xAa_{j+1} \ldots a_i \ldots a_n \gamma^R$$

and conclude that for some strings $x'$ and $\delta'$ and rule $A' \rightarrow \alpha' a_i \beta''$,

$$S' \underset{\mathrm{lm}}{\Longrightarrow}^{*} x'A'\delta' \underset{\mathrm{lm}}{\Longrightarrow} x'\alpha' a_i \beta'' \delta' = x'\alpha' a_i \ldots a_n \gamma^R \ .$$

Here we have

$$[A' \rightarrow \alpha' \cdot a_i \beta'', k{:}a_i \ldots a_n y\$] \in \mathrm{VALID}_k(\gamma a_n \ldots a_i) \ ,$$

which means that even in this case $M$ has the shift action $r_i'$. □

Now we can prove:

**Lemma 8.33** *Let $G = (V, T, P, S)$ be a grammar and $(M, \tau)$ its canonical LL($k$) parser. Further let $X_1, \ldots, X_m, Y_1, \ldots, Y_n$ be symbols in $V$ ($m, n \geqslant 0$), $x$ and $y$ strings in $T^*$, $\pi$ a rule string in $P^*$, and $[A \rightarrow \alpha \cdot \beta]$ a 0-item of the \$-augmented grammar $G'$ for $G$ such that*

$$X_m \ldots X_1 \underset{\mathrm{lm}}{\overset{\pi}{\Longrightarrow}} xY_n \ldots Y_1 \quad \text{in } G \ ,$$

$$[A \rightarrow \alpha \cdot \beta] \in \mathrm{VALID}_0(\$X_1 \ldots X_m) \ ,$$

(*a*) *$\alpha$ derives some terminal string,*
*$k{:}y\$ \in \mathrm{FIRST}_k(Y_n \ldots Y_1 \$)$, and*
*either $Y_n \ldots Y_1 = \varepsilon$ or $Y_n$ is a nonterminal .*

*Then for some action string $\pi'$*

*$\tau(\pi') = \pi$, $|\pi'| = |\pi| + |x|$, and*

(*b*) $$\$[\$]_k[\$X_1]_k \ldots [\$X_1 \ldots X_m]_k \mid xy\$$$
$$\overset{\pi'}{\Longrightarrow} \$[\$]_k[\$Y_1]_k \ldots [\$Y_1 \ldots Y_n]_k \mid y\$ \quad \text{in } M \ .$$

*Proof.* The proof is by induction on the length of rule string $\pi$. In the base case we have $\pi = \varepsilon$ and hence $X_m \ldots X_1 = xY_n \ldots Y_1$. Then $\$Y_1 \ldots Y_n x^R$ is a viable suffix of $G'$ (by Fact 8.12). Because $k{:}y\$$ is in $\mathrm{FIRST}_k(Y_n \ldots Y_1 \$)$, we conclude by

Lemma 8.32 that $M$ has an $|x|$-length string of shift actions, $\pi'$, such that

(1)
$$\begin{aligned}&\$[\$]_k[\$X_1]_k \dots [\$X_1 \dots X_m]_k \mid xy\$ \\ &= \$[\$]_k[\$Y_1]_k \dots [\$Y_1 \dots Y_n]_k \dots [\$Y_1 \dots Y_n x^R]_k \mid xy\$ \\ &\overset{\pi'}{\Longrightarrow} \$[\$]_k[\$Y_1]_k \dots [\$Y_1 \dots Y_n]_k \mid y\$ \quad \text{in } M .\end{aligned}$$

As $\tau(\pi') = \varepsilon$, statements ($b$) hold.

To prove the induction step, we assume that $\pi$ is of the form $\pi_1 r$, where $r$ is a rule $B \to \omega$. As an induction hypothesis, we assume that the lemma holds for the rule string $\pi_1$. We have:

(2)
$$X_m \dots X_1 \underset{\text{lm}}{\overset{\pi_1}{\Longrightarrow}} x_1 B Z_p \dots Z_1 \underset{\text{lm}}{\overset{r}{\Longrightarrow}} x_1 \omega Z_p \dots Z_1 = x Y_n \dots Y_1 \quad \text{in } G$$

for some string $x_1 \in T^*$ and symbols $Z_1, \dots, Z_p \in V$ ($p \geq 0$). Here $x = x_1 v$ and $\omega Z_p \dots Z_1 = v Y_n \dots Y_1$ for some $v$, because $Y_n \dots Y_1$ is empty or begins with a nonterminal. Moreover,

(3)
$$\begin{aligned}&k{:}vy\$ \in \text{FIRST}_k(v Y_n \dots Y_1 \$) = \text{FIRST}_k(\omega Z_p \dots Z_1 \$) \\ &\subseteq \text{FIRST}_k(B Z_p \dots Z_1 \$) .\end{aligned}$$

As $BZ_p \dots Z_1$ begins with a nonterminal, we can apply the induction hypothesis to the first derivation segment in (2) and conclude that for some action string $\pi_1'$

(4)
$$\begin{aligned}&\tau(\pi_1') = \pi_1, \quad |\pi_1'| = |\pi_1| + |x_1|, \text{ and} \\ &\$[\$]_k[\$X_1]_k \dots [\$X_1 \dots X_m]_k \mid xy\$ \\ &= \$[\$]_k[\$X_1]_k \dots [\$X_1 \dots X_m]_k \mid x_1 v y\$ \\ &\overset{\pi_1'}{\Longrightarrow} \$[\$]_k[\$Z_1]_k \dots [\$Z_1 \dots Z_p]_k[\$Z_1 \dots Z_p B]_k \mid vy\$ .\end{aligned}$$

On the other hand, because $[A \to \alpha \cdot \beta]$ is an item in $\text{VALID}_0(\$X_1 \dots X_m)$, we have, for some $x'$ and $\delta'$,

(5)
$$\begin{aligned}&S' \underset{\text{lm}}{\Longrightarrow}^* x' A \delta' \underset{\text{lm}}{\Longrightarrow} x' \alpha \beta \delta' = x' \alpha (\$X_1 \dots X_m)^R \\ &= x' \alpha X_m \dots X_1 \$ \quad \text{in } G' .\end{aligned}$$

As $\alpha$ was assumed to derive some terminal string, say $u$, we have, by (2),

(6)
$$\begin{aligned}&S' \underset{\text{lm}}{\Longrightarrow}^* x' u X_m \dots X_1 \$ \underset{\text{lm}}{\overset{\pi_1}{\Longrightarrow}} x' u x_1 B Z_p \dots Z_1 \$ \\ &\underset{\text{lm}}{\overset{r}{\Longrightarrow}} x' u x_1 \omega Z_p \dots Z_1 \$ = x' u x_1 (\$Z_1 \dots Z_p \omega^R)^R \quad \text{in } G' .\end{aligned}$$

Since $k{:}vy\$ \in \text{FIRST}_k(\omega Z_p \dots Z_1 \$)$, this means that

(7)
$$[B \to \cdot \omega, k{:}vy\$] \in \text{VALID}_k(\$Z_1 \dots Z_p \omega^R) .$$

Hence, by definition, $M$ has the produce action

$$(8)\quad r' = [\$Z_1 \ldots Z_p]_k[\$Z_1 \ldots Z_pB]_k \mid y' \to [\$Z_1 \ldots Z_p]_k \ldots [\$Z_1 \ldots Z_p\omega^R]_k \mid y' ,$$

where $y' = k{:}vy\$$. So we have:

$$(9)\quad \begin{aligned} &\$[\$]_k[\$Z_1]_k \ldots [\$Z_1 \ldots Z_p]_k[\$Z_1 \ldots Z_pB]_k \mid vy\$ \\ &\xRightarrow{r'} \$[\$]_k[\$Z_1]_k \ldots [\$Z_1 \ldots Z_p]_k \ldots [\$Z_1 \ldots Z_p\omega^R]_k \mid vy\$ \\ &= \$[\$]_k[\$Y_1]_k \ldots [\$Y_1 \ldots Y_n]_k \ldots [\$Y_1 \ldots Y_nv^R]_k \mid vy\$ . \end{aligned}$$

Here we can apply Lemma 8.32 and conclude that

$$(10)\quad \begin{aligned} &\$[\$]_k[\$Y_1]_k \ldots [\$Y_1 \ldots Y_n]_k \ldots [\$Y_1 \ldots Y_nv^R]_k \mid vy\$ \\ &\xRightarrow{\pi'_2} \$[\$]_k[\$Y_1]_k \ldots [\$Y_1 \ldots Y_n]_k \mid y\$ \quad \text{in } M \end{aligned}$$

for some $|v|$-length shift action string $\pi'_2$. Combining (4), (9), and (10) we get:

$$(11)\quad \begin{aligned} &\$[\$]_k[\$X_1]_k \ldots [\$X_1 \ldots X_m]_k \mid xy\$ \\ &\xRightarrow{\pi'} \$[\$]_k[\$Y_1]_k \ldots [\$Y_1 \ldots Y_n]_k \mid y\$ \quad \text{in } M , \end{aligned}$$

where $\pi' = \pi'_1 r' \pi'_2$. Here

$$(12)\quad \begin{aligned} &\tau(\pi') = \tau(\pi'_1)\tau(r')\tau(\pi'_2) = \pi_1 r = \pi, \text{ and} \\ &|\pi'| = |\pi'_1| + |r'| + |\pi'_2| = |\pi_1| + |x_1| + 1 + |v| \\ &= |\pi_1 r| + |x_1 v| = |\pi| + |x| , \end{aligned}$$

as desired. □

**Lemma 8.34** *If $(M, \tau)$ is the canonical LL(k) parser for grammar G, then $L(G) \subseteq L(M)$, and for any left parse $\pi$ of sentence w in G, $\tau(\pi') = \pi$ for some parse $\pi'$ of w in M. Moreover,* $\mathrm{TIME}_M(w) \leq \mathrm{TIME}_G(w) + |w|$.

*Proof.* Choose $m = 1, n = 0, X_1 = S, x = w, [A \to \alpha \cdot \beta] = [S' \to \$ \cdot S\$]$, and $y = \varepsilon$ in Lemma 8.33. □

By Lemmas 8.31 and 8.34 we have:

**Theorem 8.35** *The canonical LL(k) parser M for grammar G is a left parser for G. Moreover, for each sentence w in L(G), M produces all left parses of w in G, and* $\mathrm{TIME}_M(w) = \mathrm{TIME}_G(w) + |w|$. □

We conclude this section by defining the notions of "LA(k)LL(l) machine" and "LA(k)LL(l) parser", the analogs of the notions of LA(k)LR(l) machine and LA(k)LR(l) parser.

Let $G = (V, T, P, S)$ be a grammar and $k$, $l$ natural numbers, $l \leq k$. The *LA(k)LL(l) machine* for $G$ is the finite automaton obtained from the canonical LL($l$) machine of $G$ by replacing each state $q$ by the union

$$q_1 \cup \ldots \cup q_n ,$$

where

$$\{q_1, \ldots, q_n\} = \{q' \mid q' \text{ is a state in the canonical LL}(k) \text{ machine such that } \mathrm{TRUNC}_l(q') = q\} .$$

Recall that $\mathrm{TRUNC}_l(q')$ is the set of $l$-items obtained from the items in $q'$ by truncating the lookahead strings to length $l$. Obviously, the LA($k$)LL($k$) machine is the canonical LL($k$) machine. The LA($k$)LL(0) machine is called the *LALL(k) machine.*

For example, the LA(2)LL(1) machine for our grammar $G'_{abL}$ differs from the canonical LL(2) machine (Figure 8.3) in that states 11 and 15, and states 13 and 16, are united.

A rule of the form

$$\text{(pa)} \qquad [\delta]_l[\delta A]_l \mid y \to [\delta]_l[\delta X_n]_l \ldots [\delta X_n \ldots X_1]_l \mid y$$

is an *LA(k)LL(l) produce action by rule* $A \to X_1 \ldots X_n$ *on lookahead* $y$ if $\delta$ is a string in $\$V^*$, $X_1, \ldots X_n$ are symbols in $V$ $(n \geq 0)$, $A \to X_1 \ldots X_n$ is a rule in $P$, and $y$ is a string in $k{:}T^*\$$ such that

$$[A \to \cdot X_1 \ldots X_n, y] \in \mathrm{VALID}_k(\gamma) \quad \text{and} \quad [\gamma]_l = [\delta X_n \ldots X_1]_l$$

for some string $\gamma \in \$V^*$. In other words, $[A \to \cdot X_1 \ldots X_n, y]$ is LL($k$)-valid for some viable suffix LL($l$)-equivalent to $\delta X_n \ldots X_1$.

A rule of the form

$$\text{(sa)} \qquad [\delta a]_l \mid ay \to \mid y$$

is an *LA(k)LL(l) shift action on terminal a and lookahead ay* if $\delta$ is a string in $\$V^*$, $a$ is a terminal in $T$, and $y$ is a string in $\max\{k-1, 0\}{:}T^*\$$ such that

$$[A \to \alpha \cdot a\beta, k{:}ay] \in \mathrm{VALID}_k(\gamma) \quad \text{and} \quad [\gamma]_l = [\delta a]_l$$

for some rule $A \to \alpha a \beta$ in $P$ and string $\gamma \in \$V^*$.

The *LA(k)LL(l) parser* for $G$ is the pushdown transducer with stack alphabet $[G']_l$, input alphabet $T$, initial stack contents $[\$]_l[\$S]_l$, set of final stack contents $\{[\$]_l\}$, and set of actions consisting of all LA($k$)LL($l$) produce and shift actions of $G$. As usual, the output effect $\tau$ is defined to map every produce action by rule $r$ to $r$ and every shift action to $\varepsilon$. Obviously, the LA($k$)LL($k$) parser coincides with the canonical LL($k$) parser. The LA($k$)LL(0) parser is called the *LALL(k) parser.*

The properties of LA($k$)LL($l$) machines and parsers are completely analogous to those of their LR($k$) counterparts. Some of the properties are considered in the exercises.

## 8.4 LL(k) Grammars

In this section we shall characterize grammars that have a deterministic LL($k$) parser. We say that a grammar is an *LL(k) grammar* if its canonical LL($k$) parser is deterministic. A language over alphabet $T$ is an *LL(k) language* if it is the language generated by some LL($k$) grammar with terminal alphabet $T$. Grammars with deterministic LA($k$)LL($l$) parsers are called *LA(k)LL(l) grammars*, and languages generated by LA($k$)LL($l$) grammars are called *LA(k)LL(l) languages*. Grammars with deterministic LALL($k$) parsers are called *LALL(k) grammars*, and languages generated by LALL($k$) grammars are called *LALL(k) languages*. By definition, LL($k$) grammars (languages) coincide with LA($k$)LL($k$) grammars (languages), and LALL($k$) grammars (languages) coincide with LA($k$)LL(0) grammars (languages).

We shall characterize LL($k$) grammars in terms of the grammar only. We shall show that the classes of LL(1) grammars, LALL(1) grammars, and SLL(1) grammars coincide, and that the families of LL($k$) languages, LALL($k$) languages, and SLL($k$) languages coincide for all $k \geqslant 0$. We shall also compare LL($k$) grammars with LR($k$) grammars: we show that any LL($k$) grammar is an LR($k$) grammar, and we demonstrate that LALL($k$) grammars are not comparable to LALR($k$) grammars and that SLL($k$) grammars are not comparable to SLR($k$) grammars.

Let $G = (V, T, P, S)$ be a grammar, $G'$ its \$-augmented grammar, and $k$ a natural number. We say that $k$-items $[A_1 \to \cdot\omega_1, y_1]$ and $[A_2 \to \cdot\omega_2, y_2]$ of $G'$ *exhibit a produce-produce conflict* if $A_1 = A_2$, $\omega_1 \neq \omega_2$, and $y_1 = y_2$.

**Lemma 8.36** *The canonical LL(k) parser for grammar $G = (V, T, P, S)$ is nondeterministic if and only if there is a viable suffix $\delta$ and k-items $[A \to \cdot\omega_1, y]$ and $[A \to \cdot\omega_2, y]$ of $G'$ exhibiting a produce-produce conflict such that*

$$(a) \qquad [A \to \cdot\omega_1, y] \in \text{VALID}_k(\delta\omega_1^R), \text{ and} \quad [A \to \cdot\omega_2, y] \in \text{VALID}_k(\delta\omega_2^R)\ .$$

*Proof.* To prove the "if" part, assume that ($a$) holds. The definition of the canonical LL($k$) parser implies the existence of a pair of produce actions

$$[\delta]_k[\delta A]_k \mid y \to [\delta]_k[\delta X_m]_k \ldots [\delta X_m \ldots X_1]_k \mid y\ ,$$

$$[\delta]_k[\delta A]_k \mid y \to [\delta]_k[\delta Y_n]_k \ldots [\delta Y_n \ldots Y_1]_k \mid y\ ,$$

where $X_1 \ldots X_m = \omega_1$ and $Y_1 \ldots Y_n = \omega_2$. But the right-hand sides of these actions are different, because $\omega_1 \neq \omega_2$. This means that the parser is nondeterministic.

To prove the "only if" part, assume that the canonical LL($k$) parser is nondeterministic. Let therefore $\Phi$ be a configuration to which two distinct actions, $r_1$ and $r_2$, are applicable. We shall show that ($a$) holds. We have to consider three cases:

$$(1) \qquad r_1 = [\delta]_k[\delta A]_k \mid y \to [\delta]_k[\delta X_m]_k \ldots [\delta X_m \ldots X_1]_k \mid y\ , \quad r_2 = [\gamma]_k[\gamma B]_k \mid z \to [\gamma]_k[\gamma Y_n]_k \ldots [\gamma Y_n \ldots Y_1]_k \mid z\ ,$$

$$(2)\qquad \begin{aligned} r_1 &= [\delta]_k[\delta A]_k \mid y \to [\delta]_k[\delta X_m]_k \ldots [\delta X_m \ldots X_1]_k \mid y\ , \\ r_2 &= [\gamma a]_k \mid az \to \mid z\ . \end{aligned}$$

$$(3)\qquad \begin{aligned} r_1 &= [\delta a]_k \mid ay \to \mid y\ , \\ r_2 &= [\gamma b]_k \mid bz \to \mid z\ . \end{aligned}$$

As $r_1$ and $r_2$ are both applicable to the same configuration $\Phi$, we conclude that in case (1) $[\delta]_k = [\gamma]_k$, $[\delta A]_k = [\gamma B]_k$, and one of $y$ and $z$ is a prefix of the other, and in case (2) $[\delta A]_k = [\gamma a]_k$, and in case (3) $[\delta a]_k = [\gamma b]_k$ and one of $ay$ and $bz$ is a prefix of the other. Since any two LL($k$)-equivalent viable suffixes always end with the same symbol, we have in case (1) $A = B$ and in case (3) $a = b$. Moreover, case (2) cannot occur at all. As in the proof of Lemma 6.36 we conclude that in case (1) the lookahead strings $y$ and $z$ in fact are the same, because no string in $k\!:\!T^*\$$ can be a proper prefix of any other string in $k\!:\!T^*\$$. Similarly, in case (3) the strings $y$ and $z$ are the same. This rules out case (3) altogether, since $r_1$ and $r_2$ were assumed to be distinct actions. Thus, only case (1) remains. The definition of the canonical LL($k$) parser implies that

$$[A \to \cdot X_1 \ldots X_m, y] \in \mathrm{VALID}_k(\delta X_m \ldots X_1), \text{ and}$$

$$[B \to \cdot Y_1 \ldots Y_n, z] \in \mathrm{VALID}_k(\gamma Y_n \ldots Y_1)\ .$$

Here $A = B$ and $y = z$. Moreover, $X_1 \ldots X_m \neq Y_1 \ldots Y_n$ because otherwise $r_1$ and $r_2$ in (1) were not distinct actions. Since $[\delta]_k = [\gamma]_k$ and the LL($k$)-equivalence is right-invariant, we have

$$\mathrm{VALID}_k(\delta Y_n \ldots Y_1) = \mathrm{VALID}_k(\gamma Y_n \ldots Y_1)\ ,$$

which means that statement ($a$) is true. □

We say that nonterminal $A$ of grammar $G = (V, T, P, S)$ *has the LL(k) property* if

$$\mathrm{FIRST}_k(\omega_1 \delta) \cap \mathrm{FIRST}_k(\omega_2 \delta) = \varnothing$$

for all left sentential forms $xA\delta$ of $G$ and all distinct rules $A \to \omega_1$ and $A \to \omega_2$ in $P$.

**Theorem 8.37** (*Characterization of LL(k) grammars*) *The following statements are logically equivalent for all grammars $G = (V, T, P, S)$ and natural numbers k.*

(*a*) *G is an LL(k) grammar.*

(*b*) *In G′, the \$-augmented grammar for G, the conditions*

$$[A \to \cdot\omega_1, y] \in \mathrm{VALID}_k(\delta\omega_1^R),\ \textit{and}$$

$$[A \to \cdot\omega_2, y] \in \mathrm{VALID}_k(\delta\omega_2^R)$$

*always imply that $\omega_1 = \omega_2$.*

(*c*) *All nonterminals of G have the LL(k) property.*

(*d*) *In G, the conditions*

$$S \underset{lm}{\Longrightarrow}^* xA\delta \underset{lm}{\Longrightarrow} x\omega_1\delta \underset{lm}{\Longrightarrow}^* xy_1 ,$$

$$S \underset{lm}{\Longrightarrow}^* xA\delta \underset{lm}{\Longrightarrow} x\omega_2\delta \underset{lm}{\Longrightarrow}^* xy_2, \text{ and}$$

$$k{:}y_1 = k{:}y_2$$

*always imply that* $\omega_1 = \omega_2$.

*Proof.* The equivalence of statements (*a*) and (*b*) is stated in Lemma 8.36. By the definition of LL($k$)-validity, statement (*b*) is equivalent to:

($b'$) In $G'$, the conditions

$$S' \underset{lm}{\Longrightarrow}^* x_1 A\delta^R \underset{lm}{\Longrightarrow} x_1\omega_1\delta^R, \quad y \in \text{FIRST}_k(\omega_1\delta^R) ,$$

$$S' \underset{lm}{\Longrightarrow}^* x_2 A\delta^R \underset{lm}{\Longrightarrow} x_2\omega_2\delta^R, \quad y \in \text{FIRST}_k(\omega_2\delta^R)$$

always imply that $\omega_1 = \omega_2$.

Here $G'$ can be replaced by $G$ and $S'$ by $S$. Moreover, $x_2$ can be replaced by $x_1$ (observe that $S' \underset{lm}{\Longrightarrow}^* x_1 A\delta^R$ and $A \to \omega_2$ is a rule). Hence we conclude that (*b*) is equivalent to:

($b''$) In $G$, the conditions

$$S \underset{lm}{\Longrightarrow}^* xA\delta^R \underset{lm}{\Longrightarrow} x\omega_1\delta^R, \quad y \in \text{FIRST}_k(\omega_1\delta^R) ,$$

$$S \underset{lm}{\Longrightarrow}^* xA\delta^R \underset{lm}{\Longrightarrow} x\omega_2\delta^R, \quad y \in \text{FIRST}_k(\omega_2\delta^R)$$

always imply that $\omega_1 = \omega_2$.

This is obviously equivalent both to statement (*c*) and to statement (*d*). □

For all $k \geqslant l \geqslant 0$, any LA($k$)LL($l$) grammar is, obviously, also an LA($k+1$)LL($l$) grammar, and any LA($k+1$)LL($l$) grammar in turn is also an LA($k+1$)LL($l+1$) grammar. For $l \geqslant 1$ the grammar

$$S \to aAa^lb \mid bAb ,$$

$$A \to cAB \mid \varepsilon \mid a^l$$

$$B \to \varepsilon$$

is an example of an LA($k+1$)LL($l+1$) grammar, $k \geqslant l$, which is not LA($k$)LL($l$) for any $k \geqslant l$. For $k \geqslant 0$ the grammar

$$S \to a^kb \mid a^{k+1}$$

in turn is an example of an LA$(k+1)$LL(0) grammar which is not LA$(k)$LL$(l)$ for any $l \leqslant k$. We have:

**Theorem 8.38** *For all $1 \leqslant l \leqslant k$, the class of LA$(k+1)$LL$(l)$ grammars is properly contained in the class of LA$(k+1)$LL$(l+1)$ grammars. For all $0 \leqslant l \leqslant k$, the class of LA$(k)$LL$(l)$ grammars is properly contained in the class of LA$(k+1)$LL$(l)$ grammars.* □

Next we shall show that the classes of LL(1) grammars, LALL(1) grammars, and SLL(1) grammars coincide.

**Lemma 8.39** *Every LL(1) grammar is an SLL(1) grammar.*

*Proof.* Let $G = (V, T, P, S)$ be an LL(1) grammar, and let $\delta_1$ and $\delta_2$ be strings in $V^*$, $A \to \omega_1$ and $A \to \omega_2$ rules in $P$, and $x_1$, $x_2$, $y_1$, and $y_2$ strings in $T^*$ such that

$$
\begin{aligned}
&S \underset{\text{lm}}{\Longrightarrow^*} x_1 A \delta_1 \underset{\text{lm}}{\Longrightarrow} x_1 \omega_1 \delta_1 \underset{\text{lm}}{\Longrightarrow^*} x_1 y_1, \\
(1) \qquad &S \underset{\text{lm}}{\Longrightarrow^*} x_2 A \delta_2 \underset{\text{lm}}{\Longrightarrow} x_2 \omega_2 \delta_2 \underset{\text{lm}}{\Longrightarrow^*} x_2 y_2, \text{ and} \\
&1{:}y_1 = 1{:}y_2 .
\end{aligned}
$$

We show that $\omega_1 = \omega_2$, which implies, by Theorem 5.34, that $G$ is an SLL(1) grammar. The conditions (1) imply that $\omega_1 \delta_1 \underset{\text{lm}}{\Longrightarrow^*} y_1$ and $\omega_2 \delta_2 \underset{\text{lm}}{\Longrightarrow^*} y_2$, which further implies that for some strings $v_1$, $z_1$, $v_2$, and $z_2 \in T^*$

$$
\begin{aligned}
&\omega_1 \underset{\text{lm}}{\Longrightarrow^*} v_1, \quad \delta_1 \underset{\text{lm}}{\Longrightarrow^*} z_1, \quad v_1 z_1 = y_1 , \\
&\omega_2 \underset{\text{lm}}{\Longrightarrow^*} v_2, \quad \delta_2 \underset{\text{lm}}{\Longrightarrow^*} z_2, \quad v_2 z_2 = y_2 .
\end{aligned}
$$

The conditions (1) then imply that

$$
\begin{aligned}
&S \underset{\text{lm}}{\Longrightarrow^*} x_1 A \delta_1 \underset{\text{lm}}{\Longrightarrow} x_1 \omega_1 \delta_1 \underset{\text{lm}}{\Longrightarrow^*} x_1 v_1 z_1 , \\
(2) \qquad &S \underset{\text{lm}}{\Longrightarrow^*} x_1 A \delta_1 \underset{\text{lm}}{\Longrightarrow} x_1 \omega_2 \delta_1 \underset{\text{lm}}{\Longrightarrow^*} x_1 v_2 z_1 ,
\end{aligned}
$$

and that

$$
\begin{aligned}
&S \underset{\text{lm}}{\Longrightarrow^*} x_2 A \delta_2 \underset{\text{lm}}{\Longrightarrow} x_2 \omega_1 \delta_2 \underset{\text{lm}}{\Longrightarrow^*} x_2 v_1 z_2 , \\
(3) \qquad &S \underset{\text{lm}}{\Longrightarrow^*} x_2 A \delta_2 \underset{\text{lm}}{\Longrightarrow} x_2 \omega_2 \delta_2 \underset{\text{lm}}{\Longrightarrow^*} x_2 v_2 z_2 .
\end{aligned}
$$

If $v_1 \neq \varepsilon$, then $1{:}v_1 z_2 = 1{:}v_1 z_1 = 1{:}y_1 = 1{:}y_2 = 1{:}v_2 z_2$. As $G$ is an LL(1) grammar, statement (*d*) of Theorem 8.37 holds, and hence condition (3) implies that $\omega_1 = \omega_2$. Correspondingly, if $v_2 \neq \varepsilon$, then $1{:}v_1 z_1 = 1{:}y_1 = 1{:}y_2 = 1{:}v_2 z_2 = 1{:}v_2 = 1{:}v_2 z_1$, and thus (2) and statement (*d*) of Theorem 8.37 imply that $\omega_1 = \omega_2$. Finally, if $v_1 = \varepsilon = v_2$, then even $v_1 z_1 = v_2 z_1$, and again (2) and statement (*d*) of Theorem 8.37 imply that $\omega_1 = \omega_2$. □

The proof of the following lemma is left as an exercise.

**Lemma 8.40** *For all $k \geqslant 0$, any SLL($k$) grammar is an LALL($k$) grammar, and any LALL($k$) grammar is an LL($k$) grammar.* □

By Lemmas 8.39 and 8.40 we have:

**Theorem 8.41** *The classes of SLL(1), LALL(1), and LL(1) grammars coincide.* □

The classes of SLL(0), LALL(0), and LL(0) grammars contain only grammars that generate at most one sentence (see the exercises). It is also easy to see that these classes of grammars are equal.

For $k > 1$, the grammar

$$S \to aAa^{k-1}b \mid bAbb \mid ca^{2k-2}b \ ,$$

$$A \to \varepsilon \mid a^{k-1}$$

is LALL($k$) but not SLL($k$). Thus we have from Theorem 8.38 and Lemma 8.40:

**Theorem 8.42** *For $k > 1$, the class of SLL($k$) grammars is properly contained in the class of LALL($k$) grammars, which in turn is properly contained in the class of LL($k$) grammars.* □

Next we shall show that the proper containments stated in Theorem 8.42 are properties of grammars only, not properties of languages. In fact we shall show that any LL($k$) grammar can be transformed into an equivalent SLL($k$) grammar.

Let $G = (V, T, P, S)$ be a grammar and $k$ a positive natural number. We define $T_k(G)$ to be the grammar with nonterminal alphabet

$$\{[A, R] \mid A \in V \setminus T \text{ and } R \subseteq \text{FOLLOW}'_k(A)\} \ ,$$

terminal alphabet $T$, start symbol $[S, \{\$\}]$, and with set of rules consisting of all rules of the form

$$[A, R] \to X'_1 \ldots X'_m \ ,$$

where for some rule $A \to X_1 \ldots X_m$ in $P$

$$X'_i = \begin{cases} [X_i, \text{FIRST}_k(X_{i+1} \ldots X_m R)], & \text{when } X_i \text{ is a nonterminal;} \\ X_i, & \text{when } X_i \text{ is a terminal} \ , \end{cases}$$

for $i = 1, \ldots, m$.

The idea behind this transformation is much the same as that in the transformation of LR($k$) grammars into SLR($k$) grammars (Section 6.6): nonterminal $A$ is "split" into several nonterminals $[A, R_1], \ldots, [A, R_n]$, each representing an occurrence of the original nonterminal in a particular context.

As an example consider the LL(2) grammar $G_{abL}$:

$$S \rightarrow aAab \mid bAb \ ,$$

$$A \rightarrow cAB \mid \varepsilon \mid a \ ,$$

$$B \rightarrow \varepsilon \ .$$

As we saw in Section 8.1, this grammar is not SLL($k$) for any $k$. The transformed grammar $T_2(G_{abL})$ has the rules (when useless symbols have been deleted):

$$[S, \{\$\}] \rightarrow a[A, \{ab\}]ab \mid b[A, \{b\$\}]b \ ,$$

$$[A, \{ab\}] \rightarrow c[A, \{ab\}][B, \{ab\}] \mid \varepsilon \mid a \ ,$$

$$[A, \{b\$\}] \rightarrow c[A, \{b\$\}][B, \{b\$\}] \mid \varepsilon \mid a \ ,$$

$$[B, \{ab\}] \rightarrow \varepsilon \ ,$$

$$[B, \{b\$\}] \rightarrow \varepsilon \ .$$

Obviously, this grammar is SLL(2) and generates the same language as $G_{abL}$. Moreover, the grammar is structurally equivalent to the original grammar: both grammars generate sets of derivation trees that differ only in the labelling of nonterminal nodes (see Figure 8.7).

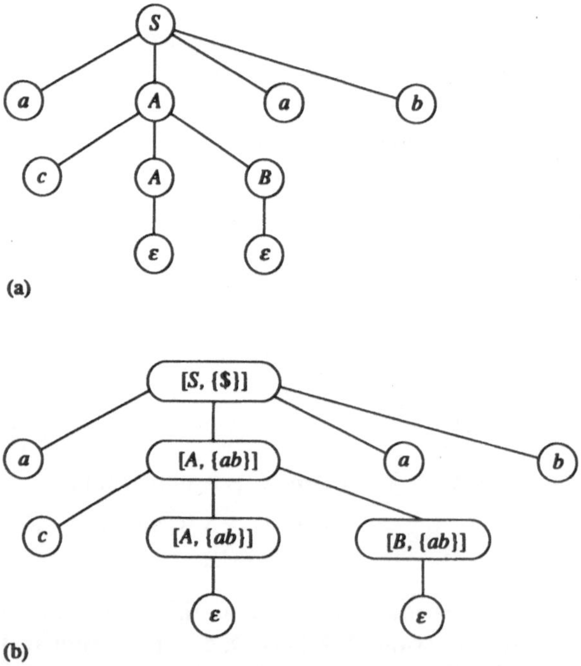


**Figure 8.7** Derivation tree of *acab*: (a) in $G_{abL}$, and (b) in the transformed grammar $T_2(G_{abL})$

Now let $h_k$ be the homomorphism from the rule strings of the transformed grammar $T_k(G)$ to the rule strings of $G$ defined by:

$$h_k([A, R] \to X'_1 \ldots X'_m) = A \to X_1 \ldots X_m \ ,$$

where, for $i = 1, \ldots, m$, $X'_i$ is $[X_i, \mathrm{FIRST}_k(X_{i+1} \ldots X_m R)]$ or $X_i$.

**Lemma 8.43** *Let $G = (V, T, P, S)$ be a grammar, $A$ a nonterminal of $G$, $R$ a subset of $\mathrm{FOLLOW}'_k(A)$, $\Phi$ a string over the alphabet of $T_k(G)$, and $\pi'$ a rule string of $T_k(G)$ such that*

(a) $$[A, R] \xRightarrow[\mathrm{lm}]{\pi'} \Phi \quad \text{in } T_k(G) \ .$$

*Then there are symbols $X_1, \ldots, X_n \in V$ $(n \geq 0)$ and a string $x \in T^*$ such that*

(b) $$\Phi = xX'_1 \ldots X'_n \quad \text{and} \quad A \xRightarrow[\mathrm{lm}]{h_k(\pi')} xX_1 \ldots X_n \quad \text{in } G \ ,$$

*where, for all $i = 1, \ldots, n$,*

(c) $$X'_i = \begin{cases} [X_i, \mathrm{FIRST}_k(X_{i+1} \ldots X_n R)], & \text{when } X_i \text{ is a nonterminal;} \\ X_i, & \text{when } X_i \text{ is a terminal .} \end{cases}$$

*Proof.* The proof is a straightforward induction on the length of rule string $\pi'$. The details are left to the exercises. □

**Lemma 8.44** *Let $G = (V, T, P, S)$ be a grammar, $A$ a nonterminal of $G$, $R$ a subset of $\mathrm{FOLLOW}'_k(A)$, $x$ a string in $T^*$, $X_1, \ldots, X_n$ symbols in $V(n \geq 0)$, and $\pi$ a rule string in $P^*$ such that*

(a) $$A \xRightarrow[\mathrm{lm}]{\pi} xX_1 \ldots X_n \text{ in } G, \text{ and}$$
$$\text{either } X_1 \ldots X_n = \varepsilon \text{ or } X_1 \text{ is a nonterminal .}$$

*Then $T_k(G)$ has a rule string $\pi'$ such that*

(b) $$h_k(\pi') = \pi \text{ and } [A, R] \xRightarrow[\mathrm{lm}]{\pi'} xX'_1 \ldots X'_n \quad \text{in } T_k(G) \ ,$$

*where, for all $i = 1, \ldots, n$,*

(c) $$X'_i = \begin{cases} [X_i, \mathrm{FIRST}_k(X_{i+1} \ldots X_n R)], & \text{when } X_i \text{ is a nonterminal;} \\ X_i, & \text{when } X_i \text{ is a terminal .} \end{cases}$$

*Proof.* The proof is a straightforward induction on the length of rule string $\pi$. The details are left to the exercises. □

**Theorem 8.45** *Let $G = (V, T, P, S)$ be a grammar and $k$ a positive natural number. Then $T_k(G)$ left-to-left covers $G$ with respect to the homomorphism $h_k$.*

*Proof.* In proving that left parses in $T_k(G)$ are mapped by $h_k$ to left parses in $G$, choose $A = S$, $R = \{\$\}$, and $\Phi = w$ in Lemma 8.43. In proving that left parses in $G$ are images under $h_k$ of left parses in $T_k(G)$, choose $A = S$, $R = \{\$\}$, $x = w$, and $n = 0$ in Lemma 8.44. □

**Corollary 8.46** *If $(M, \tau)$ is a left parser of $T_k(G)$, then $(M, \tau h_k)$ is a left parser of $G$.* □

We then show that the transformation of $G$ into $T_k(G)$ indeed produces an SLL($k$) grammar from an LL($k$) grammar.

**Theorem 8.47** *Let $G = (V, T, P, S)$ be a grammar and $k$ a positive natural number. The grammar $T_k(G)$ is SLL($k$) whenever $G$ is LL($k$). $G$ is LL($k$) whenever $T_k(G)$ is so.*

*Proof.* First we note that the language generated by nonterminal $[A, R]$ in $T_k(G)$ is always the same as the language generated by nonterminal $A$ in $G$. This follows directly from Lemmas 8.43 and 8.44.

To prove that the LL($k$)-ness of $G$ implies the SLL($k$)-ness of $T_k(G)$, let $x_1$, $x_2$, $y_1$, $y_2$ be strings in $T^*$, $X'_1, \ldots X'_p$, $Y'_1, \ldots, Y'_q$ symbols in the alphabet of $T_k(G)$, and $[A, R] \to X'_1 \ldots X'_m$ and $[A, R] \to Y'_1 \ldots Y'_n$ rules of $T_k(G)$ such that $0 \leqslant m \leqslant p$, $0 \leqslant n \leqslant q$, and

$$\begin{aligned} &[S, \{\$\}] \underset{\mathrm{lm}}{\Longrightarrow}^* x_1 [A, R] X'_{m+1} \ldots X'_p \\ &\underset{\mathrm{lm}}{\Longrightarrow} x_1 X'_1 \ldots X'_m X'_{m+1} \ldots X'_p \underset{\mathrm{lm}}{\Longrightarrow}^* x_1 y_1 , \\ (1) \qquad &[S, \{\$\}] \underset{\mathrm{lm}}{\Longrightarrow}^* x_2 [A, R] Y'_{n+1} \ldots Y'_q \\ &\underset{\mathrm{lm}}{\Longrightarrow} x_2 Y'_1 \ldots Y'_n Y'_{n+1} \ldots Y'_q \underset{\mathrm{lm}}{\Longrightarrow}^* x_2 y_2 , \\ &k{:}y_1 = k{:}y_2 . \end{aligned}$$

By definition, there are symbols $X_1, \ldots, X_p$, $Y_1, \ldots Y_q$ in $V$ such that $A \to X_1 \ldots X_m$ and $A \to Y_1 \ldots Y_n$ are rules of $G$ and for all $i = 1, \ldots, m$

$$(2) \qquad X'_i = \begin{cases} [X_i, \mathrm{FIRST}_k(X_{i+1} \ldots X_m R)], & \text{when } X_i \text{ is a nonterminal ;} \\ X_i, & \text{when } X_i \text{ is a terminal ,} \end{cases}$$

and, for all $i = 1, \ldots, n$

$$(3) \qquad Y'_i = \begin{cases} [Y_i, \mathrm{FIRST}_k(Y_{i+1} \ldots Y_n R)], & \text{when } Y_i \text{ is a nonterminal ;} \\ Y_i, & \text{when } Y_i \text{ is a terminal ,} \end{cases}$$

Moreover, for $i = m + 1, \ldots, p$, $X'_i$ is of the form $[X_i, R_i]$ when $X_i$ is a nonterminal, and $X'_i$ is $X_i$ otherwise. Similarly, for $i = n + 1, \ldots, q$, $Y'_i$ is of the form $[Y_i, R_i]$ when $Y_i$ is a nonterminal, and $Y'_i$ is $Y_i$ otherwise. From the final derivation segments in (1) we conclude the existence of strings $u_1$, $u_2$, $v_1$, $v_2$ in $T^*$ such that in

$T_k(G)$

(4)
$$X'_1 \dots X'_m \Rightarrow^* u_1, \quad X'_{m+1} \dots X'_p \Rightarrow^* v_1, \quad u_1 v_1 = y_1 ,$$
$$Y'_1 \dots Y'_n \Rightarrow^* u_2, \quad Y'_{n+1} \dots Y'_q \Rightarrow^* v_2, \quad u_2 v_2 = y_2 .$$

Since $X'_i$ and $X_i$ generate the same language for all $i = 1, \dots, p$, and since $Y'_i$ and $Y_i$ generate the same language for all $i = 1, \dots, q$, we have in $G$:

(5)
$$X_1 \dots X_m \underset{\text{lm}}{\Longrightarrow}^* u_1, \quad X_{m+1} \dots X_p \underset{\text{lm}}{\Longrightarrow}^* v_1, \quad u_1 v_1 = y_1 ,$$
$$Y_1 \dots Y_n \underset{\text{lm}}{\Longrightarrow}^* u_2, \quad Y_{n+1} \dots Y_q \underset{\text{lm}}{\Longrightarrow}^* v_2, \quad u_2 v_2 = y_2 .$$

On the other hand we can apply Lemma 8.43 to the initial derivation segments in (1) and conclude that

(6) $$\text{FIRST}_k(X_{m+1} \dots X_p\$) = R = \text{FIRST}_k(Y_{n+1} \dots Y_q\$)$$

and that in $G$

(7) $$S \underset{\text{lm}}{\Longrightarrow}^* x_1 A X_{m+1} \dots X_p .$$

By (6) and (5) we conclude that $X_{m+1} \dots X_p$ derives some terminal string $v'_2$ with $k{:}v'_2 = k{:}v_2$. Then we have:

(8) $$k{:}u_1 v_1 = k{:}y_1 = k{:}y_2 = k{:}u_2 v_2 = k{:}u_2 v'_2 .$$

By combining this with (7) and (5) we conclude that in $G$:

(8)
$$S \underset{\text{lm}}{\Longrightarrow}^* x_1 A X_{m+1} \dots X_p$$
$$\underset{\text{lm}}{\Longrightarrow} x_1 X_1 \dots X_m X_{m+1} \dots X_p \underset{\text{lm}}{\Longrightarrow}^* x_1 y_1 ,$$
$$S \underset{\text{lm}}{\Longrightarrow}^* x_1 A X_{m+1} \dots X_p$$
$$\underset{\text{lm}}{\Longrightarrow} x_1 Y_1 \dots Y_n X_{m+1} \dots X_p \underset{\text{lm}}{\Longrightarrow}^* x_1 y'_2 ,$$
$$k{:}y_1 = k{:}y'_2 ,$$

where $y'_2$ denotes the string $u_2 v'_2$. Now if $G$ is LL($k$), we conclude by Theorem 8.37($d$) that $m = n$ and $X_1 \dots X_m = Y_1 \dots Y_n$. But then (2) and (3) imply that also $X'_1 \dots X'_m = Y'_1 \dots Y'_n$, which means, by Theorem 5.34($d$), that $T_k(G)$ must be SLL($k$).

To prove that the LL($k$)-ness of $T_k(G)$ implies the LL($k$)-ness of $G$, assume that (8) is true. By definition, $T_k(G)$ has rules $[A, R] \to X'_1 \dots X'_m$ and $[A, R] \to Y'_1 \dots Y'_n$ where $R$ denotes the set $\text{FIRST}_k(X_{m+1} \dots X_p\$)$ and the symbols $X'_1, \dots, X'_m, Y'_1, \dots, Y'_n$ satisfy the conditions (2) and (3). By applying Lemma 8.44 to the initial derivation segment in (8) we conclude the existence of symbols $X'_{m+1}, \dots, X'_p$ of $T_k(G)$ such that

(9) $$[S, \{\$\}] \underset{\text{lm}}{\Longrightarrow}^* x_1 [A, R] X'_{m+1} \dots X'_p .$$

Moreover, $X_i'$ is $[X_i, \mathrm{FIRST}_k(X_{i+1} \ldots X_p\$)]$ when $X_i$ is a nonterminal, and $X_i'$ is $X_i$ otherwise ($i = m+1, \ldots, p$). Since $X_i'$ and $X_i$ generate the same language and $Y_i'$ and $Y_i$ generate the same language, we conclude by (9) and (8) that in $T_k(G)$

$$
\begin{aligned}
&[S,\{\$\}] \underset{\mathrm{lm}}{\Longrightarrow}^* x_1[A,R]X'_{m+1} \ldots X'_p \\
&\underset{\mathrm{lm}}{\Longrightarrow} x_1 X'_1 \ldots X'_m X'_{m+1} \ldots X'_p \underset{\mathrm{lm}}{\Longrightarrow} x_1 y_1 \ , \\
(10) \qquad &[S,\{\$\}] \underset{\mathrm{lm}}{\Longrightarrow}^* x_1[A,R]X'_{m+1} \ldots X'_p \\
&\underset{\mathrm{lm}}{\Longrightarrow} x_1 Y'_1 \ldots Y'_n X'_{m+1} \ldots X'_p \underset{\mathrm{lm}}{\Longrightarrow}^* x_1 y'_2 \ , \\
&k:y_1 = k:y'_2 \ .
\end{aligned}
$$

Now if $T_k(G)$ is LL($k$), we conclude that $m = n$ and $X'_1 \ldots X'_m = Y'_1 \ldots Y'_n$. This in turn implies that $X_1 \ldots X_m = Y_1 \ldots Y_n$, which means that $G$ is LL($k$). □

The transformed grammar $T_k(G)$ can be constructed from $G$. Hence we have by Theorems 8.45 and 8.47:

**Theorem 8.48** *Let $k \geqslant 1$. Any grammar can be transformed into an equivalent grammar that left-to-left covers the original grammar, and is SLL($k$) if and only if the original grammar is LL($k$). In fact, the transformed grammar is structurally equivalent to the original grammar.* □

Lemma 8.40 and Theorem 8.48 imply:

**Theorem 8.49** *For any alphabet $T$ and natural number $k$, the families of LL($k$) languages, LALL($k$) languages, and SLL($k$) languages coincide.* □

The following theorem can be proved in the same way as Theorem 5.37. Here, however, we present an alternative proof.

**Theorem 8.50** *Any LL($k$) grammar is unambiguous.*

*Proof.* Let $G = (V, T, P, S)$ be an LL($k$) grammar and let $w$ be any sentence in $L(G)$. Then let $\pi_1$ and $\pi_2$ be rule strings such that

$$S \underset{\mathrm{lm}}{\overset{\pi_1}{\Longrightarrow}} w \quad \text{and} \quad S \underset{\mathrm{lm}}{\overset{\pi_2}{\Longrightarrow}} w \ .$$

We show that $\pi_1 = \pi_2$. Assume the contrary, that $\pi_1 \neq \pi_2$. Then $\pi_1 = \pi r_1 \pi'_1$ and $\pi_2 = \pi r_2 \pi'_2$ for some distinct rules $r_1$ and $r_2$ of $G$ (note that $\pi_1$ cannot be a proper prefix of $\pi_2$ or vice versa). In other words, there are strings $\delta \in V^*$, $x$ and $y \in T^*$, and a nonterminal $A$ such that

$$
\begin{aligned}
&S \underset{\mathrm{lm}}{\overset{\pi}{\Longrightarrow}} xA\delta \underset{\mathrm{lm}}{\overset{r_1\pi'_1}{\Longrightarrow}} xy \ , \\
&S \underset{\mathrm{lm}}{\overset{\pi}{\Longrightarrow}} xA\delta \underset{\mathrm{lm}}{\overset{r_2\pi'_2}{\Longrightarrow}} xy \ ,
\end{aligned}
$$

where $xy = w$. As $G$ is LL($k$), Theorem 8.37 now implies that $r_1 = r_2$. Hence $\pi_1 = \pi_2$ and $G$ is thus unambiguous. □

Also the following result proved for SLL($k$) grammars in Section 5.4 (Corollary 5.41) holds:

**Theorem 8.51** *A reduced left-recursive grammar is not LL($k$) for any $k \geqslant 0$.* □

Now we shall compare the classes of LL($k$) and LR($k$) grammars and show that the LL($k$) grammar class is properly contained in the LR($k$) grammar class. First we give an intuitive description of these grammar classes. An LR($k$) parser detects a reduction by a rule after it has recognized the right-hand side of the rule. An LL($k$) parser performs a produce action by a rule before it has recognized the right-hand side of the rule. Moreover, a deterministic LR($k$) or LL($k$) parser is able to decide the correct parsing action at every parsing configuration, based on the text processed thus far and on the next $k$ input symbols only.

To illustrate the distinction between these parser and grammar classes, let $A \to \omega$ be a rule of grammar $G = (V, T, P, S)$, and $x$, $y$, and $z$ terminal strings such that

$$S \Rightarrow^* xAz, \quad \omega \Rightarrow^* y\ .$$

If $G$ is an LR($k$) grammar, the canonical LR($k$) parser of $G$ is able to recognize the rule $A \to \omega$ after scanning $xy$ and seeing $k{:}z$. If $G$ is an LL($k$) grammar, the canonical LL($k$) parser of $G$ is able to recognize the rule $A \to \omega$ after scanning $x$ and seeing $k{:}yz$.

This intuitive description of LR($k$) and LL($k$) grammars clearly suggests that every LL($k$) grammar is also an LR($k$) grammar. For proving this formally, we need some lemmas and definitions.

**Lemma 8.52** *Let $k$ be a natural number and $G = (V, T, P, S)$ an LL($k$) grammar. Further let $r_1 = A_1 \to \omega_1$ and $r_2 = A_2 \to \omega_2$ be rules in $P$, $\pi_1$, $\pi'_1$, $\pi_2$, and $\pi'_2$ rule strings in $P^*$, $\delta_1$ and $\delta_2$ strings in $V^*$, and $x_1, x_2, v_1, v_2, y_1, y_2$, and $v$ strings in $T^*$ such that*

$$S \underset{\mathrm{lm}}{\overset{\pi_1}{\Longrightarrow}} x_1 A_1 \delta_1 \underset{\mathrm{lm}}{\overset{r_1}{\Longrightarrow}} x_1 \omega_1 \delta_1, \quad \omega_1 \underset{\mathrm{lm}}{\overset{\pi'_1}{\Longrightarrow}} v_1, \quad \delta_1 \underset{\mathrm{lm}}{\Longrightarrow^*} y_1\ ,$$

$$S \underset{\mathrm{lm}}{\overset{\pi_2}{\Longrightarrow}} x_2 A_2 \delta_2 \underset{\mathrm{lm}}{\overset{r_2}{\Longrightarrow}} x_2 \omega_2 \delta_2, \quad \omega_2 \underset{\mathrm{lm}}{\overset{\pi'_2}{\Longrightarrow}} v_2, \quad \delta_2 \underset{\mathrm{lm}}{\Longrightarrow^*} y_2\ ,$$

$$x_2 v_2 = x_1 v_1 v, \quad \text{and} \quad k{:}y_1 = k{:}v y_2\ .$$

*Then either $\pi_1 r_1 \pi'_1$ is a prefix of $\pi_2 r_2 \pi'_2$ or $\pi_2 r_2 \pi'_2$ is a prefix of $\pi_1 r_1 \pi'_1$.*

*Proof.* For the sake of contradiction, assume that neither $\pi_1 r_1 \pi'_1$ nor $\pi_2 r_2 \pi'_2$ is a prefix of the other. Then one of the following is true: (1) $\pi_1 = \pi_2$ and $r_1 \neq r_2$;

(2) $\pi_1$ can be written as $\pi r'_1 \pi''_1$ and $\pi_2$ can be written as $\pi r'_2 \pi''_2$ where $r'_1 \neq r'_2$;
(3) $\pi_1 r_1 = \pi_2 r_2$, $\pi'_1$ can be written as $\pi r'_1 \pi''_1$ and $\pi'_2$ can be written as $\pi r'_2 \pi''_2$ where $r'_1 \neq r'_2$.

*Case 1.* $\pi_1 = \pi_2$ and $r_1 \neq r_2$. Since the string leftmost derived using a given rule string is always unique (Fact 4.5), we have $x_1 A_1 \delta_1 = x_2 A_2 \delta_2$, that is, $x_1 = x_2$, $A_1 = A_2$, and $\delta_1 = \delta_2$. The condition $r_1 \neq r_2$ in turn implies $\omega_1 \neq \omega_2$. But then we have:

$$S \underset{lm}{\Longrightarrow^*} x_1 A_1 \delta_1 \underset{lm}{\Longrightarrow} x_1 \omega_1 \delta_1 \underset{lm}{\Longrightarrow^*} x_1 v_1 y_1 \ ,$$

$$S \underset{lm}{\Longrightarrow^*} x_1 A_1 \delta_1 \underset{lm}{\Longrightarrow} x_1 \omega_2 \delta_1$$

$$\underset{lm}{\Longrightarrow^*} x_1 v_2 y_2 = x_2 v_2 y_2 = x_1 v_1 v y_2 \ ,$$

$$k{:}v_1 y_1 = k{:}v_1(k{:}y_1) = k{:}v_1(k{:}vy_2) = k{:}v_1 v y_2 \ .$$

By Theorem 8.37(*d*) this is in contradiction to the assumption that $G$ is LL($k$).

*Case 2.* $\pi_1 = \pi r'_1 \pi''_1$ and $\pi_2 = \pi r'_2 \pi''_2$ where $r'_1 \neq r'_2$. Then there are strings $\delta$, $\omega'_1$, and $\omega'_2$ in $V^*$, strings $u$, $u_1$, and $u_2$ in $T^*$, and a nonterminal $A$ such that

$$S \overset{\pi}{\underset{lm}{\Longrightarrow}} uA\delta \overset{r'_1}{\underset{lm}{\Longrightarrow}} u\omega'_1\delta \overset{\pi''_1}{\underset{lm}{\Longrightarrow}} uu_1 A_1 \delta_1 = x_1 A_1 \delta_1 \ ,$$

$$S \overset{\pi}{\underset{lm}{\Longrightarrow}} uA\delta \overset{r'_2}{\underset{lm}{\Longrightarrow}} u\omega'_2\delta \overset{\pi''_2}{\underset{lm}{\Longrightarrow}} uu_2 A_2 \delta_2 = x_2 A_2 \delta_2 \ ,$$

Since $x_1 A_1 \delta_1$ leftmost derives $x_1 v_1 y_1$ and $x_2 A_2 \delta_2$ leftmost derives $x_2 v_2 y_2$, we have:

$$S \underset{lm}{\Longrightarrow^*} uA\delta \underset{lm}{\Longrightarrow} u\omega'_1\delta \underset{lm}{\Longrightarrow^*} x_1 v_1 y_1 = uu_1 v_1 y_1 \ ,$$

$$S \underset{lm}{\Longrightarrow^*} uA\delta \underset{lm}{\Longrightarrow} u\omega'_2\delta$$

$$\underset{lm}{\Longrightarrow^*} x_2 v_2 y_2 = x_1 v_1 v y_2 = uu_1 v_1 v y_2 \ ,$$

$$k{:}u_1 v_1 y_1 = k{:}u_1 v_1(k{:}y_1) = k{:}u_1 v_1(k{:}vy_2) = k{:}u_1 v_1 v y_2 \ .$$

Here $\omega'_1 \neq \omega'_2$ because $r'_1 \neq r'_2$. This is in contradiction to the assumption that $G$ is LL($k$).

*Case 3.* $\pi_1 r_1 = \pi_2 r_2$, $\pi'_1 = \pi r'_1 \pi''_1$, and $\pi'_2 = \pi r'_2 \pi''_2$ where $r'_1 \neq r'_2$. Then $\pi_1 = \pi_2$ and $r_1 = r_2$, which implies that $x_1 = x_2$, $A_1 = A_2$, $\delta_1 = \delta_2$, and $\omega_1 = \omega_2$. Since $\omega_1$ leftmost derives $v_1$ using rule string $\pi'_1 = \pi r'_1 \pi''_1$ and $\pi_2$ leftmost derives $v_2$ using rule string $\pi'_2 = \pi r'_2 \pi''_2$, there are strings $\delta$, $\omega'_1$, and $\omega'_2$ in $V^*$, strings $u$, $u_1$, and $u_2$ in

$T^*$, and a nonterminal $A$ such that

$$\omega_1 \xRightarrow[\text{lm}]{\pi} uA\delta \xRightarrow[\text{lm}]{r'_1} u\omega'_1\delta \xRightarrow[\text{lm}]{\pi''_1} uu_1 = v_1 \ ,$$

$$\omega_2 \xRightarrow[\text{lm}]{\pi} uA\delta \xRightarrow[\text{lm}]{r'_2} u\omega'_2\delta \xRightarrow[\text{lm}]{\pi''_2} uu_2 = v_2 \ .$$

Then we have:

$$S \xRightarrow[\text{lm}]{}^* x_1uA\delta\delta_1 \xRightarrow[\text{lm}]{} x_1u\omega'_1\delta\delta_1 \xRightarrow[\text{lm}]{}^* x_1uu_1y_1 \ ,$$

$$S \xRightarrow[\text{lm}]{}^* x_1uA\delta\delta_1 \xRightarrow[\text{lm}]{} x_1u\omega'_2\delta\delta_1$$

$$\xRightarrow[\text{lm}]{}^* x_1uu_2y_2 = x_2v_2y_2 = x_1uu_1vy_2 \ ,$$

$$k{:}u_1y_1 = k{:}u_1(k{:}y_1) = k{:}u_1(k{:}vy_2) = k{:}u_1vy_2 \ .$$

Here $\omega'_1 \neq \omega'_2$ because $r'_1 \neq r'_2$. This is in contradiction to the assumption that $G$ is LL($k$). □

**Lemma 8.53** *If in an LL($k$) grammar $G = (V, T, P, S)$*

$$S \xRightarrow[\text{lm}]{}^* x_1A_1\delta_1 \xRightarrow[\text{lm}]{} x_1\omega_1\delta_1, \quad \omega_1 \Rightarrow^* v_1, \quad \delta_1 \Rightarrow^* y_1 \ ,$$

$$S \xRightarrow[\text{lm}]{}^* x_2A_2\delta_2 \xRightarrow[\text{lm}]{} x_2\omega_2\delta_2, \quad \omega_2 \Rightarrow^* v_2, \quad \delta_2 \Rightarrow^* y_2 \ ,$$

$$x_2v_2 = x_1v_1v, \quad \textit{and} \quad k{:}y_1 = k{:}vy_2 \ ,$$

*then either* $\delta_1 \Rightarrow^* v\delta_2$ *or* $v\delta_2 \Rightarrow^* \delta_1$ .

*Proof.* By Lemma 8.52, either

$$S \xRightarrow[\text{lm}]{}^* x_1A_1\delta_1 \xRightarrow[\text{lm}]{} x_1\omega_1\delta_1$$

$$\xRightarrow[\text{lm}]{}^* x_1v_1\delta_1 \xRightarrow[\text{lm}]{}^* x_2v_2\delta_2 = x_1v_1v\delta_2$$

or

$$S \xRightarrow[\text{lm}]{}^* x_2A_2\delta_2 \xRightarrow[\text{lm}]{} x_2\omega_2\delta_2$$

$$\xRightarrow[\text{lm}]{}^* x_2v_2\delta_2 = x_1v_1v\delta_2 \xRightarrow[\text{lm}]{}^* x_1v_1\delta_1 \ .$$

In the former case $\delta_1$ derives $v\delta_2$. In the latter case $v\delta_2$ derives $\delta_1$. □

In proving that LL($k$) grammars are LR($k$) grammars we have to shift from a pair of rightmost derivations to a pair of leftmost derivations, and vice versa. More specifically, given a rightmost derivation of the form

(a) $\qquad S \xRightarrow[\text{rm}]{}^+ \gamma Ay \ ,$

where $\gamma$ derives $x$, we have to find a leftmost derivation of the form

(b) $$S \underset{lm}{\Longrightarrow}^{+} xA\delta^R ,$$

where $\delta^R$ derives $y$. Conversely, given a leftmost derivation of the form (b), we have to find a rightmost derivation of the form (a).

In derivation (a) the string $\gamma$ is a viable prefix and in derivation (b) the string $\delta$ is a viable suffix. We say, informally, that $\gamma$ is a viable prefix "induced" by the leftmost derivation (b) and that $\delta$ is a viable suffix "induced" by the rightmost derivation (a). In the following we give precise definitions for these concepts. The definitions are inductive on the length of the derivations.

Let $G = (V, T, P, S)$ be a grammar, $\gamma$ a viable prefix of $G$, and $\pi$ a rule string in $P^*$. We say, inductively, that $\gamma$ is a *viable prefix induced by* $\pi$ if one of the following statements holds.

(p1) $\gamma = \varepsilon$ and $\pi = \varepsilon$.

(p2) $\gamma$ can be written as $\eta\alpha$ and $\pi$ can be written as $\pi_1 r \pi_2$ such that $\eta$ is a viable prefix induced by $\pi_1$ and

$$S \underset{lm}{\overset{\pi_1}{\Longrightarrow}} xA\phi^R \underset{lm}{\overset{r}{\Longrightarrow}} x\alpha B\beta\phi^R \quad \text{and} \quad \alpha \underset{lm}{\overset{\pi_2}{\Longrightarrow}} u$$

for some $x, u \in T^*$, $\phi, \beta \in V^*$, and $r = A \to \alpha B\beta$ in $P$.

Then let $\delta$ be a viable suffix of $G$ and $\hat{\pi}$ a rule string in $P^*$. We say that $\delta$ is a *viable suffix induced by* $\hat{\pi}$ if one of the following statements holds.

(s1) $\delta = \varepsilon$ and $\hat{\pi} = \varepsilon$.

(s2) $\delta$ can be written as $\phi\beta^R$ and $\hat{\pi}$ can be written as $\hat{\pi}_1 r \hat{\pi}_2$ such that $\phi$ is a viable suffix induced by $\hat{\pi}_1$ and

$$S \underset{rm}{\overset{\hat{\pi}_1}{\Longrightarrow}} \eta A y \underset{rm}{\overset{r}{\Longrightarrow}} \eta\alpha B\beta y \quad \text{and} \quad \beta \underset{rm}{\overset{\hat{\pi}_2}{\Longrightarrow}} v$$

for some $v, y \in T^*$, $\eta, \alpha \in V^*$, and $r = A \to \alpha B\beta$ in $P$.

The definitions are illustrated in Figures 8.8 and 8.9.

The following lemma says that the induced viable prefixes and suffixes are unique with respect to a given rule string. This will allow us to speak of "the" viable prefix or suffix induced by a rule string.

**Lemma 8.54** *Let $G = (V, T, P, S)$ be a grammar. No rule string in $P^*$ induces more than one viable prefix (resp. viable suffix).*

*Proof.* We prove the lemma for viable prefixes. The proof for viable suffixes is analogous.

For the sake of contradiction, assume that some rule string $\pi \in P^*$ induces two distinct viable prefixes $\gamma_1$ and $\gamma_2$. By definition, $\gamma_1$ can be written as $\eta_1\alpha_1$, $\gamma_2$ can be

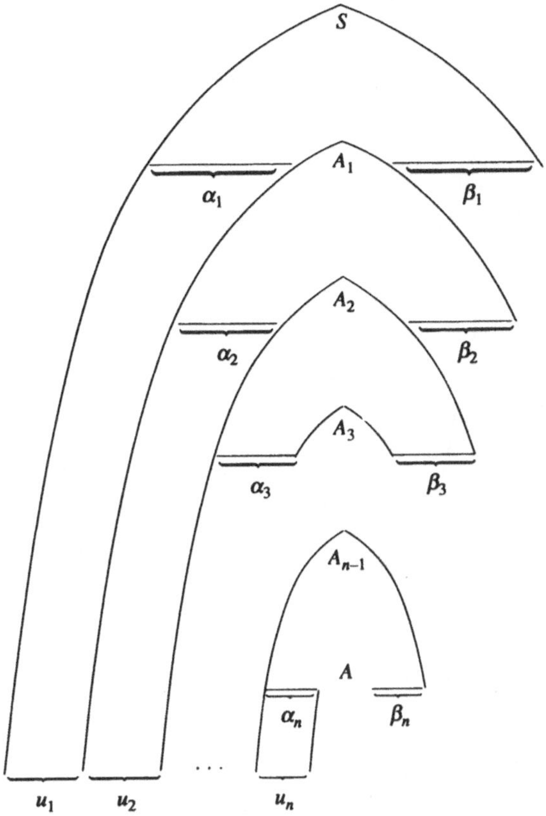


**Figure 8.8** Derivation tree of a left sentential form $xA\delta^R$, where $x = u_1u_2 \ldots u_n$ and $\delta^R = \beta_n \ldots \beta_2\beta_1$. $S \to \alpha_1 A_1 \beta_1$, $A_1 \to \alpha_2 A_2 \beta_2, \ldots, A_{n-1} \to \alpha_n A \beta_n$ are rules contained in $\pi$, the rule string used to leftmost derive $xA\delta^R$ from the start symbol $S$. The string $\gamma = \alpha_1\alpha_2 \ldots \alpha_n$ is the viable prefix induced by $\pi$

written as $\eta_2\alpha_2$, and $\pi$ can be written as $\pi_1 r_1 \pi'_1$ and as $\pi_2 r_2 \pi'_2$ such that $\eta_1$ is a viable prefix induced by $\pi_1$, $\eta_2$ is a viable prefix induced by $\pi_2$, and

$$S \underset{\text{lm}}{\overset{\pi_1}{\Longrightarrow}} x_1 A_1 \phi_1^R \underset{\text{lm}}{\overset{r_1}{\Longrightarrow}} x_1 \alpha_1 B_1 \beta_1 \phi_1^R, \quad \alpha_1 \underset{\text{lm}}{\overset{\pi'_1}{\Longrightarrow}} u_1 \ ,$$

$$S \underset{\text{lm}}{\overset{\pi_2}{\Longrightarrow}} x_2 A_2 \phi_2^R \underset{\text{lm}}{\overset{r_2}{\Longrightarrow}} x_2 \alpha_2 B_2 \beta_2 \phi_2^R, \quad \alpha_2 \underset{\text{lm}}{\overset{\pi'_2}{\Longrightarrow}} u_2$$

for some $x_1, x_2, u_1, u_2 \in T^*$, $\phi_1, \phi_2, \beta_1, \beta_2 \in V^*$, and $r_1 = A_1 \to \alpha_1 B_1 \beta_1$ and $r_2 = A_2 \to \alpha_2 B_2 \beta_2$ in $P$. Now since $\pi_1 r_1 \pi'_1 = \pi_2 r_2 \pi'_2$, we conclude that $x_1 u_1 B_1 \beta_1 \phi_1^R = x_2 u_2 B_2 \beta_2 \phi_2^R$. Hence $x_1 u_1 = x_2 u_2$, $B_1 = B_2$, and $\beta_1 \phi_1^R = \beta_2 \phi_2^R$. We shall show that $\pi_1 = \pi_2$. Observe that then $\phi_1^R = \phi_2^R$ and $r_1 = r_2$, and hence $\beta_1 = \beta_2$ and $\alpha_1 B_1 \beta_1 = \alpha_2 B_2 \beta_2$, which imply that $\alpha_1 = \alpha_2$. As $\gamma_1 = \eta_1 \alpha_1$ and $\gamma_2 = \eta_2 \alpha_2$, we may use induction on the length of $\pi$ and assume

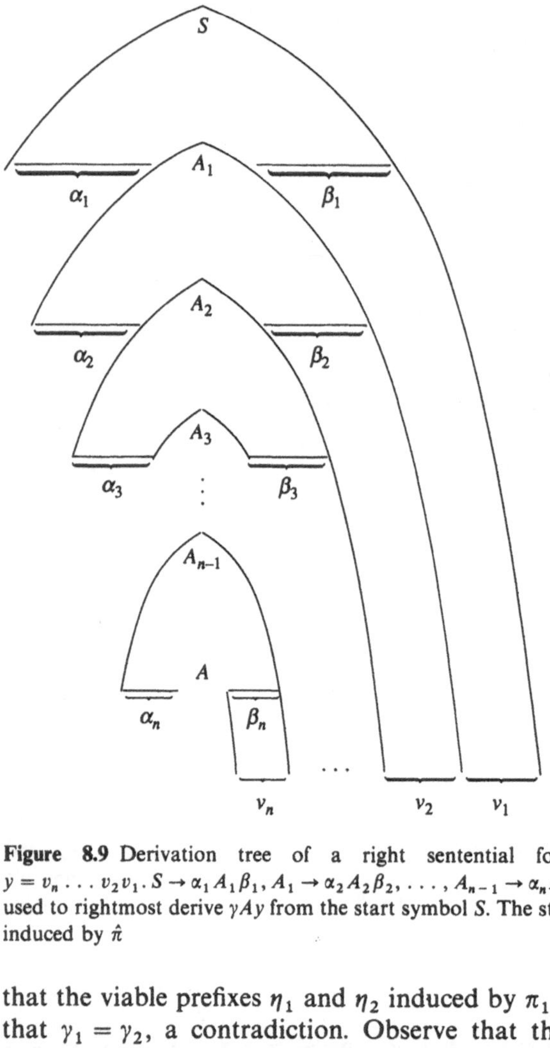


**Figure 8.9** Derivation tree of a right sentential form $\gamma A y$, where $\gamma = \alpha_1\alpha_2 \ldots \alpha_n$ and $y = v_n \ldots v_2 v_1$. $S \to \alpha_1 A_1 \beta_1, A_1 \to \alpha_2 A_2 \beta_2, \ldots, A_{n-1} \to \alpha_n A \beta_n$ are rules contained in $\hat{\pi}$, the rule string used to rightmost derive $\gamma A y$ from the start symbol $S$. The string $\delta = (\beta_n \ldots \beta_2\beta_1)^R$ is the viable suffix induced by $\hat{\pi}$

that the viable prefixes $\eta_1$ and $\eta_2$ induced by $\pi_1 = \pi_2$ are the same, thus showing that $\gamma_1 = \gamma_2$, a contradiction. Observe that the basis of the induction is true because by definition the empty rule string induces only the empty viable prefix.

Now if $\pi_1$ were not equal to $\pi_2$, the equality $\pi_1 r_1 \pi_1' = \pi_2 r_2 \pi_2'$ would imply that either $\pi_1 r_1$ is a prefix of $\pi_2$ or $\pi_2 r_2$ is a prefix of $\pi_1$. Consider the former case (the latter case is handled analogously). Then $\pi_2$ can be written as $\pi_1 r_1 \pi'$ where $\pi' r_2 \pi_2' = \pi_1'$. So we have:

$$S \xrightarrow[\text{lm}]{\pi_1 r_1} x_1\alpha_1 B_1\beta_1\phi_1^R \xrightarrow[\text{lm}]{\pi'} x_2 A_2 \phi_2^R \xrightarrow[\text{lm}]{r_2} x_2\alpha_2 B_2\beta_2\phi_2^R$$

$$\xrightarrow[\text{lm}]{\pi_2'} x_2 u_2 B_2\beta_2\phi_2^R \; .$$

Here $B_1\beta_1\phi_1^R$ cannot be involved in the derivation that uses $\pi' r_2 \pi_2'$. That is, $\pi' r_2 \pi_2'$ is only used to expand $\alpha_1$. This is because $\alpha_1$ leftmost derives a terminal string, $u_1$, using this very rule string $\pi' r_2 \pi_2' = \pi_1'$. Hence in particular $B_1\beta_1\phi_1^R$ cannot be involved in the derivation

$$x_1\alpha_1B_1\beta_1\phi_1^R \xRightarrow[\text{lm}]{\pi'} x_2A_2\phi_2^R \xRightarrow[\text{lm}]{r_2} x_2\alpha_2B_2\beta_2\phi_2^R.$$

This means that $B_1\beta_1\phi_1^R$ must be a suffix of $\phi_2^R$. But this is a contradiction because $\beta_1\phi_1^R = \beta_2\phi_2^R$. □

The following pair of lemmas show how we can shift from a leftmost derivation to a rightmost derivation, and vice versa.

**Lemma 8.55** *Let $G = (V, T, P, S)$ be a grammar that has at least one rule with left-hand side $S$. Further let $x$ and $y$ be strings in $T^*$, $\delta$ a string in $V^*$, and $\pi$ a rule string in $P^*$ such that*

(*a*) $$S \xRightarrow[\text{lm}]{\pi} xA\delta^R \quad \textit{and} \quad \delta^R \Rightarrow^* y\ .$$

*Then $\pi$ induces some viable prefix $\gamma$, and $\delta$ is a viable suffix induced by some rule string $\hat{\pi} \in P^*$. Moreover,*

(*b*) $$S \xRightarrow[\text{rm}]{\hat{\pi}} \gamma Ay \quad \textit{and} \quad \gamma \Rightarrow^* x.$$

*Proof.* The proof is by induction on the length of rule string $\pi$. If $\pi = \varepsilon$, we have $\delta = y = x = \varepsilon$ and $A = S$. Because $P$ was assumed to contain at least one rule of the form $S \to \omega$, $\varepsilon$ is a viable prefix as well as a viable suffix of $G$. If we choose $\gamma = \varepsilon$ and $\hat{\pi} = \varepsilon$, we may conclude that statement (*b*) holds and, by the definitions of induced viable prefixes and suffixes, that $\pi$ induces the viable prefix $\gamma$ and $\hat{\pi}$ induces the viable suffix $\delta$.

Then assume that $\pi \neq \varepsilon$ and, as an induction hypothesis, that the lemma holds for rule strings shorter than $\pi$. From (*a*) we can conclude by Lemma 8.5 that $\pi$ can be written as $\pi_1 r \pi_2$ such that

(1) $$S \xRightarrow[\text{lm}]{\pi_1} x_1A_1\phi^R \xRightarrow[\text{lm}]{r} x_1\alpha A\beta\phi^R = x_1\alpha A\delta^R \quad \text{and} \quad x_1\alpha \xRightarrow[\text{lm}]{\pi_2} x$$

for some $x_1 \in T^*$, $\phi \in V^*$, and $r = A_1 \to \alpha A\beta$ in $P$. Here $\alpha$ leftmost derives some suffix $u$ of $x$ using $\pi_2$. Because $\delta^R = \beta\phi^R$ and $\delta^R$ derives $y$, $y$ can be written as $vy_1$ where $v$ is derived by $\beta$ and $y_1$ is derived by $\phi^R$. So we have:

(2) $$S \xRightarrow[\text{lm}]{\pi_1} x_1A_1\phi^R \quad \text{and} \quad \phi^R \Rightarrow^* y_1\ .$$

By the induction hypothesis we may conclude that $\pi_1$ induces some viable prefix $\eta$, and $\phi$ is a viable suffix induced by some rule string $\hat{\pi}_1$. Moreover,

(3) $$S \xRightarrow[\text{rm}]{\hat{\pi}_1} \eta A_1y_1 \quad \text{and} \quad \eta \Rightarrow^* x_1\ .$$

Let $\hat{\pi}_2$ be a rule string such that $\beta$ rightmost derives $v$ using $\hat{\pi}_2$. Then we have:

(4) $$S \xRightarrow[\text{rm}]{\hat{\pi}_1} \eta A_1y_1 \xRightarrow[\text{rm}]{r} \eta\alpha A\beta y_1 \quad \text{and} \quad \beta \xRightarrow[\text{rm}]{\hat{\pi}_2} v\ .$$

As $\delta = \phi\beta^R$ and $\phi$ is a viable suffix induced by $\hat{\pi}_1$, we conclude by the definition of an induced viable suffix that $\delta$ is a viable suffix induced by $\hat{\pi}_1 r\hat{\pi}_2$. (That $\delta$ is a viable suffix of $G$ follows from (1).) We denote $\hat{\pi} = \hat{\pi}_1 r\hat{\pi}_2$ and $\gamma = \eta\alpha$. Then we have:

(5) $$S \xRightarrow[\text{rm}]{\hat{\pi}} \eta\alpha Avy_1 = \gamma Ay \quad \text{and} \quad \gamma = \eta\alpha \Rightarrow^* x_1 u = x \ .$$

Thus statement (*b*) holds. We have yet to prove that $\gamma$ is a viable prefix induced by $\pi$. First we note that $\gamma$ is indeed a viable prefix of $G$, because $S$ nontrivially rightmost derives $\gamma Ay$ (Lemmas 6.3 and 6.4). From (1) we get:

(6) $$S \xRightarrow[\text{lm}]{\pi_1} x_1 A_1 \phi^R \xRightarrow[\text{lm}]{r} x_1\alpha A\beta\phi^R \quad \text{and} \quad \alpha \xRightarrow[\text{lm}]{\pi_2} u \ .$$

As $\gamma = \eta\alpha$ and $\eta$ is a viable prefix induced by $\pi_1$, we conclude by the definition of an induced viable prefix that $\gamma$ is a viable prefix induced by $\pi_1 r\pi_2 = \pi$, as desired. □

**Lemma 8.56** *Let $G = (V, T, P, S)$ be a grammar that has at least one rule with left-hand side $S$. Further let $x$ and $y$ be strings in $T^*$, $\gamma$ a string in $V^*$, and $\hat{\pi}$ a rule string in $P^*$ such that*

(*a*) $$S \xRightarrow[\text{rm}]{\hat{\pi}} \gamma Ay \quad \text{and} \quad \gamma \Rightarrow^* x \ .$$

*Then $\hat{\pi}$ induces some viable suffix $\delta$, and $\gamma$ is a viable prefix induced by some rule string $\pi \in P^*$. Moreover,*

(*b*) $$S \xRightarrow[\text{lm}]{\pi} xA\delta^R \quad \text{and} \quad \delta^R \Rightarrow^* y \ .$$

*Proof.* The proof is completely analogous to that of Lemma 8.55 and is left as an exercise. □

Now we are able to prove:

**Theorem 8.57** *For all $k \geqslant 0$, any reduced LL(k) grammar is an LR(k) grammar.*

*Proof.* Let $G = (V, T, P, S)$ be a reduced LL($k$) grammar. First we note that $S \Rightarrow^+ S$ is impossible in $G$, because no reduced LL($k$) grammar can be left-recursive (Theorem 8.51).

Then let $\gamma$, $\gamma_1$, and $\gamma_2$ be strings in $V^*$, $y_1$, $y_2$, and $v$ strings in $T^*$, $r_1 = A_1 \to \omega_1$ and $r_2 = A_2 \to \omega_2$ rules in $P$, and $\hat{\pi}_1$ and $\hat{\pi}_2$ rule strings in $P^*$ such that

$$S \xRightarrow[\text{rm}]{\hat{\pi}_1} \gamma_1 A_1 y_1 \xRightarrow[\text{rm}]{r_1} \gamma_1\omega_1 y_1 = \gamma y_1 \ ,$$

(1) $$S \xRightarrow[\text{rm}]{\hat{\pi}_2} \gamma_2 A_2 y_2 \xRightarrow[\text{rm}]{r_2} \gamma_2\omega_2 y_2 = \gamma v y_2 \ ,$$

$$\text{and } k{:}y_1 = k{:}vy_2 \ .$$

We shall show that $\gamma_1 = \gamma_2$, $A_1 = A_2$, and $\omega_1 = \omega_2$, which implies, by Theorem 6.39, that $G$ is LR($k$).

Since $G$ was assumed to be reduced, $\gamma_1$ derives some string $x_1 \in T^*$ and $\omega_1$ derives some string $v_1 \in T^*$. Further, because $\gamma_2\omega_2 = \gamma v$, $\gamma_2$ derives some string $x_2$ and $\omega_2$ derives some string $v_2$ such that $x_2v_2 = x_1v_1v$. Then we have:

$$(2) \qquad \begin{aligned} &S \xrightarrow[\text{rm}]{\hat{\pi}_1} \gamma_1 A_1 y_1, \quad \gamma_1 \Rightarrow^* x_1 \ . \\ &S \xrightarrow[\text{rm}]{\hat{\pi}_2} \gamma_2 A_2 y_2, \quad \gamma_2 \Rightarrow^* x_2 \ . \end{aligned}$$

By Lemma 8.56 we conclude that for some rule strings $\pi_1$ and $\pi_2$ in $P^*$

$$(3) \qquad \begin{aligned} &S \xrightarrow[\text{lm}]{\pi_1} x_1 A_1 \delta_1^R, \quad \delta_1^R \Rightarrow^* y_1 \ , \\ &S \xrightarrow[\text{lm}]{\pi_2} x_2 A_2 \delta_2^R, \quad \delta_2^R \Rightarrow^* y_2 \ , \end{aligned}$$

where $\delta_1$ is the viable suffix induced by $\hat{\pi}_1$ and $\delta_2$ is the viable suffix induced by $\hat{\pi}_2$. Moreover, $\gamma_1$ is the viable prefix induced by $\pi_1$ and $\gamma_2$ is the viable prefix induced by $\pi_2$. By (3) and (1) we have:

$$(4) \qquad \begin{aligned} &S \xrightarrow[\text{lm}]{\pi_1} x_1 A_1 \delta_1^R \xrightarrow[\text{lm}]{r_1} x_1 \omega_1 \delta_1^R, \quad \omega_1 \Rightarrow^* v_1, \quad \delta_1^R \Rightarrow^* y_1 \ , \\ &S \xrightarrow[\text{lm}]{\pi_2} x_2 A_2 \delta_2^R \xrightarrow[\text{lm}]{r_2} x_2 \omega_2 \delta_2^R, \quad \omega_2 \Rightarrow^* v_2, \quad \delta_2^R \Rightarrow^* y_2 \ , \\ &x_2 v_2 = x_1 v_1 v, \quad \text{and} \quad k{:}y_1 = k{:}vy_2 \ . \end{aligned}$$

Since $G$ was assumed to be an LL($k$) grammar, we can apply Lemma 8.53 and conclude that either $\delta_1^R$ derives $v\delta_2^R$ or $v\delta_2^R$ derives $\delta_1^R$.

*Case 1.* $\delta_1^R$ derives $v\delta_2^R$. By (3) we then have:

$$(5) \qquad S \xrightarrow[\text{lm}]{\pi_1} x_1 A_1 \delta_1^R \quad \text{and} \quad \delta_1^R \Rightarrow^* v\delta_2^R \Rightarrow^* vy_2 \ .$$

Since $\gamma_1$ is the viable prefix induced by $\pi_1$, we conclude by Lemmas 8.55 and 8.54 that $S$ rightmost derives $\gamma_1 A_1 v y_2$. By (1) we then have:

$$(6) \qquad \begin{aligned} &S \underset{\text{rm}}{\Longrightarrow^*} \gamma_1 A_1 v y_2 \underset{\text{rm}}{\Longrightarrow} \gamma_1 \omega_1 v y_2 = \gamma v y_2 \ , \\ &S \underset{\text{rm}}{\Longrightarrow^*} \gamma_2 A_2 y_2 \underset{\text{rm}}{\Longrightarrow} \gamma_2 \omega_2 y_2 = \gamma v y_2 \ . \end{aligned}$$

Since $G$ is LL($k$) and hence unambiguous (Theorem 8.50), $\gamma v y_2$ cannot have more than one rightmost derivation from $S$ (this follows from Theorem 4.12 because $G$ is reduced). This means that $\gamma_1 A_1 v y_2 = \gamma_2 A_2 y_2$ and hence $\gamma_1 = \gamma_2$, $A_1 = A_2$, and $v = \varepsilon$. Then $\gamma_1\omega_1 = \gamma = \gamma v = \gamma_2\omega_2 = \gamma_1\omega_2$, which implies $\omega_1 = \omega_2$. So we have in (1) $\gamma_1 = \gamma_2$, $A_1 = A_2$, and $\omega_1 = \omega_2$, as desired.

*Case 2.* $v\delta_2^R$ derives $\delta_1^R$. By (3) we then have:

$$(7) \qquad S \xrightarrow[\text{lm}]{\pi_2} x_2 A_2 \delta_2^R \quad \text{and} \quad \delta_2^R \Rightarrow^* y_1' \ ,$$

where $vy'_1 = y_1$. Since $\gamma_2$ is the viable prefix induced by $\pi_2$, we conclude by Lemmas 8.55 and 8.54 that $S$ rightmost derives $\gamma_2 A_2 y'_1$. By (1) we then have:

$$(8) \quad \begin{aligned} S &\underset{rm}{\Longrightarrow}^* \gamma_1 A_1 y_1 \underset{rm}{\Longrightarrow} \gamma_1 \omega_1 y_1 = \gamma y_1 = \gamma v y'_1 \ , \\ S &\underset{rm}{\Longrightarrow}^* \gamma_2 A_2 y'_1 \underset{rm}{\Longrightarrow} \gamma_2 \omega_2 y'_1 = \gamma v y'_1 \ . \end{aligned}$$

Since $G$ is unambiguous, $\gamma_1 A_1 y_1 = \gamma_2 A_2 y'_1$ and hence $\gamma_1 = \gamma_2$, $A_1 = A_2$, and $y_1 = y'_1$. Then also $\omega_1 = \omega_2$. So we have also in this case $\gamma_1 = \gamma_2$, $A_1 = A_2$, and $\omega_1 = \omega_2$, as desired. □

By Theorem 8.57 the class of reduced LL($k$) grammars is contained in the class of reduced LR($k$) grammars. This containment is proper; for example, LR(0) grammars may be left-recursive but LL($k$) grammars may not, for any $k$. We have:

**Theorem 8.58** *For all $k \geqslant 0$, the class of reduced LL(k) grammars is properly contained in the class of reduced LR(k) grammars.* □

The proper containment holds also for languages:

**Proposition 8.59** (*Lewis, Rosenkrantz and Stearns,* 1970) *For all $k \geqslant 0$, the family of LL(k) languages is properly contained in the family of LR*(1) *languages.* □

Now that we have established the proper containment of the class of reduced LL($k$) grammars in the class of reduced LR($k$) grammars, a natural question to ask is whether or not SLL($k$) grammars are SLR($k$) grammars and whether or not LALL($k$) grammars are LALR($k$) grammars. Surprisingly, it turns out that there are even SLL(1) grammars that are not SLR($k$) nor LALR($k$) for any $k$.

**Theorem 8.60** *For $k \geqslant 1$, the class of SLL(k) grammars is incomparable with the class of SLR(k) grammars, and the class of LALL(k) grammars is incomparable with the class of LALR(k) grammars.*

*Proof.* The grammar

$$S \to aA \,|\, bBd \ ,$$
$$A \to Be \,|\, Cd \ ,$$
$$B \to b \,|\, \varepsilon \ ,$$
$$C \to c \,|\, \varepsilon$$

is an example of an SLL(1) grammar which is not SLR($k$) for any $k$. The grammar

$$S \to aA \,|\, bB \ ,$$
$$A \to Cc \,|\, Dd \ ,$$

$$B \to Cd|Dc \ ,$$

$$C \to FE \ ,$$

$$D \to FH \ ,$$

$$E \to \varepsilon \ ,$$

$$F \to \varepsilon \ ,$$

$$H \to \varepsilon$$

is an example of an SLL(1) grammar which is not LALR($k$) for any $k$. Conversely, the grammar

$$S \to Sa|a$$

is an example of an LALR(1) and SLR(1) grammar which is not LL($k$) (and hence not LALL($k$) or SLL($k$)) for any $k$. □

## 8.5 Construction of LL(1) Parsers

In Section 5.5 we saw how SLL(1) parsers are constructed efficiently directly from the grammar. In this section we shall consider the construction of canonical LL(1) and LALL(1) parsers in the same spirit as we considered the efficient construction of LR(1) parsers in Chapter 7. By Theorem 8.41 the classes of LL(1) grammars, LALL(1) grammars, and SLL(1) grammars coincide, and hence the SLL(1) parser of a grammar is deterministic whenever the canonical LL(1) or the LALL(1) parser is so. Therefore, the presentation of explicit construction algorithms for canonical LL(1) and LALL(1) parsers is not motivated by the goal of producing parsers for a class of grammars larger than that of SLL(1) grammars. However, canonical LL(1) parsers as well as LALL(1) parsers are more suitable for sophisticated error recovery methods than SLL(1) parsers (see Chapter 9).

Let $G = (V, T, P, S)$ be a grammar. We begin with the construction of the canonical LL(0) machine for $G$. This can be done in the same way as the construction of the canonical LR(0) machine. Let $I_0$ be the set of all 0-items of $G$. The *nondeterministic LL*(0) *machine* for $G$ is a (usually nondeterministic) finite automaton with state alphabet $I_0 \cup \{q_s\}$, $q_s \notin I_0$, input alphabet $V$, initial state $q_s$, set of final states $I_0$, and set of transitions consisting of all rules of the following forms:

(a) $q_s \to [S \to \omega \cdot]$ ,

(b) $[A \to \alpha X \cdot \beta] X \to [A \to \alpha \cdot X\beta]$, $X \in V$ ,

(c) $[A \to \alpha B \cdot \beta] \to [B \to \omega \cdot]$ .

In other words, there is a transition on symbol $X$ from any state $[A \to \alpha X \cdot \beta]$ to state $[A \to \alpha \cdot X\beta]$, and transitions on the empty string from the initial state to each state $[S \to \omega \cdot]$ and from any state $[A \to \alpha B \cdot \beta]$ to all states $[B \to \omega \cdot]$. To allow non-reduced grammars we require that in (b) $X$ and in (c) $\alpha$ derive some terminal string.

The following lemma is analogous to Lemma 7.1.

**Lemma 8.61** *The set of viable suffixes of any grammar G is the language accepted by the nondeterministic LL(0) machine of G, and for any viable suffix* $\gamma$

$$\text{VALID}_0(\gamma) = \{q \mid q \in I_0 \textit{ and } q \textit{ is accessible upon reading } \gamma \textit{ in the nondeterministic } LL(0) \textit{ machine of } G\} .$$

□

Clearly, the nondeterministic LL(0) machine of grammar $G$ is of size $O(|G|^2)$ and can be constructed from $G$ in time $O(|G|^2)$.

Lemma 8.61 implies that the canonical LL(0) machine for grammar $G$ is obtained by making the nondeterministic LL(0) machine deterministic using the standard techniques (Theorem 3.30). Because the nondeterministic LL(0) machine has $O(|G|)$ states, Theorem 3.30 implies the following:

**Theorem 8.62** *The canonical LL(0) machine for any grammar G can be constructed in time*

$$O(2^{|G| + 2\log|G|}) .$$

□

We now turn to the question of constructing the canonical LL(1) machine and the canonical LL(1) parser for a grammar $G = (V, T, P, S)$. Let $I_1$ be the set of all 1-items of $G$. We define the *nondeterministic LL(1) machine* for $G$ as the (usually nondeterministic) finite automaton with state alphabet $I_1 \cup \{q_s\}$, $q_s \notin I_1$, input alphabet $V$, initial state $q_s$, set of final states $I_1$, and with set of transitions consisting of all rules of the following forms:

(a) $q_s \to [S \to \omega \cdot, \varepsilon]$ ,

(b) $[A \to \alpha X \cdot \beta, y]X \to [A \to \alpha \cdot X\beta, z]$, $X \in V$, $z \in \text{FIRST}_1(Xy)$ ,

(c) $[A \to \alpha B \cdot \beta, y] \to [B \to \omega \cdot, y]$ .

To allow non-reduced grammars, we require that in (c) $\alpha$ derives some terminal string.

As in the LL(0) case we have:

**Lemma 8.63** *The set of viable suffixes of any grammar G is the language accepted by the nondeterministic LL(1) machine of G, and for any viable suffix* $\gamma$

$$\text{VALID}_1(\gamma) = \{q \mid q \in I_1 \textit{ and } q \textit{ is accessible upon reading } \gamma \textit{ in the nondeterministic } LL(1) \textit{ machine of } G\} .$$

□

Clearly the nondeterministic LL(1) machine for grammar $G$ is of size $O(|T|^2 \cdot |G| + |T| \cdot |G|^2) = O(|T| \cdot |G|^2)$ and it can be constructed in time $O(|T| \cdot |G|^2)$. (Recall the technique used to construct the SLL(1) parser in Section 5.5.)

Lemma 8.63 implies that we obtain the canonical LL(1) machine for $G$ by making the nondeterministic LL(1) machine deterministic. The canonical LL(1) machine is of size $O(2^{2|G| + \log|G|})$. The proof of Theorem 3.30 implies that the algorithm of Figure 3.9, when applied to the nondeterministic LL(1) machine, takes time $O(2^{2|G| + \log|G|} \cdot |Q|)$, where $|Q|$ is the number of states in the nondeterministic LL(1) machine. Because $|Q|$ is $O(|T| \cdot |G|)$, we obtain:

**Theorem 8.64** *The canonical LL*(1) *machine for any grammar G can be constructed in time*

$$O(2^{2|G| + 3\log|G|}) .$$

□

Because the size of the canonical LL(1) machine of grammar $G$ is $O(2^{2|G| + \log|G|})$ and the canonical LL(1) parser of $G$ can be constructed from this machine in time $O(2^{2|G| + 2\log|G|})$ (see Figure 8.5), we obtain from Theorem 8.64:

**Theorem 8.65** *The canonical LL*(1) *parser of any grammar G can be constructed in time*

$$O(2^{2|G| + 3\log|G|}) .$$

□

Next we shall show how the LALL(1) parser of a (reduced) grammar $G = (V, T, P, S)$ can be constructed efficiently from the canonical LL(0) machine for the \$-augmented grammar $G'$ of $G$.

For state $q$ in the canonical LL(0) machine of grammar $G'$ we define the *LALL*(1) *lookahead set* of $q$, denoted by LALL($q$), as the set

$$\text{LALL}(q) = \{b \in T \cup \{\$\} \mid [A \to \alpha \cdot \beta, b] \in \text{VALID}_1(\gamma) \text{ for some string } \gamma \text{ satisfying } \text{VALID}_0(\gamma) = q\} .$$

By the definition of the LALL(1) parser we have:

**Fact 8.66** The LALL(1) parser has a produce action of the form

$$[\delta]_0[\delta A]_0 \mid b \to [\delta]_0[\delta X_n]_0 \ldots [\delta X_n \ldots X_1]_0 \mid b$$

if and only if $[A \to \cdot X_1 \ldots X_n] \in \text{VALID}_0(\delta X_n \ldots X_1)$ and $b \in \text{LALL}(\text{VALID}_0(\delta X_n \ldots X_1))$. □

By Fact 8.13 we have:

**Lemma 8.67** *For any state q in the canonical LL*(0) *machine,*

$$\text{LALL}(q) = \{b \in \text{FIRST}_1(\gamma^R) \mid \gamma \in \$V^*, \text{VALID}_0(\gamma) = q\} .$$

*In other words,* LALL($q$) *is the union of all sets* $\text{FIRST}_1(\gamma^R)$ *where* $\gamma$ *is chosen such that* $q$ *is accessible upon reading* $\gamma$. □

To compute the LALL(1) lookahead sets we define the following relations.

$q$ **contains-item** $A \to \alpha \cdot \beta$, if $A \to \alpha \cdot \beta \in q$ .

$(q, A)$ **goes-to** GOTO$(q, A)$, if GOTO$(q, A) \neq \varnothing$ .

$q$ **has-null-transition** $(q, B)$, if GOTO$(q, B) \neq \varnothing$ and $B$ is nullable .

Here $q$ is a state in the canonical LL(0) machine of $G'$ and $A$ and $B$ are nonterminals of $G$. Note that the relations **goes-to** and **has-null-transition** are as in Section 7.3, but are now defined for the canonical LL(0) machine.

Clearly the relations **contains-item, goes-to,** and **has-null-transition** are of size $O(|G|\cdot|Q|)$ and can be computed in time $O(|G|\cdot|Q|)$, where $|Q|$ denotes the number of states in the canonical LL(0) machine.

Then consider the relational expression

**has-LALL-lookahead** =

(**goes-to**$^{-1}$ **has-null-transition**$^{-1}$)* **contains-item**

**points first-of**$^{-1}$ .

We recall from Section 5.5 that **points** is the relation defined by

$A \to \alpha \cdot X\beta$ **points** $X$

and that **first-of** is a relational expression satisfying

$a$ **first-of** $X$ if and only if $a \in \text{FIRST}_1(X)$.

We shall show that

$q$ **has-LALL-lookahead** $a$ if and only if $a \in \text{LALL}(q)$.

The relation denoted by **has-LALL-lookahead** is illustrated in Figure 8.10.

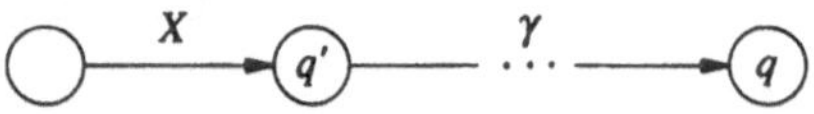


**Figure 8.10** Portion of a canonical LL(0) machine. If $\gamma$ is nullable and $a \in \text{FIRST}_1(X)$, then

$q$ (**goes-to**$^{-1}$ **has-null-transition**$^{-1}$)* $q'$

**contains-item** $A \to \alpha \cdot X\beta$ **points** $X$ **first-of**$^{-1}$ $a$ ,

that is, $q$ **has-LALL-lookahead** $a$

**Theorem 8.68** *Let G be a reduced grammar and G′ its \$-augmented grammar. Terminal a of G′ is in the LALL(1) lookahead set for state q in the canonical LL(0) machine for G′ if and only if*

$$q \textbf{ has-LALL-lookahead } a \ .$$

*Proof.* Assume first that for some state $q$ and terminal $a$, $q$ **has-LALL-lookahead** $a$, that is,

$$q \text{ (}\textbf{goes-to}^{-1} \textbf{ has-null-transition}^{-1})^* \ q' \textbf{ contains-item}$$
$$\textbf{points first-of}^{-1} \ a$$

for some state $q'$. Clearly, if $q' = \text{VALID}_0(\gamma)$ for a viable suffix $\gamma$, then $q = \text{VALID}_0(\gamma\delta)$ for some nullable string $\delta$. The condition

$$q' \textbf{ contains-item points first-of}^{-1} \ a$$

implies that $a \in \text{FIRST}_1(\gamma^R)$. Thus, because $\delta$ is nullable, $a \in \text{FIRST}_1(\delta^R\gamma^R)$. Hence $a$ is in LALL($q$), as desired (Lemma 8.67).

To prove the converse, assume that $a$ is in LALL($q$) for some terminal $a$ and state $q$. Then there is a viable suffix $\gamma$ of $G'$ such that $\text{VALID}_0(\gamma) = q$ and $a \in \text{FIRST}_1(\gamma^R)$ (Lemma 8.67). The condition $a \in \text{FIRST}_1(\gamma^R)$ implies that we may write $\gamma^R = \alpha^R X \beta^R$, where $\alpha^R$ is nullable and $a \in \text{FIRST}_1(X)$. Then

$$q \text{ (}\textbf{goes-to}^{-1} \textbf{ has-null-transition}^{-1})^* \ q'$$
$$\textbf{contains-item points first-of}^{-1} \ a \ ,$$

where $q' = \text{VALID}_0(\beta X)$. Hence

$$q \textbf{ has-LALL-lookahead } a \ ,$$

as desired. □

The relational expression **has-LALL-lookahead** is of size $O(|G| \cdot |Q|)$, where $|Q|$ is the number of states in the canonical LL(0) machine of $G'$, and has range $T \cup \{\$\}$. Thus we conclude by Theorem 2.29 that the relation denoted by **has-LALL-lookahead** can be computed in time $O(|T| \cdot |G| \cdot |Q|)$, or more specifically, in time $O(t \cdot |G| \cdot |Q|)$, where $t$ is the time needed for one set operation on subsets of $T$. Thus Theorem 8.68 implies:

**Theorem 8.69** *Let M be the canonical LL(0) machine for the \$-augmented grammar G′ of a reduced grammar G = (V, T, P, S). The collection of all LALL(1) lookahead sets* LALL(*q*), *where q is a state of M, can be computed in time* $O(t \cdot |G| \cdot |Q|)$, *where* $|Q|$ *is the number of states of M and t is the time taken by one set operation (assignment or union) on subsets of T.* □

The canonical LL(0) machine for any grammar $G$ is of size $O(2^{|G|})$, and by Theorem 8.62 it can be constructed in time $O(2^{|G| + 2\log|G|})$. Thus we obtain from Theorem 8.69 and Fact 8.66:

**Theorem 8.70** *The LALL(1) parser for any grammar $G = (V, T, P, S)$ can be constructed in time*

$$O(2^{|G| + 2\log|G| + \log|T|}) .$$

□

As an example of the LALL(1) parser construction process we apply the above techniques to the grammar

$$E \to TE' ,$$
$$E' \to \varepsilon | + TE' ,$$
$$T \to FT' ,$$
$$T' \to \varepsilon | *FT' ,$$
$$F \to a | (E) .$$

The canonical LL(0) machine for the corresponding \$-augmented grammar is given in Figure 8.11. Consider the computation of the LALL(1) lookahead sets. For state $q_6$ we have:

$$(\textbf{goes-to}^{-1}\ \textbf{has-null-transition}^{-1})^*(q_6) =$$
$$\{q_1, q_3, q_6, q_{10}\} .$$

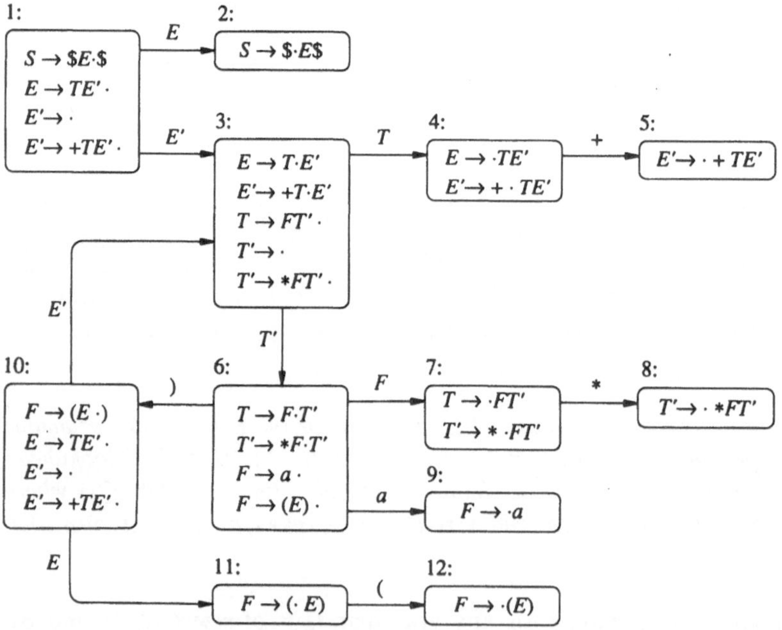


**Figure 8.11** The canonical LL(0) machine for the grammar $S \to \$E\$$, $E \to TE'$, $E' \to \varepsilon | +TE'$, $T \to FT'$, $T' \to \varepsilon | *FT'$, $F \to a | (E)$

Thus,

$$\textbf{has-LALL-lookahead}(q_6) =$$

$$\textbf{first-of}^{-1}\ (\textbf{contains-item points}\ (\{q_1, q_3, q_6, q_{10}\})) =$$

$$\textbf{first-of}^{-1}\ (\{\$, E', T', )\}) = \{\$, +, *, )\}\ ,$$

that is,

$$\mathrm{LALL}(q_6) = \{\$, +, *, )\}\ .$$

The LALL(1) lookahead sets for all states are:

$$\mathrm{LALL}(q_1) = \{\$\}\ ,$$
$$\mathrm{LALL}(q_2) = \{a, (\}\ ,$$
$$\mathrm{LALL}(q_3) = \{\$, +, )\}\ ,$$
$$\mathrm{LALL}(q_4) = \{a, (\}\ ,$$
$$\mathrm{LALL}(q_5) = \{+\}\ ,$$
$$\mathrm{LALL}(q_6) = \{\$, +, *, )\}\ ,$$
$$\mathrm{LALL}(q_7) = \{a, (\}\ ,$$
$$\mathrm{LALL}(q_8) = \{*\}\ ,$$
$$\mathrm{LALL}(q_9) = \{a\}\ ,$$
$$\mathrm{LALL}(q_{10}) = \{)\}\ ,$$
$$\mathrm{LALL}(q_{11}) = \{a, (\}\ ,$$
$$\mathrm{LALL}(q_{12}) = \{(\}\ ,$$

The produce actions of the LALL(1) parser are:

$$q_1q_2 \mid a \rightarrow q_1q_3q_4 \mid a\ ,$$
$$q_1q_2 \mid ( \rightarrow q_1q_3q_4 \mid (\ ,$$
$$q_1q_3 \mid \$ \rightarrow q_1 \mid \$\ ,$$
$$q_1q_3 \mid + \rightarrow q_1q_3q_4q_5 \mid +\ ,$$
$$q_3q_4 \mid a \rightarrow q_3q_6q_7 \mid a\ ,$$
$$q_3q_4 \mid ( \rightarrow q_3q_6q_7 \mid (\ ,$$
$$q_3q_6 \mid \$ \rightarrow q_3 \mid \$\ ,$$
$$q_3q_6 \mid + \rightarrow q_3 \mid +\ ,$$
$$q_3q_6 \mid ) \rightarrow q_3 \mid )\ ,$$
$$q_3q_6 \mid * \rightarrow q_3q_6q_7q_8 \mid *\ ,$$

$$q_6q_7 \mid a \to q_6q_9 \mid a \ ,$$

$$q_6q_7 \mid ( \to q_6q_{10}q_{11}q_{12} \mid ( \ ,$$

$$q_{10}q_3 \mid ) \to q_{10} \mid ) \ ,$$

$$q_{10}q_3 \mid + \to q_{10}q_3q_4q_5 \mid + \ ,$$

$$q_{10}q_{11} \mid a \to q_{10}q_3q_4 \mid a \ ,$$

$$q_{10}q_{11} \mid ( \to q_{10}q_3q_4 \mid ( \ .$$

The shift actions are:

$$q_5 \mid + \to \mid \ ,$$

$$q_8 \mid * \to \mid \ ,$$

$$q_9 \mid a \to \mid \ ,$$

$$q_{10} \mid ) \to \mid \ ,$$

$$q_{12} \mid ( \to \mid \ .$$

## 8.6 Non-Left-Recursive Grammatical Covers

A reduced left-recursive grammar cannot be an LL($k$) grammar (Theorem 8.51). However many constructs in programming languages are most naturally described by a left-recursive grammar. For example, arithmetic expressions are usually described by grammars like $G_{\mathrm{exp}}$:

$$E \to E + T \mid T \ ,$$

$$T \to T * F \mid F \ ,$$

$$F \to a \mid (E) \ .$$

$G_{\mathrm{exp}}$ is left-recursive and we cannot use its canonical LL($k$) parser ($k \geqslant 0$) to parse the language $L(G_{\mathrm{exp}})$ determinstically.

The language $L(G_{\mathrm{exp}})$ is an LL(1) language, however. It is generated by the LL(1) grammar $\hat{G}_{\mathrm{exp}}$:

$$E \to TE' \ ,$$

$$E' \to \varepsilon \mid + TE' \ ,$$

$$T \to FT' \ ,$$

$$T' \to \varepsilon \mid *FT' \ ,$$

$$F \to a \mid (E) \ .$$

($\hat{G}_{\mathrm{exp}}$ is the grammar considered in the previous section.)

$\hat{G}_{exp}$ is the result of the standard transformation for removing *direct left recursion* from $G_{exp}$. (We say that nonterminal $A$ is *directly left-recursive* if the grammar has a rule $A \to A\alpha$.) If the rules of a directly left-recursive nonterminal $A$ are

$$A \to A\alpha | \beta \ ,$$

these rules are replaced in the transformation by the rules

$$A \to \beta A' \ ,$$

$$A' \to \varepsilon | \alpha A' \ ,$$

where $A'$ is a new nonterminal. Thus, direct left-recursion is changed to *direct right recursion*.

The problem is that the transformation does not produce a cover. (Recall the definition of a "cover" from Section 6.6.) This means that there is no straightforward way to recover the parse of a sentence in the original grammar $G_{exp}$ from the parse of the sentence in $\hat{G}_{exp}$. This is unfortunate because it is $G_{exp}$ we prefer to use as the "semantic grammar", that is, the grammar according to which the semantics of the language are defined, while $\hat{G}_{exp}$ only plays the role of a "parsing grammar".

We shall show formally that $\hat{G}_{exp}$ does not left-to-right cover $G_{exp}$, meaning that no left parser of $G_{exp}$ can be used as a right parser of $G_{exp}$. We leave it as an exercise to show that $\hat{G}_{exp}$ in fact does not $x$-to-$y$ cover $G_{exp}$ for any $x$, $y$ in {"left", "right"}. Thus no parser of $\hat{G}_{exp}$ can be used as a parser of $G_{exp}$.

We recall that grammar $\hat{G} = (\hat{V}, T, \hat{P}, \hat{S})$ left-to-right covers grammar $G = (V, T, P, S)$ with respect to homomorphism $h$: $\hat{P}^* \to P^*$ if the following statements hold.

(1) $h$ maps left parses to right parses, that is, for all $w \in L(\hat{G})$ and left parses $\hat{\pi}$ of $w$ in $\hat{G}$, $h(\hat{\pi})$ is a right parse of $w$ in $G$.

(2) Any right parse in $G$ is an image under $h$ of some left parse in $\hat{G}$, that is, for all $w \in L(G)$ and right parses $\pi$ of $w$ in $G$, $w$ has in $\hat{G}$ a left parse $\hat{\pi}$ such that $h(\hat{\pi}) = \pi$.

Now assume for the sake of contradiction that $\hat{G}_{exp}$ left-to-right covers $G_{exp}$ with respect to some homomorphism $h$. The right parse of the sentence $a$ in $G_{exp}$ is

$$\pi_a = (F \to a)(T \to F)(E \to T)$$

and the right parse of the sentence $a + a$ in $G_{exp}$ is

$$\pi_{a+a} = (F \to a)(T \to F)(E \to T)(F \to a)(T \to F)(E \to E + T) \ .$$

The left parses of $a$ and $a + a$ in $\hat{G}_{exp}$ are:

$$\hat{\pi}_a = (E \to TE')(T \to FT')(F \to a)(T' \to \varepsilon)(E' \to \varepsilon) \ ,$$

$$\hat{\pi}_{a+a} = (E \to TE')(T \to FT')(F \to a)(T' \to \varepsilon)(E' \to +TE')$$
$$(T \to FT')(F \to a)(T' \to \varepsilon)(E' \to \varepsilon) \ .$$

Because $\hat{G}_{exp}$ was assumed to left-to-right cover $G_{exp}$ with respect to $h$, we have:

$$h(\hat{\pi}_a) = \pi_a \quad \text{and} \quad h(\hat{\pi}_{a+a}) = \pi_{a+a} \ .$$

Now $h((T' \to \varepsilon)(E' \to \varepsilon))$ must be $\varepsilon$, because otherwise the fact that $h(\hat{\pi}_a) = \pi_a$ would imply that $h((T' \to \varepsilon)(E' \to \varepsilon))$ ends with $E \to T$, and the fact that $h(\hat{\pi}_{a+a}) = \pi_{a+a}$ would imply that $h((T' \to \varepsilon)(E' \to \varepsilon))$ ends with $E \to E + T$. Thus we have:

$$h((E \to TE')(T \to FT')(F \to a)) = h(\hat{\pi}_a) = (F \to a)(T \to F)(E \to T) \ ,$$

which, together with the fact that $h(\hat{\pi}_{a+a}) = \pi_{a+a}$, implies that

$$h((T' \to \varepsilon)(E' \to +TE')(T \to FT')(F \to a)) =$$
$$(F \to a)(T \to F)(E \to E + T) \ .$$

From these equalities we conclude that $h((T \to FT')(F \to a))$ must be $\varepsilon$. Hence:

$$h(E \to TE') = (F \to a)(T \to F)(E \to T) \ .$$

But then, for example, $h$ would map the left parse

$$(E \to TE')(T \to (E))(E \to TE')(T \to F)(F \to a)(E' \to \varepsilon)(E' \to \varepsilon)$$

to a rule string that contains the rule $F \to a$ twice. No such string can be a right parse of the sentence $(a)$. We conclude that $\hat{G}_{exp}$ does not left-to-right cover $G_{exp}$.

There is however a way to remove the left recursion from $G_{exp}$ so that a left-to-right cover is obtained. First we construct a grammar $G_{exp2}$:

$$E \to E + TR_1 | TR_2 \ ,$$
$$T \to T*FR_3 | FR_4 \ ,$$
$$F \to aR_5 | (E)R_6 \ ,$$
$$R_1 \to \varepsilon,\ R_2 \to \varepsilon,\ R_3 \to \varepsilon \ ,$$
$$R_4 \to \varepsilon,\ R_5 \to \varepsilon,\ R_6 \to \varepsilon \ .$$

In this grammar each new nonterminal $R_i$ is an indication of the $i^{th}$ rule in the original grammar. Moreover, in parsing with respect to $G_{exp2}$, a rule $R_i \to \varepsilon$ is recognized at the point when a right parser of $G_{exp}$ has recognized the $i^{th}$ rule of $G_{exp}$. We now change the grammar $G_{exp2}$ using the standard transformation for removing left recursion. This yields the grammar $\hat{G}_{exp2}$:

$$E \to TR_2E' \ ,$$
$$E' \to +TR_1E' | \varepsilon \ ,$$
$$T \to FR_4T' \ ,$$
$$T' \to *FR_3T' | \varepsilon \ ,$$

$$F \to aR_5|(E)R_6 \ ,$$

$$R_1 \to \varepsilon,\ R_2 \to \varepsilon,\ R_3 \to \varepsilon \ ,$$

$$R_4 \to \varepsilon,\ R_5 \to \varepsilon,\ R_6 \to \varepsilon \ .$$

In $\hat{G}_{exp2}$ the nonterminals $R_i$ still indicate the moments when reductions by rules of $G_{exp}$ would be performed by a right parser of $G_{exp}$. For example, consider how $a + a$ is leftmost derived in $\hat{G}_{exp2}$:

$$E \underset{lm}{\Longrightarrow} TR_2E' \underset{lm}{\Longrightarrow} FR_4T'R_2E' \underset{lm}{\Longrightarrow} aR_5R_4T'R_2E'$$

$$\underset{lm}{\Longrightarrow} aR_4T'R_2E' \underset{lm}{\Longrightarrow} aT'R_2E' \underset{lm}{\Longrightarrow} aR_2E' \underset{lm}{\Longrightarrow} aE'$$

$$\underset{lm}{\Longrightarrow} a + TR_1E' \underset{lm}{\Longrightarrow} a + FR_4T'R_1E' \underset{lm}{\Longrightarrow} a + aR_5R_4T'R_1E'$$

$$\underset{lm}{\Longrightarrow} a + aR_4T'R_1E' \underset{lm}{\Longrightarrow} a + aT'R_1E' \underset{lm}{\Longrightarrow} a + aR_1E'$$

$$\underset{lm}{\Longrightarrow} a + aE' \underset{lm}{\Longrightarrow} a + a \ .$$

Here the rules for the nonterminals $R_i$ are applied in the order $R_5, R_4, R_2, R_5, R_4, R_1$. If we make up a sequence of corresponding rules of $G_{exp}$ ($R_i$ corresponds to the $i^{th}$ rule) in this order, we get:

$$(F \to a)(T \to F)(E \to T)(F \to a)(T \to F)(E \to E + T) \ .$$

But this is the right parse of $a + a$ in $G_{exp}$. In fact $(\hat{G}_{exp2}, h)$ is a left-to-right cover of $G_{exp}$ if $h$ maps $R_i \to \varepsilon$ to the $i^{th}$ rule of $G_{exp}$ for all $i$, and all other rules to $\varepsilon$. Moreover, $\hat{G}_{exp2}$ is an LL(1) grammar. Thus the LL(1) parser of $\hat{G}_{exp2}$ can be used as a right parser of $G_{exp}$.

Now we shall consider the general problem of removing left recursion from a grammar such that a cover is obtained. The standard transformation for left recursion removal is applied to a *proper* grammar, that is, to a reduced grammar which is $\varepsilon$-free and does not contain any nonterminal $A$ such that $A \Rightarrow^+ A$.

**Lemma 8.71** *Any proper grammar $G = (V, T, P, S)$ can be transformed in time $O(|G|)$ into a grammar $\hat{G} = (\hat{V}, T, \hat{P}, S)$ such that the following statements hold.*

(1) *$\hat{G}$ is not directly left-recursive.*
(2) *$V \subseteq \hat{V}$.*
(3) *$L_{\hat{G}}(X) = L_G(X)$ for all $X \in V$.*

*Proof.* We construct the grammar $\hat{G} = (\hat{V}, T, \hat{P}, S)$ as follows. For all $A \in V \setminus T$ such that for some $\alpha \in V^+$ $A \to A\alpha$ is a rule in $P$ we do the following. Let

$$A \to A\alpha_1 | \ldots | A\alpha_n | \beta_1 | \ldots | \beta_m,\ n \geqslant 1, m \geqslant 1 \ ,$$

be the set of those rules in $P$ that have $A$ as the left-hand side. Moreover, we assume that $\beta_i$ does not begin with $A$, for any $i = 1, \ldots, m$. (Note that $m \geqslant 1$, because $G$ is reduced.) We replace this set of rules by the rules

$$A \to \beta_1 A' | \ldots | \beta_m A' \ ,$$

$$A' \to \alpha_1 A' | \ldots | \alpha_n A' | \varepsilon \ ,$$

where $A'$ is a new nonterminal.

The set $\hat{V}$ is obtained by adding to $V$ all new nonterminals introduced in the above process, and the set $\hat{P}$ of rules will result from the above replacement process of rules. It is clear that for any $A \in V \setminus T$ such that the above replacement of rules is performed, the language generated by $A$ is preserved. Thus statement (3) of the lemma holds. Therefore, because the immediate left recursion is indeed eliminated, we have the lemma. □

We shall now transform a proper grammar into a grammar which is not left-recursive (neither directly nor indirectly).

**Theorem 8.72** *Any proper grammar* $G = (V, T, P, S)$ *can be transformed in time* $O(|G|^2)$ *into a grammar* $\hat{G} = (\hat{V}, T, \hat{P}, S)$ *such that the following statements hold.*

(1) $\hat{G}$ *is not left-recursive.*
(2) $V \subseteq \hat{V}$.
(3) $L_{\hat{G}}(X) = L_G(X)$ *for all* $X \in V$.

*Proof.* Let $\leqslant$ be any total order on $V \setminus T$, and let $\{A_1, \ldots, A_n\} = V \setminus T$, where $A_i < A_j$ whenever $i < j$. We shall modify the grammar $G$ such that in the resulting grammar $\hat{G}$, $A_i < A_j$ whenever $A_i \to A_j\alpha$ is a rule in $\hat{P}$. In other words, $\hat{G}$ is non-left-recursive, whenever the new nonterminals in $\hat{V}$ do not cause left recursion. An algorithm for constructing $\hat{P}$ is given in Figure 8.12. Clearly, a single replacement step in the inner loop of the algorithm always preserves the language for the nonterminal in question. This, together with Lemma 8.71, means that statement (3) holds after performing the algorithm. It is also clear that in the resulting grammar $\hat{G}$, $A_i < A_j$ whenever a rule $A_i \to A_j\alpha$ is in $\hat{P}$. Thus, because the new nonterminals

```
P̂ := P;
for i := 2 to n do begin
    for j := 1 to i − 1 do
        if A_i → A_jα for some α is in P̂ then
            replace A_i → A_jα by the set of rules
            {A_i → β_jα | A_j → β_j ∈ P̂};
        Eliminate the direct left recursion
        possibly caused by nonterminal A_i (use
        the method described in the proof of
        Lemma 8.71).
end.
```

**Figure 8.12** An algorithm for removing left recursion from a proper grammar $G = (\{A_1, \ldots, A_n\} \cup T, T, P, S)$

introduced in the elimination of direct left recursion do not cause any left recursion, we conclude that $\hat{G}$ is non-left-recursive. Finally we observe that the algorithm of Figure 8.12 runs in time $O(|G|^2)$. □

As an example of the behaviour of the algorithm of Figure 8.12 consider the grammar

$$A_1 \to A_2b \ ,$$
$$A_2 \to A_3c | A_4d \ ,$$
$$A_3 \to A_1a | A_2b \ ,$$
$$A_4 \to A_3c | a \ .$$

The first modification in the algorithm is that the rule $A_3 \to A_1a$ is replaced by the rule $A_3 \to A_2ba$. After this modification the newly added rule $A_3 \to A_2ba$ and the rule $A_3 \to A_2b$ are replaced by the rules $A_3 \to A_3cba | A_4dba$ and $A_3 \to A_3cb | A_4db$. At this point, the direct left recursion for $A_3$ is eliminated, which results in the rules

$$A_3 \to A_4dbaA'_3 | A_4dbA'_3 \ ,$$
$$A'_3 \to cbaA'_3 | cbA'_3 | \varepsilon \ .$$

Then the rule $A_4 \to A_3c$ will be replaced by the rules

$$A_4 \to A_4dbaA'_3c | A_4dbA'_3c \ ,$$

and finally the elimination of direct left recursion replaces the rules for $A_4$ by the rules

$$A_4 \to aA'_4 \ ,$$
$$A'_4 \to dbaA'_3cA'_4 | dbA'_3cA'_4 | \varepsilon \ .$$

The entire new grammar without left recursion is

$$A_1 \to A_2b \ ,$$
$$A_2 \to A_3c | A_4d \ ,$$
$$A_3 \to A_4dbaA'_3 | A_4dbA'_3 \ ,$$
$$A'_3 \to cbaA'_3 | cbA'_3 | \varepsilon \ ,$$
$$A_4 \to aA'_4 \ ,$$
$$A'_4 \to dbaA'_3cA'_4 | dbA'_3cA'_4 | \varepsilon \ .$$

Now we describe how the above techniques can be used to produce a non-left-recursive covering grammar for a proper grammar.

Given any proper grammar $G = (V, T, P, S)$, let $G_T$ be the grammar $(V \cup P, T \cup P, P_T, S)$, where

$$P_T = \{A \to \omega(A, \omega) | A \to \omega \in P\} \ .$$

That is, we add to each rule $A \to \omega$ a new terminal, the rule itself, that identifies uniquely the end of the rule.

**Lemma 8.73** *Let X be a symbol in V, w a string in* $(T \cup P)^*$, *and n a positive natural number such that*

(a) $$X \Rightarrow^n w \quad \text{in } G_T \ .$$

*Then there are strings* $y_1, \ldots, y_n \in T^*$ *and rules* $r_1, \ldots, r_n \in P$ *such that*

(b) $$w = y_1 r_1 y_2 r_2 \ldots y_n r_n, \text{ and}$$
$$X \xrightarrow[\text{rm}]{r_n \ldots r_1} y_1 y_2 \ldots y_n \quad \text{in } G \ .$$

*Proof.* The proof is a simple induction on $n$. The base case $n = 1$ is immediate, because then, by the construction of $G_T$, $w$ is of the form $yr$, where $r$ is the rule $X \to y$. The induction step $n > 0$ in turn follows directly from the construction of $G_T$ and the induction hypothesis, because statement (*a*) implies, by Lemma 4.1, the existence of a rule $X \to X_1 \ldots X_l(X, X_1 \ldots X_l)$ in $P_T$, strings $w_1, \ldots, w_l$ in $(T \cup P)^*$, and natural numbers $n_1, \ldots, n_l$ such that

$$X \Rightarrow X_1 \ldots X_l(X, X_1 \ldots X_l) \ ,$$
$$X_i \Rightarrow^{n_i} w_i \quad \text{for all } i = 1, \ldots, n \ ,$$
$$w_1 \ldots w_l(X, X_1 \ldots X_l) = w, \text{ and}$$
$$n_1 + \ldots + n_l = n - 1 \ .$$

The rule string $r_n \ldots r_1$ will be obtained so that $r_n = X \to X_1 \ldots X_l$ and $r_{n-1} \ldots r_1$ is a concatenation of $n_i$-length substrings implied by the induction hypothesis for $i = 1, \ldots, l$ $(n_i > 0)$. □

The converse of Lemma 8.73 is stated in the following:

**Lemma 8.74** *Let X be a symbol in V, y a string in* $T^*$, *n a natural number, and* $r_1, \ldots, r_n$ *rules in P,* $n \geqslant 1$, *such that*

(a) $$X \xrightarrow[\text{rm}]{r_n \ldots r_1} y \quad \text{in } G \ .$$

*Then there are strings* $y_1, \ldots, y_n \in T^*$ *such that*

(b) $$y = y_1 \ldots y_n, \quad \text{and}$$
$$X \Rightarrow^n y_1 r_1 y_2 r_2 \ldots y_n r_n \quad \text{in } G_T \ .$$

*Proof.* A straightforward induction on $n$. □

Then denote by $\hat{G}_T = (\hat{V}, T \cup P, \hat{P}_T, S)$ the grammar obtained by removing left recursion from $G_T$ by means of the algorithm given in Figure 8.12. Further, let

$\hat{G}_N = (\hat{V}, T, \hat{P}_N, S)$ be the grammar obtained from $\hat{G}_T$ by interpreting each element of $P$ appearing in the rules as a nonterminal and by adding the rule $r \to \varepsilon$ for each $r$ in $P$:

$$\hat{P}_N = \hat{P}_T \cup \{r \to \varepsilon | r \in P\} .$$

We shall show that $\hat{G}_N$ left-to-right covers $G$. (In fact $\hat{G}_N$ also right-to-right covers $G$; see the exercises.)

Let $h$ be the homomorphism from $\hat{P}_N^*$ to $P^*$ defined by:

(1) $h(r \to \varepsilon) = r$, when $r$ is a rule in $P$ .

(2) $h(A \to \omega) = \varepsilon$, when $A \to \omega$ is a rule in $\hat{P}_T$ .

**Lemma 8.75** *Let $y$ be a sentence in $L(\hat{G}_N)$ and $\hat{\pi}$ a left parse of $y$ in $\hat{G}_N$. Then $h(\hat{\pi})$ is a right parse of $y$ in $G$.*

*Proof.* By the construction of $\hat{G}_N$, there are rules $r_1, \ldots, r_n \in P$ and rule strings $\hat{\pi}_1, \ldots, \hat{\pi}_{n+1} \in \hat{P}_T^*$ such that

$$\hat{\pi} = \hat{\pi}_1(r_1 \to \varepsilon)\hat{\pi}_2(r_2 \to \varepsilon) \ldots \hat{\pi}_n(r_n \to \varepsilon)\hat{\pi}_{n+1} .$$

Because $\hat{\pi}$ is a left parse of $y$, the following must hold in $\hat{G}_N$ for some strings $y_1, \ldots, y_{n+1} \in T^*$ and $\beta_1, \ldots, \beta_n \in (\hat{V} \cup P)^*$:

$$S \overset{\hat{\pi}_1}{\underset{\text{lm}}{\Longrightarrow}} y_1 r_1 \beta_1 \underset{\text{lm}}{\Longrightarrow} y_1 \beta_1$$

$$\overset{\hat{\pi}_2}{\underset{\text{lm}}{\Longrightarrow}} y_1 y_2 r_2 \beta_2 \underset{\text{lm}}{\Longrightarrow} y_1 y_2 \beta_2$$

$$\vdots$$

$$\overset{\hat{\pi}_n}{\underset{\text{lm}}{\Longrightarrow}} y_1 y_2 \ldots y_n r_n \beta_n \underset{\text{lm}}{\Longrightarrow} y_1 y_2 \ldots y_n \beta_n$$

$$\overset{\hat{\pi}_{n+1}}{\underset{\text{lm}}{\Longrightarrow}} y_1 y_2 \ldots y_n y_{n+1} = y .$$

Here in fact $\hat{\pi}_{n+1} = \varepsilon$ and $y_{n+1} = \varepsilon = \beta_n$ because using only rules in $\hat{P}_T$ it is not possible to nontrivially derive any string in $T^*$. From the above derivation we see that

$$S \overset{\hat{\pi}_1 \ldots \hat{\pi}_n}{\underset{\text{lm}}{\Longrightarrow}} y_1 r_1 \ldots y_n r_n \quad \text{in } \hat{G}_T .$$

This in turn implies by Theorem 8.72 that

$$S \underset{\text{lm}}{\Longrightarrow}^{+} y_1 r_1 \ldots y_n r_n \quad \text{in } G_T .$$

By Lemma 8.73 we get:

$$S \xRightarrow[\text{rm}]{r_n \ldots r_1} y_1 \ldots y_n \quad \text{in } G \ .$$

This proves the lemma, because by definition $h(\hat{\pi}) = r_1 \ldots r_n$. □

**Lemma 8.76** *Let $y$ be a sentence in $L(G)$ and $\pi$ a right parse of $y$ in $G$. Then $y$ has in $\hat{G}_N$ a left parse $\hat{\pi}$ such that $h(\hat{\pi}) = \pi$.*

*Proof.* Let $\pi = r_1 \ldots r_n$, where each $r_i$ is a rule in $P$. Then we have:

$$S \xRightarrow[\text{rm}]{r_n \ldots r_1} y \quad \text{in } G \ .$$

By Lemma 8.74 there are strings $y_1, \ldots, y_n \in T^*$ such that

$$S \Rightarrow^n y_1 r_1 \ldots y_n r_n \quad \text{in } G_T \quad \text{and} \quad y_1 \ldots y_n = y \ .$$

By Theorem 8.72 we have:

$$S \Rightarrow^+ y_1 r_1 \ldots y_n r_n \quad \text{in } \hat{G}_T \ .$$

By Theorem 4.2 there is a rule string $\pi' \in \hat{P}_T^*$ such that

$$S \xRightarrow[\text{lm}]{\pi'} y_1 r_1 \ldots y_n r_n \quad \text{in } \hat{G}_T \ .$$

From $\pi'$ we get a left parse in $\hat{G}_N$ by inserting, for all $i = 1, \ldots, n$, the rule $r_i \to \varepsilon$ at that place in $\pi'$ where $r_i$ first becomes the leftmost nonterminal in the derivation. Let the resulting parse be

$$\hat{\pi} = \hat{\pi}_1 (r_1 \to \varepsilon) \ldots \hat{\pi}_n (r_n \to \varepsilon) \ .$$

Here $\hat{\pi}_1 \ldots \hat{\pi}_n = \pi'$ and we have:

$$S \xRightarrow[\text{lm}]{\hat{\pi}} y_1 \ldots y_n = y \quad \text{in } \hat{G}_N \ .$$

This proves the lemma, because $h(\hat{\pi}) = \pi$. □

Now we have:

**Theorem 8.77** *For any proper grammar $G$ there is a non-left-recursive grammar $\hat{G}$ and a homomorphism $h$ such that $(\hat{G}, h)$ is a left-to-right cover of $G$. Moreover, $(\hat{G}, h)$ can be constructed from $G$ in time $O(|G|^2)$.*

*Proof.* Lemmas 8.75 and 8.76 together state that $(\hat{G}_N, h)$ as given above is a left-to-right cover of $G$. The grammar $G_T$ is proper whenever $G$ is so, and $G_T$ can be constructed from $G$ in linear time. By Theorem 8.72, $\hat{G}_T$ is a non-left-recursive

grammar that can be constructed from $G_T$ in time $O(|G_T|^2)$. The conversion of $\hat{G}_T$ into $\hat{G}_N$ takes linear time and does not introduce any left-recursive nonterminals. □

## 8.7 Predictive LR(k) Grammars

In this section we shall describe a useful method for converting proper grammars into LL(k) form.

Let $G = (V, T, P, S)$ be a grammar. The relation **starts** on $V \cup \{\varepsilon\}$ is defined by:

$$X \textbf{ starts } A$$

if $P$ contains a rule $A \to \omega$ with $1{:}\omega = X$. For $\varepsilon$-free grammars this relation coincides with the relation **begins** considered in Section 5.5.

For grammar $G = (V, T, P, S)$, we define the *$\perp$-augmented grammar* $G_\perp$ as the grammar $G_\perp = (V \cup \{S', \perp\}, T \cup \{\perp\}, P \cup \{S' \to \perp S\}, S')$, where $S'$ and $\perp$ are new symbols.

The *LL-transformed grammar* $T_{\text{LL}}(G)$ for $G$ is then defined as the grammar with terminal alphabet $T$ and start symbol $[S', \perp]$, and with a set of rules that contains for each rule $A \to X_1 \ldots X_n$ of $G_\perp$:

(type 1) all rules of the form

$$[A, X_1 \ldots X_i] \to a[A, X_1 \ldots X_i a] ,$$

where $1 \leqslant i < n$, $a \in T$, and $a$ **starts*** $X_{i+1}$,

(type 2) all rules of the form

$$[A, X_1 \ldots X_i Y] \to [B, Y][A, X_1 \ldots X_i B] ,$$

where $1 \leqslant i < n$, $Y \in V \cup \{\varepsilon\}$, $B \in V \setminus T$, and $Y$ **starts** $B$ **starts*** $X_{i+1}$ ,

(type 3) the rule

$$[A, X_1 \ldots X_n] \to \varepsilon .$$

The number of rules of type 1 is $O(|T| \cdot |G|)$. To estimate the number of rules of type 2, first observe that there are $O(|G|^2)$ different nonterminals of the form $[A, X_1 \ldots X_i Y]$. For each occurrence of $Y$ in the rules of $G$ there is only one $B$ satisfying $Y$ **starts** $B$. Hence $O(|G|^2)$ is also an upper bound on the number of rules of type 2. As **starts*** can be computed in time $O(|G|^2)$ as a preprocessing task, we get:

**Lemma 8.78** *The grammar $T_{\text{LL}}(G)$ is of size $O(|G|^2)$ and can be constructed from $G$ in time $O(|G|^2)$.* □

As an example we apply the transformation to the grammar $G_{\text{assign}}$:

$$S \rightarrow i \leftarrow A \mid i \leftarrow B \ ,$$

$$A \rightarrow A * P \mid P \ ,$$

$$B \rightarrow A = A \ ,$$

$$P \rightarrow i \mid (A) \ .$$

The transformed grammar $T_{\text{LL}}(G_{\text{assign}})$ is:

$$[S', \bot] \rightarrow i[S', \bot i] \ ,$$

$$[S', \bot i] \rightarrow [S, i][S', \bot S] \ ,$$

$$[S', \bot S] \rightarrow \varepsilon \ ,$$

$$[S, i] \rightarrow \ \leftarrow [S, i \leftarrow] \ ,$$

$$[S, i \leftarrow] \rightarrow ([S, i \leftarrow (] \mid i[S, i \leftarrow i] \ ,$$

$$[S, i \leftarrow (] \rightarrow [P, (][S, i \leftarrow P] \ ,$$

$$[S, i \leftarrow i] \rightarrow [P, i][S, i \leftarrow P] \ ,$$

$$[S, i \leftarrow P] \rightarrow [A, P][S, i \leftarrow A] \ ,$$

$$[S, i \leftarrow A] \rightarrow [A, A][S, i \leftarrow A] \mid [B, A][S, i \leftarrow B] \mid \varepsilon \ ,$$

$$[S, i \leftarrow B] \rightarrow \varepsilon \ ,$$

$$[A, P] \rightarrow \varepsilon \ ,$$

$$[A, A] \rightarrow *[A, A*] \ ,$$

$$[A, A*] \rightarrow ([A, A*(] \mid i[A, A*i] \ ,$$

$$[A, A*(] \rightarrow [P, (][A, A*P] \ ,$$

$$[A, A*i] \rightarrow [P, i][A, A*P] \ ,$$

$$[A, A*P] \rightarrow \varepsilon \ ,$$

$$[B, A] \rightarrow \ = [B, A =] \ ,$$

$$[B, A =] \rightarrow ([B, A = (] \mid i[B, A = i] \ ,$$

$$[B, A = (] \rightarrow [P, (][B, A = P] \ ,$$

$$[B, A = i] \rightarrow [P, i][B, A = P] \ ,$$

$$[B, A = P] \rightarrow [A, P][B, A = A] \ ,$$

$$[B, A = A] \rightarrow [A, A][B, A = A] \mid \varepsilon \ ,$$

$$[P, (] \rightarrow ([P, ((] \mid i[P, (i] \ ,$$

$$[P, i] \rightarrow \varepsilon \ ,$$

$$[P, ((] \to [P, (][P, (P] \ ,$$

$$[P, (i] \to [P, i][P, (P] \ ,$$

$$[P, (P] \to [A, P][P, (A] \ ,$$

$$[P, (A] \to [A, A][P, (A] \mid )[P, (A)] \ ,$$

$$[P, (A)] \to \varepsilon \ .$$

We shall show in the sequel that $T_{\text{LL}}(G)$ for any grammar $G$ generates the language $L(G)$. We demonstrate how the sentence

$$i \leftarrow i = i*i$$

in $L(G_{\text{assign}})$ may be derived in $T_{\text{LL}}(G_{\text{assign}})$:

$$[S', \bot] \underset{\text{lm}}{\Longrightarrow} i[S', \bot i] \underset{\text{lm}}{\Longrightarrow} i[S, i][S', \bot S]$$

$$\underset{\text{lm}}{\Longrightarrow} i \leftarrow [S, i \leftarrow][S', \bot S]$$

$$\underset{\text{lm}}{\Longrightarrow} i \leftarrow i[S, i \leftarrow i][S', \bot S] \underset{\text{lm}}{\Longrightarrow} i \leftarrow i[P, i][S, i \leftarrow P][S', \bot S]$$

$$\underset{\text{lm}}{\Longrightarrow} i \leftarrow i[S, i \leftarrow P][S', \bot S] \underset{\text{lm}}{\Longrightarrow} i \leftarrow i[A, P][S, i \leftarrow A][S', \bot S]$$

$$\underset{\text{lm}}{\Longrightarrow} i \leftarrow i[S, i \leftarrow A][S', \bot S] \underset{\text{lm}}{\Longrightarrow} i \leftarrow i[B, A][S, i \leftarrow B][S', \bot S]$$

$$\underset{\text{lm}}{\Longrightarrow} i \leftarrow i = [B, A =][S, i \leftarrow B][S', \bot S]$$

$$\underset{\text{lm}}{\Longrightarrow} i \leftarrow i = i[B, A = i][S, i \leftarrow B][S', \bot S]$$

$$\underset{\text{lm}}{\Longrightarrow} i \leftarrow i = i[P, i][B, A = P][S, i \leftarrow B][S', \bot S]$$

$$\underset{\text{lm}}{\Longrightarrow} i \leftarrow i = i[B, A = P][S, i \leftarrow B][S', \bot S]$$

$$\underset{\text{lm}}{\Longrightarrow} i \leftarrow i = i[A, P][B, A = A][S, i \leftarrow B][S', \bot S]$$

$$\underset{\text{lm}}{\Longrightarrow} i \leftarrow i = i[B, A = A][S, i \leftarrow B][S', \bot S]$$

$$\underset{\text{lm}}{\Longrightarrow} i \leftarrow i = i[A, A][B, A = A][S, i \leftarrow B][S', \bot S]$$

$$\underset{\text{lm}}{\Longrightarrow} i \leftarrow i = i*[A, A*][B, A = A][S, i \leftarrow B][S', \bot S]$$

$$\underset{\text{lm}}{\Longrightarrow} i \leftarrow i = i*i[A, A*i][B, A = A][S, i \leftarrow B][S', \bot S]$$

$$\underset{\text{lm}}{\Longrightarrow} i \leftarrow i = i*i[P, i][A, A*P][B, A = A][S, i \leftarrow B][S', \bot S]$$

$$\underset{\text{lm}}{\Longrightarrow} i \leftarrow i = i*i[A, A*P][B, A = A][S, i \leftarrow B][S', \bot S]$$

$$\underset{lm}{\Longrightarrow} i \leftarrow i = i*i[B, A = A][S, i \leftarrow B][S', \perp S]$$

$$\underset{lm}{\Longrightarrow} i \leftarrow i = i*i[S, i \leftarrow B][S', \perp S]$$

$$\underset{lm}{\Longrightarrow} i \leftarrow i = i*i[S', \perp S]$$

$$\underset{lm}{\Longrightarrow} i \leftarrow i = i*i \ .$$

Observe that the rules of the form $[A, \omega] \rightarrow \varepsilon$ applied in the above derivation are (in the order of application):

$$[P, i] \rightarrow \varepsilon, \quad [A, P] \rightarrow \varepsilon, \quad [P, i] \rightarrow \varepsilon, \quad [A, P] \rightarrow \varepsilon \ ,$$

$$[P, i] \rightarrow \varepsilon, \quad [A, A*P] \rightarrow \varepsilon, \quad [B, A = A] \rightarrow \varepsilon, \quad [S, i \leftarrow B] \rightarrow \varepsilon \ ,$$

$$[S', \perp S] \rightarrow \varepsilon \ .$$

The corresponding rules of $G_{\text{assign}}$ form a right parse of the sentence $i \leftarrow i = i*i$ in $G_{\text{assign}}$:

$$(P \rightarrow i)(A \rightarrow P)(P \rightarrow i)(A \rightarrow P)(P \rightarrow i)(A \rightarrow A*P)$$

$$(B \rightarrow A = A)(S \rightarrow i \leftarrow B) \ .$$

In fact $T_{\text{LL}}(G_{\text{assign}})$ left-to-right covers $G_{\text{assign}}$.

The grammar $T_{\text{LL}}(G_{\text{assign}})$ is an LL(1) grammar, as is easily seen. The grammar may be shortened by simple substitution. That is, the rules of the forms $A \rightarrow \alpha B \beta$ and $B \rightarrow \omega$ are replaced by the rule $A \rightarrow \alpha\omega\beta$ whenever $B \rightarrow \omega$ is the only rule having $B$ as the left-hand side. The resulting grammar is:

$$[S', \perp] \rightarrow i \leftarrow [S, i \leftarrow] \ ,$$

$$[S, i \leftarrow] \rightarrow ([P, (][S, i \leftarrow A] \mid i[S, i \leftarrow A] \ ,$$

$$[S, i \leftarrow A] \rightarrow *[A, A*][S, i \leftarrow A] \mid = [B, A =] \mid \varepsilon \ ,$$

$$[A, A*] \rightarrow ([P, (] \mid i \ ,$$

$$[B, A =] \rightarrow ([P, (][B, A = A] \mid i[B, A = A] \ ,$$

$$[B, A = A] \rightarrow *[A, A*][B, A = A] \mid \varepsilon \ ,$$

$$[P, (] \rightarrow ([P, (][P, (A] \mid i[P, (A] \ ,$$

$$[P, (A] \rightarrow *[A, A*][P, (A] \mid ) \ .$$

This grammar is, of course, also an LL(1) grammar.

Now let $G = (V, T, P, S)$ be any grammar. We define a homomorphism, $h_T$, from the rule strings of the transformed grammar $T_{\text{LL}}(G)$ to the rule strings of $G$ by setting:

$$h_T([A, \alpha] \rightarrow \eta) = \begin{cases} A \rightarrow \alpha, & \text{when } \eta = \varepsilon \text{ and } A \rightarrow \alpha \text{ is in } P; \\ \varepsilon, & \text{otherwise} \ . \end{cases}$$

In other words, $h_T$ maps all type 1 and type 2 rules to $\varepsilon$ and all type 3 rules $[A, \omega] \to \varepsilon$, where $A \to \omega$ is a rule in $P$, to the rule $A \to \omega$. The type 3 rule $[S', \perp S] \to \varepsilon$ is mapped to $\varepsilon$.

We shall show that $T_{\mathrm{LL}}(G)$ left-to-right covers $G$ with respect to the homomorphism $h_T$. For simplicity, we assume in the following that $G$ is $\varepsilon$-free. We leave it to the exercises to reformulate the lemmas so that they also apply to non-$\varepsilon$-free grammars.

**Lemma 8.79** *Let $G = (V, T, P, S)$ be an $\varepsilon$-free grammar, $G_\perp$ its $\perp$-augmented grammar, $Y$ a symbol in $V \cup \{\perp\}$, $[A, \alpha Y]$ a nonterminal of the transformed grammar $T_{\mathrm{LL}}(G)$, $x$ a string in $T^*$, $\pi_T$ a rule string of $T_{\mathrm{LL}}(G)$, and $r_T$ a rule of $T_{\mathrm{LL}}(G)$ such that*

(*a*) $$[A, \alpha Y] \xRightarrow[\mathrm{lm}]{\pi_T r_T} x \quad \text{in } T_{\mathrm{LL}}(G) .$$

*Then for some symbol $X \in V \cup \{\perp\}$ and string $\beta \in V^*$*

(*b*) $$[A, \alpha Y] \xRightarrow[\mathrm{lm}]{\pi_T} x[A, \alpha X\beta] \xRightarrow{r_T} x \quad \text{in } T_{\mathrm{LL}}(G) ,$$

$$X\beta \xRightarrow[\mathrm{rm}]{h_T(\pi_T)^R} Yx \quad \text{in } G_\perp .$$

*Proof.* The proof is by induction on the length of rule string $\pi_T$. If $\pi_T = \varepsilon$, $r_T$ is the rule $[A, \alpha Y] \to x$. Because $x \in T^*$, this rule must be of type 3, that is, $x = \varepsilon$ and $A \to \alpha Y$ is a rule of $G_\perp$. Statements (*b*) then hold if we choose $X = Y$ and $\beta = \varepsilon$.

Then let $|\pi_T| > 0$ and assume, as an induction hypothesis, that the lemma holds for rule strings shorter than $\pi_T$. We have two cases to consider, depending on the type of the first rule in $\pi_T$. Observe that this rule can only be of type 1 or of type 2, not of type 3.

*Case 1.* $1{:}\pi_T$ is a type 1 rule $r'_T = [A, \alpha Y] \to a[A, \alpha Ya]$, where $a$ is a terminal in $T$. Then $\pi_T$ can be written as $r'_T \pi'_T$ and $x$ can be written as $ax'$, where

$$[A, \alpha Ya] \xRightarrow[\mathrm{lm}]{\pi'_T r_T} x' \quad \text{in } T_{\mathrm{LL}}(G) .$$

By applying the induction hypothesis to this derivation we can conclude that for some symbol $X' \in V \cup \{\perp\}$ and string $\beta' \in V^*$

$$[A, \alpha Ya] \xRightarrow[\mathrm{lm}]{\pi'_T} x'[A, \alpha YX'\beta'] \xRightarrow[\mathrm{lm}]{r_T} x' \quad \text{in } T_{\mathrm{LL}}(G) ,$$

$$X'\beta' \xRightarrow[\mathrm{rm}]{h_T(\pi'_T)^R} ax' \quad \text{in } G_\perp .$$

But then we have:

$$[A, \alpha Y] \xRightarrow[\mathrm{lm}]{\pi_T} ax'[A, \alpha YX'\beta'] \xRightarrow[\mathrm{lm}]{r_T} ax' = x \quad \text{in } T_{\mathrm{LL}}(G) ,$$

$$YX'\beta' \xRightarrow[\mathrm{rm}]{h_T(\pi_T)^R} Yax' = Yx \quad \text{in } G_\perp .$$

Observe that $h_T(\pi_T)^R = h_T(r'_T\pi'_T)^R = h_T(\pi'_T)^R$, because $h_T(r'_T) = \varepsilon$ for the type 1 rule $r'_T$. We conclude that statements (*b*) hold when we choose $X = Y$ and $\beta = X'\beta'$.

*Case 2.* $1:\pi_T$ is of type 2. Since $G$ was assumed to be $\varepsilon$-free, this rule must be of the form $r'_T = [A, \alpha Y] \to [B, Y][A, \alpha B]$. Then $\pi_T r_T$ can be written as $r'_T\pi'_T r''_T \pi''_T r_T$ and $x$ can be written as $x'x''$, where

$$[B, Y] \xRightarrow[\text{lm}]{\pi'_T r''_T} x' \quad \text{and} \quad [A, \alpha B] \xRightarrow[\text{lm}]{\pi''_T r_T} x'' \quad \text{in } T_{\text{LL}}(G) .$$

By applying the induction hypothesis to these derivations we can conclude that for some symbols $X'$ and $X$ in $V \cup \{\perp\}$ and strings $\beta'$ and $\beta$ in $V^*$

$$[B, Y] \xRightarrow[\text{lm}]{\pi'_T} x'[B, X'\beta'] \xRightarrow[\text{lm}]{r''_T} x' \quad \text{in } T_{\text{LL}}(G) ,$$

$$X'\beta' \xRightarrow[\text{rm}]{h_T(\pi'_T)^R} Yx' \quad \text{in } G_\perp ,$$

$$[A, \alpha B] \xRightarrow[\text{lm}]{\pi''_T} x''[A, \alpha X\beta] \xRightarrow[\text{lm}]{r_T} x'' \quad \text{in } T_{\text{LL}}(G) ,$$

$$X\beta \xRightarrow[\text{rm}]{h_T(\pi''_T)^R} Bx'' \quad \text{in } G_\perp .$$

Then we have (recall that $r'_T\pi'_T r''_T\pi''_T = \pi_T$):

$$[A, \alpha Y] \xRightarrow[\text{lm}]{\pi_T} x'x''[A, \alpha X\beta] \xRightarrow[\text{lm}]{r_T} x'x'' = x \quad \text{in } T_{\text{LL}}(G) .$$

Because $r''_T = [B, X'\beta'] \to \varepsilon$ is a type 3 rule of $T_{\text{LL}}(G)$ and because $B \neq S'$, $r'' = B \to X'\beta'$ is a rule of $G$ satisfying $h_T(r''_T) = r''$. We have:

$$X\beta \xRightarrow[\text{rm}]{h_T(\pi''_T)^R} Bx'' \xRightarrow[\text{rm}]{r''} X'\beta'x'' \xRightarrow[\text{rm}]{h_T(\pi'_T)^R} Yx'x'' = Yx \quad \text{in } G_\perp .$$

Here $h_T(\pi''_T)^R r'' h_T(\pi'_T)^R = (h_T(r'_T)h_T(\pi'_T)h_T(r''_T)h_T(\pi''_T))^R = h_T(\pi_T)^R$, as desired. Observe that $h_T(r'_T) = \varepsilon$ for the type 2 rule $r'_T$. □

**Lemma 8.80** *$L(T_{\text{LL}}(G)) \subseteq L(G)$. Moreover, for any left parse $\pi'$ of sentence $w$ in $T_{\text{LL}}(G)$, $h_T(\pi')$ is a right parse of $w$ in $G$.*

*Proof.* When in Lemma 8.79 we choose $A = S'$, $\alpha = \varepsilon$, $Y = \perp$, $x = w$, and $\pi_T$ and $r_T$ such that $\pi_T r_T = \pi'$, we can conclude that for some symbol $X \in V \cup \{\perp\}$ and string $\beta \in V^*$

$$[S', \perp] \xRightarrow[\text{lm}]{\pi_T} w[S', X\beta] \xRightarrow[\text{lm}]{r_T} w \quad \text{in } T_{\text{LL}}(G), \text{ and}$$

$$X\beta \xRightarrow[\text{rm}]{h_T(\pi_T)^R} \perp w \quad \text{in } G_\perp .$$

Because here $X\beta$ is a right-hand side of a rule of $S'$, $X = \bot$ and $\beta = S$. Hence we have:

$$S \xRightarrow[\text{rm}]{h_T(\pi_T)^R} w \quad \text{in } G \ .$$

Here $h_T(\pi_T)^R = h_T(\pi_T r_T)^R = h_T(\pi')^R$, because $h_T(r_T) = \varepsilon$ for the rule $r_T = [S', \bot S] \to \varepsilon$. □

**Lemma 8.81** *Let $G = (V, T, P, S)$ be an $\varepsilon$-free grammar, $G_\bot$ its $\bot$-augmented grammar, $A$ a nonterminal of $G_\bot$ $\alpha$ and $\beta$ strings in $V^*$, $X$ and $Y$ symbols in $V \cup \{\bot\}$, $x$ a string in $T^*$, and $\pi$ a rule string in $P^*$ such that*

(*a*) $$A \xRightarrow[\text{rm}]{} \alpha X\beta \quad \textit{and} \quad X\beta \xRightarrow[\text{rm}]{\pi} Yx \quad \textit{in } G_\bot \ .$$

*Then the transformed grammar $T_{\text{LL}}(G)$ has a rule string $\pi_T$ such that*

(*b*) $$[A, \alpha Y] \xRightarrow[\text{lm}]{\pi_T} x[A, \alpha X\beta] \quad \textit{in } T_{\text{LL}}(G), \quad \textit{and} \quad h_T(\pi_T) = \pi^R \ .$$

*Proof.* The proof is by induction on the length of rule string $\pi$. If $\pi = \varepsilon$, statement (*a*) implies $X\beta = Yx$. Then by the construction of $T_{\text{LL}}(G)$,

$$[A, \alpha Y] \xRightarrow[\text{lm}]{\pi_T} x[A, \alpha Yx] = x[A, \alpha X\beta] \quad \text{in } T_{\text{LL}}(G) \ ,$$

where $\pi_T$ is an $|x|$-length string of rules of type 1. By the definition of $h_T$, $h_T(\pi_T) = \varepsilon$. Hence statement (*b*) holds, as desired.

Then let $|\pi| > 0$ and assume, as an induction hypothesis, that the lemma holds for rule strings shorter than $\pi$. There are two cases to consider, depending on whether or not the derivation $X\beta \xRightarrow[\text{rm}]{\pi} Yx$ implies that $X = Y$ and $\beta \xRightarrow[\text{rm}]{\pi} x$.

*Case 1.* One of the conditions $X = Y$ and $\beta \xRightarrow[\text{rm}]{\pi} x$ does not hold. Then the rightmost derivation $X\beta \xRightarrow[\text{rm}]{\pi} Yx$ can be decomposed (recall that $G$ was assumed to be $\varepsilon$-free) as:

$$X\beta \xRightarrow[\text{rm}]{\pi'} Bz \xRightarrow[\text{rm}]{r} Y\gamma z \xRightarrow[\text{rm}]{\pi''} Yyz = Yx \ .$$

Here $\pi'$ and $\pi''$ are rule strings and $r = B \to Y\gamma$ a rule such that $\pi' r \pi'' = \pi$. Then we have:

$$A \xRightarrow[\text{rm}]{} \alpha X\beta \quad \text{and} \quad X\beta \xRightarrow[\text{rm}]{\pi'} Bz \quad \text{in } G_\bot$$

and

$$B \xRightarrow[\text{rm}]{} Y\gamma \quad \text{and} \quad Y\gamma \xRightarrow[\text{rm}]{\pi''} Yy \quad \text{in } G_\bot \ .$$

By applying the induction hypothesis to these derivations we can conclude that

$$[A, \alpha B] \xRightarrow[\text{lm}]{\pi'_T} z[A, \alpha X\beta] \quad \text{in } T_{\text{LL}}(G) \quad \text{and} \quad h_T(\pi'_T) = (\pi')^R$$

and that

$$[B, Y] \xRightarrow[\text{lm}]{\pi''_T} y[B, Y\gamma] \quad \text{in } T_{\text{LL}}(G) \quad \text{and} \quad h_T(\pi''_T) = (\pi'')^R \ ,$$

for some rule strings $\pi'_T$ and $\pi''_T$ of $T_{\text{LL}}(G)$. On the other hand, $B \xRightarrow[\text{rm}]{} Y\gamma$ implies that $Y$ **starts** $B$, and $X\beta \xRightarrow[\text{rm}]{\pi'} Bz$ implies that $B$ **starts*** $X$. This means that $T_{\text{LL}}(G)$ has the type 2 rule

$$r'_T = [A, \alpha Y] \to [B, Y][A, \alpha B] \ .$$

Because $B \to Y\gamma$ is a rule of $G$, $T_{\text{LL}}(G)$ has the type 3 rule

$$r_T = [B, Y\gamma] \to \varepsilon \ .$$

Hence we get:

$$[A, \alpha Y] \xRightarrow[\text{lm}]{r'_T} [B, Y][A, \alpha B] \xRightarrow[\text{lm}]{\pi''_T} y[B, Y\gamma][A, \alpha B]$$

$$\xRightarrow[\text{lm}]{r_T} y[A, \alpha B] \xRightarrow[\text{lm}]{\pi'_T} yz[A, \alpha X\beta] = x[A, \alpha X\beta] \quad \text{in } T_{\text{LL}}(G) \ .$$

Here $h_T(r'_T \pi''_T r_T \pi'_T) = (\pi'')^R r(\pi')^R = (\pi' r \pi'')^R = \pi^R$. Observe that $h_T(r'_T) = \varepsilon$ and $h_T(r_T) = [B, Y\gamma] \to \varepsilon = r$. We conclude that statement (*b*) holds if we choose $\pi_T = r'_T \pi''_T r_T \pi'_T$.

*Case 2.* $X = Y$ and $\beta \xRightarrow[\text{rm}]{\pi} x$. Denote by $B$ the first nonterminal in $\beta$, that is, $\beta = yB\delta$, where $y \in T^*$ and $\delta \in V^*$. Then for some $Z \in T$ and $w \in T^*$,

$$B\delta \xRightarrow[\text{rm}]{\pi} Zw \quad \text{and} \quad yZw = x \ .$$

Now $\alpha X\beta = \alpha X y B\delta$, and we can conclude from Case 1 that

$$[A, \alpha X y Z] \xRightarrow[\text{lm}]{\pi'_T} w[A, \alpha X y B\delta] = w[A, \alpha X\beta] \quad \text{in } T_{\text{LL}}(G), \text{ and}$$

$$h_T(\pi'_T) = \pi^R \ ,$$

for some rule string $\pi'_T$ of $T_{\text{LL}}(G)$. On the other hand, because $yZ$ is in $T^*$, there is a $|yZ|$-length string of type 1 rules $\pi''_T$ such that

$$[A, \alpha X] \xRightarrow[\text{lm}]{\pi''_T} yZ[A, \alpha X y Z] \quad \text{in } T_{\text{LL}}(G) \ .$$

Hence we get:

$$[A, \alpha Y] = [A, \alpha X] \xRightarrow[\text{lm}]{\pi''_T} yZ[A, \alpha XyZ] \xRightarrow[\text{lm}]{\pi'_T} yZw[A, \alpha X\beta]$$

$$= x[A, \alpha X\beta] \quad \text{in } T_{\text{LL}}(G) \ .$$

Here $h_T(\pi''_T\pi'_T) = h_T(\pi'_T) = \pi^R$. We conclude that statement ($b$) holds if we choose $\pi_T = \pi''_T\pi'_T$. □

**Lemma 8.82** $L(G) \subseteq L(T_{\text{LL}}(G))$. *Moreover, for any right parse $\pi$ of sentence $w$ in $G$ there is a left parse $\pi'$ of $w$ in $T_{\text{LL}}(G)$ such that $h_T(\pi') = \pi$.*

*Proof.* When we choose in Lemma 8.81 $A = S'$, $\alpha = \varepsilon$, $X = Y = \bot$, $\beta = S$, and $x = w$, we can conclude that $T_{\text{LL}}(G)$ has a rule string $\pi_T$ such that

$$[S', \bot] \xRightarrow[\text{lm}]{\pi_T} w[S', \bot S] \quad \text{in } T_{\text{LL}}(G), \quad \text{and} \quad h_T(\pi_T) = \pi^R \ .$$

Then

$$[S', \bot] \xRightarrow[\text{lm}]{\pi_T r_T} w \quad \text{in } T_{\text{LL}}(G) \ ,$$

where $r_T$ denotes the rule $[S', \bot S] \to \varepsilon$. Moreover, $h_T(\pi_T r_T) = \pi^R$, because $h_T(r_T) = \varepsilon$. Hence it suffices to choose $\pi' = \pi_T r_T$. □

By Lemmas 8.80 and 8.82 we have:

**Theorem 8.83** ($T_{\text{LL}}(G), h_T$) *is a left-to-right cover of the given grammar G.* □

Theorem 8.83 implies that any left parser, e.g. the SLL($k$) parser, of $T_{\text{LL}}(G)$ can be used as a right parser of $G$.

In order to be useful the defined transformation should produce LL($k$) grammars from non-LL($k$) grammars. We say that a grammar $G$ is a *predictive LR($k$) grammar* (or a *PLR($k$) grammar*, for short), $k \geqslant 1$, if the transformed grammar $T_{\text{LL}}(G)$ is LL($k$).

**Proposition 8.84** (*Soisalon-Soininen*, 1977; *Soisalon-Soininen and Ukkonen*, 1980). *For any $k \geqslant 1$, the class of PLR($k$) grammars properly contains the class of LL($k$) grammars and is properly contained in the class of LR($k$) grammars.* □

We shall give an intuitive characterization of PLR($k$) grammars such that the relationship with LL($k$) and LR($k$) grammars becomes visible. By a *PLR($k$) parser* of a grammar $G$ we mean a pushdown transducer $(M, \tau h_T)$ where $(M, \tau)$ is an LL($k$) parser of $T_{\text{LL}}(G)$ and $h_T$ is the cover homomorphism. Let $A \to X\alpha$ be a rule of $G$

and let $w$, $x$, $y$, and $z$ be terminal strings such that in $G$

$$S \Rightarrow^* wAz, \quad X \Rightarrow^* x, \quad \text{and} \quad \alpha \Rightarrow^* y .$$

If $G$ is LL($k$), then its LL($k$) parser emits the rule $A \to X\alpha$ after scanning $w$ and seeing $k{:}xyz$. If $G$ is LR($k$), then its LR($k$) parser emits the rule $A \to X\alpha$ after scanning $wxy$ and seeing $k{:}z$. If $G$ is a PLR($k$) grammar, then its PLR($k$) parser recognizes the rule $A \to X\alpha$ with certainty as in the LR($k$) case, that is, after scanning $wxy$ and seeing $k{:}z$. However, the deterministic PLR($k$) parser recognizes with certainty the left-hand side $A$ of the rule $A \to X\alpha$ already at the point when it has scanned $wx$ and seen $k{:}yz$.

As no reduced left-recursive grammar is LL($k$) (Theorem 8.51), the following proposition is important in estimating the quality of the given transformation method in converting non-LL($k$) grammars into LL($k$) grammars.

**Proposition 8.85** (*Soisalon-Soininen*, 1979) *For any proper grammar $G$, the transformed grammar $T_{\mathrm{LL}}(G)$ is non-left-recursive.* □

A grammar is *left-factored* if it has no two distinct rules $A \to \alpha\beta_1 \mid \alpha\beta_2$, where $\alpha \neq \varepsilon$.

**Fact 8.86** For any grammar $G$, the transformed grammar $T_{\mathrm{LL}}(G)$ is left-factored. □

Left-factoring, that is, transforming grammars into left-factored form, is a standard method in attempting to obtain LL($k$) grammars. For instance, we may repeat the following procedure until the grammar is left-factored: Select a group, if there is any, of rules of the form

$$A \to \alpha\beta_1 \mid \alpha\beta_2 \mid \ldots \mid \alpha\beta_n ,$$

$|\alpha| > 0$, $n \geqslant 2$, and replace them by the rules

$$A \to \alpha A' ,$$

$$A' \to \beta_1 \mid \beta_2 \mid \ldots \mid \beta_n ,$$

where $A'$ is a new nonterminal.

The following theorem, the proof of which is left as an exercise, states that the process of constructing the transformed grammar $T_{\mathrm{LL}}(G)$ also involves the process of left-factoring.

**Theorem 8.87** *Left-factoring cannot produce a PLR($k$) grammar from a non-PLR($k$) grammar, and a PLR($k$) grammar cannot be converted into a non-PLR($k$) grammar by left-factoring.* □

## Exercises

8.1 Consider the grammar

$$S \to bAbb \mid aAab \ ,$$

$$A \to \varepsilon \mid a \ .$$

Show that this grammar is not SLL(2) but is SLL(3). Construct a deterministic left parser for this grammar by introducing "lookback" symbols to the actions of the SLL(2) parser.

8.2 Consider the stack strings of the SLL(2) parser of the grammar given in the previous exercise. Divide the stack strings into equivalence classes. Can you obtain a deterministic left parser for the grammar by replacing each nonterminal appearing in the actions of the SLL(2) parser by an appropriate equivalence class?

8.3 Prove Lemma 8.2.

8.4 Consider proving Lemma 8.5.

a) Give a proof that is analogous to that of Lemma 6.2 (and does not use Lemma 6.2).
b) Prove the lemma by using Lemmas 6.2 and 8.2.

8.5 Prove Lemma 8.7 without using Lemma 6.4.

8.6 Show that $\gamma$ is a viable suffix of grammar $G = (V, T, P, S)$ if and only if there is a string $x \in T^*$, a rule $A \to \omega$ in $P$, and a string $\delta \in V^*$ such that

$$S \underset{\text{lm}}{\Rightarrow^*} xA\delta \underset{\text{lm}}{\Rightarrow} x\omega\delta \quad \text{in } G$$

and $\gamma$ is a prefix of $(\omega\delta)^R$.

8.7 Give regular expressions to denote the sets of viable suffixes of the following grammars.

a) The grammar given in Exercise 8.1.
b) The grammar $E \to TE'$. $E' \to \varepsilon \mid +TE'$, $T \to FT'$,
$T' \to \varepsilon \mid *FT'$, $F \to a \mid (E)$ .

8.8 Give right-linear grammars to denote the sets of viable suffixes of the grammars of the previous exercise.

8.9 Prove Lemma 8.9.

8.10 Give the LL(2)-valid items for all viable suffixes of the grammar of Exercise 8.1.

8.11 Prove Lemma 8.15 and Theorem 8.16.

8.12 Give the LL(1)- and LL(2)-equivalence classes of the viable suffixes of the grammar of Exercise 8.1.

8.13 Prove Lemmas 8.18 and 8.20.

8.14 Prove Lemma 8.23.

8.15 Prove Lemmas 8.25 and 8.26.

8.16 Give the canonical LL(1) and LL(2) machines for the \$-augmented grammar of the grammar of Exercise 8.1.

8.17 Give the canonical LL(1) machine for the \$-augmented grammar of the grammar of Exercise 8.7(b).

8.18 Give the canonical LL(1) and LL(2) machines for the \$-augmented grammar of the grammar $G_{\mathbf{block}}$:

$$S \to E|B \ ,$$

$$E \to \varepsilon \ ,$$

$$B \to a|\mathbf{begin}\ S\ C\ \mathbf{end} \ ,$$

$$C \to \varepsilon|;SC \ .$$

(Cf. Chapter 5.)

8.19 Give a relational expression to compute $\mathbf{passes}_1$-$X$.

8.20 Prove Theorems 8.28 and 8.29.

8.21 Give the canonical LL(1) and LL(2) parsers for the grammar of Exercise 8.1. Simulate the parsers on all sentences in the language and on some non-sentences. Identify pairs of actions that cause nondeterminism.

8.22 Show that the canonical LL($k$) parser for the grammar $S \to a|bSA$, $A \to \varepsilon|cS$ is nondeterministic for all $k \geqslant 0$. For all $k \geqslant 0$, give a pair of actions of the canonical LL($k$) parser that cause nondeterminism.

8.23 Give the canonical LL(1) parser for the grammar of Exercise 8.7(b). Simulate the parser on the strings $\varepsilon$, $a$, $aa$, $(a$, $a + a * a + a$, and $((a * (a + a))$. (Cf. Exercise 5.14.)

8.24 Give the canonical LL(1) and LL(2) parsers for the grammar $G_{\text{block}}$ of Exercise 8.18. Compare the behaviour of the parsers on some nonsentences.

8.25 Prove Lemma 8.30.

8.26 Give the canonical LL(1), LALL(1), and SLL(1) parsers for the grammar

$$S \to aABb \mid Ac \ ,$$

$$A \to B \ ,$$

$$B \to \varepsilon \ .$$

Simulate the parsers on the nonsentence $ac$.

8.27 For all $n \geqslant 1$ let $G_n$ be the grammar with nonterminal alphabet $\{A_0, A_1, \ldots, A_n, B_1, \ldots, B_n, C_1, \ldots, C_n\}$, terminal alphabet $\{a_1, \ldots, a_n, b_1, \ldots, b_n, c_1, \ldots, c_n, d_1, \ldots, d_n\}$, start symbol $A_0$, and the following rules:

$$A_i \to a_{i+1} A_{i+1} B_{i+1} \mid d_{i+1} A_{i+1} C_{i+1} \qquad (0 \leqslant i \leqslant n-1) \ ,$$

$$A_n \to b_i \mid \varepsilon \qquad (1 \leqslant i \leqslant n) \ ,$$

$$B_i \to b_i c_i \mid \varepsilon \qquad (1 \leqslant i \leqslant n) \ ,$$

$$C_i \to c_i \mid \varepsilon \qquad (1 \leqslant i \leqslant n) \ .$$

Show the following:

a) $G_n$ is LL(2) but not SLL(2).

b) There is a constant $c > 0$ such that the size of the canonical LL(2) machine for $G_n$ is at least $2^{cn}$ for all $n \geqslant 1$.

c) If $G_n$ has a deterministic left parser of size $s(n)$, then it has a deterministic right parser of size $O(s(n))$.

d) There is a constant $c > 0$ and a natural number $n_0$ such that when $n > n_0$ any deterministic right parser of $G_n$ has size at least $2^{cn}$.

e) There is a constant $c > 0$ and a natural number $n_0$ such that when $n > n_0$ any deterministic left parser of $G_n$ has size at least $2^{cn}$.

Claims (d) and (e) mean that LL($k$) grammars are exponentially more succinct language descriptions than deterministic right and left parsers.

8.28 Consider factoring out the symbols $[\delta]_k$ from produce actions

$$[\delta]_k[\delta A]_k \mid y \to [\delta]_k[\delta X_n]_k \ldots [\delta X_n \ldots X_1]_k \mid y$$

of the canonical LL($k$) parser. Show that the resulting parser remains deterministic if the original parser is so, provided that the following requirement is satisfied for all viable suffixes $\delta A$ and rules $A \to X_1 \ldots X_n$ ($n \geqslant 1$): $[\gamma X_n]_k = [\delta X_n]_k$ for all strings $\gamma$ satisfying $[\gamma A]_k = [\delta A]_k$.

8.29 Factor out the symbols $[\delta]_k$ from the produce actions of the canonical LL(1) parser of Exercise 8.23 and implement the parser using the techniques discussed in Section 5.6.

8.30 Design a recursive-descent-like technique to implement canonical LL($k$) parsers (in their general form). Apply your technique to the canonical LL(1) parser of the grammar of Figure 8.6.

8.31 Consider a simplification of the canonical LL($k$) parser obtained by replacing in the actions each class $[\delta a]_k$, $a \in T$, by the terminal $a$ itself. Show that you still get a valid left parser for the grammar and that this parser is deterministic if and only if the original parser is so. Also show that the simplification may deteriorate the error detection capability of the parser so that when $k > 1$ the simplified parser may perform more parsing actions (even shift actions) than does the original parser, before detecting an error in a nonsentence.

Consider an alternative formulation of the canonical LL($k$) parser, called the *Lewis–Stearns canonical LL*($k$) *parser*. This formulation has the advantage that in the produce actions only the topmost symbol in the stack is consulted. In implementing Lewis–Stearns canonical LL(1) parsers we can use exactly the same techniques as those used to implement SLL(1) parsers (see Section 5.6).

The stack alphabet of the Lewis–Stearns canonical LL($k$) parser for grammar $G = (V, T, P, S)$ consists of pairs $[X, R]$ in which $X$ is a symbol in $V$ and $R$ is a subset of $\text{FOLLOW}'_k(X)$. The initial stack contents are $[S, \{k{:}\$\}]$ and the set of final stack contents is $\{\varepsilon\}$. For each pair $[a, R]$, $a \in T$, and string $y$ in $\max\{k-1, 0\}{:}R$ the parser has the shift action

$$[a, R] \mid ay \rightarrow \mid y\ .$$

For each pair $[A, R]$, $A \in V \setminus T$, rule $A \rightarrow X_1 \ldots X_n$ in $P$, and string $y$ in $\text{FIRST}_k(X_1 \ldots X_n R)$ the parser has the produce action

$$[A, R] \mid y \rightarrow [X_n, R_n] \ldots [X_1, R_1] \mid y\ ,$$

where $R_n = R$ and $R_i = \text{FIRST}_k(X_{i+1} \ldots X_n R)$ for $i < n$.

8.32 Consider the Lewis–Stearns canonical LL($k$) parser defined above.
   a) Give an algorithm to construct the actions of the parser from the canonical LL($k$) machine.
   b) Apply your algorithm to the canonical LL(2) machine of the grammar $G'_{abL}$ (Figure 8.3).
   c) Simulate the parser of $G_{abL}$ on some typical sentences.

8.33 Give the Lewis–Stearns canonical LL(1) parser for the grammar of Exercise 8.7(b).

8.34 Implement the parser of the previous exercise using the techniques discussed in Section 5.6.

8.35 State and prove the counterparts of Lemmas 8.30 to 8.34 for Lewis–Stearns canonical LL($k$) parsers.

8.36 Show that a Lewis–Stearns canonical LL($k$) parser is deterministic if and only if our formulation of the canonical LL($k$) parser is so.

8.37 Derive an upper bound on the size of the Lewis–Stearns canonical LL($k$) parser. Can you obtain a sharper bound when the grammar is $\varepsilon$-free?

8.38 Define the notion of "Lewis–Stearns LA($k$)LL($l$) parser". Give the actions of the Lewis–Stearns LA(2)LL(1) parser for the grammar $G_{abL}$.

8.39 Consider a simplification of the Lewis–Stearns canonical LL($k$) parser obtained by replacing in the actions each pair $[a, R]$, $a \in T$, by the terminal $a$ itself. Show that you still get a valid left parser for the grammar and that this parser is deterministic if and only if the original parser is so. Also show that the simplification may deteriorate the error detection capability when $k > 1$.

8.40 Prove that for all $m \geqslant 1$ the grammar

$$S \to aAa^m b \mid bAb \ ,$$

$$A \to cAB \mid \varepsilon \mid a^m \ ,$$

$$B \to \varepsilon$$

is an LA($m+1$)LL($m+1$) grammar. Also prove that this grammar is not LA($k$)LL($m$) for any $k \geqslant m \geqslant 1$.

8.41 Prove or disprove the following: For any $k \geqslant 1$, any LA($k$)LL(1) grammar is LA($k$)LL(0).

8.42 Show that any LALL(0) or LL(0) grammar generates at most one sentence.

8.43 Prove Lemma 8.40.

8.44 Prove that for $k > 1$ the grammar

$$S \to aAa^{k-1}b \mid bAbb \mid ca^{2k-2}b \ ,$$

$$A \to \varepsilon \mid a^{k-1}$$

is LALL($k$) but not SLL($k$).

8.45 Prove or disprove the following: Every $\varepsilon$-free LL(2) grammar is also an SLL(2) grammar.

8.46 Construct a structurally equivalent SLL(2) grammar for the grammar given in Exercise 8.1.

8.47 Prove Lemmas 8.43 and 8.44.

8.48 Can you define a correspondence between the induced viable prefixes in grammar $G$ and the induced viable suffixes in $G^R$, the reversal of $G$? (Cf. Lemma 8.3.)

8.49 Can you characterize the LL($k$) property of grammar $G$ by means of the canonical LR($k$) machine for $G$?

8.50 Prove that the grammar $S \rightarrow aA|bBd$, $A \rightarrow Be|Cd$, $B \rightarrow b|\varepsilon$, $C \rightarrow c|\varepsilon$ is SLL(1) but is not SLR($k$) for any $k$.

8.51 Prove that the grammar $S \rightarrow aA|bB$, $A \rightarrow Cc|Dd$, $B \rightarrow Cd|Dc$, $C \rightarrow FE$, $D \rightarrow FH$, $E \rightarrow \varepsilon$, $F \rightarrow \varepsilon$, $H \rightarrow \varepsilon$ is SLL(1) but is not LALR($k$) for any $k$.

8.52 Show that every reduced $\varepsilon$-free LL(1) grammar is LR(0).

8.53 Show that every reduced LL(1) grammar in which no nonterminal derives only $\varepsilon$ is an LALR(1) grammar.

8.54 Show that for $k \geqslant 2$ there are reduced $\varepsilon$-free LL($k$) grammars that are not LALR($k$).

We say that a grammar is *left-parsable* if it has a deterministic left parser. A grammar is *right-parsable* if it has a deterministic right parser.

8.55 Show that the grammar $S \rightarrow A|B$, $A \rightarrow aaA|aa$, $B \rightarrow aaB|a$ is LR(1) and left-parsable but not LL($k$) for any $k$.

8.56 Show that the grammar $S \rightarrow Ab|Ac$, $A \rightarrow AB|a$, $B \rightarrow a$ is LR(1) but not left-parsable.

8.57 Show that the grammar $S \rightarrow Ab|Bc$, $A \rightarrow Aa|a$, $B \rightarrow Ba|a$ is both left- and right-parsable but is not LR($k$) for any $k$.

8.58 Show that the grammar $S \rightarrow Ab|Bc$, $A \rightarrow AC|a$, $B \rightarrow BC|a$, $C \rightarrow a$ is right-parsable but is neither LR($k$) for any $k$ nor left-parsable.

8.59 Show that the grammar $S \rightarrow BAb|CAc$, $A \rightarrow BA|a$, $B \rightarrow a$, $C \rightarrow a$ is left-parsable but not right-parsable.

8.60 For a grammar $G = (V, T, P, S)$ define $\hat{G} = (V \cup P, T, \hat{P}, S)$ to be the grammar where

$$\hat{P} = \{A \rightarrow (A, \omega)\omega \,|\, A \rightarrow \omega \in P\}$$
$$\cup \{(A, \omega) \rightarrow \varepsilon \,|\, A \rightarrow \omega \in P\} \ .$$

Show that $\hat{G}$ is LR($k$) if and only if $G$ is LL($k$).

8.61 Prove Lemmas 8.61 and 8.63.

8.62 Construct the nondeterministic LL(0) and LL(1) machines for the grammar $E \to TE'$, $E' \to \varepsilon \mid +TE'$, $T \to a \mid (E)$.

8.63 Define the relations **includes** and **directly-reads** for the canonical LL(0) machine for $G'$ as follows:

$q_1$ **includes** $q_2$, if for some state $q'$ and rule $A \to \omega$ of $G$,
$\text{GOTO}(q', A) = q_1$ and $\text{GOTO}(q', \omega^R) = q_2$ .

$q$ **directly-reads** $a$, if $q$ contains an item of the form $[A \to \alpha \cdot a\beta]$ .

Show that for an ε-free grammar, $a$ is in LALL($q$) if and only if $q$ **includes*** **directly-reads** $a$. Show that this statement does not always hold if the grammar is not ε-free. *Hint*: Consider the grammar $S \to ABa \mid ABb$, $A \to \varepsilon$, $B \to CD$, $C \to \varepsilon$, $D \to \varepsilon$.

8.64 Show that the grammar $E \to E + a \mid a$ is not $x$-to-$y$ covered for any $x, y \in \{$"left", "right"$\}$ by the grammar $E \to a + E \mid a$.

8.65 Consider the grammars $G_{\text{exp}}: E \to E + T \mid T$, $T \to T * F \mid F$, $F \to a \mid (E)$ and $\hat{G}_{\text{exp}}: E \to TE'$, $E' \to +TE' \mid \varepsilon$, $T \to FT'$, $T' \to *FT' \mid \varepsilon$, $F \to a \mid (E)$. Show that $\hat{G}_{\text{exp}}$ does not $x$-to-$y$ cover $G_{\text{exp}}$ for any $x, y \in \{$"left", "right"$\}$.

8.66 Modify the algorithm of Figure 8.12 for left recursion removal so that no ε-rules are introduced.

8.67 Prove Lemma 8.74.

8.68 Show that the grammar $\hat{G}_N$ (Section 8.6) right-to-right covers $G$.

8.69 Show that any left-linear grammar can be left-to-right covered by a right-linear grammar.

8.70 Show that a left-to-left and right-to-left cover can be achieved in grammatical transformations, if a marker is attached to the beginning of each right-hand side of the original rules, and the markers are then carried along in the transformations. Cf. the method in which Theorem 8.77 was derived. Explain why we cannot derive in this way the result that every proper grammar is left-to-left and right-to-left covered by a non-left-recursive grammar.

8.71 Show that for some grammars with ε-rules the algorithm of Figure 8.12 does not remove left recursion. Can you, however, relax the requirement of ε-freedom in a meaningful way such that the algorithm of Figure 8.12 still removes left recursion? Can this relaxed condition be used for Theorem 8.77, that is, does Theorem 8.77 still hold when this new condition is substituted for the requirement that the grammar is ε-free?

8.72 For the grammar $G_{exp}$ (Exercise 8.65) construct the transformed grammar $T_{LL}(G_{exp})$.

8.73 Compare the efficiencies of the SLR(1) parser and the PLR(1) parser of $G_{exp}$. To do this define suitable elementary operations each of which requires one unit of time. How do the various possible optimizations for each parser affect the comparison? What are your results for parsing the sentence $a * (a + a)$?

8.74 Reformulate Lemmas 8.79 and 8.81 so that they also apply to non-ε-free grammars.

8.75 Prove Proposition 8.84.

8.76 Prove Proposition 8.85.

8.77 Prove Theorem 8.87.

*Left-corner parsing* is another way of parsing context-free languages which is different from both left and right parsing. Left-corner parsing was used in some early compilers of programming languages. We describe this parsing method by an example. Consider the grammar

$$E \to T | E + T \ ,$$

$$T \to a | (E) \ ,$$

and the sentence $(a + a)$, whose derivation tree is depicted in Figure 8.13. The right parse of this sentence is

$$(T \to a)(E \to T)(T \to a)(E \to E + T)(T \to (E))(E \to T) \ ,$$

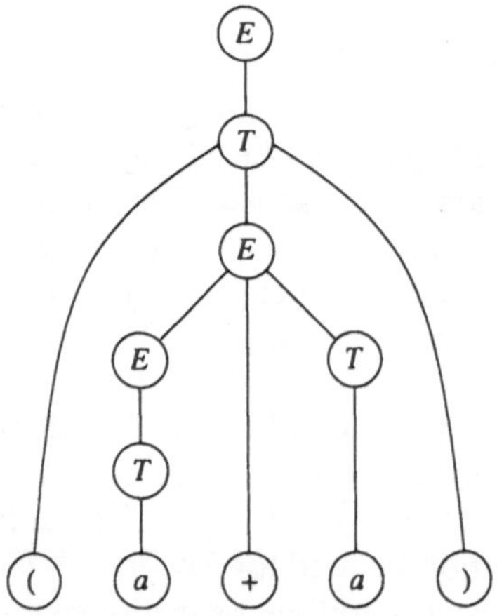


**Figure 8.13** Derivation tree of $(a + a)$

the left parse

$$(E \to T)(T \to (E))(E \to E + T)(E \to T)(T \to a)(T \to a) \ ,$$

and the *left-corner parse*

$$(T \to (E))(T \to a)(E \to T)(E \to E + T)(T \to a)(E \to T) \ .$$

In left-corner parsing the *left-corner* $X$ of each rule $A \to X\beta$ is recognized by the method of right parsing, the rule $A \to X\beta$ itself by the method of left parsing, and the suffix $\beta$ of the right-hand side of the rule by the method of left-corner parsing.

A left-corner parser of the grammar $E \to E + T | T$, $T \to a | (E)$ is given in the following. The parser uses lookahead of length 1.

| action $r$: | output $\tau(r)$: |
|---|---|
| $E \mid a \to [E, T] a \mid a$ | $T \to a$ |
| $E \mid ( \to [E, T] ) E ( \mid ($ | $T \to (E)$ |
| $[E, T] \mid + \to [E, E] \mid +$ | $E \to T$ |
| $[E, T] \mid ) \to [E, E] \mid )$ | $E \to T$ |
| $[E, T] \mid \$ \to [E, E] \mid \$$ | $E \to T$ |
| $[E, E] \mid + \to [E, E] T + \mid +$ | $E \to E + T$ |
| $[E, E] \mid ) \to \ \mid )$ | $\varepsilon$ |
| $[E, E] \mid \$ \to \ \mid \$$ | $\varepsilon$ |
| $T \mid a \to [T, T] a \mid a$ | $T \to a$ |
| $T \mid ( \to [T, T] ) E ( \mid ($ | $T \to (E)$ |
| $[T, T] \mid + \to \ \mid +$ | $\varepsilon$ |
| $[T, T] \mid ) \to \ \mid )$ | $\varepsilon$ |
| $[T, T] \mid \$ \to \ \mid \$$ | $\varepsilon$ |
| $a \mid a \to \ \mid$ | $\varepsilon$ |
| $( \mid ( \to \ \mid$ | $\varepsilon$ |
| $) \mid ) \to \ \mid$ | $\varepsilon$ |
| $+ \mid + \to \ \mid$ | $\varepsilon$ |

The sentence $(a + a)$ is parsed as follows:

| configuration: | rule output: |
|---|---|
| $\$E \mid (a + a)\$$ | |
| $\Rightarrow \$[E, T])E( \mid (a + a)\$$ | $T \to (E)$ |

| configuration: | rule output: |
|---|---|
| $\Rightarrow \$[E, T])E \mid a + a)\$$ | |
| $\Rightarrow \$[E, T])[E, T]a \mid a + a)\$$ | $T \to a$ |
| $\Rightarrow \$[E, T])[E, T] \mid + a)\$$ | |
| $\Rightarrow \$[E, T])[E, E] \mid + a)\$$ | $E \to T$ |
| $\Rightarrow \$[E, T])[E, E]T + \mid + a)\$$ | $E \to E + T$ |
| $\Rightarrow \$[E, T])[E, E]T \mid a)\$$ | |
| $\Rightarrow \$[E, T])[E, E][T, T]a \mid a)\$$ | $T \to a$ |
| $\Rightarrow \$[E, T])[E, E][T, T] \mid )\$$ | |
| $\Rightarrow \$[E, T])[E, E] \mid )\$$ | |
| $\Rightarrow \$[E, T]) \mid )\$$ | |
| $\Rightarrow \$[E, T] \mid \$$ | |
| $\Rightarrow \$[E, E] \mid \$$ | $E \to T$ |
| $\Rightarrow \$ \mid \$$ | |

Observe, for example, how the action $E \mid ( \to [E, T])E( \mid$ (demonstrates the way left-corner parsing is implemented. The parse is started from the root $E$ of the derivation tree, and when is seen as the next input symbol, the rule $T \to (E)$ is recognized. The symbol $[E, T]$ put on the pushdown stack below the reverse of the right-hand side $(E)$ contains information about the left-hand side of the rule just recognized and also about the current goal of parsing, that is, the root of the subtree to be built. The symbol $[E, T]$ indicates that $T$ must be connected with $E$ by a path in the derivation tree, and that each node in this path is labelled by the left-corner of some rule.

Also observe that in the above left-corner parser the left-hand sides of the actions always contain only one stack symbol. This means that in fact this left-corner parser is an SLL(1) parser of some grammar whose nonterminals are the stack symbols of the parser. Indeed, left-corner parsing suggests the following transformation of grammars, when non-LL($k$) grammars are to be converted into LL($k$) grammars.

Let $G = (V, T, P, S)$ be a grammar. First recall the definition of the relation **starts**:

$$X \textbf{ starts } A \ ,$$

if $G$ has a rule $A \to \omega$ with $1{:}\omega = X$. We define for $G$ the *goal-corner transformed grammar* $T_C(G)$ as the grammar with alphabet

$$V \cup \{[B, A] \mid A \in V \setminus T,\ A \textbf{ starts}^+ B, \text{ and } B \text{ does not appear only as a left corner of rules of } G\} \ ,$$

terminal alphabet $T$, start symbol $S$, and set of rules

$$\{A \to \omega[B, A] \mid A \to \omega \in P, \text{ and } 1:\omega \in T \cup \{\varepsilon\}\}$$
$$\cup \{[B, A] \to \alpha[B, A'] \mid A' \to A\alpha \in P\}$$
$$\cup \{[B, B] \to \varepsilon\} \ .$$

We say that a grammar $G$ is an *LC*($k$) *grammar*, $k \geqslant 1$, if the goal-corner transformed grammar $T_C(G)$ is LL($k$); cf. the definition of PLR($k$) grammars.

Let $h_C$ be the homomorphism from the rule strings of $T_C(G)$ to the rule strings of $G$ defined by:

$$h_C(A \to \omega[B, A]) = A \to \omega \ ,$$
$$h_C([B, A] \to \alpha[B, A']) = A' \to A\alpha \ ,$$
$$h_C([B, B] \to \varepsilon) = \varepsilon \ .$$

Now if $(M, \tau)$ is an LL($k$) parser of $T_C(G)$, the pushdown transducer $(M, \tau h_C)$ is called the *LC*($k$) *parser* of $G$.

8.78 Try to characterize the class of LC($k$) grammars intuitively in the same way as PLR($k$) grammars were characterized in Section 8.7. What is the relationship between the LC($k$) and the PLR($k$) grammar classes implied by your intuitive characterization?

8.79 Construct the goal-corner transformed grammar for the grammar $S \to i \leftarrow A \mid i \leftarrow B$, $A \to A{*}P \mid P$, $B \to A = A$, $P \to i \mid (A)$. Is the resulting grammar LL(1)? If not, can you obtain an LL(1) grammar by left-factoring?

8.80 Show that the goal-corner transformed grammar does not always *x-to-y* cover the original grammar for any $x, y \in \{$"left", "right"$\}$.

8.81 Show that a left-factored grammar is LC($k$) if and only if it is PLR($k$).

8.82 Show that for two different sentences the left-corner parse produced by a left-corner parser may be the same. That is, the left-corner parse does not always define uniquely a corresponding derivation tree. *Hint*: Consider the grammar $A \to aAb \mid Ac \mid c$.

8.83 Consider the grammar $A \to aAbB \mid AcB \mid cB$, $B \to \varepsilon$ obtained from the grammar of the previous exercise by adding a new nonterminal that marks the end of the rules and derives only the empty string. Show that in this grammar the left-corner parses and derivation trees have a unique correspondence. Also show (informally) that for any grammar, when the ending of the rules is marked in this way, the left-corner parses and derivation trees have a unique correspondence.

8.84 Show that for any proper grammar the goal-corner transformed grammar is not left-recursive.

## Bibliographic Notes

The theory of LL($k$) parsing was initiated by Lewis and Stearns (1966, 1968) and by Knuth (1967, 1971). They were the first to define the class of LL($k$) grammars. Initially, these grammars were called "TD($k$) grammars" (Top-Down grammars) by Lewis and Stearns (1966). Knuth (1967, 1971) suggested the term "LL($k$)", as an analog of his LR($k$) grammars. Soon after the introduction of LL($k$) grammars Rosenkrantz and Stearns (1970) studied extensively the constructive properties of these grammars as well as the properties of LL($k$) languages. Indeed, most of the important results on LL($k$) grammars and languages can be found in the paper by Rosenkrantz and Stearns (1970). Some of these results were independently established by Kurki-Suonio (1967, 1969) and Wood (1969b, 1970).

The presentation of LL($k$) parsing adopted in this chapter follows Sippu and Soisalon-Soininen (1982). The formulation of the canonical LL($k$) parser differs somewhat from that originally presented by Lewis and Stearns (1966, 1968). (Using our notation, we have presented the Lewis–Stearns canonical LL($k$) parser in the exercises.) Rosenkrantz and Stearns (1970) gave a transformation of LL($k$) grammars into structurally equivalent SLL($k$) grammars (Theorem 8.48) and used the SLL($k$) parser of the transformed grammar as a parser of the original grammar. The canonical LL($k$) parser presented by Aho and Ullman (1972b) is a modification of that presented by Lewis and Stearns (1966, 1968). The notions of LA($k$)LL($l$) parser and LALL($k$) parser come from Sippu and Soisalon-Soininen (1982).

The existence of deterministic left and right parsers for grammars is studied by Aho and Ullman (1973a), from whom come the grammars presented in Exercises 8.55 to 8.59. The fact that the size of the smallest deterministic left parser of an LL($k$) grammar can grow exponentially in the size of the grammar (Exercise 8.27) was observed by Ukkonen (1981, 1983). The fact that $\varepsilon$-free LL($k$) grammars have a deterministic left parser of polynomial size (Exercise 8.37) is stated in Rosenkrantz and Stearns (1970).

The result that every LL($k$) grammar is also an LR($k$) grammar was first suggested by Knuth (1967, 1971). Proofs of the result are given, for example, by Aho and Ullman (1973a), Soisalon-Soininen (1980b), and Nijholt (1982a); for a survey of the literature on the problem, see Nijholt (1982a). In our proof we have followed the ideas presented in Aho and Ullman (1973a) and Soisalon-Soininen (1980b) (also see Soisalon-Soininen, 1977b). The result that the family of LL($k$) languages is properly contained in the family of deterministic languages (Theorem 8.59) comes from Lewis and Stearns (1968) and Rosenkrantz and Stearns (1970). Theorem 8.60 and Exercises 8.50 to 8.54, which show the incomparability of SLL($k$) and LALR($k$) grammars, are from Beatty (1982) (also see Hunt and Szymanski, 1978).

The standard method for eliminating left recursion from grammars comes from Greibach (1965). Foster (1968) reports an LL(1) parser generator system in which left recursion elimination was done as a preprocessing task. Kurki-Suonio (1966) and Foster (1968) noted that semantic actions can be carried along in the transformations. In other words, for a large class of grammars left recursion can be eliminated so that a covering grammar is produced (Soisalon-Soininen, 1979). In our presentation of the results we follow Soisalon-Soininen (1979). For a survey of the results on grammatical covering, see Nijholt (1980a, 1980b).

The PLR($k$) grammars have been studied by Soisalon-Soininen and Ukkonen (1979). A similar class of grammars with the property that the grammars in the class may be transformed into LL($k$) form is given by Hammer (1974). Hammer's transformation method is even more general, though more complex, than that induced by the PLR($k$) grammars. The LC($k$) grammars by Rosenkrantz and Lewis (1970) are closely related to PLR($k$) grammars, but, in contrast to PLR($k$) grammars, the transformation for LC($k$) grammars does not produce a covering LL($k$) grammar.

Among the notable results on LL($k$) parsing not considered in this chapter is the solvability of the equivalence problem for LL($k$) languages. This was already established by Rosenkrantz and Stearns (1970). They showed that given a pair of arbitrary LL($k$) grammars $G_1$, $G_2$ it can be tested whether or not $L(G_1) = L(G_2)$. (For LR($k$) languages it is not known whether or not the equivalence problem is solvable.)

Beatty (1980) has developed iteration theorems, or "pumping lemmas", by which non-LL($k$) languages can be characterized (also see Nijholt, 1983b).

Various extensions of the LL($k$) parsing method have been proposed. Some of these are analogs of corresponding extensions of the LR($k$) parsing method. These include the LL($k$) parsing of extended context-free grammars (also called regular-right-part grammars, see the exercises of Chapter 6), which is studied by Lewi, De Vlaminck, Huens and Huybrechts (1978), Heilbrunner (1979), and Heckmann (1986). LL($k$)-like extensions of the class of strict deterministic grammars by Harrison and Havel (1973) are considered by Lomet (1969) and Pittl (1977, 1981b), and by Friede (1979). LL-like parsers using unbounded lookahead are studied by Čulik (1968), Jarzabek and Krawczyk (1975), Nijholt (1976, 1982b, 1982c), and by Poplawski (1979).

The elements of the theory of LL($k$) parsing can be found in every monograph on compiler design. However, in most of these monographs the presentation is restricted to SLL(1) parsing. A comprehensive presentation of the classical results of LL($k$) parsing can be found in Aho and Ullman (1972b, 1973a). Nijholt (1983a) has compiled an extensive bibliography on LL($k$) parsing.

# 9. Syntax Error Handling

In the previous chapters we have seen that the various parsers discussed, at least whenever they are deterministic, detect an error in any nonsentence. This means, that on any nonsentence there is a computation ending with an error configuration. For practical parsers, mere error detection is not enough; the parser should also emit a meaningful error message and recover from the error. A recovery means that the error configuration is transformed into a non-error configuration at which normal parsing can be resumed. Moreover, the transformation should be done so that as few input symbols as possible will be discarded. The goal of the error recovery is to maximize the amount of input text that can be handled in normal parsing mode and thus to detect as many errors as possible. On the other hand, the error recovery should be designed so that as few extraneous messages as possible will be emitted: only actual errors should be reported. Unfortunately, these goals are often contradictory: being able to detect and report many errors will often cause many extraneous error messages, and few extraneous error messages may imply undetected errors. Also it should be noted that a formal analysis of the quality of an error recovery method is difficult, if not impossible, because of the obvious ambiguity in the meaning of the phrase "actual error".

In Section 9.1 we shall consider the various definitions of errors and demonstrate how errors detected by parsers often differ from actual errors. Error recovery methods for LL(1) parsing are presented in Section 9.2, and for LR(1) parsing in Section 9.3. Finally, the reporting of syntax errors is discussed in Section 9.4.

## 9.1 Syntax Errors

There are two problems in defining what is meant by a syntax error. First, *actual errors*, that is, syntax errors made by the programmer when coding his program, are not a well-defined concept at all. Second, any formal definition of actual errors is likely to conflict with the way they are detected by a particular parser. Thus we have to consider two different definitions of syntax errors: one for approximating actual errors and another for describing errors encountered by a particular parser or a particular class of parsers. The former definition only depends on the language in question, whereas the latter definition reflects the behaviour of an individual parser, or more generally, the characteristics of a parsing technique.

*Minimum distance errors*

The formal definition usually agreed to yield the best approximation for actual errors is based on the concept of *Hamming distance* between two strings. The Hamming distance is the minimum number of elementary edit operations needed to transform one string into another. The edit operations usually considered are insertions, deletions, and replacements of single symbols. Sometimes also transpositions of adjacent symbols are taken as edit operations.

The number of *minimum distance errors* in string $x$ with respect to a nonempty language $L$ is defined as the Hamming distance between $x$ and the nearest sentence $y$ in $L$. For example, the erroneous Pascal statement

**begin** $A = E$ **then begin** $I := 1$ **end else** $J := 2$ **end**

has one minimum distance error: a keyword **if** is missing between **begin** and $A$.

Note that in the above example even the location of the error is uniquely defined, although all we did was to define the number of minimum distance errors. However, in the general case there are often several ways of mapping an erroneus string into the language, even when the number of edit operations used is the number of minimum distance errors. A trivial example of this is the case of unbalanced parentheses, where a correct string is obtained by either deleting or inserting a parenthesis. As another example consider the erroneous Pascal statement

$I := 3I4$ ;

in which the error can be considered to be at the number 3 or at the identifier $I4$, because a correct statement is obtained by deleting either 3 or $I4$, or by inserting an operator between 3 and $I4$.

*Correct prefix property*

Let us consider the behaviour of a right parser, such as an LR(1) parser, in the case of an erroneous string. All proper parsers have the property that when given any string not in the language they eventually detect an error in it and halt. A proof of the fact that the canonical LR($k$) parser of an LR($k$) grammar does not loop forever on any input string, that is, halts on every input, is given in Chapter 6 (Section 6.4, Theorem 6.44). This result holds for any deterministic LR($k$) parser, $k \geqslant 1$ (see the exercises in Chapter 6), as well as for any deterministic LL($k$) parser, $k \geqslant 1$ (see Chapters 5 and 8).

In the case of LR(1) parsing the error in the incorrect Pascal statement

**begin** $A = E$ **then begin** $I := 1$ **end else** $J := 2$ **end**

will be detected when **begin** and $A$ have been shifted and $A$ has been reduced to the nonterminal denoting the left-hand side of an assignment statement. We assume that the assignment statement is defined by the rule

$$AssignStatement \rightarrow Variable \text{ ':=' } Expression \ ,$$

where *Variable* has the rule *Variable* → *Identifier*. Thus the parsing configuration at the point of error detection (the stack string is denoted by the corresponding viable prefix) is:

$$\$ \textbf{ begin } Variable \mid = E \textbf{ then begin } I := 1 \textbf{ end else } J := 2 \textbf{ end } \$$$

$$* := \text{expected.}$$

Here the asterix denotes the location of the input at which the scanner would start to extract the next token. The associated text is the "declarative" error message issued by the parser. (Error messages are discussed in detail in Section 9.4.)

The point of error detection in the above example clearly disagrees with the location of the minimum distance error. The parsing has advanced up to the point in which $A$ has been reduced to *Variable*, and in this situation the parser expects to be recognizing an assignment statement and therefore announces that an assign arrow is required. The error has been detected at the token '=' because the parsing has been continued as long as possible. In general we say that the *parser-defined error* in an incorrect string is the symbol immediately following the longest sentence prefix of the string. More formally, the parser-defined error in an incorrect string $w = xy$ is the pair $(|x|, 1:y)$ or simply $1:y$, if $x$ is the longest prefix of $w$ which is a prefix of some sentence in the language. In our example the parser-defined error is clearly '='.

Let $M$ be a pushdown automaton with initial stack contents $\gamma_s$. We say that $M$ has the *correct prefix property* if the statement

$$\$\gamma_s \mid xy\$ \Rightarrow^* \$\gamma \mid y\$$$

can be true in $M$ only if $x$ is a prefix of some sentence in $L(M)$. Moreover, $M$ has the *longest correct prefix property* if $M$ has the correct prefix property and for any terminal string $xy$ in which $x$ is a prefix of some sentence in $L(M)$ there is a stack string $\gamma$ such that

$$\$\gamma_s \mid xy\$ \Rightarrow^* \$\gamma \mid y\$ \quad \text{in } M \ .$$

That is, any computation on a nonsentence can be continued up to the parser-defined error.

**Theorem 9.1** *For $k \geqslant 0$, any LR($k$) parser of a reduced grammar has the correct prefix property.*

*Proof.* Let $M$ be an LR($k$) parser of a reduced grammar $G = (V, T, P, S)$, and consider a computation

$$\$[\$] \mid xy\$ \Rightarrow^* \$\psi \mid y\$ \quad \text{in } M \ .$$

Here $\psi$ must be of the form $[\$][\$X_1] \ldots [\$X_1 \ldots X_n]$, $n \geqslant 0$, where $X_1 \ldots X_n$ is a viable prefix of $G$. Moreover, $X_1 \ldots X_n$ derives $x$ in $G$. For the canonical LR($k$) parser this fact is stated in Lemma 6.29, and for the LALR($k$) parser in Lemma 6.49.

Also for other LR($k$) parsers, Lemma 6.49 holds, as is easily seen. As any terminal string derived by a viable prefix of a reduced grammar is a prefix of some sentence, we conclude the theorem. □

Also any LL($k$) parser of a reduced grammar has the correct prefix property. Recall that by Exercise 5.11(b) even the nondeterministic produce-shift parser of a reduced grammar has the correct prefix property.

**Theorem 9.2** *For $k \geqslant 0$, any LL($k$) parser of a reduced grammar has the correct prefix property.*

*Proof.* We prove the theorem for the canonical LL($k$) parser; the cases of the SLL($k$) and LALL($k$) parsers follow similarly. Let $M$ be the canonical LL($k$) parser of a reduced grammar $G = (V, T, P, S)$, and consider a computation

$$\$[\$][\$S] \mid xy\$ \Rightarrow^* \$\psi \mid y\$ \quad \text{in } M \ .$$

Here the stack string $\psi$ is of the form $[\$][\$X_1] \ldots [\$X_1 \ldots X_n]$, $n \geqslant 0$, such that $S$ derives $xX_n \ldots X_1$ (Lemma 8.30). Thus, as $G$ is reduced, $x$ is a prefix of some sentence in $L(G)$. □

Let $M$ be a pushdown automaton with input alphabet $T$, and let $w$ be a nonsentence, that is, a string in $T^* \setminus L(M)$, and let $\Phi$ be an error configuration. We say that *$M$ detects an error in $w$ at $\Phi$*, if $M$ has on $w$ a computation that ends with $\Phi$. We say that *$M$ detects the parser-defined error in $w$*, if $M$ detects an error in $w$ at a configuration of the form $\$\gamma \mid y\$$ in which $1{:}y$ is the parser-defined error in $w$.

**Fact 9.3** Let $M$ be a pushdown automaton that detects an error in every nonsentence and has the longest correct prefix property. Then $M$ detects the parser-defined error in every nonsentence. □

We shall show that all LR(1) and LL(1) parsers detect the parser-defined error in every nonsentence. By Fact 9.3 it suffices to show that these parsers have the longest correct prefix property.

**Theorem 9.4** *Any LR(1) or LL(1) parser of a reduced grammar detects the parser-defined error in every nonsentence.*

*Proof.* We prove the theorem for LR(1) parsers; the case of LL(1) parsers follows similarly. Let $M$ be an LR(1) parser of a grammar $G = (V, T, P, S)$. We shall show that $M$ has the longest correct prefix property. Then by Fact 9.3, $M$ detects the parser-defined error in every nonsentence. (Recall that by Theorem 6.43 any canonical LR(1) parser detects an error in every nonsentence and that for other LR(1) parsers the result follows similarly.)

First, we conclude by Theorem 9.1 that $M$ has the correct prefix property. Then let $xy$ be any string in $T^*$ such that $x$ is a prefix of some sentence in $L(M) = L(G)$, that is, for some $y'$, $xy' \in L(M)$. We show that there is a configuration $\$\psi \mid y\$$ such that

$$\$[\$] \mid xy\$ \Rightarrow^* \$\psi \mid y\$ \quad \text{in } M \ .$$

If $x = \varepsilon$, then $\$\psi \mid y\$$ is the initial configuration. Otherwise, denote $x = x'a$. Then, as $xy' \in L(M)$, there is a computation

$$\$[\$] \mid x'ay'\$ \Rightarrow^* \$\psi' \mid ay'\$ \Rightarrow \$\psi \mid y'\$ \quad \text{in } M \ .$$

As the length of the lookahead is one, we may conclude by an easy induction that also

$$\$[\$] \mid x'ay\$ \Rightarrow^* \$\psi' \mid ay\$ \Rightarrow \$\psi \mid y\$ \quad \text{in } M \ .$$

□

The term "parser-defined error" is slightly misleading in that the definition only depends on the language and not on the parser. The term is, however, perfectly justified at least in the case of parsers having the longest correct prefix property, such as LR(1) and LL(1) parsers. It should be noted here that for $k > 1$ an LR($k$) or LL($k$) parser may already declare error and halt before the entire correct prefix up to the parser-defined error has been consumed. Thus these parsers may see the parser-defined error already before it appears as the first symbol in the remaining input string.

There are several classes of bottom-up parsers that do not possess the correct prefix property. These include, among others, the nondeterministic shift-reduce parsers and the simple precedence parsers defined in Sections 5.2 and 5.7. A simple example can be obtained by considering the grammar that contains only the rule

$$S \rightarrow aa \ .$$

In the case of the erroneous string $a^{k+2}$, $k \geqslant 1$, the simple precedence parser behaves as follows:

$$\$ \mid a^{k+2}\$ \Rightarrow \$a \mid a^{k+1}\$ \Rightarrow^k \$a^{k+1} \mid a\$ \Rightarrow \$a^{k+2} \mid \$ \ .$$

Thus the parser shifts the entire erroneous string $a^{k+2}$ into the stack before eventually detecting the error, although the parser-defined error is already the third $a$.

In some cases it might be useful that the parser does not detect the parser-defined error and that the error detection is delayed. For instance, if the error in the incorrect Pascal statement

**begin** $A = E$ **then begin** $I := 1$ **end else** $J := 2$ **end**

were detected at a configuration

$ **begin** . . . | **then begin** . . . **end** $ ,

the next input symbol **then** would imply that the error could be the missing keyword **if**.

*Error recovery*

We now turn to the problem of *error recovery*, that is, how to dispose of the errors detected during the parsing process. By a *recovery action* at an error configuration of a pushdown automaton we mean any effective transformation of the error configuration into a non-error configuration in which a normal parsing action is possible. The effect of a recovery action is thus to enable normal parsing to proceed for at least one step. In the case of an LR($k$) parser this means that after error recovery the parser is either at an accepting configuration, or is able to perform at least one shift or reduce action before detecting another error.

This definition of error recovery reflects the "local" nature of error recovery techniques used in practical compilers in that errors in the source program are handled one by one, as they are encountered. The recovering feature is added into the parser as a separate subroutine which is called whenever an error is detected. The definition does not, however, conveniently capture those "global" recovery techniques in which the recovering feature is embedded as an inseparable part of the parsing method itself, and the errors are handled so that the overall recovering effect is as good as possible.

## 9.2 Error Recovery in SLL(1) Parsers

In Section 5.6 we discussed two ways to implement deterministic SLL(1) parsers as RAM programs: in one approach the stack of the underlying pushdown automaton was implemented explicitly as a stack of grammar symbols, and in the other approach recursive descent procedures were used. In this section we shall demonstrate how these implementations may be augmented with error recovery. A detailed suggestion will be given for recursive descent parsers, whereas the stack implementation will only be considered briefly.

In the recursive descent implementation of a deterministic SLL(1) parser there is one procedure for each nonterminal in the grammar. The procedure for nonterminal $A$ is named "$A$" and its task is to parse a portion of the input string that is derived by $A$ (see Figures 5.6 to 5.9). Procedure $A$ is called whenever the current input symbol should start a string derived by $A$. Now when an error occurs in procedure $A$, that is, when the parsing cannot proceed according to the rules of the nonterminal $A$, control is passed to the procedure *error*, which issues an error message and should recover from the error. Note that there are two ways in which the error may be detected: either the current input symbol at the beginning of the procedure $A$ is not in $\text{FIRST}_1(A\ \text{FOLLOW}_1(A))$, or after having parsed a prefix $\alpha$ for some rule $A \rightarrow \alpha a \beta$ the current input symbol differs from $a$.

The basic strategy for error recovery could be based on the following observations. First, if the error is detected at the beginning of the procedure $A$, we may scan the remaining input string until a legal follower of the nonterminal $A$ is found. This is based on the assumption that up to this follower an instance of $A$ should have been recognized. Thus, having this follower of $A$ as the current input symbol in the procedure *error*, control may be passed back to the calling procedure $A$. In this case the procedure *error* was called at the end of the procedure $A$, and thus control is immediately passed further back to the procedure that called $A$. Second, if the error is detected at the point when a prefix $\alpha$ for some rule $A \to \alpha a \beta$ has been recognized and the current input symbol is not $a$, then the procedure *error* may search the remaining input for a terminal in $\mathrm{FIRST}_1(\beta \mathrm{FOLLOW}_1(A))$. In this case the procedure *error* was called at the point after which $\beta$ should be parsed. Thus, the parsing may proceed in the procedure $A$ as if there had not been any error when control is passed back from the procedure *error* and the current input symbol is in $\mathrm{FIRST}_1(\beta \mathrm{FOLLOW}_1(A))$.

In Figure 9.1 an implementation of the error procedure is given that follows the above recovery strategy. Now the error procedure takes two parameters, one for the error message and the other for the set of terminals on which the recovery will be based. The end marker \$ will always be included in this set in order to guarantee that the scanning will never proceed over the end of the input string. In Figures 9.2 and 9.3 schemes for generating the parsing procedure for nonterminal $A$ are given that use the new error procedure (cf. Figures 5.6 and 5.7).

A problem, however, in this error recovery scheme is that often too many input symbols will be skipped in the recovery process. This means that large portions of the program text may be left unanalyzed. As an example consider the grammar

```
procedure error (message m, terminal set W);
begin
    write m;
    while not (token.kind in W ∪ {eof-token}) do
        scan
end;
```

**Figure 9.1** Error handling procedure for the recursive descent implementation of the SLL(1) parser described in Figures 9.2 and 9.3. The procedure passes control back to the calling procedure when an input symbol in the set $W \cup \{eof\text{-}token\}$ has been found

```
procedure A;
begin
    if token.kind in FIRST'₁(ω₁ FOLLOW'₁(A)) then begin
      write "A → ω₁";
      parse(ω₁)
    end else
      ⋮
    if token.kind in FIRST'₁(ωₙ FOLLOW'₁(A)) then begin
      write "A → ωₙ";
      parse(ωₙ)
    end else
        error ("No A can start with this.", FOLLOW'₁(A))
end;
```

**Figure 9.2** Parsing procedure for nonterminal $A$ in the error recovering recursive descent SLL(1) parser. The rules for $A$ are: $A \to \omega_1 | \ldots | \omega_n$. The contents of the program segments "$parse(\omega_i)$" are given in Figure 9.3

*parse*($a\beta$) =
  *scan*;
  *check*($\beta$)
*parse*($B\beta$) =
  *B*;
  *check*($\beta$)
*check*($a\beta$) =
  **if** *token.kind* = *a* **then**
    *scan*
  **else**
    *error*("*a* expected.", $\text{FIRST}'_1(\beta\text{FOLLOW}'_1(A))$);
  *check*($\beta$)
  *check*($B\beta$) = *parse* ($B\beta$)
*parse*($\varepsilon$) = *check*($\varepsilon$) = $\varepsilon$

**Figure 9.3** Parsing programs for suffixes of right-hand sides for nonterminal $A$ in the error recovering recursive descent SLL(1) parser. Here $a$ is a terminal, $B$ a nonterminal, and $\beta$ a string in $V^*$. The equations define the meaning of "*parse*($\gamma$)" and "*check*($\gamma$)" inductively on the length of string $\gamma \in V^*$

$G_{\text{block}}$:

$$S \rightarrow E \mid B \ ,$$

$$E \rightarrow \varepsilon \ ,$$

$$B \rightarrow a \mid \textbf{begin}\ S\ C\ \textbf{end} \ ,$$

$$C \rightarrow \varepsilon \mid ;\ S\ C \ .$$

In the case of the nonsentence **begin** *a a* ; *a* ; *a* ; **end**, for example, the error in the third symbol is detected at the beginning of the procedure *C*. The only legal follower of the nonterminal *C* is **end**, and thus the search for a follower of *C* means that the remaining input string up to **end** will be skipped.

To remedy the above problem we propose the following complementary strategy. Instead of only looking for possibilities to continue parsing in the procedure in which the error was detected, we shall add the feature that portions of the input text may be parsed within the error procedure. In order to achieve this we may search for starters of some nonterminal while scanning the remaining input string in the procedure *error*. If such an input symbol is found, the corresponding parsing procedure is called. The problem here, of course, is that a given input symbol usually belongs to several sets $\text{FIRST}_1(B)$. Our strategy will be that terminal $b \in \text{FIRST}_1(B)$ will cause a call for procedure *B* in the procedure *error* only if the nonterminal *B* is in some reasonably defined subset of the set of all nonterminals, and for all other nonterminals *C* in this set, *b* does not belong to $\text{FIRST}_1(C)$.

Assume that the grammar has a rule $A \rightarrow \alpha X \beta$, where $\alpha \Rightarrow^* \varepsilon$, that is, *X* **begins** *A*. (See Section 5.5.) Assume further that here *X* is a nonterminal and that $\text{FIRST}_1(X)$ contains a terminal *b*. Then *b* also belongs to $\text{FIRST}_1(A)$. Thus in the recovering process, when encountering *b* in the remaining input string, there is seemingly a choice between trying to parse a substring to $X$ or to $A$. However, calling $A$ will capture all those parsing possibilities that arise from calling $X$.

As no (reduced) LL(1) grammar is left-recursive, we have:

**Fact 9.5** For any reduced LL(1) grammar, the relation **begins** is partial order. □

Now we are ready to describe our error recovery scheme. In the recovering process we scan the remaining input string and search for (1) symbols as defined in the scheme given in Figures 9.1 to 9.3, and (2) symbols that belong to only one set $\text{FIRST}_1(B)$ where $B$ is a maximal nonterminal with respect to the relation **begins.** In the former case we shall arrive at a situation in which passing control back to the calling procedure will allow at least one normal parsing action. In the latter case the procedure $B$ will be called. If there is a choice between these two cases, we take the former action. In Figure 9.4 this new scheme for the procedure *error* is given. Note that the parsing procedure for nonterminal $A$ given in Figures 9.2 and 9.3 needs no changes.

```
procedure error (message m, terminal set W);
begin
    write m;
    while not (token.kind in W ∪ {eof-token}) do
        if token.kind in FIRST₁(B₁) then
            B₁
        else if token.kind in FIRST₁(B₂) then
            B₂
            ⋮
        else if token.kind in FIRST₁(Bₙ) then
            Bₙ
        else
            scan
end;
```

**Figure 9.4** Revised error handling procedure. Within this procedure input text may also be parsed in normal parsing mode and not just skipped. The set $\{B_1, \ldots, B_n\}$ consists of the maximal nonterminals with respect to the partial order **begins**

The implementation of the procedure *error* given in Figure 9.4 is easy. The maximal nonterminals with respect to **begins** can be computed in time $O(|G|)$: the relation **begins** can be computed from the grammar $G$ in time $O(|G|)$ and the maximal nonterminals are those that do not appear as leftmost components in the pairs in **begins.** After computing all sets $\text{FIRST}_1(B)$, where $B$ is a maximal nonterminal, the pairwise intersections of these sets are determined. Then for any maximal $B$ we take into account only those symbols in $\text{FIRST}_1(B)$ that are in no intersection $\text{FIRST}_1(B) \cap \text{FIRST}_1(C)$, where $C$ is another maximal nonterminal.

Next we shall give the recursive descent parser with error recovery for the grammar $G_{\text{block}}$ according to the schemes given in Figures 9.2 to 9.4. The main program, which is the same for all grammars, is given in Figure 9.5, the parsing programs for all nonterminals are given in Figure 9.6, and Figure 9.7 shows the

```
scan;
S;
if token.kind ≠ eof-token then
    error ("End-of-input expected.", {eof-token});
```

**Figure 9.5** Main program for the error recovering recursive descent SLL(1) parser. Here $S$ is the parsing procedure for the start symbol of the grammar

```
procedure S;
begin
    if token.kind in {a-token, begin-keyword} then
    begin
        write "S → B";
        B;
    end else
    if token.kind in {end-keyword, semicolon,
    eof-token} then begin
        write "S → E";
        E;
    end else
        error ("No S can start with this.",
        {end-keyword, semicolon, eof-token})
end;

procedure E;
begin
    if token.kind in {end-keyword, semicolon,
    eof-token} then begin
        write "E → ε";
    end else
        error("No E can start with this.",
        {end-keyword, semicolon, eof-token});
end;

procedure B;
begin
    if token.kind = a-token then begin
        write "B → a";
        scan;
    end else
    if token.kind = begin-keyword then begin
        write "B → begin S C end";
        scan;
        S;
        C;
        if token.kind = end-keyword then
            scan
        else
            error("end-keyword expected.",
            {end-keyword, semicolon, eof-token});
```

**Figure 9.6** Parsing procedures for nonterminals in the error recovering recursive descent SLL(1) parser for $G_{block}$. The terminal set given as a parameter for the procedure *error* in parsing procedure $A$ is $FOLLOW'_1(A)$ (to be continued)

```
    end else
        error ("No B can start with this.",
        {end-keyword, semicolon, eof-token})
end;

procedure C;
begin
    if token.kind = end-keyword then begin
        write "C → ε";
    end else
    if token.kind = semicolon then begin
        write "C → ; S C";
        scan;
        S;
        C;
    end else
        error("No C can start with this.",
        {end-keyword})
end;
```

**Figure 9.6** (continued)

```
procedure error (message m, terminal set W);
begin
    write m;
    while not (token.kind in W ∪ {eof-token}) do
        if token.kind in {a-token, begin-keyword} then
            S
        else if token.kind = semicolon then
            C
        else
            scan
end;
```

**Figure 9.7** Error handling procedure for the recursive descent parser of $G_{\text{block}}$. The recovery method used is that defined by the scheme given in Figure 9.4. Observe that the maximal nonterminals with respect to **begins** are $S$ and $C$, and that $\text{FIRST}_1(S)\setminus\text{FIRST}_1(C) = \{\textit{a-token}, \textit{begin-keyword}\}$ and $\text{FIRST}_1(C)\setminus\text{FIRST}_1(S) = \{\textit{semicolon}\}$

procedure *error*. Recall that the terminal alphabet of $G_{\text{block}}$ is represented by the token class description:

*a-token* = 'a' ,

*begin-keyword* = 'begin' ,

*end-keyword* = 'end' ,

*semicolon* = ';' .

The special token class name *eof-token* represents the end marker $.

To demonstrate the behaviour of the given error recovering parser for the grammar $G_{\text{block}}$, consider the erroneous string

**begin** *a a* ; **begin** *a* **end** .

This string has two minimum distance errors; one of the possible correct sentences is

$$\textbf{begin}\ a\ ;\ a\ ;\ \textbf{begin}\ a\ \textbf{end}\ \textbf{end}\ \ .$$

The recursive descent parser given in Figures 9.5 to 9.7 works as follows. The stack of activation records for the procedures is given as a stack of procedure names, located to the left of the input string and delimited by "$\mid$", cf. the implementation of SLL(1) parsers. One step in the following sequence of configurations involves calling a procedure or returning from a procedure. Each configuration given denotes the situation immediately after a call or after a return.

| Configuration: | Rule emitted: |
|---|---|
| $S \mid \textbf{begin}\ a\ a ; \textbf{begin}\ a\ \textbf{end}\ \$\ ,$ | $S \rightarrow B$ |
| $S\ B \mid \textbf{begin}\ a\ a\ ;\ \textbf{begin}\ a\ \textbf{end}\ \$\ ,$ | $B \rightarrow \textbf{begin}\ S\ C\ \textbf{end}$ |
| $S\ B\ S \mid a\ a\ ;\ \textbf{begin}\ a\ \textbf{end}\ \$\ ,$ | $S \rightarrow B$ |
| $S\ B\ S\ B \mid a\ a\ ;\ \textbf{begin}\ a\ \textbf{end}\ \$\ ,$ | $B \rightarrow a$ |
| $S\ B\ S \mid a\ ;\ \textbf{begin}\ a\ \textbf{end}\ \$\ ,$ | |
| $S\ B \mid a\ ;\ \textbf{begin}\ a\ \textbf{end}\ \$\ ,$ | |
| $S\ B\ C \mid a\ ;\ \textbf{begin}\ a\ \textbf{end}\ \$\ ,$ | |
| $S\ B\ C\ \mathit{error} \mid a\ ;\ \textbf{begin}\ a\ \textbf{end}\ \$\ ,$ | |
| * No $C$ can start with this. | |
| $S\ B\ C\ \mathit{error}\ S \mid a\ ;\ \textbf{begin}\ a\ \textbf{end}\ \$\ ,$ | $S \rightarrow B$ |
| $S\ B\ C\ \mathit{error}\ S\ B \mid a\ ;\ \textbf{begin}\ a\ \textbf{end}\ \$\ ,$ | $B \rightarrow a$ |
| $S\ B\ C\ \mathit{error}\ S \mid ;\ \textbf{begin}\ a\ \textbf{end}\ \$$ | |
| $S\ B\ C\ \mathit{error} \mid ;\ \textbf{begin}\ a\ \textbf{end}\ \$\ ,$ | |
| $S\ B\ C\ \mathit{error}\ C \mid ;\ \textbf{begin}\ a\ \textbf{end}\ \$\ ,$ | $C \rightarrow ;\ S\ C$ |
| $S\ B\ C\ \mathit{error}\ C\ S \mid \textbf{begin}\ a\ \textbf{end}\ \$\ ,$ | $S \rightarrow B$ |
| $S\ B\ C\ \mathit{error}\ C\ S\ B \mid \textbf{begin}\ a\ \textbf{end}\ \$\ ,$ | $B \rightarrow \textbf{begin}\ S\ C\ \textbf{end}$ |
| $S\ B\ C\ \mathit{error}\ C\ S\ B\ S \mid a\ \textbf{end}\ \$\ ,$ | $S \rightarrow B$ |
| $S\ B\ C\ \mathit{error}\ C\ S\ B\ S\ B \mid a\ \textbf{end}\ \$\ ,$ | $B \rightarrow a$ |
| $S\ B\ C\ \mathit{error}\ C\ S\ B\ S \mid \textbf{end}\ \$\ ,$ | |
| $S\ B\ C\ \mathit{error}\ C\ S\ B \mid \textbf{end}\ \$\ ,$ | |
| $S\ B\ C\ \mathit{error}\ C\ S\ B\ C \mid \textbf{end}\ \$\ ,$ | $C \rightarrow \varepsilon$ |
| $S\ B\ C\ \mathit{error}\ C\ S\ B \mid \textbf{end}\ \$\ ,$ | |
| $S\ B\ C\ \mathit{error}\ C\ S \mid \$\ ,$ | |

Configuration: Rule emitted:

*S B C error C* **|** $ ,

*S B C error C C* **|** $ ,

*S B C error C C error* **|** $ ,

* No *C* can start with this.

*S B C error C C* **|** $ ,

*S B C error C* **|** $ ,

*S B C error* **|** $ ,

*S B C* **|** $ ,

*S B* **|** $ ,

*S B error* **|** $ ,

* end-keyword expected.

*S B* **|** $ ,

*S* **|** $ ,

**|** $ .

Thus the error messages issued were:

**begin** *a* *a* ; **begin** *a* **end** $

* No *C* can start with this.

* No *C* can start with this.

* end-keyword expected.

The second message can be considered extraneous. No symbols were skipped in the procedure *error*.

Our next task is to show that the error recovering recursive descent parser does not loop forever on any input string. As we are implementing a deterministic SLL(1) parser that always detects an error, the only possibilities for looping arise from the error recovery. Assume then that an error is detected in parsing procedure *A* and that the procedure *error* is called. If the recovery is based on the current input symbol, say *b*, looping forever is in principle possible. Now if the recovery action is to call parsing procedure *B*, then *b* must be in $\text{FIRST}_1(B)$ and hence the parser will be able to shift *b* before encountering the next error. On the other hand, if the recovery action is to pass control back to the procedure *A*, the parser cannot make an unbounded number of new invocations of procedures without shifting an input symbol because otherwise we would have a left-recursive nonterminal. Thus in all cases the error recovering recursive descent parser will eventually halt.

In the stack implementation of deterministic LL(1) parsers the error handling procedure may be designed in the same way as for recursive descent parsers. The differences arise from the availability of the parsing stack in the stack implementation. We shall consider here SLL(1) parsers; for other type of LL(1) parsers the error handling scheme is derived analogously.

Let us consider an error configuration

$$\$\psi X \mid y\$$$

of an SLL(1) parser. As parsing cannot proceed here, $1{:}y\$$ is not in $\text{FIRST}_1(X\psi^R\$)$. Now the recovering strategy that corresponds to the one given above for recursive descent parsers is described as follows. We pop $X$ from the parsing stack and scan the remaining input string $y\$$ until we find (1) the end marker \$ or a symbol in $\text{FIRST}_1(\psi^R\$)$, or (2) a symbol that belongs to exactly one set $\text{FIRST}_1(B)$ where $B$ is a maximal nonterminal with respect to the relation **begins**. In the former case we arrive at a configuration

$$\$\psi \mid z\$ \ ,$$

which is the accepting configuration or at which at least one parsing action is possible whenever $z \neq \varepsilon$. In the latter case we push the nonterminal $B$ onto the stack:

$$\$\psi B \mid z\$ \ ,$$

and the parsing can proceed at least one step further. If there is a choice between these two cases, we choose the former alternative, as we did in the case of the recursive descent parser.

We demonstrate the above error recovering scheme in the case of the grammar $G_{\text{block}}$, and the erroneous string **begin** $a$ $a$ ; **begin** $a$ **end**.

$\$ \ S \mid$ **begin** $a\ a$ ; **begin** $a$ **end** \$

$\Rightarrow \$ \ B \mid$ **begin** $a\ a$ ; **begin** $a$ **end** \$

$\Rightarrow \$$ **end** $C\ S$ **begin** $\mid$ **begin** $a\ a$ ; **begin** $a$ **end** \$

$\Rightarrow \$$ **end** $C\ S \mid a\ a$ ; **begin** $a$ **end** \$

$\Rightarrow \$$ **end** $C\ B \mid a\ a$ ; **begin** $a$ **end** \$

$\Rightarrow \$$ **end** $C\ a \mid a\ a$ ; **begin** $a$ **end** \$

$\Rightarrow \$$ **end** $C \mid a$ ; **begin** $a$ **end** \$

* No $C$ can start with this.

$\Rightarrow \$$ **end** $S \mid a$ ; **begin** $a$ **end** \$

$\Rightarrow \$$ **end** $B \mid a$ ; **begin** $a$ **end** \$

$\Rightarrow \$$ **end** $a \mid a$ ; **begin** $a$ **end** \$

$\Rightarrow \$$ **end** $\mid$ ; **begin** $a$ **end** \$

* end-keyword expected.

$\Rightarrow \$ \; C \,|\,$; **begin** $a$ **end** \$

$\Rightarrow \$ \; C \; S \; ; |$; **begin** $a$ **end** \$

$\Rightarrow \$ \; C \; S \,|\,$ **begin** $a$ **end** \$

$\Rightarrow \$ \; C \; B \,|\,$ **begin** $a$ **end** \$

$\Rightarrow \$ \; C$ **end** $C \; S$ **begin** | **begin** $a$ **end** \$

$\Rightarrow \$ \; C$ **end** $C \; S \,|\, a$ **end** \$

$\Rightarrow \$ \; C$ **end** $C \; B \,|\, a$ **end** \$

$\Rightarrow \$ \; C$ **end** $C \; a \,|\, a$ **end** \$

$\Rightarrow \$ \; C$ **end** $C \,|\,$ **end** \$

$\Rightarrow \$ \; C$ **end** | **end** \$

$\Rightarrow \$ \; C \,|\, \$$

* No $C$ can start with this.

$\Rightarrow \$ \,|\, \$$ .

## 9.3 Error Recovery in LR(1) Parsers

In bottom-up parsing the parsing stack contains information about partial derivation trees that are parts of the complete derivation tree. In the case of top-down parsing the situation is different: the parsing stack contains nonterminals that are predictions of segments in the remaining input string not yet even partially parsed. In bottom-up parsing information about the portion of the input string processed thus far is contained in the stack, whereas in top-down parsing no such information remains. These differences are also reflected in the design of error handling. As in bottom-up parsing there is plenty of information available, and there are several ways to design sophisticated error recovery algorithms.

*Phrase-level recovery*

One of the basic recovery techniques for bottom-up parsing, such as LR(1) parsing, is referred to as "phrase-level" recovery. The main idea in phrase-level recovery is to isolate at an error configuration an "error phrase" within which the error is assumed to lie. The error phrase consists of a suffix of the stack contents concatenated with a prefix of the remaining input string, and it is replaced by a "reduction goal" such that a non-error configuration is obtained.

Let $M$ be a deterministic LR(1) parser of a grammar $G = (V, T, P, S)$, and

$$\Phi = \$ q_0 q_1 \ldots q_m \,|\, a_1 \ldots a_n$$

an error configuration of $M$, that is, Action$[q_m, a_1]$ = "error". (We assume here that

$M$ is an LR(0)-based LR(1) parser; the case of the canonical LR(1) parser is handled in the obvious way.) We say that a substring

$$q_{i+1} \ldots q_m \mid a_1 \ldots a_{j-1}$$

of $\Phi$ is an *error phrase* in $\Phi$ if $G$ has a nonterminal $A$ such that $\text{Goto}[q_i, A] \neq \varnothing$ and $\text{Action}[\text{Goto}[q_i, A], a_j] \neq$ "error". Here $i$ may equal $m$ meaning that the stack portion of the error phrase is empty, and $j$ may equal 1 implying that the input portion is empty. We say that $q_i$ is the *recovery state*, $A$ is the (*reduction*) *goal*, $\text{Goto}[q_i, A]$ is the *goal state*, and $a_j$ is the *recovery symbol*, for the error phrase. A *phrase-level recovery action* then replaces the error configuration $\Phi$ by the non-error configuration

$$\$ q_0 q_1 \ldots q_i q_A \mid a_j \ldots a_n \ ,$$

where $q_A = \text{Goto}[q_i, A]$.

The requirements imposed by the general definition on error phrases and their reduction goals are not, as such, sufficient to guarantee unique recovery actions. Even a fixed error phrase usually has more than one reduction goal. As an example we consider the LR(1) parser given in Section 7.4 for the grammar $G_{\text{block2}}$:

$$S \rightarrow \varepsilon \mid a := E \mid \textbf{begin}\ C\ \textbf{end} \ ,$$

$$C \rightarrow C\ ;\ S \mid S \ ,$$

$$E \rightarrow E + T \mid T \ ,$$

$$T \rightarrow a \mid (E) \ .$$

Then let

$$\textbf{begin}\ a = a;\ a := a\ \textbf{end}$$

be the erroneous input string to be parsed. The error—the operator ' =' used in place of an assignment arrow—is detected at the configuration (the stack string is denoted by the corresponding viable prefix):

$$\$\ \textbf{begin}\ a \mid\ = a\ ;\ a := a\ \textbf{end}\ \$ \ .$$

Now the shortest possible error phrase is "a $\mid = a$", and it has two reduction goals, the nonterminals $S$ and $C$. However, the overall effect of the recovery action is the same no matter which of these reduction goals is chosen. This is because

$$\$\ \textbf{begin}\ S \mid;\ a := a\ \textbf{end}\ \$$$

$$\Rightarrow \$\ \textbf{begin}\ C \mid;\ a := a\ \textbf{end}\ \$ \ ,$$

that is, the configuration $\$\ \textbf{begin}\ C \mid;\ a := a\ \textbf{end}\ \$$ will be entered even if $S$ has been chosen as the reduction goal.

We say that a reduction goal $A$ of error phrase $\eta \mid x$ in error configuration $\psi\eta \mid xy$ is *important* if $\eta \mid x$ has no reduction goal $B$ that nontrivially derives $A$ by using only unit rules. In the above example, $C$ is an important reduction goal of "$a \mid = a$" but $S$ is not.

The definition of important reduction goals does not take into account the already correctly parsed portion $\eta$ of the error phrase $\eta \mid x$ in question. If we adopt the hypothesis that the contents of the stack are correct, then it is natural to require that $\eta$ corresponds to a prefix of some string derivable from the chosen reduction goal $A$. Clearly, only then can $\eta x$ be regarded as an "erroneous instance" of $A$. As an example, extend the grammar $G_{\text{block}2}$ by the rules

$$S \rightarrow \textbf{begin}\ D\ ;\ C\ \textbf{end}\ ,$$

$$D \rightarrow D\ ;\ \textbf{integer}\ a \mid \textbf{integer}\ a\ ,$$

and consider again the erroneous string "**begin** $a = a$; $a$ := $a$ **end**". For any LR(1) parser of the new grammar the error is detected, as before, at the configuration

$$\$\ \textbf{begin}\ a \mid = a\text{;}\ a := a\ \textbf{end}\ \$\ ,$$

but now the important reduction goals of the error phrase "$a \mid = a$" are $C$ and $D$. However, $D$ can be discarded because it does not derive any string having the prefix $a$.

Formally, we say that reduction goal $A$ of error phrase

$$q_{i+1} \ldots q_m \mid a_1 \ldots a_{j-1}$$

in error configuration

$$\Phi = \$ q_0 q_1 \ldots q_m \mid a_1 \ldots a_n$$

is *feasible* if there is a terminal string $z$ such that

$$A \underset{\text{rm}}{\Rightarrow^*} X_{i+1} \ldots X_m z\ ,$$

where $X_k$ is the entry symbol of the state $q_k$, $k = i + 1, \ldots, m$.

Given an error configuration $\$ q_0 q_1 \ldots q_m \mid a_1 \ldots a_n$, we shall compute the sets of feasible reduction goals:

$$F(q_{i+1} \ldots q_m) = \{A \mid A \text{ is a reduction goal of error phrase } q_{i+1} \ldots q_m \mid a_1 \ldots a_{j-1} \text{ for some } j, \text{ and } A \underset{\text{rm}}{\Rightarrow^*} X_{i+1} \ldots X_m z \text{ for some } z \in T^*, \text{ where } X_k \text{ is the entry symbol of } q_k,\ k = i + 1, \ldots, m\}$$

for all $i = 0, \ldots, m - 1$. To do this we define relations on the set of pairs of the forms $(q, A \rightarrow \alpha \cdot \beta)$ and $(q, B)$, where $q$ is a state of the LR(0) machine for grammar $G = (V, T, P, S)$, $[A \rightarrow \alpha \cdot \beta]$ is a 0-item of $G$, and $B$ is a nonterminal. For pair $(q, A \rightarrow \alpha \cdot \beta)$, the state $q$ always contains the item $[A \rightarrow \cdot \alpha\beta]$, and for pair $(q, B)$, $q$ always contains some item of the form $[A \rightarrow \alpha \cdot B\beta]$.

Then let **on-string-goes-to**, **reduces-to**, and **symbol-in** be relations defined by:

$$(q, B \to \alpha \cdot \beta) \textbf{ on-string-goes-to } \mathrm{GOTO}(q, \alpha) \ ,$$

$$(q, B \to \alpha \cdot \beta) \textbf{ reduces-to } (q, B) \ ,$$

$$(\mathrm{GOTO}(q, \alpha), B) \textbf{ symbol-in } (q, A \to \alpha B \cdot \beta) \ .$$

(Cf. the relations defined in Section 7.5.) Consider then the relational expression

$$\textbf{on-string-goes-to}^{-1} \textbf{ (reduces-to symbol-in)* reduces-to} \ .$$

It is not difficult to verify (a formal proof is left as an exercise):

**Theorem 9.6** *Nonterminal $A$ is in $F(q_{i+1} \dots q_m)$ if and only if*

$$q_m \textbf{ on-string-goes-to}^{-1} \textbf{ (reduces-to symbol-in)*}$$
$$\textbf{reduces-to } (q_i, A) \ . \quad \square$$

The computation of feasible reduction goals is illustrated in Figure 9.8.

Experiments have shown that in practice the feasibility of a reduction goal can very often be decided by inspecting only the first state $q_{i+1}$ in the stack portion of the error phrase. In other words, the property that $A$ can nontrivially rightmost derive a string of the form $X_{i+1}z$, where $X_{i+1}$ is the entry symbol of $q_{i+1}$, usually suffices to make $A$ feasible. We call this simpler property of $A$ *weak feasibility*.

Our strategy in phrase-level recovery is to find an error phrase with a unique important feasible reduction goal. The recovery routine will search the error

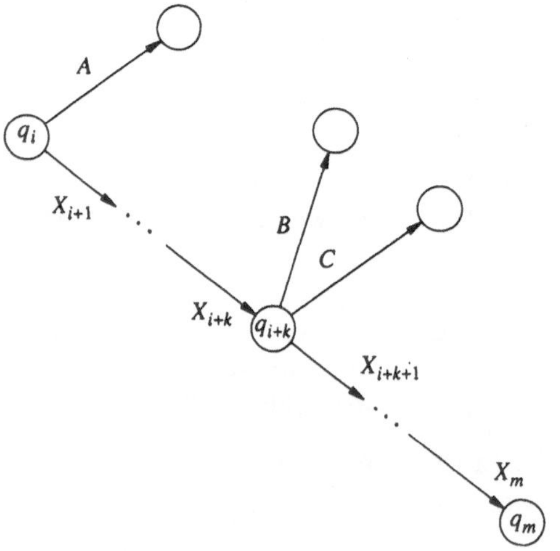


**Figure 9.8** Portion of an LR(0) machine. For some strings $\alpha$ and $\beta$, $A \to X_{i+1} \dots X_{i+k}B\alpha$ and $C \to X_{i+k+1} \dots X_m\beta$ are assumed to be rules of the grammar. Nonterminal $C$ is a feasible reduction goal for error phrases including $q_{i+k+1} \dots q_m \mathbf{I}$, as $q_m$ **on-string-goes-to**$^{-1}$ $(q_{i+k}, C \to X_{i+k+1} \dots X_m \cdot \beta)$ **reduces-to** $(q_{i+k}, C)$. Moreover, if $B \underset{rm}{\Rightarrow}^+ C\gamma$ for some $\gamma$, then $(q_{i+k}, C \to X_{i+k+1} \dots X_m \cdot \beta)$ **(reduces-to symbol-in)* reduces-to** $(q_i, A)$, and thus $A$ is feasible for error phrases including $q_{i+1} \dots q_m \mathbf{I}$

configuration for an error phrase $\eta \mid x$ that has exactly one important feasible reduction goal, and then it will perform the corresponding unique recovery action. The search for $\eta \mid x$ begins with the shortest possible error phrase, that is, with the error phrase consisting only of the vertical bar, and proceeds with larger and larger segments of the error configuration.

The ultimate recovery decision thus depends on the order in which the search for the error phrase is performed. Let us denote by pair $(i, j)$ the segment $q_{i+1} \ldots q_m \mid a_1 \ldots a_{j-1}$ in error configuration $\$q_0 q_1 \ldots q_m \mid a_1 \ldots a_n$. Then $(m, 1)$ denotes the sole vertical bar "$\mid$", and $(0, n)$ denotes the whole error configuration (without the surrounding $\$q_0$ and $a_n = \$$). We require that in any search order the pair $(m, 1)$ appears first and $(0, n)$ last. Also, whenever $(i_1, j_1)$ precedes $(i_2, j_2)$, then either $i_1 > i_2$ or $j_1 < j_2$, that is, no error phrase can precede any of its subphrases in the search order. When recovering, the pairs are tried in the prescribed order until one is found that denotes an error phrase with a unique important feasible reduction goal.

A simple order in searching for pairs $(i, j)$ is the following:

$$
\begin{array}{l}
(m, 1), (m-1, 1), \ldots, (0, 1)\ , \\
(m, 2), (m-1, 2), \ldots, (0, 2)\ , \\
\quad\quad\vdots \\
(m, n), (m-1, n), \ldots, (0, n)\ .
\end{array}
$$

According to this order, terminals in the remaining input string are successively compared with all states in the stack until a recovery action is possible. In implementing this order no input buffer is needed, because the terminal ultimately chosen as the recovery symbol is always the last token scanned.

In the above order stack symbols may be consumed excessively. If we want to save stack contents for the subsequent analysis of semantic errors, the following order has proved successful.

$$
\begin{array}{llll}
(m, 1)\ , & & & \\
(m-1, 1)\ , & & & \\
(m-2, 1), & (m, 2)\ , & & \\
(m-3, 1), & (m-1, 2)\ , & & \\
\quad . & (m-2, 2)\ , & (m, 3)\ , & \\
\quad . & \quad . & (m-1, 3)\ , & . \\
\quad . & \quad . & (m-2, 3)\ , & \ \ . \\
 & \quad . & \quad . & (m, n)\ , \\
 & & \quad . & (m-1, n)\ , \\
(0, 1) & & \quad . & (m-2, n)\ , \\
 & & & \quad . \\
 & (0, 2)\ , & & \quad . \\
 & & & \quad . \\
 & & (0, 3)\ , & \\
 & & & (0, n)\ .
\end{array}
$$

This order is oriented to consuming stack states slightly more than input tokens. Note that the input tokens must now be stored in a buffer. Because the token to be chosen as the recovery symbol is not always the last token scanned, the logic of the parser must also be modified so that after recovery the tokens remaining in the buffer are consumed before the next token is scanned.

The requirement of feasibility for reduction goals may even cause a situation in which no candidate error phrase can be chosen as a basis of the error recovery action. Such a situation occurs when the parser has recognized a complete sentence but the remaining input string is still nonempty. For example, consider the grammar $G_{\text{block2}}$ and the erroneous string

**begin end begin** $a := a$ **end** .

An LR(1) parser using default reductions detects the error at the configuration

$\$S\,|$ **begin** $a := a$ **end** $\$$ ,

for which the whole error configuration is the only possible error phrase. The start symbol $S$ is the only important reduction goal but it is not feasible. Our strategy in such situations is simply to delete the topmost stack symbol, that is, a new initial configuration is created so that the parser is again able to recognize a complete sentence. Such an action, called a *restart action*, may create an error configuration, which is then handled in the usual way.

Restart actions guarantee that at every error configuration some recovery action can be performed. However, if the current input symbol is the recovery symbol, it is not always guaranteed (see the exercises) that the recovery strategy will not cause the error recovering parser to loop forever. To avoid this, we suggest that a terminal is allowed to be used as a recovery symbol only if it is *shiftable* at the goal state, that is, the goal state has a shift action on the terminal. This means that the remaining input string will always be shortened by at least one symbol before the next error is detected, and thus termination is guaranteed.

*Local correction*

A local correction at an error configuration involves the replacement of a prefix of the remaining input string by a correct prefix, that is, a terminal string which is a valid continuation of the contents of the parsing stack. We shall consider only the simplest kind of local correction, namely insertions, deletions, and replacements of single symbols, and see how these changes at the front of the remaining input string may be incorporated into phrase-level recovery.

We shall first demonstrate the necessity of local correction. Consider again the grammar $G_{\text{block2}}$, and a string in which the first symbol is incorrect, for example:

**begim** $a := a + a \,;\, a := a$ **end** .

Now any LR(1) parser detects an error at the configuration

$\$\,|$ **begim** $a := a + a \,;\, a := a$ **end** $\$$ .

The only possible phrase-level action is to replace the whole configuration by the final configuration:

$$\$ S \mid \$ \ .$$

This is, of course, equivalent to aborting parsing: the string is scanned through for the only possible recovery symbol, the end marker \$.

The above example in a way demonstrates the sensitivity of phrase-level recovery techniques to the form of the rules in the grammar. To see this, let us assume for a moment that the grammar $G_{\mathrm{block2}}$ be transformed so that in place of each terminal $b$ there is a new nonterminal $\langle b \rangle$, and for all $\langle b \rangle$ the grammar has the new rule $\langle b \rangle \rightarrow b$. Then the misspelled **begin** could be handled by taking "$\mid$ **begim**" as the error phrase for which $\langle$**begin**$\rangle$ is the unique important feasible reduction goal. The resulting non-error configuration is:

$$\$ \ \langle \mathbf{begin} \rangle \mid a := a + a \ ; a := a \ \mathbf{end} \ \$ \ .$$

This recovery action can be considered as the replacement of the incorrect prefix **begim** by the correct prefix **begin**.

By introducing the new nonterminals $\langle b \rangle$ and the rules $\langle b \rangle \rightarrow b$ we can simulate local corrections that are either insertions or replacements of single terminals. We can generalize the transformation so that deletions can also be simulated: instead of the rules $\langle b \rangle \rightarrow b$, we introduce the rules $\langle b \rangle \rightarrow \langle \varepsilon \rangle b$, where $\langle \varepsilon \rangle$ is a new nonterminal that derives only the empty string. For example, if the erroneous string with respect to $G_{\mathrm{block2}}$ is

$$; \mathbf{begin} \ a := a \ \mathbf{end} \ ,$$

then we may replace the error configuration

$$\$ \mid ; \mathbf{begin} \ a := a \ \mathbf{end} \ \$$$

by:

$$\$ \langle \varepsilon \rangle \mid \mathbf{begin} \ a := a \ \mathbf{end} \ \$ \ .$$

The above transformation is given for conceptual purposes only. In practice, the equivalent effect is obtained more efficiently by generalizing the concept of a recovery action such that, in addition to nonterminals, also terminals and the empty string are allowable reduction goals. In the case of a terminal reduction goal the goal state and the recovery symbol are determined as in the case of a nonterminal reduction goal, whereas in the case of an empty reduction goal there is no goal state, and the recovery symbol must be a shiftable terminal at the recovery state.

As to the selection strategy for error phrases with terminal and empty reduction goals, we require that the input portion of the error phrase is at most one. The feasibility requirement in turn guarantees that the stack portion of the error phrase is empty. With these requirements the use of terminal and empty reduction goals does indeed correspond to the three simplest kinds of local correction: insertion of a single terminal, deletion of a single terminal, and replacement of a single terminal by another. However, allowing only single-token modifications does not remove the problem of selecting the ultimate local correction. Consider, for example, the grammar $G_{\text{block2}}$ and the erroneous string

$$\textbf{begin}\ a := a + \ ;\ a + a\ \textbf{end}\ .$$

The error is detected at the configuration

$$\$\ \textbf{begin}\ a := E + \mid ;\ a + a\ \textbf{end}\ \$\ ,$$

and the possible local corrections are the deletion of the semicolon and the insertion of terminal *a* in front of the semicolon. If the shortest error phrase is tried first, as in the phrase-level recovery routine, then the insertion of *a* will be selected. However, this means that insertions always have higher preference than other token modifications, and thus this strategy should be rejected in the case of local corrections. One solution is to require that only one local correction is possible at the error configuration, otherwise, a normal phrase-level recovery action is performed. However, this solution usually denies too often the possibility of local correction, and therefore many designers have suggested the use of predeclared costs for token modifications. When an error occurs, the respective cost of each allowable local correction is evaluated, and if there is only one with the lowest cost then that correction will be chosen.

*Forward-move recovery*

We shall first demonstrate some deficiencies that remain in phrase-level recovery and have led to the proposal of the recovery method called "forward-move recovery". Consider the erroneous Pascal statement

$$\textbf{begin}\ A = E\ \textbf{then begin}\ I := 1\ \textbf{end else}\ J := 2\ \textbf{end}\ ,$$

and recall from Section 9.1 that in LR(1) parsing the error will be detected at the configuration

$$\$\ \textbf{begin}\ \mathit{Variable} \mid\ = E\ \textbf{then begin}\ I := 1\ \textbf{end else}\ J := 2\ \textbf{end}\ \$\ .$$

At this error configuration a satisfactory phrase-level recovery action is possible if there is a suitable nonterminal, say *IF-THEN-Clause*, for an **if-then** construct. The error phrase is then "$\mathit{Variable} \mid\ = E$ **then**", which is replaced by *IF-THEN-Clause*:

$$\$\ \textbf{begin}\ \mathit{IF\text{-}THEN\text{-}Clause} \mid \textbf{begin}\ I := 1\ \textbf{end else}\ J := 2\ \textbf{end}\ \$\ .$$

The problem here, of course, is that *IF-THEN-Clause* is most probably not a uniquely defined important feasible reduction goal. For example, there could be a nonterminal *WHILE-DO-Clause* that would equally well suit as a reduction goal for the error phrase "$\mathit{Variable} \mid\ = E$ **then**". The correct decision might be obtained if the skipped keyword **then** could be remembered while searching for the error phrase. Another drawback is that even if the correct decision could be made the error phrase may contain many terminals that would simply be skipped and thus left unanalyzed. (Note that the local correction, to replace ' =' by ':=', would not be desirable at all.)

A *forward-move* strategy has been suggested for resolving nondeterminism in phrase-level recovery. By a forward move at an error configuration we mean passing control from the recovery routine temporarily back to the parser in order to "condense" the information around the error. The approach is fairly easy to implement in a precedence parser or in any bounded-context parser in which the elements in the stack are plain grammar symbols and the next parsing action only depends on a fixed-length string of topmost elements in the stack and the current input symbol. Since only local context is needed to determine the next move, parsing can proceed in a precedence parser even if the stack contains an improper string, that is, a string which is not a viable prefix. The local nature of a precedence parser thus seems to be an advantage as regards error recovery.

An LR(1) parser, on the contrary, has states in its stack rather than grammar symbols, and parsing works correctly only if the contents of the stack form a valid sequence of states. At an error configuration none of the parsing actions associated with the topmost state is applicable. In particular, there is no transition on the current input symbol from the topmost state. A problem arises when we try to initiate a forward move by shifting the current input symbol. This is because there may be several states that have the current input symbol as the entry symbol, and we do not know which of these is the right one to be pushed onto stack as the result of the shift action.

The problem of continuing parsing at an error configuration of an LR(1) parser can be solved by constructing a special "recovery state" for each grammar symbol. Let $G = (V, T, P, S)$ be a grammar, $M$ its LR(0) machine, and $X$ a symbol in $V$. A *recovery state for* $X$ is the union of all states in $M$ that have $X$ as the entry symbol. Successors for recovery states are then computed in the same way as successors for ordinary states in the LR(0) machine. The computation of successors proceeds until no new states (the states in $M$ are "old" states) are obtained. All states constructed in this process are classified as *recovery states*. Finally, a special new state, called the *initial recovery state*, is introduced as a state that has on each $X$ in $V$ a transition to the recovery state for $X$.

One way to define the forward-move recovery is the following: at an error configuration the whole stack contents are replaced by the initial recovery state, and then parsing proceeds with respect to the equivalence classes of viable prefixes corresponding to the recovery states. If a parsing conflict occurs in a recovery state or a reduce action would empty the whole parsing stack, a new start will be invoked by emptying the stack except for the initial recovery state. If a new error is detected at a recovery state, that is, no action of the recovery state is possible for the current input symbol, the new error is reported and the same recovery process is repeated.

We shall now define *error recovery tables*, called RGoto and RAction, that give a precise description of the above forward-move recovery. The new stack symbols have a unique correspondence to the recovery states. The stack symbol [£], $£ \notin V$, denotes the initial recovery state, and for all $X \in V$, [£$X$] denotes the recovery state for $X$. Moreover, for all $\alpha \in V^*$, the $\alpha$-successor of the recovery state for $X$ is denoted by $[£X\alpha]$. The table RGoto is then defined by:

$$\text{RGoto}[[£\delta], X] = [£\delta X] \ ,$$

for all $\delta \in V^*$, and $X \in V$.

The action table, RAction, contains the parsing actions in the error recovery mode. The entries of RAction for each recovery state of the form $[£X]$ are obtained from the Action table of the underlying LR(1) parser. If all states with entry symbol $X$ in the parser have the same parsing action on terminal $a$, then the state $[£X]$ has this action on $a$. Here we disregard possible differences due to error entries or default actions, so that a shift entry or a non-default reduce entry overrules any error entry or default reduce entry, and a default reduce entry overrules any error entry. If a unique action cannot be obtained in this way, we define:

$$\text{RAction}[[£X], a] = \text{“conflict”} \ .$$

For the other recovery states the actions are defined in the same principle as was done for the underlying LR(1) parser. If there is no unique action, the entry is marked as “conflict”.

For the initial recovery state $[£]$ we define:

$$\text{RAction}[[£], a] = \text{“shift}[£a]\text{”} \ ,$$

$a \in T$, and

$$\text{RAction}[[£], \$] = \text{“halt”} \ .$$

Using the tables RAction and RGoto we are now able to augment the table-driven implementation of an LR(1) parser (see Section 7.4) by error recovery. In order to do this we have to introduce a new Boolean variable that indicates, in conjunction with the *pop* operation, whether or not the parsing stack actually contains as many elements as are to be popped. The operation

*pop*(*m*, *emptied*)

pops all the elements from the parsing stack whenever it contains less than $m$ elements, and $m$ elements otherwise. If the stack will be empty after the operation, the Boolean valued parameter *emptied* will be assigned the value **true** (its initial value is **false**).

The error handling procedure *error* for the table-driven implementation of an LR(1) parser is given in Figure 9.9. The new procedure for performing reduce actions is given in Figure 9.10. Figure 9.11 shows the program body with the changes caused by the augmentation of error handling. Note that the Action and Goto tables are usually included in the RAction and RGoto tables. Thus we may use RAction and RGoto also for correct input strings, and it is not necessary to distinguish between the initial parsing mode and the mode entered upon error

```
procedure error (message m);
begin
    write m;
    empty;      —initialize the stack as empty
    push(initial-recovery-state)
end;
```

**Figure 9.9** Error handling procedure for LR(1) parsers. The effect of the procedure is to substitute the initial recovery state for the stack contents

```
procedure reduce(nonterminal A, length m);
begin
    pop(m, emptied);
    if not emptied then
        push(RGoto[top, A])
    else begin
        push(initial-recovery-state);
        emptied:= false
    end
end;
```

**Figure 9.10** Procedure *reduce*. If, due to error recovery, the stack does not contain enough symbols for the required reduce action, the initial recovery state will be pushed onto the stack

```
empty;
push(eof-token); push(initial-state);
accept:= halt:= emptied:= false;
scan;
repeat
    if RAction[top, token.kind] = "reduce by
    A → X1 . . . Xm" then
        reduce(A, m)
    else if RAction[top, token.kind] = "shift q" then
        shift(q)
    else if RAction[top, token.kind] = "accept" then
        accept:= true
    else if RAction[top, token.kind] = "conflict" then begin
        empty;
        push(initial-recovery-state)
    end else
    if RAction[top, token.kind] = "halt" then
        halt:= true
    else begin
        m:= ⟨error message text corresponding to the
        entry [top, token.kind]⟩;
        error(m)
    end
until accept or halt;
```

**Figure 9.11** Program body for a table-driven implementation of an error recovering LR(1) parser

detection. The new Boolean variable *halt* corresponds to the value "halt" in the RAction table. The parsing process terminates when *halt* or *accept* has the value **true**. In the former case parsing has terminated incorrectly and in the latter case the input string is in the language.

As an example we shall consider how the LR(0)-based LR(1) parser using default reductions for the grammar $G_{\mathbf{block2}}$ is augmented by the forward-move error recovery as defined above. The LR(0) machine for the \$-augmented grammar was given in Figure 7.9, and the LALR(1) parsing table was given in Figure 7.11. First we construct the recovery states for all the grammar symbols. The recovery state for $X$ is denoted by $q_X$; these are given in Figure 9.12. According to the naming of

$q_S$:
- $S' \to \$S \cdot \$$
- $C \to C; S \cdot$
- $C \to S \cdot$

$q_C$:
- $S \to \mathbf{begin}\ C \cdot \mathbf{end}$
- $C \to C \cdot ; S$

$q_E$:
- $S \to a := E \cdot$
- $E \to E \cdot + T$
- $T \to (E \cdot)$

$q_T$:
- $E \to E + T \cdot$
- $E \to T \cdot$

$q_a$:
- $S \to a \cdot := E$
- $T \to a \cdot$

$q_{:=}$:
- $S \to a := \cdot E$
- $E \to \cdot E + T$
- $E \to \cdot T$
- $T \to \cdot a$
- $T \to \cdot (E)$

$q_{\mathbf{begin}}$:
- $S \to \mathbf{begin} \cdot C\ \mathbf{end}$
- $C \to \cdot C; S$
- $C \to \cdot S$
- $S \to \cdot$
- $S \to \cdot a := E$
- $S \to \cdot \mathbf{begin}\ C\ \mathbf{end}$

$q_{\mathbf{end}}$:
- $S \to \mathbf{begin}\ C\ \mathbf{end} \cdot$

$q_;$:
- $C \to C; \cdot S$
- $S \to \cdot$
- $S \to \cdot a := E$
- $S \to \cdot \mathbf{begin}\ C\ \mathbf{end}$

$q_+$:
- $E \to E + \cdot T$
- $T \to \cdot a$
- $T \to \cdot (E)$

$q_($:
- $T \to (\cdot E)$
- $E \to \cdot E + T$
- $E \to \cdot T$
- $T \to \cdot a$
- $T \to \cdot (E)$

$q_)$:
- $T \to (E) \cdot$

**Figure 9.12** The recovery states for the grammar $G_{\mathbf{block2}}$. All the successor states are states in the LR(0) machine

the states of the LR(0) machine in Figure 7.9,

$$q_S = q_2 \cup q_{17} \cup q_{18} \ ,$$

$$q_C = q_{14} \ ,$$

$$q_E = q_5 \cup q_{10} \ ,$$

$$q_T = q_7 \cup q_{12} \ ,$$

$$q_a = q_3 \cup q_8 \ ,$$

$$q_{:=} = q_4 \ ,$$

$$q_{\mathbf{begin}} = q_{13} \ ,$$

$$q_{\mathbf{end}} = q_{15} \ ,$$

$$q_{;} = q_{16} \ ,$$

$$q_{+} = q_6 \ ,$$

$$q_{(} = q_9 \ ,$$

$$q_{)} = q_{11} \ .$$

All successors of these states are already in the LR(0) machine given in Figure 7.10. Thus the RAction and RGoto tables have four new states only, and the entries for the states in the LR(0) machine need not be repeated as they are obtained from the Action and Goto tables already. For completeness the whole RAction and RGoto tables are given in Figure 9.13. The new states $q_S$, $q_E$, $q_T$, and $q_a$ are named $q_{19}$, $q_{20}$, $q_{21}$, and $q_{22}$, respectively. Note that default reductions are applied also in the new states.

We shall now demonstrate the behaviour of the error recovering LR(1) parser for $G_{\mathrm{block2}}$ given in Figure 9.13 in the case of the erroneous string

$$\mathbf{begin}\ a := \ ;\ \mathbf{begin}\ a := a\ a := a\ \mathbf{begin}\ \mathbf{end} \ .$$

As to the error messages we refer to the next section.

$$\$q_1 \mid \mathbf{begin}\ a := ;\ \mathbf{begin}\ a := a\ a := a\ \mathbf{begin}\ \mathbf{end}\ \$$$

$$\Rightarrow \$q_1 q_{13} \mid a := ;\ \mathbf{begin}\ a := a\ a := a\ \mathbf{begin}\ \mathbf{end}\ \$$$

$$\Rightarrow \$q_1 q_{13} q_3 \mid := ;\ \mathbf{begin}\ a := a\ a := a\ \mathbf{begin}\ \mathbf{end}\ \$$$

$$\Rightarrow \$q_1 q_{13} q_3 q_4 \mid ;\mathbf{begin}\ a := a\ a := a\ \mathbf{begin}\ \mathbf{end}\ \$$$

* No $E$ can start with this.

$$\Rightarrow \$[£] \mid ;\mathbf{begin}\ a := a\ a := a\ \mathbf{begin}\ \mathbf{end}\ \$$$

$$\Rightarrow \$[£]q_{16} \mid \mathbf{begin}\ a := a\ a := a\ \mathbf{begin}\ \mathbf{end}\ \$$$

$$\Rightarrow \$[£]q_{16} q_{13} \mid a := a\ a := a\ \mathbf{begin}\ \mathbf{end}\ \$$$

$$\Rightarrow \$[£]q_{16} q_{13} q_3 \mid := a\ a := a\ \mathbf{begin}\ \mathbf{end}\ \$$$

$\Rightarrow \$[\pounds]q_{16}q_{13}q_3q_4 \mid a\ a := a$ **begin end** \$

$\Rightarrow \$[\pounds]q_{16}q_{13}q_3q_4q_8 \mid a := a$ **begin end** \$

$\Rightarrow \$[\pounds]q_{16}q_{13}q_3q_4q_{12} \mid a := a$ **begin end** \$

$\Rightarrow \$[\pounds]q_{16}q_{13}q_3q_4q_5 \mid a := a$ **begin end** \$

$\Rightarrow \$[\pounds]q_{16}q_{13}q_{18} \mid a := a$ **begin end** \$

$\Rightarrow \$[\pounds]q_{16}q_{13}q_{14} \mid a := a$ **begin end** \$

* **end** or ';' expected.

$\Rightarrow \$[\pounds] \mid a := a$ **begin end** \$

$\Rightarrow \$[\pounds]q_{22} \mid := a$ **begin end** \$

$\Rightarrow \$[\pounds]q_{22}q_4 \mid a$ **begin end** \$

$\Rightarrow \$[\pounds]q_{22}q_4q_8 \mid$ **begin end** \$

$\Rightarrow \$[\pounds]q_{22}q_4q_{12} \mid$ **begin end** \$

$\Rightarrow \$[\pounds]q_{22}q_4q_5 \mid$ **begin end** \$

$\Rightarrow \$[\pounds]q_{19} \mid$ **begin end** \$

$\Rightarrow \$[\pounds] \mid$ **begin end** \$

$\Rightarrow \$[\pounds]q_{13} \mid$ **end** \$

$\Rightarrow \$[\pounds]q_{13}q_{18} \mid$ **end** \$

$\Rightarrow \$[\pounds]q_{13}q_{14} \mid$ **end** \$

$\Rightarrow \$[\pounds]q_{13}q_{14}q_{15} \mid \$$

$\Rightarrow \$[\pounds]q_{19} \mid \$$

$\Rightarrow \$[\pounds] \mid \$$ .

Observe that the errors were detected correctly except that, because the stack contents were discarded altogether after an error, the unbalanced begin- and end-keywords were left undetected.

## 9.4 Error Reporting

In the case of each error detected, an error recovering parser should issue a comprehensive error message. The error messages may be classified as "declarative" and "operational"; the declarative message pinpoints the location of the error and describes nature of the error from the viewpoint of the parser, whereas the operational message indicates the particular recovery action performed by the recovery routine. In the case of an automatic error handling technique it is the

| | RAction/Action | | | | | | | | | RGoto/Goto | | | |
|---|---|---|---|---|---|---|---|---|---|---|---|---|---|
| | $a$ | := | **begin** | **end** | ; | + | ( | ) | \$ | $S$ | $E$ | $C$ | $T$ |
| 1 | $s3$ | $r1$ | $s13$ | $r1$ | $r1$ | $r1$ | $r1$ | $r1$ | $r1$ | 2 | | | |
| 2 | | | | | | | | | $a$ | | | | |
| 3 | | $s4$ | | | | | | | | | | | |
| 4 | $s8$ | | | | | | $s9$ | | | | 5 | | 12 |
| 5 | $r2$ | $r2$ | $r2$ | $r2$ | $r2$ | $s6$ | $r2$ | $r2$ | $r2$ | | | | |
| 6 | $s8$ | | | | | | $s9$ | | | | | | 7 |
| 7 | $r6$ | $r6$ | $r6$ | $r6$ | $r6$ | $r6$ | $r6$ | $r6$ | $r6$ | | | | |
| 8 | $r8$ | $r8$ | $r8$ | $r8$ | $r8$ | $r8$ | $r8$ | $r8$ | $r8$ | | | | |
| 9 | $s8$ | | | | | | $s9$ | | | | 10 | | 12 |
| 10 | | | | | | $s6$ | | $s11$ | | | | | |
| 11 | $r9$ | $r9$ | $r9$ | $r9$ | $r9$ | $r9$ | $r9$ | $r9$ | $r9$ | | | | |
| 12 | $r7$ | $r7$ | $r7$ | $r7$ | $r7$ | $r7$ | $r7$ | $r7$ | $r7$ | | | | |
| 13 | $s3$ | $r1$ | $s13$ | $r1$ | $r1$ | $r1$ | $r1$ | $r1$ | $r1$ | 18 | | 14 | |
| 14 | | | | $s15$ | $s16$ | | | | | | | | |
| 15 | $r3$ | $r3$ | $r3$ | $r3$ | $r3$ | $r3$ | $r3$ | $r3$ | $r3$ | | | | |
| 16 | $s3$ | $r1$ | $s13$ | $r1$ | $r1$ | $r1$ | $r1$ | $r1$ | $r1$ | 17 | | | |
| 17 | $r4$ | $r4$ | $r4$ | $r4$ | $r4$ | $r4$ | $r4$ | $r4$ | $r4$ | | | | |
| 18 | $r5$ | $r5$ | $r5$ | $r5$ | $r5$ | $r5$ | $r5$ | $r5$ | $r5$ | | | | |
| $q_S = 19$ | $c$ | $c$ | $c$ | $c$ | $c$ | $c$ | $c$ | $c$ | $c$ | | | | |
| $q_E = 20$ | $r2$ | $r2$ | $r2$ | $r2$ | $r2$ | $s6$ | $r2$ | $s11$ | $r2$ | | | | |
| $q_T = 21$ | $c$ | $c$ | $c$ | $c$ | $c$ | $c$ | $c$ | $c$ | $c$ | | | | |
| $q_a = 22$ | $r8$ | $s4$ | $r8$ | $r8$ | $r8$ | $r8$ | $r8$ | $r8$ | $r8$ | | | | |

**Figure 9.13** The parsing and error recovering table for the LR(1) parser using default reductions for the grammar $G_{\text{block}\,2}$: (1) $S \to \varepsilon$, (2) $S \to a := E$, (3) $S \to$ **begin** $C$ **end**, (4) $C \to C; S$, (5) $C \to S$, (6) $E \to E + T$, (7) $E \to T$, (8) $T \to a$, (9) $T \to (E)$. The Action and Goto tables are the first 18 rows; the RAction and RGoto tables contain all the 22 rows. In the RAction/Action tables, $a$ denotes "accept", $ri$ denotes "reduce by rule $i$", $sq$ denotes "shift $q$", $c$ denotes "conflict", and "error" is denoted by blank. In the RGoto/Goto tables blank for entry $[q, A]$ denotes the value $\varnothing$

declarative messages that present a problem, not the operational ones. Therefore we shall consider in this section only the generation of declarative messages. We also feel that good declarative messages provide sufficient information about the error, as the full understanding of the operational messages often requires some knowledge of the parsing and the error recovery method.

A declarative error message should contain explicit and concise information about the error situation. This information is to be given in terms of the language, or grammar, only; all references to parser states and internal data structures should be avoided. Because at an error configuration the current input symbol is not a valid continuation of the parsing stack, it is natural to incorporate in the associated declarative message information about the "expected" symbols, that is, symbols that are valid continuations of the stack. For example, consider the LALR(1) parser given in Figure 9.13 and the erroneous string

**begin** $a; a + a$ **end** .

The error is detected at the configuration

$$\$q_1q_{13}q_3 \,|\, ; a + a \textbf{ end} \$ \ ,$$

and the most convenient declarative error message is

":= expected" ,

because the assign arrow is the only symbol that can legally follow the contents of the stack.

In the following we shall treat separately LL(1) and LR(1) parsers. We shall give rules for the design of declarative error messages based on the expected symbols.

### *SLL*(1) *parsing*

In LL(1) parsing we always have at hand a prediction of the remaining input string. Thus, when an error occurs, we can use this prediction as the basis of the error message. Recall from Sections 5.6 and 9.2 that in SLL(1) parsing errors can only occur in two ways. First, a *shift error* occurs if a terminal cannot be shifted. In this case the topmost element in the stack is a prediction of a terminal, but the current input symbol disagrees with it. (We consider here the stack implementation; recursive descent implementation has the same types of errors and error messages.) Secondly, a *produce error* occurs if a nonterminal cannot be expanded. In this case the topmost element in the stack is a prediction of a nonterminal, but the current input symbol is neither its starter nor, in the case of a nullable nonterminal, its follower.

In SLL(1) parsing the information about the "expected" symbols at an error configuration can always be encoded by a single symbol: in the case of a shift error the only expected symbol is the terminal to be shifted, and in the case of a produce error the expected symbols are obtained as starters of the nonterminal to be expanded. Accordingly, a natural form for a declarative message is

"*a* expected"

in the case of a shift error (for terminal *a*), and, for example,

"no *A* can start with this"

in the case of a produce error (for nonterminal *A*). In fact, these kinds of error messages appear frequently in handmade production compilers implemented using the recursive descent method. As an example of the use of these messages consider the SLL(1) parsers given in Figures 5.5, 5.9, and 9.6.

### *LR*(1) *parsing*

The above rules for creating declarative error messages for LL(1) parsers are rather straightforward. Unfortunately, these rules do not readily carry over to LR(1) parsing. As we shall see, there are in the error detection state usually a great number of expected symbols, both terminals and nonterminals. This means that we have the problem of choosing suitable expected symbols for a concise declarative error message.

Let $G = (V, T, P, S)$ be a grammar and $M$ its LR(0)-based LR(1) parser. We say that $X$ in $V$ is *expected* in state $q = \text{VALID}(\gamma)$ if $q$ contains an item of the form $[A \to \alpha \cdot X\beta]$. Further, we say that $X$ is *expected* in configuration $\$\eta \mid x\$$ of $M$ if $X$ is expected in $\eta{:}1$. It follows from the construction of an LR(1) parser that if $X$ is expected in a configuration, then $X$, as well as the strings derived by it, are valid continuations of the stack. There may also be other valid continuations, namely lookahead symbols of those reduce actions that apply to the stack string. Then the *error detection state*, that is, the topmost state $q = \text{VALID}(\gamma)$ in the stack in the error configuration, contains items of the form $[A \to \omega \cdot]$. In this case the expected symbols alone do not necessarily form a sufficient basis for the declarative error message. However, this situation for the error detection states does not occur if default reductions are used. Then all the possible reductions have already been applied to the stack string before error detection, and the declarative error messages can be based solely on the expected symbols.

As an example of a situation that allows a straightforward generation of a declarative message, consider the error recovering parser given in Figure 9.13 and the erroneous string

$$\textbf{begin}\ a := a\, a := a\ \textbf{end}\ .$$

Here a semicolon is missing between the two $a$'s in the middle. As default reductions are used, the error is detected at the configuration

$$\$q_1 q_{13} q_{14} \mid a := a\ \textbf{end}\,\$\ .$$

The items in the state $q_{14}$ are:

$$[S \to \textbf{begin}\ C \cdot \textbf{end}]\ ,$$

$$[C \to C \cdot ;\ S]\ .$$

The items in the error detection state are thus incomplete, and the terminals **end** and ';' are the only expected symbols. Accordingly, we stipulate that the associated declarative message is:

"**end** or ';' expected" .

Consider again the grammar $G_{\text{block2}}$ and the erroneous string in which the left part of the latter assignment statement is missing:

$$\textbf{begin}\ a := a\ ;\ := a\ \textbf{end}\ .$$

The parser of Figure 9.13 detects the error at the configuration:

$$\$q_1 q_{13} q_{14} \mid := a\ \textbf{end}\,\$\ ,$$

and again, the error message would be "**end** or ';' expected". In contrast to the previous example, this message does not give a correct impression of the nature of the error. This is because the use of default reductions makes the parser think that there is an empty statement between the semicolon and the assignment arrow. In fact, for the generation of error messages, reductions by rules with an empty right-hand side should never be chosen as default reductions. Following this requirement the parser would detect the error already at the configuration

$$\$q_1 q_{13} q_{14} q_{16} \mid := a \ \textbf{end} \ \$ \ .$$

The items in the error detection state $q_{16}$ are:

$$[C \to C\, ;\, \cdot S] \ ,$$

$$[S \to \cdot] \ ,$$

$$[S \to \cdot a := E] \ ,$$

$$[S \to \cdot \textbf{begin}\ C\ \textbf{end}] \ ,$$

and thus the expected symbols are $S$, $a$, and **begin**. Note that also in this case the declarative error message can be based solely on the expected symbols, even though the state $q_{16}$ contains an item of the form $[A \to \omega \cdot]$, namely the item $[S \to \cdot]$. Clearly, the expected symbol $S$ captures the information about the valid continuations arising from the lookahead symbols of the reduce action by the rule $S \to \varepsilon$.

Oberve that $S$ is the only expected symbol appearing immediately after the dot in an essential item of the error detection state $q_{16}$, whereas the two other only arise from inessential, descendant items. We say that symbol $X$ expected in state $q$ is *essential* if it arises from an essential item, that is, $q$ contains an item of the form $[A \to \alpha \cdot X\beta]$ with $\alpha \neq \varepsilon$.

Clearly, the essential expected symbols capture all the information about the valid continuations obtained by all the expected symbols. Thus, for the error configuration

$$\$q_1 q_{13} q_{14} q_{16} \mid := a \ \textbf{end} \ \$$$

we stipulate that the associated declarative error message is:

"No $S$ can start with this" .

So far, we have presented two kinds of declarative messages. The format of a message depended on whether the symbol expected was a terminal or a nonterminal. However, the classification of grammar symbols into terminals and nonterminals is not refined enough for the general generation of declarative messages. We must distinguish from the nonterminals those that only behave as names for sets of single terminals. Such nonterminals should obviously be treated as terminals in error messages.

We say that symbol $X$ is *terminallike* if either (1) $X$ is itself a terminal, or (2) $X$ is a nonterminal that has only unit rules with terminallike right-hand sides, that is, every rule for $X$ is of the form $X \to Y$ where $Y$ is a terminallike symbol. A terminallike symbol can be regarded as a name for a set of terminals playing an equivalent role in a certain grammatical context. A nonterminal which is not terminallike is called *nonterminallike.*

If only essential symbols are used, this greatly reduces the number of expected symbols to be included in a declarative error message. In certain cases there may, however, still be some annoying redundancy even between the essential symbols. An essential expected symbol $Y$ may be redundant in the sense that another essential expected symbol $X$ derives $Y$ by unit rules. In each error detection state, we take into account only those essential symbols, called *maximal,* that are not derived by unit rules from other essential symbols in that state.

We are now ready to give a precise description of the automatic generation of declarative error messages for LR(1) parsers. We first consider the case in which no error detection state $q$ contains an essential item of the form $[A \to \omega \cdot]$. That is, the message associated with the error detection state is based on the expected symbols only. Suppose that $X_1, \ldots, X_n$ are the maximal essential symbols expected in error detection state $q$. If each symbol $X_i$ is terminallike, then the declarative message associated with $q$ takes one of the following forms:

(1a) "$X_1$ expected." (case $n = 1$) ;

(1b) "$X_1, \ldots, X_{n-1}$ or $X_n$ expected." (case $n > 1$) .

If, on the contrary, each symbol $X_i$ is nonterminallike, then the message takes one of the following forms:

(2a) "No $X_1$ can start with this." (case $n = 1$) ;

(2b) "Neither $X_1, \ldots, X_{n-1}$ nor $X_n$ can start with this." (case $n > 1$) .

Then we have to consider the case in which there are both terminallike and nonterminallike symbols among $X_1, \ldots, X_n$. If the symbols $X_1, \ldots, X_k (k \geqslant 1)$ are terminallike and the remaining $n - k$ symbols $X_{k+1}, \ldots, X_n (k < n)$ are nonterminallike, then the associated message takes one of the following forms:

(3a) "$X_1, \ldots, X_{n-1}$ or start of $X_n$ expected." (case $k = n - 1$) ;

(3b) "$X_1, \ldots, X_k$ or start of $X_{k+1}, \ldots, X_{n-1}$, or $X_n$ expected." (case $k < n - 1$) .

We are now left with the case in which the error detection state $q$ contains essential items of the form $[A \to \omega \cdot]$. If default reductions are allowed, this cannot occur in any error detection state. If default reductions are not allowed, for example in non-unique reduce states, then there are usually a number of error detection states with this property. For these states the expected symbols do not give sufficient information on the valid continuations of the parsing stack, and the valid lookahead symbols should also be taken into account. For practical grammars, however, there may be a large number of lookahead symbols for one reduce state.

Thus the requirement of a concise message is not fulfilled if the lookahead symbols are to be listed in an error message. Moreover, in an LR(0)-based LR(1) parser not all lookahead symbols are valid continuations of the stack, and there is no way to choose the correct ones. In this case the declarative error message is based on the unique entry symbol $X$ of the error detection state, and it takes one of the following forms:

(4a) "$X$ cannot be followed by this."
(4b) "No complete $X$ can be followed by this."
If the entry symbol $X$ is terminallike, then the form (4a) is used. Otherwise, (4b) is used.

Clearly, messages of types (1a) to (3b) are more informative, and therefore more desirable, than those of types (4a) and (4b). Paradoxically, the decreased error detection capability of an LR(1) parser using default reductions allows better error messages to be generated. Default reductions have the effect of condensing the information around the error so that a more concise declarative message is possible. For example, if default reductions are not allowed in non-unique reduce states, then the LALR(1) parser of $G_{\text{block2}}$ detects the misspelling of **end** in

**begin** $a := a$ **ned**

at the configuration

$\$q_1q_{13}q_3q_4q_5 \mid$ **ned** $\$$ .

Here the associated message is, according to (4b), "No complete $E$ can be followed by this.". On the other hand, if default reductions are allowed, then the error is detected at the configuration

$\$q_1q_{13}q_{14} \mid$ **ned** $\$$ ,

where the associated message is, according to (1b), "';' or **end** expected." This is certainly a more desirable message, because now the keyword **end** is stated explicitly.

## Exercises

9.1 Show that the location of the parser-defined error in an incorrect string may be arbitrarily far to the right from the location of a minimum distance error.

9.2 Compare the error recovering schemes given in Figure 9.1, Figure 9.4, and Exercise 5.40 in the case of the recursive descent implementation of the SLL(1) parser of $G_{\text{block}}$. To make this comparison consider the erroneous string

**begin** $a$ **begin** $a\,a$ **end** ; **end** ; **begin** $x$ **end** **begin** ,

where $x$ stands for a misspelled $a$. For each of the three error recovery methods, answer the following questions. The answers should then serve as a basis for your comparison.

a) At which point does the error recovering parser issue error messages and what are these messages?
b) Evaluate the quality of the messages. Which of the messages are misleading? Which are totally extraneous, that is, reports of nonexistent errors?
c) How large a portion of the input string is processed in the normal parsing mode?

9.3 Consider the error recovering recursive descent parser for $G_{\text{block}}$ given in Figures 9.5 to 9.7. Modify this parser so that *default produce actions* are used, that is, so that in parsing procedures one produce action is always applied without checking the lookahead (see Exercise 5.36). Does this modification affect the quality of error recovery? Compare the behaviour of the new parser with that of the original one in the case of the erroneous strings

**begin** *a a* ; **begin** *a* **end**

and

**begin** *a* **begin** *a a* **end** ; **end** ; **begin** *x* **end** **begin** .

9.4 In the error recovering scheme for SLL(1) parsers given in Figure 9.4 a procedure $B$ may be called only if the current input symbol belongs to $\text{FIRST}_1(B)$. It would basically be correct to replace this condition by the requirement that the current input symbol belongs to $\text{FIRST}_1(B\ \text{FOLLOW}_1(B))$. Show, however, that this change could cause the error recovering parser to loop forever.

9.5 When evaluating the quality of recovery actions made by an error recovering parser for a programming language, the following approach may be used. The recovery actions are divided up into four categories: "excellent", "good", "fair", and "poor", according to the overall quality of the actions. These categories only apply to recoveries from actual errors, whereas recoveries from extraneous errors are not classified at all. This is because it makes no sense in the case of an extraneous error to evaluate the extent to which the recovery action corresponds to "what the programmer had intended". A recovery action from an actual error is classified as "excellent" if it clearly corresponds to what the programmer intended. In addition, we require that it neither causes extraneous messages nor the missing of another actual error. If a recovery action probably does not correspond to what the programmer intended but still gives rise to neither extraneous messages nor missed errors, it is classified as "good". A "fair" recovery action may cause one extraneous message or one missed error (but not both at the same time). Finally, if a recovery action does not meet the requirements of a fair recovery action, then it is classified as "poor".

Consider then the error recovering recursive descent parser for $G_{\text{block}}$ given in Figures 9.5 to 9.7. Are you able to classify the performed recovery actions according to the above rules in the case of the erroneous string

**begin** *a* **begin** *a a* **end** ; **end** ; **begin** *x* **end** **begin** ?

Do this classification also in the case where the parser uses default produce actions such that a produce action by a rule with a nullable right-hand side is always preferred as default.

9.6 Give an error recovering recursive descent parser for the grammar $\hat{G}_{\mathbf{exp}}$:

$$E \to TE' \ ,$$

$$E' \to \varepsilon | +TE' \ ,$$

$$T \to FT' \ ,$$

$$T' \to \varepsilon | *FT' \ ,$$

$$F \to a | (E) \ .$$

The error handling procedure should correspond to the scheme defined in Figure 9.4. Demonstrate the behaviour of the parser in the case of the following incorrect input strings:

a) $a + a)$ b) $(a ++ (a * aa)$

9.7 Write a procedure—similar to that given in Figure 9.4—that implements the proposed error handling scheme for the stack implementation of SLL(1) parsers.

9.8 Give the error recovering SLL(1) parser for the grammar $G_{\mathbf{block}}$ as a stack implementation.

9.9 Give the error recovering SLL(1) parser for the grammar $\hat{G}_{\mathbf{exp}}$ as a stack implementation.

9.10 Design an error handling method for canonical LL(1) parsers. You may base your design on the given error handling scheme for SLL(1) parsers as stack implementation. Apply the method to the canonical LL(1) parser of the grammar $\hat{G}_{\mathbf{exp}}$. Demonstrate the behaviour of the resulting error recovering canonical LL(1) parser in the case of the input string $a) * a + aa$. What can you say about the behaviour when compared to the error recovering SLL(1) parser?

9.11 Prove Theorem 9.6.

9.12 What is the complexity of the algorithm implied by Theorem 9.6 for computing all the feasible reduction goals in an error configuration $\$q_0q_1 \ldots q_m \mid a_1 \ldots a_n$?

9.13 Construct the SLR(1) parser of the SLR(1) grammar

$$S \to A|cS|cBd \ ,$$

$$A \to Bc|aa \ ,$$

$$B \to A \ .$$

Consider then the erroneous string *ad*. Simulate the behaviour of the phrase-level recovery strategy (based on unique important feasible reduction goals) as defined in Section 9.3 except that the recovery symbols are not required to be shiftable. Observe that the recovery process will never terminate.

9.14 Consider the SLR(1) grammar

$$S \to A|B|bA|bC|cB|cD \ ,$$

$$A \to aEG \ ,$$

$$B \to aFG \ ,$$

$$C \to aFd \ ,$$

$$D \to aEd \ ,$$

$$E \to FG|e \ ,$$

$$F \to EG \ ,$$

$$G \to g \ .$$

Construct the LALR(1) parser for this grammar, and consider the effect of phrase-level recovery (based on unique important feasible reduction goals) in the case of the erroneous string *aed*. Show that the recovery actions make the error recovering parser loop forever if the recovery symbols are not required to be shiftable.

9.15 Show that phrase-level recovery as defined in Section 9.3 may never cause the error recovering parser to loop forever when the underlying parser is the canonical LR(1) parser of an LR(1) grammar, even if the recovery symbols are not required to be shiftable at the goal states.

9.16 Demonstrate the behaviour of the phrase-level recovery method as defined in Section 9.3. Consider the grammar $G_{\mathrm{block2}}$ and its LALR(1) parser (given in Figure 7.12). Use

**begin** *a* := ; *a* := *a a* := *a* **begin end**

as a sample input string. For comparison, use both of the two given search strategies for error phrases. Also compare the behaviour with and without local correction.

9.17 Give an algorithm to compute the weakly feasible reduction goals for an error phrase.

9.18 Following the scheme given in Figures 9.9 to 9.11 construct an error recovering LR(1) parser

a) for the grammar:

$E \to E + T|T$ ,

$T \to T*F|F$ ,

$F \to a|(E)$ ;

b) for the grammar:

| | |
|---|---|
| $S \to A\|I$, | $T \to T*P\|P$ , |
| $A \to a := E$, | $P \to a\|(E)$ , |
| $I \to \textbf{if } B \textbf{ then } AL$, | $B \to B \textbf{ or } a\|a$ , |
| $E \to E + T\|T$, | $L \to \textbf{else } S\|\varepsilon$ . |

(Cf. Exercise 7.21.)

9.19 In the scheme for error recovering LR(1) parsers given in Figures 9.9 to 9.11 some extra work is needed for parsing correct sentences: in all cases there is a test for the stack depth in conjunction with reduce actions. Modify the scheme so that the behaviour of the parser remains completely unaffected in the case of correct sentences.

9.20 Show that an error recovering LR(1) parser as defined in Figures 9.9 to 9.11 does not loop forever on any input string.

9.21 Give all the error detection states and the corresponding declarative error messages as prescribed in Section 9.4

a) for the LALR(1) parser of $G_{\text{block2}}$ (Figure 7.12);
b) for the error recovering LR(1) parser of $G_{\text{block2}}$ given in Figure 9.13;
c) for the error recovering LR(1) parser of $G_{\text{block2}}$ obtained from the one given in Figure 9.13 such that default reductions are not applied in the states $q_1$ and $q_{16}$.

## Bibliographic Notes

The concept of the parser-defined error originates in Peterson (1972) and Aho and Peterson (1972), who investigate the relationship between minimum-distance and parser-defined errors (cf. Exercise 9.1). The question of error detection in precedence parsing is discussed e.g. in Graham and Rhodes (1973, 1975), who argue that it may be desirable to detect errors later than the correct-prefix parser does.

The error recovery strategy for recursive descent parsers given in Section 9.2 is similar to the method by Lewi, De Vlaminck, Huens and Huybrechts (1978). Other recovery strategies for recursive descent and LL(1) parsers have been designed e.g. by Wirth (1976), Backhouse (1979, 1984), Fischer, Milton and Quiring (1980), Pai and Kieburtz (1980), and Röhrich (1980).

The basic work on phrase-level recovery is that by Leinius (1970). The principal parsing method considered is simple precedence parsing, but a phrase-level recovery strategy is also suggested for canonical LR(1) parsers. Leinius' ideas were first implemented by James (1972) in LALR(1) parsing. Peterson (1972) refines the selection strategy of error phrases and reduction goals, and also uses the method in SLR(1) parsing. The further refinement, the use of feasible reduction goals, comes from Sippu and Soisalon-Soininen (1977, 1983b).

Leinius (1970) was also the first to suggest a forward move for resolving nondeterminism in phrase-level recovery. The idea of using a forward move before eventual recovery was made popular by Graham and Rhodes (1973, 1975), whose recovery technique for simple precedence parsing is considered by many to be one of the most sophisticated. Forward-move recovery techniques in conjunction with LR(1) parsing have been developed by Mickunas and Modry (1978), Pennello and DeRemer (1978), Shields (1978), and Druseikis and Ripley (1976). Our scheme given in Figures 9.9 to 9.11 is similar to that of Druseikis and Ripley (1976).

The systematic method for generating declarative error messages presented in Section 9.4 is from Sippu (1981) and from Sippu and Soisalon-Soininen (1983b). Implementation results of Sippu and Soisalon-Soininen (1983b) indicate that the overall quality of the error messages is high: the errors are correctly pinpointed and lucidly reported. Usually very little attention has been paid to the generation of error messages even in automatic error handling, cf. Horning (1976) and Kantorowitz and Laor (1986); also see the various surveys and bibliographies on error handling (Gries, 1976; Ciesinger, 1979; Sippu, 1981; Röhrich, 1982; Hammond and Rayward-Smith, 1984).

Some authors have given experimental evaluations of their error recovery techniques (Pennello and DeRemer, 1978; Graham, Haley and Joy, 1979; Pai and Kieburtz, 1980; Sippu and Soisalon-Soininen, 1983b; Burke and Fisher, 1987). Comparison of these techniques has also been possible, to some extent, because all these authors have used in their evaluations a set of erroneous Pascal programs collected by Ripley and Druseikis (1978).

Some formal investigations of error recovery techniques have appeared in the literature. Levy (1975), Pai and Kieburtz (1980), Tai (1980) and Mauney and Fischer (1988) investigate the problem of determining sufficient lookahead for local correction. Aho and Peterson (1972) and Lyon (1974) present algorithms for global minimum-distance correction (also see Mauney and Fischer, 1982). Sippu and Soisalon-Soininen (1980) present a theoretical study of the limitations of error correcting LR($k$) parsers, and Richter (1985) takes a new step towards defining provable properties of error handling techniques.

# 10. Testing Grammars for Parsability

In the preceding chapters we have studied in detail the major methods of deterministic context-free parsing: strong LL($k$) parsing (Chapter 5), simple precedence parsing (Chapter 5), canonical LR($k$) parsing, LALR($k$) parsing, and SLR($k$) parsing (Chapters 6 and 7), and canonical LL($k$) parsing (Chapter 8). Each of these methods induces a class of grammars that are "parsable" using that method, that is, a class of grammars for which a deterministic parser employing that method can be constructed. For example, the LL($k$) grammars constitute the class of grammars parsable by the LL($k$) parsing method. By definition, a context-free grammar is an LL($k$) grammar if and only if its canonical LL($k$) parser is deterministic.

The present chapter is devoted to the problem of testing context-free grammars for parsability. We shall study how hard it is to determine whether or not a given context-free grammar is a member of grammar class C($k$), where "C($k$)" may stand for "strong LL($k$)", "LALL($k$)", "LL($k$)", "SLR($k$)", "LALR($k$)", or "LR($k$)", or some of the complement classes, for example "non-LL($k$)" or "non-LR($k$)". More specifically, we shall study the complexity of the following decision problems:

$\mathscr{P}_{C(k)}$: "Given a context-free grammar $G$, is $G$ a C($k$) grammar?"
$\mathscr{P}_{C}$: "Given a context-free grammar $G$ and a natural number $k$, is $G$ a C($k$) grammar?"

In each of the problems $\mathscr{P}_{C(k)}$, $k \geqslant 0$, the natural number $k$ is fixed and is not a parameter of the problem; an instance of $\mathscr{P}_{C(k)}$ consists only of code($G$), the encoding of grammar $G$. In the problem $\mathscr{P}_{C}$ (called the "uniform C($k$) testing problem") both $G$ and $k$ are problem parameters; an instance of $\mathscr{P}_{C}$ is a pair of the form (code($G$), code($k$)) where code($G$) is the encoding of grammar $G$ and $k$ is the representation (in unary or in binary) of natural number $k$.

From the results of the previous chapters we know that the problems $\mathscr{P}_{C}$ and $\mathscr{P}_{C(k)}$, $k \geqslant 0$, are all solvable. We can test a grammar $G$ for membership in C($k$) by constructing the C($k$) parser for $G$ and checking whether or not this parser is deterministic. However, the complexity of this kind of a test has as a lower bound the size of the parser, which is usually exponential in the size of the grammar (we recall that only the strong LL($k$) and simple precedence parsers have size polynomial in the grammar). This may be impractical in an environment in which we do not need the parser but only wish to know whether or not the grammar is C($k$). For example, this is the case when we are developing a parsing grammar for a new programming language. The grammar is obtained as the result of an iterative process in which the original, "raw" syntax taken from the language manual is transformed step by step into a grammar that possesses the desired C($k$) property. At each step we use a compiler writing system to check whether or not the current version of the grammar is C($k$), and if not, to report all the C($k$) conflicts it contains. It would be desirable that this checking and conflict reporting could be made as fast as possible.

We shall show that when C($k$) denotes the class of strong LL($k$), LL($k$), SLR($k$), or LR($k$) grammars, then the fixed-$k$ C($k$) testing problem $\mathscr{P}_{C(k)}$ is solvable in deterministic polynomial time. The algorithms for LR($k$) and SLR($k$) testing are given in Section 10.1, and the algorithms for strong LL($k$) and LL($k$) testing are given in Section 10.2. The uniform C($k$) testing problem for these classes seems not to be solvable in deterministic polynomial time. Also, the complexity of this problem depends radically on the representation chosen for $k$. We shall show that the uniform non-C($k$) testing problem is in NP when $k$ is expressed in unary, and in NE when $k$ is expressed in binary. Here NP denotes the class of decision problems solvable in nondeterministic polynomial time and NE denotes the class of decision problems solvable in nondeterministic one-level exponential time. In Section 10.3 we shall show that uniform non-C($k$) testing is NP-hard for $k$ in unary and NE-hard for $k$ in binary. This means that uniform non-C($k$) testing for $k$ in unary is among the hardest problems in NP and that uniform non-C($k$) testing for $k$ in binary is among the hardest problems in NE. Any problem in NP (NE) will reduce in polynomial time to uniform non-C($k$) testing for $k$ in unary (in binary).

In proving the hardness results for non-C($k$) testing we shall need some knowledge of the general theory of deriving lower bounds for the complexity of decision problems. We shall use a primitive model of computation, called a Turing machine. The hardness of non-C($k$) testing will follow from the fundamental result that the set of accepting Turing machine computations on a given input can be represented as the intersection of two context-free languages. From this result we shall also derive as a by-product some unsolvability results on context-free grammars, for example, the unsolvability of the problem of testing whether or not a given context-free grammar is ambiguous. Closely related to this is also the unsolvability of the decision problem

> "Given a context-free grammar $G$, is there a natural number $k$ such that $G$ is C($k$)?"

The grammar classes LALR($k$) and LALL($k$) form an exception as compared to the other classes C($k$) considered above. For LALR($k$) testing a deterministic polynomial time-bounded algorithm seems to exist only when $k = 0$, and for LALL($k$) testing only when $k = 0$ or $k = 1$. However, in Section 10.4 we shall show that for any fixed $k \geqslant 0$ these problems belong to PSPACE, the class of decision problems solvable in polynomial space. Using the result that the set of Turing machine noncomputations forms a regular language we shall show that for fixed $k \geqslant 1$ LALR($k$) testing is PSPACE-hard and that for fixed $k \geqslant 2$ LALL($k$) testing is PSPACE-hard.

## 10.1 Efficient Algorithms for LR($k$) and SLR($k$) Testing

In this section we shall show that for any fixed $k \geqslant 0$ the LR($k$) testing problem

$\mathscr{P}_{\text{LR}(k)}$: "Given a context-free grammar $G$, is $G$ an LR($k$) grammar?"

is solvable in deterministic polynomial time, and that the uniform non-LR($k$) testing problem

$\mathscr{P}_{\text{non-LR}}$: "Given a context-free grammar $G$ and a natural number $k$, is $G$ a non-LR($k$) grammar?"

is solvable in nondeterministic polynomial time when $k$ is expressed in unary, and in nondeterministic one-level exponential time when $k$ is expressed in binary. The same results will also hold when we replace "LR" by "SLR".

We recall from Chapter 1 (Section 1.5) that a decision problem is solvable in deterministic polynomial time (P) if it has a deterministic solution that runs in time $O(p(n))$, where $p$ is a polynomial. A decision problem is solvable in nondeterministic polynomial time (NP) if it has a (possibly nondeterministic) partial solution that runs in time $O(p(n))$. A decision problem is solvable in nondeterministic one-level exponential time (NE) if it has a (possibly nondeterministic) partial solution that runs in time $O(2^{p(n)})$. By a two-level exponential bound we mean $O(2^{p(2^{q(n)})})$, where both $p$ and $q$ are polynomials.

The key idea in developing efficient solutions to the LR($k$) testing problems is to represent the deterministic, canonical LR($k$) machine succinctly as an equivalent nondeterministic automaton, or, as we shall see, as a collection of nondeterministic automata that together have the effect of the original one. The size of these nondeterministic automata is only polynomial in the size of the grammar, as opposed to the exponential size of the deterministic LR($k$) machine.

In Chapter 7 we showed how the LR(0) machine can be constructed from a nondeterministic automaton whose states are single 0-items of the grammar. The LR(0) machine is obtained from this automaton using the conventional algorithm for transforming a nondeterministic finite automaton into a deterministic one (Section 3.4). The construction can easily be generalized to $k > 0$ to obtain a nondeterministic version of the canonical LR($k$) machine, $k > 0$.

Let $G = (V, T, P, S)$ be a grammar and $k$ a natural number. Denote by $I_k$ the set of all $k$-items of $G$. The *nondeterministic LR($k$) machine* for $G$ is the (usually nondeterministic) finite automaton with state alphabet $I_k \cup \{q_s\}$, $q_s \notin I_k$, input alphabet $V$, initial state $q_s$, and with set of transitions consisting of all rules of the forms:

(i) $q_s \to [S \to \cdot\omega, \varepsilon]$ ,

(ii) $[A \to \alpha \cdot X\beta, y]X \to [A \to \alpha X \cdot \beta, y]$, $\quad X \in V$ , and

(iii) $[A \to \alpha \cdot B\beta, y] \to [B \to \cdot\omega, z]$, $\quad B \in V \setminus T$, $\quad z \in \text{FIRST}_k(\beta y)$ .

In other words, there is (i) a transition on the empty string $\varepsilon$ from the initial state $q_s$ to all states $[S \rightarrow \cdot\omega, \varepsilon]$, where $S \rightarrow \omega$ is a rule of the start symbol $S$ of $G$, (ii) a transition on symbol $X$ from any state $[A \rightarrow \alpha \cdot X\beta, y]$ to the state $[A \rightarrow \alpha X \cdot \beta, y]$, and (iii) a transition on $\varepsilon$ from any state $[A \rightarrow \alpha \cdot B\beta, y]$ to all states $[B \rightarrow \cdot\omega, z]$ where $B \rightarrow \omega$ is a rule in $P$ and $z$ is a string in $\text{FIRST}_k(\beta y)$ .

The definition does not fix the set of final states of the machine. Which states are regarded as final states depends on the purpose for which the machine is used. In LR($k$) testing the set of final states will be

$$\{[A \rightarrow \omega\cdot, y] \mid A \rightarrow \omega \in P, y \in k{:}T^*\}$$
$$\cup \{[A \rightarrow \alpha \cdot a\beta, y] \mid A \rightarrow \alpha a\beta \in P, a \in T, y \in k{:}T^*\} .$$

**Theorem 10.1** *A state $[A \rightarrow \alpha \cdot \beta, y]$ in the nondeterministic LR($k$) machine of grammar G is accessible upon reading string $\gamma$ if and only if $\gamma$ is a viable prefix of G and $[A \rightarrow \alpha \cdot \beta, y]$ is an LR($k$)-valid item for $\gamma$. In other words,*

$$\{[A \rightarrow \alpha \cdot \beta, y] \mid q_s\gamma \Rightarrow^* [A \rightarrow \alpha \cdot \beta, y]\} = \text{VALID}_k(\gamma) ,$$

*for all $\gamma$ in $V^*$ .*

*Proof.* Using the results of Section 6.2 the theorem is easy to prove by means of induction. We leave the details to the exercises. □

Theorem 10.1 implies (by Theorem 6.27) that the automaton obtained by making the nondeterministic LR($k$) machine deterministic (using the algorithm of Figure 3.9) is exactly the canonical LR($k$) machine.

We recall that the number of distinct item cores $A \rightarrow \alpha \cdot \beta$ in grammar $G = (V, T, P, S)$ is bounded by $|G|$, the size of $G$. We have:

**Fact 10.2** Let $G = (V, T, P, S)$ be a grammar, $k$ a natural number, and $M$ the nondeterministic LR($k$) machine for $G$. Then

(1) $M$ has at most $|k{:}T^*| \cdot |G| + 1 = O(|T|^k \cdot |G|)$ states,
(2) $M$ has at most $|P|$ transitions of type (i),
(3) $M$ has at most $|k{:}T^*| \cdot |G| = O(|T|^k \cdot |G|)$ transitions of type (ii),
(4) $M$ has at most $|k{:}T^*|^2 \cdot |P| \cdot |G| = O(|T|^{2k} \cdot |P| \cdot |G|)$ transitions of type (iii), and
(5) the size of $M$ is $O(|G|^{2k+2})$ or, more specifically, $O(|T|^{2k} \cdot |P| \cdot |G|)$. □

It is possible to reduce further, by a factor of $|P|$, the size of the automaton by introducing additional states of the form $[B, z]$, where $B$ is a nonterminal and $z$ is a string in $k{:}T^*$. Any transition of type (iii)

$$[A \rightarrow \alpha \cdot B\beta, y] \rightarrow [B \rightarrow \cdot\omega, z]$$

is split into two transitions:

$$[A \to \alpha \cdot B\beta, y] \to [B, z], \quad \text{and}$$

$$[B, z] \to [B \to \cdot \omega, z] .$$

The number of these transitions is at most $|k{:}T^*|^2 \cdot |G| + |k{:}T^*| \cdot |P|$. The initial state $q_s$ can be identified with $[S, \varepsilon]$ .

We shall denote this modified automaton by $M_{LR(k)}(G)$, or, if no ambiguity will arise, by $M_k(G)$. Formally, $M_k(G)$ is the finite automaton with state alphabet

$$\{[A \to \alpha \cdot \beta, y] \mid A \to \alpha\beta \text{ is a rule of } G \text{ and } y \in k{:}T^*\}$$
$$\cup \{[A, y] \mid A \text{ is a nonterminal of } G \text{ and } y \in k{:}T^*\} ,$$

input alphabet $V$, initial state $[S, \varepsilon]$, and with set of transitions consisting of all rules of the forms:

(a) $[A, y] \to [A \to \cdot \omega, y]$ ,
(b) $[A \to \alpha \cdot X\beta, y]X \to [A \to \alpha X \cdot \beta, y]$, for $X \in V$, and
(c) $[A \to \alpha \cdot B\beta, y] \to [B, z]$, for $B \in V \setminus T$ and $z \in \text{FIRST}_k(\beta y)$ .

The set of final states of $M_k(G)$ is defined as the union of all sets $F_{\text{reduce}}(u)$, $u \in k{:}T^*$, and $F_{\text{shift}}(u)$, $u \in k{:}T^*$ , where

$$F_{\text{reduce}}(u) = \{[A \to \omega \cdot, u] \mid A \to \omega \text{ is a rule of } G\},$$

$$F_{\text{shift}}(u) = \{[A \to \alpha \cdot a\beta, y] \mid A \to \alpha a\beta \text{ is a rule of } G,\ y \in k{:}T^* \ a \text{ is a terminal, and } u \in \text{FIRST}_k(a\beta y)\}.$$

We shall assume that the final states are not represented as a single set but as two collections of subsets:

$$\{F_{\text{reduce}}(u) \mid u \in k{:}T^*\}, \quad \{F_{\text{shift}}(u) \mid u \in k{:}T^*\} .$$

This is because we wish that given an automaton $M_k(G)$ and an item $I$, it should be easy to determine whether or not $I$ belongs to a specific set $F_{\text{reduce}}(u)$ or $F_{\text{shift}}(u)$ .

**Fact 10.3** For any grammar $G = (V, T, P, S)$ and natural number $k$, the following statements hold in the automaton $M_k(G)$ .

(1) The number of states is at most $2 \cdot |k{:}T^*| \cdot |G| = O(|T|^k \cdot |G|)$ .
(2) The number of type (a) transitions is at most $|k{:}T^*| \cdot |P| = O(|T|^k \cdot |P|)$ .
(3) The number of type (b) transitions is at most $|k{:}T^*| \cdot |G| = O(|T|^k \cdot |G|)$ .
(4) The number of type (c) transitions is at most $|k{:}T^*|^2 \cdot |G| = O(|T|^{2k} \cdot |G|)$ .
(5) The sum of the sizes of the final state sets $F_{\text{reduce}}(u)$ and $F_{\text{shift}}(u)$, $u \in k{:}T^*$, is $O(|T|^{2k} \cdot |G|)$ .
(6) The size of the automaton $M_k(G)$ is $O(|G|^{2k+1})$ or, more specifically, $O(|T|^{2k} \cdot |G|)$ .

□

The construction of $M_k(G)$ implies that we can restate Theorem 10.1:

**Theorem 10.4** *A state of the form $[A \to \alpha \cdot \beta, y]$ in $M_k(G)$ is accessible upon reading string $\gamma$ if and only if $\gamma$ is a viable prefix of G and $[A \to \alpha \cdot \beta, y]$ is an LR(k)-valid item for $\gamma$. In other words,*

$$\{[A \to \alpha \cdot \beta, y] \mid [S, \varepsilon]\gamma \Rightarrow^* [A \to \alpha \cdot \beta, y]\} = \text{VALID}_k(\gamma) \ ,$$

*for all $\gamma$ in $V^*$.* □

As an example, consider the automaton $M_1(G'_{LR2})$, where $G'_{LR2}$ is the \$-augmented grammar for the grammar $G_{LR2}$:

$$S \to AB \ , \qquad C \to ab \ ,$$

$$A \to a \ , \qquad D \to b \ ,$$

$$B \to CDb \mid aEb \ , \qquad E \to bba \ .$$

The canonical LR(1) machine for $G'_{LR2}$ was given in Figure 6.10. $G_{LR2}$ is LR(2) but not LR(1). The automaton $M_1(G'_{LR2})$ is shown in Figure 10.1.

$G_{LR2}$ is non-LR(1) because $\text{VALID}_1(\$Aab)$ contains the pair of items $[E \to b \cdot ba, b]$, $[C \to ab \cdot, b]$, which exhibit a shift-reduce conflict. In the automaton $M_1(G'_{LR2})$ the non-LR(1)-ness of $G_{LR2}$ is shown by the fact that the conflicting items are *mutually accessible states*, that is, states that are both reachable from the initial state upon reading the same string, in this case the string $\$Aab$.

Let $G = (V, T, P, S)$ be a grammar, $G'$ its \$-augmented grammar, and $k$ a natural number. We say that distinct $k$-items $[A \to \alpha \cdot \beta, y]$ and $[B \to \omega \cdot, z]$ of $G'$ *exhibit an LR(k)-conflict* if they exhibit, for $k$, a reduce-reduce conflict or a shift-reduce conflict. That is, either (1) $\beta = \varepsilon$ and $y = z$, or (2) $1:\beta$ is a terminal in $T$ and $z$ is in $\text{FIRST}_k(\beta y)$.

**Theorem 10.5** (*Characterization of the LR(k) property via the nondeterministic automaton $M_k(G')$*) *Let $G = (V, T, P, S)$ be a grammar in which $S \Rightarrow^+ S$ is impossible. Then G is non-LR(k) if and only if the \$-augmented grammar $G'$ has a pair of distinct k-items I and J that exhibit an LR(k)-conflict and are mutually accessible states in $M_k(G')$. In other words, G is non-LR(k) if and only if there are distinct k-items $I = [A \to \alpha \cdot, y]$ and $J = [B \to \beta \cdot, y]$, or $I = [A \to \alpha \cdot a\beta, z]$ and $J = [B \to \omega \cdot, y]$ with $a \in T$ and $y \in \text{FIRST}_k(a\beta z)$, such that*

$$[S', \varepsilon]\gamma \Rightarrow^* I \quad \textit{and} \quad [S', \varepsilon]\gamma \Rightarrow^* J$$

*hold in $M_k(G')$ for some string $\gamma \in \$V^*$ .*

*Proof.* By Theorem 6.39(*b*), $G$ is non-LR($k$) if and only if for some string $\gamma \in \$V^*$, $\text{VALID}_k(\gamma)$ contains a pair of distinct items $I$, $J$ that exhibit an LR($k$)-conflict. By Theorem 10.4, $I$ and $J$ belong to $\text{VALID}_k(\gamma)$ if and only if they are states in $M_k(G')$ accessible upon reading $\gamma$. □

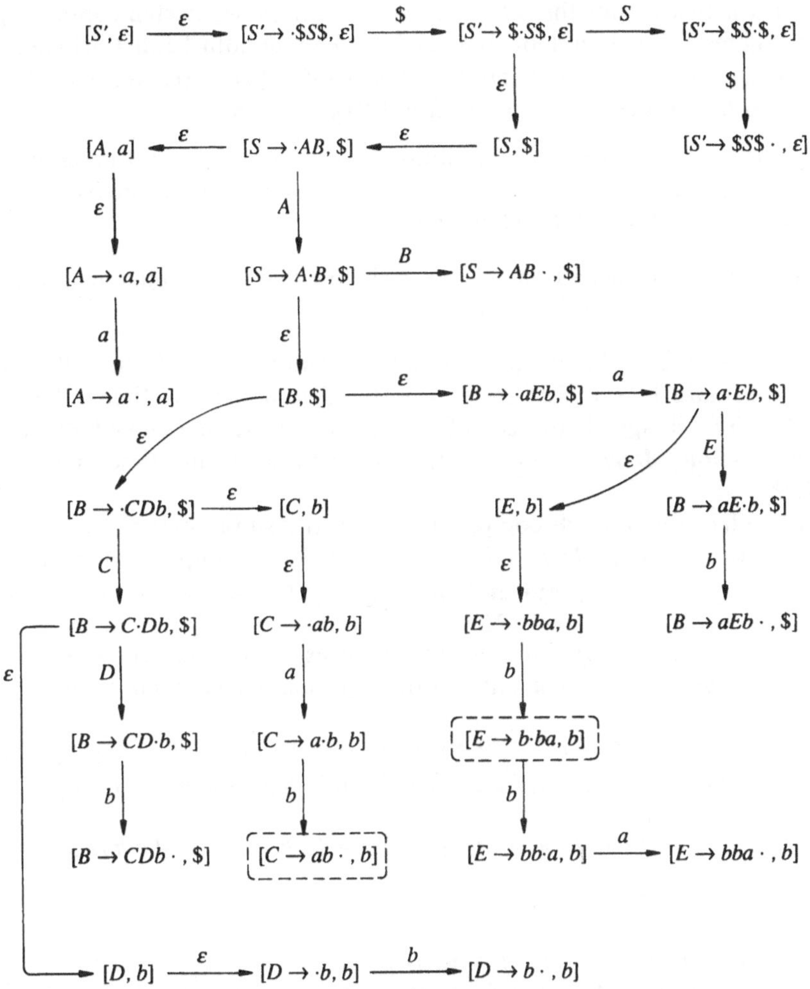


**Figure 10.1** The automaton $M_1(G'_{LR2})$ for the \$-augmented grammar $G'_{LR2}$: $S' \to \$S\$$, $S \to AB$, $A \to a$, $B \to CDb \mid aEb$, $C \to ab$, $D \to b$, $E \to bba$. The two states encircled by a broken line exhibit a shift-reduce conflict and are both accessible upon reading the string $\$Aab$

Theorem 10.5 suggests the following algorithm for testing a grammar $G = (V, T, P, S)$ for the LR($k$) property.

*Step 1.* Check whether or not $S \Rightarrow^+ S$ is possible in $G$. If yes, output "$G$ is non-LR($k$)" and halt.

*Step 2.* Construct for the \$-augmented grammar $G'$ the automaton $M_k(G')$ with collections of final state sets $F_{\text{reduce}}(u)$, $u \in k\!:\!T^*\$$, and $F_{\text{shift}}(u)$, $u \in k\!:\!T^*\$$. Remove from each $F_{\text{shift}}(u)$ the items $[S' \to \cdot\$S\$, \varepsilon]$ and $[S' \to \$S\cdot\$, \varepsilon]$.

*Step 3.* Determine in $M_k(G')$ the set of pairs of mutually accessible states.

*Step 4.* Check whether or not the set determined in the previous step contains a pair of distinct items $I$, $J$ such that for some $u \in k:T^*\$$ either both $I$ and $J$ belong to $F_{\text{reduce}}(u)$ or $I$ belongs to $F_{\text{reduce}}(u)$ and $J$ belongs to $F_{\text{shift}}(u)$. If yes, output "$G$ is non-LR($k$)" and halt. Otherwise, output "$G$ is LR($k$)" and halt.

To analyze the complexity of this algorithm, we first note that Step 1 takes only time $O(|G|)$. One just has to check whether or not $S$ belongs to the set **derives**$^+(S)$, where **derives** is the relation on $V$ defined by:

> $A$ **derives** $X$, if $G$ has a rule $A \to \alpha X \beta$ where $\alpha$ and $\beta$ are nullable, that is, $\alpha \Rightarrow^* \varepsilon$ and $\beta \Rightarrow^* \varepsilon$.

This relation is of size $O(|G|)$ and can be computed from $G$ in time $O(|G|)$. Recall that the set of nullable symbols in $G$ can be determined in time $O(|G|)$ (Theorem 4.14). The image of the set $\{S\}$ under the relation denoted by the relational expression **derives**$^+$ can then be computed in time $O(|G|)$ (Theorem 2.28).

Step 2 in the algorithm is made complicated by the transitions of type (c) and by the final state sets $F_{\text{shift}}(u)$, $u \in k:T^*\$$. Given a $k$-item $[A \to \alpha \cdot B\beta, y]$ we have to determine all strings $z \in \text{FIRST}_k(\beta y)$, and for each $u \in k:T^*\$$ we have to determine all items $[A \to \alpha \cdot a\beta, y]$ in which $\text{FIRST}_k(a\beta y)$ contains $u$. To accomplish these tasks, we need a transformed grammar in which prefixes of terminal strings derived by $\beta$ can be generated, when $\beta$ is a suffix of the right-hand side of some rule.

**Lemma 10.6** *Any grammar $G = (V, T, P, S)$ can be transformed in time $O(|G|)$ into a grammar $G_{\text{pre}} = (V_{\text{pre}}, T, P_{\text{pre}}, S_{\text{pre}})$ such that the following statements hold.*

(1) *$G_{\text{pre}}$ is in canonical two-form, so that the rules in $P_{\text{pre}}$ are of the forms*

$$A \to BC, \quad A \to B, \quad A \to a\ ,$$

*where $B$ and $C$ are nonterminals and $a$ is a terminal.*

(2) *$V \subseteq V_{\text{pre}}$ and each nonterminal $A \in V$ generates in $G_{\text{pre}}$ exactly the nonempty terminal strings derived by $A$ in $G$, that is,*

$$L_{G_{\text{pre}}}(A) = L_G(A) \setminus \{\varepsilon\}$$

*for all $A \in V \setminus T$ .*

(3) *For each nonterminal $A \in V$ there is a nonterminal $A_{\text{pre}} \in V_{\text{pre}} \setminus V$ that generates exactly the nonempty prefixes of the terminal strings derived by $A$ in $G$, that is,*

$$L_{G_{\text{pre}}}(A_{\text{pre}}) = \{x \in T^* \mid x \neq \varepsilon \text{ and } xy \in L_G(A) \text{ for some } y\}\ .$$

(4) *For each rule $A \to \alpha\beta$ in $P$ and nonempty strings $\alpha$ and $\beta$ there is a nonterminal $[\beta] \in V_{\text{pre}} \setminus V$ that generates exactly the nonempty terminal strings derived by the string $\beta$ in $G$, that is,*

$$L_{G_{\text{pre}}}([\beta]) = L_G(\beta) \setminus \{\varepsilon\}\ .$$

(5) *For each rule* $A \to \alpha\beta$ *in P and nonempty strings* $\alpha$ *and* $\beta$ *there is a nonterminal* $[\beta]_{\text{pre}} \in V_{\text{pre}} \setminus V$ *that generates exactly the nonempty prefixes of the terminal strings derived by* $\beta$ *in G, that is,*

$$L_{G_{\text{pre}}}([\beta]_{\text{pre}}) = \{x \in T^* \mid x \neq \varepsilon \text{ and } xy \in L_G(\beta) \text{ for some } y\} \ .$$

*Proof.* First we use the transformations given in Lemma 4.19 and Theorem 4.20 to transform $G$ into a canonical two-form grammar $G_1 = (V_1, T, P_1, S)$, where $V \subseteq V_1$, $L_{G_1}(A) = L_G(A) \setminus \{\varepsilon\}$, and (see the proof of Lemma 4.19) for each rule $A \to \alpha\beta$ and nonempty strings $\alpha$ and $\beta$ there is a nonterminal $[\beta] \in V_1 \setminus V$ such that $L_{G_1}([\beta]) = L_G(\beta) \setminus \{\varepsilon\}$. The desired grammar $G_{\text{pre}}$ is then $(V_{\text{pre}}, T, P_{\text{pre}}, S_{\text{pre}})$, where

$$V_{\text{pre}} = V_1 \cup \{A_{\text{pre}} \mid A \text{ is a nonterminal in } V_1\} \ ,$$

$$\begin{aligned} P_{\text{pre}} = P_1 &\cup \{A_{\text{pre}} \to A \mid A \text{ is a nonterminal in } V_1\} \\ &\cup \{A_{\text{pre}} \to BC_{\text{pre}} \mid A \to BC \text{ is a rule in } P_1\} \\ &\cup \{A_{\text{pre}} \to B_{\text{pre}} \mid \text{For some } C,\ A \to BC \text{ is a rule in } P_1 \text{ and} \\ &\quad\ C \text{ derives some terminal string}\} \\ &\cup \{A_{\text{pre}} \to B_{\text{pre}} \mid A \to B \text{ is a rule in } P_1\} \ . \end{aligned}$$

$G_{\text{pre}}$ satisfies (1) because $G_1$ does so. Each nonterminal in $V_1$ generates in $G_{\text{pre}}$ the same language as it generates in $G_1$, because $P_{\text{pre}} \setminus P_1$ contains no rules for the nonterminals in $V_1$. The rules in $P_{\text{pre}} \setminus P_1$ have the effect that each new nonterminal $A_{\text{pre}}$ generates exactly the nonempty prefixes of the sentences in $L(A)$. The size of $G_{\text{pre}}$ is linear in the size of $G_1$, and the transformation can be carried out in linear time. Recall that the nonterminals that derive some terminal string can be determined in linear time (Section 4.4). □

**Lemma 10.7** *Given a grammar* $G = (V, T, P, S)$, *a positive natural number k, and a string* $u = a_1 \ldots a_k$ *in* $T^k$, *one can compute, simultaneously in space* $O(k^2 \cdot |G|)$ *and in time* $O(k^3 \cdot |G|)$, *a* $k \times k$ *matrix* $N_u$ *containing sets of symbols of the form* $[\beta]$ *and* $[\beta]_{\text{pre}}$ *such that*

$$\begin{aligned} N_u(i,j) = \{[\beta] \mid A \to \alpha\beta \in P,\ \alpha, \beta \neq \varepsilon,\ \beta \underset{G}{\Longrightarrow^*} a_i \ldots a_j\} \\ \cup \{[\beta]_{\text{pre}} \mid A \to \alpha\beta \in P,\ \alpha, \beta \neq \varepsilon\ , \\ \beta \underset{G}{\Longrightarrow^*} a_i \ldots a_j y,\ y \in T^*\}\ , \end{aligned}$$

*for* $1 \leqslant i \leqslant j \leqslant k$ .

*Proof.* First, we construct the transformed grammar $G_{\text{pre}} = (V_{\text{pre}}, T, P_{\text{pre}}, S_{\text{pre}})$ of Lemma 10.6. This grammar is of size $O(|G|)$ and its construction takes time $O(|G|)$. As $G_{\text{pre}}$ is in canonical two-form, we can apply to it the general context-free recognition algorithm (Section 4.7, Figure 4.9). We run the algorithm on the string

$u$. The algorithm computes, in space $O(|G_{pre}|\cdot|u|^2)$ and in time $O(|G_{pre}|\cdot|u|^3)$, a $k \times k$ matrix $\hat{N}_u$ such that

$$\hat{N}_u(i,j) = \{A \in V_{pre} \setminus T \mid A \Rightarrow^* a_i \ldots a_j \text{ in } G_{pre}\} \ ,$$

for $1 \leq i \leq j \leq k$. By the construction of $G_{pre}$, $\hat{N}_u(i,j)$ contains (1) a nonterminal $[\beta]$ if and only if $\beta$ is in $V^+$ and $P$ contains a rule $A \to \alpha\beta$ where $\alpha \neq \varepsilon$ and $\beta$ derives $a_i \ldots a_j$ in $G$, and (2) a nonterminal $[\beta]_{pre}$ if and only if $\beta$ is in $V^+$ and $P$ contains a rule $A \to \alpha\beta$ where $\alpha \neq \varepsilon$ and $\beta$ derives in $G$ some string $a_i \ldots a_j y$ where $y$ is in $T^*$. Thus, we get the desired matrix $N_u$ by removing from $\hat{N}_u$ all symbols that are not of the form $[\beta]$ or $[\beta]_{pre}$. □

**Lemma 10.8** *Given a grammar $G = (V, T, P, S)$ and a natural number $k$, the automaton $M_k(G)$ (including the collections of final state sets $F_{reduce}(u)$ and $F_{shift}(u)$, $u \in k\!:\!T^*$) can be constructed in time $O((k+1)^3 \cdot |T|^{2k} \cdot |G|)$ .*

*Proof.* First, the state set, the type (a) and (b) transitions, and the final state sets $F_{reduce}(u)$, $u \in k\!:\!T^*$, are easy to determine, taking time $O(|T|^k \cdot |G|)$. If $k = 0$, also the type (c) transitions and the final state sets $F_{shift}(u)$ are easy to determine. For any 0-item $[A \to \alpha \cdot B\beta, \varepsilon]$ we add to $M_0(G)$ the transition

$$[A \to \alpha \cdot B\beta, \varepsilon] \to [B, \varepsilon]$$

whenever $\beta$ derives some terminal string. The set $F_{shift}(\varepsilon)$ we make up of all items $[A \to \alpha \cdot a\beta, \varepsilon]$ where $a$ is a terminal and $\beta$ derives some terminal string. To accomplish these tasks, we only have to precompute the set of useless symbols in $G$. This can be done in time $O(|G|)$ (Section 4.4).

In the case $k > 0$ we repeat the following for each string $u = a_1 \ldots a_l$ in $k\!:\!T^*$. We determine the final state set $F_{shift}(u)$ and all type (c) transitions of the form

$$[A \to \alpha \cdot B\beta, y] \to [B, u] \ .$$

This is done as follows. First, whenever $\beta$ is nullable, we add to $M_k(G)$ all transitions

$$[A \to \alpha \cdot B\beta, u] \to [B, u] \ ,$$

and, if $l > 0$, to $F_{shift}(u)$ all items $[A \to \alpha \cdot a_1\beta, a_2 \ldots a_l y]$ where $a_2 \ldots a_l y$ is in $k\!:\!T^*$ and $k\!:\!uy = u$. Recall that the set of nullable symbols in $G$ can be determined in time $O(|G|)$. (In fact, the determination of the nullable symbols is an initial step in the construction of the transformed grammar $G_{pre}$, which is needed in the computation of the matrix $N_u$ of Lemma 10.7; see below.) If $l = k = 1$ and $\beta$ derives some terminal string, we add to $F_{shift}(u) = F_{shift}(a_1)$ all items $[A \to \alpha \cdot a_1\beta, y]$ where $y$ is in $k\!:\!T^*$ .

When $l > 0$, we compute for $u\ (= a_1 \ldots a_l)$ the matrix $N_u$ of Lemma 10.7. For all $j = 1, \ldots, l$ and for all symbols $[\beta] \in N_u(1,j)$ we then add to $M_k(G)$ all transitions

$$[A \to \alpha \cdot B\beta, a_{j+1} \ldots a_l y] \to [B, u] \ ,$$

where $a_{j+1} \ldots a_l y$ is in $k{:}T^*$ and $k{:}uy = u$. Observe that by Lemma 10.7 $\beta$ derives $a_1 \ldots a_j$. If $l > 1$, then for all $j = 2, \ldots, l$ and for all symbols $[\beta] \in N_u(2, j)$ we add to $F_{\text{shift}}(u)$ all items $[A \to \alpha \cdot a_1 \beta, a_{j+1} \ldots a_l y]$ where $a_{j+1} \ldots a_l y$ is in $k{:}T^*$ and $k{:}uy = u$. For all symbols $[\beta]_{\text{pre}} \in N_u(1, l)$ we add to $M_k(G)$ all transitions

$$[A \to \alpha \cdot B\beta, y] \to [B, u] \ ,$$

where $y$ is a string in $k{:}T^*$ such that $y = \varepsilon$ whenever $l < k$. Observe that by Lemma 10.7, $u$ is a prefix of some terminal string derived by $\beta$. For all symbols $[\beta]_{\text{pre}} \in N_u(2, l)$ we add to $F_{\text{shift}}(u)$ all items $[A \to \alpha \cdot a_1 \beta, y]$ where $y$ is a string in $k{:}T^*$ such that $y = \varepsilon$ whenever $l < k$.

The total time spent on the construction is $O(|k{:}T^*| \cdot k^3 \cdot |G| + |T|^{2k} \cdot |G|)$, when $k > 0$. Here the term $|k{:}T^*| \cdot k^3 \cdot |G|$ comes from the computation of the matrices $N_u$, $u \in k{:}T^*$, and the term $|T|^{2k} \cdot |G|$ comes from the generation of the states and the transitions (their total number is $O(|T|^{2k} \cdot |G|)$ . □

To determine the pairs of mutually accessible states in the automaton (Step 3 in the LR($k$) testing algorithm), we define a suitable relational expression and derive the algorithm from the general results given in Chapter 2.

Assume $M$ is a finite automaton with state alphabet $Q$, input alphabet $V$, and set of transitions $P$. Further assume that $M$ is normal-form, that is, the transitions in $P$ are all of the form $q\alpha \to q'$ where $\alpha$ is in $V \cup \{\varepsilon\}$. We define on $Q \times Q$ relations **mutually-goes-to**, **by-left-passes-empty**, and **by-right-passes-empty** by setting:

$(p, q)$ **mutually-goes-to** $(p', q')$, if for some $X \in V$
$P$ contains the transitions $pX \to p'$ and $qX \to q'$ .

$(p, q)$ **by-left-passes-empty** $(p', q)$, if $P$ contains
the transition $p \to p'$ .

$(p, q)$ **by-right-passes-empty** $(p, q')$, if $P$ contains
the transition $q \to q'$ .

Then consider the relational expression

**mutually-accesses** = (**mutually-goes-to** $\cup$
**by-left-passes-empty** $\cup$ **by-right-passes-empty**)* .

By induction it is easy to show:

**Lemma 10.9** *States $p$ and $q$ are mutually accessible if and only if*

$(q_s, q_s)$ **mutually-accesses** $(p, q)$ ,

*where $q_s$ is the initial state.* □

The arguments of the relational expression **mutually-accesses** are of size $O(|M|^2)$ and can be computed from $M$ in time $O(|M|^2)$. By Theorem 2.28 we conclude that the image

$$\textbf{mutually-accesses}\ (\{(q_s, q_s)\})$$

can be computed in time $O(|M|^2)$. We have:

**Lemma 10.10** *For any finite automaton $M$, the set of pairs of mutually accessible states can be determined in time $O(|M|^2)$.* □

Now we are ready to state the complexity of the LR($k$) test outlined above in Steps 1 to 4.

**Theorem 10.11** (*LR($k$) test using the automaton $M_k(G')$*) *Grammar $G = (V, T, P, S)$ can be tested for the LR($k$) property in deterministic time $O((k+1)^3 \cdot |G|^{4k+2})$.*

*Proof.* In Step 1 of the algorithm we check whether or not $S$ can nontrivially derive itself in $G$. As explained, this checking can be carried out in time $O(|G|)$. In Step 2 we construct for the \$-augmented grammar $G'$ the automaton $M_k(G')$ and the collections of the final state sets $F_{\text{reduce}}(u)$ and $F_{\text{shift}}(u)$, $u \in k{:}T^*\$$. By Lemma 10.8 this takes time $O((k+1)^3 \cdot |T|^{2k} \cdot |G|)$. In Step 3 we determine the pairs of mutually accessible states in $M_k(G')$. By Lemma 10.10 and Fact 10.3, this takes time $O(|T|^{4k} \cdot |G|^2)$. Finally, in Step 4 we check whether or not for some pair of distinct mutually accessible states $I$, $J$ and for some string $u \in k{:}T^*\$$ we have either $I, J \in F_{\text{reduce}}(u)$, or $I \in F_{\text{reduce}}(u)$ and $J \in F_{\text{shift}}(u)$. The total time taken by this checking is not more than linear in the size of the data structures involved, that is, the set of pairs of mutually accessible states and the collections of the final state sets $F_{\text{reduce}}(u)$, and $F_{\text{shift}}(u)$, $u \in k{:}T^*\$$. Hence we conclude that the total time taken by the LR($k$) test is $O((k+1)^3 \cdot |T|^{4k} \cdot |G|^2)$. □

If we regard the natural number $k$ as fixed in Theorem 10.11, we obtain that for any $k \geqslant 0$ the problem $\mathscr{P}_{\text{LR}(k)}$ is solvable in deterministic polynomial time, or, more specifically, in deterministic time $O(n^{4k+2})$. Observe that $n$, the size of a problem instance, is proportional to $|G|$ in any of the problems $\mathscr{P}_{\text{LR}(k)}$, $k \geqslant 0$.

If we regard $k$ as free in Theorem 10.11, we obtain upper bounds on the complexity of the uniform (non-)LR($k$) testing problem. We observe that the complexity depends radically on the representation chosen for $k$. The length of the unary representation for $k$ is $O(k)$, whereas the length of the binary representation is only $O(\log k)$. This affects the complexity, because the size of problem instance (code($G$), code($k$)) is then proportional to $|G| + k$ when $k$ is expressed in unary, and proportional to $|G| + \log k$ when $k$ is expressed in binary. When choosing $n = |G| + k$ in Theorem 10.11 we obtain that for $k$ in unary the uniform (non-)LR($k$) testing problem is solvable in deterministic one-level exponential time, or, more specifically, in deterministic time $O(2^{(4n+2)\log n})$. When choosing $n = |G| + \log k$ we obtain that for $k$ in binary the problem is solvable in deterministic two-level exponential time, or, more specifically, in deterministic time $O(2^{(4 \cdot 2^n + 2)\log n})$.

Next we shall consider a more sophisticated method for LR($k$) testing. This method will yield an $O(n^{k+2})$ time-bounded deterministic LR($k$) test for any fixed $k \geqslant 0$. Moreover, this test will be very economic in space; its space complexity is only $O(n^2)$. The method will also imply a very efficient nondeterministic algorithm for non-LR($k$) testing. It will be possible, for any fixed $k \geqslant 0$, to test a grammar of size $n$ for the non-LR($k$) property simultaneously in nondeterministic space $O(n)$ and in nondeterministic time $O(n^2)$.

The key idea in the new method is to represent the automaton $M_k(G')$ as a collection of several very small automata. The collection will contain one automaton for each specific string $u \in k{:}T^*\$$. The automaton for $u$ will be denoted by $M_u(G')$. The purpose of $M_u(G')$ is to represent those, and only those, computations of $M_k(G')$ that end with $k$-items of the form $[B \rightarrow \omega\cdot, u]$, or of the form $[A \rightarrow \alpha \cdot a\beta, y]$ where $\text{FIRST}_k(a\beta y)$ contains $u$. Any LR($k$)-conflict possibly occurring for $u$ in $M_k(G')$ can be seen from $M_u(G')$, the specific automaton for $u$, but that conflict usually cannot be seen from any other automaton $M_v(G')$, $v \neq u$.

All the lookahead strings in the states of $M_u(G')$ will be suffixes of $u$. This makes the automaton very small; its size is only $O((k+1)^2 \cdot |G|)$, because for the $O(|G|)$ different item cores in $G$ there are only $k+1$ different lookahead strings to choose. The time consuming task of determining the pairs of mutually accessible states, which took time $O(|T|^{4k} \cdot |G|^2)$ for $M_k(G')$, now reduces to performing the task once for each of the small automata $M_u(G')$, $u \in k{:}T^*\$$, taking total time $O(|T|^k \cdot (k+1)^4 |G|^2)$.

Now let $G = (V, T, P, S)$ be a grammar and $u$ a string in $k{:}T^*$. We say that a $k$-item $[A \rightarrow \alpha \cdot \beta, y]$ is a *u-item*, if $y$ is a suffix of $u$. For string $\beta$ we denote by $\text{FIRST}_u(\beta)$ the set of all suffixes of $u$ that are prefixes of some terminal string derived by $\beta$. That is,

$$\text{FIRST}_u(\beta) = \{y \in T^* \mid \beta \Rightarrow^* yz \text{ and } xy = u \text{ for some } x, z\} \ .$$

We define $M_{\text{LR}(u)}(G)$ (or $M_u(G)$, for short) as the finite automaton with state alphabet

$$\{[A \rightarrow \alpha \cdot \beta, y] \mid A \rightarrow \alpha\beta \text{ is a rule of } G \text{ and } y \text{ is a suffix of } u\}$$

$$\cup \{[A, y] \mid A \text{ is a nonterminal of } G \text{ and } y \text{ is a suffix of } u\} \ ,$$

input alphabet $V$, initial state $[S, \varepsilon]$, and with set of transitions consisting of all rules of the forms:

(a) $[A, y] \rightarrow [A \rightarrow \cdot\omega, y]$ ,
(b) $[A \rightarrow \alpha \cdot X\beta, y]X \rightarrow [A \rightarrow \alpha X \cdot \beta, y]$, for $X \in V$ ,
(c) $[A \rightarrow \alpha \cdot B\beta, y] \rightarrow [B, z]$, for $B \in V \setminus T$ and $z \in \text{FIRST}_u(\beta y)$.

The set of final states of $M_u(G)$ is $F_{\text{reduce}} \cup F_{\text{shift}}$, where

$$F_{\text{reduce}} = \{[A \rightarrow \omega\cdot, u] \mid A \rightarrow \omega \text{ is a rule of } G\} \ ,$$

$$F_{\text{shift}} = \{[A \rightarrow \alpha \cdot a\beta, y] \mid A \rightarrow \alpha a\beta \text{ is a rule of } G, \ a \text{ is a terminal, and } u \in \text{FIRST}_u(a\beta y)\} \ .$$

The definition is analogous to that of $M_k(G)$. However, now all the lookahead strings are suffixes of the fixed string $u$, and in the type (c) transitions the new lookahead string $z$ is obtained from $\beta y$ via the operator $\text{FIRST}_u$. Also, the set of final states is now divided up into only two sets, $F_{\text{reduce}}$ and $F_{\text{shift}}$, corresponding to the sets $F_{\text{reduce}}(u)$ and $F_{\text{shift}}(u)$ in $M_k(G)$ for the specific string $u$.

**Fact 10.12** For any grammar $G = (V, T, P, S)$ and string $u \in T^*$, the following statements hold for the automaton $M_u(G)$.

(1) The number of states is at most $2 \cdot (|u| + 1) \cdot |G|$ .
(2) The number of type (a) transitions is at most $(|u| + 1) \cdot |P|$ .
(3) The number of type (b) transitions is at most $(|u| + 1) \cdot |G|$ .
(4) The number of type (c) transitions is at most $(|u| + 1)^2 \cdot |G|$ .
(5) The size of the automaton is $O((|u| + 1)^2 \cdot |G|)$ .

□

The automaton $M_b(G'_{\text{LR2}})$ for our grammar $G'_{\text{LR2}}$ is given in Figure 10.2. Only the interesting parts of it are shown.

Observe that $M_u(G)$ is not a subautomaton of $M_k(G)$. The computations of $M_u(G)$ are usually not computations of $M_k(G)$. This is because $\text{FIRST}_u(\beta y)$ need not be contained in $\text{FIRST}_{|u|}(\beta y)$. For example, in $M_b(G'_{\text{LR2}})$ only the computations on $\varepsilon$, \$, \$$S$, and \$$S$\$ are also computations of $M_1(G'_{\text{LR2}})$. In fact, any $M_u(G)$ always contains as a subautomaton the automaton $M_\varepsilon(G)$ (which is identical to $M_0(G)$). This is because $\text{FIRST}_u(\beta y)$ always contains the empty string $\varepsilon$ (when the grammar is reduced). Thus, whenever $G$ is non-LR(0), due to a reduce-reduce conflict, then any automaton $M_u(G')$ will inevitably contain a pair of mutually accessible states that exhibit a reduce-reduce conflict, for any $k \geqslant 0$. This need not, however, mean that $G$ is non-LR($k$). In a specific automaton $M_u(G')$ only those conflicts are true conflicts, and represent the non-LR($k$)-ness of $G$, that occur for the specific string $u$. Indeed, each automaton $M_u(G')$ is devoted entirely to representing what might be called the "non-LR($u$)-ness" of $G$, that is, whether or not the canonical LR($k$) parser of $G$ is made nondeterministic by actions having $u$ as the lookahead string. The automata $M_u(G')$, $u \in k{:}T^*\$$, together represent the entire non-LR($k$)-ness of $G$. In this sense the collection of automata $M_u(G')$ can be regarded as a representation of the single automaton $M_k(G')$.

In $M_k(G)$ states $[A \to \alpha \cdot \beta, y]$ accessible upon reading string $\gamma$ are LR($k$)-valid items for $\gamma$. Analogously, in $M_u(G)$ states $[A \to \alpha \cdot \beta, y]$ accessible upon reading $\gamma$ are what might be called "LR($u$)-valid" items for $\gamma$. The concept of "LR($u$)-validity" is obtained from the concept of LR($k$)-validity by replacing in the definition the operator $k{:}$ by the operator $\text{FIRST}_u$.

Formally, an item $[A \to \alpha \cdot \beta, y]$ of grammar $G = (V, T, P, S)$ is *LR($u$)-valid* for string $\gamma \in V^*$ if

$$S \underset{\text{rm}}{\Longrightarrow}^* \delta A z \underset{\text{rm}}{\Longrightarrow} \delta\alpha\beta z = \gamma\beta z \quad \text{and} \quad y \in \text{FIRST}_u(z)$$

hold in $G$ for some strings $\delta \in V^*$ and $z \in T^*$.

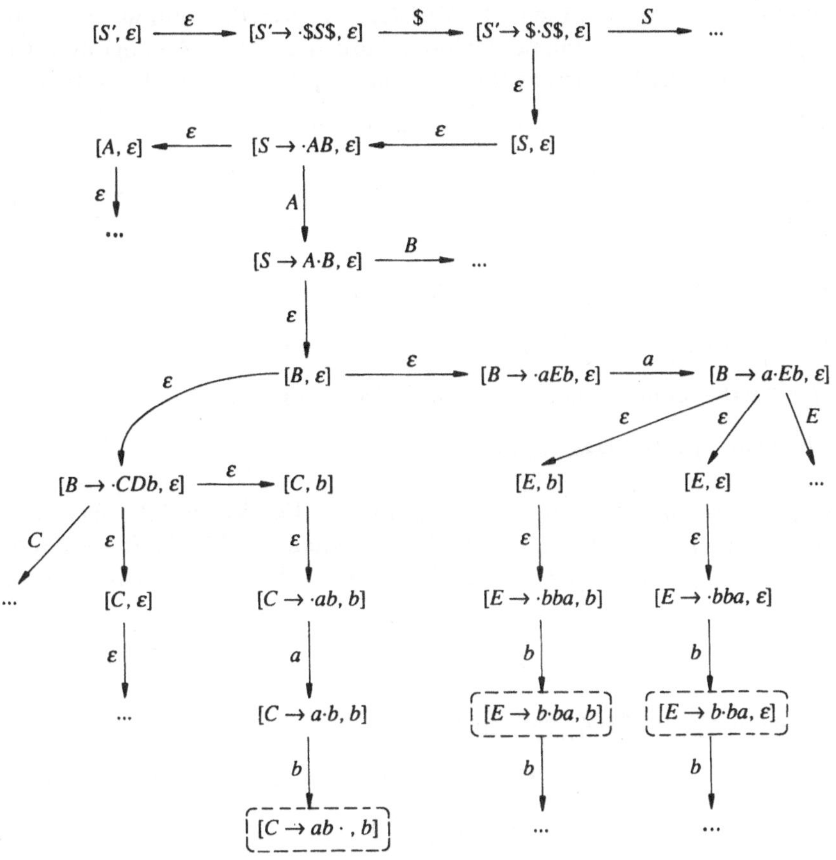


**Figure 10.2** Portions of the automaton $M_b(G'_{LR2})$ for the grammar of Figure 10.1. The states $[E \to b \cdot ba, b]$ and $[C \to ab \cdot, b]$, as well as the states $[E \to b \cdot ba, \varepsilon]$ and $[C \to ab \cdot, b]$, exhibit a shift-reduce conflict, and all three are accessible upon reading $\$Aab$

**Fact 10.13** If $[A \to \alpha \cdot \beta, y]$ is an LR($u$)-valid item for string $\gamma$, then $\gamma$ is a viable prefix, $[A \to \alpha \cdot \beta, y]$ is a $u$-item, $\alpha$ is a suffix of $\gamma$, and $y$ belongs to $\text{FOLLOW}_{|y|}(A)$ and to $\text{FOLLOW}_{|y|}(\gamma\beta)$. Conversely, if $\gamma$ is a viable prefix, then some item is LR($u$)-valid for $\gamma$. □

We denote by $\text{VALID}_{\text{LR}(u)}(\gamma)$ (or $\text{VALID}_u(\gamma)$, for short) the set of all LR($u$)-valid items for $\gamma$.

In the following we give a series of facts and lemmas, from which we shall derive the result that for any string $\gamma \in V^*$ the set $\text{VALID}_u(\gamma)$ consists exactly of those states $[A \to \alpha \cdot \beta, y]$ of the automaton $M_u(G)$ that are accessible upon reading $\gamma$. The result is correct because the operator $\text{FIRST}_u$ shares with the operator $\text{FIRST}_k$ the characteristic properties of a "lookahead operator", as defined in Chapter 6 (Exercise 6.65).

In Section 6.2 we represented $\mathrm{VALID}_k(\gamma)$ as the union of sets $\mathrm{VALID}_{k,n}(\gamma)$, $n \geq 0$. This was done to facilitate inductive proofs. Analogously, we define, for all $n \geq 0$, $\mathrm{VALID}_{u,n}(\gamma)$ as the set of items $[A \to \alpha \cdot \beta, y]$ that satisfy

$$S \underset{\mathrm{rm}}{\Longrightarrow}^{n} \delta A z \underset{\mathrm{rm}}{\Longrightarrow} \delta\alpha\beta z = \gamma\beta z \quad \text{and} \quad y \in \mathrm{FIRST}_u(z)$$

for some $\delta \in V^*$ and $z \in T^*$. Clearly, $\mathrm{VALID}_u(\gamma)$ is the union of all $\mathrm{VALID}_{u,n}(\gamma)$, $n \geq 0$.

**Lemma 10.14** *If in grammar* $G = (V, T, P, S)$

$$[A \to \alpha \cdot B\beta, y] \in \mathrm{VALID}_{u,n}(\gamma) \quad \textit{and} \quad \beta \Rightarrow^m v \in T^* ,$$

*then for all rules* $B \to \omega$ *in* $P$ *and strings* $z$ *in* $\mathrm{FIRST}_u(vy)$

$$[B \to \cdot\omega, z] \in \mathrm{VALID}_{u,n+m+1}(\gamma) .$$

*Proof.* The proof is analogous to that of Lemma 6.17. We use the fact that $\mathrm{FIRST}_u(v\mathrm{FIRST}_u(y'))$ is contained in (in fact is equal to) $\mathrm{FIRST}_u(vy')$. (Here $\mathrm{FIRST}_u(v\mathrm{FIRST}_u(y'))$ means the union of all sets $\mathrm{FIRST}_u(vw)$ where $w$ is in $\mathrm{FIRST}_u(y')$.) □

**Lemma 10.15** *If in grammar* $G = (V, T, P, S)$

$$[B \to \cdot\omega, z] \in \mathrm{VALID}_{u,n}(\gamma) \quad \textit{and} \quad n > 0 ,$$

*then for some rule* $A \to \alpha B\beta$ *in* $P$, *strings* $y$, $v$ *in* $T^*$, *and natural number* $m < n$,

$$[A \to \alpha \cdot B\beta, y] \in \mathrm{VALID}_{u,m}(\gamma),\ \beta \underset{\mathrm{rm}}{\Longrightarrow}^{n-m-1} v, \quad \textit{and}$$

$$z \in \mathrm{FIRST}_u(vy) .$$

*Proof.* The proof is analogous to that of Lemma 6.19. We use the fact that $\mathrm{FIRST}_u(vy')$ is contained in (is equal to) $\mathrm{FIRST}_u(v\mathrm{FIRST}_u(y'))$ and that $\mathrm{FIRST}_u(y')$ is nonempty for all strings $y'$. □

Corresponding to Fact 6.24 we have:

**Fact 10.16** If $[A \to \alpha \cdot \omega\beta, y]$ is an item in $\mathrm{VALID}_{u,n}(\gamma)$, then $\gamma\omega$ is a viable prefix and $[A \to \alpha\omega \cdot \beta, y]$ is in $\mathrm{VALID}_{u,n}(\gamma\omega)$. Conversely, if $[A \to \alpha\omega \cdot \beta, y]$ is an item in $\mathrm{VALID}_{u,n}(\delta)$, then there is a viable prefix $\gamma$ such that $\delta = \gamma\omega$ and $[A \to \alpha \cdot \omega\beta, y]$ is in $\mathrm{VALID}_{u,n}(\gamma)$. □

Now we can prove:

**Theorem 10.17** *Let* $G = (V. T, P, S)$ *be a grammar and* $u$ *a string in* $T^*$. *State* $[A \to \alpha \cdot \beta, y]$ *in the automaton* $M_u(G)$ *is accessible upon reading string* $\gamma$ *if and only if* $[A \to \alpha \cdot \beta, y]$ *is an LR(u)-valid item for* $\gamma$. *In other words,*

$$\mathrm{VALID}_u(\gamma) = \{[A \to \alpha \cdot \beta, y] \mid [S, \varepsilon]\gamma \Rightarrow^* [A \to \alpha \cdot \beta, y] \textit{ in } M_u(G)\} .$$

*Proof.* In the "only if" part we use induction on $m$, the length of the computation

$$[S, \varepsilon]\gamma \Rightarrow^m [A \to \alpha \cdot \beta, y] \quad \text{in } M_u(G) \ .$$

If $m = 1$, we have $\gamma = \varepsilon$ and $[A \to \alpha \cdot \beta, y] = [S \to \cdot \beta, \varepsilon]$. Here $[S \to \cdot \beta, \varepsilon]$ is an item in $\text{VALID}_u(\varepsilon)$. If $m > 1$, the computation is either of the form

$$[S, \varepsilon]\gamma = [S, \varepsilon]\gamma' X \Rightarrow^{m-1} [A \to \alpha' \cdot X\beta, y]X$$

$$\Rightarrow [A \to \alpha' X \cdot \beta, y] = [A \to \alpha \cdot \beta, y] \ ,$$

where $X \in V$, or of the form

$$[S, \varepsilon]\gamma \Rightarrow^{m-2} [A' \to \alpha' \cdot A\beta', y'] \Rightarrow [A, y]$$

$$\Rightarrow [A \to \cdot \beta, y] = [A \to \alpha \cdot \beta, y] \ ,$$

where $\text{FIRST}_u(\beta' y')$ contains $y$. In both cases we can conclude from the induction hypothesis that $[A \to \alpha \cdot \beta, y]$ is an item in $\text{VALID}_u(\gamma)$. In the former case we use Fact 10.16, and in the latter case we use Lemma 10.14.

In the "if" part we use induction on $n + |\gamma|$, where

$$[A \to \alpha \cdot \beta, y] \in \text{VALID}_{u,n}(\gamma) \ .$$

If $n + |\gamma| = 0$, we have $[A \to \alpha \cdot \beta, y] = [S \to \cdot \beta, \varepsilon]$ and $\gamma = \varepsilon$. Here $[S \to \cdot \beta, \varepsilon]$ is a state to which $M_u(G)$ has an $\varepsilon$-transition from $[S, \varepsilon]$. If $n + |\gamma| > 0$, we have either

$$[A \to \alpha \cdot \beta, y] = [A \to \alpha' X \cdot \beta, y] \in \text{VALID}_{u,n}(\gamma)$$

for some $X \in V$, or

$$[A \to \alpha \cdot \beta, y] = [A \to \cdot \beta, y] \in \text{VALID}_{u,n}(\gamma) \ ,$$

where $n > 0$. In both cases we can conclude from the induction hypothesis that $[A \to \alpha \cdot \beta, y]$ is a state in $M_u(G)$ accessible upon reading $\gamma$. In the former case we use Fact 10.16, and in the latter case we use Lemma 10.15. □

Let $u$ be a string in $k{:}T^*\$$. We say that distinct items $[A \to \alpha \cdot \beta, y]$ and $[B \to \omega \cdot, z]$ of $G'$ *exhibit an LR(u)-conflict* if either (1) $\beta = \varepsilon$ and $y = z = u$, or (2) $1{:}\beta$ is a terminal in $T$, $y$ is a suffix of $u$, and $z = u$ is in $\text{FIRST}_u(\beta y)$.

**Fact 10.18** Distinct items $[A \to \alpha \cdot \beta, y]$ and $[B \to \omega \cdot, z]$ exhibit an LR($u$)-conflict if and only if (1) the items are $u$-items, (2) they exhibit an LR($|u|$)-conflict, and (3) $z = u$. □

**Theorem 10.19** (*Characterization of the LR(k) property via the automata $M_u(G')$, $u \in k{:}T^*\$$*) *Let $G = (V, T, P, S)$ be a grammar in which $S \Rightarrow^+ S$ is impossible. Further let k be a natural number. Then G is non-LR(k) if and only if for some string $u \in k{:}T^*\$$ the \$-augmented grammar $G'$ has a pair of distinct u-items I and J that exhibit an LR(u)-conflict and are mutually accessible states in $M_u(G')$.*

*Proof.* To prove the "only if" part of the theorem, assume that $G$, and hence $G'$, is non-LR($k$). By Theorem 6.39($b$), there is a string $\gamma$ in $\$V^*$ and a pair of distinct $k$-items $[A \to \alpha \cdot \beta, y]$, $[B \to \omega \cdot, u]$ in $\text{VALID}_k(\gamma)$ that exhibit an LR($k$)-conflict. Then we have:

$$S' \underset{rm}{\Longrightarrow^*} \delta_1 A y_1 \underset{rm}{\Longrightarrow} \delta_1 \alpha\beta y_1 = \gamma\beta y_1, \quad k{:}y_1 = y \ ,$$

$$S' \underset{rm}{\Longrightarrow^*} \delta_2 B y_2 \underset{rm}{\Longrightarrow} \delta_2 \omega y_2 = \gamma y_2, \quad k{:}y_2 = u \in \text{FIRST}_k(\beta y) \ ,$$

for some strings $\delta_1, \delta_2 \in \$V^*$ and $y_1, y_2 \in T^*\$$. Then $u$ is in $k{:}T^*\$$ and in $\text{FIRST}_u(y_2)$, and hence $[B \to \omega \cdot, u]$ is in $\text{VALID}_u(\gamma)$. On the other hand, the condition $u \in \text{FIRST}_k(\beta y)$ implies that $y$ must have a prefix $y'$ such that $y'$ is a suffix of $u$ and $u \in \text{FIRST}_k(\beta y')$. This implies further that $y' \in \text{FIRST}_u(y_1)$ and $u \in \text{FIRST}_u(\beta y')$. Hence $[A \to \alpha \cdot \beta, y']$ is a $u$-item in $\text{VALID}_u(\gamma)$, and the items $[A \to \alpha \cdot \beta, y']$, $[B \to \omega \cdot, u]$ exhibit an LR($u$)-conflict. Moreover, by Theorem 10.17 they are states in $M_u(G')$ accessible upon reading $\gamma$.

To prove the "if" part of the theorem, assume that $u$ is a string in $k{:}T^*\$$ and that $[A \to \alpha \cdot \beta, y]$, $[B \to \omega \cdot, u]$ is a pair of distinct $u$-items of $G'$ that exhibit an LR($u$)-conflict and are accessible in $M_u(G')$ upon reading some string $\gamma$. Then $u$ is in $\text{FIRST}_u(\beta y)$ and, by Theorem 10.17, $[A \to \alpha \cdot \beta, y]$ and $[B \to \omega \cdot, u]$ are items in $\text{VALID}_u(\gamma)$. Then we have:

$$S' \underset{rm}{\Longrightarrow^*} \delta_1 A y_1 \underset{rm}{\Longrightarrow} \delta_1 \alpha\beta y_1 = \gamma\beta y_1, \quad y \in \text{FIRST}_u(y_1) \ ,$$

$$S' \underset{rm}{\Longrightarrow^*} \delta_2 B y_2 \underset{rm}{\Longrightarrow} \delta_2 \omega y_2 = \gamma y_2, \quad u \in \text{FIRST}_u(y_2) \ ,$$

for some strings $\delta_1, \delta_2 \in \$V^*$ and $y_1, y_2 \in T^*\$$. Here $[A \to \alpha \cdot \beta, k{:}y_1]$ and $[B \to \omega \cdot, k{:}y_2]$ are $k$-items in $\text{VALID}_k(\gamma)$. The condition $u \in \text{FIRST}_u(y_2)$ implies that $u = |u|{:}y_2$. Hence if $|u| = k$, $u = k{:}y_2$. On the other hand, if $|u| < k$, $u$ must end with \$. This is because $u$ was assumed to be in $k{:}T^*\$$. Now because $y_2 \in T^*\$$, we have $u = y_2$ when $|u| < k$. So in both cases $u = k{:}y_2$. Hence, to obtain an LR($k$)-conflict, it remains to be shown that $u$ belongs to $\text{FIRST}_k(\beta(k{:}y_1)) = \text{FIRST}_k(\beta y_1)$. Because $u \in \text{FIRST}_u(\beta y)$ and $y \in \text{FIRST}_u(y_1)$, $u$ must be in $\text{FIRST}_u(\beta y_1)$. (This follows from the equality $\text{FIRST}_u(\beta \text{FIRST}_u(y_1)) = \text{FIRST}_u(\beta y_1)$.) Hence if $|u| = k$, $u$ is in $\text{FIRST}_k(\beta y_1)$. If $|u| < k$, the condition $u \in k{:}T^*\$$ now implies that $\beta y_1$ derives $u$. Note that $y_1 \in k{:}T^*\$$ and that $\beta \in V^*$. So in both cases $u$ belongs to $\text{FIRST}_k(\beta y_1)$, as desired. By Theorem 6.39($b$), we conclude that $G$ is non-LR($k$). □

**Lemma 10.20** *Given a grammar $G = (V, T, P, S)$ and a string $u \in T^*$, the automaton $M_u(G)$ (including the final state sets $F_{\text{reduce}}$ and $F_{\text{shift}}$) can be constructed simultaneously in space $O((|u| + 1)^2 \cdot |G|)$ and in time $O((|u| + 1)^3 \cdot |G|)$.*

*Proof.* The proof is very similar to that of Lemma 10.8. First, the state set, the type (a) and (b) transitions, and the final state set $F_{\text{reduce}}$ can be determined in space and time $O((|u| + 1) \cdot |G|)$. Also, if $u = \varepsilon$, the type (c) transitions and the final state set

$F_{shift}$ can be determined in space and time $O((|u| + 1)\cdot|G|)$. If $|u| = 1$, the set $F_{shift}$ is composed of all items $[A \to \alpha \cdot u\beta, y]$ where $y$ is a suffix of $u$ and $\beta$ derives some terminal string. Whenever $\beta$ is nullable, we add to $M_u(G)$ all transitions

$$[A \to \alpha \cdot B\beta, vy] \to [B, v] \ ,$$

where $vy$ and $v$ are suffixes of $u$, and, if $u = av$ for $a \in T$, we add to $F_{shift}$ all items $[A \to \alpha \cdot a\beta, vy]$ where $vy$ is a suffix of $u$.

In the case $u = a_1 \ldots a_l \neq \varepsilon$ we compute, in space $O(|u|^2 \cdot |G|)$ and in time $O(|u|^3 \cdot |G|)$, the matrix $N_u$ of Lemma 10.7. For all $1 \leqslant i \leqslant j \leqslant l$ and for all symbols $[\beta] \in N_u(i,j)$ we add to $M_u(G)$ all transitions

$$[A \to \alpha \cdot B\beta, a_{j+1} \ldots a_l y] \to [B, a_i \ldots a_l] \ ,$$

where $a_{j+1} \ldots a_l y$ is a suffix of $u$. If $l > 1$, then for all $j = 2, \ldots, l$ and for all symbols $[\beta] \in N_u(2,j)$ we add to $F_{shift}$ all items $[A \to \alpha \cdot a_1\beta, a_{j+1} \ldots a_l y]$ where $a_{j+1} \ldots a_l y$ is a suffix of $u$. For all $i = 1, \ldots, l$ and symbols $[\beta]_{pre} \in N_u(i, l)$ we add to $M_u(G)$ all transitions

$$[A \to \alpha \cdot B\beta, y] \to [B, a_i \ldots a_l] \ ,$$

where $y$ is a suffix of $u$. If $l > 1$, then for all symbols $[\beta]_{pre} \in N_u(2, l)$ we add to $F_{shift}$ all items $[A \to \alpha \cdot a_1\beta, y]$ where $y$ is a suffix of $u$. □

**Theorem 10.21** (*Deterministic LR($k$) test using the automata $M_u(G')$, $u \in k{:}T^*\$$; Hunt, Szymanski and Ullman, 1975*) *Grammar $G = (V, T, P, S)$ can be tested for the LR($k$) property simultaneously in deterministic space $O((k + 1)^2 \cdot |G|^2)$ and in deterministic time $O((k + 1)^3 \cdot |T|^k \cdot |G|^2)$.*

*Proof.* Here we show that the LR($k$) test can be carried out in space $O((k+1)^4 \cdot |G|^2)$ and in time $O((k+1)^4 \cdot |T|^k \cdot |G|^2)$. We leave to the exercises the establishment of the sharper bounds $O((k + 1)^2 \cdot |G|^2)$ and $O((k + 1)^3 \cdot |T|^k \cdot |G|^2)$.

For each string $u \in k{:}T^*\$$ we perform the following. First, we construct for the \$-augmented grammar $G'$ the automaton $M_u(G')$ and the final state sets $F_{reduce}$ and $F_{shift}$ (from $F_{shift}$ we remove the items $[S' \to \cdot \$S\$, \varepsilon]$ and $[S' \to \$S \cdot \$, \varepsilon]$). By Lemma 10.20 this can be done in space $O((|u| + 1)^2 \cdot |G|)$ and in time $O((|u| + 1)^3 \cdot |G|)$. Then we determine in $M_u(G')$ the pairs of mutually accessible states. As the size of $M_u(G')$ is $O((|u| + 1)^2 \cdot |G|)$, this takes time $O((|u| + 1)^4 \cdot |G|^2)$ (Lemma 10.10 and Fact 10.12). Finally, we check whether or not for some pair of distinct mutually accessible states $I$, $J$ we have either $(I, J) \in F_{reduce} \times F_{reduce}$ or $(I, J) \in F_{shift} \times F_{reduce}$. If for some $u$ such a pair of states $I$, $J$ is found, $G$ is not LR($k$). Otherwise, it is.

As there are $O(|T|^k)$ different strings $u \in k{:}T^*\$$, we conclude that the entire LR($k$) test can be carried out in time $O(|T|^k \cdot (|u| + 1)^4 \cdot |G|^2)$. As only one of the automata $M_u(G')$ need be present at a time, space $O((|u| + 1)^4 \cdot |G|^2)$ suffices for the entire test. □

If we regard the natural number $k$ as fixed in Theorem 10.21, we get:

**Corollary 10.22** *For any fixed natural number k, the LR(k) testing problem $\mathscr{P}_{LR(k)}$ is solvable simultaneously in deterministic space $O(n^2)$ and in deterministic time $O(n^{k+2})$.* □

For uniform LR($k$) testing we get:

**Corollary 10.23** *The uniform LR(k) testing problem $\mathscr{P}_{LR}$ is solvable simultaneously in deterministic polynomial space and in deterministic one-level exponential time when k is expressed in unary, and simultaneously in deterministic one-level exponential space and in deterministic two-level exponential time when k is expressed in binary.* □

The automata $M_u(G')$ allow us to make use of nondeterminism in deriving an efficient algorithm for non-LR($k$) testing. Since by Theorem 10.19 a grammar $G$ (in which $S \Rightarrow^+ S$ is impossible) is non-LR($k$) if and only if a conflicting pair of items is found in some automaton $M_u(G')$, it suffices to guess this automaton and to check whether or not the guess was right. More specifically, given a grammar $G = (V, T, P, S)$ and a natural number $k$, we do the following.

*Step 1.* Check whether or not $S \Rightarrow^+ S$ is possible in $G$. If yes, output "$G$ is non-LR($k$)" and halt.

*Step 2.* Guess a string $u \in k{:}T^*\$$.

*Step 3.* Construct for the \$-augmented grammar $G'$ the automaton $M_u(G')$ with final state sets $F_{\text{reduce}}$ and $F_{\text{shift}}$. Remove from $F_{\text{shift}}$ the items $[S' \to \cdot \$S\$, \varepsilon]$ and $[S' \to \$S \cdot \$, \varepsilon]$.

*Step 4.* Determine in $M_u(G')$ the set of pairs of mutually accessible states.

*Step 5.* Check whether or not the set determined in the previous step contains a pair of distinct items $I$, $J$ such that $(I, J)$ belongs either to $F_{\text{reduce}} \times F_{\text{reduce}}$ or to $F_{\text{shift}} \times F_{\text{reduce}}$. If yes, output "$G$ is non-LR($k$)" and halt. Otherwise, halt.

Observe that this algorithm provides a partial solution (as defined in Section 1.4) to the problem of non-LR($k$) testing, not to the problem of LR($k$) testing.

The time taken by Step 1 is $O(|G|)$. The time taken by a "guess" is proportional to the size of the guessed value. Hence Step 2 can be executed in time $O(k)$. By Lemma 10.20, Step 3 takes space $O((k+1)^2 \cdot |G|)$ and time $O((k+1)^3 \cdot |G|)$. By Lemma 10.10, Step 4 takes space and time $O((k+1)^4 \cdot |G|^2)$. Hence it follows that the algorithm runs in space and time $O((k+1)^4 \cdot |G|^2)$. This implies that for any fixed $k \geqslant 0$ the non-LR($k$) testing problem $\mathscr{P}_{\text{non-LR}(k)}$ is solvable in nondeterministic time $O(n^2)$.

The space bound of the algorithm can readily be sharpened by a factor of $(k+1)^2 \cdot |G|$. This is made possible by the observation that it is not necessary to retain the entire set of pairs of mutually accessible states of $M_u(G')$. It suffices to generate, nondeterministically, two computations of $M_u(G')$ on some string $\gamma \in \$V^*$. We represent these computations as corresponding strings of states $I_1 \ldots I_m$ and $J_1 \ldots J_n$. The generation proceeds step by step; at each step one or both of the computations are advanced by a move to a new state. At the beginning we have $m = n = 1$ and $I_1 = J_1 = [S', \varepsilon]$. After the execution of the $p^{\text{th}}$ step, for some $p \geq 1$, we have generated some computations $I_1 \dots I_m$ and $J_1 \dots J_n$, where $m, n \leq p$. Then at the $(p + 1)^{\text{th}}$ step we first check whether or not $I_m$ and $J_n$ exhibit a conflict. If not, we choose one from three possibilities to advance the computations: (1) $X$-transitions from $I_m$ to $I_{m+1}$ and from $J_n$ to $J_{n+1}$; (2) an $\varepsilon$-transition from $I_m$ to $I_{m+1}$; (3) an $\varepsilon$-transition from $J_n$ to $J_{n+1}$. The algorithm is space-efficient because at any step only the latest pair of states, $I_m$, $J_n$, so far generated need be present.

The entire algorithm is shown in Figure 10.3. It should be clear that the algorithm produces output "$G$ is non-LR($k$)" if and only if $G$ is non-LR($k$). It can be shown by a simple induction that at any moment the pair of states $I, J$ reached so far are mutually accessible and, conversely, that for any pair of mutually accessible states $I, J$ the algorithm can make such a sequence of guesses that this pair of states is reached.

The time complexity of the **while**-loop of the algorithm is proportional to the maximum of the lengths of the shortest paths in the relation **mutually-accesses** from the node $([S', \varepsilon], [S', \varepsilon])$ to nodes $(I, J)$, taken over all pairs of states $I, J$ in

```
Check whether or not S ⇒+ S is possible in G; if yes, output "G is non-LR(k)" and halt;
guess a string u ∈ k:T*$;
construct the automaton M_u(G') and the final state sets F_reduce and F_shift;
remove from F_shift the items [S' → ·$S$, ε] and [S' → $S·$, ε];
I := [S', ε]; J := [S', ε];
while true do
    if I and J are distinct final states of M_u(G') such that
    (I, J) ∈ F_reduce × F_reduce or (I, J) ∈ F_shift × F_reduce then
        output "G is non-LR(k)" and halt
    else begin
        guess choice ∈ {1, 2, 3};
        case choice of
        1: guess in M_u(G') a transition on some symbol X from
           I to some state I' and a transition on some symbol
           Y from J to some state J';
           if this guessing succeeded and X ⇒ Y then begin
               I := I'; J := J'
           end else
               halt;
        2: guess in M_u(G') an ε-transition from I to some state I';
           if this guessing succeeded then
               I := I'
           else
               halt;
        3: guess in M_u(G') an ε-transition from J to some state J';
           if this guessing succeeded then
               J := J'
           else
               halt
        end case
    end.
```

**Figure 10.3** A nondeterministic algorithm for non-LR($k$) testing

$M_u(G')$. Since there are $O((k+1)^2 \cdot |G|^2)$ such pairs, we conclude that the algorithm runs in time $O((k+1)^3 \cdot |G| + (k+1)^2 \cdot |G|^2)$.

The space complexity of the algorithm is $O((k+1)^2 \cdot |G|)$, because $M_u(G')$ can be constructed within this space and because at any moment in the execution of the **while**-loop no more than an $O(|G| + k)$ space is needed besides the space taken by $M_u(G')$.

It is possible to reduce even further the space and time spent in a nondeterministic non-LR($k$) test. This is obtained by avoiding the explicit construction of the automaton $M_u(G')$ and by considering only computations of a certain kind. The complexity of this improved test is stated in the following theorem, the proof of which is left to the exercises.

**Theorem 10.24** (*Nondeterministic non-LR($k$) test using the automata $M_u(G')$, $u \in k{:}T^*\$$; Hunt, Szymanski and Ullman,* 1975) *Grammar $G = (V, T, P, S)$ can be tested for the non-LR($k$) property simultaneously in nondeterministic space $O(|G| + k)$ and in nondeterministic time $O((k+1) \cdot |G|^2)$.* □

**Corollary 10.25** *For any fixed natural number $k$, the non-LR($k$) testing problem $\mathscr{P}_{\text{non-LR}(k)}$ is solvable simultaneously in nondeterministic space $O(n)$ and in nondeterministic time $O(n^2)$.* □

**Corollary 10.26** *The uniform non-LR($k$) testing problem $\mathscr{P}_{\text{non-LR}}$ is solvable in nondeterministic polynomial time when $k$ is expressed in unary, and in nondeterministic one-level exponential time when $k$ is expressed in binary.* □

We conclude this section with results obtained using the automata $M_u(G')$ for SLR($k$) testing. The following theorem says how we can characterize the SLR($k$) property by the automata $M_u(G')$, $u \in k{:}T^*\$$, and by the automaton $M_\varepsilon(G')$ $(= M_0(G'))$. This characterization is illustrated in Figure 10.4(b). In Figure 10.4(a) is illustrated the characterization of the LR($k$) property (Theorem 10.19).

**Theorem 10.27** (*Characterization of the SLR($k$) property*) *Let $G = (V, T, P, S)$ be a grammar in which $S \Rightarrow^+ S$ is impossible. Further let $k$ be a natural number. Then $G$ is non-SLR($k$) if and only if there is some string $u \in k{:}T^*\$$ such that the \$-augmented grammar $G'$ has a pair of distinct $u$-items $[A \to \alpha \cdot \beta, y]$ and $[B \to \omega \cdot, u]$ that exhibit an LR($u$)-conflict and are (not necessarily mutually) accessible states in $M_u(G')$ and where $[A \to \alpha \cdot \beta]$ and $[B \to \omega \cdot]$ are mutually accessible states in $M_\varepsilon(G')$.*

*Proof.* Exercise. □

**Theorem 10.28** (*Deterministic SLR($k$) test*) *Grammar $G = (V, T, P, S)$ can be tested for the SLR($k$) property simultaneously in deterministic space $O((k+1)^2 \cdot |G| + |G|^2)$ and in deterministic time $O((k+1)^3 \cdot |T|^k \cdot |G|^2)$.*

*Proof.* Exercise. □

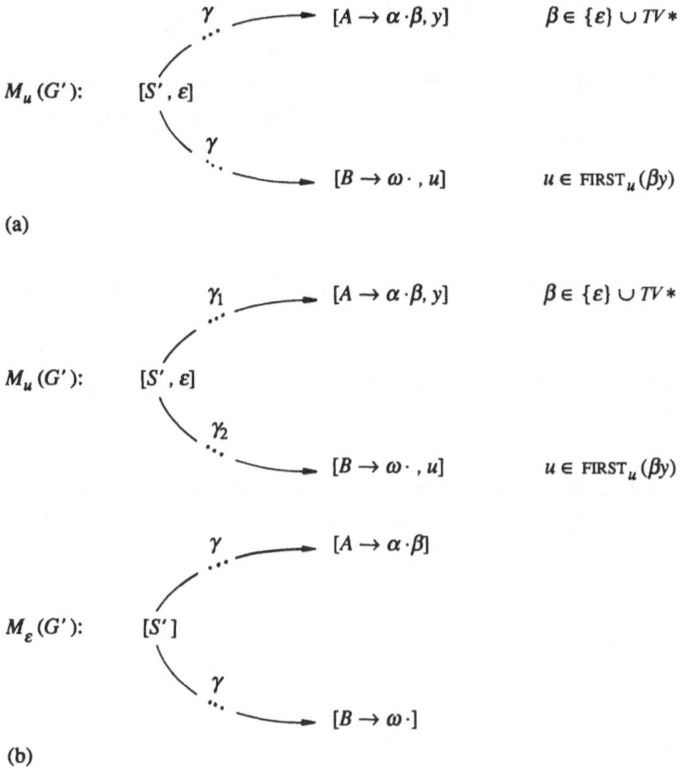


**Figure 10.4** Characterization of (a) the non-LR($k$) property, and (b) the non-SLR($k$) property

**Corollary 10.29** *For any fixed natural number k, the SLR(k) testing problem* $\mathscr{P}_{\text{SLR}(k)}$ *is solvable simultaneously in deterministic space* $O(n^2)$ *and in deterministic time* $O(n^{k+2})$. □

For $k \leqslant 2$ the time bound in Corollary 10.29 can be sharpened into $O(n^{k+1})$ (see the exercises).

**Theorem 10.30** (*Nondeterministic non-SLR(k) test*) *Grammar* $G = (V, T, P, S)$ *can be tested for the non-SLR(k) property simultaneously in nondeterministic space* $O(|G| + k)$ *and in nondeterministic time* $O((k + 1)\cdot|G| + |G|^2)$.

*Proof.* Exercise. □

Theorem 10.30 implies immediately that Corollaries 10.25 and 10.26 also hold when we replace "LR" by "SLR".

## 10.2 Efficient Algorithms for LL($k$) and SLL($k$) Testing

In this section we shall apply the ideas of the previous section to develop efficient algorithms for LL($k$) and strong LL($k$) testing. We shall show (among other things) that for any fixed natural number $k$ the LL($k$) testing problem

$\mathscr{P}_{\mathrm{LL}(k)}$: "Given a context-free grammar $G$, is $G$ an LL($k$) grammar?"

is solvable in deterministic polynomial time, and that the uniform non-LL($k$) testing problem

$\mathscr{P}_{\text{non-LL}}$: "Given a context-free grammar $G$ and a natural number $k$, is $G$ a non-LL($k$) grammar?"

is solvable in nondeterministic polynomial time when $k$ is expressed in unary, and in nondeterministic one-level exponential time when $k$ is expressed in binary. The same results will also hold when we replace "LL" by "SLL".

The above results can be obtained in two ways. First, we may dualize the constructions of the previous section and represent the canonical LL($k$) machine as a collection of automata $M_{\mathrm{LL}(u)}(G')$, $u \in k{:}T^*\$$, the analogs of the automata $M_{\mathrm{LR}(u)}(G')$. Secondly, we may carry our results on LR($k$) testing over to LL($k$) testing by reducing the problem of LL($k$) testing to the problem of LR($k$) testing. This is possible, because it turns out that any (reduced) grammar can be transformed in linear time into a grammar which is LR($k$) if and only if the original grammar is LL($k$). Thus, whenever we have an algorithm for LR($k$) testing, we can use this algorithm for LL($k$) testing by applying it to the transformed grammar. Because the transformation is linear-time, the asymptotic complexity of the LL($k$) test is identical to that of the LR($k$) test. We begin by presenting this transformation.

Let $G = (V, T, P, S)$ be a grammar. The *LR-transformed grammar* for $G$ is the grammar $G_{\mathrm{LR}} = (V \cup P, T, P_{\mathrm{LR}}, S)$, where

$$P_{\mathrm{LR}} = \{A \to (A, \omega)\omega \mid A \to \omega \in P\}$$
$$\cup \{(A, \omega) \to \varepsilon \mid A \to \omega \in P\} \ .$$

That is, we add to each rule $A \to \omega$ in the original grammar a new "marker" nonterminal $(A, \omega)$, the rule itself, that identifies uniquely the beginning of the rule. These new nonterminals $(A, \omega)$ have as their only rule the rule $(A, \omega) \to \varepsilon$.

The size of $G_{\mathrm{LR}}$ is at most $3 \cdot |G|$, and $G_{\mathrm{LR}}$ can be constructed from $G$ in linear time.

We shall show that $G$ is LL($k$) if and only if $G_{\mathrm{LR}}$ is LR($k$) (provided that $G$ is reduced). We first give an intuitive argument for this. Suppose that $G = (V, T, P, S)$ is a grammar, $A \to \omega$ is a rule in $P$, and $x$, $y$, and $z$ are strings in $T^*$ such that

(1) $S \Rightarrow^* xAz$ and $\omega \Rightarrow^* y$ in $G$ .

Then the construction of $G_{LR}$ implies that

(2) $$S \Rightarrow^* xAz \Rightarrow x(A, \omega)\omega z \Rightarrow^* x(A, \omega)yz \quad \text{in } G_{LR} .$$

Now if $G$ is LL($k$), then in (1) the canonical LL($k$) parser of $G$ recognizes the rule $A \to \omega$ after scanning $x$ and seeing $k{:}yz$. In other words, in deriving $xyz$ from $xAz$ in $G$ the appropriate rule $A \to \omega$ is determined uniquely by $x$ and $k{:}yz$. But then in deriving $xyz$ from $xAz$ in $G_{LR}$ the rule $A \to (A, \omega)\omega$ must be determined uniquely by $x$ and $k{:}yz$. This means that in (2) the canonical LR($k$) parser of $G_{LR}$ must be able to recognize the rule $(A, \omega) \to \varepsilon$ after scanning $x$ and seeing $k{:}yz$. This in turn implies immediately that the canonical LR($k$) parser of $G_{LR}$ is also able to recognize the rule $A \to (A, \omega)\omega$ after scanning $xy$ and seeing $k{:}z$. (Observe that the rule $A \to (A, \omega)\omega$ will already be determined uniquely once the unique left corner $(A, \omega)$ has been determined.) So the LL($k$)-ness of $G$ seems to imply the LR($k$)-ness of $G_{LR}$.

Conversely, if $G_{LR}$ is LR($k$), then in (2) the canonical LR($k$) parser of $G_{LR}$ recognizes the rule $(A, \omega) \to \varepsilon$ after scanning $x$ and seeing $k{:}yz$. This means that in deriving $xyz$ from $xAz$ in $G_{LR}$ the appropriate rule $A \to (A, \omega)\omega$ is determined uniquely by $x$ and $k{:}yz$. But then in deriving $xyz$ from $xAz$ in $G$ the rule $A \to \omega$ must also be determined uniquely by $x$ and $k{:}yz$. Hence in (1) the canonical LL($k$) parser of $G$ must be able to recognize the rule $A \to \omega$ after scanning $x$ and seeing $k{:}yz$. So the LR($k$)-ness of $G_{LR}$ seems to imply the LL($k$)-ness of $G$.

For a rigorous proof of the fact we need some lemmas.

**Lemma 10.31** *Let $G = (V, T, P, S)$ be a grammar, $G_{LR}$ the LR-transformed grammar for $G$, and $h$ a homomorphism from the rule strings of $G_{LR}$ to the rule strings of $G$ defined by:*

$$h(A \to (A, \omega)\omega) = \varepsilon ,$$

$$h((A, \omega) \to \varepsilon) = A \to \omega .$$

*If $X$ is a symbol in $V$, $\phi$ a string in $V^*$, and $\pi$ a rule string in $P^*$ such that*

$$X \overset{\pi}{\underset{lm}{\Longrightarrow}} \phi \quad \textit{in } G ,$$

*then $G_{LR}$ has a unique rule string $\pi'$ such that*

$$X \overset{\pi'}{\underset{lm}{\Longrightarrow}} \phi \quad \textit{in } G_{LR} \quad \textit{and} \quad h(\pi') = \pi .$$

*Conversely, if $X$ is a symbol in $V$, $\phi$ a string, and $\pi'$ a rule string of $G_{LR}$ such that*

$$X \overset{\pi'}{\underset{lm}{\Longrightarrow}} \phi \in V^* \quad \textit{in } G_{LR} ,$$

*then*

$$X \overset{h(\pi')}{\underset{lm}{\Longrightarrow}} \phi \quad \textit{in } G .$$

*Moreover, if $X$ is a symbol in $V$, $x$ a string in $T^*$, $A$ a nonterminal in $V$, and $\delta$ a string over the alphabet of $G_{LR}$ such that*

$$X \underset{lm}{\Longrightarrow^*} xA\delta ,$$

*then $\delta \in V^*$.*

*Proof.* Two simple inductions on derivation length. The details are left to the exercises. □

**Lemma 10.32** *Let $G = (V, T, P, S)$ be a grammar and $G_{LR}$ its LR-transformed grammar. Then the following statements hold for all $k \geqslant 0$.*

*(a) $G$ is $LL(k)$ if and only if $G_{LR}$ is $LL(k)$ .*
*(b) $G$ is $SLL(k)$ if and only if $G_{LR}$ is $SLL(k)$ .*

*Proof.* We shall only prove statement (a); the proof of statement (b) is analogous and is left to the exercises.

Assume first that $G$ is not LL($k$). Then by Theorem 8.37 there are leftmost derivations

$$S \underset{lm}{\Longrightarrow^*} xA\delta \underset{lm}{\Longrightarrow} x\omega_1\delta \underset{lm}{\Longrightarrow^*} xy_1 \quad \text{in } G ,$$

$$S \underset{lm}{\Longrightarrow^*} xA\delta \underset{lm}{\Longrightarrow} x\omega_2\delta \underset{lm}{\Longrightarrow^*} xy_2 \quad \text{in } G ,$$

where $\omega_1 \neq \omega_2$ and $k{:}y_1 = k{:}y_2$. By Lemma 10.31 we have:

$$S \underset{lm}{\Longrightarrow^*} xA\delta, \quad x\omega_1\delta \underset{lm}{\Longrightarrow^*} xy_1, \quad \text{and} \quad x\omega_2\delta \underset{lm}{\Longrightarrow^*} xy_2 \quad \text{in } G_{LR} .$$

Because by definition $A \to (A, \omega_1)\omega_1, (A, \omega_1) \to \varepsilon, A \to (A, \omega_2)\omega_2$, and $(A, \omega_2) \to \varepsilon$ are rules of $G_{LR}$, we have:

$$S \underset{lm}{\Longrightarrow^*} xA\delta \underset{lm}{\Longrightarrow} x(A, \omega_1)\omega_1\delta \underset{lm}{\Longrightarrow} x\omega_1\delta \underset{lm}{\Longrightarrow^*} xy_1 \quad \text{in } G_{LR} ,$$

$$S' \underset{lm}{\Longrightarrow^*} xA\delta \underset{lm}{\Longrightarrow} x(A,\omega_2)\omega_2\delta \underset{lm}{\Longrightarrow} x\omega_2\delta \underset{lm}{\Longrightarrow^*} xy_2 \quad \text{in } G_{LR} .$$

Here $A \to (A, \omega_1)\omega_1$ and $A \to (A, \omega_2)\omega_2$ are distinct rules, since $\omega_1 \neq \omega_2$. Hence by Theorem 8.37 $G_{LR}$ is not LL($k$).

Assume then that $G_{LR}$ is not LL($k$). Then there are leftmost derivations

$$S \underset{lm}{\Longrightarrow^*} xA\delta \underset{lm}{\Longrightarrow} x\omega_1'\delta \underset{lm}{\Longrightarrow^*} xy_1 \quad \text{in } G_{LR} ,$$

$$S \underset{lm}{\Longrightarrow^*} xA\delta \underset{lm}{\Longrightarrow} x\omega_2'\delta \underset{lm}{\Longrightarrow^*} xy_2 \quad \text{in } G_{LR} ,$$

where $\omega_1' \neq \omega_2'$ and $k{:}y_1 = k{:}y_2$. Because $A \to \omega_1'$ and $A \to \omega_2'$ are distinct rules of the same nonterminal, $A$ must be a nonterminal of $G$, $\omega_1'$ must be of the form $(A, \omega_1)\omega_1$ and $\omega_2'$ must be of the form $(A, \omega_2)\omega_2$, where $A \to \omega_1$ and $A \to \omega_2$ are rules of $G$. (Recall that nonterminals of the form $(A, \omega)$ have only the rule $(A, \omega) \to \varepsilon$.) By Lemma 10.31 we then conclude that $\delta \in V^*$ and that

$$S \underset{\text{lm}}{\Longrightarrow}^* xA\delta \underset{\text{lm}}{\Longrightarrow} x\omega_1\delta \underset{\text{lm}}{\Longrightarrow}^* xy_1 \quad \text{in } G ,$$

$$S \underset{\text{lm}}{\Longrightarrow}^* xA\delta \underset{\text{lm}}{\Longrightarrow} x\omega_2\delta \underset{\text{lm}}{\Longrightarrow}^* xy_2 \quad \text{in } G ,$$

where $\omega_1 \neq \omega_2$, which means that $G$ is not LL($k$). Observe that the derivations $x(A, \omega_1)\omega_1\delta \underset{\text{lm}}{\Longrightarrow}^* xy_1$ and $x(A, \omega_2)\omega_2\delta \underset{\text{lm}}{\Longrightarrow}^* xy_2$ imply that $\omega_1\delta \underset{\text{lm}}{\Longrightarrow}^* y_1$ and $\omega_2\delta \underset{\text{lm}}{\Longrightarrow}^* y_2$ in $G_{\text{LR}}$, and hence, by Lemma 10.31, these derivations also hold in $G$. □

**Lemma 10.33** *Let $G_{\text{LR}}$ be the LR-transformed grammar for a reduced grammar $G = (V, T, P, S)$ and let $k \geq 0$. If $G_{\text{LR}}$ is LR($k$), then it is also LL($k$).*

*Proof.* Assume $G_{\text{LR}}$ is not LL($k$). Then there are in $G_{\text{LR}}$ leftmost derivations

$$S \overset{\pi}{\underset{\text{lm}}{\Longrightarrow}} xA\delta \underset{\text{lm}}{\Longrightarrow} x(A, \omega_1)\omega_1\delta \underset{\text{lm}}{\Longrightarrow} x\omega_1\delta \underset{\text{lm}}{\Longrightarrow}^* xv_1y_1 ,$$

$$S \overset{\pi}{\underset{\text{lm}}{\Longrightarrow}} xA\delta \underset{\text{lm}}{\Longrightarrow} x(A, \omega_2)\omega_2\delta \underset{\text{lm}}{\Longrightarrow} x\omega_2\delta \underset{\text{lm}}{\Longrightarrow}^* xv_2y_2 ,$$

where $\omega_1 \neq \omega_2$, $k{:}v_1y_1 = k{:}v_2y_2$, and $\omega_1$ derives $v_1$, $\omega_2$ derives $v_2$, and $\delta$ derives $y_1$ and $y_2$. By Lemma 8.55 the rule string $\pi$ induces some viable prefixes $\gamma$ and $\gamma'$ such that $S$ rightmost derives $\gamma Ay_1$ and $\gamma' Ay_2$. Because no rule string can induce two distinct viable prefixes (Lemma 8.54), we have $\gamma = \gamma'$. Hence there are in $G_{\text{LR}}$ the rightmost derivations

$$S \underset{\text{rm}}{\Longrightarrow}^* \gamma Ay_1 \underset{\text{rm}}{\Longrightarrow} \gamma(A, \omega_1)\omega_1y_1 \underset{\text{rm}}{\Longrightarrow}^* \gamma(A, \omega_1)v_1y_1 \underset{\text{rm}}{\Longrightarrow} \gamma v_1y_1 ,$$

$$S \underset{\text{rm}}{\Longrightarrow}^* \gamma Ay_2 \underset{\text{rm}}{\Longrightarrow} \gamma(A, \omega_2)\omega_2y_2 \underset{\text{rm}}{\Longrightarrow}^* \gamma(A, \omega_2)v_2y_2 \underset{\text{rm}}{\Longrightarrow} \gamma v_2y_2 .$$

Because here $k{:}v_1y_1 = k{:}v_2y_2$ and $(A, \omega_1) \to \varepsilon$ and $(A, \omega_2) \to \varepsilon$ are distinct rules, we conclude by Theorem 6.39 that $G_{\text{LR}}$ is not LR($k$). □

Lemma 10.32(*a*), Lemma 10.33, and Theorem 8.57 now imply that for any reduced grammar $G$ the LR-transformed grammar $G_{\text{LR}}$ is LR($k$) if and only if $G$ is LL($k$). The result can be stated more generally as:

**Theorem 10.34** (*Brosgol*, 1974; *Hunt and Szymanski*, 1978) *Let $k$ be a natural number and let $\mathscr{C}$ be any class of grammars that lies between the class of reduced LL($k$) grammars and the class of reduced LR($k$) grammars, that is,*

$$\{G \mid G \text{ is reduced } LL(k)\} \subseteq \mathscr{C} \subseteq \{G \mid G \text{ is reduced } LR(k)\} .$$

*Then any reduced grammar G can be transformed in time $O(|G|)$ into a grammar $f(G)$ such that G is LL(k) if and only if $f(G) \in \mathscr{C}$. Moreover, the transformation f is independent of $\mathscr{C}$.*

*Proof.* $f(G)$ is the LR-transformed grammar $G_{LR}$ for $G$. As noted earlier, $G_{LR}$ is of size at most $3 \cdot |G|$ and is easily constructed from $G$. If $G$ is reduced LL($k$), then $G_{LR}$ is also reduced and LL($k$) by Lemma 10.32. Since $\mathscr{C}$ includes all the reduced LL($k$) grammars, $G_{LR}$ is in $\mathscr{C}$. Conversely, if $G$ is not reduced LL($k$), then $G_{LR}$ is not reduced LL($k$) by Lemma 10.32, and hence, by Lemma 10.33, $G_{LR}$ is not reduced LR($k$). But since every member of $\mathscr{C}$ is reduced LR($k$), we conclude that $G_{LR}$ is not in $\mathscr{C}$. □

Observe that because by Theorem 8.57 every reduced LL($k$) grammar is also an LR($k$) grammar, we can choose in Theorem 10.34 for example $\mathscr{C} = \{G \mid G \text{ is reduced LR}(k)\}$.

Theorem 10.34 states that, when only reduced grammars are considered, the problem of LL($k$) testing reduces in linear time to the problem of $\mathscr{C}$ testing, that is, to the decision problem "Is grammar $G$ in $\mathscr{C}$?", where $\mathscr{C}$ is any class of grammars lying between the class of reduced LL($k$) grammars and the class of reduced LR($k$) grammars. Of course, the same is also true for the complements of these problems.

**Corollary 10.35** *Assume only reduced grammars are considered. Then the problem of LL(k) testing reduces in linear time to the problem of LR(k) testing, and the problem of non-LL(k) testing reduces in linear time to the problem of non-LR(k) testing.* □

Now Corollary 10.35 implies (by Lemma 1.42) that Theorems 10.21 and 10.24 also hold for LL($k$) testing. Hence we can conclude, for example, that for any fixed $k \geqslant 0$ the LL($k$) testing problem $\mathscr{P}_{LL(k)}$ (for reduced grammars) is solvable simultaneously in deterministic space $O(n^2)$ and in deterministic time $O(n^{k+2})$ (cf. Corollary 10.22), and that the uniform non-LL($k$) testing problem $\mathscr{P}_{\text{non-LL}}$ (for reduced grammars) is solvable in nondeterministic polynomial time when $k$ is expressed in unary, and in nondeterministic one-level exponential time when $k$ is expressed in binary (cf. Corollary 10.26).

Next we shall consider the second approach to LL($k$) testing mentioned at the beginning. We shall represent the canonical LL($k$) machine succinctly as a collection of small nondeterministic automata $M_{LL(u)}(G')$, $u \in k{:}T^*\$$, constructed in a way analogous to the automata $M_{LR(u)}(G')$ considered in the previous section. It turns out that a strictly analogous construction yields exactly the same asymptotic complexity bounds as those for LR($k$) testing. However, a modification is possible that yields a deterministic LL($k$) test with space complexity $O(n)$ and time complexity $O(n^{k+1})$ for fixed $k$. In other words, the bounds obtained via the reduction to LR($k$) testing can be sharpened by a factor of $n$.

First we consider the straightforward construction. This is motivated by the fact that it will readily yield an $O(n)$ space-bounded and $O(n^{k+1})$ time-bounded deterministic SLL($k$) test.

Let $G = (V, T, P, S)$ be a grammar and $u$ a string in $T^*$. We define $M_{\mathrm{LL}(u)}(G)$ (or $M_u(G)$, if no ambiguity arises) as the finite automaton with state alphabet

$$\{[A \to \alpha \cdot \beta, y] \mid A \to \alpha\beta \text{ is a rule of } G \text{ and } y \text{ is a suffix of } u\}$$
$$\cup \{[A, y] \mid A \text{ is a nonterminal of } G \text{ and } y \text{ a suffix of } u\} ,$$

input alphabet $V$, initial state $[S, \varepsilon]$, and with set of transitions consisting of all rules of the forms:

(a) $[A, y] \to [A \to \omega \cdot, y]$,

(b) $[A \to \alpha X \cdot \beta, y]X \to [A \to \alpha \cdot X\beta, z]$, for $X \in V$ and $z \in \mathrm{FIRST}_u(Xy)$, and

(c) $[A \to \alpha B \cdot \beta, y] \to [B, y]$, for $B \in V \setminus T$ .

The set of final states of $M_u(G)$ is

$$F_{\mathrm{produce}} = \{[A \to \cdot\, \omega, u] \mid A \to \omega \text{ is a rule of } G\} .$$

To allow grammars that are not reduced, we require in addition that in type (c) transitions the string $\alpha$ derives some terminal string (cf. the definition of the relation $\mathbf{desc}_{\mathrm{LL}(k)}$ in Section 8.2).

**Fact 10.36** For any grammar $G = (V, T, P, S)$ and string $u \in T^*$ the following statements hold for the automaton $M_{\mathrm{LL}(u)}(G)$.

(1) The number of states is at most $2 \cdot (|u| + 1) \cdot |G|$.
(2) The number of type (a) transitions is at most $(|u| + 1) \cdot |P|$.
(3) The number of type (b) transitions is at most $(|u| + 1)^2 \cdot |G|$.
(4) The number of type (c) transitions is at most $(|u| + 1) \cdot |G|$.
(5) The size of the automaton is $O((|u| + 1)^2 \cdot |G|)$. □

As an example consider the grammar $G_{\mathrm{LL3}}$:

$$S \to AB, \quad A \to \varepsilon \mid a, \quad B \to ab \mid bc .$$

This grammar is LL(3) but not LL(2). The automaton $M_{ab}(G'_{\mathrm{LL3}})$ for the \$-augmented grammar is given in Figure 10.5. Only the interesting portions are shown.

Now $G_{\mathrm{LL3}}$ is not LL(2) because in $M_{ab}(G'_{\mathrm{LL3}})$ the states $[A, b]$ and $[A, ab]$ are mutually accessible and because the final state $[A \to \cdot\, a, ab]$ is reachable from $[A, b]$ upon reading $a^R$, the reversal of the right-hand side of $A \to a$, and the final state $[A \to \cdot, ab]$ is reachable from $[A, ab]$ upon reading $\varepsilon^R$, the reversal of the right-hand side of $A \to \varepsilon$.

Let $G = (V, T, P, S)$ be a grammar and $u$ a string in $T^*$. We say that an item $[A \to \alpha \cdot \beta, y]$ of $G$ is *LL(u)-valid* for string $\gamma \in V^*$ if

$$S \underset{\mathrm{lm}}{\Longrightarrow^*} xA\delta \underset{\mathrm{lm}}{\Longrightarrow} x\alpha\beta\delta = x\alpha\gamma^R \quad \text{and} \quad y \in \mathrm{FIRST}_u(\gamma^R)$$

hold in $G$ for some strings $x \in T^*$ and $\delta \in V^*$.

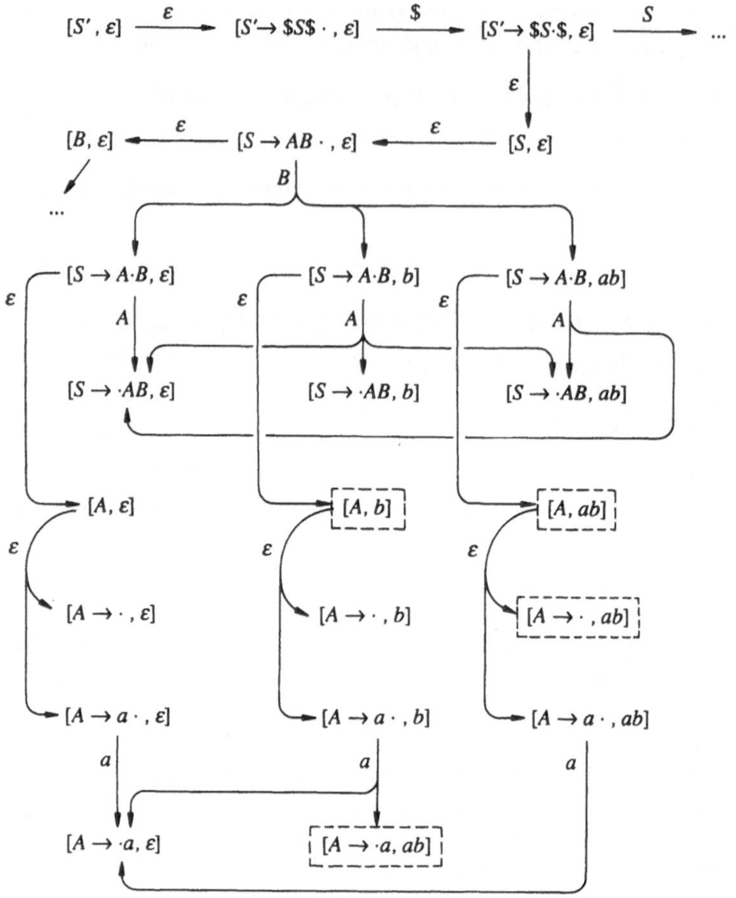


**Figure 10.5** Portions of the automaton $M_{ab}(G'_{LL3})$ for the \$-augmented grammar $S' \to \$S\$$, $S \to AB$, $A \to \varepsilon | a$, $B \to ab | bc$. The states encircled by a broken line give rise to an LL($ab$)-conflict

**Fact 10.37** If $[A \to \alpha \cdot \beta, y]$ is an LL($u$)-valid item for $\gamma$, then $\gamma$ is a viable suffix, $[A \to \alpha \cdot \beta, y]$ is a $u$-item, $\beta^R$ is a suffix of $\gamma$, and $y$ belongs to $\text{FIRST}_{|y|}(\beta\text{FOLLOW}_{|y|}(A))$. Conversely, if $\gamma$ is a viable suffix, then some item is LL($u$)-valid for $\gamma$, provided that the grammar is reduced. □

We denote by $\text{VALID}_{\text{LL}(u)}(\gamma)$ (or $\text{VALID}_u(\gamma)$, for short) the set of LL($u$)-valid items for $\gamma$. For $n \geq 0$ we denote by $\text{VALID}_{u,n}(\gamma)$ the set of items $[A \to \alpha \cdot \beta, y]$ that satisfy

$$S \underset{\text{lm}}{\Longrightarrow}^n xA\delta \underset{\text{lm}}{\Longrightarrow} x\alpha\beta\delta = x\alpha\gamma^R \quad \text{and} \quad y \in \text{FIRST}_u(\gamma^R)$$

for some $x \in T^*$ and $\delta \in V^*$ .

The following lemmas are the "LL($u$) analogs" of Lemmas 8.18, 8.20, and 8.25. The first two lemmas follow immediately from Lemmas 8.18 and 8.20. The third lemma is true because the operator $\text{FIRST}_u$ shares with the operator $\text{FIRST}_k$ the characteristic properties of a "lookahead operator".

**Lemma 10.38** *If in grammar* $G = (V, T, P, S)$

$$[A \to \alpha B \cdot \beta, y] \in \text{VALID}_{u,n}(\gamma) \quad \textit{and} \quad \alpha \Rightarrow^m v \in T^* ,$$

*then for all rules* $B \to \omega$ *in* $P$

$$[B \to \omega \cdot, y] \in \text{VALID}_{u,n+m+1}(\gamma) .$$

□

**Lemma 10.39** *If in grammar* $G = (V, T, P, S)$

$$[B \to \omega \cdot, y] \in \text{VALID}_{u,n}(\gamma) \quad \textit{and} \quad n > 0 ,$$

*then for some rule* $A \to \alpha B \beta$ *in* $P$, *string* $v$ *in* $T^*$, *and natural number* $m < n$

$$[A \to \alpha B \cdot \beta, y] \in \text{VALID}_{u,m}(\gamma) \quad \textit{and} \quad \alpha \Rightarrow^{n-m-1} v .$$

□

**Lemma 10.40** *If* $[A \to \alpha\omega \cdot \beta, y]$ *is an item in* $\text{VALID}_{u,n}(\gamma)$, *then* $\gamma\omega^R$ *is a viable suffix and* $[A \to \alpha \cdot \omega\beta, z]$ *is in* $\text{VALID}_{u,n}(\gamma\omega^R)$ *for all* $z \in \text{FIRST}_u(\omega y)$. *Conversely, if* $[A \to \alpha \cdot \omega\beta, z]$ *is an item in* $\text{VALID}_{u,n}(\delta)$, *then there is a viable suffix* $\gamma$ *such that* $\delta = \gamma\omega^R$ *and* $\text{VALID}_{u,n}(\gamma)$ *contains an item* $[A \to \alpha\omega \cdot \beta, y]$ *where* $\text{FIRST}_u(\omega y)$ *contains* $z$. □

Using the above lemmas it is easy to prove the following theorem. The theorem is a restatement of Theorem 10.17, but now for LL($u$)-valid items and the automaton $M_{\text{LL}(u)}(G)$.

**Theorem 10.41** *Let* $G = (V, T, P, S)$ *be a grammar and* $u$ *a string in* $T^*$. *State* $[A \to \alpha \cdot \beta, y]$ *in the automaton* $M_u(G)$ *is accessible upon reading string* $\gamma$ *if and only if* $[A \to \alpha \cdot \beta, y]$ *is an LL(u)-valid item for* $\gamma$. *In other words,*

$$\text{VALID}_u(\gamma) = \{[A \to \alpha \cdot \beta, y] \mid [S, \varepsilon]\gamma \Rightarrow^* [A \to \alpha \cdot \beta, y] \quad \textit{in } M_u(G)\} .$$

□

Let $G'$ be the \$-augmented grammar for grammar $G = (V, T, P, S)$, $k$ a natural number, and $u$ a string in $k{:}T^*\$$. We say that items $[A_1 \to \cdot\omega_1, y_1]$ and $[A_2 \to \cdot\omega_2, y_2]$ *exhibit an LL(u)-conflict* if $A_1 = A_2$, $\omega_1 \neq \omega_2$, and $y_1 = y_2 = u$.

**Theorem 10.42** (*Characterization of the SLL(k) property*) *Let* $G = (V, T, P, S)$ *be a grammar,* $G'$ *its \$-augmented grammar, and* $k$ *a natural number. Then* $G$ *is non-SLL(k) if and only if there is a string* $u$ *in* $k{:}T^*\$$ *and accessible states* $I$, $J$ *in* $M_u(G')$ *that exhibit an LL(u)-conflict.*

*Proof.* To prove the "only if" part of the theorem, assume that $G$, and hence $G'$, is non-SLL($k$). By Theorem 5.34, there are leftmost derivations

$$S' \underset{\text{lm}}{\Longrightarrow}^* x_1 A\delta_1 \underset{\text{lm}}{\Longrightarrow} x_1\omega_1\delta_1 \underset{\text{lm}}{\Longrightarrow}^* x_1 y_1 ,$$

$$S' \underset{\text{lm}}{\Longrightarrow}^* x_2 A\delta_2 \underset{\text{lm}}{\Longrightarrow} x_2\omega_2\delta_2 \underset{\text{lm}}{\Longrightarrow}^* x_2 y_2 ,$$

where $k{:}y_1 = k{:}y_2$ and $\omega_1 \neq \omega_2$. Let $u = k{:}y_1$. Then $u$ is in $k{:}T^*\$$, in $\text{FIRST}_u(\omega_1\delta_1)$, and in $\text{FIRST}_u(\omega_2\delta_2)$. Hence by definition $[A \to \cdot\omega_1, u]$ is an LL($u$)-valid item for $(\omega_1\delta_1)^R$ and $[A \to \cdot\omega_2, u]$ is an LL($u$)-valid item for $(\omega_2\delta_2)^R$. By Theorem 10.41, $[A \to \cdot\omega_1, u]$ is a state in $M_u(G')$ accessible upon reading $(\omega_1\delta_1)^R$ and $[A \to \cdot\omega_2, u]$ is a state in $M_u(G')$ accessible upon reading $(\omega_2\delta_2)^R$. As $\omega_1 \neq \omega_2$, these states exhibit an LL($u$)-conflict.

To prove the "if" part of the theorem, assume that $u$ is a string in $k{:}T^*\$$ and that $[A \to \cdot\omega_1, u]$ and $[A \to \cdot\omega_2, u]$ are states in $M_u(G')$ such that $\omega_1 \neq \omega_2$, $[A \to \cdot\omega_1, u]$ is accessible upon reading some string $\gamma_1$, and $[A \to \cdot\omega_2, u]$ is accessible upon reading some string $\gamma_2$. Then by Theorem 10.41, $[A \to \cdot\omega_1, u]$ is an LL($u$)-valid item for $\gamma_1$ and $[A \to \cdot\omega_2, u]$ is an LL($u$)-valid item for $\gamma_2$. By definition there are leftmost derivations

$$S' \underset{\text{lm}}{\Longrightarrow}^* x_1 A\delta_1 \underset{\text{lm}}{\Longrightarrow} x_1\omega_1\delta_1 = x_1\gamma_1^R, \quad u \in \text{FIRST}_u(\gamma_1^R) ,$$

$$S' \underset{\text{lm}}{\Longrightarrow}^* x_2 A\delta_2 \underset{\text{lm}}{\Longrightarrow} x_2\omega_2\delta_2 = x_2\gamma_2^R, \quad u \in \text{FIRST}_u(\gamma_2^R) .$$

Because $u$ was assumed to belong to $k{:}T^*\$$, we conclude that the condition $u \in \text{FIRST}_u(\gamma_i^R)$ implies $u \in \text{FIRST}_k(\gamma_i^R)$, $i = 1, 2$ (cf. the proof of Theorem 10.19). But then we have for some strings $y_1$ and $y_2$ in $T^*\$$

$$S' \underset{\text{lm}}{\Longrightarrow}^* x_1 A\delta_1 \underset{\text{lm}}{\Longrightarrow} x_1\omega_1\delta_1 \underset{\text{lm}}{\Longrightarrow}^* x_1 y_1$$

$$S' \underset{\text{lm}}{\Longrightarrow}^* x_2 A\delta_2 \underset{\text{lm}}{\Longrightarrow} x_2\omega_2\delta_2 \underset{\text{lm}}{\Longrightarrow}^* x_2 y_2 ,$$

$$k{:}y_1 = u = k{:}y_2 .$$

Since here $\omega_1 \neq \omega_2$, we conclude by Theorem 5.34 that $G'$, and hence $G$, is non-SLL($k$). □

**Theorem 10.43** (*Characterization of the LL(k) property*) *Let $G = (V, T, P, S)$ be a grammar, $G'$ its \$-augmented grammar, and $k$ a natural number. Then $G$ is non-LL($k$) if and only if there is a string $u$ in $k{:}T^*\$$, a string $\gamma$ in $\$V^*$, and states $[A, y_1]$, $[A, y_2]$, $[A \to \cdot\omega_1, u]$, $[A \to \cdot\omega_2, u]$ in $M_u(G')$ such that the following statements hold.*

(1) *$[A, y_1]$ and $[A, y_2]$ are both accessible upon reading $\gamma$.*
(2) *$[A \to \cdot\omega_1, u]$ is reachable from $[A, y_1]$ upon reading $\omega_1^R$.*
(3) *$[A \to \cdot\omega_2, u]$ is reachable from $[A, y_2]$ upon reading $\omega_2^R$.*
(4) *The items $[A \to \cdot\omega_1, u]$ and $[A \to \cdot\omega_2, u]$ exhibit an LL($u$)-conflict, that is, $\omega_1 \neq \omega_2$.*

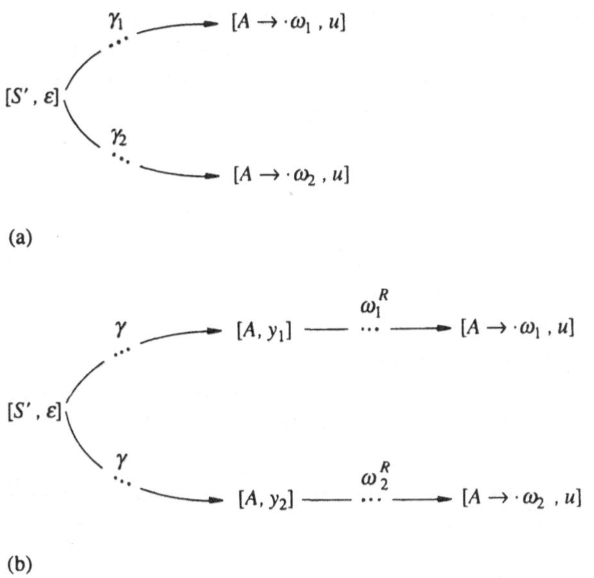


**Figure 10.6** Portions of the automaton $M_u(G')$ indicating (a) that $G$ is non-SLL($k$), and (b) that $G$ is non-LL($k$)

*Proof.* The proof is similar to that of Theorem 10.42. In place of Theorem 5.34 we use Theorem 8.37. Observe that $[A \to \cdot\omega, u]$ is an accessible state in $M_u(G')$ if and only if there is an accessible state $[A \to \omega\cdot, y]$ such that $u$ is in $\text{FIRST}_u(\omega y)$. □

Theorems 10.42 and 10.43 are illustrated in Figure 10.6.

**Lemma 10.44** *Given a grammar $G = (V, T, P, S)$ and a string $u \in T^*$, the automaton $M_u(G)$ can be constructed simultaneously in space $O((|u| + 1)^2 \cdot |G|)$ and in time $O((|u| + 1)^3 \cdot |G|)$.*

*Proof.* The proof is very similar to that of Lemma 10.20. The state set, the type (a) transitions, and the final state set $F_{\text{produce}}$ are trivial to construct. In constructing the type (c) transitions we need the set of useful symbols in $G$, which can be determined in linear time. In constructing the type (b) transitions we need the fact that in the grammar $G_{\text{pre}}$ of Lemma 10.6 any nonterminal $A$ in $V$ generates all (nonempty) sentences in $L_G(A)$ and that for any nonterminal $A$ in $V$ there is in $G_{\text{pre}}$ a nonterminal $A_{\text{pre}}$ that generates the set of all (nonempty) prefixes of sentences in $L_G(A)$. □

**Theorem 10.45** (*Deterministic SLL(k) test using the automata $M_u(G')$*) *Grammar $G = (V, T, P, S)$ can be tested for the SLL($k$) property simultaneously in deterministic space $O((k + 1)^2 \cdot |G|)$ and in deterministic time $O((k + 1)^3 \cdot |T|^k \cdot |G|)$.*

*Proof.* For each string $u \in k{:}T^*\$$ we perform the following. First, we construct for the \$-augmented grammar $G'$ the automaton $M_u(G')$. By Lemma 10.44 this can be done in space $O((k+1)^2 \cdot |G|)$ and in time $O((k+1)^3 \cdot |G|)$. Then we determine in $M_u(G')$ the set of accessible states. This can be done in time $O((k+1)^2 \cdot |G|)$, that is, in time linear in the size of $M_u(G')$. Observe that the set of accessible states in any finite automaton is obtained as the image **accesses***$(q_s)$, where $q_s$ is the initial state and **accesses** is a relation defined by:

$$q_1 \textbf{ accesses } q_2 \text{ if there is some transition from } q_1 \text{ to } q_2 \ .$$

Finally, we check whether or not for some nonterminal $A$ there are two accessible final states $[A \to \cdot\omega_1, u]$ and $[A \to \cdot\omega_2, u]$. This checking can be done in linear time. If such a pair of states is found, $G$ is not SLL($k$). Otherwise, it is. As there are $O(|T|^k)$ strings $u$ in $k{:}T^*\$$ to be considered, we conclude that the entire test can be carried out in time $O(|T|^k \cdot (k+1)^3 \cdot |G|)$. As only one of the automata $M_u(G')$ need be present at a time, space $O((k+1)^2 \cdot |G|)$ suffices for the entire test. □

**Corollary 10.46** *For any fixed $k \geqslant 0$, the SLL($k$) testing problem $\mathscr{P}_{\mathrm{SLL}(k)}$ is solvable simultaneously in deterministic space $O(n)$ and in deterministic time $O(n^{k+1})$.* □

For nondeterministic non-SLL($k$) testing we may prove:

**Theorem 10.47** (*Nondeterministic non-SLL($k$) test using the automata $M_u(G')$*) *Grammar $G = (V, T, P, S)$ can be tested for the non-SLL($k$) property simultaneously in nondeterministic space $O(|G| + k)$ and in nondeterministic time $O((k+1) \cdot |G|)$.*

*Proof.* Exercise. □

**Corollary 10.48** *For any fixed $k \geqslant 0$, the non-SLL($k$) testing problem $\mathscr{P}_{\text{non-SLL}(k)}$ is solvable in nondeterministic time $O(n)$.* □

**Corollary 10.49** *The uniform non-SLL($k$) testing problem $\mathscr{P}_{\text{non-SLL}}$ is solvable in nondeterministic polynomial time when $k$ is expressed in unary, and in nondeterministic one-level exponential time when $k$ is expressed in binary.* □

We now turn to the problem of LL($k$) testing. From the characterization of the LL($k$) property given in Theorem 10.43 we can readily derive both a deterministic algorithm for LL($k$) testing and a nondeterministic algorithm for non-LL($k$) testing. The deterministic algorithm works as follows. For each string $u \in k{:}T^*\$$ the algorithm performs four steps. First, the automaton $M_u(G')$ is constructed. Second, the set of pairs of mutually accessible states in $M_u(G')$ is determined. Third, the algorithm determines the set of all states $[A \to \omega\cdot, y]$ in $M_u(G')$ from which the state $[A \to \cdot\omega, u]$ is reachable using only type (b) transitions. Fourth, it is checked whether or not the set determined in the previous step contains a pair of states of the form $[A \to \omega_1\cdot, y_1]$, $[A \to \omega_2\cdot, y_2]$ that are mutually accessible and such that $\omega_1 \neq \omega_2$. If yes, the grammar is non-LL($k$).

The first step takes space $O((k+1)^2 \cdot |G|)$ and time $O((k+1)^3 \cdot |G|)$ by Lemma 10.44. The second step can be carried out in space and time $O((k+1)^4 \cdot |G|^2)$ by Lemma 10.10. The time taken by the third step is not more than linear in the size of

$M_u(G')$. Observe that the desired set is obtained as the image

$$(\textbf{type-b-trans}^{-1})^* \ \textbf{is-last-item}(\{[A \to \cdot\omega, u] \mid A \to \omega \text{ is a rule of the grammar}\}) \ ,$$

where **type-b-trans** and **is-last-item** are relations defined by:

$I$ **type-b-trans** $J$, if $M_u(G')$ has a type (b) transition from $I$ to $J$ .

$I$ **is-last-item** $I$, if $I$ is of the form $[A \to \omega\cdot, y]$ .

Finally, the fourth step takes time linear in the size of the set of pairs of mutually accessible states. We conclude that the entire LL($k$) test can be carried out in space $O((k+1)^4 \cdot |G|^2)$ and in time $O((k+1)^4 \cdot |T|^k \cdot |G|^2)$. Here the space bound can in fact be sharpened to $O((k+1)^2 \cdot |G|^2)$ (cf. Theorem 10.21 and the exercises). We have:

**Theorem 10.50** (*Deterministic LL($k$) test using the automata $M_u(G')$*) *Grammar $G = (V, T, P, S)$ can be tested for the LL($k$) property simultaneously in deterministic space $O((k+1)^2 \cdot |G|^2)$ and in deterministic time $O((k+1)^4 \cdot |T|^k \cdot |G|^2)$.* □

For nondeterministic non-LL($k$) testing we may prove:

**Theorem 10.51** (*Nondeterministic non-LL($k$) test using the automata $M_u(G')$*) *Grammar $G = (V, T, P, S)$ can be tested for the non-LL($k$) property simultaneously in nondeterministic space $O(|G| + k)$ and in nondeterministic time $O((k+1) \cdot |G|^2)$.*

*Proof.* Exercise. □

The bounds obtained are essentially the same as those for LR($k$) testing. This is because the major tasks performed for a single string $u \in k{:}T^*\$$ are analogous to those performed for $u$ in LR($k$) testing. In the deterministic LR($k$) and LL($k$) tests the most time and space consuming task performed for $u$ is the determining of the set of pairs of mutually accessible states in $M_u(G')$. The space and time complexity of this task is quadratic in the size of $M_u(G')$, while the other tasks performed for $u$ have complexity only linear in the size of the grammar. In the nondeterministic non-LR($k$) and non-LL($k$) tests two computations of $M_u(G')$ are generated. Because these computations have to be computations on the same string $\gamma$, their length can be quadratic in the number of states in $M_u(G')$.

It turns out that for LL($k$) testing the automata $M_u(G')$ can be modified so that in the deterministic test it will no longer be necessary to determine the pairs of mutually accessible states and that in the nondeterministic test it will suffice to generate only one, and therefore a shorter, computation. This is made possible by the observation that in the automaton $M_{\mathrm{LL}(u)}(G')$ for a non-LL($k$) grammar the conflicting items $[A \to \cdot\omega_1, u]$ and $[A \to \cdot\omega_2, u]$ are essentially "closer" to each other than are the conflicting items $[A \to \alpha\cdot\beta, y]$ $[B \to \omega\cdot, u]$ in the automaton $M_{\mathrm{LR}(u)}(G')$ for a non-LR($k$) grammar. In $M_{\mathrm{LL}(u)}(G')$ the items $[A \to \cdot\omega_1, u]$ and

$[A \to \cdot\omega_2, u]$ originate from nearby states of the form $[A, y]$, where only the lookahead string $y$ may vary. In $M_{\mathrm{LR}(u)}(G')$ on the contrary the items $[A \to \alpha\cdot\beta, y]$ and $[B \to \omega\cdot, u]$ may not have such a nearby, common origin. This difference between the LL($k$) and LR($k$) properties is also apparent in the grammatical characterizations of these properties. In the LL($k$) characterization (Theorem 8.37($d$)) the initial segments in the two leftmost derivations are the same, both ending with the same left sentential form $xA\delta$, while in the LR($k$) characterization (Theorem 6.39($c$)) the initial segments in the two rightmost derivations end with distinct right sentential forms $\delta_1 A_1 y_1$ and $\delta_2 A_2 y_2$.

We shall modify the automata $M_{\mathrm{LL}(u)}(G')$ so that the "origins" of any pair of conflicting items $[A \to \cdot\omega_1, u]$, $[A \to \cdot\omega_2, u]$ will be embedded into a single state. More specifically, if $[A \to \cdot\omega_1, u]$ is reachable from state $[A, y_1]$ upon reading $\omega_1^R$ and $[A \to \cdot\omega_2, u]$ is reachable from state $[A, y_2]$ upon reading $\omega_2^R$, where $[A, y_1]$ and $[A, y_2]$ are reachable from the initial state upon reading viable suffix $\gamma$, then the modified automaton will have a single state, denoted by $[A, W]$, that represents both $[A, y_1]$ and $[A, y_2]$. Here $W$ is a set of lookahead strings defined by:

$$W = \{y \mid [A, y] \text{ is a state in } M_u(G') \text{ accessible upon reading } \gamma\} .$$

The modified automaton will be denoted by $M_{u\text{-set}}(G')$.

Let $G = (V, T, P, S)$ be a grammar and $u$ a string in $T^*$. We define $M_{u\text{-set}}(G)$ as the finite automaton with state alphabet

$$\{[A \to \alpha\cdot\beta, W] \mid A \to \alpha\beta \text{ is a rule of } G \text{ and } W \subseteq \mathrm{SUFFIX}(u)\}$$
$$\cup \{[A, W] \mid A \text{ is a nonterminal of } G \text{ and } W \subseteq \mathrm{SUFFIX}(u)\} ,$$

input alphabet $V$, initial state $[S, \{\varepsilon\}]$, and with set of transitions consisting of all rules of the forms:

(a) $[A, W] \to [A \to \omega\cdot, W]$ ,

(b) $[A \to \alpha X\cdot\beta, W]X \to [A \to \alpha\cdot X\beta, \mathrm{FIRST}_u(XW)]$, for $X \in V$ ,

(c) $[A \to \alpha B\cdot\beta, W] \to [B, W]$, for $B \in V\backslash T$ .

Here $W$ denotes any subset of SUFFIX($u$), and $\mathrm{FIRST}_u(XW)$ denotes the union of all $\mathrm{FIRST}_u(Xy)$ where $y \in W$. As before, we require that in (c) the string $\alpha$ derives some terminal string. The set of final states of $M_{u\text{-set}}(G)$ is

$$F_{\mathrm{produce}} = \{[A \to \cdot\omega, W] \mid A \to \omega \text{ is a rule of } G \text{ and } u \in W \subseteq \mathrm{SUFFIX}(u)\} .$$

**Fact 10.52** For any grammar $G = (V, T, P, S)$ and string $u \in T^*$ the following statements are true for the automaton $M_{u\text{-set}}(G)$.

(1) The number of states is at most $2\cdot 2^{|u|+1}\cdot|G|$.
(2) The number of type (a) transitions is at most $2^{|u|+1}\cdot|P|$.
(3) The number of type (b) transitions is at most $2^{|u|+1}\cdot|G|$.
(4) The number of type (c) transitions is at most $2^{|u|+1}\cdot|G|$.
(5) The size of the automaton is $O(2^{|u|}\cdot|G|)$.

□

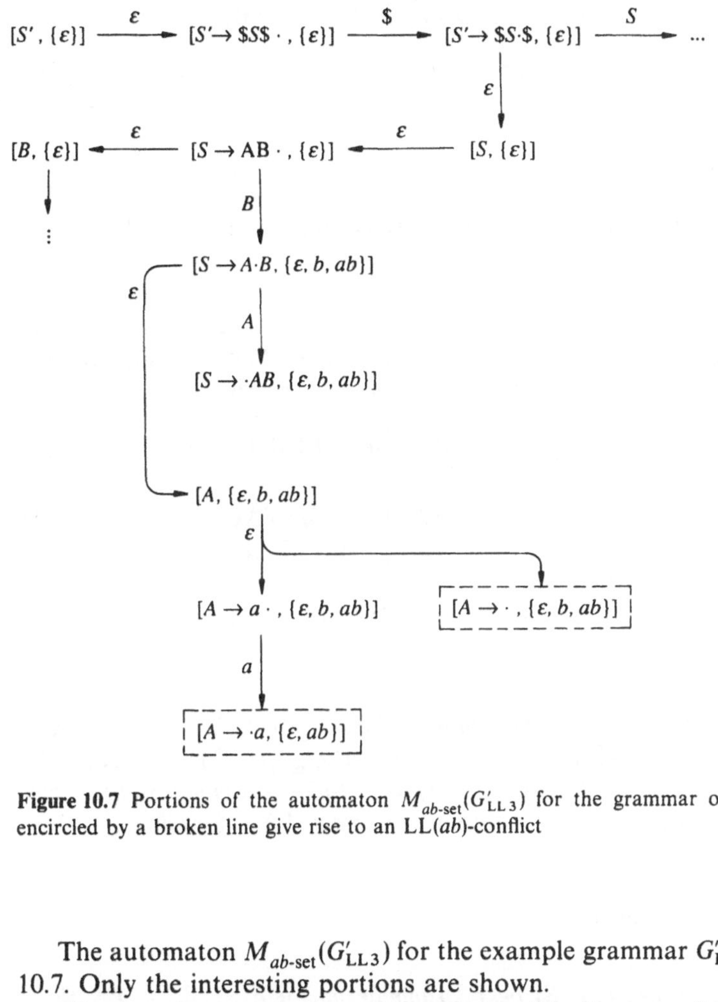


**Figure 10.7** Portions of the automaton $M_{ab\text{-set}}(G'_{\text{LL}3})$ for the grammar of Figure 10.5. The states encircled by a broken line give rise to an LL($ab$)-conflict

The automaton $M_{ab\text{-set}}(G'_{\text{LL}3})$ for the example grammar $G'_{\text{LL}3}$ is given in Figure 10.7. Only the interesting portions are shown.

Observe that in the automaton $M_{u\text{-set}}(G)$ the type (b) transitions are all deterministic. From state $[A \to \alpha X \cdot \beta, W]$ there is in $M_{u\text{-set}}(G)$ an $X$-transition to the state $[A \to \alpha \cdot X\beta, \text{FIRST}_u(XW)]$ only, while in $M_u(G)$ there are usually several $X$-transitions from a state $[A \to \alpha X \cdot \beta, y]$. Also observe that since the type (b) transitions are the only transitions in $M_{u\text{-set}}(G)$ that can change the lookahead strings, any pair of mutually accessible states in $M_{u\text{-set}}(G)$ must have as its second component the same set of lookahead strings. So if $[A, W_1]$ and $[A, W_2]$ are mutually accessible states in $M_{u\text{-set}}(G)$ then in fact $[A, W_1] = [A, W_2]$. This means that in LL($k$) testing we only need to check whether or not $M_{u\text{-set}}(G)$ has accessible states $[A, W]$, $[A \to \cdot\omega_1, W_1]$, and $[A \to \cdot\omega_2, W_2]$ where $[A \to \cdot\omega_1, W_1]$ is reachable from $[A, W]$ upon reading $\omega_1^R$ and $[A \to \cdot\omega_2, W_2]$ is reachable from $[A, W]$ upon reading $\omega_2^R$, and $\omega_1 \neq \omega_2$ and $u$ is in $W_1 \cap W_2$ (see Figure 10.8). Hence in the deterministic test there is no longer any need to compute the pairs of mutually accessible states in the automaton, and in the nondeterministic test it suffices to generate only one computation.

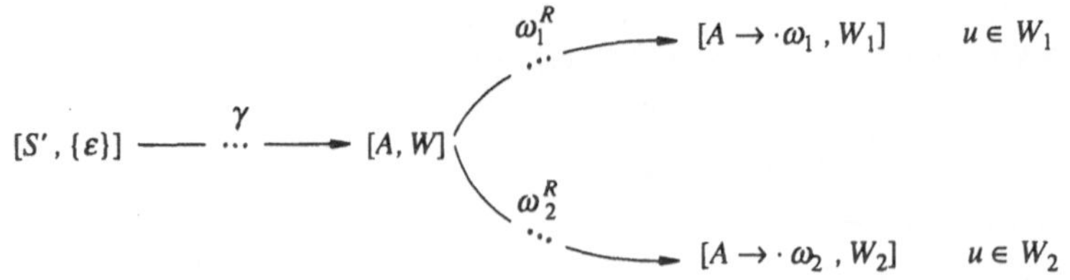


**Figure 10.8** Portions of the automation $M_{u\text{-set}}(G')$ indicating that $G$ is not LL($k$)

Let $G = (V, T, P, S)$ be a grammar and $u$ a string in $T^*$. We say that a pair of the form $[A \rightarrow \alpha \cdot \beta, W]$ is a *u-set-item* if $A \rightarrow \alpha\beta$ is a rule in $P$ and $W$ is a subset of SUFFIX($u$). An item $[A \rightarrow \alpha \cdot \beta, W]$ is *LL(u-set)-valid* for string $\gamma \in V^*$ if

$$S \underset{\text{lm}}{\Longrightarrow}^* xA\delta \underset{\text{lm}}{\Longrightarrow} x\alpha\beta\delta = x\alpha\gamma^R \quad \text{and} \quad W = \text{FIRST}_u(\gamma^R)$$

hold in $G$ for some strings $x \in T^*$ and $\delta \in V^*$. We denote by $\text{VALID}_{u\text{-set}}(\gamma)$ the set of LL($u$-set)-valid items for $\gamma$. As before, $\text{VALID}_{u\text{-set}}(\gamma)$ is obtained as the union of subsets $\text{VALID}_{u\text{-set},n}(\gamma)$, $n \geqslant 0$ (cf. $\text{VALID}_{u,n}(\gamma)$).

Now Lemmas 10.38 and 10.39 hold immediately when we replace "$u$" by "$u$-set" and "$y$" by "$W$". Lemma 10.40 reads as follows.

**Lemma 10.53** *If* $[A \rightarrow \alpha\omega \cdot \beta, W]$ *is an item in* $\text{VALID}_{u\text{-set},n}(\gamma)$, *then* $\gamma\omega^R$ *is a viable suffix and* $[A \rightarrow \alpha \cdot \omega\beta, \text{FIRST}_u(\omega W)]$ *is in* $\text{VALID}_{u\text{-set},n}(\gamma\omega^R)$. *Conversely, if* $[A \rightarrow \alpha \cdot \omega\beta, W']$ *is an item in* $\text{VALID}_{u\text{-set},n}(\delta)$, *then there is a viable suffix* $\gamma$ *such that* $\delta = \gamma\omega^R$ *and* $\text{VALID}_{u\text{-set},n}(\gamma)$ *contains an item* $[A \rightarrow \alpha\omega \cdot \beta, W]$ *where* $\text{FIRST}_u(\omega W) = W'$. □

Theorem 10.41 now reads as:

**Theorem 10.54** *Let* $G = (V, T, P, S)$ *be a grammar and* $u$ *a string in* $T^*$. *State* $[A \rightarrow \alpha \cdot \beta, W]$ *in the automaton* $M_{u\text{-set}}(G)$ *is accessible upon reading string* $\gamma$ *if and only if* $[A \rightarrow \alpha \cdot \beta, W]$ *is an LL(u-set)-valid item for* $\gamma$. *In other words,*

$$\text{VALID}_{u\text{-set}}(\gamma) = \{[A \rightarrow \alpha \cdot \beta, W] \mid [S, \{\varepsilon\}]\gamma \Rightarrow^* [A \rightarrow \alpha \cdot \beta, W] \text{ in } M_{u\text{-set}}(G)\} \ .$$

□

Let $G'$ be the \$-augmented grammar for grammar $G = (V, T, P, S)$, $k$ a natural number, and $u$ a string in $k{:}T^*\$$. We say that $u$-set-items $[A \rightarrow \cdot\omega_1, W_1]$ and $[A \rightarrow \cdot\omega_2, W_2]$ *exhibit an LL(u)-conflict* if $\omega_1 \neq \omega_2$ and $u \in W_1 \cap W_2$.

**Theorem 10.55** (*Characterization of the LL(k) property via the automata* $M_{u\text{-set}}(G')$) *Let* $G = (V, T, P, S)$ *be a grammar,* $G'$ *its \$-augmented grammar, and* $k$ *a natural number. Then* $G$ *is non-LL(k) if and only if there is a string* $u$ *in* $k{:}T^*\$$ *and states*

*$[A, W]$, $[A \to \cdot\omega_1, W_1]$, and $[A \to \cdot\omega_2, W_2]$ in $M_{u\text{-set}}(G')$ such that the following statements are true.*

(1) *$[A, W]$ is accessible.*
(2) *$[A \to \cdot\omega_1, W_1]$ is reachable from $[A, W]$ upon reading $\omega_1^R$.*
(3) *$[A \to \cdot\omega_2, W_2]$ is reachable from $[A, W]$ upon reading $\omega_2^R$.*
(4) *The items $[A \to \cdot\omega_1, W_1]$ and $[A \to \cdot\omega_2, W_2]$ exhibit an LL($u$)-conflict, that is, $\omega_1 \neq \omega_2$ and $u \in W_1 \cap W_2$.*

*Proof.* To prove the "only if" part of the theorem, assume that $G$, and hence $G'$, is non-LL($k$). By Theorem 8.37, there are leftmost derivations

$$S' \underset{\text{lm}}{\Longrightarrow^*} xA\delta \underset{\text{lm}}{\Longrightarrow} x\omega_1\delta \underset{\text{lm}}{\Longrightarrow^*} xy_1 \ ,$$

$$S' \underset{\text{lm}}{\Longrightarrow^*} xA\delta \underset{\text{lm}}{\Longrightarrow} x\omega_2\delta \underset{\text{lm}}{\Longrightarrow^*} xy_2 \ ,$$

where $k{:}y_1 = k{:}y_2$ and $\omega_1 \neq \omega_2$. Let $u = k{:}y_1(= k{:}y_2)$. Further let $W = \text{FIRST}_u(\delta)$, $W_1 = \text{FIRST}_u(\omega_1\delta)$, and $W_2 = \text{FIRST}_u(\omega_2\delta)$. Then $u$ is in $k{:}T^*\$$ and in $W_1 \cap W_2$. Moreover, $[A \to \omega_1\cdot, W]$ and $[A \to \omega_2\cdot, W]$ are LL($u$-set)-valid for $\delta^R$, $[A \to \cdot\omega_1, W_1]$ is LL($u$-set)-valid for $\delta^R\omega_1^R$, and $[A \to \cdot\omega_2, W_2]$ is LL($u$-set)-valid for $\delta^R\omega_2^R$. By Theorem 10.54, $[A \to \omega_1\cdot, W]$ and $[A \to \omega_2\cdot, W]$ are states in $M_{u\text{-set}}(G')$ accessible upon reading $\delta^R$, $[A \to \cdot\omega_1, W_1]$ is a state in $M_{u\text{-set}}(G')$ accessible upon reading $\delta^R\omega_1^R$, and $[A \to \cdot\omega_2, W_2]$ is a state in $M_{u\text{-set}}(G')$ accessible upon reading $\delta^R\omega_2^R$.

By construction, $[A, W]$ is a state of $M_{u\text{-set}}(G')$ accessible upon reading $\delta^R$. Moreover, $M_{u\text{-set}}(G')$ has states $[A \to \omega_1\cdot, W'_1]$ and $[A \to \omega_2\cdot, W'_2]$ accessible upon reading $\delta^R$ such that $[A \to \cdot\omega_1, W_1]$ is reachable from $[A \to \omega_1\cdot, W'_1]$ upon reading $\omega_1^R$ and using only type (b) transitions and $[A \to \cdot\omega_2, W_2]$ is reachable from $[A \to \omega_2\cdot, W'_2]$ upon reading $\omega_2^R$ and using only type (b) transitions. By Theorem 10.54, $[A \to \omega_1\cdot, W'_1]$ and $[A \to \omega_2\cdot, W'_2]$ are LL($u$-set)-valid for $\delta$. But then $W'_1 = W'_2 = \text{FIRST}_u(\delta^R) = W$, which means that $[A \to \cdot\omega_1, W_1]$ is reachable from $[A, W]$ upon reading $\omega_1^R$ using one type (a) transition and $|\omega_1|$ type (b) transitions and that $[A \to \cdot\omega_2, W_2]$ is reachable from $[A, W]$ upon reading $\omega_2^R$ using one type (a) transition and $|\omega_2|$ type (b) transitions. We conclude that statements (1) to (4) are true.

To prove the "if" part of the theorem, assume that $u$ is a string in $k{:}T^*\$$, $\delta$ is a string in $V^*\$$, and $[A, W]$, $[A \to \cdot\omega_1, W_1]$ and $[A \to \cdot\omega_2, W_2]$ are states in $M_{u\text{-set}}(G')$ such that $[A, W]$ is accessible upon reading $\delta^R$ and statements (2) to (4) hold. Then $[A \to \omega_1\cdot, W]$ and $[A \to \omega_2\ , W]$ are states in $M_{u\text{-set}}(G')$ accessible upon reading $\delta^R$, and $[A \to \cdot\omega_1, W_1]$ is accessible upon reading $\delta^R\omega_1^R$, and $[A \to \cdot\omega_2, W_2]$ is accessible upon reading $\delta^R\omega_2^R$. By Theorem 10.54, $[A \to \omega_1\cdot, W]$ and $[A \to \omega_2\cdot, W]$ are LL($u$-set)-valid items for $\delta^R$, $W_1 = \text{FIRST}_u(\omega_1\delta)$, and $W_2 = \text{FIRST}_u(\omega_2\delta)$. By (4) we then have in $G'$:

$$S' \underset{\text{lm}}{\Longrightarrow^*} xA\delta \underset{\text{lm}}{\Longrightarrow} x\omega_1\delta, \quad u \in \text{FIRST}_u(\omega_1\delta) \ ,$$

$$S' \underset{\text{lm}}{\Longrightarrow^*} xA\delta \underset{\text{lm}}{\Longrightarrow} x\omega_2\delta, \quad u \in \text{FIRST}_u(\omega_2\delta) \ ,$$

where $\omega_1 \neq \omega_2$. Because $u$ was assumed to belong to $k{:}T^*\$$, the condition $u \in \mathrm{FIRST}_u(\omega_i\delta)$ implies $u \in \mathrm{FIRST}_k(\omega_i\delta)$, $i = 1, 2$ (cf. the proof of Theorem 10.19). Hence by Theorem 8.37 $G'$ (and therefore $G$, too) is non-LL($k$). □

The following lemma is proved as Lemma 10.44.

**Lemma 10.56** *Given a grammar $G = (V, T, P, S)$ and a string $u \in T^*$, the automaton $M_{u\text{-set}}(G)$ can be constructed simultaneously in space $O(2^{|u|} \cdot |G|)$ and in time $O((|u| + 1) \cdot 2^{|u|} \cdot |G|)$.* □

Observe that once the matrix $N_u$ of Lemma 10.7 has been computed for the grammar $G'_{\mathrm{pre}}$, then the type (b) transition starting from a fixed state $[A \to \alpha X \cdot \beta, W]$ can be determined in time $O(|u| + 1)$.

Now we can state the main results of this section.

**Theorem 10.57** (*Deterministic LL($k$) test using the automata $M_{u\text{-set}}(G')$*) *Grammar $G = (V, T, P, S)$ can be tested for the LL($k$) property simultaneously in deterministic space $O(2^k \cdot |G|)$ and in deterministic time $O((k + 1) \cdot 2^k \cdot |T|^k \cdot |G|)$.*

*Proof.* For each $u \in k{:}T^*\$$ perform the following. First, construct the automaton $M_{u\text{-set}}(G')$. By Lemma 10.56 this takes space $O(2^k \cdot |G|)$ and time $O((k + 1) \cdot 2^k \cdot |G|)$. Second, determine the set of accessible states in $M_{u\text{-set}}(G')$. As explained in the proof of Theorem 10.45, this can be carried out in time linear in the size of automaton, that is, in time $O(2^k \cdot |G|)$. Third, determine the set of all states $[A \to \omega\cdot, W]$ in $M_{u\text{-set}}(G')$ from which some final state $[A \to \cdot\omega, W']$, $u \in W'$, is reachable using only type (b) transitions. (In fact here $W' = \mathrm{FIRST}_u(\omega W)$.) As explained, this can be done in time linear in the size of $M_{u\text{-set}}(G')$ using the relational expression (**type-b-trans**$^{-1}$)* **is-last-item**. Finally, check whether or not the set determined in the previous step contains two distinct states of the form $[A \to \omega_1\cdot, W]$ and $[A \to \omega_2\cdot, W]$. □

**Corollary 10.58** *For any fixed $k \geq 0$, the LL($k$) testing problem $\mathscr{P}_{\mathrm{LL}(k)}$ is solvable simultaneously in deterministic space $O(n)$ and in deterministic time $O(n^{k+1})$.* □

**Theorem 10.59** (*Nondeterministic non-LL($k$) test using the automata $M_{u\text{-set}}(G')$*) *Grammar $G = (V, T, P, S)$ can be tested for the non-LL($k$) property simultaneously in nondeterministic space $O((k + 1)^2 \cdot |G|)$ and in nondeterministic time $O((k + 1) \cdot 2^k \cdot |G|)$.*

*Proof.* Exercise. □

**Corollary 10.60** *For any fixed $k \geq 0$, the non-LL($k$) testing problem $\mathscr{P}_{\text{non-LL}(k)}$ is solvable in nondeterministic time $O(n)$.* □

## 10.3 Hardness of Uniform LR(k) and LL(k) Testing

In the previous sections we have derived upper bounds on the complexity of the problems of C(k) testing and non-C(k) testing, when C(k) is one of the grammar classes LR(k), SLR(k), LL(k), or SLL(k). In the case in which the natural number $k$ is not a parameter of the problems we have determined the exact complexity of the problems in that we have shown that for any fixed $k \geqslant 0$ the problems $\mathscr{P}_{C(k)}$ and $\mathscr{P}_{\text{non-}C(k)}$ are in P, the class of decision problems solvable in deterministic polynomial time. However, for free $k$ (that is, $k$ is a parameter of the problem) we have only derived some superpolynomial upper bounds on the complexity. We have shown that the uniform non-C(k) testing problem $\mathscr{P}_{\text{non-C}}$ belongs to NP when $k$ is expressed in unary, and to NE when $k$ is expressed in binary. Here NP denotes the class of decision problems solvable in nondeterministic polynomial time, and NE denotes the class of decision problems solvable in nondeterministic one-level exponential time.

In this section we shall derive lower bounds on the complexity of uniform non-C(k) testing. We shall show that for $k$ in unary the uniform non-C(k) testing problem $\mathscr{P}_{\text{non-C}}$ is among the "hardest" problems in NP, when we regard two decision problems as equally "hard" if they reduce to each other in polynomial time (cf. Section 1.5). More specifically, we shall show that any decision problem in NP reduces in polynomial time to the problem of uniform non-C(k) testing when $k$ is expressed in unary. This means (recall Lemma 1.42) that whenever we have an algorithm for uniform non-C(k) testing (for $k$ in unary) that has time complexity $T(n)$, then for any decision problem $\mathscr{P}$ in NP there is a polynomial $p$ and an algorithm for solving $\mathscr{P}$ in time $O(T(p(n)))$. Similarly, we shall show that for $k$ in binary the uniform non-C(k) testing problem is among the hardest problems in NE. That is, any decision problem in NE reduces in polynomial time to $\mathscr{P}_{\text{non-C}}$ when $k$ is expressed in binary.

We say that a decision problem $\mathscr{P}$ is *hard for* NP (or *NP-hard*) if every decision problem in NP reduces in polynomial time to $\mathscr{P}$. $\mathscr{P}$ is *hard for* NE (or *NE-hard*) if every decision problem in NE reduces in polynomial time to $\mathscr{P}$. $\mathscr{P}$ is *complete for* NP (or *NP-complete*) if $\mathscr{P}$ is in NP and is NP-hard. $\mathscr{P}$ is *complete for* NE (or *NE-complete*) if $\mathscr{P}$ is in NE and is NE-hard. More generally, decision problem $\mathscr{P}$ is *hard for* decision problem class $\mathscr{C}$ (or *$\mathscr{C}$-hard*) if every decision problem in $\mathscr{C}$ reduces in polynomial time to $\mathscr{P}$. $\mathscr{P}$ is *complete for* $\mathscr{C}$ (or *$\mathscr{C}$-complete*) if $\mathscr{P}$ is in $\mathscr{C}$ and is $\mathscr{C}$-hard.

Problems that are complete for some class of decision problems (most notably NP) play an important role in complexity theory. The most famous open question in complexity theory is whether or not P = NP, that is, whether or not every decision problem which is solvable nondeterministically in polynomial time in fact is solvable deterministically in polynomial time. By Lemma 1.42, P = NP if and only if some NP-complete problem, for example uniform non-C(k) testing, is in *P*. It is generally believed that P $\neq$ NP. Hence it is probable that $\mathscr{P}_{\text{non-C}}$ cannot be solved deterministically in polynomial time.

In showing the NP-hardness (resp. NE-hardness) of uniform non-C(k) testing for $k$ in unary (resp. $k$ in binary) we have two approaches to choose. The easier approach might be to select from the literature some specific decision problem which is known to be NP-hard (resp. NE-hard) and reduce this problem to uniform non-C($k$) testing. Observe that because the relation "reduces-in-polynomial-time-to" is transitive, uniform non-C($k$) testing must then be NP-hard (resp. NE-hard). However, to make the presentation more self-contained and instructive, we shall take the more arduous approach and present what is called a "generic" reduction. This means that we shall base the proof directly on the definition of hardness. We consider an arbitrary decision problem $\mathscr{P}$ in NP and show that there exists a polynomial time-bounded reduction of $\mathscr{P}$ to $\mathscr{P}_{\text{non-C}}$. In doing this the only thing we may assume is the existence of some (nondeterministic) partial solution $M_{\mathscr{P}}$ to $\mathscr{P}$ and a polynomial $p$ such that $M_{\mathscr{P}}$ runs in time $O(p(n))$. From the algorithm $M_{\mathscr{P}}$ and the polynomial $p$ we have to design a polynomial time-bounded deterministic algorithm $M$ that transforms each yes-instance of $\mathscr{P}$ into some yes-instance of $\mathscr{P}_{\text{non-C}}$ and each no-instance of $\mathscr{P}$ into some no-instance of $\mathscr{P}_{\text{non-C}}$.

If we are going to present the generic reduction of $\mathscr{P}$ to $\mathscr{P}_{\text{non-C}}$ rigorously, we have to rely on some formal model of computation. That is, we have to assume that the algorithm $M_{\mathscr{P}}$ is expressed in some formally defined and concise enough language. For this purpose we take the Turing machine, which is a generally accepted formal model of computation. We begin with some basic definitions pertaining to Turing machines.

Let $M = (V, P)$ be a rewriting system and let $Q$, $\Sigma$, and $\Gamma$ be subsets of the alphabet $V$, $q_s$ an element in $Q$, $F$ a subset of $Q$, $B$ a symbol in $\Gamma \setminus \Sigma$, and \$ a symbol in $V \setminus (Q \cup \Gamma)$ such that $V = Q \cup \Gamma \cup \{\$\}$, $Q \cap \Gamma = \varnothing$, and $\Sigma \subseteq \Gamma$. We say that $M$ is a *Turing machine* (or *Turing machine program*) *with state alphabet*, $Q$, *input alphabet* $\Sigma$, *tape alphabet* $\Gamma$, *set of actions* $P$, *initial state* $q_s$, *set of final states* $F$, *blank symbol* $B$, and *end marker* \$, denoted by

$$M = (Q, \Sigma, \Gamma, P, q_s, F, B, \$) ,$$

if each rule in $P$ has one of the following forms:

| | |
|---|---|
| (a) $q_1 a_1 \to q_2 a_2$ | "print $a_2$"; |
| (b) $q_1 a_1 \to a_2 q_2$ | "print $a_2$ and move to the right"; |
| (c) $d q_1 a_1 \to q_2 d a_2$ | "print $a_2$ and move to the left"; |
| (d) $q_1 \$ \to q_2 \$$ | "record the end of tape"; |
| (e) $q_1 \$ \to q_2 B \$$ | "record the end of tape and extend workspace"; |
| (f) $d q_1 \$ \to q_2 d \$$ | "record the end of tape and move to the left" |

Here $a_1$, $a_2$, and $d$ are tape symbols in $\Gamma$, and $q_1$ and $q_2$ are states in $Q$.

A *configuration* (or an *instantaneous description*) of Turing machine $M$ is a string of the form

$$\$\alpha q \beta \$ ,$$

where $\alpha$ and $\beta$ are tape symbol strings in $\Gamma^*$ and $q$ is a state in $Q$. The string $\alpha\beta$ is called the *tape contents*, and $1{:}\beta\$$ is the *tape symbol scanned* at $\$\alpha q \beta \$$.

Configuration $\$\alpha q\beta\$$ is *initial for* an input string $w \in \Sigma^*$ if $\alpha = \varepsilon$, $\beta = w$, and $q$ is the initial state $q_s$. Configuration $\$\alpha q\beta\$$ is *accepting* if $q$ is some final state in $F$. A nonaccepting configuration to which no rule in $P$ is applicable is called an *error configuration.*

A *computation* (or *process*) *of* Turing machine $M$ *on* input string $w$ is any derivation in $M$ from the initial configuration for $w$. A computation is *accepting* if it ends with an accepting configuration. $M$ *accepts* $w$ if it has an accepting computation on $w$. The *language accepted* (or *recognized* or *described*) by $M$, denoted by $L(M)$, is the set of input strings accepted by $M$. In other words,

$$L(M) = \{w \in \Sigma^* \mid \$q_s w\$ \underset{M}{\Longrightarrow^*} \$\alpha q\beta\$ \text{ for some } \alpha,\ \beta \in \Gamma^* \text{ and } q \in F\} \ .$$

As an example we give a Turing machine that accepts the non-context-free language

$$\{wcw \mid w \in \{0, 1\}^*\} \ ,$$

where $c \notin \{0, 1\}$. The Turing machine has state alphabet $\{q_s, q_0, q_0', q_1, q_1', q_2, q_2', q_3, q_f\}$, input alphabet $\{0, 1, c\}$, tape alphabet $\{0, 1, c, B\}$, initial state $q_s$, set of final states $\{q_f\}$, and the following actions:

$q_s 0 \rightarrow B q_0$ "remember 0";

$q_s 1 \rightarrow B q_1$ "remember 1";

$q_s c \rightarrow B q_3$ "begin the check for blank tape";

$$\left.\begin{array}{l} q_0 0 \rightarrow 0 q_0 \\ q_0 1 \rightarrow 1 q_0 \\ q_0 c \rightarrow c q_0' \end{array}\right\}$$
"remembering 0, scan the right until $c$ is found";

$$\left.\begin{array}{l} q_0' B \rightarrow B q_0' \\ q_0' 0 \rightarrow q_2 B \end{array}\right\}$$
"check that the first non-blank symbol after $c$ is 0";

$$\left.\begin{array}{l} q_1 0 \rightarrow 0 q_1 \\ q_1 1 \rightarrow 1 q_1 \\ q_1 c \rightarrow c q_1' \end{array}\right\}$$
"remembering 1, scan to the right until $c$ is found";

$$\left.\begin{array}{l} q_1' B \rightarrow B q_1' \\ q_1' 1 \rightarrow q_2 B \end{array}\right\}$$
"check that the first non-blank symbol after $c$ is 1";

$$\left.\begin{array}{ll} d q_2 B \rightarrow q_2 d B, & \text{for } d \in \{0, 1, c, B\} \\ d q_2 c \rightarrow q_2' d c, & \text{for } d \in \{0, 1, c, B\} \end{array}\right\}$$
"scan to the left until $c$ is found";

$$\left.\begin{array}{ll} d q_2' 0 \rightarrow q_2' d 0, & \text{for } d \in \{0, 1, c, B\} \\ d q_2' 1 \rightarrow q_2' d 1, & \text{for } d \in \{0, 1, c, B\} \\ q_2' B \rightarrow B q_s & \end{array}\right\}$$
"scan to the left until a blank is found";

$$\left.\begin{array}{l} q_3 B \rightarrow B q_3 \\ q_3 \$ \rightarrow q_f \$ \end{array}\right\}$$
"check for blank tape and accept".

The following hold in the above Turing machine.

$$\$q_s c\$ \Rightarrow \$Bq_3\$ \Rightarrow \$Bq_f\$ \ .$$

$$\$q_s 10c10\$ \Rightarrow \$Bq_1 0c10\$ \Rightarrow \$B0q_1 c10\$ \Rightarrow \$B0cq'_1 10\$$$
$$\Rightarrow \$B0cq_2 B0\$ \Rightarrow \$B0q_2 cB0\$ \Rightarrow \$Bq'_2 0cB0\$ \Rightarrow \$q'_2 B0cB0\$$$
$$\Rightarrow \$Bq_s 0cB0\$ \Rightarrow \$BBq_0 cB0\$ \Rightarrow \$BBcq'_0 B0\$ \Rightarrow \$BBcBq'_0 0\$$$
$$\Rightarrow \$BBcBq_2 B\$ \Rightarrow \$BBcq_2 BB\$ \Rightarrow \$BBq_2 cBB\$ \Rightarrow \$Bq'_2 BcBB\$$$
$$\Rightarrow \$BBq_s cBB\$ \Rightarrow \$BBBq_3 BB\$ \Rightarrow \$BBBBq_3 B\$ \Rightarrow \$BBBBBq_3\$$$
$$\Rightarrow \$BBBBBq_f\$ \ .$$

Turing machine $M$ is *nondeterministic* if to some configuration two actions are applicable. Otherwise, $M$ is *deterministic.* For example, the Turing machine presented above is deterministic.

Turing machine $M$ *halts correctly on* input string $w$ if $M$ accepts $w$. $M$ *halts incorrectly on* $w$ if $M$ has on $w$ a computation that ends with an error configuration. $M$ *loops forever on* $w$ if $M$ has arbitrarily long computations on $w$.

For all $w$ in $L(M)$ we define:

$$\mathrm{TIME}_M(w) = \min\{\mathrm{TIME}_M(\$q_s w\$, \$\alpha q\beta\$) \mid \alpha, \beta \in \Gamma^*, q \in F\} \ .$$
$$\mathrm{SPACE}_M(w) = \min\{\mathrm{SPACE}_M(\$q_s w\$, \$\alpha q\beta\$) \mid \alpha, \beta \in \Gamma^*, q \in F\} \ .$$

Here $\mathrm{TIME}_M(\gamma_1, \gamma_2)$ and $\mathrm{SPACE}_M(\gamma_1, \gamma_2)$, for configurations $\gamma_1$ and $\gamma_2$, denote the time complexity and the space complexity of deriving $\gamma_2$ from $\gamma_1$ (see Section 1.6). $\mathrm{TIME}_M(w)$ is called the *time complexity*, and $\mathrm{SPACE}_M(w)$ the *space complexity, of accepting* $w$ *in* $M$. $M$ *accepts* $w$ *in time* $t$ if $\mathrm{TIME}_M(w) \leqslant t$. $M$ *accepts* $w$ *in space* $s$ if $\mathrm{SPACE}_M(w) \leqslant s$. $M$ *accepts* $w$ *simultaneously in time* $t$ *and in space* $s$ if $M$ has on $w$ an accepting computation $\mathscr{C} = (\gamma_0, \gamma_1, \ldots, \gamma_n)$ with $\mathrm{TIME}(\mathscr{C}) \leqslant t$ and $\mathrm{SPACE}(\mathscr{C}) \leqslant s$, that is, $n \leqslant t$ and $|\gamma_i| \leqslant s$ for all $i = 0, 1, \ldots, n$ (recall Section 1.6).

Turing machine $M$ is $T(n)$ *time-bounded*, or *runs in time* $T(n)$, if $M$ accepts every sentence of length $n$ in time $T(n)$. $M$ is $S(n)$ *space-bounded*, or *runs in space* $S(n)$, if $M$ accepts every sentence of length $n$ in space $S(n)$. $M$ is *simultaneously* $T(n)$ *time-bounded and* $S(n)$ *space-bounded*, or *runs simultaneously in time* $T(n)$ *and in space* $S(n)$, if $M$ accepts every sentence of length $n$ simultaneously in time $T(n)$ and in space $S(n)$.

For example, the Turing machine given above accepts each sentence $wcw$ simultaneously in time $O(|w|^2)$ and in space $O(|w|)$. Hence the machine is simultaneously $O(n^2)$ time-bounded and $O(n)$ space-bounded.

It is clear that any deterministic Turing machine can be simulated by a deterministic random-access machine. Moreover, if the Turing machine is $T(n)$ time-bounded and $S(n)$ space-bounded, then there exists a natural number $k$ such that the simulating random-access machine is $O(T(n)^k)$ time-bounded and $O(S(n)^k)$ space-bounded when the logarithmic cost criterion is used (see Section 1.5). It is also clear that nondeterministic Turing machines can be simulated by nondeterministic random-access machines. (A nondeterministic random-access machine is one whose instruction set contains the nondeterministic instruction **guess** $a$; see Section 1.3.) The following proposition states the converse result, that is, that any random-access machine can be simulated by a Turing machine.

**Proposition 10.61** *Let $M$ be any language recognizer (random-access machine) with input alphabet $\Sigma$. Then there exists a Turing machine $M'$ with input alphabet $\Sigma$ such that the following statements hold for some natural number $k$.*

(1) $L(M) = L(M')$.
(2) *If $M$ runs in time $O(T(n))$, then $M'$ runs in time $O(T(n)^k)$.*
(3) *If $M$ runs in space $O(S(n))$, then $M'$ runs in space $O(S(n)^k)$.*
(4) *If $M$ runs simultaneously in time $O(T(n))$ and in space $O(S(n))$, then $M'$ runs simultaneously in time $O(T(n)^k)$ and in space $O(S(n)^k)$.*
(5) *If $M$ is deterministic, then so is $M'$.*
(6) *If $M$ halts on input $w$, then so does $M'$.*

*Here the time and space complexities for $M$ are stated using the logarithmic cost criterion.* □

Proposition 10.61 states that the Turing machines are just as powerful language recognizers as the random-access machines, regarding both the extent of the family of languages recognized and the complexity of recognition. For any language accepted by a random-access machine there is a Turing machine accepting the same language and having complexity that differs only polynomially from that of the random-access machine. Hence in deriving lower bounds for the complexity of decision problems we may assume a Turing machine in place of a random-access machine, when we are only concerned with superpolynomial differences in complexities.

Next we shall show that the set of accepting computations of any Turing machine on a fixed input string can be represented as the intersection of two context-free languages. Moreover, we shall show that any Turing machine can easily be transformed into an equivalent Turing machine for which these two context-free languages are $s$-languages (see Section 5.2) and hence LL(1). This fundamental result will be crucial in establishing the polynomial time reduction of the problems in NP (NE) to uniform non-C($k$) testing.

Let $M$ be a Turing machine with state alphabet $Q$, input alphabet $\Sigma$, tape alphabet $\Gamma$, set of actions $P$, initial state $q_s$, set of final states $F$, and end marker \$. Further let $w$ be an input string in $\Sigma^*$ and

$$\mathscr{C} = (\gamma_0, \gamma_1, \ldots, \gamma_{n+1})$$

be a computation of $M$ on $w$. Assume $\mathscr{C}$ is *nontrivial*, meaning that it has length

$n + 1 \geqslant 1$. Then we may represent $\mathscr{C}$ as the string

$$\text{repr}(\mathscr{C}) = \gamma_0 \# \gamma_1^R \# \gamma_1 \# \gamma_2^R \# \ \ldots \ \gamma_n \# \gamma_{n+1}^R \# \# \ .$$

Here $\#$ is a symbol not belonging to $Q \cup \Gamma \cup \{\$\}$. Obviously, nontrivial computations $\mathscr{C}$ and strings $\text{repr}(\mathscr{C})$ are in one-to-one correspondence with each other. We shall show that the set

$$\{\text{repr}(\mathscr{C}) | \mathscr{C} \text{ is a nontrivial accepting computation of } M \text{ on } w\}$$

is the intersection of languages $L(G_1(M))$ and $L(G_2(M, w))$, where $G_1(M)$ is a certain context-free grammar constructed from $M$ and $G_2(M, w)$ is a certain context-free grammar constructed from $M$ and $w$.

We define $G_1(M)$ as the grammar with nonterminal alphabet $\{S_1, A_1, B_1\}$, terminal alphabet $Q \cup \Gamma \cup \{\$, \#\}$, start symbol $S_1$, and the following rules:

(1) $S_1 \to \$ A_1 \$ \# S_1$ ,

(2) $S_1 \to \#$ ,

(3) $A_1 \to a A_1 a$ for all tape symbols $a \in \Gamma$ ,

(4) $A_1 \to \omega_1 B_1 \omega_2^R$ for all actions $\omega_1 \to \omega_2$ in $P$ where $\omega_1$ and $\omega_2$ do not contain \$ ,

(5) $A_1 \to \omega_1 \$ \# (\omega_2 \$)^R$ for all actions $\omega_1 \$ \to \omega_2 \$$ in $P$ ,

(6) $B_1 \to a B_1 a$ for all tape symbols $a \in \Gamma$ ,

(7) $B_1 \to \$ \# \$$ .

In $G_1(M)$ the following hold.

$$L(B_1) = \{\beta \$ \# \$ \beta^R | \beta \in \Gamma^*\} \ .$$

$$\begin{aligned} L(A_1) = {} & \{\alpha \omega_1 \gamma \omega_2^R \alpha^R | \alpha \in \Gamma^*, \omega_1 \to \omega_2 \text{ is in } P, \omega_1 \text{ and} \\ & \quad \omega_2 \text{ do not contain \$, and } \gamma \in L(B_1)\} \\ & \quad \cup \{\alpha \omega_1 \$ \# (\omega_2 \$)^R \alpha^R | \alpha \in \Gamma^* \text{ and } \omega_1 \$ \to \omega_2 \$ \text{ is in } P\} \\ = {} & \{\alpha \omega_1 \beta \$ \# \$ \beta^R \omega_2^R \alpha^R | \alpha, \beta \in \Gamma^*, \omega_1 \to \omega_2 \text{ is in } P, \text{ and} \\ & \quad \omega_1 \text{ and } \omega_2 \text{ do not contain } \$\} \\ & \quad \cup \{\alpha \omega_1 \$ \# \$ \omega_2^R \alpha^R | \alpha \in \Gamma^* \text{ and } \omega_1 \$ \to \omega_2 \$ \text{ is in } P\} \\ = {} & \{\alpha \omega_1 \beta \$ \# (\alpha \omega_2 \beta \$)^R | \alpha, \beta \in \Gamma^*, \omega_1 \to \omega_2 \text{ is in } P, \\ & \quad \text{and } \omega_1 \text{ and } \omega_2 \text{ do not contain } \$\} \\ & \quad \cup \{\alpha \omega_1 \$ \# (\alpha \omega_2 \$)^R | \alpha \in \Gamma^* \text{ and } \omega_1 \$ \to \omega_2 \$ \text{ is in } P\} \\ = {} & \{\gamma \$ \# (\delta \$)^R | \gamma, \delta \in \Gamma^* Q \Gamma^* \text{ and } \gamma \$ \Rightarrow \delta \$ \text{ in } M\} \ . \end{aligned}$$

$$L(S_1) = (\$L(A_1)\$\#)^*\#$$
$$= \{\$\gamma\$\#(\delta\$)^R\$\# \mid \gamma, \delta \in \Gamma^*Q\Gamma^* \text{ and } \gamma\$ \Rightarrow \delta\$ \text{ in } M\}^*\#$$
$$= \{\$\gamma\$\#\$\delta^R\$\# \mid \gamma, \delta \in \Gamma^*Q\Gamma^* \text{ and } \$\gamma\$ \Rightarrow \$\delta\$ \text{ in } M\}^*\#$$
$$= \{\phi\#\psi^R\# \mid \phi, \psi \in \$\Gamma^*Q\Gamma^*\$ \text{ and } \phi \Rightarrow \psi \text{ in } M\}^*\#$$
$$= \{\#\} \cup \{\phi_0\#\psi_1^R\#\phi_1\#\psi_2^R\# \dots \phi_n\#\psi_{n+1}^R\#\# \mid n \geq 0,\ \phi_i, \psi_{i+1} \in \$\Gamma^*Q\Gamma^*\$ \text{ and } \phi_i \Rightarrow \psi_{i+1} \text{ in } M \text{ for all } i = 0, \dots, n\}\ .$$

We have

**Lemma 10.62** *For any Turing machine M,*

$$L(G_1(M)) = \{\#\} \cup \{\phi_0\#\psi_1^R\#\phi_1\#\psi_2^R\# \dots \phi_n\#\psi_{n+1}^R\#\# \mid n \geq 0,\ \phi_i \textit{ and } \psi_{i+1} \textit{ are configurations of } M \textit{ and } \phi_i \Rightarrow \psi_{i+1} \textit{ in } M \textit{ for all } i = 0, \dots, n\}\ .$$

*Moreover, the grammar $G_1(M)$ is of size $O(|M|)$ and can be constructed from M in time $O(|M|)$.* □

Then let $w$ be any input string in $\Sigma^*$. For $M$ and $w$ we define $G_2(M, w)$ as the grammar with nonterminal alphabet $\{S_2, A_2, B_2, C, D, E\}$, terminal alphabet $Q \cup \Gamma \cup \{\$, \#\}$, start symbol $S_2$, and the following rules:

(1) $S_2 \to \$q_s w\$\#A_2\#$ ,

(2) $A_2 \to \$B_2\$\#A_2$ ,

(3) $A_2 \to \$D$ ,

(4) $B_2 \to aB_2a$ for all tape symbols $a \in \Gamma$ ,

(5) $B_2 \to qCq$ for all states $q \in Q$ ,

(6) $C \to aCa$ for all tape symbols $a \in \Gamma$ ,

(7) $C \to \$\#\$$ ,

(8) $D \to aD$ for all tape symbols $a \in \Gamma$ ,

(9) $D \to qE$ for all final states $q \in F$ ,

(10) $E \to aE$ for all tape symbols $a \in \Gamma$ ,

(11) $E \to \$\#$ .

In $G_2(M, w)$ the following hold.

$$L(E) = \Gamma^*\$\#\ .$$
$$L(D) = \Gamma^*FL(E) = \Gamma^*F\Gamma^*\$\#\ .$$

$$L(C) = \{\beta\$\#\$\beta^R \mid \beta \in \Gamma^*\} \ .$$

$$\begin{aligned}
L(B_2) &= \{\alpha q \gamma q \alpha^R \mid \alpha \in \Gamma^*, q \in Q, \text{ and } \gamma \in L(C)\} \\
&= \{\alpha q \beta\$\#\$\beta^R q \alpha^R \mid \alpha, \beta \in \Gamma^* \text{ and } q \in Q\} \\
&= \{\alpha q \beta\$\#\$(\alpha q \beta)^R \mid \alpha, \beta \in \Gamma^* \text{ and } q \in Q\} \\
&= \{\delta^R\$\#\$\delta \mid \delta \in \Gamma^* Q \Gamma^*\} \ .
\end{aligned}$$

$$\begin{aligned}
L(A_2) &= (\$L(B_2)\$\#)^*\$L(D) \\
&= \{\$\delta^R\$\#\$\delta\$\# \mid \delta \in \Gamma^* Q \Gamma^*\}^*\$\Gamma^* F \Gamma^*\$\# \\
&= \{\gamma^R\#\gamma\# \mid \gamma \in \$\Gamma^* Q \Gamma^*\$\}^*\$\Gamma^* F \Gamma^*\$\# \\
&= \{\gamma_1^R\#\gamma_1\#\gamma_2^R\#\gamma_2\# \ldots \gamma_n^R\#\gamma_n\#\gamma_{n+1}^R\# \mid n \geqslant 0, \\
&\qquad \gamma_i \in \$\Gamma^* Q \Gamma^*\$ \text{ for all } i = 1, \ldots, n, \text{ and} \\
&\qquad \gamma_{n+1} \in \$\Gamma^* F \Gamma^*\$\} \ .
\end{aligned}$$

$$\begin{aligned}
L(S_2) &= \$q_s w\$\#L(A_2)\# \\
&= \{\$q_s w\$\#\gamma_1^R\#\gamma_1\#\gamma_2^R\#\gamma_2\# \ldots \gamma_n^R\#\gamma_n\#\gamma_{n+1}^R\#\# \mid n \geqslant 0 \ , \\
&\qquad \gamma_i \in \$\Gamma^* Q \Gamma^*\$ \text{ for all } i = 1, \ldots, n, \text{ and} \\
&\qquad \gamma_{n+1} \in \$\Gamma^* F \Gamma^*\$\} \ .
\end{aligned}$$

**Lemma 10.63** *For any Turing machine $M$ and input string $w$,*

$$\begin{aligned}
L(G_2(M, w)) = \{&\gamma_0\#\gamma_1^R\#\gamma_1\#\gamma_2^R\#\gamma_2\# \ldots \gamma_n^R\#\gamma_n\#\gamma_{n+1}^R\#\# \mid n \geqslant 0, \\
&\gamma_0 \textit{ is the initial configuration of } M \textit{ for } w, \gamma_i \textit{ is a} \\
&\textit{configuration of } M \textit{ for all } i = 1, \ldots, n, \textit{ and } \gamma_{n+1} \textit{ is} \\
&\textit{an accepting configuration of } M\} \ .
\end{aligned}$$

*Moreover, the grammar $G_2(M, w)$ is of size $O(|M| + |w|)$ and can be constructed from $M$ and $w$ in time $O(|M| + |w|)$.* □

**Theorem 10.64** *Let $M$ be a Turing machine and $w$ an input string. Then*

(*a*) $L(G_1(M)) \cap L(G_2(M, w)) =$
$\{\text{repr}(\mathscr{C}) \mid \mathscr{C}$ *is a nontrivial accepting computation of $M$ on $w$*$\}$ .

*Furthermore, for any natural number $k > |w| + 3$,*

(*b*) $k{:}L(G_1(M)) \cap k{:}L(G_2(M, w)) \subseteq$
$\{k{:}\text{repr}(\mathscr{C}) \mid \mathscr{C}$ *is a nontrivial computation of $M$ on $w$*$\}$ .

*Moreover, if* repr($\mathscr{C}$) *belongs to $k{:}L(G_2(M, w))$, then the computation $\mathscr{C}$ is an accepting computation.*

*Proof.* Consider claim (a). Let $\mathscr{C}$ be a nontrivial accepting computation of $M$ on $w$. By definition, there is a natural number $n$ and configurations $\gamma_0, \gamma_1, \ldots, \gamma_{n+1}$ of $M$ such that

$$\mathscr{C} = (\gamma_0, \gamma_1, \ldots, \gamma_{n+1}), \text{ and}$$

$$\text{repr}(\mathscr{C}) = \gamma_0 \# \gamma_1^R \# \gamma_1 \# \gamma_2^R \# \ldots \gamma_n \# \gamma_{n+1}^R \# \# \ ,$$

where $\gamma_0$ is the initial configuration for $w$, $\gamma_{n+1}$ is an accepting configuration, and $\gamma_i \Rightarrow \gamma_{i+1}$ for all $i = 0, \ldots, n$. But then by Lemma 10.62 repr($\mathscr{C}$) belongs to $L(G_1(M))$, and by Lemma 10.63 repr($\mathscr{C}$) belongs to $L(G_2(M, w))$. This means that the set of all strings repr($\mathscr{C}$), where $\mathscr{C}$ is a nontrivial accepting computation of $M$ on $w$, is contained in $L(G_1(M)) \cap L(G_2(M, w))$.

Conversely, assume that $\Phi$ is a string in $L(G_1(M)) \cap L(G_2(M, w))$. By Lemma 10.62 any string in $L(G_1(M))$ is either $\#$ or of the form

$$\phi_0 \# \psi_1^R \# \phi_1 \# \psi_2^R \# \phi_2 \# \ \ldots \ \psi_n^R \# \phi_n \# \psi_{n+1}^R \# \# \ ,$$

where $n \geqslant 0$, $\phi_i$ and $\psi_{i+1}$ are configurations of $M$ and $\phi_i \Rightarrow \psi_{i+1}$ for all $i = 0, \ldots, n$. By Lemma 10.63 any string in $L(G_2(M, w))$ is of the form

$$\gamma_0 \# \gamma_1^R \# \gamma_1 \# \gamma_2^R \# \gamma_2 \# \ \ldots \ \gamma_m^R \# \gamma_m \# \gamma_{m+1}^R \# \# \ ,$$

where $m \geqslant 0$, $\gamma_0$ is the initial configuration of $M$ for $w$, $\gamma_i$ is a configuration of $M$ for all $i = 1, \ldots, m$, and $\gamma_{m+1}$ is an accepting configuration of $M$. Clearly, $\Phi$ cannot be $\#$. Because no configuration of $M$ can contain the symbol $\#$, the only way the above two strings can be equal is that $n = m$, $\phi_0 = \gamma_0$, $\psi_1^R = \gamma_1^R$, $\phi_1 = \gamma_1$, $\psi_2^R = \gamma_2^R$, $\phi_2 = \gamma_2, \ldots, \psi_n^R = \gamma_m^R$, $\phi_n = \gamma_m$, and $\psi_{n+1}^R = \gamma_{m+1}^R$. But then $\mathscr{C} = (\gamma_0, \gamma_1, \ldots, \gamma_{n+1})$ is a nontrivial accepting computation of $M$ on $w$ and repr($\mathscr{C}$) $= \Phi$. Hence we conclude that $L(G_1(M)) \cap L(G_2(M, w))$ is contained in the set of strings repr($\mathscr{C}$) where $\mathscr{C}$ is a nontrivial accepting computation of $M$ on $w$. This proves claim (a).

Next, consider claim (b). Let $\Phi$ be a string in $k{:}L(G_1(M)) \cap k{:}L(G_2(M, w))$. By Lemma 10.62, any string in $k{:}L(G_1(M))$ is either $k{:}\,\#$ or of the form

$$k{:}\phi_0 \# \psi_1^R \# \phi_1 \# \psi_2^R \# \phi_2 \# \ \ldots \ \psi_n^R \# \phi_n \# \psi_{n+1}^R \# \# \ ,$$

where $n \geqslant 0$, $\phi_i$ and $\psi_{i+1}$ are configurations of $M$ and $\phi_i \Rightarrow \psi_{i+1}$ in $M$ for all $i = 0, \ldots, n$. By Lemma 10.63, any string in $k{:}L(G_2(M, w))$ is of the form

$$k{:}\gamma_0 \# \gamma_1^R \# \gamma_1 \# \gamma_2^R \# \gamma_2 \# \ \ldots \ \gamma_m^R \# \gamma_m \# \gamma_{m+1}^R \# \# \ ,$$

where $m \geqslant 0$, $\gamma_0 = \$q_s w\$$, $\gamma_i$ is a configuration of $M$ for all $i = 1, \ldots, m + 1$. Because $k > 0$, $\Phi$ cannot be $k{:}\,\#$. Because $k > |w| + 3 = |\gamma_0|$, $\phi_0$ must be equal to $\gamma_0$. But this means that $\Phi$ must be of the form $k{:}$repr($\mathscr{C}$), where $\mathscr{C}$ is some nontrivial computation of $M$ on $w$. This proves claim (b).

Finally, it is clear that if an entire string repr($\mathscr{C}$) belongs to $k{:}L(G_2(M, w))$, then it must also belong to $L(G_2(M, w))$, which means that $\mathscr{C}$ is an accepting computation. □

**Theorem 10.65** (*Hartmanis*, 1967) *Given any Turing machine $M$ and input string $w$, the pair $(M, w)$ can be transformed in polynomial time into a pair of context-free grammars $(G_1, G_2)$ such that the following statements are logically equivalent.*

(1) *$M$ accepts $w$.*
(2) $L(G_1) \cap L(G_2) \neq \varnothing$ .

*Proof.* We may assume that the initial state $q_s$ of $M$ is not a final state. Observe that if $q_s$ is a final state, then $M$ accepts every input, and we can first transform $M$ into an equivalent Turing machine $M'$ having state alphabet $\{q_s, q_f\}$, initial state $q_s$, set of final states $\{q_f\}$, and set of actions $\{q_s a \rightarrow q_f a \mid a \in \Sigma \cup \{\$\}\}$. When $q_s$ is not a final state, it follows that every accepting computation must be nontrivial. Hence if we choose $G_1 = G_1(M)$ and $G_2 = G_2(M, w)$, we may conclude by Theorem 10.64 that $M$ accepts $w$ if and only if $L(G_1) \cap L(G_2)$ is nonempty. As $G_1(M)$ and $G_2(M, w)$ can be constructed from $(M, w)$ in polynomial time (see Lemmas 10.62 and 10.63), we have the theorem. □

The decision problem

$\mathscr{P}_{\text{accept}}$: "Does Turing machine $M$ accept input $w$?"

is called the *acceptance problem* for Turing machines. Theorem 10.65 states that this problem reduces in polynomial time to the decision problem

$\mathscr{P}_{\text{non-}\cap}$: "Given two context-free grammars $G_1$ and $G_2$, is $L(G_1) \cap L(G_2) \neq \varnothing$?"

The problem is called the *nonemptiness of intersection problem* for context-free grammars.

In Section 1.4 we showed that for random-access machines the acceptance problem is unsolvable. By Proposition 10.61, the acceptance problem must also be unsolvable for Turing machines. Hence we conclude (by Lemma 1.30) that the nonemptiness of intersection problem for context-free languages is unsolvable as well.

Next we shall show that in Theorem 10.64 the grammars $G_1(M)$ and $G_2(M, w)$ can be replaced by two $s$-grammars, when $M$ satisfies some additional conditions. We recall that a grammar is an $s$-grammar when it is in Greibach normal-form, that is, all the rules begin with a terminal, and when there is no pair of rules $A \rightarrow a\beta_1 \mid a\beta_2$ where $\beta_1 \neq \beta_2$. We say that a nonterminal $A$ of a context-free grammar *has the s-property* if (1) all the rules of $A$ begin with a terminal and (2) there is no pair of rules $A \rightarrow a\beta_1 \mid a\beta_2$ where $\beta_1 \neq \beta_2$.

First consider the grammar $G_1(M)$. Clearly, the nonterminals $S_1$ and $B_1$ of $G_1(M)$ always have the $s$-property, and hence the SLL(1) property. For the nonterminal $A_1$ the $s$-property (and the SLL(1) property) may be violated in the following cases:

(1) $G_1(M)$ has rules $A_1 \rightarrow dA_1d$ and $A_1 \rightarrow dq_1a_1B_1a_2dq_2$ where $dq_1a_1 \rightarrow q_2da_2$ is an action of $M$.

(2) $G_1(M)$ has rules $A_1 \to dA_1d$ and $A_1 \to dq_1\$\#\$dq_2$ where $dq_1\$ \to q_2d\$$ is an action of $M$.

(3) $G_1(M)$ has rules $A_1 \to qa_1B_1\omega_1^R$ and $A_1 \to qa_2B_1\omega_2^R$ where $qa_1 \to \omega_1$ and $qa_2 \to \omega_2$ are actions of $M$.

(4) $G_1(M)$ has rules $A_1 \to q\$\#\$\omega_1^R$ and $A_1 \to q\$\#\$\omega_2^R$ where $q\$ \to \omega_1\$$ and $q\$ \to \omega_2\$$ are actions of $M$.

(5) $G_1(M)$ has rules $A_1 \to qa_1B_1\omega_1^R$ and $A_1 \to q\$\#\$\omega_2^R$ where $qa_1 \to \omega_1$ and $q\$ \to \omega_2\$$ are actions of $M$.

(6) $G_1(M)$ has rules $A_1 \to dq_1a_1B_1a_2dq_2$ and $A_1 \to dq_3a_3B_1a_4dq_4$ where $dq_1a_1 \to q_2da_2$ and $dq_3a_3 \to q_4da_4$ are actions of $M$.

(7) $G_1(M)$ has rules $A_1 \to dq_1\$\#\$dq_2$ and $A_1 \to dq_3\$\#\$dq_4$ where $dq_1\$ \to q_2d\$$ and $dq_3\$ \to q_4d\$$ are actions of $M$.

(8) $G_1(M)$ has rules $A_1 \to dq_1a_1B_1a_2dq_2$ and $A_1 \to dq_3\$\#\$dq_4$ where $dq_1a_1 \to q_2da_2$ and $dq_3\$ \to q_4d\$$ are actions of $M$.

We can avoid the above conflicts by left factoring (see Section 8.7) the grammar $G_1(M)$. We denote the resulting grammar $\hat{G}_1(M)$.

$\hat{G}_1(M)$ is obtained from $G_1(M)$ as follows. First, the rules of $S_1$ and $B_1$ are as in $G_1(M)$. Second, the rules of $A_1$ are changed to:

$$A_1 \to a[A_1, a] \qquad \text{for all } a \in \Gamma ,$$

$$A_1 \to q[A_1, q] \qquad \text{for all } q \in Q .$$

Here $[A_1, X]$, $X \in \Gamma \cup \{\$\} \cup Q$, are new nonterminals. Third, for all $a_1, a_2 \in \Gamma$ the nonterminal $[A_1, a_1]$ will have (among others) the rule

$$[A_1, a_1] \to a_2[A_1, a_2]a_1 .$$

Fourth, each rule of the form $A_1 \to X_1 \ldots X_mB_1Y_1 \ldots Y_n$ in $G_1(M)$ is replaced by the following rules:

$$[A_1, X_1] \to X_2[A_1, X_1X_2] ,$$

$$\vdots$$

$$[A_1, X_1 \ldots X_{m-1}] \to X_mB_1[A_1, X_1 \ldots X_mB_1] ,$$

$$[A_1, X_1 \ldots X_mB_1] \to Y_1[A_1, X_1 \ldots X_mB_1Y_1] ,$$

$$\vdots$$

$$[A_1, X_1 \ldots X_mB_1Y_1 \ldots Y_{n-1}] \to Y_n .$$

For example, the rule $A_1 \to dq_1a_1B_1a_2dq_2$ is replaced by the rules

$$[A_1, d] \to q_1[A_1, dq_1] ,$$

$$[A_1, dq_1] \to a_1B_1[A_1, dq_1a_1B_1] ,$$

$$[A_1, dq_1a_1B_1] \to a_2[A_1, dq_1a_1B_1a_2] ,$$

$$[A_1, dq_1a_1B_1a_2] \to q_2 .$$

The resulting grammar $\hat{G}_1(M)$ is in Greibach normal-form and obviously generates the same language as $G_1(M)$. Also, $\hat{G}_1(M)$ is of size $O(|G_1(M)|^2)$ and can be constructed from $G_1(M)$ in time $O(|G_1(M)|^2)$. Furthermore, it is not hard to see that the grammar is an *s*-grammar. First, the nonterminals $S_1$ and $B_1$ have the *s*-property. So has any nonterminal $[A_1, \gamma]$ where $|\gamma| > 1$. Second, the rules of any nonterminal $[A_1, q]$, where $q \in Q$, are all of the form $[A_1, q] \to a[A_1, qa]$. Third, the rules of any nonterminal $[A_1, a]$, where $a \in \Gamma$, are of the forms $[A_1, a] \to b[A_1, b]a$ where $b \in \Gamma$, and $[A_1, a] \to q[A_1, aq]$ where $q \in Q$.

We have:

**Lemma 10.66** *For any Turing machine M,*

$$L(\hat{G}_1(M)) = \{\#\} \cup \{\phi_0 \# \psi_1^R \# \phi_1 \# \psi_2^R \# \ \ldots\ \phi_n \# \psi_{n+1}^R \# \# \mid n \geqslant 0,\ \phi_i \text{ and } \psi_{i+1} \text{ are configurations of } M \text{ and } \phi_i \Rightarrow \psi_{i+1} \text{ in } M \text{ for all } i = 0, \ldots, n\}\ .$$

*Moreover, $\hat{G}_1(M)$ is an s-grammar of size $O(|M|^2)$ and can be constructed from M in time $O(|M|^2)$.* □

Then consider the grammar $G_2(M, w)$. The grammar is in Greibach normal-form and the nonterminals $S_2$, $B_2$, $C$, $D$, and $E$ have the *s*-property. However, the grammar is not LL($k$) for any $k$ because the nonterminal $A_2$ does not have the LL($k$) property for any $k$. Observe that for any $k \geqslant 1$ the following holds for the rules $A_2 \to \$B_2\$\#A_2$ and $A_2 \to \$D$:

$$\text{FIRST}_k(\$B_2\$\#A_2) \cap \text{FIRST}_k(\$D) =$$
$$k{:}\{\gamma^R \# \gamma \# \mid \gamma \in \$\Gamma^* Q \Gamma^* \$\}^+ \$\Gamma^* F \Gamma^* \$ \# \cap k{:}\$\Gamma^* F \Gamma^* \$ \#\ .$$

This set contains for example all strings in $\$\Gamma^{k-1}$ and in $\$\Gamma^m F \Gamma^n$, $m \geqslant n \geqslant 0$, $m + n = k - 2$.

We can remove the above conflict if we impose some additional requirements on the underlying Turing machine. Making use of these requirements we may rewrite $G_2(M, w)$ such that the above conflict will be removed. Most of this rewriting will be just removing some rules from $G_2(M, w)$.

The purpose of the rule $A_2 \to \$D$ is to generate the reversals of all the accepting configurations of $M$. Assume that $M$ were designed so that it accepts only at the extreme right end of its tape, that is, every accessible accepting configuration of $M$ is of the form $\$\gamma q\$$ where $q \in F$. Then we may restrict the language generated by $\$D$ to $\$F\Gamma^*\$\#$. This is obtained by removing from $G_2(M, w)$ all the rules $D \to aD$ where $a \in \Gamma$. Now every string in $\text{FIRST}_k(\$D)$, $k \geqslant 2$, begins with $\$q$ where $q$ is a final state. However, this will not remove all the conflicts, because the intermediate configurations $\gamma$ occurring in strings $\gamma^R \# \gamma \#$ derived by $\$B_2\$\#$ may contain states belonging to $F$. This source of conflicts can be removed if we assume that $M$ can make no move out of a final state, that is, in every action of $M$ the state contained in the left-hand side belongs to $Q \backslash F$. Then we may restrict the language generated by $\$B_2\$ \# A_2$ to

$$\{\gamma^R \# \gamma \# \mid \gamma \in \$\Gamma^*(Q \setminus F)\Gamma^*\$\}^+ \$F\Gamma^*\$ \# \ .$$

This is obtained by removing from $G_2(M, w)$ all the rules $B_2 \to qCq$ where $q \in F$. The resulting grammar is SLL(2). By left factoring and simple substitution we can transform this grammar further into an $s$-grammar. We denote this $s$-grammar by $\hat{G}_2(M, w)$.

In conclusion, $\hat{G}_2(M, w)$ is the grammar with nonterminal alphabet $\{S_2, A'_2, A_2, B_2, C, E\}$, terminal alphabet $Q \cup \Gamma \cup \{\$, \#\}$, start symbol $S_2$, and the following rules:

(1) $S_2 \to \$q_s w\$ \# A_2 \#$ ,

(2) $A_2 \to \$A'_2$ ,

(3) $A'_2 \to aB_2a\$ \# A_2$ for all tape symbols $a \in \Gamma$ ,

(4) $A'_2 \to qCq\$ \# A_2$ for all states $q \in Q \setminus F$ ,

(5) $A'_2 \to qE$ for all states $q \in F$ ,

(6) $B_2 \to aB_2a$ for all tape symbols $a \in \Gamma$ ,

(7) $B_2 \to qCq$ for all states $q \in Q \setminus F$ ,

(8) $C \to aCa$ for all tape symbols $a \in \Gamma$ ,

(9) $C \to \$ \# \$$ ,

(10) $E \to aE$ for all tape symbols $a \in \Gamma$ ,

(11) $E \to \$ \#$ .

We have:

**Lemma 10.67** *For any Turing machine M and input string w,*

$$L(\hat{G}_2(M, w)) = \{\gamma_0 \# \gamma_1^R \# \gamma_1 \# \gamma_2^R \# \gamma_2 \# \dots \gamma_n^R \# \gamma_n \# \gamma_{n+1}^R \# \# \mid n \geq 0,$$
*$\gamma_0$ is the initial configuration of M for w, $\gamma_i$ is a configuration in $\$\Gamma^*(Q \setminus F)\Gamma^*\$$ for all $i = 1, \dots, n$, and $\gamma_{n+1}$ is a configuration in $\$\Gamma^* F\$\}$ .*

*Moreover, $\hat{G}_2(M, w)$ is an s-grammar of size $O(|M| + |w|)$ and can be constructed from M and w in time $O(|M| + |w|)$.* □

By Lemmas 10.66 and 10.67 and by Theorem 10.64 we have:

**Theorem 10.68** *Let M be a Turing machine such that the following statements hold.*

(1) *The initial state $q_s$ of M is not a final state.*
(2) *M can make no move out of a final state.*
(3) *M accepts only at the extreme right end of its tape.*

*Then for any input string w*

$$L(\hat{G}_1(M)) \cap L(\hat{G}_2(M, w)) =$$
$$\{\text{repr}(\mathscr{C}) | \mathscr{C} \textit{ is an accepting computation of } M \textit{ on } w\} \; .$$

*Furthermore, for any natural number* $k > |w| + 3$,

$$k{:}L(\hat{G}_1(M)) \cap k{:}L(\hat{G}_2(M, w)) \subseteq$$
$$\{k{:}\text{repr}(\mathscr{C}) | \mathscr{C} \textit{ is a nontrivial computation of } M \textit{ on } w\} \; .$$

*Moreover, if* repr($\mathscr{C}$) *belongs to* $k{:}L(\hat{G}_2(M, w))$, *then* $\mathscr{C}$ *is an accepting computation.* □

The following lemma states that the requirements imposed in Theorem 10.68 on the Turing machine $M$ are justified.

**Lemma 10.69** *Any Turing machine* $M = (Q, \Sigma, \Gamma, P, q_s, F, B, \$)$ *can be transformed in time* $O(|M|)$ *into a Turing machine* $M' = (Q', \Sigma, \Gamma, P', q_s, F', B, \$)$ *such that the following statements hold.*

(1) $q_s$ *does not belong to* $F'$.
(2) $M'$ *can make no move out of states in* $F'$.
(3) $M'$ *accepts only at the extreme right end of its tape.*
(4) $L(M') = L(M)$.
(5) *If* $M$ *is* $T(n)$ *time-bounded,* $M'$ *is* $O(\max\{n, T(n)\})$ *time-bounded.*
(6) *If* $M$ *is* $S(n)$ *space-bounded,* $M'$ *is* $S(n)$ *space-bounded.*
(7) *If* $M$ *is simultaneously* $T(n)$ *time-bounded and* $S(n)$ *space-bounded,* $M'$ *is simultaneously* $O(\max\{n, T(n)\})$ *time-bounded and* $S(n)$ *space-bounded.*

*Proof.* For all $q \in F$ let $q'$ be a new symbol not found in $Q \cup \Gamma$. Further let $q_f$ be another new symbol. The state alphabet $Q'$, the set of actions $P'$, and the set of final states $F'$ of $M'$ are defined by:

$$Q' = Q \cup \{q' | q \in F\} \cup \{q_f\} \; .$$
$$P' = P \cup \{qa \to q'a | q \in F \text{ and } a \in \Gamma \cup \{\$\}\}$$
$$\cup \{q'a \to aq' | q \in F \text{ and } a \in \Gamma\}$$
$$\cup \{q'\$ \to q_f\$\} \; .$$
$$F' = \{q_f\} \; .$$

□

By Theorem 10.68 and Lemma 10.69 we have:

**Theorem 10.70** *Given any Turing machine M and input string w, the pair* $(M, w)$ *can be transformed in polynomial time into a pair of s-grammars* $(G_1, G_2)$ *such that the following statements are logically equivalent.*

(1) *M accepts w.*
(2) $L(G_1) \cap L(G_2) \neq \varnothing$ . □

Theorem 10.70 states that the acceptance problem for Turing machines reduces in polynomial time to the nonemptiness of intersection problem for s-languages. We have:

**Theorem 10.71** *The nonemptiness of intersection problem for s-languages is unsolvable.* □

Then let $\hat{G}(M, w)$ be the grammar obtained by uniting the s-grammars $\hat{G}_1(M)$ and $\hat{G}_2(M, w)$ and by adding a new start symbol $S$ with the rules

$$S \rightarrow S_1 \mid S_2 \ .$$

In other words, $\hat{G}(M, w)$ is the grammar in which the nonterminal alphabet contains $S$ and all the nonterminals of $\hat{G}_1(M)$ and $\hat{G}_2(M, w)$, the terminal alphabet is $\hat{Q} \cup \Gamma \cup \{\$, \#\}$, the start symbol is $S$, and the set of rules consists of all the rules of $\hat{G}_1(M)$ and $\hat{G}_2(M, w)$ with the above two rules added.

**Theorem 10.72** *Given any Turing machine M and input string w, the pair (M, w) can be transformed in polynomial time into a context-free grammar G such that the following statements are logically equivalent.*

(*a*) *M accepts w.*
(*b*) *G is ambiguous.*

*Proof.* By Lemma 10.69 we may assume that $M$ satisfies conditions (1), (2), and (3) of Theorem 10.68. $G$ is the grammar $\hat{G}(M, w)$. As the component grammars $\hat{G}_1(M)$ and $\hat{G}_2(M, w)$ can be constructed from $M$ and $w$ in polynomial time, then so can $\hat{G}(M, w)$. Now because the nonterminal alphabets of the component grammars are disjoint and because the grammars are s-grammars, no ambiguity can occur in derivations from their start symbols $S_1$ and $S_2$. The only way $\hat{G}(M, w)$ can be ambiguous is that some sentence $w$ can be derived both via $S_1$ and via $S_2$:

$$S \underset{\text{lm}}{\Longrightarrow} S_1 \underset{\text{lm}}{\Longrightarrow}^* w \ ,$$

$$S \underset{\text{lm}}{\Longrightarrow} S_2 \underset{\text{lm}}{\Longrightarrow}^* w \ .$$

But by Theorem 10.68 such a sentence $w$ exists if and only if $M$ accepts $w$. □

The decision problem

$\mathscr{P}_{\text{amb}}$: "Given a context-free grammar $G$, is $G$ ambiguous?"

is called the *ambiguity problem* for context-free grammars. Theorem 10.72 states that the acceptance problem for Turing machines reduces in polynomial time to $\mathscr{P}_{\text{amb}}$. We have:

**Theorem 10.73** *The ambiguity problem for context-free grammars is unsolvable.* □

Next we shall show that when the computations of Turing machine $M$ are of a bounded length, then for a sufficiently great $k$ the ambiguity of $\hat{G}(M, w)$ will in fact be equivalent to the non-C($k$)-ness of $\hat{G}(M, w)$, where C($k$) denotes any of the grammar classes LR($k$), LALR($k$), SLR($k$), LL($k$), LALL($k$), or SLL($k$). First we note:

**Lemma 10.74** *If $\mathscr{C} = (\gamma_0, \gamma_1, \ldots, \gamma_t)$, $t \geqslant 1$, is a computation of Turing machine $M$ on input string $w$, then*

$$|\text{repr}(\mathscr{C})| \leqslant 2t \cdot (|w| + t + 4) + 1 \ .$$

*Proof.* By definition,

$$\text{repr}(\mathscr{C}) = \gamma_0 \# \gamma_1^R \# \gamma_1 \# \gamma_2^R \# \ \ldots \ \gamma_{t-1} \# \gamma_t^R \# \# \ .$$

Here $|\gamma_0| = |\$q_s w\$| = |w| + 3$. The length of any $\gamma_i$, $i = 1, \ldots, t$, is at most $|\gamma_0| + t$, because the application of $t$ actions of $M$ can increase the length of $\gamma_0$ by at most $t$. Hence we have:

$$\begin{aligned}|\text{repr}(\mathscr{C})| &= |\gamma_0 \#| + 2|\gamma_1 \#| + \ \ldots \ + 2|\gamma_{t-1} \#| + |\gamma_t \#| + 1 \\ &\leqslant 2t(|\gamma_0| + 1 + t) + 1 = 2t(|w| + 4 + t) + 1 \ .\end{aligned}$$

□

**Theorem 10.75** *Let $M$ be a Turing machine such that the following statements hold.*

(1) *The initial state $q_s$ of $M$ is not a final state.*
(2) *$M$ can make no move out of a final state.*
(3) *$M$ accepts only at the extreme right end of its tape.*

*Further let $w$ be an input string and assume that there is a natural number $t > |w|$ such that*

(4) *$M$ makes no more than $t$ moves on $w$, that is, $M$ has no computation on $w$ with length greater than $t$.*

*Then for all $k \geqslant 13 \cdot t^2$ the following statements are logically equivalent.*

(a) *$M$ accepts $w$ in time $t$.*
(b) *$\hat{G}(M, w)$ is ambiguous.*
(c) *$\hat{G}(M, w)$ is not $C(k)$, where $C(k)$ denotes any of the grammar classes $LR(k)$, $LALR(k)$, $SLR(k)$, $LL(k)$, $LALL(k)$, or $SLL(k)$.*

*Proof.* Assume that statement (*a*) is true. As in the proof of Theorem 10.72 we can conclude that $\hat{G}(M, w)$ must then be ambiguous. This in turn implies that $\hat{G}(M, w)$ is non-LR($k$), non-LALR($k$), non-SLR($k$), non-LL($k$), non-LALL($k$), and non-SLL($k$) for all $k \geq 0$. In other words, statement (*a*) implies statements (*b*) and (*c*).

Conversely, assume that statement (*a*) is not true. Then $M$ has on $w$ no accepting computation of length $\leq t$. On the other hand, since $M$ was assumed never to make more than $t$ moves on $w$, all computations on $w$ have length at most $t$. Now if $\mathscr{C} = (\gamma_0, \gamma_1, \ldots, \gamma_{m+1})$, $m \geq 0$, is a computation on $w$, then by Lemma 10.74 the length of the string repr($\mathscr{C}$) is at most $2t(t + t + 4) + 1 = 4t^2 + 8t + 1 \leq 13t^2$. But then we conclude by Theorem 10.68 that for all $k \geq 13t^2$

$$k{:}L(S_1) \cap k{:}L(S_2) \subseteq$$
$$\{\text{repr}(\mathscr{C}) \mid \mathscr{C} \text{ is an accepting computation on } w\} \ .$$

Here $S_1$ is the start symbol of $\hat{G}_1(M)$ and $S_2$ is the start symbol of $\hat{G}_2(M, w)$. Since $M$ does not accept $w$, we conclude that the intersection $k{:}L(S_1) \cap k{:}L(S_2)$ must be empty. This means that the start symbol $S$ of $\hat{G}(M, w)$ has the SLL($k$) property. But then $\hat{G}(M, w)$ is an SLL($k$) grammar because the nonterminal alphabets of the component grammars $\hat{G}_1(M)$ and $\hat{G}_2(M, w)$ are disjoint and because all the nonterminals in the component grammars have the *s*-property. Then $\hat{G}(M, w)$ is also LALL($k$), LL($k$), LR($k$), and unambiguous. It is not hard to see that $\hat{G}(M, w)$ is also SLR($k$) and LALR($k$) (we leave the details of proving this to the exercises). Thus we conclude that the converse of statement (*a*) implies the converses of statements (*b*) and (*c*). □

A function $T$ from the set of natural numbers to the set of positive natural numbers is *time-constructible* if there is a deterministic $T(n)$ time-bounded Turing machine $M$ such that for all $n$ there is an input $w$ of length $n$ on which $M$ actually makes $T(n)$ moves and halts. We leave it as an exercise to show that any natural-number-valued polynomial $p$ and the exponent function $2^{p(n)}$ are time-constructible.

**Proposition 10.76** *Let $T$ be any time-constructible function. Then for any $T(n)$ time-bounded Turing machine $M$ there are constants $c$ and $k$ and an equivalent $cT(n)^k$ time-bounded Turing machine $M'$ that never makes more than $cT(n)^k$ moves on input of length $n$. Moreover, $M'$ is deterministic whenever $M$ is so.* □

Now we can state the main result of this section.

**Theorem 10.77** (*Hunt, Szymanski and Ullman*, 1975) *Let $C(k)$*, for all $k \geq 0$, *denote the class of SLL($k$), LL($k$), SLR($k$), or LR($k$) grammars. Then the problem of uniform non-$C(k)$ testing is NP-complete when $k$ is expressed in unary, and NE-complete when $k$ is expressed in binary. When $C(k)$ denotes the class of LALR($k$) or LALL($k$) grammars, the problem of uniform non-$C(k)$ testing is NP-hard when $k$ is expressed in unary, and NE-hard when $k$ is expressed in binary.*

*Proof.* In the previous sections we have shown that for the grammar classes $C(k) = SLL(k)$, $LL(k)$, $SLR(k)$, $LR(k)$ the uniform non-$C(k)$ testing problem is in NP when $k$ is expressed in unary, and in NE when $k$ is expressed in binary. To show that the problem is NP-hard for $k$ in unary and NE-hard for $k$ in binary we have to establish polynomial-time reductions to this problem from arbitrary decision problems in NP and in NE.

Let $\mathscr{P}$ be any decision problem in NP. By Proposition 10.61 there exists a polynomial $p$ and a $p(n)$ time-bounded Turing machine $M$ such that $M$ accepts input string $w$ if and only if $w$ is a yes-instance of $\mathscr{P}$. By Lemma 10.69 we may assume that (1) the initial state of $M$ is not a final state, (2) $M$ can make no move out of a final state, and (3) $M$ accepts only at the extreme right end of its tape. By Proposition 10.76 we may assume that (4) $M$ never makes more than $p(n)$ moves on input of length $n$. Now any instance $w$ of $\mathscr{P}$ can be transformed into the pair

$$(\hat{G}(M, w), un(13 \cdot p(|w|)^2)) ,$$

where $un(k)$, for natural number $k$, denotes the unary representation of $k$. As explained earlier, the grammar $\hat{G}(M, w)$ can be constructed from $M$ and $w$ in polynomial time. It is also clear that the natural number $13 \cdot p(|w|)^2$ and its unary representation can be computed in time polynomial in $|w|$. Observe that for $n$ in binary the value $p(n)$ (in binary) can be determined in time polynomial in $\log n$. Hence the transformation is a polynomial-time transformation. Moreover, by Theorem 10.75 $M$ accepts $w$ if and only if $\hat{G}(M, w)$ is non-$C(13 \cdot p(|w|)^2)$. Hence the transformation is a reduction of $\mathscr{P}$ to the problem of non-$C(k)$ testing for $k$ in unary. By definition, uniform non-$C(k)$ testing is NP-hard for $k$ in unary.

The proof that uniform non-$C(k)$ testing is NE-hard for $k$ in binary is analogous. We leave the details to the exercises. □

We have now determined the complexity of $C(k)$ testing when $k$ is a fixed natural number and the complexity of non-$C(k)$ testing when the natural number $k$ is a parameter of the test. Here $C(k)$ may denote any of the grammar classes $LR(k)$, $SLR(k)$, $LL(k)$, or $SLL(k)$. Another interesting decision problem for these grammar classes is:

> "Given a context-free grammar $G$, is there a natural number $k$ such that $G$ is $C(k)$?"

As might be expected we have:

**Theorem 10.78** (*Knuth*, 1965; *Rosenkrantz and Stearns*, 1970) *Let $C(k)$ denote one of the grammar classes $LR(k)$, $LALR(k)$, $SLR(k)$, $LL(k)$, $LALL(k)$, or $SLL(k)$. It is unsolvable whether or not a given context-free grammar $G$ is $C(k)$ for some $k \geqslant 0$.* □

## 10.4 Complexity of LALR($k$) and LALL($k$) Testing

In the previous sections we have determined the complexity of LR($k$), SLR($k$), LL($k$), and SLL($k$) testing for fixed $k$ as well as the complexity of uniform non-LR($k$), non-SLR($k$), non-LL($k$), and non-SLL($k$) testing. However, for LALR($k$) and LALL($k$) testing we have only shown that uniform non-LALR($k$) and non-LALL($k$) testing is NP-hard when $k$ is expressed in unary, and NE-hard when $k$ is expressed in binary (Theorem 10.77).

In this section we shall show that for any fixed $k \geqslant 1$ the decision problem

$\mathscr{P}_{\mathrm{LALR}(k)}$: "Given a context-free grammar $G$, is $G$ an LALR($k$) grammar?"

is complete for PSPACE, the class of decision problems solvable in (deterministic or nondeterministic) polynomial space. Similarly we shall show that for any fixed $k \geqslant 2$ the decision problem

$\mathscr{P}_{\mathrm{LALL}(k)}$: "Given a context-free grammar $G$, is $G$ an LALL($k$) grammar?"

is complete for PSPACE.

The above results are in contrast to the results of Sections 10.1 and 10.2. Recall that for any fixed $k \geqslant 0$ the problems of LR($k$), SLR($k$), LL($k$), and SLL($k$) testing are in P, the class of decision problems solvable in deterministic polynomial time. Observe that (by Lemma 1.33) the class PSPACE contains the class NP. (Currently it is not known whether or not this containment is proper.)

For $k = 0$ we know that the problems $\mathscr{P}_{\mathrm{LALR}(k)}$ and $\mathscr{P}_{\mathrm{LALL}(k)}$ are in P, because the class of LALR(0) grammars coincides with the class of LR(0) ( = SLR(0)) grammars and the class of LALL(0) grammars coincides with the class of LL(0) ( = SLL(0)) grammars. Also, as the classes of LL(1), LALL(1), and SLL(1) grammars coincide (Theorem 8.41), we know that the problem $\mathscr{P}_{\mathrm{LALL}(1)}$ is in P.

The uniform non-LALR($k$) and non-LALL($k$) testing problems turn out to be PSPACE-complete for $k$ in unary, and NE-complete for $k$ in binary.

We start by showing that for all fixed $k \geqslant 1$ the problem of LALR($k$) testing is in PSPACE. We shall do this by giving a polynomial space-bounded nondeterministic algorithm for non-LALR($k$) testing. This is sufficient because by Savitch's Theorem (Proposition 1.38) the class of decision problems solvable in nondeterministic polynomial space coincides with the class of decision problems solvable in deterministic polynomial space. If we can establish a nondeterministic polynomial space-bounded partial solution for non-LALR($k$) testing, then by Savitch's Theorem there is some deterministic polynomial space-bounded partial solution for non-LALR($k$) testing. Because of the polynomial space-boundedness this partial solution can be converted into a total solution which is also deterministic and polynomial space-bounded. This total solution can then be used as a solution to the complement problem, the problem of LALR($k$) testing.

The idea in the nondeterministic non-LALR($k$) test is simple. Starting from the initial state of the canonical LR($k$) machine for the augmented grammar, the

$Q_1 := Q_2 := \{[S' \to \cdot \$S\$, \varepsilon]\}$;
**while true do begin**
  **if** CORE($Q_1$) = CORE($Q_2$) **then**
    **if** $Q_1 \cup Q_2$ contains a pair of distinct
    items exhibiting an LR($k$)-conflict **then**
      output "$G$ is non-LALR($k$)" and halt;
  **guess** strings $X$ and $Y \in V \cup \{\$, \varepsilon\}$;
  $Q_1 :=$ GOTO($Q_1$, $X$);
  $Q_2 :=$ GOTO($Q_2$, $Y$)
**end**

**Figure 10.9** A nondeterministic algorithm for non-LALR($k$) testing

algorithm generates, nondeterministically, two states, $Q_1$ and $Q_2$, of the canonical LR($k$) machine. If $Q_1$ and $Q_2$ happen to have the same set of item cores and if $Q_1 \cup Q_2$ happens to contain a pair of distinct items exhibiting an LR($k$) conflict, the algorithm accepts its input. The algorithm is shown in Figure 10.9. For $k$-item set $Q$, CORE($Q$) denotes the set of all $A \to \alpha \cdot \beta$ where $[A \to \alpha \cdot \beta, y]$ is an item in $Q$ for some $y$.

It is clear that the algorithm is a partial solution to non-LALR($k$) testing. It is also clear that the algorithm runs in polynomial space when $k$ is a fixed natural number. Observe that only the current pair of states $Q_1$, $Q_2$ need be present at a time, taking space $O(|G| \cdot |T|^k)$. In the computation of the successor states GOTO($Q_1$, $X$) and GOTO($Q_2$, $Y$) the algorithm uses the matrices $N_u$, $u \in k{:}T^*\$$, of Lemma 10.7. These matrices are precomputed for all $u \in k{:}T^*\$$, taking total space $O(k^2 \cdot |G| \cdot |T|^k)$. We have:

**Theorem 10.79** *For any fixed $k \geq 0$, the problems of non-LALR($k$) testing and LALR($k$) testing are in PSPACE.* □

To show that non-LALR($k$) testing and LALR($k$) testing are PSPACE-complete problems we have to establish a polynomial-time reduction from an arbitrary decision problem in PSPACE to (non-)LALR($k$) testing. We shall do this by first showing that another problem, called regular expression nonuniversality, is PSPACE-hard and then establishing a polynomial-time reduction from this problem to non-LALR($k$) testing.

*Regular expression nonuniversality* is the decision problem

$\mathscr{P}_{\text{nonuniv}}$: "Given a regular expression $E$ over alphabet $V$, is $L(E) \neq V^*$?"

In other words, $(E, V)$ is a yes-instance of $\mathscr{P}_{\text{nonuniv}}$ if and only if $E$ does not denote all the strings over its alphabet $V$.

That $\mathscr{P}_{\text{nonuniv}}$ is a PSPACE-hard problem will follow from the observation that the set of noncomputations of a space-bounded Turing machine can be represented as a regular language. By a noncomputation of Turing machine $M$ on input $w$ we mean any string (over the alphabet used to represent computations) that does not represent a valid computation of $M$ on $w$. We shall show that given any polynomial $p$, a $p(n)$ space-bounded Turing machine $M$, and an input string $w$, the pair $(M, w)$ can be transformed in polynomial time into a regular expression $E(M, p, w)$ that denotes the set of those strings that are not representations of accepting computations of $M$ on $w$ (or are computations having space complexity greater than $P(|w|)$). Then $M$ accepts $w$ if and only if $L(E(M, p, w)) \neq V^*$, where $V$ is the alphabet used to represent computations.

We choose $V = \Gamma \cup Q \cup \{\$\}$, where $\Gamma$ is the tape alphabet and $Q$ is the state alphabet of Turing machine $M$. That is, $V$ is the alphabet of $M$. We represent a computation $(\gamma_0, \ldots, \gamma_n)$, $n \geqslant 0$, of $M$ simply as the string $\gamma_0 \ldots \gamma_n$. Recall that any configuration $\gamma_i$ of $M$ is a string in $\$\Gamma^*Q\Gamma^*\$$, where the end marker does not belong to $\Gamma \cup Q$.

The expression $E(M, p, w)$ will be the union of fourteen regular expressions, each of which denotes a particular subset of noncomputations. We start by defining a regular expression that denotes the set of those strings in $V^*$ that are not concatenations of configurations and hence definitely cannot be computations of $M$ on any input $w$. This expression, denoted by $E_1(M)$, is defined by:

$$\begin{aligned} E_1(M) = \varepsilon &\cup (\$\Gamma^*Q\Gamma^*\$)^*(\Gamma \cup Q)V^* \\ &\cup (\$\Gamma^*Q\Gamma^*\$)^*\$(\Gamma \cup Q)^* \\ &\cup (\$\Gamma^*Q\Gamma^*\$)^*\$\Gamma^*\$V^* \\ &\cup (\$\Gamma^*Q\Gamma^*\$)^*\$\Gamma^*Q(\Gamma \cup Q)^*Q\Gamma^*\$V^* \ . \end{aligned}$$

For brevity, we have used $\Gamma$, $Q$, $\Gamma \cup Q$, and $V$ in place of regular subexpressions that denote exactly the symbols in these sets. In general, we shall write $W$ in place of the expression $(X_1 \cup X_2 \cup \ldots \cup X_n)$ when $W$ is the subset $\{X_1, X_2, \ldots, X_n\}$ of $V$.

It should be clear that a string belongs to $L(E_1(M))$ if and only if it is not of the form $\gamma_0 \ldots \gamma_n$ where $n \geqslant 0$ and each $\gamma_i$ is a configuration of $M$. Each of the five major subexpressions in $E_1(M)$ denotes a particular subset of "erroneous" strings, that is, strings in $V^*$ that for some specific reason are not of the desired form $\gamma_0 \ldots \gamma_n$. First, the empty string $\varepsilon$ is not of this form, and belongs to $L(E_1(M))$. The second subexpression denotes those erroneous strings whose first error is a missing \$ at the beginning of a configuration. The third subexpression denotes those erroneous strings whose error is due to a missing \$ at the end of a configuration. The fourth subexpression denotes those erroneous strings whose first error is a missing state in some configuration. The last subexpression denotes those erroneous strings whose first error is a configuration that contains more than one state. Obviously, $E_1(M)$ is of size $O(|M|)$ and can be constructed from $M$ in time $O(|M|)$.

Next we define for $M$ a regular expression that denotes those strings in $V^*$ that begin with a noninitial configuration. This expression is:

$$E_2(M) = \$\Gamma^+Q\Gamma^*\$V^* \cup \$(Q\backslash\{q_s\})\Gamma^*\$V^* \cup \$q_s\Gamma^*(\Gamma\backslash\Sigma)\Gamma^*\$V^* \ .$$

Here $\Sigma$ is the input alphabet of $M$. $E_2(M)$ is of size $O(|M|)$ and can be constructed from $M$ in time $O(|M|)$.

For $M$ and input string $w = a_1 \ldots a_n$ in $\Sigma^n$, $n \geqslant 0$, we define:

$$E_3(M, w) = \$q_s\$V^* \cup \$q_s\Sigma\$V^* \cup \ldots \cup \$q_s\Sigma^{n-1}\$V^*$$
$$\cup \$q_s\Sigma^{n+1}\Sigma^*\$V^*$$
$$\cup \$q_s(\Sigma\backslash\{a_1\})\Sigma^*\$V^* \cup \$q_s\Sigma(\Sigma\backslash\{a_2\})\Sigma^*\$V^* \cup \ldots$$
$$\cup \$q_s\Sigma^{n-1}(\Sigma\backslash\{a_n\})\Sigma^*\$V^* \ .$$

For $k \geqslant 0$, $\Sigma^k$ means the expression for $\Sigma$ written $k$ times. ($\Sigma^0$ means $\varepsilon$.) Obviously, $E_3(M, w)$ denotes those strings in $V^*$ that begin with an initial configuration of $M$ for some input string distinct from $w$. $E_2(M, w)$ is of size $O(|M| \cdot |w|^2)$ and can be constructed from $M$ and $w$ in time $O(|M| \cdot |w|^2)$.

For $M$ we define:

$$E_4(M) = V^*\$\Gamma^*(Q\backslash F)\Gamma^*\$ \ .$$

Here $F$ is the set of final states of $M$. Clearly, $E_4(M)$ denotes those strings in $V^*$ that end with a nonaccepting configuration.

At this point let us summarize what we have done so far. From the above discussion, it follows that the expression

$$E_1(M) \cup E_2(M) \cup E_3(M, w) \cup E_4(M)$$

denotes the set of those strings in $V^*$ that are not of the form $\gamma_0 \ldots \gamma_n$ where $n \geqslant 0$, $\gamma_0$ is the initial configuration of $M$ for $w$, $\gamma_i$ is a configuration of $M$ for all $i = 1, \ldots, n-1$, and $\gamma_n$ is an accepting configuration of $M$.

We have yet to construct expressions to denote those strings that are of the form $\gamma_0 \ldots \gamma_n$ but are noncomputations because for some $i < n$ the configuration $\gamma_{i+1}$ does not follow from $\gamma_i$ using an action of $M$. This is possible only if we can restrict our attention to configurations of bounded length. If $M$ is of space complexity $s(n)$, we may first rule out all strings containing configurations longer than $s(n)$. This is done by means of the expression

$$E_5(M, s, w) = V^*\$(\Gamma \cup Q)^{s(|w|)-1}(\Gamma \cup Q)^*\$V^* \ .$$

The size of this expression is $O(|M| \cdot s(|w|))$. If $s(n)$ can be computed in time polynomial in $\log n$, then the expression can be constructed from $M$ and $w$ in time polynomial in $|M| \cdot s(|w|)$. This is true for example when $s$ is a polynomial or $s(n)$ is of the form $2^{p(n)}$ where $p$ is a polynomial. When $s$ is a polynomial, we conclude that $E_5(M, s, w)$ can be constructed from $M$ and $w$ in time polynomial in $|M| + |w|$.

Then we define for $M$, $s$, and $w$ the expression

$$E_6(M, s, w) = \cup \{V^*\$\Gamma^m Q\Gamma^n\$\$\Gamma^k Q\Gamma^l\$V^* \mid m, n, k, l \geqslant 0,$$
$0 \leqslant m + n \leqslant s(|w|) - 3$, and $0 \leqslant k + l \leqslant s(|w|) - 3$,
but none of the following conditions are satisfied:
(a) $k = m$ and $l = n > 0$,
(b) $k = m + 1$ and $l = n - 1$,
(c) $k = m - 1$ and $l = n + 1 > 1$,

(d) $k = m$ and $l = n = 0$, (e) $k = m$ and $l = n + 1 = 1$,
(f) $k = m - 1$ and $l = n + 1 = 1\}$ .

For finite set $W$ of regular expressions, $\cup W$ denotes the union of the expressions in $W$. Conditions (a) to (f) correspond to the six types of actions that a Turing machine can have. The expression $E_6(M, s, w)$ rules out all those strings that contain two consecutive configurations (of length at most $s(|w|)$) in which the difference in tape length is wrong, or the positioning of the states is wrong, regardless of what the set of actions of $M$ is. The expression is of size $O(|M| \cdot s(|w|)^5)$. When $s$ is a polynomial, the expression can be constructed from $M$ and $w$ in time polynomial in $|M| + |w|$.

From now on we may restrict our attention to strings denoted by the following expressions.

(a) $V^*\$\Gamma^m Q\Gamma^n\$\$\Gamma^m Q\Gamma^n\$V^*$, where $m \geqslant 0$ and $n > 0$ .

(b) $V^*\$\Gamma^m Q\Gamma^n\$\$\Gamma^{m+1} Q\Gamma^{n-1}\$V^*$, where $m \geqslant 0$ and $n > 0$ .

(c) $V^*\$\Gamma^m Q\Gamma^n\$\$\Gamma^{m-1} Q\Gamma^{n+1}\$V^*$, where $m > 0$ and $n > 0$ .

(d) $V^*\$\Gamma^m Q\$\$\Gamma^m Q\$V^*$, where $m \geqslant 0$ .

(e) $V^*\$\Gamma^m Q\$\$\Gamma^m Q\Gamma\$V^*$, where $m \geqslant 0$ .

(f) $V^*\$\Gamma^m Q\$\$\Gamma^{m-1} Q\Gamma\$V^*$, where $m > 0$ .

In (a), (b), and (c) we may assume that $m + n \leqslant s(|w|) - 3$, and in (d), (e), and (f) we may assume that $m \leqslant s(|w|) - 3$.

The following expressions will rule out all strings of the above forms in which tape symbols not involved in actions are illegally changed.

$$E_7(M, s, w) = \cup\{V^*\$\Gamma^m a\Gamma^* Q\Gamma^*\$\$\Gamma^m(\Gamma\backslash\{a\})\Gamma^* Q\Gamma^*\$V^* \mid a \in \Gamma \text{ and } 0 \leqslant m \leqslant s(|w|) - 4\} .$$

$$E_8(M, s, w) = \cup\{V^*\$\Gamma^* Q\Gamma^+ a\Gamma^n\$\$\Gamma^* Q\Gamma^*(\Gamma\backslash\{a\})\Gamma^n\$V^* \mid a \in \Gamma \text{ and } 0 \leqslant n \leqslant s(|w|) - 4\} .$$

These expressions are of size $O(|M| \cdot s(|w|)^2)$ and (when $s$ is a polynomial) can be constructed from $M$ and $w$ in time polynomial in $|M| + |w|$.

Finally we take into account the specific set of actions $M$ has, and rule out the rest of those strings that cannot be accepting computations of $M$ on $w$ (of space complexity at most $s(|w|)$). For each of the six types of action there is an expression of its own. Observe that each of the string forms (a) to (f) listed above defines uniquely the type of action that can possibly change the former configuration to the latter configuration. The six expressions for (a) to (f) are:

$$E_a(M, s, w) = \cup\{V^*\$\Gamma^m q_1 a_1 \Gamma^*\$\$\Gamma^m q_2 a_2 \Gamma^*\$V^* \mid 0 \leqslant m \leqslant s(|w|) - 4, q_1, q_2 \in Q, \text{ and } a_1, a_2 \in \Gamma, \text{ but } q_1 a_1 \to q_2 a_2 \text{ is not an action of } M\} .$$

$$E_b(M, s, w) = \cup\{V^*\$\Gamma^m q_1 a_1 \Gamma^*\$\$\Gamma^m a_2 q_2 \Gamma^*\$V^* \mid 0 \leqslant m \leqslant s(|w|) - 4,\ q_1, q_2 \in Q, \text{ and } a_1, a_2 \in \Gamma, \text{ but } q_1 a_1 \to a_2 q_2 \text{ is not an action of } M\}\ .$$

$$E_c(M, s, w) = \cup\{V^*\$\Gamma^m d_1 q_1 a_1 \Gamma^*\$\$\Gamma^m q_2 d_2 a_2 \Gamma^*\$V^* \mid 0 \leqslant m \leqslant s(|w|) - 5,\ q_1, q_2 \in Q, \text{ and } a_1, a_2, d_1, d_2 \in \Gamma, \text{ but } d_1 q_1 a_1 \to q_2 d_2 a_2 \text{ is not an action of } M\}\ .$$

$$E_d(M, s, w) = \cup\{V^*\$\Gamma^m q_1 \$\$\Gamma^m q_2 \$V^* \mid 0 \leqslant m \leqslant s(|w|) - 3, \text{ and } q_1, q_2 \in Q, \text{ but } q_1\$ \to q_2\$ \text{ is not an action of } M\}\ .$$

$$E_e(M, s, w) = \cup\{V^*\$\Gamma^m q_1 \$\$\Gamma^m q_2 a\$V^* \mid 0 \leqslant m \leqslant s(|w|) - 3,\ q_1, q_2 \in Q, \text{ and } a \in \Gamma, \text{ but } q_1\$ \to q_2 a\$ \text{ is not an action of } M\}\ .$$

$$E_f(M, s, w) = \cup\{V^*\$\Gamma^m d_1 q_1 \$\$\Gamma^m q_2 d_2 \$V^* \mid 0 \leqslant m \leqslant s(|w|) - 4,\ q_1, q_2 \in Q, \text{ and } d_1, d_2 \in \Gamma, \text{ but } d_1 q_1 \$ \to q_2 d_2 \$ \text{ is not an action of } M\}\ .$$

Each expression has size at most $O(|M|^7 \cdot s(|w|)^2)$ and (when $s$ is a polynomial) can be constructed from $M$ and $w$ in time polynomial in $|M| + |w|$.

Finally let $E(M, s, w)$ be the union of all the expressions so far defined, That is,

$$\begin{aligned} E(M, s, w) = {} & E_1(M) \cup E_2(M) \cup E_3(M, w) \cup E_4(M) \cup E_5(M, s, w) \\ & \cup E_6(M, s, w) \cup E_7(M, s, w) \cup E_8(M, s, w) \\ & \cup E_a(M, s, w) \cup E_b(M, s, w) \cup E_c(M, s, w) \\ & \cup E_d(M, s, w) \cup E_e(M, s, w) \cup E_f(M, s, w)\ . \end{aligned}$$

We have:

**Theorem 10.80** *Let $p$ be a polynomial, $M$ a Turing machine that runs in space $p(n)$, and $w$ an input string. Then*

$$L(E(M, p, w)) = V^* \setminus \{\gamma_0 \ldots \gamma_n \mid n \geqslant 0, (\gamma_0, \ldots, \gamma_n) \text{ is an accepting computation of } M \text{ on } w \text{ having space complexity at most } p(|w|)\}\ ,$$

*where $V$ is the alphabet of $M$. Moreover, the regular expression $E(M, p, w)$ can be constructed from $M$ and $w$ in time polynomial in $|M| + |w|$.* □

Now we can prove:

**Theorem 10.81** (*Stockmeyer and Meyer*, 1973) *$\mathscr{P}_{\text{nonuniv}}$, regular expression non-universality, is PSPACE-complete.*

*Proof.* We only show that $\mathscr{P}_{\text{nonuniv}}$ is PSPACE-hard, because only this part of the result will be needed in the proof of the PSPACE-hardness of LALR($k$) testing. (In fact, when we establish a reduction of $\mathscr{P}_{\text{nonuniv}}$ to non-LALR($k$) testing, this will readily imply (by Theorem 10.79) that $\mathscr{P}_{\text{nonuniv}}$ belongs to PSPACE.)

To show that $\mathscr{P}_{\text{nonuniv}}$ is PSPACE-hard, we choose an arbitrary decision problem $\mathscr{P}$ in PSPACE and establish a polynomial-time reduction of $\mathscr{P}$ to $\mathscr{P}_{\text{nonuniv}}$. Since $\mathscr{P}$ is in PSPACE it has a polynomial space-bounded solution. By Proposition 10.61 there exists a polynomial $p$ and a $p(n)$ space-bounded Turing machine $M$ such that $M$ accepts input string $w$ if and only if $w$ is a yes-instance of $\mathscr{P}$. By Theorem 10.80 there exists a polynomial time-bounded algorithm that transforms any input string $w$ of $M$ into a regular expression $E$ over alphabet $V$ such that $L(E) \neq V^*$ if and only if $M$ has on $w$ an accepting computation of space complexity at most $p(|w|)$. In other words, any instance $w$ of $\mathscr{P}$ can be transformed in polynomial time into an instance $(E, V)$ of $\mathscr{P}_{\text{nonuniv}}$ such that $(E, V)$ is a yes-instance of $\mathscr{P}_{\text{nonuniv}}$ if and only if $w$ is a yes-instance of $\mathscr{P}$. □

Then we turn to the task of establishing a polynomial-time reduction of regular expression nonuniversality to non-LALR($k$) testing. We shall show that for any fixed $k \geqslant 1$ there exists a polynomial time-bounded algorithm that transforms any regular expression $E$ over alphabet $T$ into a context-free grammar $\hat{G}(E, k)$ such that $L(E) \neq T^*$ if and only if $\hat{G}(E, k)$ is non-LALR($k$).

In establishing the reduction we shall use in place of the expression $E$ a right-linear grammar $G$ with terminal alphabet $T$. Moreover, we assume that the rules in $G$ are of the forms $A \to aB$, $A \to \varepsilon$, where $a$ is a terminal in $T$. (This assumption is not absolutely necessary, but it will somewhat simplify the arguments.) Recall that in Chapter 3 we have shown the following. First, any regular expression over alphabet $T$ can be transformed in linear time into an equivalent (nondeterministic) finite automaton with input alphabet $T$ (Theorem 3.16). Second, any finite automaton can be transformed in polynomial time into an equivalent $\varepsilon$-free normal-form finite automaton, that is, an automaton containing only actions of the form $q_1 a \to q_2$, $a \in T$ (Theorems 3.13 and 3.14). Third, any finite automaton with input alphabet $T$ can be transformed in linear time into an equivalent right-linear grammar with terminal alphabet $T$ (Theorem 3.19). Moreover, as can be seen from the proof of Theorem 3.19, the right-linear grammar obtained from an $\varepsilon$-free normal-form finite automaton contains only rules of the forms $A \to aB$, $A \to \varepsilon$, where $a \in T$.

Hence, regular expression nonuniversality reduces in polynomial time to "right-linear grammar nonuniversality", or, more specifically, to the decision problem

> "Given a right-linear grammar $G$ with terminal alphabet $T$ and with set of rules containing only rules of the forms $A \to aB$ and $A \to \varepsilon$, is $L(G) \neq T^*$?"

If we manage to show that this problem reduces in polynomial time to non-LALR($k$) testing, we have established a polynomial-time reduction of regular expression nonuniversality to non-LALR($k$) testing.

Let $k \geqslant 1$ be a natural number and $G$ a right-linear grammar with nonterminal alphabet $N$, terminal alphabet $T$, set of rules $P$, and start symbol $S$. Further assume that the rules in $P$ are of the forms $A \to aB$, $A \to \varepsilon$. We define $\hat{G}(G, k)$ as the grammar with nonterminal alphabet

$$\{\hat{S}, E_1, E_2, H_1, H_2, H_3\} \cup N \ ,$$

terminal alphabet

$$T \cup \{c, d, f, g, h, (\hat{S}, S)\} \cup P \ ,$$

start symbol $\hat{S}$, and with the following set of rules:

$$\hat{S} \to E_1 | S(\hat{S}, S) | gE_2 \ ,$$

$$E_1 \to aE_1 \quad \text{for all terminals } a \in T \ ,$$

$$E_1 \to H_1 d^k | H_2 c^k \ ,$$

$$E_2 \to H_1 c^k | H_2 d^k \ ,$$

$$A \to aB(A, aB) \quad \text{for all rules } A \to aB \quad \text{in } P \ ,$$

$$A \to H_3 f^k(A, \varepsilon) \quad \text{for all rules } A \to \varepsilon \quad \text{in } P \ ,$$

$$H_1 \to h \ ,$$

$$H_2 \to h \ ,$$

$$H_3 \to h \ .$$

Here $\hat{S}, E_1, E_2, H_1, H_2, H_3, c, d, f, g, h$ are distinct new symbols not found in $N \cup T$. When a terminal of $\hat{G}(G, k)$ belonging to $P$ occurs in a rule of $\hat{G}(G, k)$, we use the pair notation $(A, \omega)$ instead of $A \to \omega$.

The rules of the start symbol $\hat{S}$ divide the grammar $\hat{G}(G, k)$ into three parts. The first part, starting with $E_1$, generates in $\hat{G}(G, k)$ the language

$$L(E_1) = T^* h\{c^k, d^k\} \ .$$

This part of the grammar guarantees that for any $w \in T^*$ the state $\text{VALID}_k(\$w)$ in the canonical LR($k$) machine (for the \$-augmented grammar) is nonempty and contains a $k$-item of the form $[C \to \alpha \cdot E_1 \beta, y]$. Observe that the state $\text{VALID}_k(\$wh)$ then always contains the pair of items $[H_1 \to h\cdot, d^k]$ and $[H_2 \to h\cdot, c^k]$.

The second part of the grammar, starting with $S(\hat{S}, S)$, where $S$ is the start symbol of $G$, generates in $\hat{G}(G, k)$ the language

$$L(S(\hat{S}, S)) = \{whf^k \pi^R(\hat{S}, S) | S \overset{\pi}{\Longrightarrow} w \text{ in } G\} \ .$$

This part of the grammar has the effect that for any string $w \in T^*$ the state $\text{VALID}_k(\$w)$ contains an item of the form $[A \to \cdot H_3 f^k(A, \varepsilon), y]$ if and only if $w \in L(G)$. Note that this means that $\text{VALID}_k(\$wh)$ contains the item $[H_3 \to h\cdot, f^k]$ if and only if $w \in L(G)$.

The augmenting terminals $(A, \omega) \in P$ and $(\hat{S}, S)$ have been introduced so as to circumvent any "unwanted" conflicts that would possibly arise if the rules $\hat{S} \to S$,

$A \to aB$, and $A \to H_3 f^k$ were used. Note that these unaugmented rules would make the grammar ambiguous whenever $G$ is ambiguous. And we must certainly allow $G$ to be ambiguous: the equivalence problem for unambiguous regular language descriptors is solvable in deterministic polynomial time (Proposition 3.47). Indeed, the regular expression $E(M, p, w)$ constructed above is highly ambiguous, as is easily seen.

The third part of the grammar, starting with $gE_2$, is finally used to introduce the "wanted" conflict into the grammar. Observe that this part of the grammar gives rise to the state VALID$_k$(\$$gh$), which contains the pair of items $[H_1 \to h\cdot, c^k]$, $[H_2 \to h\cdot, d^k]$. This state has the same set of item cores as the set VALID$_k$(\$$wh$), $w \in T^*$, whenever VALID$_k$(\$$wh$) contains only the items $[H_1 \to h\cdot, d^k]$ and $[H_2 \to h\cdot, c^k]$, that is, whenever $w \in T^* \backslash L(G)$. This makes the grammar non-LALR($k$), because the items $[H_1 \to h\cdot, c^k]$ and $[H_2 \to h\cdot, c^k]$ (as well as the items $[H_1 \to h\cdot, d^k]$ and $[H_2 \to h\cdot, d^k]$) exhibit an LR($k$)-conflict. In the case in which $w \in L(G)$ the state VALID$_k$(\$$wh$) also contains the item $[H_3 \to h\cdot, f^k]$, which prevents the occurrence of conflicts. Thus $\hat{G}(G, k)$ is non-LALR($k$) if and only if $L(G) \neq T^*$.

The grammar $\hat{G}(G, k)$ and the interesting portions of the canonical LR($k$) machine for the \$-augmented grammar for $\hat{G}(G, k)$ are illustrated in Figure 10.10.

Now we make the above reasoning more precise. The following lemma states that no "unwanted" conflicts can occur.

**Lemma 10.82** *Let $\gamma$ be a string such that the state* VALID$_0(\gamma)$ *in the LR(0) machine of the \$-augmented grammar for $\hat{G}(G, k)$ contains a pair of distinct items $[C \to \alpha \cdot \beta]$ and $[D \to \omega\cdot]$, where $\alpha \neq \varepsilon$. Then $\gamma{:}1 = h$.*

*Proof.* We base the proof on the fact that one of the strings $\alpha$ and $\omega$ must be a suffix of the other, and that both $\alpha$ and $\omega$ must be suffixes of $\gamma$ (recall Fact 6.12). In particular, we have $\gamma{:}1 = \alpha{:}1 = \omega{:}1$ (note that $\omega \neq \varepsilon$ because $\hat{G}(G, k)$ is $\varepsilon$-free). We denote $\gamma{:}1$ by $X$ and prove that $X$ can only be $h$.

First, $X$ can be neither $\hat{S}'$, $\hat{S}$, $H_1$, $H_2$, $H_3$, $f$, $g$, nor any symbol in $N \cup T$ (the alphabet of $G$), because in no rule of the \$-augmented grammar for $\hat{G}(G, k)$ does the right-hand side end with any of these symbols (recall that $k \geqslant 1$). Second, $X$ can be neither $E_2$, \$, $(\hat{S}, S)$, $(A, \varepsilon)$, nor $(A, aB)$ for any $A, B \in N$ and $a \in T$, because each of these symbols occurs immediately in front of the dot only in a single 0-item of the grammar (recall that $[C \to \alpha \cdot \beta]$ and $[D \to \omega\cdot]$ were assumed to be distinct). Third, $X$ can be neither $c$ nor $d$, because VALID$_0(\gamma)$ can contain no pair of distinct items $[E_i \to H_j c^m \cdot c^{k-m}]$, $[E_l \to H_r c^k\cdot]$, $0 \leqslant m \leqslant k$, and no pair of items $[E_i \to H_j d^m \cdot d^{k-m}]$, $[E_l \to H_r d^k\cdot]$, $0 \leqslant m \leqslant k$. Observe that if these items were to be in the same state, then $m = k$ and $H_j = H_r$, and hence also $E_i = E_l$ (see the grammar). Finally, $X$ cannot be $E_1$, because the items $[E_1 \to aE_1\cdot]$ and $[E_1 \to bE_1\cdot]$, $a \neq b$, cannot simultaneously be in VALID$_0(\gamma)$ and because the item $[\hat{S} \to E_1\cdot]$ belongs only to VALID$_0$(\$$E_1$), which cannot contain $[E_1 \to aE_1\cdot]$. Thus, we conclude that $X$ can only be $h$. □

The following lemma characterizes the basic properties of the three parts of the grammar $\hat{G}(G, k)$.

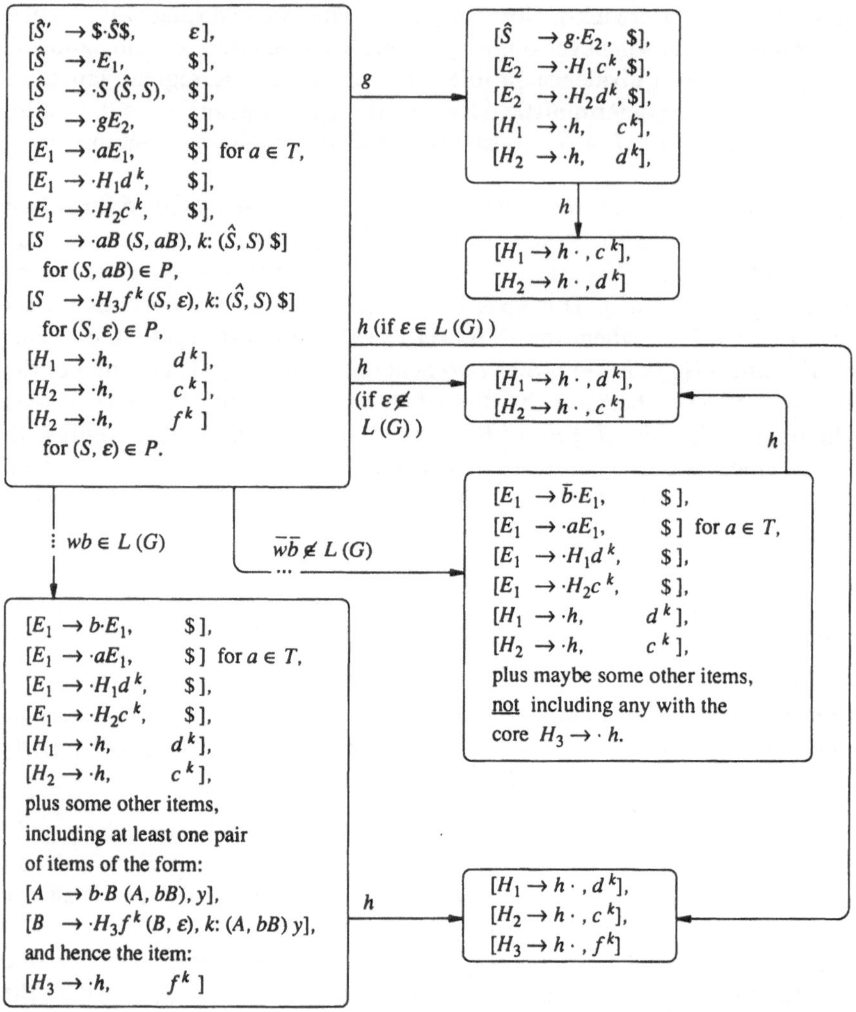


**Figure 10.10** Portions of the canonical LR($k$) machine ($k \geqslant 1$) for the \$-augmented grammar of $\hat{G}(G, k)$

**Lemma 10.83** *For all $0 \leqslant n \leqslant k$ and strings $\gamma$ the following hold for the \$-augmented grammar of $\hat{G}(G, k)$.*

*(a) $\text{VALID}_n(\gamma)$ contains an item of the form $[C \to \alpha \cdot E_1 \beta, y]$ if and only if $\gamma \in \$T^*$.*

*(b) $\text{VALID}_n(\gamma)$ contains an item of the form $[C \to \alpha \cdot A\beta, y]$, $A \in N$, if and only if $\gamma$ is of the form $\$w$ where $w \in T^*$ and $S \Rightarrow^* wA$ in $G$.*

*(c) $\text{VALID}_n(\gamma)$ contains an item of the form $[C \to \alpha \cdot E_2 \beta, y]$ if and only if $C = \hat{S}$, $\alpha = g$, $\beta = \varepsilon$, $y = \$$, and $\gamma = \$g$.*

*Proof.* The proof is by a series of simple inductions, using the results of Section 6.2 In (*a*) the induction is on $|\gamma|$. In the "if" part of (*b*) the induction is on the length of the derivation $S \Rightarrow^* wA$, and in the "only if" part on $|\gamma|$ plus the number of applications of the descendant relation $\mathbf{desc}_k$. We leave the details to the exercises. Claim (*c*) follows immediately from the construction of $\hat{G}(G, k)$. □

The following lemma delineates the potential conflicts in $\hat{G}(G, k)$.

**Lemma 10.84** *Let* $0 \leqslant n \leqslant k$ *and let* $\gamma$ *be a string such that in the* \$*-augmented grammar of* $\hat{G}(G, k)$, $\text{VALID}_n(\gamma h) \neq \varnothing$. *Then* $\gamma \in \$T^* \cup \$g$. *Moreover,* $\text{VALID}_n(\gamma h)$ *equals*

(1) $\{[H_1 \rightarrow h\cdot, d^n], [H_2 \rightarrow h\cdot, c^n], [H_3 \rightarrow h\cdot, f^n]\}$ *if* $\gamma \in \$L(G)$ ,
(2) $\{[H_1 \rightarrow h\cdot, d^n], [H_2 \rightarrow h\cdot, c^n]\}$ *if* $\gamma \in \$T^* \setminus \$L(G)$ ,
(3) $\{[H_1 \rightarrow h\cdot, c^n], [H_2 \rightarrow h\cdot, d^n]\}$ *if* $\gamma = \$g$ .

*Proof.* First observe that $\text{VALID}_n(\gamma h)$ can only contain the items $[H_1 \rightarrow h\cdot, d^n]$, $[H_1 \rightarrow h\cdot, c^n]$, $[H_2 \rightarrow h\cdot, c^n]$, $[H_2 \rightarrow h\cdot, d^n]$, $[H_3 \rightarrow h\cdot, f^n]$, because these five items are the only LR($n$)-valid items having a core of the form $C \rightarrow \alpha h \cdot \beta$. The items $[H_1 \rightarrow h\cdot, d^n]$ and $[H_2 \rightarrow h\cdot, c^n]$ can belong to $\text{VALID}_n(\gamma h)$ if and only if $\text{VALID}_n(\gamma)$ contains an item of the form $[C \rightarrow \alpha \cdot E_1\beta, y]$. By Lemma 10.83 (*a*), this can happen if and only if $\gamma \in \$T^*$. The item $[H_3 \rightarrow h\cdot, f^n]$ can belong to $\text{VALID}_n(\gamma h)$ if and only if $\text{VALID}_n(\gamma)$ contains an item of the form $[C \rightarrow \alpha \cdot A\beta, y]$ where $A$ is a nonterminal of $G$ having the rule $A \rightarrow \varepsilon$. By Lemma 10.83(*b*), this can happen if and only if $\gamma$ is of the form $\$w$ where $w \in T^*$, $S \Rightarrow^* wA$, and $A \Rightarrow \varepsilon$ in $G$. Finally, the items $[H_1 \rightarrow h\cdot, c^n]$ and $[H_2 \rightarrow h\cdot, d^n]$ can belong to $\text{VALID}_n(\gamma h)$ if and only if $\text{VALID}_n(\gamma)$ contains an item of the form $[C \rightarrow \alpha \cdot E_2\beta, y]$. By Lemma 10.83(*c*), this can happen if and only if $C = \hat{S}$, $\alpha = g$, $\beta = \varepsilon$, $y = \$$, and $\gamma = \$g$. □

Now we can prove:

**Theorem 10.85** *Let G be any right-linear grammar with terminal alphabet T and with a set of rules containing only rules of the forms* $A \rightarrow aB$, $A \rightarrow \varepsilon$. *Then for all natural numbers* $k \geqslant 1$, *the grammar* $\hat{G}(G, k)$ *is LR*(1). *Moreover,* $\hat{G}(G, k)$ *is LALR*(1) *if* $L(G) = T^*$, *and non-LALR*($k$) *if* $L(G) \neq T^*$.

*Proof.* Let $\gamma_1'$ and $\gamma_2'$ be strings, $[C' \rightarrow \alpha' \cdot \beta', y']$ an item in $\text{VALID}_1(\gamma_1')$, and $[C \rightarrow \omega\cdot, z]$ an item in $\text{VALID}_1(\gamma_2')$ such that $C \rightarrow \omega\cdot$ is distinct from $C' \rightarrow \alpha' \cdot \beta'$ (that is, $[C' \rightarrow \alpha' \cdot \beta']$ and $[C \rightarrow \omega\cdot]$ possibly exhibit an LR(0)-conflict). Then $\text{VALID}_1(\gamma_1')$ must contain an item $[A \rightarrow \alpha \cdot \beta, y]$ such that $A \rightarrow \alpha \cdot \beta$ is distinct from $C \rightarrow \omega\cdot$ and $\alpha \neq \varepsilon$. (Recall that any item of the form $[C' \rightarrow \cdot\beta', y']$ in $\text{VALID}(\gamma')$, $\gamma' \neq \varepsilon$, is a descendant of some essential item in $\text{VALID}(\gamma')$.) Now if $\text{VALID}_0(\gamma_1') = \text{VALID}_0(\gamma_2')$, then by Lemma 10.82 $\gamma_1'$ is of the form $\gamma_1 h$ and $\gamma_2'$ is of the form $\gamma_2 h$. But then Lemma 10.84 shows that $\hat{G}(G, k)$ is LR(1). Indeed, $\hat{G}(G, k)$ is actually LALR(1) if $L(G) = T^*$. On the other hand, Lemma 10.84 shows that whenever $L(G) \neq T^*$, then $\hat{G}(G, k)$ cannot even be LALR($k$). □

Because for each fixed $k$ the grammar $\hat{G}(G, k)$ can obviously be constructed from $G$ in time linear in $|G|$, we conclude that for each fixed $k \geqslant 1$, regular expression nonuniversality reduces in polynomial time to non-LALR($k$) testing. By Theorems 10.81 and 10.79 we then have:

**Theorem 10.86** *For each fixed natural number $k \geqslant 1$, the problems of non-LALR($k$) testing and LALR($k$) testing are PSPACE-complete.* □

Observe that because PSPACE is a deterministic problem class, the PSPACE-hardness of problem $\mathscr{P}$ implies the PSPACE-hardness of the complement of $\mathscr{P}$.

The proof of the PSPACE-completeness of non-LALL($k$) testing and LALL($k$) testing, $k \geqslant 2$, is very similar to the above, and we will not repeat it in detail. First, non-LALL($k$) testing belongs to PSPACE, because a nondeterministic algorithm analogous to that given in Figure 10.9 exists. Second, regular expression non-universality can be shown to reduce in polynomial time to non-LALL($k$) testing. The grammar $\hat{G}(G, k)$, for a right-linear grammar $G = (N \cup T, T, P, S)$ and $k \geqslant 2$, now takes the form:

$$\hat{S} \to E \mid S \mid hHhf^k \ ,$$

$$E \to (E, a)Ea \quad \text{for all } a \in T \ ,$$

$$E \to fHf^k \ ,$$

$$H \to \varepsilon \mid h \ ,$$

$$A \to (A, aB)Ba \quad \text{for all } A \to aB \text{ in } P \ ,$$

$$A \to (A, \varepsilon)hf^k \quad \text{for all } A \to \varepsilon \text{ in } P \ .$$

This grammar is LL(2) for all $k \geqslant 2$. Moreover, the grammar is LALL(2) if $L(G) = T^*$, and non-LALL($k$) if $L(G) \neq T^*$. We leave the details of showing this to the exercises. We have:

**Theorem 10.87** *For each fixed natural number $k \geqslant 2$, the problems of non-LALL($k$) testing and LALL($k$) testing are PSPACE-complete.* □

For uniform non-LALR($k$) and non-LALL($k$) testing one can show the following.

**Theorem 10.88** *Grammar $G = (V, T, P, S)$ can be tested for the non-LALR($k$) and non-LALL($k$) properties simultaneously in nondeterministic space $O(|G| + k)$ and in nondeterministic time $O((k+1) \cdot |G|^2 \cdot 2^{|G|})$.*

*Proof.* Exercise. □

Theorem 10.88 implies that the problems of uniform non-LALR($k$), LALR($k$), non-LALL($k$), and LALL($k$) testing belong to PSPACE when $k$ is expressed in unary, and that the problems of non-LALR($k$) and non-LALL($k$) testing belong to

**Table 10.1** Complexity of non-C($k$) testing

| Grammar class non-C($k$) | Role of $k$: fixed $k = 1$ | fixed $k \geqslant 2$ | free $k$ in unary | free $k$ in binary | existence of $k$ such that $G$ is C($k$) |
|---|---|---|---|---|---|
| non-SLL($k$) | in P | in P | NP-complete | NE-complete | unsolvable |
| non-LL($k$) | in P | in P | NP-complete | NE-complete | unsolvable |
| non-SLR($k$) | in P | in P | NP-complete | NE-complete | unsolvable |
| non-LR($k$) | in P | in P | NP-complete | NE-complete | unsolvable |
| non-LALL($k$) | in P | PSPACE-complete | PSPACE-complete | NE-complete | unsolvable |
| non-LALR($k$) | PSPACE-complete | PSPACE-complete | PSPACE-complete | NE-complete | unsolvable |

**Table 10.2** Upper bounds on the complexity of non-C($k$) testing when $k \geqslant 2$ is fixed

| Grammar class non-C($k$) | Resource: deterministic time | deterministic space | nondeterministic time | Size of the C($k$) parser |
|---|---|---|---|---|
| non-SLL($k$) | $O(n^{k+1})$ | $O(n)$ | $O(n)$ | $O(n^{k+1})$ |
| non-LL($k$) | $O(n^{k+1})$ | $O(n)$ | $O(n)$ | $O(2^{n^{k+1}+(k+1)\log n})$ |
| non-SLR($k$) | $O(n^{k+2})$* | $O(n^2)$ | $O(n^2)$ | $O(2^{n+(k+1)\log n})$ |
| non-LR($k$) | $O(n^{k+2})$ | $O(n^2)$ | $O(n^2)$ | $O(2^{n^{k+1}+(k+1)\log n})$ |
| non-LALL($k$) | parser construction time | $O(n^2)$ | $O(2^{n+2\log n})$ | $O(2^{n+(k+1)\log n})$ |
| non-LALR($k$) | parser construction time | $O(n^2)$ | $O(2^{n+2\log n})$ | $O(2^{n+(k+1)\log n})$ |

* For (non-)SLR(2) testing an $O(n^3)$ time-bounded algorithm is known.

NE when $k$ is expressed in binary. Previously we have shown (Theorem 10.77) that uniform non-LALR($k$) and non-LALL($k$) testing are NE-hard for $k$ in binary. On the other hand, because (non-)LALR(1) testing and (non-)LALL(2) testing trivially reduce to uniform (non-)LALR($k$) testing and (non-)LALL($k$) testing, Theorems 10.86 and 10.87 imply that the problems of non-LALR($k$), LALR($k$), non-LALL($k$), and LALL($k$) testing are PSPACE-hard (for $k$ either in unary or in binary). Hence we have:

**Theorem 10.89** *The problems of uniform non-LALR($k$), LALR($k$), non-LALL($k$), and LALL($k$) testing are PSPACE-complete when $k$ is expressed in unary. The problems of non-LALR($k$) and non-LALL($k$) testing are NE-complete when $k$ is expressed in binary.* □

We conclude by summarizing the complexities of different C($k$) testing problems. Basic results are given in Table 10.1. More detailed complexity bounds for non-C($k$) testing for $k \geqslant 2$ are given in Table 10.2. In Table 10.2 are also given the sizes of the corresponding parsers. For (non-)LALL($k$) and (non-)LALR($k$) testing no deterministic time bound better than that implied by the parser construction algorithm is known when $k \geqslant 2$. Deriving an upper bound on the time complexity of constructing the canonical LR($k$) parser and the LALR($k$) parser for general $k$ has been left to the exercises. The same time bounds will also hold for canonical LL($k$) and LALL($k$) parser construction. Finally in Table 10.3 are given bounds on the complexity of C(1) testing and on the complexity of constructing C(1) parsers.

**Table 10.3** Upper bounds on the complexity of C(1) testing and on parser construction

| Grammar class C(1) | C(1) testing in deterministic time | C(1) parser size | C(1) parser construction time |
|---|---|---|---|
| SLL(1) | $O(n^2)$ | $O(n^2)$ | $O(n^2)$ |
| LL(1) | $O(n^2)$ | $O(2^{n^2 + 2\log n})$ | $O(2^{n^2 + 4\log n})$ |
| SLR(1) | $O(n^2)$ | $O(2^{n + 2\log n})$ | $O(2^{n + 3\log n})$ |
| LR(1) | $O(n^3)$ | $O(2^{n^2 + 2\log n})$ | $O(2^{n^2 + 4\log n})$ |
| LALL(1) | $O(n^2)$ | $O(2^{n + 2\log n})$ | $O(2^{n + 3\log n})$ |
| LALR(1) | $O(2^{n + 3\log n})$ | $O(2^{n + 2\log n})$ | $O(2^{n + 3\log n})$ |

## Exercises

10.1 Prove Theorem 10.4 (without using Theorem 10.1).

10.2 Consider the grammar (see Exercise 6.25)

$$S \to AB,\ A \to a,\ B \to CD \,|\, aE,\ C \to ab\ ,$$

$$D \to bb,\ E \to bba\ .$$

Give the automata $M_1(G')$ and $M_2(G')$ for the \$-augmented grammar of this grammar. Explain why the grammar is LR(2) but not LR(1).

10.3 Show that the equivalence induced by the automaton $M_{\mathrm{LR}(k)}(G)$ on the set of viable prefixes of $G$ is LR($k$)-equivalence. (For the definition of the equivalence induced by a finite automaton, see Exercise 3.32.)

10.4 Give the grammar $G_{\mathrm{pre}}$ of Lemma 10.6 for the grammar given in Exercise 10.2.

10.5 Give a tight upper bound on the space complexity of constructing $M_{\mathrm{LR}(k)}(G)$.

10.6 Derive upper bounds on the time and space complexity of constructing for grammar $G$ (a) the canonical LR($k$) parser, and (b) the LALR($k$) parser.

*Hint*: Recall Theorem 3.30, which states the complexity of making an arbitrary nondeterministic finite automaton deterministic.

10.7 Give a string $u$ in $\{a, b, \$\}$ such that the non-LR(1)-ness of the grammar of Exercise 10.2 can be seen from the automaton $M_u(G')$. Give $M_u(G')$ in its entirety.

10.8 For alphabet $T$ and string $u \in T^*$ define on $2^{T^*}$ a relation $\lambda_u$ by setting:

$$W \lambda_u \{y\} \text{ whenever } W \subseteq T^* \text{ and } y \in \mathrm{FIRST}_u(W) \ .$$

Show that $\lambda_u$ is a lookahead operator (as defined in Exercise 6.65). Observe that a $u$-item $[A \to \alpha \cdot \beta, y]$ is LR($u$)-valid for $\gamma$ if and only if $[A \to \alpha \cdot \beta, \{y\}]$ is an LR($\lambda_u$)-valid $\lambda_u$-item for $\gamma$ (as defined in Exercise 6.66).

10.9 For grammar $G = (V, T, P, S)$ and an arbitrary lookahead operator $\lambda$ over $T$, define the notion of an automaton $M_{\mathrm{LR}(\lambda)}(G)$. Your definition should yield $M_{\mathrm{LR}(\lambda_k)}(G) = M_{\mathrm{LR}(k)}(G)$ and $M_{\mathrm{LR}(\lambda_u)}(G) = M_{\mathrm{LR}(u)}(G)$, where $\lambda_k$ is the lookahead operator defined in Exercise 6.65 and $\lambda_u$ is the lookahead operator defined in Exercise 10.8. Also show the correspondence between $M_{\mathrm{LR}(\lambda)}(G)$ and LR($\lambda$)-validity. In other words, state and prove generalizations of Theorems 10.4 and 10.17 for arbitrary $\lambda$.

10.10 Show that in the automaton $M_{\mathrm{LR}(u)}(G)$ the set of pairs of mutually accessible states can be determined simultaneously in space $O((|u| + 1)^2 \cdot |G|^2)$ and in time $O((|u| + 1)^3 \cdot |G|^2)$. Recall that the general result (Lemma 10.10) yields the space and time bound $O((|u| + 1)^4 \cdot |G|^2)$.

*Hint*: Devise an algorithm that uses a stack to store the set of pairs of states whose successors have not yet been determined.

10.11 Give a complete proof for Theorem 10.21.

10.12 We say that a transition in $M_{\mathrm{LR}(u)}(G)$ is *monotonic* if it is a type (a) or (b) transition, or if it is a type (c) transition

$$[A \to \alpha \cdot B\beta, y] \to [B, vy] \ ,$$

where $v$ is a string derived by $\beta$, or a type (c) transition

$$[A \to \alpha \cdot B\beta, \varepsilon] \to [B, v] \ ,$$

where $v$ is prefix of some string derived by $\beta$. The string $v$ is called the *addition string* for the transition. (For a type (a) or (b) transition the addition string is $\varepsilon$.) A computation $(I_0\gamma_0, \ldots, I_m\gamma_m)$ is *monotonic* if all the transitions applied in it are monotonic.

a) Find nonmonotonic computations in $M_b(G'_{\mathrm{LR}2})$ (Figure 10.2).
b) Show that in a monotonic computation $(I_0\gamma_0, \ldots, I_m\gamma_m)$ of $M_u(G)$ the lookahead string of $I_m$ is of the form $v_m v_{m-1} \ldots v_1$, where $v_i$ is the addition string for the transition from $I_{i-1}$ to $I_i$.
c) Show that for any computation $(I_0\gamma_0, \ldots, I_m\gamma_m)$ of $M_u(G)$ on string $\gamma$ there is a monotonic computation $(I'_0\gamma_0, \ldots, I'_m\gamma_m)$ on $\gamma$ where $I'_m = I_m$ (and of course $I'_0 = I_0 = [S, \varepsilon]$).

10.13 Consider the nondeterministic generation of monotonic computations in $M_u(G)$, assuming that $M_u(G)$ has not been constructed beforehand. Show that given any state of the form $[A \to \alpha \cdot B\beta, y]$ in $M_u(G)$ it is possible to guess, simultaneously in space $O(|G| + |v|)$ and in time $O(|v| \cdot |G|)$, any transition of the form

$$[A \to \alpha \cdot B\beta, y] \to [B, vy] \ ,$$

where $\beta$ derives $v$. Also show that given any state of the form $[A \to \alpha \cdot B\beta, \varepsilon]$ in $M_u(G)$ it is possible to guess, simultaneously in space $O(|G| + |v|)$ and in time $O(|v| \cdot |G|)$, any transition of the form

$$[A \to \alpha \cdot B\beta, \varepsilon] \to [B, v] \ ,$$

where $v$ is a prefix of some terminal string derived by $\beta$.

*Hint*: Recall the complexity of deriving sentences in an $\varepsilon$-free grammar (Theorem 4.21).

10.14 Show that in $M_u(G)$ any monotonic computation of length $m$ can be guessed in time $O(m + |u| \cdot |G|)$. Also show that any accessible state in $M_u(G)$ can be guessed simultaneously in space $O(|G| + |u|)$ and in time $O(|u| \cdot |G|)$. (In both cases we assume $M_u(G)$ has not been constructed beforehand.)

10.15 Prove Theorem 10.24.

10.16 Give a nondeterministic non-LR($k$) testing algorithm that is based on the automaton $M_k(G')$. What is the complexity of your algorithm?

10.17 Prove Theorem 10.27.

10.18 Prove Theorem 10.28.

10.19 Prove the following improvement of Theorem 10.28 for the cases $k = 1$ and $k = 2$: Grammar $G = (V, T, P, S)$ can be tested for the SLR(1) property in deterministic time $O(|G|^2)$ and for the SLR(2) property in deterministic time $O(|T| \cdot |G|^2)$.

*Hint*: Use relational expressions. For SLR(1) testing derive a relational expression that denotes the set of all pairs of item cores that may take part in an LR(1) conflict. Generalize your construction to the SLR(2) case by defining for each fixed terminal $a \in T$ a relational expression that can handle those LR(2)-conflicts that may occur in the case of lookahead strings beginning with $a$.

10.20 Derive an upper bound on the complexity of constructing the SLR($k$) parser for grammar $G$.

10.21 Prove Theorem 10.30.

10.22 Let $G$ be a right-linear grammar such that $L(G)$ is prefix-free (that is, no proper prefix of a sentence in $L(G)$ belongs to $L(G)$; see Exercise 6.57). Show that $G$ is unambiguous if and only if $G$ is LR(0) (cf. Exercise 6.31).

10.23 Consider showing that the unambiguity problems for finite automata, regular expressions, and regular grammars are in P, or more specifically, are solvable in deterministic time $O(n^2)$ (Theorem 3.48). Provide a linear-time reduction from these problems to LR(0) testing.

10.24 Prove Lemma 10.31.

10.25 Prove part (b) of Lemma 10.32.

10.26 Consider the grammar (see Exercise 8.1)

$$S \to bAbb \mid aAab \ ,$$

$$A \to \varepsilon \mid a \ .$$

Give the automaton $M_{\text{LL}(ab)}(G')$ for the \$-augmented grammar of this grammar. Identify the states that indicate the non-SLL(2)-ness of the grammar.

10.27 Let $G = (V, T, P, S)$ be a grammar and $\lambda$ a lookahead operator over $T$ (see Exercise 6.65). Further let $[A \to \alpha \cdot \beta, W]$ be a $\lambda$-item of $G$, that is, $A \to \alpha\beta$ is a rule in $P$ and $W$ is a lookahead set in $\lambda(2^{T^*})$. Say that $[A \to \alpha \cdot \beta, W]$ is *LL(λ)-valid for* string $\gamma$ if

$$S \underset{\text{lm}}{\Rightarrow}^* xA\delta \underset{\text{lm}}{\Rightarrow} x\alpha\beta\delta = x\alpha\gamma^R \quad \text{and} \quad L(\gamma^R)\lambda W$$

hold in $G$ for some strings $x \in T^*$ and $\delta \in V^*$. Denote by $\text{VALID}_{\text{LL}(\lambda)}(\gamma)$ (or $\text{VALID}_\lambda(\gamma)$, for short) the set of all LL($\lambda$)-valid items for $\gamma$. Observe that a $u$-item $[A \to \alpha \cdot \beta, y]$ is LL($u$)-valid for $\gamma$ if and only if the $\lambda_u$-item $[A \to \alpha \cdot \beta, \{y\}]$ is LL($\lambda_u$)-valid for $\gamma$, where $\lambda_u$ is the lookahead operator defined in Exercise 10.8. State and prove the generalizations of Lemmas 10.38, 10.39, and 10.40 for an arbitrary lookahead operator $\lambda$.

10.28 For grammar $G = (V, T, P, S)$ and an arbitrary lookahead operator $\lambda$ over $T$, define the notion of an automaton $M_{\text{LL}(\lambda)}(G)$. Your definition should yield $M_{\text{LL}(\lambda_u)}(G) = M_{\text{LL}(u)}(G)$, where $\lambda_u$ is the lookahead operator defined in Exercise 10.8. Also show the correspondence between $M_{\text{LL}(\lambda)}(G)$ and LL($\lambda$)-validity. In other words, state and prove a generalization of Theorem 10.41 for arbitrary $\lambda$.

10.29 Define the notions of a monotonic transition and a monotonic computation in $M_{\text{LL}(u)}(G)$ (cf. Exercise 10.12). Show that for any computation $(I_0\gamma_0, \ldots, I_m\gamma_m)$ of $M_{\text{LL}(u)}(G)$ on string $\gamma$ there is a monotonic computation $(I'_0\gamma_0, \ldots, I'_m\gamma_m)$ on $\gamma$ where $I'_m = I_m$.

10.30 Prove Theorem 10.47.

10.31 Show that in the automaton $M_{\text{LL}(u)}(G)$ the set of pairs of mutually accessible states can be determined simultaneously in space $O((|u| + 1)^2 \cdot |G|^2)$ and in time $O((|u| + 1)^4 \cdot |G|^2)$. Can you obtain the tighter time bound $O((|u| + 1)^3 \cdot |G|^2)$? (Cf. Exercise 10.10.)

10.32 Give a complete proof for Theorem 10.50.

10.33 Prove Theorem 10.51.

10.34 Give the automaton $M_{ab\text{-set}}(G')$ for the \$-augmented grammar of the grammar given in Exercise 10.26.

10.35 For alphabet $T$ and string $u \in T^*$ define on $2^{T^*}$ a relation $\lambda_{u\text{-set}}$ by setting:

$$W_1 \lambda_{u\text{-set}} W_2 \text{ whenever } W_1 \subseteq T^* \text{ and } W_2 = \text{FIRST}_u(W_1) .$$

Show that $\lambda_{u\text{-set}}$ is a lookahead operator. Observe that a $u$-set-item $[A \to \alpha \cdot \beta, W]$ is LL($u$-set)-valid for string $\gamma$ if and only if $[A \to \alpha \cdot \beta, W]$ is an LL($\lambda_{u\text{-set}}$)-valid $\lambda_{u\text{-set}}$-item for $\gamma$ (as defined in Exercise 10.27).

10.36 Prove Lemma 10.56.

10.37 Prove Theorem 10.59.

10.38 Derive an LL($k$) testing algorithm using the automaton $M_{\mathrm{LL}(k)}(G') = M_{\mathrm{LL}(\lambda_k)}(G')$. What is the complexity of your algorithm?

10.39 For $k \geqslant 0$ define the lookahead operator $\lambda_{k\text{-set}}$. Derive an LL($k$) testing algorithm using the automaton $M_{\mathrm{LL}(\lambda_{k\text{-set}})}(G')$ and an LR($k$) testing algorithm using the automaton $M_{\mathrm{LR}(\lambda_{k\text{-set}})}(G')$. What is the complexity of your algorithms?

10.40 Give a deterministic Turing machine that accepts the set of palindromes over $\{0, 1\}$ and runs in time $O(n^2)$ and in space $O(n)$.

10.41 Consider Theorem 10.64. In statement (b), only the containment $\subseteq$ is claimed to hold. Does the converse containment also hold? That is, are the two sets in fact equal?

10.42 Show that the nonemptiness of intersection problem for context-free languages and the ambiguity problem for context-free grammars are partially solvable.

10.43 Show that for any deterministic Turing machine $M$ the grammar $G_1(M)$ is an SLL(3) grammar.

10.44 Consider Theorem 10.75. Show that the converse of statement (a) implies the SLR($k$)-ness and the LALR($k$)-ness of $\hat{G}(M, w)$.

10.45 Show that any natural-number-valued polynomial $p(n)$ and the exponent function $2^{p(n)}$ are time-constructible.

10.46 Sketch a proof for Proposition 10.76.

10.47 Consider Theorem 10.77. Prove that uniform non-C($k$) testing is NE-hard when $k$ is expressed in binary.

10.48 *Post's correspondence problem* is the decision problem

"Given an alphabet $\Sigma$ and a finite relation $R$ on $\Sigma^*$, are there a natural number $n \geqslant 1$ and pairs $(x_1, y_1), \ldots, (x_n, y_n)$ in $R$ such that $x_1 \ldots x_n = y_1 \ldots y_n$?"

Show that the problem is partially solvable.

10.49 Establish a reduction from the acceptance problem for Turing machines to Post's correspondence problem, hence showing that Post's correspondence problem is unsolvable.

*Hint*: Given a Turing machine $M$ with alphabet $V$ and an input string $w$, construct a finite relation $R(M, w)$ on $V^*$ such that for any $n \geqslant 1$ and any sequence of pairs $(x_1, y_1), \ldots, (x_n, y_n)$ in $R(M, w)$ the equality $x_1 \ldots x_n = y_1 \ldots y_n$ holds if and only if $x_1 \ldots x_n$ and $y_1 \ldots y_n$ have as a common prefix an accepting computation of $M$ on $w$. $R(M, w)$ will contain the pair $(\$, \$q_s w\$)$, all the actions of $M$, and some additional pairs.

10.50 Give a new proof for Theorems 10.71 and 10.73 by establishing a reduction from Post's correspondence problem.

*Hint*: Given an alphabet $\Sigma$ and a finite relation $R$ on $\Sigma^*$, construct grammars for the following *s*-languages over $\Sigma \cup R$:

$$L_1 = \{(x_i, y_i) \ldots (x_1, y_1)x_1 \ldots x_i | i \geqslant 1, (x_1, y_1), \ldots, (x_i, y_i) \in R\} \ ,$$

$$L_2 = \{(x_i, y_i) \ldots (x_1, y_1)y_1 \ldots y_i | i \geqslant 1, (x_1, y_1), \ldots, (x_i, y_i) \in R\} \ .$$

10.51 The *partial correspondence problem* is the decision problem

"Given an alphabet $\Sigma$ and a finite relation $R$ on $\Sigma^*$, are there, for all $n \geqslant 1$, pairs $(x_1, y_1), \ldots, (x_n, y_n)$ in $R$ such that $n{:}x_1 \ldots x_n = n{:}y_1 \ldots y_n$?"

Establish a reduction from the complement of the halting problem for Turing machines to the partial correspondence problem, hence showing that the partial correspondence problem is unsolvable. Is the problem partially solvable?

10.52 Prove Theorem 10.78 by establishing a reduction from the partial correspondence problem.

10.53 Consider the following "time-bounded" variant of Post's correspondence problem.

"Given an alphabet $\Sigma$ and a finite relation $R$ on $\Sigma^*$, are there a natural number $n$, $1 \leqslant n \leqslant k$, and pairs $(x_1, y_1), \ldots, (x_n, y_n)$ in $R$ such that $x_1 \ldots x_n = y_1 \ldots y_n$?"

Show that this problem is

a) in P, when $k$ is a fixed natural number;
b) NP-complete, when $k$ is a parameter of the problem and expressed in unary;
c) NE-complete, when $k$ is a parameter of the problem and expressed in binary.

10.54 Consider the decision problem

"Given two *s*-grammars $G_1$ and $G_2$, does $L(G_1) \cap L(G_2)$ contain a string of length at most $k$?"

Show that this problem is

a) in P, when $k$ is fixed;
b) NP-complete, when $k$ is expressed in unary;
c) NE-complete, when $k$ is expressed in binary.

10.55 Another "time-bounded" variant of Post's correspondence problem is stated as follows:

"Given an alphabet $\Sigma$ and a finite relation $R$ on $\Sigma^*$, are there a natural number $n \geqslant 1$ and pairs $(x_1, y_1), \ldots, (x_n, y_n)$ in $R$ such that $k{:}x_1 \ldots x_n = k{:}y_1 \ldots y_n$?"

Show that this problem is

a) in P, when $k$ is fixed;
b) NP-complete, when $k$ is expressed in unary;
c) NE-complete, when $k$ is expressed in binary.

10.56 Give a new proof for Theorem 10.77 by establishing a polynomial-time reduction from the problem stated in the previous exercise to the problem of non-C($k$) testing.

10.57 Show that given two finite automata $M_1$ and $M_2$ with input alphabet $T$, it is solvable in nondeterministic space $O(|M_1| + |M_2|)$ whether or not $L(M_1) \neq L(M_2)$. Observe that this implies in particular that regular expression nonuniversality is in PSPACE.

10.58 Consider the transformation of regular expression nonuniversality to non-LALR($k$) testing. How do you write the grammar $\hat{G}(G, k)$ if a finite automaton is used in the place of the right-linear grammar $G$?

10.59 Give a detailed proof for Lemma 10.83.

10.60 Restate Lemmas 10.83 and 10.84 for the case in which a finite automaton is used in place of a right-linear grammar.

10.61 Give a detailed proof for Theorem 10.87.

10.62 A *regular expression with exponentation* is an expression over the set of operators $\{\cup, \cdot, {}^*, {}^2\}$, where $\cup$, $\cdot$, and $*$ are the usual operators of regular expressions and $^2$ is an operator defined by:

$$L(E^2) = L(E)^2 .$$

That is, $E^2$ denotes the language $L(E)L(E)$, where $L(E)$ is the language denoted by $E$. Show that nonuniversality of regular expressions with exponentation is complete for ESPACE, the class of decision problems solvable in one-level exponential space.

10.63 Prove Theorem 10.88.

*Hint*: Guess a string $u \in k{:}T^*\$$ and generate, nondeterministically, a computation (state string) $I_0 \ldots I_m$ of $M_u(G')$ on some string $\gamma_1 \ldots \gamma_m$ and a computation (state string) $J_0 \ldots J_n$ of $M_u(G')$ on some string $\delta_1 \ldots \delta_n$. (Here $I_i\gamma_{i+1} \to I_{i+1}$ and $J_j\delta_{j+1} \to J_{j+1}$ are transitions in $M_u(G')$, $i = 0, \ldots, m-1, j = 0, \ldots, n-1$.) Along with the generation, keep track of the 0-item sets $\text{VALID}_0(\gamma_1 \ldots \gamma_i)$ and $\text{VALID}_0(\delta_1 \ldots \delta_j)$. Finally, check whether or not $I_m$ and $J_n$ exhibit a conflict. Observe that the computations need not be longer than $2(|u|+1)\cdot|G'|\cdot 2^{|G'|}$.

10.64 Consider the following "space-bounded" variant of Post's correspondence problem:

"Given an alphabet $\Sigma$ and a finite relation $R$ on $\Sigma^*$, are there a natural number $n \geq 1$ and pairs $(x_1, y_1), \ldots, (x_n, y_n)$ in $R$ such that $x_1 \ldots x_n = y_1 \ldots y_n$ and $||x_1| - |y_1|| + \ldots + ||x_n| - |y_n|| \leq k$?"

Show that this problem is

a) PSPACE-complete, when $k \geq |R|$ is fixed;
b) PSPACE-complete, when $k$ is expressed in unary;
c) ESPACE-complete, when $k$ is expressed in binary.

## Bibliographic Notes

The fundamental result that for any fixed natural number $k$ there exists a polynomial time-bounded deterministic algorithm for testing a context-free grammar for the LR($k$) property is already present in the paper by Knuth (1965). The algorithm given by Knuth is essentially that implied by the nondeterministic finite automaton $M_k(G')$ (Theorem 10.11). In place of a finite automaton Knuth used a right-linear grammar. The idea of using in place of $M_k(G')$ a collection of more succinct automata $M_u(G')$ was suggested by Hunt, Szymanski and Ullman (1975). From them comes Theorem 10.21. Hunt, Szymanski and Ullman were also the first to investigate the nondeterministic complexity of non-LR($k$) testing and the effect of the role of $k$ in the complexity. From their paper come Theorem 10.24 and the results for SLR($k$) testing (Theorems 10.28 and 10.30). The improved time bound for SLR(1) testing (Exercise 10.19) is from Hunt, Szymanski and Ullman (1974, 1977), and the improved time bound for SLR(2) testing is from Sippu and Soisalon-Soininen (1985).

The linear-time reduction of LL($k$) testing to LR($k$) testing comes from Brosgol (1974). The more general formulation of the result (Theorem 10.34) was stated by Hunt and Szymanski (1978). The results for SLL($k$) testing (Theorems 10.45 and 10.47) and the results for LL($k$) testing obtained via the use of the automata $M_{u\text{-set}}(G')$ (Theorems 10.57 and 10.59) come from Sippu and Soisalon-Soininen (1983a). Reductions between different grammar classes are considered by Hunt and Szymanski (1978), who also study the complexity of relative decision problems, for example, the complexity of determining for an LR($k$) grammar whether or not the grammar is LL($k'$) for some $k'$.

The notion of a Turing machine comes from Turing (1936). The version of a Turing machine defined in Section 10.3 is what is usually called a "nondeterministic Turing machine with one semi-infinite tape". The formulation as a rewriting system has been adopted from Salomaa (1973). For the basic results on Turing machines and computational complexity, see Salomaa (1973), Aho, Hopcroft and Ullman (1974), and Hopcroft and Ullman (1979).

The idea of embedding Turing machine computations in context-free languages (Theorems 10.64 and 10.65) comes from Hartmanis (1967) (also see Hunt, 1982). The hardness of uniform non-LR($k$), non-LALR($k$), non-SLR($k$), non-LL($k$), and non-SLL($k$) testing (Theorems 10.75 and 10.77) was established by Hunt, Szymanski and Ullman (1975). The unsolvability of the existence of $k$ such that a given context-free grammar is LR($k$) or LL($k$) (Theorem 10.78) comes from Knuth (1965) and from Rosenkrantz and Stearns (1970). Rosenkrantz and Stearns proved the result for LL($k$) by presenting a generic transformation. Knuth proved the result for LR($k$) via a reduction from a variant of Post's correspondence problem (Exercise 10.51). The original formulation of Post's correspondence problem comes from Post (1946). The hardness of bounded variants of the problem (Exercise 10.53) is considered by Constable, Hunt and Sahni (1974). The variant given in Exercise 10.55 was suggested by Otto Nurmi and is especially suitable for proving the hardness of the uniform testing problems.

The results on the hardness of regular expression nonuniversality (Theorem 10.81 and Exercise 10.62) come from Meyer and Stockmeyer (1972) and Stockmeyer and Meyer (1973). Other decision problems on regular languages are considered by Hunt, Rosenkrantz and Szymanski (1976), Hunt and Rosenkrantz (1978), and Hunt (1979). The reduction of regular expression nonuniversality to non-LALR($k$) testing (Theorem 10.85) and the hardness result for the fixed $k \geqslant 1$ case (Theorem 10.86) are from Ukkonen and Soisalon-Soininen (1981) and from Sippu, Soisalon-Soininen and Ukkonen (1983). The corresponding reduction for LALL($k$) testing (Theorem 10.87) can be found in Sippu and Soisalon-Soininen (1983a). The upper bounds for uniform non-LALR($k$) and non-LALL($k$) testing (Theorem 10.88) can be found in Sippu, Soisalon-Soininen and Ukkonen (1983) and in Sippu and Soisalon-Soininen (1983a).

The solvability and complexity of diffferent kinds of decision problems on context-free grammars are studied by Hunt, Rosenkrantz and Szymanski (1976), Hunt and Szymanski (1976), Hunt and Rosenkrantz (1977, 1978, 1980), Hunt (1982), Heilbrunner (1983), and Rosenkrantz and Hunt (1985, 1987).

# Bibliography to Volume II


Aho AV, Johnson SC (1974) LR parsing. Comput. Surveys 6: 99–124

Aho AV, Peterson TG (1972) A minimum distance error-correcting parser for context-free languages. SIAM J. Comput. 1: 305–312

Aho AV, Ullman JD (1972a) Optimization of LR(*k*) parsers. J. Computer System Sci. 6: 573–602

Aho AV, Ullman JD (1972b) The theory of parsing, translation, and compiling, Vol. I: parsing. Prentice-Hall, Englewood Cliffs, N.J.

Aho AV, Ullman JD (1973a) The theory of parsing, translation, and compiling, Vol. II: compiling. Prentice–Hall, Englewood Cliffs, N.J.

Aho AV, Ullman JD (1973b) A technique for speeding up LR(*k*) parsers. SIAM J. Comput. 2: 106–127

Aho AV, Ullman JD (1977) Principles of compiler design. Addison-Wesley, Reading, Mass.

Aho AV, Hopcroft JE, Ullman JD (1974) The design and analysis of computer algorithms. Addison-Wesley, Reading, Mass.

Aho AV, Johnson SC, Ullman JD (1975) Deterministic parsing of ambiguous grammars. Comm. ACM 18: 441–452

Aho AV, Sethi R, Ullman JD (1986) Compilers: principles, techniques, and tools. Addison-Wesley, Reading, Mass.

Ancona M, Gianuzzi V (1981) A new method for implementing LR(*k*) tables. Inform. Proc. Letters 13: 171–176

Anderson T (1972) Syntactic analysis of LR(*k*) languages. Thesis, University of Newcastle upon Tyne

Anderson T, Eve J, Horning JJ (1973) Efficient LR(1) parsers. Acta Inform. 2: 12–39

Backhouse RC (1979) Syntax of programming languages: theory and practice. Prentice-Hall International, London

Backhouse R (1984) Global data flow analysis problems arising in locally least-cost error recovery. ACM Trans. Prog. Lang. Syst. 6: 192–214

Baker TP (1981) Extending lookahead for LR parsers. J. Computer System Sci. 22: 243–259

Bauer FL, Eickel J, eds. (1976) Compiler construction: An advanced course, 2nd ed. Springer, Berlin Heidelberg New York (Lecture notes in computer science, vol 21)

Beatty JC (1980) Two iteration theorems for the LL(*k*) languages. Theor. Computer Sci. 12: 193–228

Beatty JC (1982) On the relationship between the LL(1) and LR(1) grammars. J. Assoc. Comput. Mach. 29: 1007–1022

Bermudez ME, Logothetis G (1989) Simple computation of LALR(1) lookahead sets. Inform. Proc. Letters 31: 233–238

Brosgol BM (1974) Deterministic translation grammars. Thesis and TR 3-74, Center for Research in Computing Technology, Harvard University, Cambridge, Mass.

Burke MG, Fisher GA (1987) A practical method for LR and LL syntactic error diagnosis and recovery. ACM Trans. Prog. Lang. Syst. 9: 164–197

Celentano A (1978) Incremental LR parsers. Acta Inform. 10: 307–321

Chapman NP (1984) LALR(1, 1) parser generation for regular right part grammars. Acta Inform. 21: 29–45

Ciesinger J (1979) A bibliography of error-handling. ACM SIGPLAN Notices 14, Nr. 1: 16–26

Constable RL, Hunt HB III, Sahni S (1974) On the computational complexity of scheme equivalence. Report 74-201, Dept. of Computer Science, Cornell University, Ithaca, N.Y.

Čulik K II (1968) Contribution to deterministic top-down analysis of context-free languages. Kybernetika 4: 422–431

Čulik K, Cohen R (1973) LR-regular grammars—an extension of LR(*k*) grammars. J. Computer System Sci. 7: 66–96

Degano P, Mannucci S, Mojana B (1988) Efficient incremental LR parsing for syntax-directed editors. ACM Trans. Prog. Lang. Syst. 10: 345–373

Demers AJ (1974) Skeletal LR parsing. In: 15th Annual IEEE Symp. on Switching and Automata Theory, Oct 1974. IEEE, New York, pp 185–198

Demers AJ (1975) Elimination of single productions and merging nonterminal symbols of LR(1) grammars. Computer Lang. 1: 105–119

Dencker P, Durre K, Heuft J (1984) Optimization of parser tables for portable compilers. ACM Trans. Prog. Lang. Syst. 6: 546–572

DeRemer FL (1969) Practical translators for LR(*k*) languages. Thesis, Massachusetts Institute of Technology, Cambridge, Mass.

DeRemer FL (1971) Simple LR(*k*) grammars. Comm. ACM 14: 453–460

DeRemer FL, Pennello TJ (1982) Efficient computation of LALR(1) lookahead sets. ACM Trans. Prog. Lang. Syst. 4: 615–649

Drossopoulou S (1982) Verschmelzen von Aktionen in Zerteilern. Thesis, University of Karlsruhe

Druseikis FC, Ripley GD (1976) Error recovery for simple LR(*k*) parsers. In: ACM'76 Annual Conference, Houston, Texas, Oct 1976. ACM, New York, pp 396–400

Earley J (1968) An efficient context-free parsing algorithm. Thesis, Carnagie-Mellon University, Pittsburgh, Pa.

Fischer CN, Milton DR, Quiring SB (1980) Efficient LL(1) error correction and recovery using only insertions. Acta Inform. 13: 141–154

Fischer CN, Tai KC, Milton DR (1979) Immediate error detection in strong LL(1) parsers. Inform. Proc. Letters 8: 261–266

Foster JM (1968) A syntax improving program. Computer J. 11: 31–34

Friede D (1979) Partitioned LL(*k*) grammars. In: Maurer HA (ed.) Automata, Languages and Programming, 6th Colloquium, Graz, July 1979. Springer, Berlin Heidelberg New York, pp 245–255 (Lecture notes in computer science, vol 71)

Garey MR, Johnson DS (1979) Computers and intractability: a guide to the theory of NP-completeness. Freeman, San Francisco, Calif.

Geller MM, Harrison MA (1977a) On LR(*k*) grammars and languages. Theor. Computer Sci. 4: 245–276

Geller MM, Harrison MA (1977b) Characteristic parsing: a framework for producing compact deterministic parsers. J. Computer System Sci. 14: 265–317 (Part 1), 318–343 (Part 2)

Ghezzi C, Mandrioli D (1979) Incremental parsing. ACM Trans. Prog. Lang. Syst. 1: 58–70

Ghezzi C, Mandrioli D (1980) Augmenting parsers to support incrementality. J. Assoc. Comput. Mach. 27: 564–579

Graham SL (1970) Extended precedence languages, bounded right context languages and deterministic languages. In: 11th Annual IEEE Symp. on Switching and Automata Theory, 1970. IEEE, New York, pp 175–180

Graham SL (1971) Precedence languages and bounded right context languages. Thesis, Department of Computer Science, Stanford University, Stanford, Calif.

Graham SL (1974) On bounded right context languages and grammars. SIAM J. Comput. 3: 224–254

Graham SL, Rhodes SP (1973) Practical syntactic error recovery in compilers. In: ACM Symp. on Principles of Programming Languages, Boston, Massachusetts, Oct 1973. ACM, New York, pp 52–58

Graham SL, Rhodes SP (1975) Practical syntactic error recovery. Comm. ACM 18: 639–650

Graham SL, Haley CB, Joy WN (1979) Practical LR error recovery. In: ACM SIGPLAN Symp. on Compiler Construction, Denver, Colorado, Aug 1979. ACM SIGPLAN Notices 14, Nr. 8: 168–175

Gray JN, Harrison MA (1972) On the covering and reduction problems for context-free grammars. J. Assoc. Comput. Mach. 19: 675–698

Greibach SA (1965) A new normal form theorem for context-free phrase structure grammars. J. Assoc. Comput. Mach. 12: 42–52

Gries D (1971) Compiler construction for digital computers. Wiley, New York
Gries D (1976) Error recovery and correction: an introduction to the literature. In: Bauer FL, Eickel J (eds) Compiler Construction: An Advanced Course, 2n ed. Springer, Berlin Heidelberg New York, pp 627–638 (Lecture notes in computer science, vol 21)
Hammer MM (1974) A new grammatical transformation into LL($k$) form. In: 6th Annual ACM Symp. on Theory of Computing, 1974. ACM, New York, pp 266–275
Hammond K, Rayward-Smith VJ (1984) A survey on syntactic error recovery and repair. Computer Lang. 9: 51–67
Harris LA (1987) SLR(1) and LALR(1) parsing for unrestricted grammars. Acta Inform. 24: 191–209
Harrison MA (1978) Introduction to formal language theory. Addison-Wesley, Reading, Mass.
Harrison MA, Havel IM (1973) Strict deterministic grammars. J. Computer System Sci. 7: 237–277
Hartmanis J (1967) Context-free languages and Turing machine computations. In: Proc. Symp. Appl. Math. Vol 19, Amer. Math. Soc., Providence, 1967, pp 45–51
Heckmann R (1986) An efficient ELL(1)-parser generator. Acta Inform. 23: 127–148
Heilbrunner S (1979) On the definition of ELR($k$) and ELL($k$) grammars. Acta Inform. 11: 169–176
Heilbrunner S (1981) A parsing automata approach to LR theory. Theor. Computer Sci. 15: 117–157
Heilbrunner S (1983) A metatheorem for undecidable properties of formal languages and its application to LRR and LLR grammars and languages. Theor. Computer Sci. 23: 49–68
Heilbrunner S (1985) Truly prefix-correct chain-free LR(1) parsers. Acta Inform. 22: 475–498
Hopcroft JE, Ullman JD (1979) Introduction to automata theory, languages, and computation. Addison-Wesley, Reading, Mass.
Horning JJ (1976) What the compiler should tell the user. In: Bauer FL, Eickel J (eds) Compiler Construction: An Advanced Course, 2nd ed. Springer, Berlin Heidelberg New York, pp 525–548 (Lecture notes in computer science, vol 21)
Hunt HB III (1979) Observations on the complexity of regular expression problems. J. Computer System Sci. 19: 222–236
Hunt HB III (1982) On the decidability of grammar problems. J. Assoc. Comput. Mach. 29: 429–447
Hunt HB III, Rosenkrantz DJ (1977) Complexity of grammatical similarity relations. In: Conf. on Theoretical Computer Science, Univ. of Waterloo, Waterloo, Ontario, Aug 1977, pp 139–145
Hunt HB III, Rosenkrantz DJ (1978) Computational parallels between the regular and context-free languages. SIAM J. Comput. 7: 99–114
Hunt HB III, Rosenkrantz DJ (1980) Efficient algorithms for structural similarity of grammars. In: 7th ACM Symp. on Principles of Programming Languages, Las Vegas, Nevada, Jan 1980. ACM, New York, pp 213–219
Hunt HB III, Szymanski TG (1976) Complexity metatheorems for context-free grammar problems. J. Computer System Sci. 13: 318–334
Hunt HB III, Szymanski TG (1978) Lower bounds and reductions between grammar problems. J. Assoc. Comput. Mach. 25: 32–51 (Corrigendum: ibid, pp 687–688)
Hunt HB III, Rosenkrantz DJ, Szymanski TG (1976) On the equivalence, containment, and covering problems for the regular and context-free languages. J. Computer System Sci. 12: 222–268
Hunt HB III, Szymanski TG, Ullman JD (1974) Operations on sparse relations and efficient algorithms for grammar problems. In: 15th Annual IEEE Symp. on Switching and Automata Theory, Oct 1974. IEEE, New York, pp 127–132
Hunt HB III, Szymanski TG, Ullman JD (1975) On the complexity of LR($k$) testing. Comm. ACM 18: 707–716
Hunt HB III, Szymanski TG, Ullman JD (1977) Operations on sparse relations. Comm. ACM 20: 171–176
Ichbiah JD, Morse SP (1970) A technique for generating almost optimal Floyd-Evans productions for precedence grammars. Comm. ACM 13: 501–508
James LR (1972) A syntax directed error recovery method. Technical Report CSRG-13, Computer Systems Research Group, University of Toronto
Jarzabek S, Krawczyk T (1975) LL-regular grammars. Inform. Proc. Letters 4: 31–37
Johnson DB, Sethi R (1975) Efficient construction of LL(1) parsers. Technical Report No. 164, Computer Science Department, The Pennsylvania State University, University Park, Penn.

Johnson DB, Sethi R (1976) A characterization of LL(1) grammars. BIT 16: 275–280
Johnson SC (1975) YACC: Yet another compiler-compiler. Computing Science Technical Report Nr. 32, Bell Laboratories, Murray Hill, N.J.
Jalili F, Gallier JH (1982) Building friendly parsers. In: 9th ACM Symp. on Principles of Programming Languages, Albuquerque, New Mexico, Jan 1982. ACM, New York, pp 196–206
Joliat ML (1973) On the reduced matrix representation of LR($k$) parsing tables. Thesis and Technical Report CSRG-28, University of Toronto
Joliat ML (1974) Practical minimization of LR($k$) parser tables. In: Information Processing 74. North-Holland, Amsterdam, pp 376–380
Kantorowitz E, Laor H (1986) Automatic generation of useful syntax error messages. Software—Practice and Experience 16: 627–640
Knuth DE (1965) On the translation of languages from left to right. Inform. Control 8: 607–639
Knuth DE (1967) Top-down syntax analysis. Lecture notes, International Summer School on Computer Programming, Copenhagen, Denmark
Knuth DE (1971) Top-down syntax analysis. Acta Inform. 1: 79–110
Koskimies K, Soisalon-Soininen E (1979) On a method for optimizing LR parsers. Intern. J. Computer Math. 7: 287–295
Koskimies K, Nurmi O, Paakki J, Sippu S (1988) The design of a language processor generator. Software — Practice and Experience 18: 107–135
Kristensen BB, Madsen OL (1981) Methods for computing LALR($k$) lookahead. ACM Trans. Prog. Lang. Syst. 3: 60–82
Kurki-Suonio R (1966) On top-to-bottom recognition and left recursion. Comm. ACM 9: 527–528
Kurki-Suonio R (1967) A note on LL(1) languages. International Summer School on Computer Programming, Copenhagen, Denmark
Kurki-Suonio R (1969) Notes on top-down languages. BIT 9: 225–238
LaLonde WR (1971) An efficient LALR parser generator. Technical Report CSRG-2, University of Toronto
LaLonde WR (1976a) On directly constructing LR($k$) parsers without chain reductions. In: 3rd ACM Symp. on Principles of Programming Languages, Atlanta, Georgia, Jan 1976. ACM, New York, pp 127–133
LaLonde WR (1976b) On directly constructing LA($k$)LR($m$) parsers without chain reductions. Technical Report No. SE&CS 76-9, Department of Systems Engineering and Computer Science, Carleton University, Ottawa
LaLonde WR (1977) Regular right part grammars and their parsers. Comm. ACM 20: 731–741
LaLonde WR (1979) Constructing LR parsers for regular right part grammars. Acta Inform. 11: 177–193
LaLonde WR (1981) The construction of stack-controlling LR parsers for regular right part grammars. ACM Trans. Prog. Lang. Syst. 3: 168–207
LaLonde WR (1984) Comments on Soisalon-Soininen's "Inessential error entries". ACM Trans. Prog. Lang. Syst. 6: 432–439
Leinius RP (1970) Error detection and recovery for syntax directed compiler systems. Thesis, Computer Science Department, University of Wisconsin, Madison
Levy JP (1975) Automatic correction of syntax errors in programming languages. Acta Inform. 4: 271–292
Lewi J, De Vlaminck K, Huens J, Huybrechts M (1978) The ELL(1) parser generator and the error recovery mechanism. Acta Inform. 10: 209–228
Lewis PM II, Stearns RE (1966) Syntax-directed transduction. In: 7th Annual IEEE Symp. on Switching and Automata Theory, Oct 1966. IEEE, New York, pp 21–35
Lewis PM II, Stearns RE (1968) Syntax-directed transduction. J. Assoc. Comput. Mach. 15: 465–488
Lewis PM II, Rosenkrantz DJ, Stearns RE (1976) Compiler design theory. Addison-Wesley, Reading, Mass.
Lomet DB (1969) The construction of efficient deterministic language processors. Thesis, University of Pennsylvania, Philadelphia, Penn.
Lyon G (1974) Syntax-directed least-errors analysis for context-free languages: a practical approach. Comm. ACM 17: 3–14

Madsen OL, Kristensen BB (1976) LR-parsing of extended context free grammars. Acta Inform. 7: 61–73

Mauney J, Fischer CN (1982) A forward move algorithm for LL and LR parsers. In: ACM SIGPLAN'82 Symp. on Compiler Construction, Boston, Massachusetts, June 1982. ACM SIGPLAN Notices 17, Nr. 6: 79–87

Mauney J, Fischer CN (1988) Determining the extent of lookahead in syntactic error repair. ACM Trans. Prog. Lang. Syst. 10: 456–469

McKeeman WM, Horning JJ, Wortman DB (1970) A compiler generator. Prentice-Hall, Englewood Cliffs, N.J.

Meyer AR, Stockmeyer LJ (1972) The equivalence problem for regular expressions with squaring requires exponential space. In: 13th Annual IEEE Symp. on Switching and Automata Theory, Oct 1972. IEEE, New York, pp 125–129

Mickunas MD (1976) On the complete covering problem for LR(*k*) grammars. J. Assoc. Comput. Mach. 23: 17–30

Mickunas MD, Modry JA (1978) Automatic error recovery for LR parsers. Comm. ACM 21: 459–465

Mickunas MD, Lancaster RL, Schneider VB (1976) Transforming LR(*k*) grammars into LR(1), SLR(1), and (1,1) bounded right-context grammars. J. Assoc. Comput. Mach. 23: 511–533

Nakata I, Sassa M (1986) Generation of efficient LALR parsers for regular right part grammars. Acta Inform. 23: 149–162

Nijholt A (1976) On the parsing of LL-regular grammars. In: Mazurkiewicz A (ed) Mathematical Foundations of Computer Science 1976, Proceedings, 5th Symposium, Gdansk, September 1976. Springer, Berlin Heidelberg New York, pp 446–452 (Lecture notes in computer science, vol 45)

Nijholt A (1977) On the covering of parsable grammars. J. Computer System Sci. 15: 99–110

Nijholt A (1980a) Context-free grammars: covers, normal forms, and parsing. Springer, Berlin Heidelberg New York (Lecture notes in computer science, vol 93)

Nijholt A (1980b) A survey of normal-form covers for context free grammars. Acta Inform. 14: 271–294

Nijholt A (1982a) On the relationship between the LL(*k*) and LR(*k*) grammars. Inform. Proc. Letters 15: 97–101.

Nijholt A (1982b) From LL-regular to LL(1) grammars: transformations, covers and parsing. R.A.I.R.O. Theor. Informatics 16: 387–406

Nijholt A (1982c) The equivalence problem for LL- and LR-regular grammars. J. Computer System Sci. 24: 149–161

Nijholt A (1983a) Deterministic top-down and bottom-up parsing: historical notes and bibliographies. Mathematical Centre, Amsterdam

Nijholt A (1983b) On satisfying the LL-iteration theorem (note). Theor. Computer Sci. 23: 91–94

Pager D (1970) A solution to an open problem by Knuth. Inform. Control 17: 462–473

Pager D (1974) On eliminating unit productions from LR(*k*) parsers. In: Loeckx J (ed) Automata, Languages and Programming, 2nd Colloquium, University of Saarbrucken, July–August 1974. Springer, Berlin Heidelberg New York, pp 242–254 (Lecture notes in computer science, vol 14)

Pager D (1977a) A practical general method for constructing LR(*k*) parsers. Acta Inform. 7: 249–268

Pager D (1977b) Eliminating unit productions from LR parsers. Acta Inform. 9: 31–59

Pai AB, Kieburtz RB (1980) Global context recovery: A new strategy for syntactic error recovery by table-driven parsers. ACM Trans. Prog. Lang. Syst. 2: 18–41

Park JCH, Choe KM, Chang CH (1985) A new analysis of LALR formalisms. ACM Trans. Prog. Lang. Syst. 7: 159–175

Pennello TJ, DeRemer F (1978) A forward move algorithm for LR error revovery. In: 5th Annual ACM Symp. on Principles of Programming Languages, Tucson, Arizona, Jan 1978. ACM, New York, pp 241–254

Peterson TG (1972) Syntax error detection, correction and recovery in parsers. Thesis, Stevens Institute of Technology, Hoboken, N.J.

Pittl J (1977) Exponential optimization for the LLP(*k*) parsing method. In: Gruska J (ed) Mathematical Foundations of Computer Science 1977, Proceedings, 6th Symposium, Tatranska Lomnica, September, 1977. Springer, Berlin Heidelberg New York, pp 435–442 (Lecture notes in computer science, vol 53)

Pittl J (1981a) Negative results on the size of deterministic right parsers. In: Gruska J, Chytil M (eds) Mathematical Foundations of Computer Science, Tenth International Symposium, Strbske Pleso, 1981. Springer, Berlin Heidelberg New York, pp 442–451 (Lecture notes in computer science, vol 118)

Pittl J (1981b) On LLP(*k*) grammars and languages. Theor. Computer Sci. 16: 149–175

Poplawski DA (1979) On LL-regular grammars. J. Computer System Sci. 18: 218–227

Post EL (1946) A variant of a recursively unsolvable problem. Bull. Amer. Math. Soc. 52: 264–268

Purdom P (1974) The size of LALR(1) parsers. BIT 14: 326–337

Purdom P Jr, Brown CA (1981) Parsing extended LR(*k*) grammars. Acta Inform. 15: 115–127

Räihä K-J, Saarinen M, Sarjakoski M, Sippu S, Soisalon-Soininen E, Tienari M (1983) Revised report on the compiler writing system HLP78. Report A-1983-1, Department of Computer Science, University of Helsinki

Richter H (1985) Noncorrecting syntax error recovery. ACM Trans. Prog. Lang. Syst. 7: 478–489

Ripley GD (1978) A simple recovery-only procedure for simple precedence parsers. Comm. ACM 21: 928–930

Ripley GD, Druseikis FC (1978) A statistical analysis of syntax errors. Computer Lang. 3: 227–240

Röhrich J (1980) Methods for the automatic construction of error correcting parsers. Acta Inform. 13: 115–139

Röhrich J (1982) Behandlung syntaktischer Fehler. Informatik-Spektrum 5: 171–184

Rosenkrantz DJ, Hunt HB III (1985) Testing for grammatical coverings. Theor. Computer Sci. 38: 323–341

Rosenkrantz DJ, Hunt HB (1987) Efficient algorithms for automatic construction and compactification of parsing grammars. ACM Trans. Prog. Lang. Syst. 9: 543–566

Rosenkrantz DJ, Lewis PM II (1970) Deterministic left corner parsing. In: 11th Annual IEEE Symp. on Switching and Automata Theory, 1970. IEEE, New York, pp 139–152

Rosenkrantz DJ, Stearns RE (1970) Properties of deterministic top-down grammars. Inform. Control 17: 226–256

Rushby JM (1977) LR(*k*) sparse-parsers and their optimization. Thesis, Department of Computer Science, University of Newcastle upon Tyne

Sager TJ (1986) A short proof of a conjecture of DeRemer and Pennello. ACM Trans. Prog. Lang. Syst. 8: 264–271

Salomaa A (1973) Formal languages. Academic Press, New York

Schmitz L (1984) On the correct elimination of chain productions from LR parsers. Intern. J. Computer Math. 15: 99–116

Shields TE (1978) Syntax directed error analysis in automatically constructed parsers. Thesis, Rice University, Houston, Texas

Sippu S (1981) Syntax error handling in compilers. Report A-1981-1, Department of Computer Science, University of Helsinki

Sippu S, Soisalon-Soininen E (1977) On defining error recovery in context-free parsing. In: Salomaa A, Steinby M (eds) Automata, Languages and Programming, Fourth Colloquium, University of Turku, Finland, July 1977. Springer, Berlin Heidelberg New York, pp 492–503 (Lecture notes in computer science, vol 52)

Sippu S, Soisalon-Soininen E (1980) A scheme for LR(*k*) parsing with error recovery, Part 1: LR(*k*) parsing, Part 2: Error recovery, Part 3: Error correction. Intern. J. Computer Math. 8: 27–42 (Part 1), 107–119 (Part 2), 189–206 (Part 3)

Sippu S, Soisalon-Soininen E (1982) On LL(*k*) parsing. Inform. Control 53: 141–164

Sippu S, Soisalon-Soininen E (1983a) On the complexity of LL(*k*) testing. J. Computer System Sci. 26: 244–268

Sippu S, Soisalon-Soininen E (1983b) A syntax-error-handling technique and its experimental analysis. ACM Trans. Prog. Lang. Syst. 5: 656–679

Sippu S, Soisalon-Soininen E (1985) On the use of relational expressions in the design of efficient algorithms. In: Brauer W (ed) Automata, Languages and Programming, Twelfth Colloquium, Nafplion, Greece, July 1985. Springer, Berlin Heidelberg New York Tokyo, pp 456–464 (Lecture notes in computer science, vol 194)

Sippu S, Soisalon-Soininen E, Ukkonen E (1983) The complexity of LALR(*k*) testing. J. Assoc. Comput. Mach. 30: 259–270
Soisalon-Soininen E (1977a) Elimination of single productions from LR parsers in conjunction with the use of default reductions. In: 4th ACM Symp. on Principles of Programming Languages, Los Angeles, California, Jan 1977. ACM, New York, pp 183–193
Soisalon-Soininen E (1977b) Characterization of LL(*k*) languages by restricted LR(*k*) grammars. Report A-1977-3, Department of Computer Science, University of Helsinki
Soisalon-Soininen E (1979) On the covering problem for left-recursive grammars. Theor. Computer Sci. 8: 1–11
Soisalon-Soininen E (1980a) On the space optimizing effect of eliminating single productions from LR parsers. Acta Inform. 14: 157–174
Soisalon-Soininen E (1980b) On comparing LL(*k*) and LR(*k*) grammars. Math. Syst. Theory 13: 323–329
Soisalon-Soininen E (1982) Inessential error entries and their use in LR parser optimization. ACM Trans. Prog. Lang. Syst. 4: 179–195
Soisalon-Soininen E,Ukkonen E (1979) A method for transforming grammars into LL(*k*) form. Acta Inform. 12: 339–369
Stockmeyer LJ, Meyer AR (1973) Word problems requiring exponential time. In: 5th Annual ACM Symp. on Theory of Computing, April–May, 1973. ACM, New York, pp 1–9
Szymanski TG (1973) Generalized bottom-up parsing. Thesis, Cornell University, Ithaca, N.Y.
Szymanski TG, Williams JH (1976) Noncanonical extensions of bottom-up parsing techniques. SIAM J. Comput. 5: 231–250
Tai K-C (1979) Noncanonical SLR(1) grammars. ACM Trans. Prog. Lang. Syst. 1: 295–320
Tai K-C (1980) Predictors of context-free grammars. SIAM J. Comput. 9: 653–664
Tokuda T (1981) Eliminating unit reductions from LR(*k*) parsers using minimum contexts. Acta Inform. 15: 447–470
Turing AM (1936) On computable numbers with an application to the Entscheidungsproblem. Proc. London Math. Soc. 2–42: 230–265
Ukkonen E (1981) On size bounds for deterministic parsers. In: Even S, Kariv O (eds) Automata, Languages and Programming, Eighth Colloquium, Acre (Akko), July 1981. Springer, Berlin Heidelberg New York, pp 218–228 (Lecture notes in computer science, vol 115)
Ukkonen E (1983) Lower bounds on the size of deterministic parsers. J. Computer System Sci. 26: 153–170
Ukkonen E (1985) Upper bounds on the size of LR(*k*) parsers. Inform. Proc. Letters 20: 99–103
Ukkonen E, Soisalon-Soininen E (1981) LALR(*k*) testing is PSPACE-complete. In: 13th Annual ACM Symp. on Theory of Computing, May 1981. ACM, New York, pp 202–206
Waite WM, Goos G (1984) Compiler construction. Springer, New York Berlin Heidelberg Tokyo
Wegman M (1980) Parsing for structural editors. In: 21st IEEE Symp. on Foundations of Computer Science. IEEE, New York, pp 320–327
Wirth N (1976) Algorithms + Data Structures = Programs. Prentice-Hall, Englewood Cliffs, N.J.
Wood D (1969a) A note on top-down deterministic languages. BIT 9: 387–399
Wood D (1969b) The theory of left factored languages, Part I. Computer J. 12: 349–356
Wood D (1970) The theory of left factored languages, Part II. Computer J. 13: 55–62
Wood D (1971) A further note on top-down deterministic languages. Computer J. 14: 396–403
Wyrostek P (1986) Precedence technique is not worse than SLR(1). Acta Inform. 23: 361–392

# Index to Volume II

## EATCS Monographs on Theoretical Computer Science

Vol. 1: K. Mehlhorn
**Data Structures and Algorithms 1:**
**Sorting and Searching**

Vol. 2: K. Mehlhorn
**Data Structures and Algorithms 2:**
**Graph Algorithms and NP-Completeness**

Vol. 3: K. Mehlhorn
**Data Structures and Algorithms 3:**
**Multidimensional Searching and Computational Geometry**

Vol. 4: W. Reisig
**Petri Nets**
**An Introduction**

Vol. 5: W. Kuich, A. Salomaa
**Semirings, Automata, Languages**

Vol. 6: H. Ehrig, B. Mahr
**Fundamentals of Algebraic Specification 1**
**Equations and Initial Semantics**

Vol. 7: F. Gécseg
**Products of Automata**

Vol. 8: F. Kröger
**Temporal Logic of Programs**

Vol. 9: K. Weihrauch
**Computability**

Vol. 10: H. Edelsbrunner
**Algorithms in Combinatorial Geometry**

Vol. 11: J. L. Balcázar, J. Díaz, J. Gabarró
**Structural Complexity I**

Vol. 12: J. Berstel, C. Reutenauer
**Rational Series and Their Languages**

Vol. 13: E. Best, C. Fernàndez C.
**Nonsequential Processes**
**A Petri Net View**

Vol. 14: M. Jantzen
**Confluent String Rewriting**

Vol. 15: S. Sippu, E. Soisalon-Soininen
**Parsing Theory**
**Volume I: Languages and Parsing**

Vol. 16: P. Padawitz
**Computing in Horn Clause Theories**

Vol. 17: J. Paredaens, P. De Bra, M. Gyssens, D. Van Gucht
**The Structure of the Relational Database Model**

Vol. 18: J. Dassow, G. Pâun
**Regulated Rewriting in Formal Language Theory**

Vol. 19: M. Tofte
**Compiler Generators**
**What they can do, what they might do, and what they will probably never do**

Vol. 20: S. Sippu, E. Soisalon-Soininen
**Parsing Theory**
**Volume II: LR(k) and LL(k) Parsing**

Vol. 21: H. Ehrig, B. Mahr
**Fundamentals of Algebraic Specification 2**
**Module Specifications and Constraints**

Vol. 22: J. L. Balcázar, J, Díaz, J. Gabarró
**Structural Complexity II**